The War of the Roses—This black comedy about Douglas and Turner battling their way physically and emotionally through their property settlement stops being a comedy after a certain point and just feels black. Not a date movie, unless you're planning for it to be the last one.

You and Me—One of the most incontrovertibly strange movies of the thirties, this brooding Expressionist musical comedy about a department store owner taken to hiring ex-cons comes off as a Capraesque version of The Threepenny Opera. But with Fritz Lang directing, Bertolt Brecht working (uncredited) on the story, and Kurt Weill composing the score, what do you expect?

The Rocking Horse Winner—This focused and most satisfying film adaptation of Lawrence's work centers on a boy who can predict racetrack winners. Instead of getting all tangled up in sexual politics, fecund dirt, and the rest of the usual blather, this sad and eerie movie drives ahead on emotion and the strength of its plot. An unheralded classic.

Reservoir Dogs—A gang of handpicked professionals in Blues Brothers suits comes together for a diamond heist. Unfortunately, one of them's a cop. Stunning, ferocious, original portrait of bonding and betrayal with the men reduced to the level of wild dogs when things go sour. Brilliantly conceived and executed on a shoestring by first-time writer/director Quentin Tarantino, who plays one of the mongrels. The relentless intensity of the violence is strangely set off by the absurd seventies pop-culture junkie humor and detached irony of the approach. The performances cut so deep, nothing can stop the bleeding.

Nuns on the Run—Things get really hot for Idle and Coltrane as bungling crooks who pick up strange habits in order to avoid the murderous thugs who want them dead. Adding a twist of faith to the Lemmon/Curtis solution, they hide in a convent dressed up as nuns. Absolutely hilarious, it lacks the depth and style of the Wilder film, but, hey, nobody's perfect.

AND MANY MORE!

THE
REEL LIST

A Categorical Companion
to Over 2,000 Memorable Films

Lynne Arany, Tom Dyja, and Gary Goldsmith

With an Introduction by Andrew Sarris

Delta
Trade
Paperbacks

A Delta Book
Published by
Dell Publishing
a division of
Bantam Doubleday Dell Publishing Group, Inc.
1540 Broadway
New York, New York 10036

Library of Congress Cataloging in Publication Data

Arany, Lynne.
    The reel list : a categorical companion to over 2,000 memorable films /
Lynne Arany, Tom Dyja, and Gary Goldsmith.
        p.   cm.
    ISBN: 0–385–31362–4
    1. Motion pictures—Catalogs. I. Dyja, Tom. II. Goldsmith, Gary, 1950–
III. Title.
PN1998.A665 1995
016.79143'75—dc20   94–28066
                                                                 CIP

Produced by Ink Projects. Book design by Lynne Arany.

Manufactured in the United States of America
Published simultaneously in Canada

February 1995
10 9 8 7 6 5 4 3 2 1

CONTENTS

Authors' Note ix
Acknowledgments xi
A Rationale for Lists
  by Andrew Sarris xiii

THE REAL WORLD 1

WORKING STIFFS 3

Up the Corporation 3
Look for the Union Label 4
Madison Avenue 6
Teachers 7
The Butler Did It 8
Cab Fare 10
Farmers 11

MEDICINE 13

Doctor, Doctor 13
Diseases 15
Blindness 16
Plastic Surgery 18
You Must Remember This 19
On the Couch 21
Over the Edge 22

CRIME & PUNISHMENT 24

The Legend of Bonnie & Clyde 24
Hot Rock Rip-Offs
  & Other Capers 27
Order in the Court 29
Watching the Detectives: 32
  Hard-Boiled Eggs:
    The Private Eyes 32
  Well-Cooked Cops 34
  Otherwise-Occupied Eggs 37
  Soft-Boiled Eggs 39
The Big House 41

POLITICS 42

On the Campaign Trail 42
Capitol Games 44

Well-Greased Machines
  & Other Political Dirt 46
Hail to the Chiefs 48
Assassinations 50

DIVERSIONS 53

HOLIDAYS 55

Auld Lang Syne 55
Erin Go Bragh 56
The Last Supper
  & Other Seders 57
The Fourth of July 59
Tricks & Treats 60
'Tis the Season 62

TRAVEL 63

On the Road 64
On Track 65
Up in the Air 67
By the Sea 69

PLACES 71

Gotham 71
Inside the Beltway 72
Cajun Cooking 74
Under the Golden Gate 76
London Fog 77
City of Light 79
Roma 80
Out of Africa 82
South America 84
The Polar Regions 85

VICES 86

Food 86
Drink 88
Gambling 90
Cons & Scams 91
Drugs 93
Oldest Profession 95

WONDERFUL WORLD
  OF FASHION 97

Does Macy's Tell Gimbels?   97
Down the Runway   99
If the Shoe Fits   100

SPORTS   **102**

Cooperstown Classics   102
Slam Dunk   103
The Popcorn Bowl   104
KO's   106
The Checkered Flag   107
The Wide World of Sports   109

ANIMALS   **110**

Celluloid Kitties   110
Movie Mutts   112
Film Fish   113
Hollywood Horses   114
Wild Kindgom   116

MAKING MOVIES   **119**

AUTEUR   **121**

Screenwriters: 121
   The Algonquin Round Table   121
   Screenwriting Playwrights   122
Cinematographers: 124
   James Wong Howe   124
   Gregg Toland   126
   John Alton   129
Writers: 130
   Written, but Not Directed,
     by Preston Sturges   130
   Written, but Not Directed,
     by Billy Wilder   132
   Written, but Not Directed,
     by John Huston   134
   By Hecht   136
Hollywood Composers: 140
   Max Steiner   140
   Bernard Herrmann   142
   Dimitri Tiomkin   144
Credit Where Credit Is Due   146

CUTTING ROOM FLOOR   **148**

Hollywood Women (and their
   Men): Before the Code   148
Enabling Kane   150
Howard Hughes   152
The Aesthetics of Elvis   153
The Rat Pack   156
Pre-*Star Wars* Special Effects   158
Uncredited Remakes   159
Kid Stuff   161

CULTURE   **165**

LITERARY ADAPTATIONS   **167**

The Bard   167
The Bard Bowdlerized   168
English Lit:
   18th & 19th Centuries   170
English Lit: 20th Century   172
American Lit: 19th Century   173
American Lit: 20th Century   175
Lit Française   177
Steppe Class   179
The Lost Generation   181
The Women's Room   182

FINE ARTS   **184**

Art History   184
Photography   185
The Art Scene   187

MUSIC   **189**

Tin Pan Alley Tunesmiths   189
S'Wonderful   191
He's the Top   193
All That Jazz   195
Rock Around the Clock:
   1950s Rock 'n' Roll   197
The British Are Coming   199
A Box at the Opry   201
Classical Music   203
One of a Musical Kind   204

LIVELY ARTS   **206**

On Your Radio Dial   206

On the Tube 208

Movies About the Movies:

   Behind the Scenes 210

The Moviegoers 213

Stand-Up Comedy 214

Big Tops & Midways 215

Dance Card: 217

   Fred, Ginger & Gene 217

   Gotta Dance 219

   Best of Busby 221

FAMILY VALUES 223

A QUESTION OF GENDER 225

The First Sex 225

Boys to Men 227

Opening the Closet 230

Just Like a Woman 232

LOVE & MARRIAGE 235

Nymphets 235

Paging Dr. Ruth 237

I Do, I Do 239

I Did, I Did 241

Adulteries to Remember 242

Divorce, Hollywood Style 244

Killing Your Spouse 246

Obstetrics & Pediatrics 247

Old Age 248

RELIGION 250

God & the Devil 250

Cherubim & Seraphim 251

Men of the Cloth 252

Nuns 254

The Chosen People 255

The Afterlife 257

HISTORY 259

THE WAY WE WERE 261

Hail Caesar 261

Knights & Castles 262

The British Raj 264

The Civil War 266

Cowpersons &

   Indigenous Peoples 267

WWI 270

The Great Depression 271

Wars in History 272

Submarines 274

WWII: Europe & the Atlantic 275

WWII: The Pacific & Elsewhere 277

WWII: The Homefront 279

Korea: The Forgotten War 280

The Red Menace 282

Vietnam 285

Black in America 286

Black & White 288

Pride & Prejudice 290

THINGS TO COME 292

Alien Presence 292

Robots, 'Droids & Other

   Sentient Beings 294

Cautionary Tales 296

Post-Apocalypse 299

INDEX 301

AUTHORS' NOTE

In film's hundred year history thousands of books have attempted to define, decode, or delineate the art of cinema or at least some part of the moviegoing experience. Every worthy film critic that ever put pen to paper has come out with a collection of his or her reviews; theories and "isms" abound. There are books on each genre, from the western to nouveau noir. And to fill your more encyclopedic needs, bookstores are stocked with a mountain of Maltinesque compendiums, providing basic info and a soupçon of insight into most every movie ever made. Convenient? Of course they are. Even essential. Don't throw those away to make room on your shelf for this. What we're serving up is something completely different.

The Reel List is neither theoretical nor historical; it's not, strictly speaking, a reference or a guide book. We've attempted, instead, to fill in a gap—to create a companion for the general reader and movie cultist alike, a companion that sorts movies into relatively uncommon categories, making connections, distinctions, and a host of associations that will make you look at many movies that you know and love in a whole new context, remind you of others you'd always meant to see, and lead you to some you never knew about.

This is a book of movie lists. There is no single governing theory here, no thumbs up-thumbs down, two, three, or four star rating system; no "top tens" or "all time bests." *The Reel List* looks for common ground, kindred spirits, birds of a feather, and the ties that bind. You won't find catch-all categories like "Action," "Comedy," "Drama," etc. Our focus is much more selective.

Some lists are straight-on, some sneak up from around the bend. You'll find lists built around lifestyles, musical modes, and literary heritage. *The Reel List* explores the world of medicine, the world of fashion, and the world at war. It spotlights cinematographers and film composers. One list illuminates the Gershwin touch, another is Shakespearean, another chases Bonnie and Clyde through a dozen different movies. *The Reel List* links Eric Idle to R.W. Fassbinder because both have a feel for cross dressing; it digs into the *oeuvre* of Elvis and discovers an auteurist aesthetic; it finds a red-baiting parable at the core of one of the most beloved children's movies of all time; it unites *King Kong* and John Wayne through the music of Max Steiner; it reminds you that *Tom Jones* and *Eating Raoul* both give you food for thought. There's a list of films about dogs, a list of films about football, and a list of films that were shot by the same cinematographer as *Citizen Kane*.

Each individual list blends straightforward choices with a solid offering of subtleties and surprises. For us, the idea behind the book is the connective tissue in the list, the combinations and juxtapositions that might send you back to the movies or your VCR for another, perhaps deeper look at an old favorite . . .

or a first look at a new find. Take *The Reel List* along when you rent a movie and for once you'll be looking for specific movies and not just waiting for something to jump off the rack. Every film listed comes complete with commentary, cast rundown, and pertinent data. A cube above the review means a film is not available on video at this time, but with new releases coming every day, it's worth double-checking at your video store.

The Reel List is a book we think you'll want to spend some time with. We want to give you something to read as much as a list of titles to choose from. What we have written is obviously more than a guide book . . . it's also a book to play with, to rail against, to talk back to. Whether you're a casual fan or a film student, you'll be coming up with your own additions to our lists and lists in addition to ours. As firmly as we expect you'll agree with some of our quirkier picks, we expect you to quibble with others, to delight in unexpected inclusions, and bristle at sins of omission. Debate is inevitable. Plenty of it went into the writing of this book. Don't forget, these lists were compiled by three individual writers. And while our sensibilities are generally in synch, we each have our own bents and biases.

What distinguishes *The Reel List* from any other book of lists is range and critical perspective. Where else will you find films about fish listed side by side with films from French literary sources? So whether you're feeling hard-boiled and cynical or hopelessly romantic, shamelessly sexual, or vaguely intellectual, or if you just happen to feel a song coming on . . . have we got a list for you.

ACKNOWLEDGMENTS

Thanks to Howard Salen and Charles Brandt for input and insight, and to Barbara Penna for love, support, and invaluable feedback. Thanks to Channel Video on Columbus for service with a smile.

—G.G.

Thanks to the Hon. Seymour Schwartz, Molly Pomerance, Ruth Pomerance; to E.J. and the rest of the staff of the Video Room; and especially to my wife, Suzanne, who always makes me pick the movies.

—T.D.

Thanks to Cary, Clark, and *The Thin Man* . . . and to Don Larsen, who always had the answers, and Jill Weiner, Jane Kepp, Ron Perfit, and Joelle Hertel for always being there. And with special thanks to John Gaffney and the ever-helpful and informed staff at World of Video.

—L.A.

And a big round of thanks to all the people who helped in the production of the book—some of whom have been there since the beginning, some of whom appeared like magic at key moments and proved invaluable. Any flaws that remain are not for want of their diligent efforts. Gail Weiss, Michael Cooper, Meredith Storer, Lorie Young, Chuck Berry, Andrew Freund, Carole Desnoes, Tina Thompson, Karen Van Craenenbroeck, Robert Gampert, Greg Villepique, Tracey Lander, Archie Hobson, Eden Fahlen, and Hilla Shavitt—thank you all.

And to everyone at Delacorte whose help and attention has been most appreciated, notably Susan Schwartz, Mary Fischer, Judy Young, and especially Jenny Minton; to Leslie Schnur who was always thinking of what was best for the book; and most of all to our wonderful editor, Jackie Cantor, whose enthusiasm, encouragement, and support helped us through some rough spots and made the good ones even better.

A RATIONALE FOR LISTS

BY ANDREW SARRIS

Pauline Kael, my ever esteemed colleague and eternal antagonist, once asked me to my face in her maddeningly rhetorical manner if I were some sort of list queen. What could I say? Lists are my life. Yet as much as I bristled at her imputation of effeminacy to my list-making proclivity, I could not think of a suitable retort on the spot. It had never occurred to me that lists in themselves could be objectionable to anyone. I did note after my encounter with Ms. Kael that she was the only regular movie reviewer who had never published a 10-best list. Obviously, she considered herself superior to any such menial journalistic task. Anyway, that was almost 30 years ago, and I had not given the matter much thought until I was approached by the authors in the summer of 1994 to write an introduction to their book, *The Reel List: A Categorical Companion to Over 2000 Memorable Films*. Under the circumstances, how could I refuse? Here at last was my long deferred opportunity to answer Ms. Kael's outrageous question with the benefit of smoldering hindsight and *l'esprit d'escalier*.

First of all, list-making and numbers-crunching, far from being categorizable solely as effete endeavors, are a quintessential boy-guy thing from the earliest license plates one copies to the statistics one computes day-by-day from boxscores. I still remember a fall afternoon in 1941 at P.S. 146 in Howard Beach, Queens, a time in which Ted Williams, Cecil Travis of the Washington Senators, and Joe DiMaggio were running 1-2-3 in the race for the batting crown. Two of my more statistically addicted classmates were hunched together conferring on possible scenarios that would enable DiMaggio to pass Travis and Williams. If they had worked half as hard on their studies as they did on batting averages, they would have been class valedictorians instead of the class roughnecks they happened to be.

For my own part I feasted on not only all the numerical minutiae of baseball, but also *World Almanac* population figures for countries, states, and cities. I was an ear-glued-to-the-radio convention and election fanatic. I still remember that Robert A. Taft received 337 votes at the 1940 Republican convention making it possible for Wendell L. Willkie to surge past Thomas E. Dewey and win the nomination to contest the third-term bid of FDR.

Meanwhile, down in San Antonio, Texas, a little boy named Samuel Eugene Archer was making up his own movie 10-best lists. When we met years later in Roger Tilton's winter 1954–55 class in film studies at Columbia, we began comparing our 10-best lists, mine of much more recent vintage. Our four-year collaboration on movie lists eventually bore fruit in the spring 1963 issue of *Film Culture,* devoted to my critical evaluation of the American Cinema. By then Archer and I had parted company, but that is another story. The point I want to make, and it may be disputed, is that boys and men, seem to me to be even more entranced by lists and numbers than girls and women. I would go further and suggest that males are born Platonists, females born Aristotelians; males born romanticists and females born realists. But that's one man's opinion.

Now that I have established a rationale for list-making, I am pleased to endorse the Arany-Dyja-Goldsmith enterprise in its entirety. What they've accomplished, I'm convinced, will appeal equally to both men and women. Theirs is not simply a process of making mere lists within what one philosopher derogated as "bloodless categories." These are instead mnemonic stimuli to invoke the living, breathing, moving images on the screen. The authors are audacious in their groupings, confronting head on the touchy issues of repetitions, clichés, stereotypes, Manichaean simplistics, etc., and then tackling the thematic and stylistic variations that give the best movies their unique texture, rhythm, and impact. The movie buff in me embraces the movie buff in them.

Nor is the altar of "fun" before which Ms. Kael has always professed to worship neglected by the authors. Indeed, they must have had great fun with sub-categories like Does Macy's Tell Gimbels?, Celluloid Kitties, Movie Mutts, Film Fish, Hollywood Horses—hey, alliteration is my most notorious vice, if not my deadliest sin—Nymphets, Paging Dr. Ruth, Killing Your Spouse, Cooperstown Classics, Slam Dunk, The Checkered Flag, London Fog, City of Light, Gotham, Inside the Beltway, Cajun Cooking, Under the Golden Gate, Out of Africa, The Polar Regions. On a more somber note there are Diseases, On the Couch, Over the Edge, The Big House, and Assassinations.

Curiously, the section entitled "Auteur" seems to be more Kaelian than Sarrisian in its orientation, what with lists like "The Algonquin Round Table" and "Screenwriting Playwrights" in the Screenwriters section; "James Wong Howe," "Gregg Toland," and "John Alton" under Cinematography; "Written, but Not Directed by Preston Sturges," "Written, but Not Directed by John Huston," and "Written by Ben Hecht" under Writers; "Max Steiner," "Bernard Herrmann," and "Dimitri Tiomkin" under Hollywood Composers; and an additional category entitled "Credit Where Credit Is Due."

I can only applaud. As I have said many times in the past, directorial auteurism is the first step rather than the last step in a coherent and comprehensive film criticism and film history. Nonetheless, the spirit of auteurism gallops across every text of the authors on individual movies. The important thing is to get people to look at a great many more movies than they would have if they had listened to old-fashioned sociological critics who preached social significance at all costs, including the pleasure principle. This is not to say that our seemingly facile categorizers are mindless sybarites. Far from it. *The Reel List* is a missionary work preaching the gospel of cinema from many different vantage points. Read the text, and get the video. You'll be glad you did. On many occasions, you'll be enchanted and edified. Now enjoy.

THE
REEL LIST

THE
REAL
WORLD

WORKING
STIFFS

UP THE CORPORATION

After a long day at the office, the first thing you want to see is a film about corporate intrigue and back-stabbing, right? Actually, watching some of these movies may have a cathartic effect. Though the little guy almost always gets crushed, he does get off the big speech that you keep wishing you were insane enough to lay on your boss.

The Apartment (1960, U.S., 125 mins., b/w) Dir: Billy Wilder; Cast: Jack Lemmon, Shirley MacLaine, Fred MacMurray, Ray Walston, Jack Kruschen, Edie Adams, David Lewis, Joan Shawlee.

Lemmon scrambles up the corporation by letting the big shots use his apartment. All goes well until he falls in love with his boss's latest girlfriend. Like most Billy Wilder films, it's truly funny, mean, and brilliant.

How to Succeed in Business Without Really Trying (1967, U.S., 119 mins.) Dir: David Swift; Cast: Robert Morse, Michele Lee, Rudy Vallee, Sammy Smith.

Rousing musical starring Robert Morse as a window-washer who moves inside and connives his way to the top, from the days when conniving your way to the top was your duty as an American. Wait, wasn't that the eighties?

Wall Street (1987, U.S., 125 mins.) Dir: Oliver Stone; Cast: Charlie Sheen, Michael Douglas, Daryl Hannah, Martin Sheen, Terence Stamp, Hal Holbrook, James Spader, James Karen, Sean Young.

Now it comes back. The eighties were untrammeled greed and 23-year-olds deciding the fate of corporations; kids like Sheen here, who checks out of humanity to get into the inner circle of his brokerage firm. Stone's film, for all its flaws, will probably be used in your grandchildren's history classes to explain the phrase "Die, Yuppie Scum."

Roger & Me (1989, U.S., 90 mins.) Dir: Michael Moore.

Humorous and sad documentary by Michael Moore that chronicles his attempts to track down General Motors chairman Roger Smith for a discussion about plant closings in Flint, Michigan. Moore comes down very hard, and rightfully so, on Smith and the privileged few of the Flint area, but he also has more than enough laughs at the expense of those hit by the closings, leaving the impression that Moore is the only smart guy around.

Tucker: The Man and His Dream (1988, U.S., 110 mins.) Dir: Francis Ford Coppola; Cast: Jeff Bridges, Joan Allen, Martin Landau, Frederic Forrest, Mako, Dean Stockwell, Lloyd Bridges.

The true story of Preston Tucker, who in the forties challenged the Big Three with a visionary new car. Instead of hitting us on the head like Oliver Stone, Coppola shows a master's hand by telling a parable relevant to the present and giving us as much to look at as he does for us to think about.

The Man in the White Suit (1951, Great Britain, 84 mins., b/w) Dir: Alexander Mackendrick; Cast: Alec Guinness, Joan Greenwood, Cecil Parker.

Meek inventor Alec Guinness creates a fabric that never wears out, much to the dismay of the fabric industry. An amusing movie about David taking on Goliath.

Working Girl (1988, U.S., 114 mins.) Dir: Mike Nichols; Cast: Melanie Griffith, Harrison Ford, Sigourney Weaver, Joan Cusack, Alec Baldwin.

Secretary Griffith tries to wheel and deal her way up past bitchy boss Sigourney Weaver. An entertaining film, but it's a sad commentary that the two images of working women seemingly presented are airhead and hellbeast.

Patterns (1956, U.S., 83 mins., b/w) Dir: Fielder Cook; Cast: Van Heflin, Everett Sloane, Beatrice Straight, Ed Begley.

Hard-nosed drama about a power play at a huge corporation. The gripping and unnervingly realistic Rod Serling script will bring back those vague stomach pains you get when the boss calls you to her office.

Executive Suite (1954, U.S., 104 mins., b/w) Dir: Robert Wise; Cast: William Holden, June Allyson, Fredric March, Barbara Stanwyck, Shelley Winters, Nina Foch, Paul Douglas, Walter Pidgeon.

Another power play at a huge corporation, but not quite up to *Patterns*. Still, the cast is great. If you don't recognize the upper management of your own company here, you're not paying enough attention at meetings.

Citizen Kane (1941, U.S., 119 mins., b/w) Dir: Orson Welles; Cast: Orson Welles, Joseph Cotten, Dorothy Comingore, Ruth Warrick, Everett Sloane, Agnes Moorehead, George Coulouris.

The Big Daddy of them all, based on the life of press baron William Randolph Hearst. Aside from all the cinematic reasons for seeing this, *Citizen Kane* is an unmatched view of greed, loyalty, ambition, and friendship in big business.

Glengarry Glen Ross (1992, U.S., 100 mins.) Dir: James Foley; Cast: Al Pacino, Jack Lemmon, Alec Baldwin, Ed Harris, Alan Arkin.

Film adaptation of David Mamet's play about lowlife real estate salesmen trying to stay alive lacks the punch of the stage version, despite its big-name cast. Though Lemmon seems perfect for his role, he's almost too perfect and his performance comes off more as outtakes from *Save the Tiger* than as ensemble work. Pacino, on the other hand, makes this worth seeing. As much as we associate Robards with O'Neill, Malkovich with Shepard, and Olivier with Shakespeare, no one will ever top Pacino at interpreting Mamet's work.

LOOK FOR THE UNION LABEL

Though all those Jaguars and Beverly Hills mansions didn't come from the company store, Hollywood can seem a lot like a company town. Just ask one of the writers or directors blacklisted in the fifties. But given that the studios' customers are mostly working stiffs like us, Hollywood has usually sided with labor when it comes to presenting unions.

Matewan (1987, U.S., 132 mins.) Dir: John Sayles; Cast: Chris Cooper, Will Oldham, Mary McDonnell, Bob Gunton, James Earl Jones.

An epic tale of an early confrontation between West Virginia coal miners and their greedy management. If John Sayles was French or German, we'd all call him the greatest thing since Kurosawa. Instead, he's American; so while we keep wondering when he's going to have a box-office hit, he makes great films, writes novels, and probably cures diseases on the side.

The Devil and Miss Jones (1941, U.S., 92 mins., b/w) Dir: Sam Wood; Cast: Jean Arthur, Robert Cummings, Charles Coburn, S. Z. Sakall, William Demarest.

A little gem of a comedy about a tycoon who goes to work in one of his own department stores to ferret out union organizers. Clearly pre-McCarthy, with its strong labor sympathies, it balances screwball laughs with romance and a taste of working-class life in forties New York.

Last Exit to Brooklyn (1989, West Germany, 110 mins.) Dir: Uli Edel; Cast: Stephen Lang, Jennifer Jason Leigh, Burt Young, Peter Dobson, Jerry Orbach, Ricki Lake, Alexis Arquette.

This depressing and sometimes unpleasant version of Hubert Selby, Jr.'s novel includes a subplot involving a union organizer trying to control a strike and his own gender confusion at the same time. Not a walk in the park, but it's nice to know that a movie like this can still shock us. Jennifer Jason Leigh stands out.

On the Waterfront (1954, U.S., 108 mins., b/w) Dir: Elia Kazan; Cast: Marlon Brando, Eva Marie Saint, Karl Malden, Lee J. Cobb, Rod Steiger.

Elia Kazan's classic movie about New York City longshoremen and their crooked union. Scripted by Budd Schulberg, with an amazing cast. One of the greatest American movies ever made.

Hoffa (1992, U.S., 140 mins.) Dir: Danny DeVito; Cast: Jack Nicholson, Danny DeVito, Armand Assante, J. T. Walsh, John C. Reilly.

Sympathetic biography of former Teamsters boss Jimmy Hoffa. David Mamet is arguably the finest American playwright of our generation, but his screenwriting is spotty. Remember *We're No Angels*?

Harlan County U.S.A. (1977, U.S., 103 mins.) Dir: Barbara Kopple.

Oscar-winning documentary by Barbara Kopple covers a strike by Kentucky coal-mine workers. A searing, fascinating film that's considered one of the best documentaries ever made.

American Dream (1989, U.S., 100 mins.) Dir: Barbara Kopple.

Kopple returns to organized labor a dozen years later in this documentary about the long strike against Hormel, but here the answers aren't as clearcut as they were in Harlan County. A strong reflection of the ambivalence Kopple shares with many Americans about organized labor.

How Green Was My Valley (1941, U.S., 118 mins., b/w) Dir: John Ford; Cast: Walter Pidgeon, Maureen O'Hara, Donald Crisp, Anna Lee, Roddy McDowall, Sara Allgood, Barry Fitzgerald, John Loder, Patric Knowles.

This story of 50 years in the life of a Welsh coal-mining family beat out *Citizen Kane* for Best Picture at the 1941 Academy Awards. The fact that no one makes much of that tells you how fine a movie John Ford created. As in all coal-mining films, strikes and unions figure prominently.

I'm All Right, Jack (1960, Great Britain, 104 mins., b/w) Dirs: John and Roy Boulting; Cast: Ian Carmichael, Peter Sellers, Terry-Thomas.

Sellers plays an obnoxious communist labor leader in this enjoyable British satire about a crooked business scheme gone awry.

Norma Rae (1979, U.S., 113 mins.) Dir: Martin Ritt; Cast: Sally Field, Ron Leibman, Beau Bridges, Pat Hingle.

Sally Field won an Oscar for her portrayal of a southern textile worker who teams up with New York union man Leibman to organize her factory. Field finally made people forget, or at least forgive, her *Flying Nun* days with this performance.

MADISON AVENUE

Expending massive amounts of time, money, and creative energy to convince people to buy things they don't need—what could be more American? We know we're being brainwashed, but we defend advertising as a basic tenet of capitalism and the dirty not-so-secret secret is that we love it. Why else would there be so many movies—and so many good movies—about advertising?

The Hucksters (1947, U.S., 115 mins., b/w) Dir: Jack Conway; Cast: Clark Gable, Deborah Kerr, Sydney Greenstreet, Adolphe Menjou, Ava Gardner, Keenan Wynn, Edward Arnold.

Clark Gable tries to keep his integrity and still please Greenstreet, a hateful soap magnate and the biggest client of Gable's firm. The film sags at points, but some stellar moments from the cast, especially Greenstreet, make this worth seeing.

Lover Come Back (1961, U.S., 107 mins.) Dir: Delbert Mann; Cast: Doris Day, Rock Hudson, Tony Randall, Edie Adams.

Ad exec Doris Day battles rival Rock Hudson for a client. It's no coincidence that during the height of American power, advertising was THE job to have. And you have to admit, Doris and Rock make it look like a lot of fun. Bright pastels and cheesy jazz music; the sixties weren't all Iron Butterfly and Peter Max, you know.

Good Neighbor Sam (1964, U.S., 130 mins.) Dir: David Swift; Cast: Jack Lemmon, Romy Schneider, Dorothy Provine.

Another sixties paean to the ad game, this time with adman Lemmon forced

to pretend neighbor Romy Schneider is his wife. All that nostalgia about rebellious sixties youth may be misplaced because the grown-ups appear to have had a much better time. Tom Collins, anyone?

The Man in the Gray Flannel Suit (1956, U.S., 153 mins.) Dir: Nunnally Johnson; Cast: Gregory Peck, Jennifer Jones, Fredric March, Marisa Pavan.

All right, advertising wasn't always so easy, at least not before Kennedy took office. Here, Gregory Peck struggles to move up the corporate ladder and stay sane at the same time. This film, along with *To Kill a Mockingbird,* really defined Peck as the American everyman.

It Should Happen to You (1953, U.S., 81 mins., b/w) Dir: George Cukor; Cast: Judy Holliday, Jack Lemmon, Peter Lawford, Michael O'Shea.

Aspiring actress Judy Holliday uses the power of advertising to make a name for herself in New York. The fact is, all of Holliday's five films are wonderful, so don't miss this one. Plus, Jack Lemmon makes his screen debut.

Putney Swope (1969, U.S., 84 mins., b/w) Dir: Robert Downey; Cast: Allen Garfield, Alan Abel, Mel Brooks.

"African-Americans take over an ad agency." That premise rings offensive now, but most of us didn't think so in 1969. This is a bit like one of your old Firesign Theater albums—it was definitely funny then and it still might be funny now with some "help," but is it really worth it?

Boomerang (1992, U.S., 118 mins.) Dir: Reginald Hudlin; Cast: Eddie Murphy, Halle Berry, Robin Givens, David Alan Grier, Martin Lawrence, Grace Jones, Geoffrey Holder.

Eddie Murphy plays a hotshot exec who gets taken down a few pegs by new boss Robin Givens. So what if it's not *Beverly Hills Cop;* it's raunchy and funny and worth a rental. It's also nice to have an enormous black-owned business presented as a given and not a plot point.

Crazy People (1990, U.S., 90 mins.) Dir: Tony Bill; Cast: Dudley Moore, Daryl Hannah, Paul Reiser, Mercedes Ruehl, J. T. Walsh, Ben Hammer, Floyd Vivino, John Terlesky.

Comedy about an institutionalized adman who employs his fellow patients to work on his new campaign. The film doesn't have much of an edge, but somehow the lack of both false sincerity and cultivated cynicism give it a strange innocence. The fake ads are funny, too.

How to Get Ahead in Advertising (1989, Great Britain, 96 mins.) Dir: Bruce Robinson; Cast: Richard E. Grant, Rachel Ward, Richard Wilson.

This is the film you want if you're looking for an edge. While struggling with ideas for a pimple-cream spot, an ad exec starts to believe a boil he's developed is speaking to him. The first two-thirds roars along with black comedy, but then it slows down into a mystery of sorts. Still, it's a winner.

Lost in America (1985, U.S., 91 mins.) Dir: Albert Brooks; Cast: Albert Brooks, Julie Hagerty, Garry Marshall, Art Frankel.

Albert Brooks quits his job, buys a Winnebago, and takes wife Julie Hagerty out to find meaning in America. Brooks's best and funniest film and the last word on all the lip service most of us give to dropping out of the rat race.

TEACHERS

Come September, you may feel the primordial urge to buy new folders and notebooks; maybe even one of those metal lunch boxes with a thermos. It usually passes as soon as you picture yourself explaining the Snoopy pencil case to the CEO, but if you still can't shake the urge, these films about teachers may do the trick.

To Sir, With Love (1967, Great Britain, 105 mins.) Dir: James Clavell; Cast: Sidney Poitier, Judy Geeson, Suzy Kendall, Faith Brook, Lulu.

Might as well start at the top. Sidney Poitier turns his class of racist, lowlife London youths into proper ladies and gentlemen. Watching this, you can see why Poitier was such a huge star. Big question: Does Natalie Merchant do the title song better than Lulu?

The Blackboard Jungle (1955, U.S., 101 mins., b/w) Dir: Richard Brooks; Cast: Glenn Ford, Anne Francis, Vic Morrow, Louis Calhern, Sidney Poitier, Richard Kiley, Warner Anderson, Paul Mazursky, John Hoyt, Jamie Farr.

Groundbreaking film about tough times for a young teacher in a New York City public school. One of the first honest looks at troubled urban youths and also the first film to use a rock-and-roll score.

The Prime of Miss Jean Brodie (1969, Great Britain, 116 mins.) Dir: Ronald Neame; Cast: Maggie Smith, Robert Stephens, Pamela Franklin, Celia Johnson.

Maggie Smith won an Oscar for her portrayal of a Scottish teacher who has maybe too great of an effect on her students. A tour de force by Smith, based on Muriel Spark's novel. You'll agree afterward that the Scots have the best accent in the world.

Goodbye, Mr. Chips (1939, Great Britain, 114 mins., b/w) Dir: Sam Wood; Cast: Robert Donat, Greer Garson, John Mills, Paul Henreid.

No, not the Peter O'Toole/Petula Clark

musical version—the Robert Donat one. Withdrawn headmaster finds life and love with Greer Garson. Note to Oscar-hungry stars: Donat also won an Oscar playing a teacher. Hint, hint.

Dead Poets Society (1989, U.S., 128 mins.) Dir: Peter Weir; Cast: Robin Williams, Robert Sean Leonard, Ethan Hawke, Kurtwood Smith.

Another guru teacher whose students go a little too far, this time in a boys' boarding school in the fifties. Apparently everyone who has ever written more than a laundry list has had a teacher like the one Robin Williams plays here, full of love for poetry and *carpe diem*ing all over. God bless them. Plays better with the younger crowd, but you might get teary, too.

Stand and Deliver (1988, U.S., 102 mins.) Dir: Ramon Menendez; Cast: Edward James Olmos, Lou Diamond Phillips, Rosana de Soto, Andy Garcia.

Edward James Olmos stars as a tough calculus instructor who drives his class of East L.A. students to excellence. A good film; uplifting, inspiring, well-intentioned, but so much so that it feels like an after-school special. We HAVE to like it. Maybe it's just math-phobia. . . .

Educating Rita (1983, Great Britain, 110 mins.) Dir: Lewis Gilbert; Cast: Michael Caine, Julie Walters.

Drunkard/professor Michael Caine tutors working-class heroine Julie Walters. Trinity College setting may have you looking at course guides for next semester. Caine is very good (sorry, no Oscar), but why hasn't Julie Walters worked more since then?

Conrack (1974, U.S., 107 mins.) Dir: Martin Ritt; Cast: Jon Voight, Paul Winfield, Hume Cronyn, Madge Sinclair, Tina Andrews, Antonio Fargas.

Adaptation of *The Water Is Wide*, Pat Conroy's novel about a young teacher, played by Jon Voight, who tries to bring the world to one of the isolated shore islands off the South Carolina coast. The Beethoven scene is worth the price of the rental.

Up the Down Staircase (1967, U.S., 124 mins.) Dir: Robert Mulligan; Cast: Sandy Dennis, Patrick Bedford, Eileen Heckart, Jean Stapleton.

It ain't *Blackboard Jungle*, but this adaptation of Bel Kaufman's bestseller about teaching in a New York City public school still has its moments.

Diabolique (1955, France, 107 mins., b/w) Dir: Henri-Georges Clouzot; Cast: Simone Signoret, Vera Clouzot, Charles Vanel.

The wife and mistress of a sadistic headmaster team up to kill him, but did they really finish him off? The missing link between Grand Guignol and John Carpenter, this French chiller will let you vicariously knock off your least favorite teacher.

THE BUTLER DID IT

As Zoë Baird taught us, good help is very hard to find, especially if what you need is someone to watch the kids while you're at work or doing some laundry. Hollywood servants are usually of the butler and maid variety and their skills don't extend far beyond the ability to make a positively arid martini, but if that's the kind of help you're looking for, hire one of the following for a night.

My Man Godfrey (1936, U.S., 90 mins., b/w) Dir: Gregory La Cava; Cast: Carole Lombard, William Powell, Eugene Pallette, Mischa Auer, Gail Patrick, Alan Mowbray, Alice Brady.

Of course he's a good butler; he went to Harvard. A sublime screwball comedy about "forgotten man" Powell, who's hired and wooed by young socialite Lombard. The family scenes are among the funniest ever filmed, and Eugene Pallette as the beleaguered father and Mischa Auer as a pianist/leech are brilliant. If you haven't seen this, now's the time.

Thank You, Jeeves (1936, U.S., 68 mins., b/w) Dir: Arthur Collins; Cast: Arthur Treacher, Virginia Field, David Niven.

Arthur Treacher as P. G. Wodehouse's impeccable Mr. Jeeves and Niven as his hapless charge pull this one out of the pack. Treacher and Niven teamed up for a sequel—*Step Lively, Jeeves*—and there was a great little BBC series of Wodehouse adaptations worth checking into if you're a fan. It doesn't boast the big-name cast, but it's extremely faithful. David Niven also went "downstairs" once, playing Godfrey in a 1957 remake of our first entry.

The Remains of the Day (1993, U.S., 134 mins.) Dir: James Ivory; Cast: Anthony Hopkins, Emma Thompson, Christopher Reeve, James Fox.

Though Hopkins is quite good here as a perfect butler who surrenders his entire life to a beneficent, yet pliantly fascist, master in pre-World War II England, this film is in many ways a step backward for Merchant-Ivory after their triumph with *Howards End*. Since restraint and emotions both undisplayed and unspoken are the point, not much happens to the characters, so the set design steps in to provide something to watch. A visually beautiful, if unimaginative, film with fine performances and poor pacing.

The Servant (1963, Great Britain, 115 mins., b/w) Dir: Joseph Losey; Cast: Dirk Bogarde, Sarah Miles, James Fox, Wendy Craig.

Talk about a servant in control. Bogarde stands out as the evil butler who

takes over his employer's life in this chilling film written by Harold Pinter.

The Maids (1975, Great Britain, 95 mins.) Dir: Christopher Miles; Cast: Glenda Jackson, Susannah York, Vivien Merchant.

Jean Genet's play is not a classic for the ages, but Jackson and York as two disgruntled maids are fun to watch.

Sunset Boulevard (1950, U.S., 110 mins., b/w) Dir: Billy Wilder; Cast: Gloria Swanson, William Holden, Erich von Stroheim, Nancy Olson, Jack Webb, Cecil B. DeMille, Hedda Hopper, Buster Keaton, Fred Clark.

Billy Wilder's flawless film about a forgotten silent-picture star and the young writer she keeps. Von Stroheim's performance as the butler established the archetype of the menacing Teutonic servant and it's one of the dozens of reasons to see this film.

Arthur (1981, U.S., 97 mins.) Dir: Steve Gordon; Cast: Dudley Moore, Liza Minnelli, John Gielgud, Geraldine Fitzgerald, Jill Eikenberry, Stephen Elliott.

Gielgud won the Best Supporting Actor Oscar for his role as faithful and caustic valet to Moore's drunkard millionaire. There's a hysterical scene with another servant that will not be spoiled by the telling here, but know that it's consistent in taste with a comedy about an alcoholic.

Diary of a Chambermaid (1964, France-Italy, 97 mins., b/w) Dir: Luis Buñuel; Cast: Jeanne Moreau, Michel Piccoli, Georges Geret, Françoise Lugagne.

Jeanne Moreau stars as a Parisian maid pulled into the political and sexual perversions of her new provincial employers. Buñuel's political remake has a much greater impact than Renoir's sedate original. The evil current of fascism runs throughout and it's as valuable, and compelling, now as it was 30 years ago.

Gone With the Wind (1939, U.S., 219 mins.) Dir: Victor Fleming; Cast: Clark Gable, Vivien Leigh, Leslie Howard, Olivia de Havilland, Hattie McDaniel, Butterfly McQueen, Thomas Mitchell, Ona Munson, Ann Rutherford, Evelyn Keyes, George Reeves, Laura Hope Crews.

Though it is stretching things to call slaves servants, it's fair to say that Hattie McDaniel as Mammy is the most memorable film maid ever. She was named Best Supporting Actress for her performance, and Butterfly McQueen's famous scene is a classic, too.

Imitation of Life (1959, U.S., 124 mins.) Dir: Douglas Sirk; Cast: Lana Turner, John Gavin, Sandra Dee, Dan O'Herlihy, Susan Kohner, Juanita Moore, Troy Donahue, Robert Alda.

Melodrama of the highest order, with Turner as a driven actress and Moore as her kindly maid. Sirk turns what could have been pure soap into brilliance. Don't bother with the 1934 version, in which Louise Beavers as the maid is forced to appear grateful that boss Claudette Colbert makes tons of money by ripping off her pancake recipe.

The Fallen Idol (1948, Great Britain, 94 mins., b/w) Dir: Carol Reed; Cast: Ralph Richardson, Michele Morgan, Bobby Henrey.

A terrific thriller about a little boy whose love for his butler friend leads to the man being suspected of murder. Richardson is top-notch as the butler and for once a child actor behaves like a child. The thrills keep going until the final seconds. A must.

CAB FARE

Are all cabbies required to be just a bit, well, unusual? Before this devolves into a stand-up routine, be assured that cabbies have provided movies with some of their most memorable characters. Hail one of these on a rainy night.

Taxi Driver (1976, U.S., 112 mins.) Dir: Martin Scorsese; Cast: Robert De Niro, Cybill Shepherd, Jodie Foster, Peter Boyle, Albert Brooks, Leonard Harris.

De Niro and Scorsese team up for this violent tale of a deranged cabbie. A thoroughly unpleasant, harrowing, and brilliant film. Share this cab with someone.

Taxi (1953, U.S., 77 mins., b/w) Dir: Gregory Ratoff; Cast: Dan Dailey, Constance Smith, Neva Patterson, Blanche Yurka, Stubby Kaye.

John Cassavetes makes his first film appearance in this light comedy about a taxi driver trying to help a woman find her husband on the streets of New York.

Midnight (1939, U.S., 94 mins., b/w) Dir: Mitchell Leisen; Cast: Claudette Colbert, Don Ameche, John Barrymore, Mary Astor, Francis Lederer.
■ A charming eclair of a film with Colbert as a down-on-her-luck American passing herself off as Hungarian royalty and Ameche as the Parisian cab driver who loves her. The ending doesn't quite work, but who cares—the wit and romance of writers Billy Wilder and Charles Brackett and Barrymore's superb performance conquer all.

Scrooged (1988, U.S., 101 mins.) Dir: Richard Donner; Cast: Bill Murray, Karen Allen, Bobcat Goldthwait, Carol Kane, David Johansen, Robert Mitchum, John Forsythe.

Buster Poindexter, aka David Johansen, former cross-dressing lead singer of the New York Dolls, plays a metaphysical cabbie who ferries Murray back and forth through time in this updating of Charles Dickens's *A Christmas Carol*.

Night on Earth (1991, U.S., 125 mins.) Dir: Jim Jarmusch; Cast: Winona Ryder, Gena Rowlands, Giancarlo Esposito, Armin Mueller-Stahl, Rosie Perez, Beatrice Dalle.

Jim Jarmusch takes us on cab rides through five different places on earth. Typical Jarmusch, torn between pretension and an infectious, good-natured humor. Don't quit after the first episode in L.A.; New York and Rome are the best and well worth the watch.

The Yellow Cab Man (1950, U.S., 85 mins., b/w) Dir: Jack Donohue; Cast: Red Skelton, Gloria De Haven, Walter Slezak.

Cabbie Red Skelton invents an unbreakable glass and sleazy businessmen go after him. The concept is dated—ever hear of Plexiglas?—but Red does his part toward extending the film's appeal beyond the velvet-painting crowd.

Taxi! (1932, U.S., 70 mins., b/w) Dir: Roy Del Ruth; Cast: James Cagney, Loretta Young, George E. Stone.
Rival hacks take their battle to New York's streets. Cagney stars as a feisty cabbie in this Depression-era action film.

Taxi Blues (1990, U.S.S.R.-France, 110 mins.) Dir: Pavel Lounguine; Cast: Piotr Mamonov, Piotr Zaitchenko, Vladimir Kachpour, Natalia Koliakanova, Hal Singer, Elena Saphonova.

Another international cabbie film, this time in Moscow, that follows the relationship between an old-line Russian cabdriver and a Jewish musician. Lounguine was named Best Director at Cannes for this, so think art film.

Love in a Taxi (1980, U.S., 90 mins.) Dir: Robert Sickinger; Cast: Diane Sommerfield, James H. Jacobs, Earl Monroe, Malik Murray, Lisa Jane Persky.

A Jewish cabbie falls for a black sales-clerk in this sweet, small film that takes place in New York. Look for former basketball star Earl "The Pearl" Monroe.

FARMERS

Acre after acre of swaying wheat. Cobs of fresh sweet corn and the earthy smell of old Bessie the cow. Sometimes the idea of pulling up stakes and working the land seems like the best solution to the frustrations of modern life. Before you commit to waking up at 4:30 every morning to milk Bessie, however, watch a few of these movies. You might decide to settle for a vegetable garden in the yard.

The Egg and I (1947, U.S., 108 mins., b/w) Dir: Chester Erskine; Cast: Claudette Colbert, Fred MacMurray, Marjorie Main, Louise Allbritton.

City mouse Colbert and husband MacMurray try to realize his dream of running a successful chicken farm. An ancestor of *Green Acres,* this has loads of corny humor and marks the screen debut of Ma and Pa Kettle.

The Tree of Wooden Clogs (1978, Italy, 186 mins.) Dir: Ermanno Olmi; Cast: Luigi Ornaghi, Francesca Moriggi, Omar Brignoli.

One of the best movies ever made. A chronicle of the everyday struggles and miracles of a farming community in turn-of-the-century northern Italy. Real citizens of the Bergamo area do the acting; they give freshness to even the smallest scene and contribute to the constant sense of wonder the film creates.

Places in the Heart (1984, U.S., 110 mins.) Dir: Robert Benton; Cast: Sally Field, Lindsay Crouse, Ed Harris, Amy Madigan, John Malkovich, Danny Glover.

John Malkovich's performance as a blind man steals this film about a young widow raising cotton in Depression-era Texas. Field won her second Best Actress Oscar for her work here and the film succeeds despite its Hollywood slickness.

God's Little Acre (1958, U.S., 110 mins., b/w) Dir: Anthony Mann; Cast: Robert Ryan, Aldo Ray, Tina Louise.

A campy potboiler based on Erskine Caldwell's novel of lust and greed among a family of poor Georgia farmers. What can you say about a movie that co-stars Buddy Hackett and Jack Lord, features Michael Landon as an albino, and introduces Tina Louise to the world? Any one of the above would earn it a place on this list, but all three, well . . .

Days of Heaven (1978, U.S., 95 mins.) Dir: Terrence Malick; Cast: Richard Gere, Brooke Adams, Linda Manz, Sam Shepard, Robert Wilke.

Arguably the most visually beautiful film, period. Nestor Almendros shot this tale of a tragic love triangle between two migrants and the owner of the farm they're working. The remarkable images complement the rich biblical resonances Malick weaves throughout. Please come back Terrence Malick, wherever you are.

Country (1984, U.S., 108 mins.) Dir: Richard Pierce; Cast: Jessica Lange, Wilford Brimley, Sam Shepard, Matt Clark.

Jessica Lange and boyfriend Sam Shepard star as modern farmers pushed to ruin by the withdrawal of a government loan. A solid, unromantic view of farming the way it really is now.

State Fair (1945, U.S., 100 mins.) Dir: Walter Lang; Cast: Jeanne Crain, Dana Andrews, Dick Haymes, Vivian Blaine, Charles Winninger, Fay Bainter, Donald Meek.

There have been three versions of this story of a farm family in search of love and blue ribbons at the Iowa State Fair. You want the one from 1945 with Jeanne Crain, Dana Andrews, and the Rogers and Hammerstein score. Somehow they packed everything good about American farm life into 100 minutes. Beware the 1962 version starring Pat Boone—need we explain?

Jean de Florette (1986, France, 122 mins.) Dir: Claude Berri; Cast: Yves Montand, Gerard Depardieu, Daniel Auteuil.

Manon of the Spring (1986, France, 113 mins.) Dir: Claude Berri; Cast: Yves Montand, Daniel Auteuil, Emmanuelle Béart.

The first film begins Claude Berri's adaptation of Marcel Pagnol's tale of an avaricious uncle and nephew who conspire to drive out their neighbor, a city dweller new to farming, so they can buy his land. *Manon* picks up the story years later, as the farmer's daughter plots her revenge. Yves Montand caps his career with these performances.

The Field (1990, Ireland, 110 mins.) Dir: Jim Sheridan; Cast: Richard Harris, John Hurt, Tom Berenger, Sean Bean, Francis Tomelty, Brenda Fricker.

Richard Harris towers above everyone else here, starring as an Irish farmer driven mad by the sale of land he's cultivated into valuable property.

Of Mice and Men (1992, U.S., 110 mins.) Dir: Gary Sinise; Cast: John Malkovich, Gary Sinise, Alexis Arquette, Sherilyn Fenn, Joe Morton, Ray Walston.

Like *State Fair,* there are three versions of Steinbeck's tragic tale of migrant worker George and his idiot charge Lenny, but this time the choice is harder. The 1939 rendition stars Burgess Meredith and Lon Chaney, Jr. and has a better taste of the time than Gary

Sinise's 1992 version. Yet Malkovich goes all out as Lenny in the latter. Sinise's film also has a sense of the definitive to it, which some say makes it feel like classroom viewing. It's a tough call. Take Sinise and the points.

MEDICINE

DOCTOR, DOCTOR

The ability to save lives gives doctors an unusual power and also makes them very interesting to Hollywood. Though most medical movies deal with specific ailments and let the patients have all the really good scenes, there have been films that look more closely at doctors themselves. Here are several memorable doctors, and they all make house calls.

Doctor in the House (1954, Great Britain, 92 mins.) Dir: Ralph Thomas; Cast: Kay Kendall, Dirk Bogarde.

Hysterical English romp about a group of medical students in the fifties. Always good-natured and bright, with some truly funny moments. Comparing this to the recent med-student film *Gross Anatomy* shows you just how seriously Hollywood takes itself now.

Awakenings (1990, U.S., 121 mins.) Dir: Penny Marshall; Cast: Robert De Niro, Robin Williams, Julie Kavner, Ruth Nelson, Penelope Ann Miller, John Heard, Anne Meara, Judith Malina, Richard Libertini, Dexter Gordon, Max von Sydow.

Good movie based on the great book about a doctor reviving patients frozen for decades by a Parkinson's-related illness. Though Hollywood has taken its usual liberties, the story is factual. The too-good-to-be-true Dr. Oliver Sacks really exists and Robin Williams captures the essence of this brilliant, idiosyncratic man who questions the value of his work when the experiment begins to show signs of failure.

Dr. Jekyll and Mr. Hyde (1932, U.S., 99 mins., b/w) Dir: Rouben Mamoulian; Cast: Fredric March, Miriam Hopkins, Rose Hobart.

Robert Louis Stevenson's famous tale of medical genius of more evil bent has been done a few times, but this is the one you want. Whereas most other adaptations view the story as a vague battle between good and bad, March and Mamoulian take a psychosexual approach to it all, emphasizing the specifics of Jekyll's motivations and dark side. The whipping scene makes clear the relationship they're drawing to Victorian sexuality and erotica.

Dead Ringers (1988, Canada, 113 mins.) Dir: David Cronenberg; Cast: Jeremy Irons, Genevieve Bujold, Heidi von Palleske.

We promise this chilling story about perverse twins who become gynecologists is the last depraved doctor film on the list. Jeremy Irons's tour de force performance as both twins makes it a must, though. You may have heard how disgusting this film is, with strange tools and all, but the fact is that while it will certainly make you uncomfortable, it's not visually graphic.

M*A*S*H (1970, U.S., 116 mins.) Dir: Robert Altman; Cast: Donald Sutherland, Elliott Gould, Tom Skerritt, Sally Kellerman, Robert Duvall, Jo Ann Pflug, Gary Burghoff.

Back to comedy with Altman's classic about a mobile surgical unit during the Korean War. Now that all 53,000 episodes of the TV show have dulled your memory of the film, take another look. The film has none of the sappiness of the television version. It's mean and sharp and doesn't care if it wins an Emmy.

Fantastic Voyage (1966, U.S., 100 mins.) Dir: Richard Fleischer; Cast: Stephen Boyd, Arthur Kennedy, Raquel Welch, Donald Pleasence.

The tiniest doctors ever pile aboard an inner-spaceship and cruise around the innards of an important scientist. Thrill as they pass the dreaded eardrum to battle the ferocious antibodies! Neato fun and great special effects.

The Doctor (1991, U.S., 125 mins.) Dir: Randa Haines; Cast: William Hurt, Christine Lahti, Elizabeth Perkins, Mandy Patinkin, Adam Arkin, Charlie Korsmo.

A hotshot doctor learns he has cancer and finds out just how awful doctors can be. Pretentious and ponderous at times with the standard brave and annoying dying-woman theme added in, but valuable for showing how far we've come from the friendly old doc who takes your doll's temperature.

The Hospital (1971, U.S., 103 mins.) Dir: Arthur Hiller; Cast: George C. Scott, Diana Rigg, Richard Dysart, Barnard Hughes.

Paddy Chayevsky won an Oscar for the screenplay of this black comedy about a disillusioned doctor at a chaotic urban hospital. Like M*A*S*H, despite all the laughs, it's not a happy film. Scott's performance rates as one of his best.

Not as a Stranger (1955, U.S., 135 mins., b/w) Dir: Stanley Kramer; Cast: Olivia de Havilland, Frank Sinatra, Robert Mitchum, Charles Bickford, Gloria Grahame, Lee Marvin.

The great cast makes sure that Kramer's first directorial outing is a successful one. Mitchum is a devoted med student who marries plain nurse de Havilland so she can support him through school. Could have been a fairly standard melodrama, but the curves keep coming so quickly that you're always interested. And boy, did those doctors smoke! Even Kramer makes a joke about it here.

House Calls (1978, U.S., 96 mins.) Dir: Howard Zieff; Cast: Walter Matthau, Glenda Jackson, Richard Benjamin, Art Carney.

A snappy comedy featuring Matthau as a swinging widower/doctor courting the very English and very tough Glenda Jackson. The repartee between the two is priceless, as is Carney in a supporting role.

The Citadel (1938, Great Britain, 113 mins., b/w) Dir: King Vidor; Cast: Robert Donat, Rosalind Russell, Rex Harrison, Ralph Richardson.

Broke doctor Donat sells out his principles and everyone around him by shifting his practice to serve rich, and none too sick, patients. Top-notch adaptation of A. J. Cronin's novel has renewed resonance in these days of the health-care crisis.

Article 99 (1992, U.S., 99 mins.) Dir: Howard Deutch; Cast: Ray Liotta, Kiefer Sutherland, Forest Whitaker, Lea Thompson, John C. McGinley, John Mahoney, Keith David, Kathy Baker, Eli Wallach.

Sutherland's a slick young doctor at a VA hospital where he encounters an all but impenetrable bureaucracy and a surgeon named Sturges who's willing to fight the system. While the film never captures the anarchic quality of the original M*A*S*H, and Liotta seems determined to undermine every comic moment in the script, director Deutch turns the piece into an impassioned plea for justice and veterans' rights, building to a powerful, emotionally affecting conclusion. And Wallach's turn as a dying old soldier is, in itself, worth the price of a rental.

DISEASES

The golden age of the TV Movie of the Week was a festival of disease. People were dropping like flies in particularly pathetic ways so often that the value of a good tearjerker plummeted. Sorry, but John Travolta as *The Boy in the Plastic Bubble* doesn't stack up against the kind of powerful experience that intelligent, well-acted films like the following can provide.

Panic in the Streets (1950, U.S., 96 mins., b/w) Dir: Elia Kazan; Cast: Richard Widmark, Jack Palance, Paul Douglas, Barbara Bel Geddes, Zero Mostel.

Richard Widmark is a military doctor who must hunt down a gangster carrying the bubonic plague. One of Kazan's favorite films, it's a tense search through New Orleans against the clock. A classic thriller.

My Left Foot (1989, Ireland, 103 mins.) Dir: Jim Sheridan; Cast: Daniel Day-Lewis, Brenda Fricker, Ray McAnally, Hugh O'Conor, Fiona Shaw.

A brilliant film about Irish writer and painter Christy Brown, who suffered from cerebral palsy. Daniel Day-Lewis won an Oscar as much for the contortions he put himself through for this demanding role as for his acting. What saves the film from being a typical against-all-odds sort of thing is that Christy is an immensely complex and believable character. Brenda Fricker also won an Oscar for her role as Brown's heroic mother.

Sister Kenny (1946, U.S., 116 mins., b/w) Dir: Dudley Nichols; Cast: Ros-alind Russell, Alexander Knox, Philip Merivale, Dean Jagger.

Mary McCarthy co-wrote the script for this biography of the Australian nurse who pushed for the treatment of polio. Rosalind Russell was nominated for Best Actress for her performance in this intelligent, moving film.

Longtime Companion (1990, U.S., 96 mins.) Dir: Norman Rene; Cast: Bruce Davison, Campbell Scott, Stephen Caffrey, Mark Lamos, Patrick Cassidy, Mary-Louise Parker, Dermot Mulroney, Michael Schoeffling.

The best movies and plays about AIDS came very early in the crisis, years before red ribbons could substitute for thought, compassion, and action. This film focuses on a group of gay friends in New York City and follows them from rumors of the virus in the early eighties to its devastation of the gay community only a few years later.

Dark Victory (1939, U.S., 106 mins., b/w) Dir: Edmund Goulding; Cast: Bette Davis, George Brent, Humphrey Bogart, Geraldine Fitzgerald, Ronald Reagan, Henry Travers.

Bette Davis is so high-strung in this film about a young socialite dying of brain cancer that she's almost visibly vibrating. A classic tearjerker, though, with a stately, unforgettable ending.

A Matter of WHO (1961, Great Britain, 90 mins., b/w) Dir: Don Chaffey; Cast: Terry-Thomas, Alex Nicol, Sonja Zie-mann, Honor Blackman.

A little comic relief. Terry-Thomas stars as an officer of the World Health Organization searching for someone carrying a deadly disease. If you go for Thomas's English-style humor, this could be for you.

Dr. Ehrlich's Magic Bullet (1940, U.S., 103 mins., b/w) Dir: William Dieterle; Cast: Edward G. Robinson, Ruth Gordon, Donald Crisp, Maria Ouspenskaya, Otto Kruger.

Edward G. Robinson as Dr. Ehrlich and an intelligent script co-written by John Huston make this story of the search for a cure to venereal disease a lot more interesting than you'd ever guess.

Terms of Endearment (1983, U.S., 132 mins.) Dir: James L. Brooks; Cast: Shirley MacLaine, Jack Nicholson, Debra Winger, Danny DeVito, Jeff Daniels, John Lithgow.

James Brooks made quite a nice start as a screenwriter and a director with this comedy turned soaper about a mother and daughter over 30 years. The film won Best Picture and Best Adapted Screenplay from Larry McMurtry's book, as well as Oscars for Shirley MacLaine and Jack Nicholson. What really gets the tears going is Winger's fatal battle with cancer.

The Elephant Man (1980, U.S., 125 mins., b/w) Dir: David Lynch; Cast: John Hurt, Anne Bancroft, Anthony Hopkins, Freddie Jones, Wendy Hiller.

The one film that merges David Lynch's dark vision with his strange innocence. Cribbing liberally from Tod Browning's *Freaks*, Lynch creates a nightmarish black-and-white fantasy about John Merrick, horrifyingly disfigured by a disease, and the doctor who profited personally from hospitalizing him and improving his life. Haunting and beautiful. John Hurt, burdened by makeup, will bring you to tears with his performance as the smart, yet childlike, Merrick.

Ikiru (1952, Japan, 143 mins., b/w) Dir: Akira Kurosawa; Cast: Takashi Shimura, Nabuo Kaneko, Kyoko Seki, Miki Odagiri.

There are thousands of sad movies, but this movie is so sad, so wrenching, that watching it is actually a cathartic experience. Bureaucrat Shimura learns he has stomach cancer and tries to figure out what to do with the six months remaining in his life. A very carefully crafted film, with composed shots and wonderful performances melded with overwhelming emotion. No other film has ever caught the impulse to life that imminent death brings. If you can understand where Mr. Watanabe goes, this film can take you beyond the depression of this earth and into the joy of the ineffable.

Lorenzo's Oil (1992, U.S., 135 mins.) Dir: George Miller; Cast: Nick Nolte, Susan Sarandon, Peter Ustinov, Kathleen Wilhoite, Zack O'Malley Greenburg.

Grueling film based on the true story of Michaela and Augusto Odone, who relentlessly pursued a cure for their young son's mysterious disease in spite of long odds and opposition from the medical community. Excruciating at times, in need of cutting, and Nolte's Italian accent is baffling, but *Mad Max* director Miller keeps you watching with his distinctive camerawork and an even-handed take on the complex characters.

BLINDNESS

To an art form based on visual images, blindness is the worst possible tragedy and the source of great stories. To performers, it's an opportunity for some serious acting. Here's a selection of memorable movies that should keep you from taking for granted the fact that you're watching them.

The Miracle Worker (1962, U.S., 107 mins.) Dir: Arthur Penn; Cast: Anne Bancroft, Patty Duke, Victor Jory, Inga Swenson.

Patty Duke stars as the young Helen Keller and Anne Bancroft as her teacher Annie Sullivan in this tough, moving film about bringing a blind, deaf, and mute girl out of her silent, dark world. Both Bancroft and Duke won Oscars for their performances. No soppiness here, no pathos, so the triumphant ending really has an impact. A film that gets better and better.

The Light That Failed (1939, U.S., 97 mins., b/w) Dir: William Wellman; Cast: Ronald Colman, Ida Lupino, Walter Huston.
■
Adaptation of Rudyard Kipling story about a painter going blind who rushes to finish a portrait of a lower-class girl he's fallen in love with. The juxtaposition of the veddy British Colman and Lupino's cockney scene-stealing gives this some real chemistry. Melodrama of the highest order.

A Patch of Blue (1965, U.S., 105 mins., b/w) Dir: Guy Green; Cast: Sidney Poitier, Elizabeth Hartman, Shelley Winters, Wallace Ford, Ivan Dixon.

Shelley Winters steals the show with an Oscar-winning performance as a bigoted woman whose blind daughter falls in love with Sidney Poitier. Obviously more controversial in its day, but it never sinks to polemic or smarm and hasn't dated like some "important" films of past decades.

Butterflies Are Free (1972, U.S., 109 mins.) Dir: Milton Katselas; Cast: Goldie Hawn, Edward Albert, Eileen Heckart, Mike Warren.

Screen version of the Broadway comic drama about a young blind man trying to get away from his overprotective mother and start his own life. Goldie Hawn skims close to the legally allowed level of perkiness as the next-door neighbor who helps him become his own man. Another terribly meaningful product of the sixties and seventies that has enough in the way of acting and, here, humor to keep it fresh.

City Lights (1931, U.S., 90 mins., b/w) Dir: Charlie Chaplin; Cast: Charlie Chaplin, Virginia Cherrill, Florence Lee.

One of Chaplin's finest films has him wooing a sweet blind girl and doing some hilarious things to help her pay the rent. A sign of Chaplin's true brilliance is that he's able to create funny scenes about her blindness that neither offend nor pander. The boxing sequence is tremendous, too.

Proof (1992, Australia, 91 mins.) Dir: Jocelyn Moorhouse; Cast: Hugo Weaving, Genevieve Picot, Russell Crowe, Heather Mitchell, Jeffrey Walker, Frank Gallacher.

A bizarre little film about a blind man who takes photographs and then hires people to describe what's in them. As much of a "blindness as metaphor" film as an examination of character, this is a fascinating discussion of trust, honesty, and friendship.

Wait Until Dark (1967, U.S., 108 mins.) Dir: Terence Young; Cast: Audrey Hepburn, Alan Arkin, Jack Weston, Richard Crenna, Efrem Zimbalist, Jr.

Best of the Blind Woman Pursued by Killers films, written by the author of *Dial M for Murder*. Hepburn received an Oscar nomination as the blind woman in question, who is terrorized by hoodlums hunting for drugs they believe are in her apartment. Mia Farrow's *See No Evil* and the recent *Jennifer 8* are of the same ilk, but start here.

On Dangerous Ground (1951, U.S., 82 mins., b/w) Dir: Nicholas Ray; Cast: Robert Ryan, Ida Lupino, Ward Bond, Ed Begley.

Gritty noir film starring Ryan as a cop who's become too tough for his own good. When he's sent upstate to solve a murder in a small town, he meets Ida Lupino, a gentle blind woman who brings him back to life. No soft edges here; it's grim stuff all the way, which makes Ryan's eventual transformation that much more meaningful.

Scent of a Woman (1992, U.S., 137 mins.) Dir: Martin Brest; Cast: Al Pacino, Chris O'Donnell, James Rebhorn, Gabrielle Anwar, Philip S. Hoffman.

Some people loved this story of a prep-school student alternately abused and mentored by the blind ex-military man he's been hired to care for. Others hated it. Two things are certain: Pacino's Oscar-winning acting job is worth seeing, and doing the tango on an empty ballroom floor isn't so hard if you know the steps.

Pride of the Marines (1945, U.S., 119 mins., b/w) Dir: Delmer Daves; Cast: John Garfield, Eleanor Parker, Dane Clark, Rosemary DeCamp, John Ridgely.
John Garfield checks in with his usual fine job in this true story of a marine blinded in battle by the Japanese. Again, like all the films on this list, it avoids the kind of maudlin sentiment that would be easy to sink to given the subject matter.

Day of the Triffids (1963, Great Britain, 93 mins.) Dir: Steve Sekely; Cast: Howard Keel, Nicole Maurey, Janette Scott, Kieron Moore.

Superb and creepy sci-fi film. A meteor shower blinds the earth's population so that carnivorous alien plants can feast on human prey, and a man whose eyes were bandaged during the sky show is the planet's only hope.

PLASTIC SURGERY

Given all the implanted breasts and collagened lips you see in movies now, it's hard to believe that there was once a time when plastic surgery was a reasonable subject matter and not just another aspect of the production. Here are 10 films to see before you make the decision about that tummy tuck or rhinoplasty.

Ash Wednesday (1973, U.S., 99 mins.) Dir: Larry Peerce; Cast: Elizabeth Taylor, Henry Fonda, Helmut Berger.

Elizabeth Taylor gets herself redone to please nasty hubby Fonda. The subject is perfect for Liz and it's played out against le monde du beautiful people of seventies Europe. It would be comedy if anyone else was the star, but you know that she's taking all of this very seriously. How they ever got the Vaseline off those lenses, we'll never know. Pair with any Pia Zadora film for a camp double feature.

Dark Passage (1947, U.S., 106 mins., b/w) Dir: Delmer Daves; Cast: Humphrey Bogart, Lauren Bacall.

Bogart escapes from prison after he's framed for a murder, then gets a new face so he can hunt down the person who sent him up the river. Interesting point-of-view start, which avoids any bad makeup tricks on pre-surgery Bogey, and the best creepy surgery scene of the whole group.

Rabid (1977, Canada, 91 mins.) Dir: David Cronenberg; Cast: Marilyn Chambers, Frank Moore, Joe Silver.

Early David Cronenberg effort has motorcycle accident victim Marilyn Chambers receiving skin grafts that turn her into a rabid, blood-sucking monster. Not much more than a gross horror flick, but you can see where Cronenberg is heading.

Johnny Handsome (1989, U.S., 95 mins.) Dir: Walter Hill; Cast: Mickey Rourke, Ellen Barkin, Forest Whitaker, Elizabeth McGovern, Lance Henrickson, Morgan Freeman.

Genetically disfigured criminal Rourke gets a new face from the prison's plastic surgeon (Louisiana is a very enlightened state), then tries to set up the two accomplices who double-crossed him and killed his buddy. An odd film, with some good performances. Imagine if surgery to make you look like Mickey Rourke was available in France.

Circus of Horrors (1960, Great Britain, 89 mins.) Dir: Sidney Hayers; Cast: Anton Diffring, Erica Remberg, Donald Pleasence.

Solid British horror flick about an evil plastic surgeon and his nurse who run a circus full of former patients in order to escape one who was not too happy with the doctor's work.

Seconds (1966, U.S., 106 mins., b/w) Dir: John Frankenheimer; Cast: Rock Hudson, Salome Jens, John Randolph, Jeff Corey, Murray Hamilton, Will Geer.
A supremely eerie and terrific film about a middle-aged man who is transformed into a new and enviable form. Camerawork by James Wong Howe and gritty direction by Frankenheimer give this all a quasi-documentary feel and presage the currently stylish handheld shots. Even at its happiest moments, the terror and suspense of a completely new life chew at the edges.

Darkman (1990, U.S., 95 mins.) Dir: Sam Raimi; Cast: Liam Neeson, Frances McDormand, Larry Drake.

Excellent comic-book-type revenge film with Neeson as a scientist blown up by bad guys just as he's about to perfect a way to create new body parts. Now brutally disfigured, he uses his new technology on himself to get even. Good and gory, with *Phantom of the Opera* overtones and an enviable knack for knowing just when to place its tongue in its cheek and when not to.

Tomorrow Is Forever (1946, U.S., 105 mins., b/w) Dir: Irving Pichel; Cast: Claudette Colbert, Orson Welles, George Brent, Lucille Watson, Richard Long, Natalie Wood.

Welles is injured and thought dead in the first war, so wife Colbert goes on with her life. He returns with a new face on the brink of the second, and she has a new family. The political speeches are dated, but the scenes with Welles and Colbert are gold.

The Girl Most Likely to . . . (1973, U.S., 74 mins.) Dir: Lee Philips; Cast: Stockard Channing, Edward Asner, Warren Berlinger, Jim Backus, Fred Grandy.

Joan Rivers co-wrote this black comedy about an unattractive woman who has plastic surgery and then proceeds to exact revenge on all the men who were mean to her before. Major early role for Channing.

Death Becomes Her (1992, U.S., 104 mins.) Dir: Robert Zemeckis; Cast: Meryl Streep, Goldie Hawn, Bruce Willis, Isabella Rossellini, Ian Ogilvy.

Lifelong rivals Streep and Hawn both use some very radical procedures to make themselves look younger. A playful, cheerfully disgusting comedy with fabulous special effects.

YOU MUST REMEMBER THIS

Shell shock can do it. A good thwack on the head with an Indian club can do it. All sorts of things can make you lose your memory. If you have a vague memory of seeing any of these films, take a look at your birth certificate just to make sure you really are who you think you are. Maybe you saw them in another life.

Random Harvest (1942, U.S., 124 mins., b/w) Dir: Mervyn LeRoy; Cast: Ronald Colman, Greer Garson, Susan Peters, Philip Dorn.

Forties melodrama of the highest order. World War I soldier Colman loses his memory because of a battlefield injury and actress Garson helps him create a new life. That's only the first half. Contrived, manipulative, and enormously entertaining, as all great tearjerkers are.

Mirage (1965, U.S., 109 mins., b/w) Dir: Edward Dmytryk; Cast: Gregory Peck, Diane Baker, Walter Matthau.

Gregory Peck wakes up one day and finds out that he doesn't exist anymore. For much of the way the film can't decide if it's ripping off Kafka or Hitchcock, but by the end it's definitely Hitch who receives the sincerest form of flattery. Even so, it's fun in a *Twilight Zone* sort of way and the off-center Walter Matthau balances Peck, who, after Pat Boone, is the world's whitest man.

Spellbound (1945, U.S., 111 mins., b/w) Dir: Alfred Hitchcock; Cast: Gregory Peck, Ingrid Bergman, Michael Chekhov, Leo G. Carroll, Wallace Ford, John Emery, Rhonda Fleming, Regis Toomey.

All right, if you're going to split hairs, this should go on the "On the Couch" list or next to *Marnie,* on the "Over the Edge" list, but all of Gregory Peck's hunting around in his memory for the clues to his past gives it an equal kinship to these amnesia films. In fact, the amnesia aspects work better than the amateur Freud that Hitchcock was so fond of promulgating.

Anastasia (1956, U.S., 105 mins.) Dir: Anatole Litvak; Cast: Ingrid Bergman, Yul Brynner, Helen Hayes.

Bergman won an Oscar for her performance as an amnesiac who claims to be Anastasia, the daughter of Tsar Nicholas II and only survivor of the Bolshevik massacre of the Romanoffs. Is she being used to get to the tsar's riches, or could she really be . . . ? Grand, stylish entertainment.

Regarding Henry (1991, U.S., 107 mins.) Dir: Mike Nichols; Cast: Harrison Ford, Annette Bening, Bill Nunn, Mikki Allen, Donald Moffat, Nancy Marchand.

Nasty lawyer Ford sustains brain damage when he's shot during a robbery, has no memory of who he is, and turns into a nice guy. A slick film with some definite Capraesque social overtones about trying to forget those greedy Reagan years.

Overboard (1987, U.S., 112 mins.) Dir: Garry Marshall; Cast: Goldie Hawn, Kurt Russell, Edward Herrman, Katherine Helmond.

This successful eighties attempt at screwball comedy has rich woman Hawn falling off her yacht and suffering amnesia. Russell, a carpenter, picks her up at the hospital, claiming that she's his wife and mother of his bratty kids. Let's face it, with Hawn and Russell you're not expecting wonders, but this one works well enough for a rental.

Desperately Seeking Susan (1985, U.S., 104 mins.) Dir: Susan Seidelman; Cast: Rosanna Arquette, Madonna, Aidan Quinn, Laurie Metcalf, Richard Hell, Ann Magnuson, John Lurie, Steven Wright, John Turturro.

This enjoyable comedy follows a suburban housewife's growing obsession with a Downtown woman (played by Madonna, of course) whom she reads about in the personal ads. After a conk on the noggin, the housewife begins to take over Madonna's life. A very talented cast, a look at some genuine mid-eighties New York bohemia, and lots of Madonna when she really *was* sexy.

As You Desire Me (1931, U.S., 71 mins., b/w) Dir: George Fitzmaurice; Cast: Greta Garbo, Melvyn Douglas, Erich von Stroheim, Owen Moore, Hedda Hopper.

Garbo stars in this sometimes creaky adaptation of Pirandello's play about a flamboyant singer who allows herself to be convinced that she is actually the wife of a wealthy count. As usual, Garbo acts up in a big way, but the real story is von Stroheim as the man she leaves. His performance is sort of proto-method; he doesn't waste a single moment he's on film. If he's not speaking, he's doing something—a facial expression, a fidget—something that further builds his character.

ON THE COUCH

If you've ever known someone whose mother or father was a psychiatrist, you know that there's a good chance the person sitting in the chair taking notes while you're on the couch is probably crazier than you are. This has clearly dawned on Hollywood, too. Here are some of the best movie psychiatrists, most of whom could use a little help themselves.

Freud (1962, U.S., 139 mins., b/w) Dir: John Huston; Cast: Montgomery Clift, Susannah York, Susan Kohner, David McCallum, Larry Parks.
Whether or not people in the 21st century will chuckle about Freud the way we do about Mesmer is beside the point. You have to admire Montgomery Clift as a seriously on-the-brink Freud. His intensity fuels Huston's sensible depiction of a powerful theory in the process of being created by a very fallible man. Huston is on Freud's side, but he's not adoring. Worth a watch, no matter where you stand.

Lilith (1964, U.S., 114 mins., b/w) Dir: Robert Rossen; Cast: Warren Beatty, Jean Seberg, Peter Fonda, Kim Hunter, Gene Hackman.

Beatty plays a young doctor at an institution who has an affair with patient Seberg. This turgid, moody relic of the 1960s has its following and it is compelling at times, but it smacks too often of a college sophomore's idea of high romance to make much of a statement about the mind or psychotherapy. Peter Fonda steals every scene he's in.

The President's Analyst (1967, U.S., 104 mins.) Dir: Theodore J. Flicker; Cast: James Coburn, Godfrey Cambridge.

One of Second City's unheralded founders, Theodore J. Flicker, wrote and directed this black comedy about a psychiatrist who is hunted by just about every intelligence agency in the world because he knows all the president's dark secrets. Excessive, violent, absurd, and hysterical. Another 1960s relic, but brilliant. Where *Lilith* invites unintentional laughs by taking the whole sixties thing very seriously, Flicker knew the decade was funny while it was going on.

On a Clear Day You Can See Forever (1970, U.S., 129 mins.) Dir: Vincente Minnelli; Cast: Barbra Streisand, Yves Montand, Jack Nicholson, Bob Newhart.

First off, what an outfit Streisand's wearing in the early scenes! Since this isn't much more than a two-hour *Vogue* layout with music, it's an appropriate observation. The absurd story is that psychiatrist Montand hypnotizes Barbra, who was some sexy psychic tart in Regency England, and then falls in love with the regressed Babs. Her voice, like butter. Her acting? Who cares? Montand's got a nice voice too, but he was not meant to sing in English. A curiosity of a film whose charm depends on how much you like Scaasi.

The Prince of Tides (1991, U.S., 132 mins.) Dir: Barbra Streisand; Cast: Nick Nolte, Barbra Streisand, Blythe Danner, Kate Nelligan, Melinda Dillon, George Carlin, Jason Gould.

This time Streisand plays the shrink who behaves inappropriately in her one-woman adaptation of Pat Conroy's novel about a man finding himself by helping his sister's doctor reconstruct their family history. No shrink has ever had an office that looked like hers, and not many have legs like that either. Not a classic movie, but it draws you in enough to warrant a viewing.

What's New, Pussycat? (1965, U.S.-France, 108 mins.) Dir: Clive Donner; Cast: Peter Sellers, Peter O'Toole, Woody Allen, Romy Schneider, Ursula Andress, Paula Prentiss, Capucine.

Boy, did they ever love psychiatrists in those wacky 1960s. From the moment you hear Tom Jones singing and see Peter Sellers's velvet suit, you know you're in for something, though it's hard to say what that something actually is. We know these things for sure: it is Woody Allen's first screenplay; it is Sellers as a crazed shrink trying to cure commitmentphobe/satyr O'Toole; and it is a mess of the most exuberant sort. Don't expect wall-to-wall laughs and you'll be pleasantly amused.

House of Games (1987, U.S., 102 mins.) Dir: David Mamet; Cast: Lindsay Crouse, Joe Mantegna, Mike Nussbaum, Lilia Skala.

This and *Things Change* are Mamet's two best film outings, and this is the one that is most in keeping with Mamet's stage style. Mamet's ex-wife Crouse plays a psychiatrist who falls in with a con man, with many surprises and deceptions resulting. Mamet elicits clipped, overenunciated performances that heighten the overall sense of unreality. Fascinating to most, cold and manipulating to a few.

High Anxiety (1977, U.S., 94 mins.) Dir: Mel Brooks; Cast: Mel Brooks, Madeline Kahn, Harvey Korman.

Not Mel Brooks's best by far, but the Hitchcock/psychiatrist connection is astute and it has its moments. Brooks stars as the new head of an institution run by an evil staff. An admiring send-up of Hitchcock is worth any number of DePalma rip-offs.

What About Bob? (1991, U.S., 97 mins.) Dir: Frank Oz; Cast: Bill Murray, Richard Dreyfuss, Julie Hagerty, Charlie Korsmo, Kathryn Erbe, Tom Aldredge, Susan Willis.

Though the movie loses speed when it turns away from Murray, Dreyfuss plays the kind of pompous, self-involved shrink that's most common in the real world. You'll either get this or not, but if you don't think Murray is great in this comedy of a nut who follows his doctor on vacation, maybe you should consider counseling.

OVER THE EDGE

The movies are full of crazed slashers and mad doctors digging up bodies, but that's not the kind of insanity we're concerned with here. This list looks at Hollywood's serious attempts to treat the multifaceted issue of mental illness.

Gaslight (1944, U.S., 114 mins., b/w) Dir: George Cukor; Cast: Charles Boyer, Ingrid Bergman, Joseph Cotten, Angela Lansbury, Dame May Whitty.

You have to ask yourself why Charles Boyer is trying to drive Ingrid Bergman insane. Would *you* trade Bergman for some jewels? For saucy maid Angela Lansbury in her first screen role? That part doesn't make sense; still, it's grand entertainment. Some say the earlier version is better, but Bergman's scene with Boyer at the very end can't be topped.

Frances (1982, U.S., 139 mins.) Dir: Graeme Clifford; Cast: Jessica Lange,

Kim Stanley, Sam Shepard, Jeffrey DeMunn.

After her first few movies, who could be blamed for thinking that Jessica Lange was just another blonde? Then she came up with this great portrayal of actress Frances Farmer and her descent into mental illness. Lange keeps enough of an edge on Farmer that she never becomes pathetic and the film manages to do the same.

One Flew Over the Cuckoo's Nest (1975, U.S., 129 mins.) Dir: Milos Forman; Cast: Jack Nicholson, Louise Fletcher, Brad Dourif, William Redfield, Will Sampson.

Ironically, the greatest performance by someone in a movie about insanity was given by an actor portraying a character who's *not* insane. Jack Nicholson won an Oscar for his work as the criminal who fakes insanity to avoid jail and finds himself someplace even worse. Just about everyone else involved with this adaptation of Ken Kesey's novel won an Oscar, too. The best of this bunch by far.

The Snake Pit (1948, U.S., 108 mins., b/w) Dir: Anatole Litvak; Cast: Olivia de Havilland, Leo Genn, Mark Stevens, Celeste Holm, Beulah Bondi.

Unlike Lange and Nicholson, Olivia de Havilland begs for pity as a young woman suffering a nervous breakdown. Given that, the film still has some strong scenes and the depictions of the asylum's various wards are harrowing. This was about as sensitive a look at mental illness as you could get at the time.

The Three Faces of Eve (1957, U.S., 91 mins., b/w) Dir: Nunnally Johnson; Cast: Joanne Woodward, David Wayne, Lee J. Cobb, Nancy Kulp, Vince Edwards.

Another Oscar-winning lead. This time it's Joanne Woodward in the best of all multiple-personality films. Producer, director, and screenwriter Nunnally Johnson lets Woodward act, but unlike other movies on this topic, the point is her character and not her versatility as an actress.

The Prisoner of Second Avenue (1975, U.S., 99 mins.) Dir: Melvin Frank; Cast: Jack Lemmon, Anne Bancroft.

Neil Simon's play about a middle-aged New Yorker driven to a nervous breakdown is never quite sure if it's a comedy or a drama, but the laughs come as welcome relief from Jack Lemmon's intense and sometimes moving performance. At the time it was probably viewed as a midlife worst-case scenario, but nowadays it's too close for comfort. Or maybe we're all just that much older.

I Never Promised You a Rose Garden (1977, U.S., 96 mins.) Dir: Anthony Page; Cast: Bibi Andersson, Kathleen Quinlan, Ben Piazza, Lorraine Gary, Reni Santori.

Teen classic about a 16-year-old's battle with schizophrenia brought to the screen with all the gruesome details intact. Not a cheery triumph of youth by any means, it has some almost gothic scenes. You can see why kids of a certain generation gravitated to the story—it certainly puts your zits into perspective.

The Ruling Class (1971, Great Britain, 155 mins.) Dir: Peter Medak; Cast: Peter O'Toole, Alastair Sim, Harry Andrews, Arthur Lowe, Coral Browne.

An often hysterical film about a schizophrenic English lord who believes that he is Jesus Christ. Though slightly dated, somewhat stagy, and guilty of trying to make too much of a statement, it has some very funny moments and O'Toole is wonderful.

Man Facing Southeast (1987, Argentina, 105 mins.) Dir: Eliseo Subiela; Cast: Lorenzo Quinteros, Hugo Soto, Ines Vernengo.

A man suddenly appears in an Argentine asylum claiming to be an alien, and, despite the obvious doubts of the doctor he works with, he may very well be. A fine film with a vague ending that will let you debate things afterward, and though its message is nothing new, it's delivered in a fresh and measured way. Try it.

An Angel at My Table (1990, New Zealand, 150 mins.) Dir: Jane Campion; Cast: Kerry Fox, Alexian Keogh, Karen Ferguson, Iris Churn.

Re-edited version of a television series based on the autobiography of New Zealand's most famous writer, Janet Frame, whose troubled childhood and artistic nature led to her being wrongly institutionalized. The wonder is that she became an award-winning writer while in the asylum. Like most TV series packaged into films, the pacing tends to be sluggish and there are some hard-to-watch scenes early on, but Jane Campion's direction and fine acting all around make this worth your time.

Marnie (1964, U.S., 129 mins.) Dir: Alfred Hitchcock; Cast: Tippi Hedren, Sean Connery, Diane Baker, Louise Latham, Martin Gable, Bruce Dern.

Hitchcock gives a brief seminar on Freud, as Connery marries thieving Tippi Hedren and then tries to solve the mystery of why she steals. In fact, the real mystery he's trying to solve is why she won't sleep with him. The film has a kinship with *Vertigo* and *Rear Window* in its overall style and its examination of sexual deviancy. Like the other two films, the music is too rich and so are the colors, but they're irresistible. Underrated Hitchcock, if there is such a thing.

Shock Corridor (1963, U.S., 101 mins., b/w) Dir: Sam Fuller; Cast: Peter Breck, Constance Towers, Gene Evans, James Best, Hari Rhodes.

A bizarre Sam Fuller curiosity in which a journalist fakes insanity so he can go undercover into an asylum and solve the mystery of a patient's murder. What's really going on, though, is an investigation of America circa 1963, with racism, Communism, and the Bomb its main subjects. Over the top and fascinating; no other film on this list features a striptease by the main character's girlfriend.

CRIME & PUNISHMENT

THE LEGEND OF BONNIE & CLYDE

In the roaring twenties, America's most notorious criminals were bootleggers, mobsters, and syndicate bosses who held entire cities in their vise-like grip. But the coming of the Depression affected everyone, even the criminals. The best-known bandits of the thirties were reckless, colorful desperadoes—and the most colorful of all were Bonnie and Clyde. Heirs to the outlaw tradition of Jesse James and the Daltons—robbing banks, killing people, making their getaways in Model T Fords instead of on horseback—they became folk heroes. Poems were written, songs were sung, movies were made ... and remade, time and again. Only one can lay claim to biography; the rest descend from the legend.

Bonnie and Clyde (1967, U.S., 111 mins.) Dir: Arthur Penn; Cast: Warren Beatty, Faye Dunaway, Estelle Parsons, Gene Hackman, Michael J. Pollard.

Groundbreaking work of astonishing originality. Its violence is audacious and sensual; its tenderness moving. It's also very funny. Script by Robert Benton and David Newman (with uncredited help from Robert Towne) delivers the sheer storytelling that legend demands; Penn's pyrotechnics and compassion turn it into art. Beatty (he also produced) makes his non-acting style work quite well—though it's tough to think of Warren as impotent. Dunaway's Bonnie is achingly sexy, vulnerable, and extremely dangerous. Support from Hackman, Parsons (Oscar), and Pollack is superb. Based on actual accounts, it's as close as we ever get to the truth.

You Only Live Once (1937, U.S., 90 mins., b/w) Dir: Fritz Lang; Cast: Henry Fonda, Sylvia Sidney, William Gargan, Barton MacLane, Margaret Hamilton.

Lang's tragic melodrama was Hollywood's first stab at the legend. Visually dense with shadows, night, and fog, it's an expressionist masterpiece. Sidney is the most innocent of all screen Bonnies (Joan in this film) and Fonda's Clyde (here, Eddie Taylor) is a victim of fate. They rob out of necessity; killing causes them pain and stirs up spiritual torment. More outcasts than outlaws, in the Langian universe Bonnie and Clyde are two lost souls, running from the law and looking for redemption.

Gun Crazy (1949, U.S., 86 mins., b/w) Dir: Joseph H. Lewis; Cast: Peggy Cummins, John Dall, Morris Carnovsky.

John Dall and Peggy Cummins (sexiest of all B-movie femme fatales) are the gun-crazed lovers in this delirious plunge into the world of film noir. Their first encounter at a carnival shooting match is charged with eroticism and Freudian implications. Similarities to the story of Bonnie and Clyde abound, but *Gun Crazy* stands on its own. Directed with hair-trigger intensity and amazing economic invention by Lewis. More than just a cult classic, it's the undisputed king of the B's.

Guncrazy (1992, U.S., 97 mins.) Dir: Tamra Davis; Cast: Drew Barrymore, James LeGros, Billy Drago, Rodney Harvey.

Most youthful Bonnie and Clyde-like pairing, this lurid little remake of the film noir classic cherry-picks scenes and conceits from the original, then spins out in its own deadly direction. Barrymore takes her trash-queen slut persona to a new level, giving a performance that combines "duh," depth, and teenage angst. Her ex-con lover (LeGros) uses guns as a substitute for what he (like Beatty's Clyde) can't get up in bed. Novice director Davis works with a sharp eye for B-movie tawdriness and a feel for all the Bonnies and Clydes that came before.

They Live by Night (1949, U.S., 95 mins., b/w) Dir: Nicholas Ray; Cast: Farley Granger, Cathy O'Donnell, Howard da Silva, Helen Craig, Jay C. Flippen.

Adapted from Edward Anderson's novel *Thieves Like Us,* this tale of doomed lovers is plainly cut from Bonnie and Clyde cloth. That the couple is part of a gang of dust-bowl bank robbers makes them closer to the real Clyde Barrow and Bonnie Parker than their contemporaries in *Gun Crazy.* O'Donnell's Keechie (a great noir name) is a much warmer Bonnie than her cold-blooded counterpart Cummins. Granger is the sweetest, most romantic of Clydes. First time out of the box for Ray, he imbues the film with the kinetic energy and adolescent intensity that are hallmarks of his directorial style.

Thieves Like Us (1974, U.S., 123 mins., b/w) Dir: Robert Altman; Cast: Keith Carradine, Shelley Duvall, John Schuck, Louise Fletcher, Bert Remsen, Tom Skerritt.

Robert Altman's underappreciated remake of *They Live by Night* goes back to the book for its title as well as much of its dialogue. His view of the fugitive lovers, running through the back roads and backwater towns of Mississippi, is the softest, most reflective retelling of the Bonnie and Clyde story and one of Altman's loveliest films. Carradine and Duvall as the desperadoes seem genuinely, desperately, deeply in love.

Breathless (aka: *A Bout de Souffle*, 1959, France, 89 mins.) Dir: Jean-Luc Godard; Cast: Jean Seberg, Jean-Paul Belmondo, Daniel Boulanger.

Benton and Newman cite Godard's new-wave masterpiece (from a story by François Truffaut) as a direct source of inspiration and they offered the *Bonnie and Clyde* script to both French directors. Truffaut was unavailable and Godard didn't click with producers. As for *Breathless*, the film is Godard's valentine to American noir classics. If Seberg and Belmondo aren't immediately related to Bonnie Parker and Clyde Barrow, they are certainly kissing cousins.

Breathless (1983, U.S., 105 mins.) Dir: Jim McBride; Cast: Richard Gere, Valerie Kaprisky, Art Metrano.

Director Jim *(The Big Easy)* McBride's pedal-to-the-metal style brings this rock 'n' roll remix of the new-wave classic closer to the mythos of Bonnie and Clyde than Godard ever gets. Unlike Belmondo and Seberg, who spend most of their time in a Paris apartment, gun-crazy Gere and his hot-blooded girlfriend take it on the lam. Gere's ditty-bop hood wears on the nerves, and Kaprisky, though stunning

to look at, can't act at all. Still, the film is full of fancy footwork and its killer leap from the Godard title to the Jerry Lee Lewis song is a kick and a half.

The Bonnie Parker Story (1958, U.S., 80 mins., b/w) Dir: William Whitney; Cast: Dorothy Provine, Richard Bakalyan, Joseph Turkel, Jack Hogan.

Relatively obscure 1950s cheapie with Provine as pistol-packin' bank-robbin' mama sans any reference to Clyde. Lurid little melodrama has a TV look, a notch or two below an *Untouchables* episode—which is a long way from terrible. Interesting in that this so-called biopic is further from the true story than most of the others. Worth a peek if you can find it, but still, we can't help but wonder what happened to Clyde.

Badlands (1974, U.S., 95 mins.) Dir: Terrence Malick; Cast: Sissy Spacek, Martin Sheen, Warren Oates, Ramon Bieri, Alan Vint.

First-time writer/director Malick drew his inspiration from the factual case of teenagers Charles Starkweather and Caril Fugate and their interstate murder spree in the 1950s. Kit and Holly (Sheen and Spacek) are their screen incarnations; their killing is motivated by little more than the desire to escape from boredom. Even though based on entirely different real-life criminals, this extraordinary film, with its renegades-on-the-run motif, fits the Bonnie and Clyde mold. Besides, any movie that features the late, great Warren Oates needs no further recommendation.

The Getaway (1972, U.S., 122 mins.) Dir: Sam Peckinpah; Cast: Steve McQueen, Ali MacGraw, Ben Johnson, Sally Struthers.

A bank heist gone wrong and a series of double crosses serve as the springboard for McQueen and MacGraw's flight from the law. Walter Hill's script captures the brutality of Jim Thompson's novel, but Peckinpah's direction is uncharacteristically tame; the renegade lovers take too long to get where they're going. And while Sally Struthers is good as a hot, bouncy babe who can't get enough, mistreatment of women throughout makes this the most misogynistic mutation of the Bonnie and Clyde story.

Thelma and Louise (1991, U.S., 128 mins.) Dir: Ridley Scott; Cast: Susan Sarandon, Geena Davis, Harvey Keitel, Michael Madsen, Christopher McDonald, Brad Pitt, Stephen Tobolowsky, Timothy Carhart, Lucinda Jenney.

Callie Khourie's Oscar-winning script is a fatally feminist variation on the theme—the perfect response to Peckinpah. Best friends Sarandon and Davis become wanted women when one stops a man from raping the other . . . with a bullet in the chest. Their tear across the western plains has the racy rhythm and yearning undertow we associate with the Bonnie and Clyde tradition. With what they go through and how they end up, the legacy resonates with new-found relevance.

True Romance (1993, U.S., 121 mins.) Dir: Tony Scott; Cast: Christian Slater, Patricia Arquette, Dennis Hopper, Val Kilmer, Gary Oldman, Brad Pitt, Christopher Walken.

Comicbook store clerk Slater and gold-hearted hooker Arquette meet sweet, fall in love, and wind up with a satchel of skag, on the run from the mob. Written by pulp-culture junkie Quentin Tarantino, this is an X generation Bonnie and Clyde where the icons are Elvis, Sonny Chiba, and Spiderman. Cross references to other Bonnie and Clyde films abound; the Hans Zimmer score seems lifted whole-cloth from *Badlands*. Director Scott, with his ad agency sensibility, seems unable to distinguish between gritty and pretty, but the film basically works. And the supporting cast is unbelievably good.

HOT ROCK RIP-OFFS & OTHER CAPERS

. . . in which planners, schemers, dreamers, and thieves come together with the hope of scoring the big score.

Rififi (1954, France, 89 mins., b/w) Dir: Jules Dassin; Cast: Jean Servais, Carl Mohner, Magali Noel, Robert Manuel, Perlo Vita (Jules Dassin).

The title comes from French underworld slang for "trouble," with the rififi in this case revolving around a gang of thieves who come apart at the seams after pulling a jewelry store heist—a masterfully executed 25-minute sequence, rendered in almost total silence. Dassin, working in France in the wake of the Hollywood blacklist, co-wrote, directed, and acted (under the name Perlo Vita) in this low-budget bijou that became a huge international hit and a blueprint for films of the genre.

Topkapi (1964, U.S., 119 mins.) Dir: Jules Dassin; Cast: Melina Mercouri, Maximilian Schell, Robert Morley, Peter Ustinov.

Supersuave Schell and ultrachic Mercouri hatch an ingenious scheme to lift a jewel-encrusted dagger from a theft-proof case in an Istanbul museum. Morley is delightful as the eccentric inventor who figures out how to circumvent the alarm, but Ustinov's rumpled guide-hustler-historian-schmo steals the movie and copped an Oscar. Dassin borrows a trick or two from his own *Rififi*, lightens up the tone, and pulls it all off with style and wit.

Big Deal on Madonna Street (1958, Italy, 91 mins.) Dir: Mario Monicelli; Cast: Marcello Mastroianni, Vittorio Gassman, Renato Salvatori, Carla Gravina, Rossana Rory.

Gassman and Mastroianni head up a

stupefyingly inept gang of thieves plotting to rob a store. Full of hilarious slapshtick, the film is designed as a spoof of the genre but goes wider and deeper than that—we can't help caring about this motley but irresistible crew of misfits. Oscar nominated for Best Foreign Film. The sequel, *Big Deal on Madonna Street . . . 20 Years Later,* was actually made 27 years later, and the American remake, *Crackers* (1984), directed by Louis Malle, is way off the mark.

The Hot Rock (1972, U.S., 101 mins.) Dir: Peter Yates; Cast: Robert Redford, George Segal, Ron Liebman, Paul Sand, Zero Mostel.

William Goldman's adaptation of Donald Westlake's first Dortmunder novel is a Flatbush variation on the *Topkapi* theme, with the blunderbuss band of small-time thieves after a priceless diamond in the Brooklyn Museum. Redford is the beleaguered mastermind, Segal his pest of a sidekick, Liebman the wheelman with a street map for a brain, Sand the space cadet, and Mostel his lowlife lawyer dad. Yates may not be the world's most inspired director, but he brings it home; it's hard to have more fun watching a movie.

Bank Shot (1974, U.S., 83 mins.) Dir: Gower Champion; Cast: George C. Scott, Joanna Cassidy, Clifton James.

Follow-up to *The Hot Rock* with Scott as Dortmunder, this time figuring the best way to rob a bank is to get more than what's in the vault . . . a lot more. Lacks the street-smart kick of the Yates/Goldman approach, but fun nonetheless, thanks to another nifty Westlake setup.

Sneakers (1992, U.S., 125 mins.) Dir: Phil Alden Robinson; Cast: Robert Redford, Dan Aykroyd, Ben Kingsley, Mary McDonnell, River Phoenix, Sidney Poitier, David Strathairn.

Former sixties subversive Redford, currently running a high-tech private investigating agency comprised of an oddball assortment of hackers, geeks, and wizards, is forced by the feds into deploying his troops in a dubious heist with highly charged political overtones. Writer/director Phil *(Field of Dreams)* Robinson neatly blends hardware, software, characters, and plot into a cutting-edge comic caper that pays its respects to the hot-rock tradition and pays off handsomely on its own.

Gambit (1966, U.S., 108 mins.) Dir: Ronald Neame; Cast: Shirley MacLaine, Michael Caine, Herbert Lom, Roger C. Carmel, John Abbott.

Clever cockney Caine gets a Eurasian lovely, amusingly played by Shirley, to help him nab a prized statuette from the private collection of a millionaire . . . but the crime isn't nearly as perfect as it seems. The lighthearted script by Alvin Sargent and Jack Davies does a neat job crisscrossing the plot while the characters double-cross each other. Smooth, sophisticated, suspenseful fun.

The Asphalt Jungle (1950, U.S., 112 mins., b/w) Dir: John Huston; Cast: Sterling Hayden, Sam Jaffe, Marc Lawrence, Jean Hagen, Louis Calhern, James Whitmore, Marilyn Monroe.

Huston's extremely cynical film noir classic about a gang of experienced criminals who come together to pull a job. Jaffe is the brains of the outfit, Hayden the brawn. Monroe, in an early screen role, has a few hot minutes. Crime-doesn't-pay theme is explored through exceptional characterizations, each participant in the robbery evincing a tragic flaw that will do him in. Remade as a western—*The Badlanders;* an international adventure—*Cairo;* and a 1970s black action vehicle—*Cool Breeze.* From a novel by W. R. Burnett.

The Great Escape (1963, U.S., 168 mins.) Dir: John Sturges; Cast: Steve McQueen, James Garner, Charles Bronson, James Coburn, David McCallum,

Donald Pleasence, Richard Attenborough.

Genre-wise this classic WWII P.O.W. movie might not appear to belong on the list. But when you think about it, the planning and execution of the escape from the Nazi prison camp—the big "score" here is freedom, not money or jewels—is handled with the same kind of crime-prep construction and personality blending of the participants as the best caper films. And W. R. *(The Asphalt Jungle)* Burnett co-wrote the screenplay. Entertaining as all get out.

The Killing (1956, U.S., 83 mins., b/w) Dir: Stanley Kubrick; Cast: Sterling Hayden, Coleen Gray, Elisha Cook, Timothy Carey.

Early Kubrick, adapted from the novel *Clean Break* by Lionel White, is very much from the *Asphalt Jungle* school, bearing down, with a film noir camera, on a gang of hard guys who join forces for a racetrack robbery—with Hayden again playing a pivotal role. What sets this apart is the unique narrative structure that follows each character separately up to the climactic moment of the heist, then skips back in time and follows someone else. Solid performances all around, but Cook and Carey stand out.

Bob le Flambeur (1955, France, 97 mins., b/w) Dir: Jean-Pierre Melville; Cast: Roger Duchesne, Isabel Corey, Daniel Cauchy.

Exceptional film that sits on the cusp between classical French cinema and the new wave is the story of an inveterate gambler (Duchesne) who decides there are more profitable ways of working the Deauville casino than playing the tables—for instance, robbing the place. An homage to American *policiers* and crime films like *The Asphalt Jungle,* it is also a valentine to a Paris that never really existed, a city of imagination and dreams—a place where the time of day always seems to be a couple of deals before dawn. Dark, ironic, entertaining poetry from writer/director Melville. Isabel Corey adds a serious dose of petulant sensuality.

Ocean's Eleven (1960, U.S., 127 mins.) Dir: Lewis Milestone; Cast: Frank Sinatra, Dean Martin, Sammy Davis, Jr., Joey Bishop, Peter Lawford, Angie Dickinson.

Sinatra and his pack o' rats are old army buddies gathering in Vegas for a reunion with ulterior motives—they're planning to knock over four casinos on New Year's Eve. While it never approaches the poetic depth of *Bob le Flambeur* or expresses the fatalism of *The Asphalt Jungle,* the film does have a strange dark cloud hanging over it, making it more than just a slick celebrity vehicle.

Reservoir Dogs (1992, U.S., 100 mins.) Dir: Quentin Tarantino; Cast: Harvey Keitel, Tom Roth, Chris Penn, Steve Buscemi, Lawrence Tierney, Michael Madsen.

A gang of handpicked professionals in Blues Brothers suits comes together for a diamond heist. Unfortunately, one of them's a cop. Stunning, ferocious, original portrait of bonding and betrayal with the men reduced to the level of wild dogs when things go sour. Brilliantly conceived and executed on a shoestring by first-time writer/director Tarantino, who plays one of the mongrels. The relentless intensity of the violence is strangely set off by the absurd seventies pop-culture-junkie humor and detached irony of the approach. The performances cut so deep, nothing can stop the bleeding.

ORDER IN THE COURT

When Shakespeare said, "The first thing we do, let's kill all the lawyers," we think he was getting a lit-

tle out of hand. We know of many real-life lawyers who should be allowed to live—unfortunately they both live in Delaware. In the movies, however, it's a different story. Lawyers make for dynamic heroes and courtrooms are grand arenas in which sensational, gut-wrenching emotional battles are fought. The outcome often hinges on dramatic twists supplied by fate or a surprise witness, invariably manipulated for the good of all concerned by a consummately clever attorney who almost never comes from Delaware. Here are some favorites.

Young Mr. Lincoln (1939, U.S., 100 mins., b/w) Dir: John Ford; Cast: Henry Fonda, Alice Brady, Richard Cromwell, Donald Meek, Marjorie Weaver.

Ford's foray into biographical myth-making—much heavier on the myth than the bio—is built around a murder trial, which may or may not have actually happened, at which young Mr. Lawyer appears for the defense. Aside from what this extraordinarily beautiful film says about Ford's sensibility and Lincoln's place in America's memory, it makes for a whopping good courtroom drama.

Adam's Rib (1949, U.S., 101 mins., b/w) Dir: George Cukor; Cast: Spencer Tracy, Katharine Hepburn, Judy Holliday, Jean Hagen, Tom Ewell, David Wayne.

Tracy and Hepburn are married lawyers on opposite sides of a legal situation with feminist implications. Ditzy Judy Holliday, brilliant in her first major screen role, has shot her philandering slug of a husband (Ewell) and is on trial for attempted murder. One of seven screenplays written by husband-and-wife team Garson Kanin and Ruth Gordon for director Cukor progresses neatly from a chemistry-of-the-couple bedroom comedy to a battle-of-the-sexes farce where the field of conflict is

a public courtroom. Light-years ahead of its time and extremely funny to boot.

Force of Evil (1949, U.S., 78 mins., b/w) Dir: Abraham Polonsky; Cast: John Garfield, Beatrice Pearson, Thomas Gomez.

Garfield is Joe Morse, an ambitious lawyer with warped values working with the mob on a "policy" scam. The situation takes a tragic turn when Joe's brother (Gomez), a small-time numbers banker, refuses to relinquish control of his mom-and-pop-style operation to the all-encompassing syndicate. Writer/director Abraham Polonsky blends social realism and cinematic poetry to create a blistering critique of a socio-economic system in which the law can be easily bent to serve society's blood-suckers.

Knock on Any Door (1949, U.S., 100 mins., b/w) Dir: Nicholas Ray; Cast: Humphrey Bogart, John Derek, Allene Roberts.

First film produced by Bogart's company, Santana Pictures, stars Bogie as a slum-bred lawyer defending a kid with a similar background, accused of killing a cop. Impassioned plea for justice and social awareness is deepened by a surprising spin of the plot, but the impact is blunted by Ray's uncharacteristically pedestrian handling of the material.

Anatomy of a Murder (1959, U.S., 160 mins., b/w) Dir: Otto Preminger; Cast: James Stewart, Lee Remick, Ben Gazzara, Joseph Welch, Arthur O'Connell, Eve Arden, George C. Scott, Murray Hamilton.

When Lieutenant Frederick Manion (Gazzara) is hit with a murder rap for killing the bartender who raped his wife (Remick), he makes a wise decision—he hires easygoing, piano-pumping former prosecutor Paul Biegler (Stewart) to defend him. An enigmatic courtroom mystery where the question at hand is not who done it, but why did it happen. The film, one of Preminger's best, caused quite a stir in its day, hinging as it does on a complex view of sexuality, rage, and Mrs. Manion's panties. Great performances by the entire cast. Duke Ellington did the score.

Witness for the Prosecution (1957, U.S., 116 mins., b/w) Dir: Billy Wilder; Cast: Tyrone Power, Charles Laughton, Marlene Dietrich, John Williams, Elsa Lanchester.

An American gigolo living in London is accused of murdering the wealthy widow he's been hanging out with. Billy Wilder applies his cynical wit to Agatha Christie's novel and transforms it into a masterpiece. Laughton, exhibiting his extraordinary range and power in the role of the waddling barrister, meets his match in Lanchester and Dietrich; Power, whose matinee-idol looks often obscure his weakness as an actor, rises to the occasion as the accused. Tricky, disturbing, and a great deal of fun.

Inherit the Wind (1960, U.S., 127 mins.) Dir: Stanley Kramer; Cast: Spencer Tracy, Fredric March, Gene Kelly.

Stanley Kramer production of the hit Broadway play—a semifictional account of the 1925 Scopes monkey trial in which William Jennings Bryan prosecuted, and Clarence Darrow defended, a Tennessee high school teacher who dared to teach Darwin's theory of evolution. Tracy gives a sincere performance as the Darrow-derivative, but March's Bryan-like Bible-thumping zealot is a ham sandwich slathered with way too much mayo. Shallow characterizations and sledgehammer direction notwithstanding, with one of the great courtroom battles of the century as its basis, and two colorful historical figures duking it out philosophically, the film grabs and holds from start to finish.

To Kill a Mockingbird (1962, U.S., 129 mins., b/w) Dir: Robert Mulligan; Cast: Gregory Peck, Mary Badham, Philip Alford, Brock Peters.

Peck's performance as Atticus Finch, a Lincolnesque lawyer defending a southern black man accused of raping a white woman, is a trifle less wooden than usual and it earned him an Academy Award. Horton Foote's screenplay, from Harper Lee's Pulitzer Prize-winning book, filled with wonderful human touches—the story is narrated by the lawyer's daughter, Scout—gets somewhat bogged down in early sixties political correctness. But Mulligan's evocative direction makes it as much about the imaginings, fears, and memories of childhood as it is about social justice.

The Verdict (1982, U.S., 129 mins.) Dir: Sidney Lumet; Cast: Paul Newman, Charlotte Rampling, Jack Warden, James Mason, Milo O'Shea, Edward Binns, Julie Bovasso.

Frank Galvin (Newman) is a Boston lawyer with a problem—he's much more likely to be found at the local pub stooped over his favorite pinball machine with a beer in front of him than at his trash heap of an office. It takes the case of a young woman turned into a vegetable by a medical mistake at a huge Catholic hospital to put some glide back in his stride. David Mamet's screenplay is ripe with good dialogue, three-dimensional characters, and grade-A suspense. Director Lumet gets as much mileage out of the human drama as he does from the courtroom theatrics, and Newman's performance has as many layers as any he's ever given.

True Believer (1989, U.S., 102 mins.) Dir: Joseph Ruben; Cast: James Woods, Robert Downey, Jr., Margaret Colin, Kurtwood Smith.

Woods brings his usual razor-sharp

edge to the role of Eddie Dodge. A seriously burnt Bill Kunstler-type former champion of 1960s radical causes, Dodge spends his time smoking pot and crusading on behalf of lowlife drug dealers, until his hero-worshiping clerk hypes him up on the case of an Asian-American in prison for a crime he didn't commit. Good, tough little thriller; wraps the fine points of law in explosive action, packing a serious message with an effective punch.

WATCHING THE DETECTIVES
■

HARD-BOILED EGGS: THE PRIVATE EYES

They stepped out of the pulp magazine stories and novels of writers like Hammett and Chandler, into the shadowy world of film noir. They had a special way of smoking a cigarette, of turning up the collar of a trench coat, of turning down the brim of a hat. They knew how to handle a rod, a dame, or a cheap hood in a dark alley. They lived and died by an unwritten code. They came in many guises—police detectives, newspapermen, insurance investigators, World War II vets, and private eyes whose business was murder. Their heyday was the forties and fifties, but just when you think they've fallen into extinction, a new one shows up on screen. These are the hard-boiled heroes, the twenty-minute eggs, the tough guys who set things straight—though their sense of justice sometimes means watching a beautiful blonde put a slug in the belly of a two-timing rat, then letting her walk away. Sometimes. You never know till the final fadeout.

The Maltese Falcon (1941, U.S., 100 mins., b/w) Dir: John Huston; Cast: Humphrey Bogart, Mary Astor, Peter Lorre, Sydney Greenstreet, Walter Huston, Lee Patrick, Elisha Cook, Jr., Barton MacLane.

Opening paragraph of classic hard-boiled Hammett novel on which this film is based describes the detective as "a blonde Satan." But ever since John Huston's masterful adaptation hit the screen, when you think of Sam Spade, you think of Humphrey Bogart. The rest of the ensemble—Lorre, Greenstreet, Astor, et al.—is just as memorable. Their scavenger hunt for the precious black bird is a deadly game of greed and deception and the film remains the most important work in any medium in shaping the poetics of the private eye.

The Big Sleep (1946, U.S., 114 mins., b/w) Dir: Howard Hawks; Cast: Humphrey Bogart, Lauren Bacall, Martha Vickers, John Ridgely, Regis Toomey, Elisha Cook, Jr., Bob Steele, Dorothy Malone.

Raymond Chandler's first and most confusing novel makes an even more convoluted film; neither Hawks nor the screenwriting team, which includes William Faulkner, are able to unravel the plot . . . not that they seem to care. Chandler himself said he didn't have any idea "who done it." But Bogart is far and away the best Philip Marlowe—the guy doesn't need a gun to be tough—and the witty, insolent Bogie/Bacall banter positively sizzles. Entire enterprise is like well-cooked bacon: crisp, lean, smoky, and delicious.

Murder, My Sweet (1944, U.S., 95 mins., b/w) Dir: Edward Dmytryk; Cast: Dick Powell, Claire Trevor, Anne Shirley, Otto Kruger, Mike Mazurki.

Song-and-danceman Powell trades tap shoes for gumshoes in first "serious role" as Philip Marlowe, but his petulant little boy performance softens the core of the character. Which doesn't matter all that much. Shadows, fog, and rain-soaked streets are the real protagonists in this superbly atmospheric adaptation of Raymond Chandler's *Farewell, My Lovely*. Dmytryk constantly finds visual equivalents for Chandler's prose and the end result is one of the defining achievements of the film noir genre.

The Long Goodbye (1973, U.S., 111 mins.) Dir: Robert Altman; Cast: Elliott Gould, Sterling Hayden, Mark Rydell, Henry Gibson, Jim Bouton, Nina van Pallandt, David Arkin, Warren Berlinger, Arnold Schwarzenegger.

In Altman's film noir redux Elliott Gould plays Philip Marlowe as a man living in the wrong time—the hippie girls next door walk around naked and bake hash brownies. Script by Leigh Brackett (co-writer of *The Big Sleep*) has the detective muttering to himself constantly—a running stream of semiconscious commentary that functions as a clever substitute for the classic first-person narration of the old movies. Amazingly, Chandler's original novel (arguably his best) is extremely well-served.

Kiss Me Deadly (1955, U.S., 105 mins., b/w) Dir: Robert Aldrich; Cast: Ralph Meeker, Albert Dekker, Paul Stewart, Wesley Addy, Maxine Cooper, Cloris Leachman, Gaby Rodgers, Jack Elam, Strother Martin.

Mickey Spillane's Mike Hammer lives in an unstable universe that is far more malevolent than Chandler's. In this film, Hammer's hunt for a deadly Pandora's box begins when a loony half-naked dame jumps in front of his car, and ends with the world on the brink of disaster. Director Aldrich thickens every frame with menace, discharging it with quicksilver bursts of savage brutality and searing flashes of heat and light, raising the hard-boiled detective melodrama to the level of apocalyptic vision. Fave of French new wavers, touted by Truffaut as the "cinema event of 1955."

I, the Jury (1982, U.S., 109 mins.) Dir: Richard T. Heffron; Cast: Armand Assante, Barbara Carrera, Alan King, Geoffrey Lewis.

Brando wannabe Assante applies the Method to Mike Hammer, mumbling and sulking his way through the Larry Cohen script and N.Y. locations as he tracks his friend's killer. Surprisingly good, very sexy '80s take on Mickey Spillane's cheesy '50s detective meller; Cohen's unashamedly trashy style and inexhaustible flair for the nervous rhythms of contemporary speech are perfectly suited to the material. The 1953 version, made in 3-D, is well worth catching if you can find it.

Out of the Past (1947, U.S., 97 mins., b/w) Dir: Jacques Tourneur; Cast: Robert Mitchum, Kirk Douglas, Jane Greer, Rhonda Fleming.

Mitchum is at his best as Jeff Markham, a private eye with a past he's trying desperately to escape, but can't—Mr. Big (Douglas) and bad-girl Greer won't let him. One of the most fatalistic films of the forties with a superbly crafted script built around a stunning flashback and classic voice-over narration, the direction by Mr. Tourneur is as evocative as the title. Remade in 1984 as *Against All Odds*.

Chinatown (1974, U.S., 130 mins.) Dir: Roman Polanski; Cast: Jack Nicholson, Faye Dunaway, John Huston, Diane Ladd, Perry Lopez, John Hillerman.

Polanski and screenwriter Robert Towne step back into the past for this period piece that brilliantly captures the spirit of the genre while creating a completely contemporary film. Not the least bit nostalgic or campy, this is the genuine article—Nicholson's Jake Gittes could sit down for a drink with Marlowe or Spade at any gin mill in town and feel at home. Dunaway's pale, neurotic dame walks a fine line between femme fatale and vulnerable victim. And Huston's appearance as her demonic dad somehow completes the cycle. Yessss.

8 Million Ways to Die (1986, U.S., 115 mins.) Dir: Hal Ashby; Cast: Jeff Bridges, Rosanna Arquette, Alexandra Paul, Randy Brooks, Andy Garcia, Lisa Sloan.

Adaptation of novel by Lawrence Block, genuine heir to the Hammett/Chandler tradition, features a bravura performance by Bridges as hard-drinking shamus Matt Scudder. Film does a nifty job of changing the book's locale from New York to L.A. and establishing a solid "backstory" for the character—a modern-day movie detective whose battle with the bottle is just as tough as his fight against crime. Screenplay, co-written by Oliver *(JFK)* Stone, was doctored by Robert Towne (uncredited).

Night Moves (1975, U.S., 100 mins.) Dir: Arthur Penn; Cast: Gene Hackman, Susan Clark, Jennifer Warren, Melanie Griffith.

Harry Mosby (Hackman), a private eye whose private life is a mess, is hired by a fading film star to find her runaway daughter, a role that gives a very young Melanie Griffith her first opportunity to bare her breasts on film. Penn filters the genre through his modernist sensibility, turning the detective into an emotionally crippled creature with none of the Bogart wit. Haunting film owes as much of a debt to Antonioni as it does to Howard Hawks.

The Conversation (1974, U.S., 113 mins.) Dir: Francis Ford Coppola; Cast: Gene Hackman, John Cazale, Allen Garfield, Cindy Williams.

Speaking of Antonioni, this is a sort of audio *Blow-Up* . . . with a decidedly post-Watergate paranoid spin. Hackman is Harry Caul, less a private eye than a private ear, an expert at the art of bugging, and the taped conversation

he's piecing together just may hold the key to a murder plot . . . or it may not. We haven't actually figured it out. Still, it's Coppola's most personal and disturbing film and Hackman is sensational.

The Last Boy Scout (1991, U.S., 105 mins.) Dir: Tony Scott; Cast: Bruce Willis, Damon Wayans, Chelsea Field, Noble Willingham, Taylor Negron, Danielle Harris.

L.A. gumshoe Willis is a hard-boiled egg with the look and smell of rotting egg salad—he needs a shave and a bath, his wife is bopping his best friend, and his daughter swears like a truck driver. When he buddies up with ex-grid star Wayans, he finds his way back to the land of the living. Shane *(Lethal Weapon)* Black got megabucks for the screenplay, and the steady stream of snappy patter is sharp, fast, and funny. But the sports gambling plot misses the uprights and the overblown action owes more to comic books than it does to tough-guy fiction.

WATCHING THE DETECTIVES

■

WELL-COOKED COPS

Here are some hard-boiled heroes who draw their paychecks from local law-enforcement agencies—police detectives.

The Narrow Margin (1952, U.S., 70 mins., b/w) Dir: Richard Fleischer; Cast: Charles McGraw, Marie Windsor, Jacqueline White, Queenie Leonard.

Supremely cynical cop is assigned to escort a mobster's wife from Chicago to L.A. so she can rat on her husband in court. The bad guys, natch, will stop at nothing to prevent this from happening. Incredibly tight, twisty melodrama where every component clicks. A suspenseful and claustrophobic B-movie train ride—take it and skip the overblown remake.

The Big Heat (1953, U.S., 90 mins., b/w) Dir: Fritz Lang; Cast: Glenn Ford, Gloria Grahame, Lee Marvin, Carolyn Jones, Jocelyn Brando, Jeanette Nolan.

Lang's blistering masterpiece of revenge and redemption features Ford as a happily married homicide detective whose nice little life goes up in flames when he looks into a suspicious suicide. Marvin is brilliant as a sadistic hood whose use for hot coffee extends well beyond dunking a donut, and Grahame is more than his match as the moll who isn't about to get burned without burning back. One of the darkest, most nihilistic of all film noirs.

Laura (1944, U.S., 88 mins., b/w) Dir: Otto Preminger; Cast: Gene Tierney, Dana Andrews, Clifton Webb, Vincent Price, Judith Anderson, Grant Mitchell, Lane Chandler, Dorothy Adams.

Preminger's classic exploration of the neurotic fringes of human emotion where passion becomes obsession, stars Andrews as a hard-boiled cop turned into mush by the image of a woman (Tierney) whose murder he is investigating—he falls in love with a painting! Webb's Waldo Lydecker is a marvelously precise and prickly creation and David Raskin's musical theme haunts the film like a ghost. One of the greats.

Where the Sidewalk Ends (1950, U.S., 95 mins., b/w) Dir: Otto Preminger; Cast: Dana Andrews, Gene Tierney, Gary Merrill, Karl Malden.
■
Superb naturalistic melodrama about an overheated cop with a penchant for police brutality who cooks his own goose when he beats a suspect to death. Fox's attempt to cash in on the casting combo of Tierney and Andrews under the firm hand of director Pre-

minger makes this a close relation to *Laura*, but Ben Hecht's hard-edged screenplay takes it into a much rougher neighborhood, replacing upper-crust decadence with underworld grit. Aces all the way.

Dirty Harry (1971, U.S., 102 mins.) Dir: Don Siegel; Cast: Clint Eastwood, Harry Guardino, Andy Robinson, John Vernon, John Larch.

First and best in series built around the violent exploits of inspector Harry Callahan brings the old-fashioned detective into the modern era, where cops are handcuffed by Supreme Court rulings and police brutality seems a reasonable response to crime run amok. Armed with a .44 Magnum and a bad attitude, Eastwood's Harry speaks English as a third language—after snarling and shooting people. Siegel's masterful direction paints a disturbing, reactionary vision of a changing world on the edge of oblivion.

The French Connection (1971, U.S., 104 mins.) Dir: William Friedkin; Cast: Gene Hackman, Fernando Rey, Roy Scheider, Eddie Egan, Sonny Grosso.

Popeye Doyle is a New York City detective whose repugnance for the sewer in which he works is tempered only by the pleasure he gets in brutalizing the scum who inhabit it and bringing them to justice. The plot (based on a true story) revolves around the largest heroin bust in the city's history, but the highlight of the film is a deftly designed, heart-pounding car chase—a sequence that set new standards for movie action. Film won Oscars for Best Picture, Actor, Director, Screenplay, and Editing.

Deep Cover (1992, U.S., 112 mins.) Dir: Bill Duke; Cast: Larry Fishburne, Jeff Goldblum, Victoria Dillard, Charles Martin Smith, Sidney Lassick, Clarence Williams III.

Director Bill Duke puts a techno-pop spin on the tough-cop genre in this hip-hop, hard-boiled, socially relevant nouveau noir about a narcotics investigation with startling political implications. Fishburne (the dad from *Boyz N the Hood*) is impressive as the narc whose heart was hardened during childhood, and Goldblum's drug-dealing lawyer is a wholly original movie villain. This little sleeper is well worth catching.

Blade Runner (1982, U.S., 117 mins.) Dir: Ridley Scott; Cast: Harrison Ford, Rutger Hauer, Sean Young, Edward James Olmos, Joanna Cassidy, Daryl Hannah.

Ridley Scott version of Philip K. Dick novel about 21st-century L.A. cop on the trail of humanistic robots who are up to no good blends set decoration and sound design into a digitized assault on the senses that's alternately stimulating and snooze-inducing. The script, which is basically an out-of-control mess, leans heavily on the hard-boiled tradition—the character played by Ford is a futuristic Philip Marlowe with a badge. When the film gets out of its own way, it's actually fun to be with. Note: Released in multiple versions. Earlier versions have a first-person hard-boiled voiceover narration that is eliminated in the director's cut.

Cry of the City (1948, U.S., 96 mins., b/w) Dir: Robert Siodmak; Cast: Richard Conte, Victor Mature, Shelley Winters, Debra Paget.
∎
Classic Manhattan melodrama hinges on conflict between two men—boyhood pals now on opposite sides of the law. But the line between right and wrong, good-guy/bad-guy, is blurred. Mature's obsessive cop has an almost metaphysical hardness and Conte's troubled hood is genuinely sympathetic. And the city seethes with the same unrest as the characters. Siodmak uses both location and studio sets, mixing documentary and expressionistic techniques to create a somber, poetic vision of New York. The Gershwinesque score by Alfred Newmann audibly captures the city's cry.

The Killer (1989, Hong Kong, 110 mins.) Dir: John Woo; Cast: Chow Yun Fat, Sally Yeh, Danny Lee.

Cream of Hong Kong action crop lifts a plot point or two from *Cry of the City:* a killer and a cop who share a common bond are involved in a deadly game of cat and mouse. Did we say deadly? Writer/director Woo (Asia's answer to Leone and Peckinpah) has created a plasma bath that makes *The Wild Bunch* seem tame. It's a shocking, absurdly beautiful, bullet-ridden ballet bolstered by a surprisingly moving script and rich characterizations. If you're too squeamish to sit through it, you'll be missing one hell of a cinematic spectacle.

Hard-Boiled (1991, Hong Kong, 127 mins.) Dir: John Woo; Cast: Chow Yun Fat, Tony Chiu Wai Leung, Teresa Mo.

Though this one by Woo leans more on comic books than film noir, the cop-hero is, as the title implies, one tough cookie. And tough cookies don't crumble. "Tequila" Yuen bounces off cars, skids across floors, slides down banisters, falls out of windows, and keeps coming back for more. The blazing pistols, which appear to be attached to his hands, never run out of bullets; the toothpick sticking insolently out of his mouth never seems to fall. The plot involves gunrunning in Hong Kong, but that's irrelevant—the story here is action. There's more firepower on display in this movie than the U.S. expended in the Gulf War.

Die Hard (1988, U.S., 127 mins.) Dir: John McTiernan; Cast: Bruce Willis, Alan Rickman, Bonnie Bedelia, Alexander Godunov, Paul Gleason, William Atherton.

An L.A. office building is taken over by a terrorist gang and the only man who can save the day is wisecracking, tough-as-nails N.Y.C. detective Willis, in town trying to patch things up with his estranged wife (Bedelia). Action scenes, stamped by producer Joel Silver's propensity for excess, are tempered by clever, surprisingly literate script and it all adds up to exhilarating entertainment.

WATCHING THE
DETECTIVES
■
OTHERWISE-OCCUPIED
EGGS

Not cops, not private eyes, the hard guys on this list have slightly different job descriptions . . . but their work is much the same.

The Undercover Man (1949, U.S., 85 mins., b/w) Dir: Joseph H. Lewis; Cast: Glenn Ford, Nina Foch, James Whitmore, Barry Kelley, Howard St. John.

The hero here (Ford) is, believe it or not, an accountant! But this particular numbers-cruncher is tougher than most—he works undercover for the Treasury Department and the case at hand involves the overcooked books of a major league mobster (Whitmore in his film debut) loosely based on Al Capone. Rare opportunity for B-movie champ Lewis to direct A-level cast; the result is a solid B+.

T-Men (1947, U.S., 96 mins., b/w) Dir: Anthony Mann; Cast: Dennis O'Keefe, June Lockhart, Alfred Ryder, Charles McGraw, Wallace Ford, Mary Meade.

Treasury agents again, this time going undercover to bring down a counterfeiting ring. Superior to the Lewis film, this B-movie masterpiece rates serious attention by anyone interested in the art of visual expression.

Double Indemnity (1944, U.S., 106 mins., b/w) Dir: Billy Wilder; Cast: Fred MacMurray, Barbara Stanwyck, Edward G. Robinson.

Insurance agent MacMurray schemes with femme fatale Stanwyck to kill her husband, make it look like an accident, and collect the insurance money, but company bloodhound Robinson smells fish. Script by Wilder and Raymond Chandler via James M. Cain's classic novel is so hard-boiled a trip hammer couldn't put a dent in the dialogue. Full of dark nights and darker implications, the film transcends its own tawdriness and resonates long after the final fadeout. Perfect.

Crack-Up (1946, U.S., 93 mins., b/w) Dir: Irving Reis; Cast: Pat O'Brien, Claire Trevor, Herbert Marshall, Wallace Ford.

George Steele, tour guide and lecturer for a metropolitan art museum, stumbles onto a forgery plot and plunges into a nightmare. As played by O'Brien and written by John (*Murder, My Sweet*) Paxton, the character is not only able to wax eloquent on the beauty of old-master paintings, he can toss off a tough stream of patter and handle himself in a pinch. Odd, affecting, neglected little thriller with a socialist slant, takes a poke or two at modern art and thoroughly trashes the cultural elite.

Ride the Pink Horse (1947, U.S., 101 mins., b/w) Dir: Robert Montgomery; Cast: Robert Montgomery, Wanda Hendrix, Thomas Gomez, Andrea King, Fred Clark, Art Smith.

An ex-GI named Lucky Gagin (Montgomery) arrives in Mexico at fiesta time intent on blackmailing a big-time gangster, but F.B.I. man Smith tugs at the more heroic side of his nature and sweet señorita Hendrix tugs at his heart. Crafty, literate script by Ben Hecht and Charles Lederer is well-served by Montgomery's performance and direction, and the finished film is as evocative as the title.

Experiment in Terror (1962, U.S., 123 mins., b/w) Dir: Blake Edwards; Cast: Glenn Ford, Lee Remick, Stefanie Powers, Ross Martin, Roy Poole, Ned Glass.

Heavy-breathing psycho-killer Martin terrorizes bankteller Remick. Ford is the tough yet tender FBI guy who comes to her rescue . . . but not before you sit through a serious dose of good old-fashioned nail-biting suspense. Director Edwards, known primarily for comedy *(The Pink Panther)*, romance *(Breakfast at Tiffany's)*, and the occasional drama *(Days of Wine and Roses)*, may not be Hitchcock but he makes the experiment work just fine.

The Enforcer (1951, U.S., 87 mins., b/w) Dir: Bretaigne Windust; Cast: Humphrey Bogart, Zero Mostel, Ted de Corsia, Everett Sloane, Roy Roberts.

Taut, realistic melodrama based on the true story of hit-for-hire gang, Murder Inc., features Bogart as the doggedly determined D.A. dead set on bringing them down. Sloane is a worthy opponent as the crime boss and de Corsica is a find as the tough guy who turns, but the real treat in the cast is Mostel as a big dumb blubbering slob who melts when Bogie cranks up the heat. Director Windust was the beneficiary of an uncredited assist from Warner's ace Raoul Walsh.

The Harder They Fall (1956, U.S., 109 mins., b/w) Dir: Mark Robson; Cast: Humphrey Bogart, Rod Steiger, Jan Sterling, Mike Lane, Max Baer, Edward Andrews.

Bogie gives one of his most complete performances (his last) as a world-weary sportswriter hired by slimy promoter Steiger to push the career of a gigantic childlike brawler whose road to a title shot is paved with payola. From a book by Budd Schulberg, based

on the real-life story of Primo Carnera, this hard-hitting exposé takes off the gloves and rips big-time boxing so wide open no cut-man in the business could possibly stop the bleeding.

Call Northside 777 (1948, U.S., 111 mins., b/w) Dir: Henry Hathaway; Cast: James Stewart, Richard Conte, Lee J. Cobb, Helen Walker, Moroni Olsen, E. G. Marshall.

A cynical newspaper reporter (Stewart) looks into a classified ad offering $500 for info on an 11-year-old killing and turns a human-interest story into a crusade for truth and justice. Working from a series of articles by James McGuire, Hathaway's direction employs an arrestingly flat documentary style, real locations, and striking attention to detail. Stewart's subdued intensity, and exceptional supporting work by Conte and Cobb, lend credence and weight to the proceedings.

While the City Sleeps (1956, U.S., 100 mins., b/w) Dir: Fritz Lang; Cast: Dana Andrews, Ida Lupino, Rhonda Fleming, George Sanders, Vincent Price, John Drew Barrymore, Sally Forrest.

A serial murderer is on the loose and effete newspaper publisher Walter Kyne, Jr., creates a competition for his staff—whoever finds "the lipstick killer" becomes executive editor of the paper. Andrews is the rugged reporter who starts out as a detached observer, but gets sucked so completely into the game he winds up dangling his girlfriend (Forrest) as bait. Last American film by Fritz Lang is clean, lean, mean, and hard.

Shock Corridor (1963, U.S., 101 mins., b/w) Dir: Sam Fuller; Cast: Peter Breck, Constance Towers, Gene Evans, James Best, Hari Rhodes.

Wild descent into deranged delirium courtesy of Sam Fuller begins when a Pulitzer-hungry hard-boiled reporter attempts to solve a mental hospital murder mystery by posing as an inmate. Fuller—the tabloid cineaste par excellence—is forever walking the line between trash and art, profane and profound, lunacy and lucidity, and this film, more than any other, defines his view of the world as one big lunatic asylum. A lurid, sexual, visceral jolt from one of the screen's genuine originals.

WATCHING THE DETECTIVES
■
SOFT-BOILED EGGS

Generally gentlemen, often piss-elegant to boot, the sleuths on this list sport canes, smoke pipes, wear smoking jackets, ascots, and distinctive hats, live in expensive digs, own cute little dogs, travel in cosmopolitan circles and, British or not, have superb command of the king's English. Even when they're not of the trust-fund variety, they have a certain *je ne sais quoi* capacity for sophistication. "Shoot first, ask questions later," is not part of their vocabulary. In fact, most of these guys don't even carry a gun. Detection, deductive reasoning is their weapon of choice—they are far less likely to slap suspects around than to simply outsmart them.

Bulldog Drummond (1929, U.S., 80 mins., b/w) Dir: F. Richard Jones; Cast: Ronald Colman, Joan Bennett, Lilyan Tashman.

One of the first great Hollywood murder mysteries, with a delightfully debonair Colman as H. C. McNeile's dogged detective out to save an American girl and her uncle from a dastardly nursing-home scam the N.Y. tabloids would love. Extremely satisfying, influential early talkie boasts a script by Sidney (*They Knew What They Wanted, Gone*

With the Wind) Howard, sets by William Cameron Menzies, and photography by Gregg Toland.

The Thin Man (1934, U.S., 93 mins., b/w) Dir: W. S. Van Dyke; Cast: William Powell, Myrna Loy, Maureen O'Sullivan, Nat Pendleton, Minna Gombell, Porter Hall.

Based on Dashiell Hammett's novel (which means a hard-boiled touch or two), this first and best in the series of six MGM films featuring crime detection by husband-and-wife team Nick and Nora Charles (Powell and Loy) and their dog Asta is a breezy, boozy, pleasingly unpredictable murder mystery that is alternately comic and suspenseful. Oscar nominated for Picture, Script, Actor, and Director. James Wong Howe shot it.

The Kennel Murder Case (1933, U.S., 73 mins., b/w) Dir: Michael Curtiz; Cast: William Powell, Mary Astor, Eugene Pallette.

Powell, obviously Hollywood's gentleman sleuth of choice, is superb as S. S. Van Dyne's Philo Vance. Set in society's crusty regions where the denizens value pets more than people, the case at hand involves the locked-room murder of a blue-ribbon-dog owner and collector of Chinoiserie. Director Curtiz keeps the action moving at a lightning-quick pace with a stunning assortment of pans, wipes, split screens, unusual angles, and moving cameras. A must for whodunit lovers and anyone interested in the fine art of film.

Green for Danger (1946, Great Britain, 93 mins., b/w) Dir: Sidney Gilliat; Cast: Alastair Sim, Trevor Howard, Sally Gray, Leo Genn.

Alastair Sim is Inspector Cockrill, a seemingly addle-brained but deceptively shrewd British detective with a penchant for cracking wise while sorting through clues and questioning suspects. Here he investigates the case of a mailman whose death during a medical operation appears to be murder. Written and directed by Sidney Gilliat, co-writer and producer of Hitchcock's *The Lady Vanishes*, this smooth, macabre little mystery is visually exciting and full of suspense.

The Stranger (1946, U.S., 95 mins., b/w) Dir: Orson Welles; Cast: Edward G. Robinson, Orson Welles, Loretta Young.

Nazi clock-maniac Welles hides out in New England town and sweeps WASP princess Young off her feet. Robinson is the mild-mannered war-crimes investigator willing to make pawns out of anyone who can help bag his prey. Too easily dismissed as minor Welles . . . the director is at the top of his game and having some fun while playing it. John Huston worked on the screenplay without credit. Great, great, great.

The Woman in the Window (1944, U.S., 99 mins., b/w) Dir: Fritz Lang; Cast: Edward G. Robinson, Joan Bennett, Raymond Massey, Dan Duryea.
■
Sedentary middle-aged professor Robinson succumbs to the charms of a mysterious woman and commits a murder on her behalf. His regular lunchtime companion just happens to be the police inspector working the case. Lang laces the simple crime story with his Expressionist vision and turns it into a rich psychoanalytic criminal melodrama about the eruption of repressed desire. Wow.

Dial M for Murder (1954, U.S., 105 mins., b/w) Dir: Alfred Hitchcock; Cast: Ray Milland, Grace Kelly, Robert Cummings, John Williams, Anthony Dawson.

Former tennis star Milland blackmails a vulnerable sleaze into killing his cheating-but-wealthy wife (Kelly). But the plan misfires and she kills the would-be killer, so hubby sets wifey up as a mur-

deress. It's up to quintessential Scotland Yard bloodhound Williams to sort things out before Gracie goes to the gallows. Basically faithful adaptation of Frederick Knot's algebraic formula of a stage play made multidimensional by Sir Alfred. Shot in 3-D but not seen that way until recently.

Midnight Lace (1960, U.S., 108 mins.) Dir: David Miller; Cast: Doris Day, Rex Harrison, John Gavin, Myrna Loy, Roddy McDowall, Herbert Marshall.

Poor Mrs. Preston (Doris) is receiving terrifying phone calls and getting chased through the London fog by a ghostlike figure. If super-suave husband Harrison can't figure out who's doing it, perhaps wily Scotland Yard Inspector Williams (virtually reprising his role from *Dial M for Murder*) can. Imitation Hitchcock and fun all the way.

Bunny Lake Is Missing (1965, U.S., 107 mins., b/w) Dir: Otto Preminger; Cast: Laurence Olivier, Keir Dullea, Carol Lynley, Noel Coward.
■
American mom Lynley loses daughter in London and the British detective (Olivier) assigned to the case is not at all convinced that the little girl even exists. Last great film by Preminger, his relentlessly mobile camera takes us over, under, around, and through an artificial plot strewn with red herrings into deep pathological territory. As disturbing as it is entertaining.

The Private Life of Sherlock Holmes (1970, U.S., 125 mins.) Dir: Billy Wilder; Cast: Robert Stephens, Colin Blakely, Genevieve Page, Stanley Holloway, Clive Revill.

A far cry from Basil Rathbone, this intimate portrait of Arthur Conan Doyle's master sleuth presents him as a cerebral, passionate, compulsive, cynical man, susceptible to boredom, seeking solace in music and drugs; and a man with tremendous psychological ambivalence toward women. A tender, sensual, romantic puzzle rendered with exquisite sensitivity by Wilder. Even though butchered by an hour when released, what remains may well be the director's most personal artistic statement and beautifully crafted work.

THE BIG HOUSE

You can't come and go as you please. You're told what to eat, when to sleep. You can't have sex. No, you're not married. You're in prison. Here are some frightening reminders of what can happen if you tear off that little tag on your mattress.

Cool Hand Luke (1967, U.S., 126 mins.) Dir: Stuart Rosenberg; Cast: Paul Newman, George Kennedy, Strother Martin, Dennis Hopper.

"Cool" is definitely the operative word here. Newman stars as the Christ-like prisoner on a chain gang who gives new life to his fellow inmates. Strother Martin and George Kennedy provide great support through scene after memorable scene. A movie worth seeing over and over, though you may never eat hard-boiled eggs again.

I Am a Fugitive From a Chain Gang (1932, U.S., 100 mins., b/w) Dir: Mervyn LeRoy; Cast: Paul Muni, Glenda Farrell, Helen Vinson, Preston Foster.

The other classic chain-gang film has Paul Muni imprisoned for a crime he did not commit. Even though it's a chestnut, this harrowing film (especially the last scene) will give you the shivers.

The Glass House (1972, U.S./MTV, 73 mins.) Dir: Tom Gries; Cast: Vic Morrow, Alan Alda, Clu Gulager.

Based on a story by Truman Capote, this is a better-than-average tale of a college professor sent to the big house on a manslaughter rap. Because Alda is

a normal guy, if not a bit wimpy, he acts as an intermediary figure and we can see how we might react if we found ourselves in the worst situation imaginable. For once prison isn't a fishbowl; it's a terrible possibility.

American Me (1992, U.S., 126 mins.) Dir: Edward James Olmos; Cast: Edward James Olmos, William Forsythe, Pepe Serna, Danny De La Paz, Sal Lopez.

A moving and violent film by Edward James Olmos about the rise of Mexican gangs in the California prison system. Tough, realistic prison scenes resonate throughout and give weight to the transformation of Olmos's character from folk hero to thug. The best parts show his difficult adaptation to life and love outside prison walls.

Papillon (1973, U.S., 153 mins.) Dir: Franklin J. Schaffner; Cast: Steve McQueen, Dustin Hoffman, Victor Jory, William Smithers.

A cartoon adventure about suave thief McQueen trying to escape from Devil's Island with the help of fidgeting swindler Hoffman. Graphic and gripping all the way, with lepers, mean guards, roach-eating, and a Ratso Rizzo reprise from Hoffman. What more could you ask for? A rugged subject treated with great flair.

Runaway Train (1985, U.S., 107 mins.) Dir: Andrei Konchalovsky; Cast: Jon Voight, Eric Roberts, Rebecca DeMornay, Kyle Heffner, John Ryan, T. K. Carter, Kenneth McMillan.

Staying with the escape theme, this Konchalovsky movie about two escaped convicts hijacking a train through the Alaskan wilderness is one of the best. Voight actually manages to seem tough and the prison scenes are so disgusting and brutal that they're fun. The whole thing successfully rides a fine line between heart-pounding and comic book. Also in this vein, be sure to see *Escape From New York,* in which all of Manhattan is turned into a prison. As if it wasn't already.

Slammer (aka: *Short Eyes,* 1977, U.S., 104 mins.) Dir: Robert M. Young; Cast: Bruce Davison, José Perez, Joseph Carberry, Nathan George, Don Blakeley, Shawn Elliott, Curtis Mayfield, Freddy Fender.

"Short Eyes" is prison slang for a child molester, and prisoners don't like child molesters very much, as Davison learns in this powerful drama filmed on location at the now unused Tombs of New York City. As well as being a fine movie, it also gives you a chance to see Freddy Fender and Curtis Mayfield act.

Jailhouse Rock (1957, U.S., 96 mins., b/w) Dir: Richard Thorpe; Cast: Elvis Presley, Judy Tyler, Dean Jones, Vaughn Taylor.

Long before Nixon named Elvis a special agent to combat drugs, the King played a teenager in prison who learns how to pluck a guitar and becomes a big star. While not a particularly realistic look at life in prison, it's arguably Elvis's best film and that's something.

The Bird Man of Alcatraz (1962, U.S., 147 mins., b/w) Dir: John Frankenheimer; Cast: Burt Lancaster, Karl Malden, Thelma Ritter, Betty Field, Neville Brand, Telly Savalas, Edmund O'Brien, Hugh Marlowe.

No film captures the tedium, the loneliness, the boredom, and suffocating dread of prison life as this one does. Lancaster matches the atmosphere and pacing with an underplayed, but terrific, performance as the lifer who becomes an authority on birds while locked up at Alcatraz. A must-see, even if you're not into prison films.

20,000 Years in Sing Sing (1933, U.S., 81 mins., b/w) Dir: Michael Curtiz;

Cast: Spencer Tracy, Bette Davis, Lyle Talbot, Louis Calhern, Grant Mitchell.
■
Tracy stars as a tough con in this classic early prison film. Bette Davis co-stars as his moll. The film doesn't seem out of the ordinary now, but Curtiz's direction keeps things moving along and it was definitely fresh then.

Each Dawn I Die (1939, U.S., 84 mins., b/w) Dir: William Keighley; Cast: James Cagney, George Raft, Jane Bryan, George Bancroft, Maxie Rosenbloom.

Reporter Cagney gets framed and ends up in the Big House, where he befriends mobster Raft and gets involved in an ill-advised escape plot. Another of the early prison brutality films, you'll have to suspend your disbelief more than a little bit at the ending, but Cagney and Raft make it all worth it.

POLITICS

ON THE CAMPAIGN TRAIL

Campaign promises are made to be broken. But we stand by our promise that these campaign films will deliver the goods.

The Candidate (1972, U.S., 109 mins.) Dir: Michael Ritchie; Cast: Robert Redford, Melvyn Douglas, Peter Boyle, Karen Carlson, Allen Garfield.

An idealistic yet intellectually vacant pretty-boy lawyer (Redford) is hand-picked by California Democrats to toss his hat into the Senatorial ring. Caustic McLuhan-age critique of political hype and hoopla makes the point that when the media is properly manipulated, the message doesn't matter. Oscar-winning screenplay by Jeremy Larner and jittery direction by Michael Ritchie walk an interesting line between satire and pseudo-doc. Good film suffers from an absence of human emotion.

Bob Roberts (1992, U.S., 101 mins.) Dir: Tim Robbins; Cast: Tim Robbins, Giancarlo Esposito, Ray Wise, Rebecca Jenkins, Harry J. Lennix, John Ottavino, Robert Stanton, Alan Rickman, Gore Vidal, David Straithairn, Anita Gillette.

Writer/director/star Tim Robbins developed this project while working with Robert Altman on *The Player,* and it shows. Altman's influence is all over this mock doc about the rise of country-western crypto fascist political wannabe Roberts (Robbins) and his race for the U.S. Senate. The film is clever and thought-provoking, yet misses the mark. The world it creates is almost believable, but not quite; the characters almost work, but fall short. Robbins's first film is impressively ambitious, but artistic ambition and artistic achievement are two different things.

Tanner 88 (1988, U.S., 11 episodes, 40 mins. each) Dir: Robert Altman; Cast: Michael Murphy, Pamela Reed, Cynthia Nixon, Kevin J. O'Connor.

Anticipating the lively Hegedus-Pennebaker Clinton campaign documentary *The War Room,* this video hybrid is a collection of episodes from an HBO series by Altman and Garry *(Doonesbury)* Trudeau. Following fictional candidate Jack Tanner through actual 1988 presidential primaries, script is a hysterically funny collage of political insight and pop-culture observation. Altman's use of video and television is truly inspired—a signal of health in a medium that all too often seems braindead. Michael Murphy is perfect as the candidate and Pamela Reed is a revelation as his manager. The words "tour de force" don't do it justice.

The Best Man (1964, U.S., 102 mins., b/w) Dir: Franklin J. Schaffner; Cast: Cliff Robertson, Henry Fonda, Lee Tracy, Edie Adams.

Fonda and Robertson are the men who would be president, duking it out at a national convention. Gore Vidal's screen adaptation of his own play has a reputation as scathing political satire and its pointed wit does pop a few balloons, but the whole enterprise is dated and predictable. Schaffner's direction lacks dimension. Haskell Wexler's medium-cool cinematography gives it an edge. Oscar-nominated Tracy steals the show as party elder statesman who knows that in the game of political one-upmanship there are no ends, only means.

Hail the Conquering Hero (1944, U.S., 101 mins., b/w) Dir: Preston Sturges; Cast: Eddie Bracken, William Demarest, Ella Raines, Raymond Walburn, Franklin Pangborn.

Woodrow Truesmith (Bracken) is discharged from the Marine Corps during WWII because of his hay fever. Lamenting his fate in a N.Y. bar, he encounters six marines who bring him home, stuff him sneezing and wheezing into a uniform, and convince the townsfolk he's a hero. Woodrow, unable to quell the rising tide, is drafted to run for mayor. Gloriously impudent madcap satire by writer/director Sturges, the film turns hero worship, patriotism, small-town life and politics upside down and inside out. This is the flip side of Capra. Not to be missed.

State of the Union (1948, U.S., 124 mins., b/w) Dir: Frank Capra; Cast: Spencer Tracy, Katharine Hepburn, Angela Lansbury, Van Johnson, Adolphe Menjou.

Dying tycoon bequeaths chain of newspapers to his daughter (Lansbury), urging her to use power of the press to elect a Republican president.

Idealistic, highly successful business-man Tracy becomes her choice as well as the object of her affections. But the candidate's relationship with his ex-wife (Hepburn) complicates matters greatly. Overly talky and insufficiently screwy screwball comedy is far from Capra's best, but a lucid statement of his politics—benevolent capitalism and populist demagoguery that anticipate Ross Perot by 45 years.

The Last Hurrah (1958, U.S., 121 mins., b/w) Dir: John Ford; Cast: Spencer Tracy, Jeffrey Hunter, Pat O'Brien, Dianne Foster, Basil Rathbone, John Carradine, Jane Darwell, Donald Crisp, James Gleason.

Story of big-city mayor Frank Skeffing-ton (Tracy), the last of the great old-line Irish-Catholic pols, and his final foray in the political arena. John Ford's most overtly political film tries hard to cap-ture the look and feel of big-city poli-tics. One of those films that Hollywood and the critics of the day deemed important, but in retrospect it's stodgy and slow. Ford is surprisingly off his game here. Still, solid Tracy and famil-iar faces from the John Ford stock com-pany make the film worth a look.

Judge Priest (1934, U.S., 71 mins., b/w) Dir: John Ford; Cast: Will Rogers, Anita Louise, Stepin Fetchit.

Will Rogers is the mint-julep-sipping southern jurist up for re-election in this wonderful patchwork Americana sewn together from a handful of sto-ries by Irwin S. Cobb. One of Ford's lesser-known films, this warmhearted comedy/drama is the director's rumi-nation on life and politics in an 1890s Kentucky town haunted by ghosts of the Civil War. Rogers slips into the role of Billy Priest as if into a pair of well-worn shoes—it's a remarkably natural performance. Ford was so fond of the material that he remade it 20 years later as *The Sun Shines Bright*.

The Man Who Shot Liberty Valance (1962, U.S., 122 mins., b/w) Dir: John Ford; Cast: John Wayne, James Stew-art, Lee Marvin, Woody Strode, Vera Miles.

Surprised to find this John Ford west-ern on a list of political entries? Don't be. A substantial aspect of this remark-able movie hinges on the territorial election that sends Jimmy Stewart from the wild-west town of Shinbone to Washington, D.C. One of John Ford's most important films, it's a political western, a murder mystery, and a med-itation on American mythology. It's about appearance and reality, legend and fact, the discrepancy between recorded history and what actually happened. Stewart, John Wayne, and Lee Marvin form a triangle trapped by time in what amounts to a memory play for the ages.

CAPITOL GAMES

Oscar Wilde once said that "Ameri-can democracy means simply the bludgeoning of the people, by the people for the people." Any close inspection of the goings-on in Wash-ington reveals him to be right. But every once in a while a lone voice rings out from the very top of Capitol Hill and convinces us not to give up hope. There actually are people who go to Washington to fight the good fight. No, wait a minute—that only happens in the movies.

Mr. Smith Goes to Washington (1939, U.S., 130 mins., b/w) Dir: Frank Capra; Cast: James Stewart, Jean Arthur, Claude Rains, Guy Kibbee, Eugene Pal-lette, Beulah Bondi, Harry Carey, H. B. Warner, Charles Lane, Porter Hall.

Capra classic kicks hard and lands squarely on the seat of the U.S. govern-ment. Jimmy Stewart stars as wide-eyed eager-beaver Jefferson Smith who takes on the entire Senate—with an able assist from love-interest Arthur—and climbs to Christ-like heights in the process. The film, which caused quite a stir in Congress when it was released, manages to deliver a searing critique of the system and champion its basic values at the same time. Artful blending of D.C. landmarks with studio sets combine with top-flight ensemble acting and brilliant direction to create one of the enduring works of the American cinema. It makes lost causes seem well worth fighting for.

Protocol (1984, U.S., 96 mins.) Dir: Herbert Ross; Cast: Goldie Hawn, Chris Sarandon, Richard Romanus, Ed Begley, Jr., Gail Strickland, Andre Gregory, Cliff De Young.

We-the-people populism with Hawn as ditzy waitress who gets shot in the gluteus maximus thereby saving the life of an Arab emir. She becomes a national hero and government pawn who brings new meaning to the words "political party." Script by Buck Henry cleverly sets up the premise but disintegrates into silliness. Intended as a throwback to *Mr. Smith,* this "Goldie goes to Washington" fable falls miles short of Capra. Still, direction by Ross is smooth and the film delivers some warmhearted fun.

The Senator Was Indiscreet (1947, U.S., 81 mins., b/w) Dir: George S. Kaufman; Cast: William Powell, Ella Raines, Peter Lind Hayes.

Only film with celebrated wit, playwright, and Broadway director Kaufman at the helm concerns lame-duck senator (Powell) with his sights set on the presidency. A bumbling innocent, the schnook is compromised when his politically embarrassing diary gets into the wrong hands. Mildly engaging, rather innocuous spoof of American politics, the film was denounced by witch-hunting Senator Joe McCarthy as "un-American" and "downright trai-

torous." Proof positive that McCarthy was out of his mind.

The Seduction of Joe Tynan (1979, U.S., 107 mins.) Dir: Jerry Schatzberg; Cast: Alan Alda, Meryl Streep, Barbara Harris, Rip Torn, Melvyn Douglas.

Public and private affairs of wishy-washy senator whose love and loyalty are up for grabs. Writer/star Alda leans ever so correctly to the left while walking carefully down the middle of the road. Streep, Torn, Harris, and especially Douglas elevate the proceedings considerably, but Alda's smug liberalism and shallow personal perspective are tough to take. Given the range of existing choices, his Senator Tynan is someone we might feel compelled to vote for; we'd just hate to hang out with the guy.

True Colors (1991, U.S., 111 mins.) Dir: Herbert Ross; Cast: John Cusack, James Spader, Imogen Stubbs, Mandy Patinkin, Richard Widmark, Dina Merrill, Philip Bosco, Paul Guilfoyle.

Screenwriter Kevin Wade *(Working Girl)* takes us inside the corridors of power for a penetrating but painfully obvious look at big-time politics. Cusack and Spader are both strong as law school roomies who start out together but choose alternate routes on the road to Washington. Widmark helps the proceedings as a powerful senator, but Imogen Stubbs misses the mark as his daughter.

Advise and Consent (1962, U.S., 139 mins.) Dir: Otto Preminger; Cast: Henry Fonda, Walter Pidgeon, Charles Laughton, Don Murray, Lew Ayres, Gene Tierney, Franchot Tone, Paul Ford, Burgess Meredith.

Preminger version of Alan Drury's prize-winning novel was made with the intention of rattling the foundation of the Washington establishment. The president picks a controversial candidate for secretary of state (Fonda) and his Senate confirmation is in doubt. Strong work by all-star cast includes standout performances by Burgess Meredith and the great Charles Laughton in his final role. Lurid plot runs the gamut from strange bedfellows in a senator's closet to perjury, blackmail, and suicide. Sensationalistic? Yes. Turgid? Perhaps. But now, in the post Clarence Thomas-Anita Hill atmosphere on Capitol Hill, prophetic, *n'est-ce pas?*

The Distinguished Gentleman (1992, U.S., 112 mins.) Dir: Jonathan Lynn; Cast: Eddie Murphy, Lane Smith, Sheryl Lee Ralph, Joe Don Baker, Kevin McCarthy, James Garner.

Guess who's going to Washington now. Eddie is Thomas Jefferson Johnson, a low-plains grifter who cons his way to Capitol Hill—he runs for Congress and wins. Marty Kaplan's script has just enough Sturges snap and a feel for the flip side of Capra to make it work, and Murphy proves that, as obnoxious as he can be on screen, he's able to reach beyond his usual shtick and come up with a rounded performance. A screwball surprise.

No Way Out (1987, U.S., 114 mins.) Dir: Roger Donaldson; Cast: Kevin Costner, Gene Hackman, Sean Young, Will Patton, Howard Duff, George Dzunda, Jason Bernard, Iman, David Paymer, Fred Dalton Thompson.

Naval officer Costner hunts for killer of his girlfriend (Young), and the secretary of defense (Hackman) is the most likely suspect. But complications arise, tables are turned, and the hunter winds up as the prey. This pounding, sexy political thriller careens through the corridors of power in Washington and doesn't let up till the letdown at the end. The heat generated by Costner and Young's "inaugural ball" in the back of a limo makes it the kind of movie you should see with a friend.

WELL-GREASED MACHINES & OTHER POLITICAL DIRT

If power corrupts, and absolute power corrupts absolutely . . . then the path to power must be paved with a pretty fair share of dishonesty, chicanery, fraud, and deceit. None of these films focus on a single campaign or election; each in its own way looks deeper than that. When all is said and done, very few stones are left unturned.

The Great McGinty (1940, U.S., 81 mins., b/w) Dir: Preston Sturges; Cast: Brian Donlevy, Akim Tamiroff, Muriel Angelus, William Demarest, Allyn Joslyn.

Preston Sturges's brawling screwball satire about a bum named McGinty (Donlevy), hired to stuff ballot boxes, who falls under the wing of a corrupt political boss (Tamiroff) and winds up as governor. Sturges's directorial debut after penning a string of studio scripts, this marked the beginning of one of the great, if short-lived, writer-director careers in movie history. For *McGinty*, Sturges snared the first-ever Original Screenplay Oscar, besting Ben Hecht, John Huston, and Charles Chaplin.

The Glass Key (1942, U.S., 85 mins., b/w) Dir: Stuart Heisler; Cast: Alan Ladd, Veronica Lake, Brian Donlevy, Robert Preston, William Bendix.

Strong adaptation of Dashiell Hammett novel with Ladd as right-hand man to a big-time political wardhealer (Donlevy). The pulpy plot twists and turns around dirty doings of the political machine and the machinations of a mysterious dame (Veronica Lake). Heisler's noirish direction neatly matches the hardboiled script by Jonathan Latimer. And frankly, dialogue that is peppered with lines like "He throwed another Joe," "Gimme the roscoe," and "Get out, you heel, this is the kiss-off" is simply irresistible. See the movie, then read the book.

Meet John Doe (1941, U.S., 132 mins., b/w) Dir: Frank Capra; Cast: Gary Cooper, Barbara Stanwyck, Walter Brennan, Edward Arnold, Spring Byington, James Gleason.

Stanwyck's the wisecracking reporter and Cooper the dupe and ultimate martyr in this political parable about the threat of fascism. Capra imagines a political process where the powers-that-would-be are corrupt beyond belief, but trusts so deeply in the human spirit that good cannot help but triumph over evil. An expert blend of screwball comedy and grim drama (almost tragedy), the film is also a visual masterpiece. The John Doe convention in the rain at Yankee Stadium is exquisite. Ending was reshot five times and some critics insist wrong one was chosen. Question remains: How far can a martyr actually go in Hollywood?

Boomerang (1947, U.S., 88 mins., b/w) Dir: Elia Kazan; Cast: Dana Andrews, Jane Wyatt, Lee J. Cobb.
■
Courtroom drama has D.A. Andrews faced with trying an innocent man because the powers that be and the back-room boys that prop them up need a conviction. Based on a true story, this early Kazan employs strikingly innovative, influential, pseudo-documentary approach. Has a real feel for the knot of political corruption twisting away in the underbelly of American urban life.

A Face in the Crowd (1957, U.S., 125 mins., b/w) Dir: Elia Kazan; Cast: Andy Griffith, Patricia Neal, Anthony Franciosa, Walter Matthau, Lee Remick.

Kazan 10 years later, working with *On the Waterfront* partner, writer Budd Schulberg, created this in-your-face harangue charting the rise of a guitar-picking yokel to megalomaniacal TV star with dangerous political ambitions. Griffith's Lonesome Rhodes is a far cry from Sheriff Andy Taylor—this is Andy in overdrive. Admired by many (it was one of Truffaut's favorites), the film suffers under the weight of heavy-handed script and direction. Neal and Matthau are good in co-starring roles and Lee Remick makes an impressive screen debut as a sexy, baton-twirling slut.

All the King's Men (1949, U.S., 109 mins., b/w) Dir: Robert Rossen; Cast: Broderick Crawford, Joanne Dru, John Ireland, Mercedes McCambridge, John Derek, Shepherd Strudwick, Anne Seymour.

Dark, disturbing political drama based on Robert Penn Warren's Pulitzer Prize-winning *roman à clef* about Louisiana legend Huey Long. Crawford won a well-deserved Academy Award as Willie Stark, a Long-like politician—full of bombast and bluster—who bullies his way into the governor's mansion. It's a character of awesome complexity, energy, ambition, and power. Beautifully shot and cut, every frame of the film (Best Picture Oscar) explodes with QUALITY. Too bad it moves like a lumbering ox.

Blaze (1989, U.S., 120 mins.) Dir: Ron Shelton; Cast: Paul Newman, Lolita Davidovitch, Robert Wuhl, Jeffrey DeMunn.

Story of Earl Kemp Long—Huey's younger brother, governor of Louisiana, the most investigated man in state history and proud of it—and his relationship with Miss Spontaneous Combustion ("and we do mean bustion") herself, Bourbon Street stripper Blaze Starr. Newman plays Long as a cross between Dr. John, Dr. Zorba, and Harpo Marx—it's his most original characterization. Writer/director Shelton *(Bull Durham, White Men Can't Jump)*, working from Starr's autobiography, has concocted a wonderfully comic love story and as affectionate a portrait of political machinery as one is likely to find.

City of Hope (1991, U.S., 129 mins.) Dir: John Sayles; Cast: Vincent Spano, Tony Lo Bianco, Joe Morton, John Sayles, Angela Bassett, David Strathairn.

Writer/director Sayles labors hard to expose corruption on every level of municipal government and reveal the pain of the human condition, and winds up trying to make this multi-tiered urban melodrama transcend itself. Ambitious effort gets bogged down in bumper stickers masquerading as dialogue and direction that doesn't know quite how to get where it wants to go. Many good performances get lost along the way. Fiercely independent Sayles gets credit for honorable intentions, but like the pols in this film, we're looking for a bigger payoff.

HAIL TO THE CHIEFS

There are many roads to the White House. And many angles from which to view the presidency. Here are some biographies, fables, and speculations about men who became president, before, during, and after they took up residence at 1600 Pennsylvania Avenue.

Young Mr. Lincoln (1939, U.S., 100 mins., b/w) Dir: John Ford; Cast: Henry Fonda, Alice Brady, Richard Cromwell, Donald Meek, Marjorie Weaver.

Director Ford (who crafted the script with Lamar Trotti) works in bold, mythic strokes on a historical canvas to paint this richly textured portrait of Honest Abe (Henry Fonda) as youthful country lawyer on his way to becoming our most revered political icon. A fundamentally Fordian fiction centering around a tumultuous small-town murder trial, the film is ripe with religious symbolism and resonant with meaning, feeling, and faith in the American spirit. Less about the political process than its spiritual foundation, it's a deeply personal, deceptively simple film with epic implications and much to say about the fundamental belief system of this country.

Abe Lincoln in Illinois (1940, U.S., 110 mins., b/w) Dir: John Cromwell; Cast: Raymond Massey, Ruth Gordon.

Based on the play by Sherwood Anderson, this rather typical Hollywood biopic stars Raymond Massey as Lincoln, the role he considered his most memorable. If he hadn't left such an indelible mark as Dr. Gillespie in TV's *Dr. Kildare,* we would have to agree. Suffice it to say, when Americans think of their 16th president, they likely picture Massey or Fonda. The debate has long raged as to who was the better Lincoln. We give the nod to Hank.

Wilson (1944, U.S., 154 mins.) Dir: Henry King; Cast: Alexander Knox, Geraldine Fitzgerald, Charles Coburn, Vincent Price.

Boring bio of America's World War I president made in 1944 is only of interest when seen in the light of WWII propaganda. Lamar Trotti's Oscar-winning screenplay (doctored extensively by producer Darryl Zanuck) portrays Wilson as a regular Joe with enormous integrity and an almost prophetic instinct for great issues. Zanuck lards the production with ponderous detail and ridiculous characters, and the end result is an unhappy convergence of politics and popular culture.

Sunrise at Campobello (1960, U.S., 143 mins.) Dir: Vincent J. Donehue; Cast: Ralph Bellamy, Greer Garson.

Adaptation of Broadway play about Franklin Delano Roosevelt's battle with polio and his courageous struggle to take first steps on one of the most remarkable political journeys in American history. Released during Nixon-Kennedy race for the White House, the film reflects writer/producer Dore Schary's political concerns. FDR monologue on the issue of Al Smith's Catholicism responds directly to questions voters had about JFK . . . who became, of course, our first Catholic president.

Eleanor and Franklin (1976, U.S./MTV, 208 mins.) Dir: Daniel Petrie; Cast: Jane Alexander, Edward Herrmann, Ed Flanders, Rosemary Murphy.
■ Made-for-TV adaptation of Joseph Lash's Pulitzer Prize-winning book, which was based on the private papers of Eleanor Roosevelt. More about her than him, it's the intimate chronicle of a woman and a marriage, a union that had an enormous impact on the ebb and flow of the American Century. The stunning performances by Edward Herrmann and Jane Alexander capture not only the figures of history but the frailties and foibles of the human beings.

Eleanor and Franklin: The White House Years (1977, U.S./MTV, 144 mins.) Dir: Daniel Petrie; Cast: Jane Alexander, Edward Herrmann, Priscilla Pointer.
■ While *Eleanor and Franklin* covers the expanse from FDR's salad days to his death in 1945, this equally effective sequel zeros in on his presidency and Eleanor's stint as First Lady.

Gabriel Over the White House (1933, U.S., 87 mins., b/w) Dir: Gregory La Cava; Cast: Walter Huston, Karen Morley, Franchot Tone, Jean Parker, Dickie Moore.

Huston is a corrupt politician who bluffs his way to the presidency at the height of the Great Depression. Confronted with collapse and despair everywhere, the wheeler-dealer turns a new leaf and offers the people a new deal. Released on the eve of Roosevelt's first inauguration, the film fulfilled the Depression-era audience's demands for escapist comedy and, at the same time, touched seriously on important issues. Rare, hard-to-find gem.

Wild in the Streets (1968, U.S., 97 mins.) Dir: Barry Shear; Cast: Shelley Winters, Christopher Jones, Diane Varsi, Hal Holbrook, Bert Freed, Millie Perkins, Richard Pryor.

Far-out sixties fable plays on notion that no one over 30 can be trusted. When voting age is lowered to 14, rock and roller Max Frost (Jones) is elected president and everyone over the big three-oh is carted away and force-fed LSD. Script by Robert Thom is trippy political popcorn—think Orwell on orange sunshine. Depending on how you relate to the sixties, tune in and turn on at your own risk.

All the President's Men (1976, U.S., 136 mins.) Dir: Alan J. Pakula; Cast: Dustin Hoffman, Robert Redford, Jason Robards, Jr., Jane Alexander, Martin Balsam, Jack Warden.

Redford and Hoffman star as Woodward and Bernstein, the *Washington Post* investigative reporters who first realized that the Nixon White House was a house of cards ready to tumble. Scenarist William Goldman (Oscar) turns the events that led to the Watergate scandal into a pulsating political thriller. Director Pakula doesn't miss a beat. Story grabs and holds from start to finish. Even though we know the ending, watching Tricky Dickie fall is one of the screen's great political pleasures.

Secret Honor (1984, U.S., 90 mins.) Dir: Robert Altman; Cast: Philip Baker Hall.

Nixon's the one in this one-man play— a nifty mix of biographical detail, historical fact, and psychological flight of fancy, brilliantly brought to the screen by Altman. But the real triumph here is Philip Baker Hall's. His mad, rambling Nixon is neither caricature nor impersonation—it's acting of the highest order. Let loose on a sea of memory and scotch, this is the unindicted co-conspirator in search of release and redemption for a life of political crimes. If Nixon never spent a night like this, the film makes you feel that he damn well should have.

ASSASSINATIONS

On November 22, 1963, when Walter Cronkite, voice choked with emotion, interrupted a CBS broadcast of *As the World Turns* with a news flash from Dallas, it changed forever the way we'd react to the word "assassination." Many of the films on this list relate directly to that day. But rounding it out are a number of films about leaders and assassins, real and imaginary, foreign as well as domestic, which add much to our insight into this most heinous of all political crimes.

JFK (1991, U.S., 188 mins., c & b/w) Dir: Oliver Stone; Cast: Kevin Costner, Sissy Spacek, Kevin Bacon, Tommy Lee Jones, Laurie Metcalf, Gary Oldman, Michael Rooker, Jay O. Sanders.

The age of innocence that ended when President Kennedy was killed gave way to an age of conspiracy and cover-up that is still with us. *JFK* is Oliver Stone's attempt to get to the bottom of a seemingly bottomless pit of unanswered questions. Using New Orleans D.A. Jim Garrison (Costner) as his point man, Stone sets out in search of the truth. The blend of documentary footage and drama is dazzling. The acting is a marvel from top to bottom. And whether or not you buy the conclusion, you're bound to rethink the meaning of truth, justice, and the American way.

Ruby (1992, U.S., 110 mins.) Dir: John MacKenzie; Cast: Danny Aiello, Sherilyn Fenn, Arliss Howard, Tobin Bell, David Duchovny.

On Sunday, November 24, 1963, two days after Kennedy was shot, Jack Ruby walked into the basement of Dallas police headquarters and murdered the only man ever officially accused of killing the president. Ruby's life of crimes and criminal connections, his actions and motives on and around that infamous weekend, are mysterious and pertinent enough to warrant a movie. This particular blend of fact and conjecture, largely unseen when first released, is worth catching up with. Aiello as Ruby makes it that way.

Winter Kills (1979, U.S., 97 mins.) Dir: William Richert; Cast: Jeff Bridges, John Huston, Belinda Bauer, Anthony Perkins, Richard Boone, Sterling Hayden, Toshiro Mifune, Eli Wallach, Dorothy Malone, Elizabeth Taylor.

Obvious parallels to the Kennedy assassination form the basis for this over-the-top black comedy starring Bridges as the dead prexy's brother trying to crack the conspiracy. Butchered by the producers, this baby was a box-office bomb when first released, but the director's cut exists on tape. In adapting Richard Condon's novel, writer/director William Richert has fashioned a sly, sexy, stylish movie. Spirited work by a wonderful cast features inspired turns by Tony Perkins as a military loon and John Huston as the powerful pater familias.

The Parallax View (1974, U.S., 102 mins.) Dir: Alan J. Pakula; Cast: Warren Beatty, William Daniels, Hume Cronyn, Paula Prentiss.

Paranoia runs rampant in this political thriller about the assassination of a U.S. senator. Beatty gives his patented dreamboat/somnambulist performance as an investigative reporter who stumbles and mumbles his way into a conspiracy buff's worst nightmare. Director Pakula creates an intricate geometric web of doubt and fear; it's a stunning, modernist vision of America. While the action sequences are hit and miss, the ending is blindingly brilliant.

The Manchurian Candidate (1962, U.S., 126 mins., b/w) Dir: John Frankenheimer; Cast: Frank Sinatra, Laurence Harvey, Janet Leigh, Angela Lansbury.

Wild melange of satire, mystery, and political tract, this adaptation of Richard Condon's novel actually brings right-wing extremists and commies together in a conspiracy to kill a presidential candidate. Harvey is the brainwashed war hero set up by his megalomaniacal mom (Lansbury) to do the deed. Francis Albert is the army intelligence major whose nightmares help him figure things out. Director Frankenheimer mixes traditional film noir elements with innovative technique and the result is stimulating fun. Made the year before Kennedy was shot, it stakes a claim on political as well as artistic vision.

Seven Days in May (1964, U.S., 118 mins., b/w) Dir: John Frankenheimer; Cast: Burt Lancaster, Kirk Douglas, Ava Gardner, Fredric March, Edmond O'Brien.

Fredric March is the pacifist prez in this intricately plotted thriller about Pentagon plan to take him out—not by assassination, but with a coup d'état. Rod Serling's script from best-selling novel is less *Twilight Zone* fantasy than "it can happen here" warning. The raging conflict in America in 1964 was between those who wanted to ban the Bomb and those who wanted to drop it. Frankenheimer's taut direction captures the Cold War climate quite well. But, hell, in an age where Barry Goldwater was a viable alternative, you didn't need a weatherman to know which way the wind was blowing.

Nashville (1975, U.S., 159 mins.) Dir: Robert Altman; Cast: Lily Tomlin, Shelley Duvall, Henry Gibson, Ronee Blakley, Karen Black, Barbara Harris, Allen Garfield, Geraldine Chaplin, Keenan Wynn, Keith Carradine.

Altman deftly orchestrates dozens of characters, story lines, and leitmotivs into a cinematic symphony of country and western sights and sounds. The violent convergence of music, politics, hopes, and dreams at the campaign rally conclusion is remarkable in its scope and vision. When little Barbara Harris picks up the microphone to sing, she becomes the embodiment of America's ability to transcend national tragedy. Kennedy references throughout pave the way for what's coming. An extraordinary achievement from start to finish, it was named Best Picture by the New York Film Critics and National Board of Review. Keith Carradine's "I'm Easy" won the Oscar for Best Song.

Taxi Driver (1976, U.S., 112 mins.) Dir: Martin Scorsese; Cast: Robert De Niro, Cybill Shepherd, Jodie Foster, Peter Boyle, Albert Brooks, Leonard Harris.

Scorsese's nightmare vision about New York cabbie Travis Bickle (De Niro in a scorching performance) and how his obsession with straight-laced campaign worker (Shepherd) leads to an assassination attempt on a presidential candidate. When that fails, he transfers his fixation to a 12-year-old hooker played by Jodie Foster, which leads to a shocking explosion of violence. In one of history's sick, twisted ironies, real-life would-be assassin John Hinckley (who obviously felt De Niro was talking directly to him) shot Ronald Reagan based on his own obsession with Foster and this film—adding new and perverse dimension to the notion that life imitates art.

All the King's Men (1949, U.S., 109 mins., b/w) Dir: Robert Rossen; Cast:

Broderick Crawford, Joanne Dru, John Ireland, Mercedes McCambridge, John Derek, Shepherd Strudwick, Anne Seymour.

Sorry to tip the ending, but if you know that the Crawford character is based on Huey Long, and that Long was killed by an assassin's bullet, then you might want to watch this film for the light it sheds on the first major American political assassination of modern times.

Suddenly (1954, U.S., 77 mins., b/w) Dir: Lewis Allen; Cast: Frank Sinatra, Sterling Hayden, Nancy Gates, James Gleason.

Trio of bad guys led by Sinatra invades an average American home overlooking a railroad station in small-town America. Their purpose: gun down the president of the United States when he stops to change trains. Tough, compact, claustrophobic thriller hits quick and hard, like a punch in the gut. An assassination melodrama that's not really about assassination—it's about unexpected violence "suddenly" (the name of the town) shattering the peaceful existence of one particular family.

In the Line of Fire (1993, U.S., 127 mins.) Dir: Wolfgang Peterson; Cast: Clint Eastwood, John Malkovich, Rene Russo, Dylan McDermott, Gary Cole, Fred Dalton Thompson, John Mahoney.

Secret Service dinosaur (Eastwood) who failed JFK in '63 goes one on one with a modern-day maniac bent on killing the current prez. Clint trades on his aging hero image and cashes it in for one of the best performances of his career. Malkovich was nominated for an Oscar as the bad guy and we think

he should have won—his would-be assassin is one of the outstanding screen villains in movie history. Peterson nails the action perfectly without losing sight of the deeper implications in Jeff Maguire's script. The blend of suspense with the theme of guilt and redemption gives the film a decidedly Hitchcockian air, though it never feels the least bit derivative.

The Prisoner of Shark Island (1936, U.S., 94 mins., b/w) Dir: John Ford; Cast: Warner Baxter, Gloria Stuart, John Carradine, Harry Carey.

Fordian "biography" of Samuel Mudd, physician condemned to prison after unwittingly aiding Lincoln's assassin. Opens with tender evocation of Lincoln as national healer, and the Ford's Theatre sequence is a marvelous bit of historic reconstruction. The rest centers around Mudd's time in jail and uses the good doctor as a Lincoln surrogate. A significant piece of Lincoln lore— American history selectively told to help create American myth.

The Day of the Jackal (1973, Great Britain-France, 141 mins.) Dir: Fred Zinnemann; Cast: Edward Fox, Cyril Cusack, Delphine Seyrig.

Director Zinnemann turns Frederick Forsyth's best-selling novel into a smooth, clinical cinematic thriller. "Jackal" is the code name for the expert assassin (Fox) hired by a group of disgruntled Frenchmen to eliminate President Charles De Gaulle. Goes beyond mere suspense as it examines the complex methodology of a political hit in painstaking detail. A cold, calculating film, it involves you in its story, but you walk away feeling very little.

DIVERSIONS

HOLIDAYS

AULD LANG SYNE

Names like the Marx Brothers and Fred and Ginger bring to mind classic films with laughs and romance and champagne. They're also classic films that you have seen a hundred times. If you're not out celebrating in some more public fashion, here are some fresh choices for New Year's Eve viewing.

Peter's Friends (1992, Great Britain, 100 mins.) Dir: Kenneth Branagh; Cast: Kenneth Branagh, Emma Thompson, Rita Rudner, Steven Fry, Hugh Laurie.

An English *Big Chill,* with Branagh and his old college chums getting together for a holiday weekend. Light fun mixes well with some serious themes right up to the rather clunky ending.

When Harry Met Sally (1989, U.S., 95 mins.) Dir: Rob Reiner; Cast: Billy Crystal, Meg Ryan, Carrie Fisher.

Not much champagne until the New Year's Eve scene at the end, but lots of laughs and romance. Ryan uses her limited skills to great effect, especially in her bit at Katz's Deli. A very good pick for a romantically fraught evening.

The Poseidon Adventure (1972, U.S., 117 mins.) Dir: Ronald Neame; Cast: Gene Hackman, Ernest Borgnine, Shelley Winters, Stella Stevens, Jack Albertson, Carol Lynley, Red Buttons, Roddy McDowall, Leslie Nielsen, Pamela Sue Martin.

A tidal wave flips over a big ocean liner in mid-New Year's Eve party and the survivors struggle their way to the bottom (now the top). Sound like any parties you've ever been to? Tied with *The*

Towering Inferno for best disaster movie, it blends campiness, great effects, drama, and an apparently shameless Shelley Winters.

Holiday Inn (1942, U.S., 101 mins., b/w) Dir: Mark Sandrich; Cast: Bing Crosby, Fred Astaire, Marjorie Reynolds, Virginia Dale, Walter Abel, Louise Beavers.

Der Bingle and Fred vie for the same girl at Crosby's holidays-only club in Connecticut. The year-round settings and balance between Bing's crooning and Astaire's dancing keep it in here despite the movie's overexposure.

Happy New Year (1973, France, 112 mins.) Dir: Claude Lelouch; Cast: Lino Ventura, Françoise Fabian, Charles Gerard, Andre Falcon.

Two ex-cons get snared by love as they plan to knock over a Cannes jewelry store. Lelouch pokes fun at his own movie *A Man and a Woman* in this very likable, funny film. The exposition is torturous at first, but hang in there and you'll see that this is a great New Year's film.

Get Crazy (1983, U.S., 92 mins.) Dir: Allan Arkush; Cast: Malcolm McDowell, Allen Gorowitz, Daniel Stern, Lou Reed, Franklin Ajaye.

A perfect choice for New Year's Eve. A rock promoter tries to put on a huge New Year's Eve concert at a Fillmore East-type of hall, but everything goes wrong in very funny ways. Lots of cameos from familiar faces, including Bobby Sherman (!) and Lou Reed.

Holiday (1938, U.S., 93 mins., b/w) Dir: George Cukor; Cast: Katharine Hepburn, Cary Grant, Doris Nolan, Lew Ayres, Edward Everett Horton, Binnie Barnes, Ruth Donnelly, Henry Daniell.

Love among the blue bloods. Grant and socialite Hepburn find each other as well as countless witty things to say in this sophisticated screwball comedy, the second film version of Philip Barry's play. The first stars Ann Harding and Robert Ames and would make a nice substitute if you've seen Cary and Kate once too often.

Ocean's Eleven (1960, U.S., 127 mins.) Dir: Lewis Milestone; Cast: Frank Sinatra, Dean Martin, Sammy Davis, Jr., Joey Bishop, Peter Lawford, Angie Dickinson.

Sinatra lines up his cronies to knock over five Vegas casinos on New Year's Eve. The Rat Pack was actually more of a Rat Herd. Sammy, Peter, Joey, Dino, Angie, and more all stand around and display fantastic amounts of attitude. The political discussion they have about midway through is hysterical considering what we now know about what these guys were actually doing then and what they did later. Excessive, goofy, filled with laughs both intentional and unintentional—what more could you ask for on New Year's Eve?

ERIN GO BRAGH

Along with New Year's Eve, St. Patrick's Day is one of the best days of the year to stay tucked in at home, safe from the revellers. Here are some films about the ould sod that should go well with a potful of corned beef and a six-pack of green beer.

The Dead (1987, U.S.-Great Britain-West Germany, 83 mins.) Dir: John Huston; Cast: Anjelica Huston, Donal McCann, Helena Carroll, Cathleen Delany, Dan O'Herlihy, Donal Donnelly.

John Huston's last film is an adaptation of Joyce's short story about a quietly unhappy marriage. Affecting, beautiful, and slight; the Irish cast and rich atmosphere cover the fact that there's not much of a plot.

The Quiet Man (1952, U.S., 129 mins., b/w) Dir: John Ford; Cast: John Wayne, Maureen O'Hara, Barry Fitzgerald, Victor McLaglen, Mildred Natwick.

This is the Irish movie that you probably watch every year. The Duke plays an Irish-American boxer who returns to Ireland and wins the hand of the comely Maureen O'Hara. The fact is, it's a wonderful John Ford movie and unless your viewings of it number in the double digits, the film deserves another look.

The Playboys (1992, U.S., 110 mins.) Dir: Gillies MacKennon; Cast: Albert Finney, Aidan Quinn, Robin Wright, Milo O'Shea, Alan Devlin, Niamh Cusack.

Policeman Albert Finney and actor Aidan Quinn battle for the hand of Robin Wright, who has scandalized her small village by having a child out of wedlock. No matter how cruel time has been to Finney's face, the man can act with the best of them. Nice for the look at traveling theater and the bond the Irish have with it.

Parnell (1937, U.S., 118 mins., b/w) Dir: John M. Stahl; Cast: Clark Gable, Myrna Loy, Edmund Gwenn, Donald Crisp.

■
You just can't separate Ireland from politics. This biography stars Clark Gable as the great Irish nationalist leader Charles Parnell. The film bombed. Still, it may stir some patriotic feelings in hard-core Irishmen and it's a handy refresher on history you may have forgotten.

The Informer (1935, U.S., 100 mins., b/w) Dir: John Ford; Cast: Victor McLaglen, Preston Foster.

A John Ford classic about friendship and betrayal during the Irish Rebellion of 1922. The screenplay won an Oscar, as did Victor McLaglen for Best Actor. A must-see.

Ryan's Daughter (1970, Great Britain, 192 mins.) Dir: David Lean; Cast: Robert Mitchum, Trevor Howard, Sarah Miles, John Mills, Christopher Jones.

A sluggish tale of a love triangle in Northern Ireland between a young woman, her schoolteacher husband, and a British soldier. Visually lush, but with such a cast, such a director, and a Robert Bolt script, you keep wanting more. Great for atmospherics, though.

Cal (1984, Great Britain, 102 mins.) Dir: Pat O'Connor; Cast: Helen Mirren, John Lynch, Donal McCann, John Kavenhagh.

An absolutely heartbreaking film that tells the story of a young IRA wheelman who falls in love with the widow of a British soldier he helped to kill. This should be required viewing for every knee-jerk IRA sympathizer and Orangeman. Helen Mirren is fabulous and, yes, the score by Mark Knopfler of Dire Straits is available at your record store.

The Crying Game (1992, Great Britain, 112 mins.) Dir: Neil Jordan; Cast: Stephen Rea, Miranda Richardson, Forest Whitaker, Jim Broadbent, Jaye Davidson.

IRA man Rea falls for the lover of the British soldier he has just kidnapped. A film that questions all your assumptions about life, love, and politics. By the way, don't rent this one with the kids around; you'll spend the next three months answering questions.

The Commitments (1991, Great Britain, 117 mins.) Dir: Alan Parker; Cast: Robert Arkins, Michael Aherne, Angeline Ball, Maria Doyle, Dave Finnegan.

Alan Parker, of *Fame* fame, whipped up this bit of Irish cotton candy about a group of working-class Dublin 20-somethings who start their own soul band. The down-and-out in Dublin details are strong and it's fun to watch as long as you keep believing that it's a real movie, not just the collection of music videos it really is. The one reason to hate the film is that some people now think *The Commitments* introduced songs like "Mustang Sally" and "Try a Little Tenderness" to the world. Maybe they should do an album with Michael Bolton.

THE LAST SUPPER & OTHER SEDERS

We'll assume you've seen *The Robe* and *Ben-Hur*. If you haven't, you should put this book down and scamper off to the video store before you even consider any of the following for holiday viewing.

The Ten Commandments (1956, U.S., 219 mins.) Dir: Cecil B. DeMille; Cast: Charlton Heston, Edward G. Robinson, Yul Brynner, Cedric Hardwicke, Debra Paget, John Derek, Anne Baxter.

This is required watching along with the two mentioned above, but we're listing it here because it's always worth seeing again. Heston and Brynner and the water flowing red and the parting of the Red Sea and the plagues and Edward G. Robinson and on and on. This "Classics Illustrated" version of Exodus is simply great.

King of Kings (1961, U.S., 161 mins.) Dir: Nicholas Ray; Cast: Jeffrey Hunter, Robert Ryan, Siobhan McKenna, Viveca Lindfors.

The 1961 version gets the nod over the 1927 *King of Kings* and *The Greatest Story Ever Told* (1965) because Nicholas Ray directed it, it's very effective visually, and it's actually about Christ and not the number of stars per scene Ray could fit in. You're not likely to have a spiritual awakening, but it is a good film.

Barabbas (1962, U.S., 134 mins.) Dir: Richard Fleischer; Cast: Anthony

Quinn, Silvana Mangano, Arthur Kennedy, Jack Palance, Ernest Borgnine, Katy Jurado.

Anthony Quinn stars as the criminal released so that Jesus could take his place on the cross. Another epic film sure to be on during the Easter season and worth your time if you're willing to commit the two plus hours involved. Keep in mind that the eclipse during the crucifixion is an actual eclipse, the first ever filmed.

The Last Temptation of Christ (1988, U.S., 160 mins.) Dir: Martin Scorsese; Cast: Willem Dafoe, Harvey Keitel, Barbara Hershey, Harry Dean Stanton, David Bowie, Verna Bloom, Andre Gregory, Victor Argo.

If you're offended by the very idea of Christ having thoughts of sex and marriage, move along. Scorsese's adaptation of Nikos Kazantzakis's novel raised many hackles when it was released, but many viewers found it a moving examination of Christ's humanity.

Godspell (1973, U.S., 103 mins.) Dir: David Greene; Cast: Victor Garber, David Haskell.

■
Jesus Christ Superstar (1973, U.S., 107 mins.) Dir: Norman Jewison; Cast: Ted Neeley, Carl Anderson, Joshua Mostel, Yvonne Elliman.

As they are inextricably linked in your mind, so they will remain in this list. Definitely products of their time, both films are dated and are more interesting as nostalgia than as either religious experience or fine movie-making. Still, a lot of us can't get through an Eastertide without humming "Day by Day" or "All for the Best." And, sadly, the *Godspell* look is back.

The Last Supper (1977, Cuba, 110 mins.) Dir: Tomás Gutiérrez Alea; Cast: Silvanno Rey, Luis Alberto García, Nelsom Villagra, José Antonio Rodríguez.

A Cuban slaveholder repents and tries to bring his servants to the church by having them reenact the Last Supper.

Jesus of Montreal (1989, Canada, 118 mins.) Dir: Denys Arcand; Cast: Lothaire Bluteau, Catherine Wilkening, Johanne-Marie Tremblay, Remy Girard, Robert Lepage.

An Easter movie for grown-ups. The drama surrounding an avant-garde production of the Passion in Montreal begins to resemble the Passion itself. A thought-provoking film and not for archconservatives, but a clear statement of Christ's message and the values of faith and action.

Monty Python's Life of Brian (1979, Great Britain, 91 mins.) Dir: Terry Jones; Cast: Graham Chapman, Terry Gilliam, John Cleese, Terry Jones, Michael Palin, Eric Idle.

This Monty Python version of the New Testament chronicles the life of a man who is constantly mistaken for Christ. Some may say it's offensive and sacrilegious, but the fact is, all the jokes are about those exploiting Jesus, not Jesus himself. A perfect antidote if you've watched too many religious epics.

Easter Parade (1948, U.S., 103 mins.) Dir: Charles Walters; Cast: Judy Garland, Fred Astaire, Ann Miller, Peter Lawford.

The bonnet, eggs, bunny, etc., say Easter to many and this Astaire/Garland musical is perfect for them. There's not much real Easter in here, but you weren't looking for that anyway if you're watching this.

Avalon (1990, U.S., 127 mins.) Dir: Barry Levinson; Cast: Armin Mueller-Stahl, Aidan Quinn, Elizabeth Perkins, Kevin Pollak, Joan Plowright, Lou Jacobi, Elijah Wood, Leo Fuchs, Israel Rubinek.

A moving story of a family of Jewish

immigrants in Baltimore, with some important scenes taking place at Passover. A sad and lovely film by Levinson. The fact is, after *The Ten Commandments,* there aren't many other Passover films.

THE FOURTH OF JULY

Every other day of the year, most of us grumble about how this country is going right down the toilet along with our tax dollars. On July 4th, though, we do manage to shut up for a few hours and give some thought to why we're Americans. Here are some films about the Revolution and the American experience to watch between the wienies and the fireworks.

Yankee Doodle Dandy (1942, U.S., 126 mins., b/w) Dir: Michael Curtiz; Cast: James Cagney, Walter Huston, Joan Leslie, Jeanne Cagney, Richard Whorf, Rosemary De Camp.

It's going to be on, so tune in if you haven't seen it in a while. Cagney was never better than he is here as composer George M. Cohan. It's getting harder to find the original black-and-white version since it's been colorized, but this is one film that doesn't suffer from a dose of unnaturally bright red, white, and blue.

1776 (1972, U.S., 150 mins.) Dir: Peter H. Hunt; Cast: William Daniels, Howard Da Silva, Ken Howard, Blythe Danner.

The image of John Adams, Ben Franklin, and Tom Jefferson dancing about, singing of the Declaration of Independence may strike you as odd, but this film works. It's a solid American musical and not syrupy at all; the performances and settings are first-rate and the drama builds effectively to the climactic signing of the Declaration.

Consider emigrating if the ending doesn't give you goose bumps.

Mr. Smith Goes to Washington (1939, U.S., 130 mins., b/w) Dir: Frank Capra; Cast: James Stewart, Jean Arthur, Claude Rains, Guy Kibbee, Eugene Pallette, Beulah Bondi, Harry Carey, H. B. Warner, Charles Lane, Porter Hall.

Young Senator Stewart finds little but corruption when he takes his seat in Congress. Capra could be the one filmmaker who best understood what America is all about. This movie expresses the fears and hopes that we felt then and still feel about this country.

Johnny Tremain (1957, U.S., 80 mins.) Dir: Robert Stevenson; Cast: Hal Stalmaster, Luana Patten, Sebastian Cabot.

Disney version of Esther Forbes's novel about a boy in the Revolutionary War. Solid fare for the kids in the house. If the kids are very young, try to find *Ben and Me,* a wonderful Disney cartoon about the adventures of Ben Franklin's mouse pal Amos.

The Music Man (1962, U.S., 151 mins.) Dir: Morton Da Costa; Cast: Robert Preston, Shirley Jones, Buddy Hackett, Pert Kelton, Ronny Howard, Paul Ford, Hermione Gingold.

This is America in all its small-town splendor, as conman Preston falls in love with River City while he's trying to fleece its citizens. "Seventy-six Trombones" are here, along with brass-band concerts in the park, nosy neighbors, and a sweet librarian named Marian. Have a glass of lemonade and enjoy, because by now, River City is probably a strip of fast-food joints and a mall.

Moscow on the Hudson (1984, U.S., 115 mins.) Dir: Paul Mazursky; Cast: Robin Williams, Maria Conchita Alonso, Cleavant Derricks.

Somewhere along the way, many of us have forgotten that all of our ancestors were in one form or another immigrants to America. Mazursky's serio-comic film about a Russian musician defecting to the U.S. will make you consider what being an American means, which seems an appropriate activity for the day.

The Howards of Virginia (1940, U.S., 122 mins., b/w) Dir: Frank Lloyd; Cast: Cary Grant, Martha Scott, Cedric Hardwicke, Alan Marshal.

A longish costume drama about a famous Virginia family during the Revolutionary War. Fine if you're interested in the period.

Drums Along the Mohawk (1939, U.S., 103 mins.) Dir: John Ford; Cast: Claudette Colbert, Henry Fonda, Edna May Oliver, John Carradine.

Ford lent his master's touch to this film about colonial life in upstate New York. This one has all the action and drama that *The Howards of Virginia* lacks, though it might not satisfy a desire for views of early American finery. A good choice any time of the year.

The Devil's Disciple (1959, Great Britain, 82 mins.) Dir: Guy Hamilton; Cast: Kirk Douglas, Burt Lancaster, Laurence Olivier.

A nice change from the standard good guy/bad guy look at the Revolution. George Bernard Shaw's caustic satire on the war for American independence leaves no one unscathed and provides a vehicle for memorable performances from Olivier, Douglas, and Lancaster. You won't find a better script or cast on this list.

The Time of Their Lives (1946, U.S., 82 mins., b/w) Dir: Charles Barton; Cast: Bud Abbott, Lou Costello, Marjorie Reynolds, Binnie Barnes.

You may not believe it, but there actually is a funny Abbott and Costello movie and this is it. Costello plays the ghost of a patriot wrongly labeled a traitor who haunts a house inhabited by Abbott, a descendant of the man who did him in during the Revolutionary War. The kids will like it and if you let yourself, you will too.

TRICKS & TREATS

Talk all you want about witches and Dracula and Frankenstein, but the scariest things, the whole point of the Halloween celebration, are ghosts. So what better to watch on this day than a ghost story? Not all of the following will frighten, but worrying about your kids out trick-or-treating is probably scary enough.

Blithe Spirit (1945, Great Britain, 96 mins.) Dir: David Lean; Cast: Rex Harrison, Constance Cummings, Kay Hammond, Margaret Rutherford.

Elegant and funny adaptation of Noel Coward's play about a man whose long-dead first wife comes back to haunt him and his new marriage. A quintessential English comedy with great performances by Margaret Rutherford and Rex Harrison.

Doña Flor and Her Two Husbands (1978, Brazil, 106 mins.) Dir: Bruno Barreto; Cast: Sonia Braga, José Wilker, Mauro Mendoca.

Another spouse returns. This time a lusty late husband reappears with certain corporeal abilities intact to bring love to his wife, now trapped in an unsatisfying marriage. Based on Jorge Amado's novel, it's full of good Brazilian pop and is definitely too spicy for the younger ghouls in the house. You'll enjoy it, though.

Ghost (1990, U.S., 127 mins.) Dir: Jerry Zucker; Cast: Patrick Swayze, Demi Moore, Whoopi Goldberg, Tony Goldwyn, Rick Aviles, Gail Boggs, Armelia McQueen, Vincent Schiavelli.

Hopefully the very last dead-lover-comes-back movie. Swayze's ghost returns to help his wife find his killer. Whoopi Goldberg steals every scene she's in. Like *The Bodyguard,* the critics wrote it off and America loved it.

The Uninvited (1944, U.S., 98 mins., b/w) Dir: Lewis Allen; Cast: Ray Milland, Ruth Hussey, Cornelia Otis Skinner, Gail Russell.

A rich and very scary ghost story, done as only the English can. Ray Milland and sister Ruth Hussey move into a haunted mansion in Cornwall. The plot relies on mystery more than special effects for its chills and is all the more effective because of that.

The Haunting (1963, U.S., 112 mins., b/w) Dir: Robert Wise; Cast: Julie Harris, Claire Bloom, Richard Johnson, Russ Tamblyn, Lois Maxwell, Fay Compton.

Worth its weight in ectoplasm. Four people move into the dreaded Hill House to determine once and for all whether it's haunted. A perfect choice for Halloween or any other night you're in the mood to sit around the house with all the lights on.

Topper (1937, U.S., 96 mins., b/w) Dir: Norman Z. McLeod; Cast: Cary Grant, Roland Young, Constance Bennett.

Countless sequels and remakes later, the original version still stands out as a classic. The ghosts of Grant and Bennett haunt nerdy Roland Young in only the most sophisticated ways.

The Canterville Ghost (1944, U.S., 96 mins., b/w) Dir: Jules Dassin; Cast: Charles Laughton, Robert Young, Margaret O'Brien, William Gargan.

This is all Laughton's show, as he plays a 17th-century ghost who will be forced to forever haunt his castle unless American descendant Young can help him display some courage. Any resemblance to Oscar Wilde's short story of the same name is entirely coincidental.

Ugetsu (1953, Japan, 96 mins., b/w) Dir: Kenji Mizoguchi; Cast: Machiko Kyo, Masayuki Mori, Kinyo Tanaka.

Two peasants in 16th-century Japan go in search of success. One finds horrors of an earthly nature and the other encounters the supernatural. The Japanese music and the shadowy cinematography create an unsettling mood that you don't need subtitles to appreciate.

Beetlejuice (1988, U.S., 96 mins.) Dir: Tim Burton; Cast: Alec Baldwin, Geena Davis, Michael Keaton, Catherine O'Hara, Jeffrey Jones, Winona Ryder, Sylvia Sidney.

*Topper*esque comedy about young ghost couple who rely on the unsavory spirit Betelgeuse for help in making their transition to the afterlife. Fabulous special effects and Danny Elfman music, plus an over-the-top performance from Michael Keaton. He may be remembered as Batman, but this is the movie where he shows all his talents.

The Ghost and Mrs. Muir (1947, U.S., 104 mins., b/w) Dir: Joseph L. Mankiewicz; Cast: Rex Harrison, Gene Tierney, George Sanders, Edna Best.

Sea-captain ghost Harrison falls in love with Gene Tierney, the new occupant of his home. Stylish, romantic, and lovely, this would probably be appropriate for a Valentine's Day list, too.

■

NOTE: *Ghostbusters* lies fallow right now, as *Monty Python and the Holy Grail* did for a decade, but in a few more years you'll have forgotten most of the lines and it will be funny again.

'TIS THE SEASON

Just when *It's a Wonderful Life* was about to slip over into the netherworld of overexposed chestnuts, Turner finally put some restrictions on its showing. While this does not fully atone for the film's colorization, one or two presentations a Christmas will go a long way toward making this film fresh again. Now we have to worry about *Miracle on 34th Street* and the Alastair Sim version of *A Christmas Carol.* All three are great films and if you ever expect to enjoy them again in your life, watch some of the following instead this Christmas.

Holiday Affair (1949, U.S., 87 mins., b/w) Dir: Don Hartman; Cast: Robert Mitchum, Janet Leigh, Wendell Corey.

Passionate Mitchum and lawyerly Corey both set their sights on Leigh, a war widow with a young son. Funny and touching, with a smart script and just enough tugging at the heartstrings. The Mitchum factor gives it the extra tension it needs to be more than just a reworking of themes from *Miracle on 34th Street.*

Fanny and Alexander (1983, West Germany, 197 mins.) Dir: Ingmar Bergman; Cast: Gunn Wallgren, Allan Edwall, Jarl Kulle, Borje Ahlstedt, Bertil Guva, Jan Malmsjo, Ewa Froling.

The crowning touch to Bergman's career is this lovely feast for the senses that chronicles the life of a Swedish family through the year 1907. The Christmas scene is a high point, but virtually every scene has magic.

The Ref (1994, US, 92 mins) Dir: Ted Demme; Cast: Dennis Leary, Judy Davis, Kevin Spacey, Glynis Johns, Christine Baranski.

Nasty thief Leary finds himself spending Christmas Eve with a family full of sparring eccentrics even nastier than he is. A cheerily mean-spirited film that loses its vigor when it suddenly tries to become nice. There's a studio executive somewhere who deserves to be locked in a room with Dennis Leary for spoiling what could have been a fine dose of bitters.

The Lion in Winter (1968, Great Britain, 135 mins.) Dir: Anthony Harvey; Cast: Peter O'Toole, Katharine Hepburn, John Castle, Anthony Hopkins, Jane Merrow.

One for the grown-ups. Henry II, his wife Eleanor of Aquitaine, and their adult sons join to celebrate Christmas and to battle over who will wear the crown of England after Henry. A thoughtful costume drama with fabulous settings and brilliant work by O'Toole and Hepburn.

A Christmas Story (1983, U.S., 98 mins.) Dir: Bob Clark; Cast: Melinda Dillon, Darren McGavin, Peter Billingsley, Ian Petrella.

Clark brings together some of humorist Jean Shepherd's finest stories about growing up in thirties Indiana. Like Shepherd at his best, the film only nibbles at the edge of sentimental and gives us much more true warmth and family humor than we're used to expecting from Hollywood. An instant Christmas classic; let's hope it doesn't get overexposed.

Christmas in Connecticut (1945, U.S., 101 mins., b/w) Dir: Peter Godfrey; Cast: Barbara Stanwyck, Dennis Morgan, Sydney Greenstreet, Reginald Gardiner.

One of the minor Christmas standards that you may not have seen yet. Housekeeping columnist Stanwyck—who's actually not so hot with oven or broom—is forced to pretend she's great at keeping house when her boss comes over for Christmas. A light comedy, mercifully free of messages.

3 Godfathers (1948, U.S., 105 mins.) Dir: John Ford; Cast: John Wayne, Ward Bond, Pedro Armendariz, Harry Carey, Jr., Ben Johnson, Mildred Natwick, Jane Darwell, Hank Worden.

Wayne, Armendariz, and Carey are a trio of not-so bad guys on the lam after a bank job who stumble into a Christian parable in the middle of the Arizona desert. When they find a dying woman (Natwick) and her newborn baby (born on Christmas Day), the outlaws promise to deliver the child to safety, and set out for the town of New Jerusalem. One of John Ford's simplest, most overtly religious films, the story is told with a childlike innocence and grace that resonates with faith, feeling, and the director's perennial quest for redemption. A genuinely moving experience.

The Holly and the Ivy (1953, Great Britain, 80 mins., b/w) Dir: George More O'Ferrall; Cast: Ralph Richardson, Celia Johnson, Margaret Leighton, Denholm Elliott.
▪
If you're not in the mood for another mug of forced cheer, this drama about a minister in a small English town and his three adult children makes for a more serious holiday pick.

Metropolitan (1990, U.S., 98 mins.) Dir: Whit Stillman; Cast: Edward Clements, Christopher Eigeman, Taylor Nichols, Carolyn Farina, Allison Rutledge-Parisi, Dylan Hundley.

A low-budget charmer about a group of upper-class New York teens during the debutante season, a period known to the rest of us as Christmastime. Stillman's script and direction, as well as the understated acting by the new performers, make us care about people we might otherwise write off as rich snobs.

Scrooged (1988, U.S., 101 mins.) Dir: Richard Donner; Cast: Bill Murray, Karen Allen, Bobcat Goldthwait, Carol

Kane, David Johansen, Robert Mitchum, John Forsythe.

Funny contemporary reworking of *A Christmas Carol* stars Murray as a disgusting TV exec who finds, yes, the true meaning of Christmas. The movie's sarcastic spirit speaks to that little Grinch inside us all, and still manages to give us a happy ending.

Hail Mary (*Je Vous Salue Marie*, 1984, Switzerland-France, 100 mins.) Dir: Jean-Luc Godard; Cast: Myriem Roussel, Thierry Rode, Philippe Lacoste, Manon Anderson.

Don't get this one if Aunt Mary is coming over, unless Aunt Mary is a real freethinker. Godard's modern retelling of the Nativity was banned in some countries. Many hated it; others loved it. It helps if you like long, moody French movies.

▪

NOTE: The very best animated Christmas film was shown on PBS years ago. It was called *Simple Gifts* and featured vignettes with Christmas themes ranging from a chapter in Virginia Woolf's *Orlando* to a Christmas Day armistice on the western front during WWI. If you ever see it listed, set the VCR.

TRAVEL

ON THE ROAD

The American love affair with cross-country travel, while started perhaps in a stagecoach, reached full tilt in a train, but became truly American in a car—with a radio. It's not all Route 66, it's not even all American (or cars, for that matter), but grab your hat and come along.

Something Wild (1986, U.S., 113 mins.) Dir: Jonathan Demme; Cast: Jeff Daniels, Melanie Griffith, Ray Liotta, Margaret Colin.

Funny *and* suspenseful (remember Demme's dark side) East Coast road trip with lots of hip zip, has straight-arrow Daniels uncovering his wild side, as he's lured out of town for a few days by his new friend, the flaky and mysterious Lulu (Griffith). The music's a lot of fun; so are the credits. Watch for John Sayles and John Waters in some good bits.

Two for the Road (1967, Great Britain, 112 mins.) Dir: Stanley Donen; Cast: Audrey Hepburn, Albert Finney, Eleanor Bron, William Daniels, Jacqueline Bisset.

Motoring in France, the super team of Finney and Hepburn play back their 12-year marriage and find that despite the difficulties, they still want to find a common ground.

The Road Warrior (1982, Australia, 94 mins.) Dir: George Miller; Cast: Mel Gibson, Emile Minty, Virginia Hay, Bruce Spence.

Not a road movie in any traditional sense, and Mel sounds like a barking seal, but this wild, post-apocalyptic vision of high-desert nuclear waste down under is a well-crafted cop and chase film with some truly remarkable stunts and action shooting.

Ishtar (1987, U.S., 108 mins.) Dir: Elaine May; Cast: Warren Beatty, Dustin Hoffman, Isabelle Adjani, Charles Grodin, Jack Weston, Tess Harper, Carol Kane.

All the press about being over budget (OK, *way* over budget) ignored the fact that this *Road to . . .* -style movie about a neurotic American song act (Beatty and Hoffman) on the road to Saudi Arabia is actually very enjoyable. You won't hum the Paul Williams tunes but you'll remember the camels. By the way, *Road to Singapore* was the first, and *Morocco* and *Rio* probably the best, of the seven amusing Crosby/Hope/Lamour formulas, and they were almost cast with Fred MacMurray and Jack Oakie instead.

It Happened One Night (1934, U.S., 110 mins., b/w) Dir: Frank Capra; Cast: Clark Gable, Claudette Colbert, Walter Connolly, Roscoe Karns.

The consummate screwball comedy pits reporter Gable against runaway society-girl Colbert on a cross-country bus trip. Absolutely timeless and it doesn't get better than that hitchhiking scene. A true gem.

Easy Rider (1969, U.S., 94 mins.) Dir: Dennis Hopper; Cast: Dennis Hopper, Peter Fonda, Jack Nicholson, Karen Black, Robert Walker, Jr.

We're talking about major disaffection with American society; as filtered through the American South, that is. Long hair or otherwise, outsiders were not welcome, as Fonda, Hopper, and Nicholson show us as they travel through. Vehicle of choice: choppers. Dated? Probably, but worth a look for the photography, the resonant music (used almost as a script), the early Nicholson, its insight into guns, paranoia, and the American psyche, and your chance to note whether things have changed.

Thelma and Louise (1991, U.S., 128 mins.) Dir: Ridley Scott; Cast: Susan Sarandon, Geena Davis, Harvey Keitel, Michael Madsen, Christopher McDonald, Brad Pitt.

As much a complex and action-driven buddy movie as a road trip, a lot of reviewers thought this was just too hard on men. Well, it is terrifically written by Callie Khouri, with Sarandon and Davis shining as two women who, needing a change of scene, leave town and wind up as fugitives. It's just a really good movie. Keitel is pretty special here also.

Stranger Than Paradise (1984, U.S., 90 mins., b/w) Dir: Jim Jarmusch; Cast: John Lurie, Eszter Balint, Richard Edson.

When your pre-*glasnost* Hungarian cousin comes to visit in Brooklyn, what better way to show her the country than that traditional American road trip to Florida, tacky pink flamingos, sleazy roadside motels, and all. In true Jarmusch fashion, there's a somewhat surreal side to how the events unfold; the characters may seem eccentric, but they are very real. In beautiful black and white, it kind of looks like how we imagined that barren Soviet Bloc would look.

Harry and Tonto (1974, U.S., 115 mins.) Dir: Paul Mazursky; Cast: Art Carney, Ellen Burstyn, Larry Hagman, Geraldine Fitzgerald, Josh Mostel, Barbara Rhoades, Arthur Hunnicutt, Melanie Mayron.

Oscar-winning performance for aging Carney, as he makes a last trip cross-country with his loyal cat, Tonto. Enjoyably sentimental study of a man seeking to fully experience the later days of his life.

ON TRACK

Trains. Romance, adventure, the building of empires—always something more than just a way to get from point A to point B.

The Lady Vanishes (1938, Great Britain, 97 mins., b/w) Dir: Alfred Hitchcock; Cast: Margaret Lockwood, Paul Lukas, Michael Redgrave, Cecil Parker, Catherine Lacey, Dame May Whitty.

Hitchcock at his witty and suspenseful best. A young woman (Lockwood) on a long train trip gets tangled in a spy plot when she tries to locate the charming older woman (Whitty) she'd befriended earlier. As always, Hitchcock makes the most of sound and visuals (even when he only had models to shoot from) as the train hurtles on. The 1979 Cybill Shepherd/Elliott Gould remake is a waste of time, but go back to Hitchcock for a different tale of murder and twisted psyches, the superbly acted *Strangers on a Train.*

Throw Momma From the Train (1987, U.S., 88 mins.) Dir: Danny DeVito; Cast: Danny DeVito, Billy Crystal, Kim Greist, Anne Ramsey.

Worth seeing for Ramsey's inspired performance alone, this is the DeVito/Crystal take on *Strangers on a Train.* DeVito is the weak-willed son driven to extremes; Crystal is a writing professor, who becomes DeVito's reluctant co-conspirator in a murder plot.

Some Like It Hot (1959, U.S., 122 mins.) Dir: Billy Wilder; Cast: Tony Curtis, Marilyn Monroe, Jack Lemmon, Joe E. Brown, George Raft, Joan Shawlee, Mike Mazurki, Pat O'Brien.

Brilliant and hysterical with Lemmon and Curtis trying to bluff their way out of a tight spot by passing as part of an all-girl traveling band whose members include a luminous Monroe. The memorable scenes for *this* review are the bedtime-in-the-sleeper-cars—but check out this film under Just Like a Woman also.

Closely Watched Trains (1966, Czechoslovakia, 89 mins., b/w) Dir: Jiri Menzel; Cast: Vaclav Neckar, Jitka Bendova.

Beautifully shot, compelling, and wry WWII-story (and Academy Award winner) about appealingly shy, sexually insecure train-station conductor who becomes a, perhaps unwitting, hero in occupied Czechoslovakia. Film has an acutely European sensibility, daring to express sexual situations in simultaneously arousing, tender, and farcical ways. Jean Renoir's superb *La Bête Humaine* takes a similar setting and applies a far more fatalistic twist.

The General (1927, U.S., 74 mins., b/w) Dir: Buster Keaton; Cast: Buster Keaton, Marion Mack.

No train list would be complete without Keaton's silent Civil War great. Meticulous battle and stunt detail rages in the background in antically told true story of Confederate general determined to recapture his stolen locomotive from Union forces. The photography is exquisite.

Union Pacific (1939, U.S., 135 mins., b/w) Dir: Cecil B. DeMille; Cast: Joel McCrea, Barbara Stanwyck, Akim Tamiroff, Robert Preston, Brian Donlevy.
■
All aboard. Cecil B.'s grand and glorious epic about the sinking of that last golden nail to join the East and West by rail, replete with heroes, villains, and a great train wreck. You'll want to see the classic silent film, *The Iron Horse*, for the John Ford version of the same and the granddaddy of this genre.

Something Wicked This Way Comes (1983, U.S., 94 mins.) Dir: Jack Clayton; Cast: Jason Robards, Jonathan Pryce, Pam Grier, Shawn Carson, Vidal Peterson.

You might like this one better if you read Ray Bradbury's novel first. While he also wrote the screenplay, the film misses just a bit. But it's still a nicely eerie tale about a carnival that rolls into a small American town, the train whistle in the distance ominously announcing its approach for days.

The Narrow Margin (1952, U.S., 70 mins., b/w) Dir: Richard Fleischer; Cast: Charles McGraw, Marie Windsor.

Short, fast, and dated "B" trip on the Golden West Limited westbound from Chicago. Straight-arrow L.A. cop must protect a key female witness while transporting her to a grand-jury hearing. Standard tough-guy lines, but some good plot twists and fine photography. Remade, far less successfully, in 1990 as *Narrow Margin* with Gene Hackman.

Murder on the Orient Express (1974, Great Britain, 127 mins.) Dir: Sidney Lumet; Cast: Albert Finney, Lauren Bacall, Martin Balsam, Ingrid Bergman, Jacqueline Bisset, Sean Connery, John Gielgud, Wendy Hiller, Anthony Perkins, Vanessa Redgrave, Richard Widmark, Michael York.

Wonderfully entertaining 1930s period piece with exotic group of travelers in this Agatha Christie/Hercule Poirot murder mystery. Great cast, nice plot build, very atmospheric.

Twentieth Century (1934, U.S., 91 mins., b/w) Dir: Howard Hawks; Cast: John Barrymore, Carole Lombard, Walter Connolly, Roscoe Karns.
■
Also set in the 1930s, when train travel was at its most glamorous. This one is screwball at its best, with whacked-out, egomaniacal producer Barrymore trying to woo back his protégé-turned-big-star (Lombard) on the famous run between New York and Chicago. For more screwball on a train, see Preston Sturges's hilarious run to sunny Florida, *The Palm Beach Story*.

Von Ryan's Express (1965, U.S., 117 mins.) Dir: Mark Robson; Cast: Frank Sinatra, Trevor Howard, Edward Mulhare, James Brolin.

Excitement! Adventure! WWII! Sinatra doesn't even need to drink. In fact, he's terrific, along with most of the cast, in this high-tension P.O.W. escape film that peaks with a daring hijack of a German freight train. The same year brought *The Train*, Frankenheimer's gripping tale of the efforts of the French Resistance to reclaim art treasures that have fallen into German hands.

Shanghai Express (1932, U.S., 84 mins., b/w) Dir: Josef von Sternberg; Cast: Marlene Dietrich, Clive Brook, Anna May Wong, Warner Oland.

La Dietrich is Shanghai Lily, a woman who uses her lack of virtue to good advantage on a train ride to Shanghai through war-torn China. Oscar-winning photography (Lee Garmes) and von Sternberg's acute sense of the star's appeal keep this camp classic sharp.

Runaway Train (1985, U.S., 107 mins.) Dir: Andrei Konchalovsky; Cast: Jon Voight, Eric Roberts, Rebecca DeMornay, Kyle Heffner, John Ryan, T. K. Carter, Kenneth McMillan.

Voight's at his very best in this pulse-pounding psycho-existential runaway train ride across the Alaskan tundra. Escaped-con story with wild action footage is based on an unused Akira Kurosawa script.

Zentropa (1992, Denmark-Sweden-France-Germany, 114 mins., c & b/w) Dir: Lars von Trier; Cast: Barbara Sukowa, Jean-Marc Barr.

Surreal allegory or flat-out thriller entertainment—it depends on how hard you want to work at this Cannes prize-winning journey into post-WWII German guilt. Black and white and color are mixed effectively, heightening the experience of the young American train conductor working on board the German Zentropa.

Sun Valley Serenade (1941, U.S., 86 mins.) Dir: H. Bruce Humberstone; Cast: Sonja Henie, Lynn Bari, Joan Davis, John Payne, Milton Berle, Glenn Miller and His Orchestra.

Not really a train movie, but it does have one of the best train songs ever written, "Chattanooga Choo-Choo," performed by the great Glenn Miller band. A very pleasant musical comedy set in an Idaho resort. Check out Milton Berle as Miller's manager.

UP IN THE AIR

Flight is a wonderful thing. And planes show up in so many movies, it was very hard to pick. Two you must see for specific scenes: *King Kong*, swatting those small planes buzzing the Empire State Building, and Hitchcock's *North by Northwest* for the unforgettable shot of the low-flying crop duster casting its shadows in the cornfields, and Cary in its sights. Then there are plane crashes: *Foreign Correspondent* (great Pan Am clipper), *Lost Horizon*, *The Buddy Holly Story*, *La Bamba*, *A Matter of Life and Death* (a magnificent parable that addresses airplanes *and* the afterlife, aka: *Stairway to Heaven*), and *Voyager* (a moody Volker Schlondorff movie starring Sam Shepard) deserve special notice, among many.

The Spirit of St. Louis (1957, U.S., 138 mins., b/w) Dir: Billy Wilder; Cast: James Stewart, Murray Hamilton, Patricia Smith.

Jimmy Stewart's turn as Lucky Lindy in his pioneering solo flight across the Atlantic. A very long flight, but still charged with the wonder of it.

Airplane! (1980, U.S., 88 mins.) Dirs: Jim Abrahams, David Zucker, Jerry Zucker; Cast: Robert Hays, Leslie Nielsen, Kareem Abdul Jabbar, Lloyd Bridges, Peter Graves, Julie Hagerty, Robert Stack.

The consummate airline nightmare spoof. Neilsen and Hagerty are hilarious, as is the rest of the cast, in this totally whacked take on the *Airport*-type disaster films. For the best of these, see William Wellman's *The High and the Mighty,* with a young Robert Stack.

Twilight Zone—The Movie (1983, U.S., 100 mins.) Dirs: John Landis, Steven Spielberg, Joe Dante, George Miller; Cast: Vic Morrow, Scatman Crothers, Kathleen Quinlan, Patricia Barry, Abbe Lane, John Lithgow, Dan Aykroyd.

Based on the classic TV show, this movie consists of four segments. The best by far is George Miller's, with a super Lithgow in mid-flight and the only witness to a terrifying creature out on the wing in a blinding storm.

Melvin and Howard (1980, U.S., 95 mins.) Dir: Jonathan Demme; Cast: Paul LeMat, Jason Robards, Jr., Mary Steenburgen, Elizabeth Cheshire, Michael J. Pollard, Pamela Reed, Dabney Coleman.

Howard Hughes, that is. This is a wonderful tale about the possible relationship between blue-collar Melvin Dummar and aviation and media magnate Hughes.

Flying Down to Rio (1933, U.S., 72 mins., b/w) Dir: Thornton Freeland; Cast: Dolores Del Rio, Gene Raymond, Fred Astaire, Ginger Rogers, Raul Roulien, Franklin Pangborn.

Fred & Ginger's first. The story's the usual confection involving a big band, fantastic clothes, the suave and the swank, their private planes, and of course, dancing and romance. The twist is, it's not F&G's flirtation, yet. What you're here for are the remarkable pre-code flying choreography scenes of girls on the wing, and we mean *on* the wing, and the very enjoyable Vincent Youmans music.

The Lost Squadron (1932, U.S., 90 mins., b/w) Dir: George Archainbaud; Cast: Joel McCrea, Richard Dix, Erich von Stroheim, Mary Astor.

Von Stroheim's tyrannical film director

is slightly off-kilter—perfect for Mr. von S; here he willfully endangers his flying-film-stunt crew made up of former WWI flying aces. Adventure and intrigue, with great aerial shots, tells the story of the crew's attempt to stop him.

Twelve O'Clock High (1949, U.S., 132 mins., b/w) Dir: Henry King; Cast: Gregory Peck, Gary Merrill, Hugh Marlowe, Dean Jagger.

The classic WWII high-tension action tale focuses on the huge pressures of flight command, as a perfectly cast Peck finds it impossible to maintain distance from his England-based crew.

Christopher Strong (1933, U.S., 77 mins., b/w) Dir: Dorothy Arzner; Cast: Katharine Hepburn, Colin Clive, Billie Burke, Helen Chandler.

Sincere drama and respectable story of independent spirit, pioneering aviatrix Lady Cynthia Carrington, plummets with its morality-laden closing. (We don't know why this adaptation of the novel was named after the lesser character; nevertheless, Hepburn is magnetic in her first major role.) Interesting slice about wealth, privilege, sexual politics, and, of course, the swell planes of the era.

The Right Stuff (1983, U.S., 191 mins.) Dir: Philip Kaufman; Cast: Sam Shepard, Scott Glenn, Fred Ward, Ed Harris, Dennis Quaid, Veronica Cartwright, Barbara Hershey, Pamela Reed, Levon Helm, Jeff Goldblum.

Long, but always interesting interpretation of Tom Wolfe's book about the race for space and the almost mythological men who would be astronauts, focuses especially on superpilot Chuck Yeager (Shepard). Fine casting overall, and spectacular photography shows off both the air- and spacecraft that were truly built for speed.

Brewster McCloud (1970, U.S., 104 mins.) Dir: Robert Altman; Cast: Bud

Cort, Sally Kellerman, Michael Murphy, William Windom, Shelley Duvall, René Auberjonois, Stacy Keach, Margaret Hamilton.

This sort of warped flight-of-Icarus with a sense of humor has the odd and unusual characters (and sensibility) that we've come to expect from Altman. Bud Cort is determined to fly; statuesque Sally Kellerman is his guide.

Only Angels Have Wings (1939, U.S., 121 mins., b/w) Dir: Howard Hawks; Cast: Cary Grant, Jean Arthur, Richard Barthelmess, Thomas Mitchell, Sig Ruman, John Carroll, Rita Hayworth.

Cary has to wear this big white hat (he's the boss), but once you get used to it, this saga of a low-budget mail-run airline in the Peruvian Andes will win you over. Romantic subtext of course with Jean and Rita; lots of harrowing flights in impossible weather and wings held on with Krazy Glue.

The Absent-Minded Professor (1961, U.S., 104 mins.) Dir: Robert Stevenson; Cast: Fred MacMurray, Nancy Olson, Tommy Kirk, Ed Wynn, Keenan Wynn.

The history of aviation would not be complete without a tip of the aileron to Flubber. That inspired invention not only lifted full basketball teams to pre-Jordan glory, but forever set a standard of wishful thinking for any motorist who's been stuck in terminal gridlock. Great fun for the whole family.

BY THE SEA

On the high seas or floating down a lazy river, travel at sea can be simply romantic, or fraught with danger—it depends on who you're traveling with, but even more, it's about respecting the forces at work and knowing that the water itself is the most powerful character.

Ship of Fools (1965, U.S., 149 mins., b/w) Dir: Stanley Kramer; Cast: Simone Signoret, Oskar Werner, Lee Marvin, Vivien Leigh, Michael Dunn, George Segal, Elizabeth Ashley, José Ferrer, Lilia Skala, Kaaren Verne.

Grand-scale soap-drama adaptation of Katherine Anne Porter novel brings together an international cast of characters sailing to 1933 Germany from Mexico under the gathering storm clouds of WWII. Leigh is best in her last movie. Oscars for Art Direction and Cinematography.

River of No Return (1954, U.S., 91 mins.) Dir: Otto Preminger; Cast: Marilyn Monroe, Robert Mitchum, Rory Calhoun, Tommy Rettig.

Mitchum, Monroe, CinemaScope. The bigger your screen the better, but gorgeous western location shots hold up regardless, as Mitchum rescues saloon-singer Monroe and mean and useless gambler-hubby Calhoun from a leaky raft. Indians attack, Calhoun slimes away, and Monroe, Mitchum's young son, and Mitchum ride down the river—hot on a perilous trail of revenge.

History Is Made at Night (1937, U.S., 110 mins., b/w) Dir: Frank Borzage; Cast: Charles Boyer, Jean Arthur.

Jean runs away from her rather unpleasant husband and falls in love with Boyer. The vindictive cuckold tries framing the charming Charles for murder, then sets out to destroy both Boyer and Arthur in the stunning shipwreck climax. Melodramatic, yes, but it has its humorous side too.

Fitzcarraldo (1982, West Germany, 158 mins.) Dir: Werner Herzog; Cast: Klaus Kinski, Claudia Cardinale, Paul Hittscher, José Lewgoy.

Turn-of-the-century Enrico Caruso-obsessed Irishman is determined to build a grand-opera house along an inaccessible stretch of the Amazon

River in Peru. To realize his goal he must first gain access to a shipping route by hauling his supply boat through the jungle and over the top of an interfering mountain. This remarkable fictionalized document of his endeavor is mesmerizing. The making of *Fitzcarraldo* was almost as remarkable. Les Blank documents Herzog's obsession in the equally fascinating *Burden of Dreams*.

The Mosquito Coast (1986, U.S., 118 mins.) Dir: Peter Weir; Cast: Harrison Ford, Helen Mirren, River Phoenix, Conrad Roberts, Andre Gregory.

Modern obsession in the jungle as Paul Theroux's novel becomes a powerful movie about eccentric U.S. inventor dropout who brings his family to remote Central America to build an ice-making factory and live off the land. This is not the endearing Ford we know, and his alienation becomes quite dangerous in this flawed but resonant production.

Dead Calm (1989, U.S., 97 mins.) Dir: Phillip Noyce; Cast: Sam Neill, Nicole Kidman, Billy Zane.

Successfully stylish thriller-turned-slasher about bereaved Australian family off to sea for a bit of reflection and escape only to be victimized by psychotic shipwreck survivor they've picked up. The end jolts unnecessarily, but the film's overall intelligence wins out.

Knife in the Water (1962, Poland, 94 mins.) Dir: Roman Polanski; Cast: Leon Niemczyk, Jolanta Umecka, Zygmunt Malanowicz.

Polanski's fully developed first feature has you expecting a slasher in this atmosphere-crackling triangle drama. Story about a disaffected couple who spend a day sailing with a hitchhiker they picked up is understated yet cumulatively jarring.

Monkey Business (1931, U.S., 77 mins., b/w) Dir: Norman McLeod; Cast: Groucho, Harpo, Chico, and Zeppo Marx, Thelma Todd.

This is the zaniest luxury liner on the ocean with the Marx Brothers stowing away and dispensing sight gags, Depression puns, and no end of riotous havoc in their fabulous first script written (with S. J. Perelman) just for film. *A Night at the Opera*, another ocean-going Marx vehicle, features that famous stateroom scene with the one and only Margaret Dumont.

Das Boot (*The Boat*, 1982, Germany, 150 mins.) Dir: Wolfgang Petersen; Cast: Jurgen Prochnow, Herbert Gronemeyer, Klaus Wennemann, Hubertas Bengsch.

Perception-changing WWII antiwar action masterpiece reveals the humans (and the gruesome conditions) inside a Nazi U-boat during the course of a mission in 1941. Submarine warfare footage is spectacular. Subtitled version is preferable—there's more impact when you hear the sailors speaking German.

Operation Petticoat (1959, U.S., 124 mins.) Dir: Blake Edwards; Cast: Cary Grant, Tony Curtis, Dina Merrill.

A WWII submarine of a different stripe in a romp across the Pacific with Cary at the helm and a perfectly cast Curtis as his street-smart first officer. A tumble of fast gags and eyebrow-raising misadventures add up to a lot of nostalgic fun.

■

NOTE: High-seas honorable mentions: Roaring ocean, sea air, the wind, and adventure; they're all here, stirringly photographed in the marginal *1492: Conquest of Paradise; Mutiny on the Bounty;* John Huston's masterwork of Melville's *Moby Dick; Billy Budd;* and Hitchcock's unforgettable *Lifeboat*.

PLACES

GOTHAM

Hundreds, maybe thousands, of films have been shot in New York, but in most of them the city is simply a very loud and very dirty stage set. The truth is that New York is many cities; as many cities as there are people living in it, which is somewhere around 7 million. The following is a highly subjective collection of films that show the Big Apple in some of its different attires.

Manhattan (1979, U.S., 93 mins., b/w) Dir: Woody Allen; Cast: Woody Allen, Diane Keaton, Mariel Hemingway, Michael Murphy, Meryl Streep.

One of the finest Valentines to a place ever made. This is the New York of late-night cab rides and the Sunday *Times* and romantic walks in Central Park and smart, beautiful people being exceptionally witty. About four days a year, New York actually resembles the city Woody Allen shows in this comedy; on the other 361 it can be as nasty and insufferable as the characters in this film.

On the Town (1950, U.S., 98 mins.) Dirs: Gene Kelly, Stanley Donen; Cast: Gene Kelly, Frank Sinatra, Betty Garrett, Ann Miller, Vera Ellen, Jules Munchin.

The way New York used to be. Three sailors on leave hit the big town and see the sights as they fall in love with three New York women. The Comden-Green-Bernstein music keeps everything rolling along at a crisp pace and the travelogue of a New York long gone is fun.

After Hours (1985, U.S., 97 mins.) Dir: Martin Scorsese; Cast: Griffin Dunne, Rosanna Arquette, Teri Garr, Linda Fiorentino, John Heard, Catherine O'Hara, Cheech & Chong.

While Wall Street was printing money in the eighties, another section of downtown Manhattan was also growing. Here, Griffin Dunne takes a Dante-esque journey into the bowels of SoHo when he goes on one of the world's worst dates. *Slaves of New York,* based on Tama Janowitz's collection of stories, is another view of the downtown scene of the time.

Quick Change (1990, U.S., 89 mins.) Dirs: Howard Franklin, Bill Murray; Cast: Bill Murray, Geena Davis, Randy Quaid, Jason Robards, Bob Elliot, Phillip Bosco, Tony Shalhoub.

Anyone who's lived in New York understands the need to get out of it once in a while. Here, Bill Murray and his gang of bank robbers have a very tough time leaving New York after they pull off a big heist. Though much of the humor depends on knowing the city, if you want a sense of what it's really like to live there and how many New Yorkers feel about it, this is your film.

The Brother From Another Planet (1984, U.S., 110 mins.) Dir: John Sayles; Cast: Joe Morton, Darryl Edwards, Dee Dee Bridgewater, John Sayles, David Strathairn.

A wonderful film by John Sayles about an alien fleeing other alien bad guys, who lands in New York and moves into Harlem. A small and rewarding comedy that shows life on 125th Street as it is today.

Do the Right Thing (1989, U.S., 120 mins.) Dir: Spike Lee; Cast: Danny Aiello, Spike Lee, Ossie Davis, Ruby Dee, John Turturro.

New York is also famous for its constant racial tension, and no film has captured it as well as this Spike Lee movie about a white-owned pizza parlor in the heart of black Brooklyn. The city isn't all skyscrapers and fountains; it's places like Bed-Stuy, too, and the kinds of memorable characters Lee presents. The same goes for his *Jungle Fever,* and its view of buppies in Harlem.

Saturday Night Fever (1977, U.S., 119 mins.) Dir: John Badham; Cast: John Travolta, Karen Lynn Gorney, Joseph Cali, Barry Miller, Julie Bovasso, Donna Pescow.

The BBQ—Brooklyn, Bronx, Queens—crowd is another important face of New York. Though there are many films that take place in the outer boroughs, this story of an ordinary Joe whose only moments to shine come on the dance floor may top the list. Now that disco is creeping back you should probably watch it again.

The Taking of Pelham One Two Three (1974, U.S., 102 mins.) Dir: Joseph Sargent; Cast: Walter Matthau, Robert Shaw, Martin Balsam, Hector Elizondo.

The subway is New York's bloodstream. Though everyone complains about it, the city would stop dead without underground transportation. Of course this is no consolation when a track fire keeps you standing in a crowded car for half an hour. This taut thriller about a gang of thugs holding a loaded train hostage for a million dollars should be a nice reminder that it could be worse.

Breakfast at Tiffany's (1961, U.S., 115 mins.) Dir: Blake Edwards; Cast: Audrey Hepburn, George Peppard, Patricia Neal, Buddy Ebsen, Mickey Rooney.

Like any great performer, Audrey Hepburn makes her partner look good, and in this charming film her partner is the suave, swinging New York of the early sixties. Edwards does a nice job as well in bringing a taste of Capote's many years chronicling the lives of wealthy Upper East Siders to the screen.

Miracle on 34th Street (1947, U.S., 96 mins., b/w) Dir: George Seaton; Cast: Edmund Gwenn, John Payne, Maureen O'Hara, Natalie Wood.

The magic of New York, its grandeur, occasional charm, and romance are all distilled into this old favorite about Macy's very special Santa. Though Seaton doesn't make as big a deal about it as Woody, this film is a loving vision of an incomparable city.

INSIDE THE BELTWAY

If you've ever been to our nation's capital during cherry-blossom time, you know from painful experience that the city is one of America's favorite tourist destinations. Given the long lines at the Air and Space Museum and the Smithsonian, renting some of the following films about Washington, D.C., might be a reasonable alternative.

Mr. Smith Goes to Washington (1939, U.S., 130 mins., b/w) Dir: Frank Capra; Cast: James Stewart, Jean Arthur, Claude Rains, Guy Kibbee, Eugene Pallette, Beulah Bondi, Harry Carey, H. B. Warner, Charles Lane, Porter Hall.

Stewart plays an idealistic young senator who—gasp!—finds corruption in the Senate and tries to remain idealistic in the face of it. A pre-visit must, mainly because it will remind you of why Washington, D.C., and this country, are special places. Wouldn't it be nice to drop off a copy for your senator or representative?

All the President's Men (1976, U.S., 136 mins.) Dir: Alan J. Pakula; Cast: Dustin Hoffman, Robert Redford, Jason

Robards, Jr., Jane Alexander, Martin Balsam, Jack Warden.

As well as being the center of our government, Washington is also one of the nation's media capitals and here we see the greatest confrontation ever between government and the press. Redford and Hoffman play Woodward and Bernstein, the investigative reporters at the *Washington Post* who brought down the Nixon government. Good look at Washington exteriors and a frightening look at the interiors, too.

Broadcast News (1987, U.S., 131 mins.) Dir: James L. Brooks; Cast: William Hurt, Holly Hunter, Albert Brooks, Joan Cusack, Lois Chiles, Jack Nicholson (cameo).

A lighter take on the Washington media corps starring Holly Hunter as a relentless young television news producer who falls in love with a shallow reporter. Albert Brooks plays another reporter and the scene when he fills in at the anchor desk is the movie's best. Nice, smarter-than-average comedy.

Heartburn (1986, U.S., 108 mins.) Dir: Mike Nichols; Cast: Meryl Streep, Jack Nicholson, Stockard Channing, Maureen Stapleton, Catherine O'Hara, Karen Akers, Jeff Daniels, Richard Masur.

Our final look at the press is based on Nora Ephron's *roman à clef* about her rocky marriage to *Post* reporter Carl Bernstein. If you think the press within the Beltway has no idea about how most of America lives, watch these folks at their spiffy Georgetown parties and have your worst fears confirmed.

The Exorcist (1973, U.S., 122 mins.) Dir: William Friedkin; Cast: Ellen Burstyn, Max von Sydow, Lee J. Cobb, Kitty Winn, Jason Miller, Linda Blair.

At least little Megan has an excuse for her Georgetown excesses—she's possessed by the devil. This spooky classic caused quite an upsurge in Mass attendance in its day and while the special effects aren't so amazing now, it still packs a punch.

The President's Analyst (1967, U.S., 104 mins.) Dir: Theodore J. Flicker; Cast: James Coburn, Godfrey Cambridge, Severn Darden, Joan Delaney.

An odd, black comedy about the president's shrink, who is pursued by the world's intelligence communities for his knowledge of the president's secrets. The film's funniest scenes involve Coburn kidnapping a family of tourists so he can sneak out of the city.

Being There (1979, U.S., 107 mins.) Dir: Hal Ashby; Cast: Peter Sellers, Melvyn Douglas, Shirley MacLaine, Jack Warden, Richard Dysart, Richard Basehart.

A long, but still thought-provoking, film about a simple gardener who gains access to Washington's circle of power when his ignorance is mistaken for cryptic brilliance. One of Sellers's last films, it also features an Oscar-winning performance by Douglas.

The Day the Earth Stood Still (1951, U.S., 92 mins., b/w) Dir: Robert Wise; Cast: Patricia Neal, Michael Rennie, Hugh Marlowe, Sam Jaffe, Billy Gray.

Science fiction classic about an alien who comes to Washington to warn the Earth against its dangerous nuclear future. The message remains valuable even after the Cold War, and the shots of Washington, D.C., are top-notch.

D.C. Cab (1983, U.S., 104 mins.) Dir: Joel Schumacher; Cast: Mr. T, Adam Baldwin, Max Gail, Gary Busey, Charlie Barnett, Irene Cara.

There's a lot more to Washington, D.C., than marble buildings and government types, and this is one of the only films to show it. A solid comedy that follows a motley group of Washington cabbies as they try to straighten up and drive right. A must for Mr. T fans.

The More the Merrier (1943, U.S., 104 mins., b/w) Dir: George Stevens; Cast: Jean Arthur, Joel McCrea, Charles Coburn, Richard Gaines, Bruce Bennett, Ann Savage, Ann Doran, Frank Sully, Grady Sutton.

A real wartime charmer. Jean Arthur stars as a single woman forced by the housing shortage to share her apartment with two men. One is the quirky but sweet Coburn and the other is Joel McCrea, who annoys the heck out of Jean, even after she falls in love with him.

Dave (1993, U.S., 105 mins.) Dir: Ivan Reitman; Cast: Kevin Kline, Sigourney Weaver, Frank Langella, Ben Kingsley, Charles Grodin, Faith Prince, Laura Linney, Anna Deavere Smith, Bonnie Hunt, Parley Baer, Stefan Gierasch.

Political comedy has Kline playing both the president and his double, who takes over the Oval Office in a pinch and manages to do a better job as a president and as a husband to the First Lady. Lots of great D.C. visuals and a reasonably enjoyable film.

Born Yesterday (1951, U.S., 103 mins., b/w) Dir: George Cukor; Cast: Judy Holliday, William Holden, Broderick Crawford, Howard St. John.

Judy Holliday gives maybe the finest performance ever by a comedic actress in this tale of a crooked businessman trying to throw his weight around Washington, losing his moll in the process. Extremely funny and unsentimental, with a short travelogue through D.C. with Judy and William Holden for good measure.

∎

NOTE: *In Country* has the best and most moving scene you'll see about the Vietnam Memorial.

CAJUN COOKING

Outside of New York, no American city is as decidedly un-American as New Orleans. With its French flavors and smells and fabulous music, it would be a shame to experience the city only on film, so think of these movies as postcards from a place you have to see yourself.

The Big Easy (1986, U.S., 108 mins.) Dir: Jim McBride; Cast: Dennis Quaid, Ellen Barkin, Ned Beatty, John Goodman, Ebbe Rose Smith, Charles Ludlam, Marc Lawrence, Lisa Jane Persky.

The film to start with, for reasons other than the great sex scene between Quaid and Barkin. From the Beausoleil song over the credits to Aaron Neville singing "Tell It Like It Is," the score of this otherwise standard mystery captures one of New Orleans's best aspects. The movie also gives us the most complete tour of the town as it is today.

Panic in the Streets (1950, U.S., 96 mins., b/w) Dir: Elia Kazan; Cast: Richard Widmark, Jack Palance, Paul Douglas, Barbara Bel Geddes, Zero Mostel.

This tense winner features Widmark as a military doctor who must scramble through the streets and alleys of New Orleans to track down a criminal infected with the plague. Not your usual travelogue, but a heck of a lot more exciting.

A Streetcar Named Desire (1951, U.S., 125 mins., b/w) Dir: Elia Kazan; Cast: Marlon Brando, Vivien Leigh, Karl Malden, Kim Hunter.

Tennessee Williams's classic of American theater becomes a classic of American film. Wearing his ripped T-shirt and bellowing "Stella!" Brando created an archetype with his performance as the brutal Stanley Kowalski, and Vivien

Leigh as his neurotic sister-in-law Blanche DuBois does pretty well, too. In fact, she's the one who won an Oscar for this film.

Angel Heart (1987, U.S., 113 mins.) Dir: Alan Parker; Cast: Mickey Rourke, Robert De Niro, Lisa Bonet, Charlotte Rampling.

For some reason this film has the reputation of being a bomb, but it's actually quite watchable. Schlub detective Rourke goes to New Orleans to investigate the whereabouts of a disappeared singer and finds himself sinking into an eerie morass of voodoo. Solid atmospherics and the much-vaunted sex scene with Bonet are pretty good, too. You'll figure out half of this in the first 10 minutes, but hang on, because there are surprises in store.

JFK (1991, U.S., 188 mins., c & b/w) Dir: Oliver Stone; Cast: Kevin Costner, Sissy Spacek, Kevin Bacon, Tommy Lee Jones, Laurie Metcalf, Gary Oldman, Michael Rooker.

Like him or hate him, Oliver Stone managed to make three hours of goofy conspiracy theories a fast, fascinating movie-going experience. Since the film centers around New Orleans D.A. Jim Garrison, we get lots of local color between quick cuts of the Zapruder film.

Pretty Baby (1978, U.S., 109 mins.) Dir: Louis Malle; Cast: Keith Carradine, Brooke Shields, Susan Sarandon, Antonio Fargas.

Though most famous as the high point of Brooke Shields's acting career, this Louis Malle film has more going for it than that. Carradine plays Hillaire Bellocq, a photographer who at the turn of the century chronicled the community of prostitutes in New Orleans's Storyville district. Shields plays his child bride. Given its subject matter, it's sometimes hard to watch, but that's not the fault of Sven Nykvist's cinematography or its beautiful Crescent City setting. A disturbing, slow, yet interesting film, rich in New Orleans flavor.

Walk on the Wild Side (1962, U.S., 114 mins., b/w) Dir: Edward Dmytryk; Cast: Laurence Harvey, Capucine, Jane Fonda, Anne Baxter, Barbara Stanwyck.

Nelson Algren rarely gets the respect he deserves as a writer and he certainly never got it from those who turned his books into films. *The Man With the Golden Arm* bears no resemblance to the Algren book, and this screen adaptation spins away from him too, but not quite as blatantly. Screenwriter John Fante seems to have at least tried to inject Algren into the story of a man who finds his long-lost love working in a New Orleans bordello. Algren aside, the film has its moments, especially when the predatory lesbian madam Stanwyck puts the moves on love-object Capucine. Melodrama, and amusing in its way.

Tightrope (1984, U.S., 114 mins.) Dir: Richard Tuggle; Cast: Clint Eastwood, Genevieve Bujold, Alison Eastwood, Dan Hedaya, Jennifer Beck.

An intriguing psychological thriller about New Orleans detective Eastwood tracking a serial killer who frequents the same kinky sex dives in the French Quarter that Eastwood does. Engrossing, but it goes on for at least half an hour more than it should.

Tune in Tomorrow . . . (1990, U.S., 105 mins.) Dir: Jon Amiel; Cast: Barbara Hershey, Keanu Reeves, Peter Falk, Peter Gallagher, Buck Henry, Hope Lange, Elizabeth McGovern, Danny Aiello III, Patricia Clarkson.

So what if the filmmakers moved the setting of Mario Vargas Llosa's novel from South America to fifties New Orleans? What does matter is that the movie, surprisingly enough, is almost as entertaining as the book. Reeves plays a young man trying to make his way up the ladder in the New Orleans radio business and Hershey is the lusty aunt he falls in love with. Falk's role as a bizarre writer provides some strong laughs. A solid rental.

UNDER THE GOLDEN GATE

With the fog rolling in over the Golden Gate Bridge and the cable cars crawling up and down the hills, San Francisco has a feel all its own. Tony Bennett left his heart there and you might want to do that as well after you watch some of these films.

Bullitt (1968, U.S., 113 mins.) Dir: Peter Yates; Cast: Steve McQueen, Robert Vaughn, Jacqueline Bisset.

Even apart from the car chase, which is absolutely the best ever, this Steve McQueen thriller about a cop guarding a witness will keep you glued to the screen. It'll also make you want to buy a Mustang and move to San Francisco. A seriously cool movie.

The Conversation (1974, U.S., 113 mins.) Dir: Francis Ford Coppola; Cast: Gene Hackman, John Cazale, Allen Garfield, Cindy Williams.

A classic from Coppola about a surveillance expert who gets more involved in a case than he should and finds himself tangled in something much larger than he bargained for. A terrific film that you should see for reasons beyond its San Francisco location.

Barbary Coast (1935, U.S., 100 mins., b/w) Dir: Howard Hawks; Cast: Joel McCrea, Edward G. Robinson, Miriam Hopkins, Walter Brennan.

Robinson stands out among a great cast in this top-notch costumer about an evil club owner who tries to force one of his lovely singing attractions to fall for him. The rough-and-tumble 19th-century settings show San Francisco in the days when it had a reputation for crime, not football and the Grateful Dead.

Chan Is Missing (1982, U.S., 80 mins., b/w) Dir: Wayne Wang; Cast: Wood Moy, Marc Hayashi, Laureen Chew, Judy Mihei, Peter Wang, Presco Tabios.

America's most famous Chinatown gets its due in this small film about two Chinese-American cab drivers hunting through the city for the man who stole their savings. Good acting, a smart script, and inventive directing again prove that a big budget isn't necessary to make a great film.

Dirty Harry (1971, U.S., 102 mins.) Dir: Don Siegel; Cast: Clint Eastwood, Harry Guardino, Andy Robinson, John Vernon, John Larch.

Violent, tense winner stars Eastwood as a detective who cares more about getting the job done than he does about whether it's done by the book. Followed by a whole batch of sequels, but this is where it all started. If you can tear your eyes away from the action, you'll see some solid San Francisco scenery.

Vertigo (1958, U.S., 128 mins.) Dir: Alfred Hitchcock; Cast: Kim Novak, James Stewart, Tom Helmore, Barbara Bel Geddes, Ellen Corby, Raymond Bailey, Lee Patrick, Henry Jones.

Many thought Hitchcock had gone totally bonkers when this came out. You might think so too after you see it, but it's more likely that you'll be blown away. Stewart plays a detective who has to leave the force when his fear of heights causes the death of his partner. From there on, you're on your own. Hitchcock uses San Francisco and all its quirks to feed the film's odd vision.

The Maltese Falcon (1941, U.S., 100 mins., b/w) Dir: John Huston; Cast: Humphrey Bogart, Mary Astor, Peter Lorre, Sydney Greenstreet, Walter Huston, Lee Patrick, Elisha Cook, Jr., Barton MacLane.

John Huston's first film, based on Dashiell Hammett's novel about San Francisco detective Sam Spade and the strange cast of characters searching for a valuable sculpture. If you haven't seen this by now, you've been missing something. Tense, tough, and smart and it hasn't aged a bit.

Invasion of the Body Snatchers (1978, U.S., 114 mins.) Dir: Philip Kaufman; Cast: Donald Sutherland, Brooke Adams, Leonard Nimoy, Veronica Cartwright, Jeff Goldblum.

Though not the classic that the original is, this remake manages to get many solid thrills out of the story about aliens taking over the planet by planting substitutes. The subtext has to do with the mind-numbing late seventies lifestyle that took over San Francisco. Team this up with the Martin Mull comedy *Serial* for an alternative SF double bill.

Star Trek IV: The Voyage Home (1986, U.S., 119 mins.) Dir: Leonard Nimoy; Cast: William Shatner, Leonard Nimoy, DeForest Kelley, James Doohan, Walter Koenig, Nichelle Nichols, George Takei.

The crew of the *Enterprise* travel to 20th-century San Francisco to solve the mystery of some strange transmissions that sound a lot like humpback whales. For once, the whole *Star Trek* phenomenon is treated with a sense of humor to match its middle-brow philosophies and the result is a charming film that still has enough space thrills to please Trekkies.

San Francisco (1936, U.S., 120 mins., b/w) Dir: W. S. Van Dyke; Cast: Clark Gable, Spencer Tracy, Jeanette MacDonald.

Re-creation of the 1906 San Francisco earthquake, along with documentary footage, highlights this historical drama about a romance between a singer and a bar owner. More than just another costume romp; it was nominated for five Oscars and has a screenplay by Anita Loos.

LONDON FOG

Paris is known for romance and the Eiffel Tower. Rome has the Vatican and the ruins of the Empire. London has fog and bad food. To be fair, the city can be fairly romantic and it does have the ruins of its own Empire living in Buckingham Palace. Here's a selection of films set in London that use the city to great effect.

The Long Good Friday (1980, Great Britain, 105 mins.) Dir: John MacKenzie; Cast: Bob Hoskins, Helen Mirren, Eddie Constantine.

Bob Hoskins powered onto the scene with his performance here as a London gangster under siege from unknown enemies. Strong and gory, it's up there with the best mob films and it's full of London flavor. Check out *Mona Lisa* for another strong job by Bob Hoskins and a look at more contemporary London mobsters.

Mary Poppins (1964, U.S., 140 mins.) Dir: Robert Stevenson; Cast: Julie Andrews, Dick Van Dyke, David Tomlinson, Glynis Johns, Elsa Lanchester, Ed Wynn.

Julie Andrews powered onto the scene with her performance here as a London nanny under siege from, whoops. Seriously, this is classic Disney, with magic, wholesome songs, animation, and a terrific travelogue of London that's a major part of the appeal.

A Hard Day's Night (1964, Great Britain, 85 mins., b/w) Dir: Richard

Lester; Cast: The Beatles, Wilfrid Brambell, Victor Spinetti.

John, George, Paul, and Ringo scamper about London singing up a storm. As shallow, frenetic, and thoroughly entertaining as anything you'll see on MTV tonight, but if you're interested, you're probably in the VH1 demographic.

An American Werewolf in London (1981, U.S., 98 mins.) Dir: John Landis; Cast: David Naughton, Griffin Dunne, Jenny Agutter, John Woodvine.

A terrific chiller/comedy about a young American attacked by a werewolf who finds himself howling at the London moon too. A perfect balance between scariness and laughs, it pulls off the very tricky task of giving you goose bumps while winking at the same time.

My Beautiful Laundrette (1985, Great Britain, 94 mins.) Dir: Stephen Frears; Cast: Daniel Day-Lewis, Gordon Warnecke, Saeed Jaffrey, Roshan Seth, Shirley Anne Field.

A young and eager East Indian man gets involved in the family business and tries to make a go of a beat-up laundrette in a South London slum to prove his value. An early effort by both Frears and Day-Lewis that had much to do with their rise.

My Fair Lady (1964, U.S., 170 mins.) Dir: George Cukor; Cast: Rex Harrison, Audrey Hepburn, Stanley Holloway, Wilfrid Hyde-White, Gladys Cooper, Jeremy Brett, Theodore Bikel.

One of the perfect musicals. Harrison plays a professor who bets that he can turn a Covent Garden flower girl into a lady, as if Hepburn wasn't one already. The film won a boxful of Oscars and has enough elegance and wit to satisfy any Anglophile. The Leslie Howard version of Shaw's *Pygmalion* is equally worth seeing.

High Hopes (1988, Great Britain, 110 mins.) Dir: Mike Leigh; Cast: Philip Davis, Ruth Sheen, Edna Dore, Philip Jackson.

Two remnants of the counterculture try to keep their heads above water in an England they believe has sold its soul. Though Mike Leigh's more recent film, *Life Is Sweet,* is superior to this one, *High Hopes* stands out as the best look at Thatcher's Britain we'll get.

The Krays (1990, Great Britain, 119 mins.) Dir: Peter Medak; Cast: Gary Kemp, Martin Kemp, Billy Whitelaw, Kate Hardie, Gary Love, Susan Fleetwood, Tom Bell, Charlotte Cornwall.

A stylish and hyperviolent movie about two London brothers in the sixties who become gangsters. A bloody film, and we mean that literally, but the character studies of Ronnie and Reggie Kray are fascinating. If you like this, you might also be interested in *Scandal,* an equally perverse examination of the Profumo affair that rocked Parliament during roughly the same period.

Blow-Up (1966, Great Britain-Italy, 111 mins.) Dir: Michelangelo Antonioni; Cast: David Hemmings, Vanessa Redgrave, Sarah Miles, Verushka.

Swinging London was one of the world's trendsetting places in the sixties, and this Antonioni film about a London photographer who thinks he may have witnessed a murder was one of its most trendsetting products. Inexplicable at times, always compelling, and arguably the sharpest vision of the period.

Alfie (1966, Great Britain, 114 mins.) Dir: Lewis Gilbert; Cast: Michael Caine, Shelley Winters, Millicent Martin, Vivien Merchant, Shirley Anne Field, Denholm Elliott, Julia Foster.

Caine's first great role has him as an amoral playboy who is brought down to earth with a thud. A terrific, sad, and funny film told with constant asides from Caine that John Hughes obviously ripped off in *Ferris Bueller's Day Off.* Also note that in the special Joan Collins Collection edition, she introduces the film and says that Alfie is "a playwright who would rather play than write." Since Alfie is a driver, one has to wonder why Joan didn't even bother to watch one of her favorite films. Hmmm.

Passport to Pimlico (1949, Great Britain, 72 mins., b/w) Dir: Henry Cornelius; Cast: Stanley Holloway, Hermione Baddeley, Margaret Rutherford.

Lightweight comedy about a neighborhood that decides to secede from London when it discovers an ancient treaty that gives it the right to declare its independence. A harmless period piece set in post-World War II London, it shows the London that the royals probably never got to much during the Blitz. Also for historical interest, see any of the David Lean adaptations of Dickens, like *Oliver Twist,* for 19th-century London.

CITY OF LIGHT

There's much to be said for renting a movie trip to Paris over actually going there. No one will be rude to you for speaking poorly accented French in your living room and it's a lot cheaper. Of course the food is better there and, unless you've got some secrets, it's a good deal more romantic than a night in front of the VCR. If you actually have a choice, watch some of these so you can make an informed decision.

An American in Paris (1951, U.S., 113 mins.) Dir: Vincente Minnelli; Cast: Gene Kelly, Leslie Caron, Oscar Levant, Nina Foch, Georges Guetary.

The Hollywood version of Paris, as Gene Kelly studies art, tears his heart between Caron and Foch, and dances up a regular old storm to Gershwin's music. Not much real Paris here since most of what you see are sets, but you'll get the picture on the romance side.

Paris Blues (1961, U.S., 98 mins., b/w) Dir: Martin Ritt; Cast: Paul Newman, Joanne Woodward, Sidney Poitier, Diahann Carroll, Louis Armstrong.

Woodward and Carroll are tourists courted by expatriate jazz musicians Newman and Poitier. When the guys aren't playing, they're giving the ladies a fairly extensive tour of Paris while a terrific Duke Ellington score plays on the soundtrack. A good film, and if you can beat lots of crisp black-and-white shots of Paris and music by Ellington, let us know.

Children of Paradise (*Les Enfants du Paradis,* 1945, France, 188 mins., b/w) Dir: Marcel Carne; Cast: Jean Louis Barrault, Arletty, Pierre Brasseur, Maria Casares.

A much beloved and remarkably romantic movie about lifelong love between a Parisian actor and a beautiful, seemingly unattainable woman. Some say it's the best movie ever made; it doesn't just capture the romantic spirit of Paris—it helped create it. Filmed during the German occupation, many of the performers were active in the Resistance.

Under the Roofs of Paris (1930, France, 86 mins., b/w) Dir: René Clair; Cast: Albert Prejean, Gaston Modot, Pola Illery, Edmond Gréville.

This much-acclaimed early talkie about a love triangle is also notable for its use of Paris. Clearly made by someone who loves the city, the movie has a real feeling of place and, given when it was made, it's almost a documentary view of Hemingway's Paris.

The Man on the Eiffel Tower (1949, U.S., 97 mins.) Dir: Burgess Meredith; Cast: Charles Laughton, Franchot Tone, Burgess Meredith.

Burgess Meredith's first directorial effort is based on one of George Simenon's Maigret novels. Here, Laughton as Maigret tries to snare suspected killer Tone. If you can get past the poor-quality video, you'll get some nice views of Paris.

Charade (1963, U.S., 114 mins.) Dir: Stanley Donen; Cast: Cary Grant, Audrey Hepburn, Walter Matthau, James Coburn, George Kennedy, Ned Glass.

Hepburn and Grant in Paris with Henry Mancini music. Need we say more? If you're not convinced by that, you'll go for the Oscar-winning screenplay full of twists about a widow trying to find her husband's ill-gotten fortune before bad guys get it. Charming and fun.

Playtime (1968, France, 108 mins.) Dir: Jacques Tati; Cast: Jacques Tati.

Jacques Tati takes on the modern Paris of skyscrapers in this comedy about a man attempting to keep an appointment despite the city's best efforts to stop him. Mostly played without dialogue, Tati lets the sounds of Paris and his great gifts as a physical comedian tell the story. If you like Buster Keaton, you'll like this.

Breathless (*A Bout de Souffle*, 1959, France, 89 mins., b/w) Dir: Jean-Luc Godard; Cast: Jean Seberg, Jean-Paul Belmondo, Daniel Boulanger.

A classic film and certainly the best introduction to French New Wave cinema. Belmondo plays a French hood who takes up with American girl Seberg and proceeds to steal a car and knock off a *gendarme*. Besides its place in film history, it's a good look at everyday life in Paris.

Zazie dans le Métro (1960, France, 92 mins.) Dir: Louis Malle; Cast: Catherine Demonget, Philippe Noiret, Carla Marlier, Hubert Deschamps.

An early Malle film based on Raymond Queneau's novel about a little girl visiting her uncle in Paris and whose greatest wish is to ride the Métro. A jumpy, offbeat, and generally cheery film shot in rich color all over Paris.

Last Tango in Paris (1972, Italy-France, 129 mins.) Dir: Bernardo Bertolucci; Cast: Marlon Brando, Maria Schneider, Jean-Pierre Léaud, Catherine Sola.

Another American in Paris, but this time he does more than just dance. Though critics loved this film about widower Brando coming to Paris and trying to forget his wife's death with an affair, most of the talk around it had to do with how explicitly the affair is portrayed. Make no mistake, this is a dirty movie, but Bertolucci delves so deeply into the psyches of his characters that you're as affected by them as you are by the sex scenes. And Paris looks nice, too.

ROMA

Ah, bella Roma! The Eternal City. Though it's hard to beat ruling the planet for a few centuries, Rome has had some wonderful days since the Empire, and the city's history—imperial, Catholic, and plebian—is on display everywhere. St. Peter's, the Coliseum, the Spanish Steps; the list goes on. If you're in the mood for some red wine, tinny mandolin music, and a taste of Rome, watch one of these.

Rome Adventure (1962, U.S., 119 mins.) Dir: Delmer Daves; Cast: Troy Donahue, Suzanne Pleshette, Angie Dickinson, Rossano Brazzi.

There's no reason to watch this other

than to get a guided tour of Rome. The plot, such as it is, revolves around prissy Pleshette going to Rome to find *amore* and being torn between two men, but Rome is the real star here. Since Pleshette goes on some guided tours in the film, we get to tag along and listen as the guide takes us through some lovely parts of the city.

Roman Holiday (1953, U.S., 119 mins., b/w) Dir: William Wyler; Cast: Gregory Peck, Audrey Hepburn, Eddie Albert.

A sweet, romantic tale of a princess tired of the royal life who takes a brief and secret holiday and falls in love with a reporter. Hepburn won an Oscar for her performance as did the story, and Rome probably deserved one too. The city comes across as the most romantic place in the world, but then again Audrey Hepburn could make Buffalo romantic.

The Bicycle Thief (1949, Italy, 90 mins., b/w) Dir: Vittorio De Sica; Cast: Enzo Staiola, Lamberto Maggiorani, Lianella Carell.

If you have more than a passing interest in film, you've probably heard of this and relegated it to some back drawer of your mind reserved for boring things you're supposed to see. Forget it. At first you'll wonder what the big deal is about a man and his son searching through Rome for a stolen bicycle, but after 45 minutes you'll realize your eyes haven't left the screen and after 90 minutes you'll be crying.

The Roof (1957, Italy, 91 mins., b/w) Dir: Vittorio De Sica; Cast: Gabriella Pallotti, Giorgio Listuzzi.

Another De Sica, not up to the level of *The Bicycle Thief,* yet still a good view of a Rome that you most likely wouldn't see if you were visiting. A young couple gets married and struggles to find a place to live. Think of it as an Italian Realist version of *Barefoot in the Park.*

La Dolce Vita (1960, Italy, 180 mins., b/w) Dir: Federico Fellini; Cast: Marcello Mastroianni, Anita Ekberg, Yvonne Furneaux, Anouk Aimee, Lex Barker, Annibale Nincni, Alain Cuny.

Reporter Mastroianni looks for meaning through the beautifully shot streets, clubs, and houses of Rome. Fellini's long film about depraved, empty lives in the Eternal City sounds much more exciting and prurient than it is, though you still haven't been to many parties like these. Despite the image most people have of Fellini and his visual pyrotechnics, this is a very intellectual movie. Rewarding if you have the patience.

The Roman Spring of Mrs. Stone (1961, Great Britain, 104 mins.) Dir: José Quintero; Cast: Vivien Leigh, Warren Beatty, Jill St. John, Lotte Lenya, Coral Browne.

Strange but engrossing drama based on a novella by Tennessee Williams about a widow living in Rome who has a last fling of sorts with an Italian gigolo. Another terrific view of Rome, but here the stars come first. Leigh is quite convincing as the widow and Lotte Lenya sufficiently evil as the procuress. Warren as the gigolo is hysterically bad, sounding throughout as if he used his barber as his accent coach. Campy and fascinating in that Williams way.

Open City (1946, Italy, 105 mins., b/w) Dir: Roberto Rossellini; Cast: Aldo Fabrizi, Anna Magnani.

Rossellini's classic about the Resistance in Rome during World War II. Always gripping and human, it's an interesting contrast to the kinds of flag-waving films America was producing then. This is about real people suffering horribly and behaving with supreme courage because they can't imagine acting in any other way. The Nazis, though cartoons, are insidious, hateful characters. No wonder Italy had such a strong Communist Party.

Love in the City (1953, Italy, 90 mins., b/w) Dirs: Federico Fellini, Michelangelo Antonioni, Cesare Zavattini, Dino Risi, Alberto Lattuada, Francesco Maselli; Cast: Livia Venturini, Antonio Cifariello, nonprofessional cast.

A curiosity for fans of Italian film. A series of shorts by directors like Fellini and Antonioni were stitched together under the concept of an *Argosy*-type magazine of the screen about love in Rome. English voiceovers give completely different, fairly judgmental spins to the films. The result is somewhere between early *Playboy* and a high school hygiene movie. It's terrible, but it's funny terrible.

Fellini's Roma (1972, Italy-France, 113 mins.) Dir: Federico Fellini; Cast: Peter Gonzales, Stefano Majore, Anna Magnani, Gore Vidal.

A loving pastiche of images and reflections on Rome that loosely follows Fellini's lifelong relationship with the city. There's no plot here—he admits it up front—but that's not the point anyway. Silly at times, serious at others, this film sums up Rome yesterday and Rome today and gives the single finest taste of what the place is like.

OUT OF AFRICA

Until recently, films about Africa meant brave white hunters in safari togs ordering about bearers and shooting at stock footage of lions and elephants. But now we're so enlightened that the animal footage is usually shot on location. Let's hope that Hollywood continues to learn more about the second largest continent. Here's some of the best so far.

Mountains of the Moon (1990, U.S., 135 mins.) Dir: Bob Rafelson; Cast: Patrick Bergin, Iain Glen, Richard E. Grant, Bernard Hill, Fiona Shaw, Paul Onsongo.

A beautifully shot, intelligently written, and reasonably accurate account of the journey taken by Sir Richard Francis Burton and John Speke to find the source of the Nile. Through Burton, who is well-played by Bergin, we see African cultures as valid and not the curiosities they are usually presented as in Western films. Plus, the action sequences are terrific. A grand epic. Also of interest, *Stanley and Livingston,* starring Spencer Tracy.

Zulu (1964, Great Britain, 138 mins.) Dir: Cy Endfield; Cast: Stanley Baker, Jack Hawkins, James Booth, Michael Caine.

A minus 12 on the political correctness scale, as a small band of English soldiers try to stave off an attack by a huge army of Zulu warriors. Two points in the film's defense. First, unlike many films about the Empire, the Zulus are shown as great warriors and not craven animals. Second, it's one of the most exciting, rousing movies ever made.

Out of Africa (1985, U.S., 155 mins.) Dir: Sydney Pollack; Cast: Meryl Streep, Robert Redford, Klaus Maria Brandauer, Michael Gough.

Lush photography and Meryl Streep make this adaptation of Isak Dinesen's book worth watching, even more than the story itself. Dinesen was hardly a great admirer of indigenous East African cultures and very little really happens. It's just a love story in a beautiful place. If you like the Ralph Lauren ads, you'll love this movie.

Chocolat (1988, France, 105 mins.) Dir: Claire Denis; Cast: Issach de Bankole, Giulia Boschi, Francois Cluzet.

Another slowly paced film, this time about a young girl growing up in French West Africa and the charged relationship between her mother and a male servant. Strong on sweltering atmospherics, both personal and meteorological.

Mogambo (1953, U.S., 116 mins.) Dir: John Ford; Cast: Clark Gable, Ava Gardner, Grace Kelly, Donald Sinden, Laurence Naismith.

John Ford directs a great cast in this remake of *Red Dust*. Gardner, Kelly, and Gable are the three corners of a love triangle, with Gable as the great white hunter. Ford shows the same appreciation for the African countryside as he does for Monument Valley, so it's lovely to watch without being artsy.

Something of Value (1957, U.S., 113 mins., b/w) Dir: Richard Brooks; Cast: Rock Hudson, Dana Wynter, Sidney Poitier, Wendy Hiller.

A surprisingly good adaptation of Robert Ruark's novel about the Mau Mau Rebellion in Kenya. Hudson and Poitier play boyhood friends who find themselves on opposite sides of the machete. At least an attempt was made to avoid awful stereotypes and the scene of the Mau Mau raid is exceptional.

Cry Freedom (1987, U.S., 157 mins.) Dir: Richard Attenborough; Cast: Kevin Kline, Denzel Washington, Penelope Wilton.

Though Attenborough's epic telling of the relationship between murdered South African activist Steven Biko and white reporter Donald Woods is well-meaning, the fact that Biko dies half-way through and we're left with Woods to worry about should tell you some-thing. Lite politics, made reassuring with a white hero. Still, moving and grand at times.

Sarafina! (1992, U.S.-Great Britain-France, 115 mins.) Dir: Darrell James Roodt; Cast: Whoopi Goldberg, Leleti Khumalo, Miriam Makeba, John Kani.

The only apartheid musical around manages to be affecting despite its sim-ple politics, and, over a lilting sound-track, offers a tough view of growing up in Soweto. Whoopi gives a restrained performance and seems the better for it.

The Sheltering Sky (1990, U.S., 137 mins.) Dir: Bernardo Bertolucci; Cast: Debra Winger, John Malkovich, Camp-bell Scott, Jill Bennett, Timothy Spall, Eric Vu-An, Paul Bowles.

The Sahara is the world's largest desert and you'll certainly feel as though you've been there after sitting through Bertolucci's version of Paul Bowles's novel about an American couple sucked into and destroyed by North Africa. Visually stunning, but be pre-pared for long stretches of desert tor-por. If you can restrain yourself from the desire to pop the main characters upside the head, you may even enjoy it.

The African Queen (1951, U.S., 103 mins.) Dir: John Huston; Cast: Kath-arine Hepburn, Humphrey Bogart, Robert Morley, Theodore Bikel.

Africa here is simply a stage set for the immense talents of Hepburn and Bogey, but what talents and what a stage set. Bogart won an Oscar as the drunk who takes spinster Hepburn up the Congo during World War I. On the way they fight each other, they fight Germans, they pick leeches off each other, and have a generally nasty time until they realize that they're in love. A classic. If you like this film, you'll be interested in *White Hunter, Black Heart,* a fictional treatment of John Huston and the tumult leading up to the filming of *The African Queen.* Clint Eastwood makes a sincere effort at por-traying Huston, and the film itself works by never becoming pretentious.

Samba Traore (1993, Burkina Faso, 85 mins.) Dir: Iderissa Ouedrango; Cast: Bakary Sangare, Miriam Kaba, Abdoulaye Komboudri, Irene Tassem-bedo.

Once you're finished seeing everything

Hollywood has to show of Africa, then it's time to begin sampling the brilliant films Africans themselves have produced, and here's a fine place to start. This simple story of a man returning to his small village in the bush after a stint in the city and a brush with crime has the lean power of a folk tale and some very fine, very human performances by its mixed cast of professionals and locals. No safaris or politics; just a moving look at everyday life in Burkina Faso.

SOUTH AMERICA

Continent of the tango and the proud capybara; home of Evita, Pelé, and Gabriel García Márquez; land of the Amazon and Angel Falls. Though just as exotic and rich as Africa, South America has never quite entered the North American consciousness in the same way. Maybe that's why we have more hard-hitting, interesting films about the place.

At Play in the Fields of the Lord (1991, U.S., 187 mins.) Dir: Hector Babenco; Cast: Tom Berenger, Aidan Quinn, Kathy Bates, John Lithgow, Daryl Hannah.

Based on Peter Mathiessen's novel, it's a long, wrenching, and rewarding look at the conflict between an Amazonian tribe and the North American missionaries come to convert them. Stunning scenery and a truthful portrayal of tribal life in the rain forest. The story seems too slight to justify three hours, but you'll be hard-pressed to find anything to cut.

Black Orpheus (1959, France-Portugal, 98 mins.) Dir: Marcel Camus; Cast: Breno Mello, Marpessa Dawn.

This beautiful retelling of the Orpheus myth is set during Carnival in Rio and is justly famous for its unforgettable samba score. As sweet and rich as coconut milk, with all the colors of a jungle bird.

Pixote (1981, Brazil, 127 mins.) Dir: Hector Babenco; Cast: Fernando Ramos da Silva, Mariba Peña, Jorge Juliano.

Babenco's unromantic view of life in Rio follows a 10-year-old child of the streets who lives to steal and sniff glue and kill. A terribly graphic movie that slaps you in the face—hard—with the horrific circumstances of this child's life. Tough and brilliant.

Doña Flor and Her Two Husbands (1978, Brazil, 106 mins.) Dir: Bruno Barreto; Cast: Sonia Braga, José Wilker, Mauro Mendoca.

Sonia Braga misses her dead good-for-nothing husband so much that he comes back from the grave to keep her company. Bawdy and explicit; you can see why she'd miss him.

Kiss of the Spider Woman (1985, Brazil-U.S., 119 mins., c & b/w) Dir: Hector Babenco; Cast: William Hurt, Raul Julia, Sonia Braga, José Lewgoy.

Babenco's third entry here is based on Manuel Puig's novel about a revolutionary and a homosexual who are cellmates in a South American prison. Hurt won an Oscar as the gay prisoner. Slow going at times, yet enthralling at others.

Fitzcarraldo (1982, West Germany, 158 mins.) Dir: Werner Herzog; Cast: Klaus Kinski, Claudia Cardinale, Paul Hittscher, José Lewgoy.

A fascinating, overwhelming film from the true story of a railroad baron obsessed with building an opera house in the middle of the Peruvian rain forest. Equally fascinating is Kinski, whose brilliant performance belies his large body of work in schlock films.

Aguirre, the Wrath of God (1972, West Germany, 95 mins.) Dir: Werner Herzog; Cast: Klaus Kinski, Ruy Guerra, Helena Rojo.

Herzog's other film about obsession and madness in the Amazon tells the story of Spanish conquistadors in the 16th century on a fatal search for El Dorado, the City of Gold. An intense and gripping viewing experience. This and *Fitzcarraldo* are the finest moments on film for both Herzog and Kinski to date.

Erendira (1984, Mexico-France-Germany, 103 mins.) Dir: Ruy Guerra; Cast: Irene Papas, Claudia Ohana.

Strange film about a girl who is forced by her grandmother to wander the desert prostituting herself. The strangeness is explained by the fact that it's based on a novel by Gabriel García Márquez. The movie does well in capturing the bizarre and lyrical qualities of the master of magical realism.

State of Siege (1973, France, 120 mins.) Dir: Constantin Costa-Gavras; Cast: Yves Montand, Renato Salvatori, O. E. Hasse.

South America is also the home of some truly terrifying political terrorism by those both in and out of power. This tense film about the assassination of an American official in Uruguay has, like all of Costa-Gavras's work, a decidedly leftist slant. Your interest in this will depend more on your sympathies with that point of view than it will with his movie-making skills or Montand's great acting.

Missing (1982, U.S., 122 mins.) Dir: Constantin Costa-Gavras; Cast: Jack Lemmon, Sissy Spacek, John Shea, Melanie Mayron, David Clennon, Janice Rule, Charles Cioffi.

Costa-Gavras again, this time with an American cast to tell the true story of a journalist who disappeared during a Chilean coup and the struggles his wife and father encounter in trying to find him. Many great scenes between Lemmon as the right-wing dad and Spacek as the left-wing wife keep this on a human level. Scary stuff that makes you happy to be an American until you realize that the point is that our government is complicit. Political theater at its best.

The Official Story (1985, Argentina, 110 mins.) Dir: Luis Puenzo; Cast: Hector Alterio, Norma Aleandro, Chela Ruiz, Analia Castro.

For once the Academy went out on a limb in 1985 and gave the award for Best Foreign Language Film to this challenging Argentinian movie about a pampered woman who believes that the child she has just adopted was taken from one of the thousands of political prisoners being held in the nation's jails. Storytelling and politics get equal attention in the riveting film.

THE POLAR REGIONS

You may wonder why we bothered with this list, but remember last August? 103 in the shade; broken air conditioner. You're sticking to the chair, praying for a breeze. . . . Rent one of these, add ice, and stir.

Antarctica (1983, Japan, 112 mins.) Dir: Koreyoshi Kurahara; Cast: Ken Takakura, Masako Natsume.

Japanese film about a scientific expedition to the South Pole forced to abandon its dog teams. The best authentic footage of Antarctica, but if you have a soft spot for dogs, keep some hankies nearby.

Scott of the Antarctic (1948, Great Britain, 110 mins.) Dir: Charles Frend; Cast: John Mills, Derek Bond, Kenneth More, Christopher Lee.

Earnest re-creation of Captain Robert Scott's fatal race to the South Pole against Norwegian Roald Amundsen. Cleaves to the official whitewash version of Scott as a hero, but a sturdy drama all the same. See the British television series *The Last Place on Earth,* based on Roland Huntford's *Scott and Amundsen,* for the best version of this story and the most realistic portrayal of a polar expedition.

The Thing (aka: *The Thing From Another World,* 1951, U.S., 87 mins., b/w) Dir: Christian Nyby; Cast: Kenneth Tobey, Margaret Sheridan, Robert Cornthwaite, James Arness, George Fenneman.

The original. Scientists in the Arctic accidentally thaw out a deadly alien, played by Arness. Produced by Howard Hawks, who is often credited with directing (untrue). Good sci-fi/horror, though not the best look at the Arctic. The kids in John Carpenter's *Halloween* are watching this movie when Michael drops by.

Forbidden Quest (1993, The Netherlands, 75 mins.) Dir: Peter Delpeut; Cast: Joseph O'Conor, Roy Ward.

Clips from film shot during actual early expeditions were cut together to create this new and fictional tale about the frightening, otherworldly limits of polar exploration. A tad overwrought at times, but the footage is priceless and tells the eerie story well enough to raise a good crop of goose bumps.

Nanook of the North (1922, U.S., 65 mins., b/w) Dir: Robert Flaherty.

Now this is a travelogue of the Arctic. Flaherty's groundbreaking documentary about Inuit life early in the century.

The Perfect Furlough (1958, U.S., 93 mins.) Dir: Blake Edwards; Cast: Tony Curtis, Janet Leigh, Keenan Wynn, Linda Cristal, Elaine Stritch, Troy Donahue.

Curtis is picked out of 104 men stationed in the Arctic to go on furlough in Paris to relieve their collective cabin fever. Early Blake Edwards, but already his style is evident. The only strange note is the 104 beautifully groomed beards on the men at the base.

Ice Station Zebra (1968, U.S., 148 mins.) Dir: John Sturges; Cast: Rock Hudson, Patrick McGoohan, Ernest Borgnine, Jim Brown, Tony Bill.

Spies and submarines at the North Pole. As often happens in the polar regions, not a woman in sight. Nice scenes underneath the ice and a colorful shoot-out at the end.

VICES

FOOD

Food glorious food. From basic sustenance, to tantalizer of the senses, to gluttony and excess. From the simple to the symbolic, or just trying to diet and then hearing the siren call of that pint of Rocky Road from the fridge. The short of it is, you just can't live without it, so dig in.

The Discreet Charm of the Bourgeoisie (1972, France, 100 mins.) Dir: Luis Buñuel; Cast: Delphine Seyrig, Fernando Rey, Stephane Audran, Jean-Pierre Cassel, Michel Piccoli.

Part of the charm of these particular bourgeois is they never do seem to sit down to their dinner. Political radicals, the social elite, Buñuel takes jabs at them all in an accessibly surreal—but somewhat too long—dig at pompous self-importance and the class system.

Babette's Feast (1987, Denmark, 102 mins.) Dir: Gabriel Axel; Cast: Stephane Audran, Birgitte Federspiel, Bodil Kjer, Jarl Kulle.

Set in deepest northern Denmark, this is the story of a grand gustatory gesture served up in a setting of apparent sensory impoverishment. The richness and overwhelming detail of a meal prepared for a group of old acquaintances by a former chef who sought refuge as a servant in an austere Danish home, brings to the surface the hidden depth and complexity of a seemingly simple community. The subtlety of smells and flavors are palpable from the screen. You'll also be completely seduced by the preparation and dining scenes in *The Dead,* Christmas dinner in *Fanny and Alexander,* and throughout Ang Lee's *Eat Drink Man Woman.*

Tampopo (1987, Japan, 117 mins.) Dir: Juzo Itami; Cast: Tsutomu Yamazaki, Nobuko Miyamoto, Koji Yakusho, Ken Watanabe.

A witty yet winding contemporary Japanese food and sex cult classic about one woman's goal to open the perfect noodle shop. Sushi served provocatively *sur la torso* is one of the main courses offered here.

Like Water for Chocolate (1992, Mexico, 113 mins.) Dir: Alfonso Arau; Cast: Lumi Cavazos, Marco Leonardi, Regina Torne, Mario Ivan Martinez, Ada Carrasco.

A spirited interpretation of Laura Esquivel's mystical novel about a Mexican family's tradition that the youngest daughter must stay home to care for the mother as she ages. All of the daughter's passion for her life and the man she must not have is channeled into her meal preparations and we see the magical effects on everyone. More lightweight than García Márquez though comparable in mood, the film is as much about the power of love as the strength of the women portrayed here.

Five Easy Pieces (1970, U.S., 96 mins.) Dir: Bob Rafelson; Cast: Jack Nicholson, Karen Black, Susan Anspach, Fannie Flagg, Billy Green Bush.

Finely drawn character portrait of a disaffected middle-class 1960s "dropout." Nicholson's classical musician turned oil-rig roustabout has one of his best scenes in an all-time best short-order moment. Hilarious and memorable, he and Black are perfect together.

Cool Hand Luke (1967, U.S., 126 mins.) Dir: Stuart Rosenberg; Cast: Paul Newman, George Kennedy, Strother Martin, Dennis Hopper.

You'll say "no" to hard-boiled eggs after seeing this intense chain-gang drama with Newman at war against his shackles, the system, and Martin's beyond-nasty white-trash prison warden.

Diner (1982, U.S., 110 mins.) Dir: Barry Levinson; Cast: Steve Guttenberg, Daniel Stern, Mickey Rourke, Kevin Bacon, Timothy Daly, Ellen Barkin.

Of course just about every scene ends up back at the local diner, the center of all social activity and transaction imaginable in this fun and poignant view of teen hopes and dreams in 1950s Baltimore. The most memorable food scene is still the box of popcorn, however.

Eating Raoul (1982, U.S., 83 mins.) Dir: Paul Bartel; Cast: Paul Bartel, Mary Woronov, Robert Beltran.

Seemingly predictable, repressed suburban couple have a dream to open a restaurant, but how to raise cash? They succeed in a very funny, black kind of way when they're inspired to commit some robberies—that happen to involve murder. Highlighted with inventive body-disposal techniques and quirky sex.

My Dinner With Andre (1982, U.S., 110 mins.) Dir: Louis Malle; Cast: Andre Gregory, Wallace Shawn.

The stunningly simple premise—two old friends who haven't seen each other in a while dine together in an elegant restaurant—is powerfully developed through the bright, brilliant, wholly eclectic, realistic, and urbane conversation between playwright/actor Shawn and theater director Gregory that makes the ordinary extraordinary.

Life Is Sweet (1991, Great Britain, 102 mins.) Dir: Mike Leigh; Cast: Alison Steadman, Jim Broadbent, Claire Skinner, Jane Horrocks, Stephen Rea, Timothy Spall.

Leigh portrays another close-in slice of modern, barely subsisting British life in this tough family farce. Terrific acting reveals some fabulously unique characters as they encounter and cope with anorexia, the restaurant business, hot-dog wagons (that's Stephen Rea), lust, and other cravings.

Delicatessen (1991, France, 95 mins.) Dirs: Jean-Pierre Jeunet, Marc Caro; Cast: Marie-Laure Dougnac, Dominique Pinon, Karin Viard, Jean Claude Dreyfus.

Sort of a cannibalistic-eye-view of the food industry. Hilarious not-quite-too-graphic tale of life at a deli of the future. Check out *Soylent Green* which, while it takes itself far more seriously, does its best to look at ways to deal with futuristic food-shortage problems as well.

Easy Living (1937, U.S., 90 mins.) Dir: Mitchell Leisen; Cast: Jean Arthur, Edward Arnold, Ray Milland.

This fabulous screwball comedy has Jean taking up with the son of her wealthy benefactor. But you're here for the hysterical flying food at the Automat scene.

The Baker's Wife (1938, France, 124 mins., b/w) Dir: Marcel Pagnol; Cast: Raimu, Ginette Laclerc, Charles Moulin, Robert Vattier, Robert Brassa.

A warm and bittersweet story of a baker's love for his beautiful wife, her betrayal, and their reconciliation. Charmingly told with wit and humor, the conversations are gems of subtlety and perception.

DRINK

That demon alcohol. Mostly, it only looks like fun. But we've tried to present a range.

Thunder Road (1958, U.S., 92 mins.) Dir: Arthur Ripley; Cast: Robert Mitchum, Keely Smith, Gene Barry.

Moonshine and bootlegger Mitchum make a swell combo against the revenuers. By the way, Mitchum wrote the title song *and* the story this zippy backwoods tale is based on; and, that's his son James playing his brother.

The Lost Weekend (1945, U.S., 101 mins.) Dir: Billy Wilder; Cast: Ray Milland, Jane Wyman, Philip Terry, Howard Da Silva.

Milland is completely believable as a writer who cannot believe in himself and turns to the bottle, rejecting everyone who tries to help him. Brilliant in its revelation of the alcoholic's skill at hiding his problem—especially from himself. Only the end is a little pat and dissatisfying. For the equally painful, middle-class-couple version of this, see Blake Edwards's *Days of Wine and Roses,* with its stellar performances by Lee Remick and Jack Lemmon.

S.O.B. (1981, U.S., 121 mins.) Dir: Blake Edwards; Cast: Julie Andrews, William Holden, Richard Mulligan, Robert Vaughn, Robert Webber, Robert Preston, Rosanna Arquette, Larry Hagman.

Edwards continues his uneven directorial career with this sometimes very funny, sometimes misfiring inside-Hollywood satire featuring a hard-drinking and otherwise self-indulgent producer and his whacked ploys to save a bomb.

The Verdict (1982, U.S., 129 mins.) Dir: Sidney Lumet; Cast: Paul Newman, Charlotte Rampling, Jack Warden, James Mason, Milo O'Shea, Edward Binns, Julie Bovasso.

Boston lawyer Newman gets a chance to redeem his career from his drinking "problem." Playwright David Mamet's screenplay interpreted with Lumet's eloquent direction and razor-sharp performances by Newman and Mason. Rampling is also interesting to watch.

The Thin Man (1934, U.S., 93 mins., b/w) Dir: W. S. Van Dyke; Cast: William Powell, Myrna Loy, Maureen O'Sullivan, Nat Pendleton, Minna Gombell, Porter Hall.

Well, the Nick and Nora Charles version of a drinking problem would be running out of champagne glasses. This first *Thin Man* is absolutely the best of a series that celebrates drinking (and smoking) as the quintessential prop of the most urbanely sophisticated. No couple was ever more insouciant, dapper, elegant, hysterically funny, and constantly loaded as Nick and Nora, wryly played by Powell and Loy. Of course it's their unique wit and mutual attraction that make it all so appealing; the excessive wealth just provides the atmosphere. There is actually a plot here—Nick and Nora (and Asta) investigate the mysterious death of a kindly inventor. The first two sequels are worth a look, too: *After the Thin Man* and *Another Thin Man*.

Smash-Up: The Story of a Woman (1947, U.S., 103 mins., b/w) Dir: Stuart Heisler; Cast: Susan Hayward, Lee Bowman, Eddie Albert, Marsha Hunt.

Sensationalist soaper with Oscar-nomination performance by Hayward (and script co-written by Dorothy Parker) as a nightclub singer who gives up her career for her husband's, then turns to drink. This was good practice for her identifying role in the landmark bio of actress Lillian Roth, *I'll Cry Tomorrow*, in 1955.

Barfly (1987, U.S., 100 mins.) Dir: Barbet Schroeder; Cast: Mickey Rourke, Faye Dunaway, Alice Krige, Jack Nance, J. C. Quinn, Frank Stallone.

Mickey and Faye never looked so bad (well, Faye anyway) in voyeuristically compelling semi-autobio of wildman poet Charles Bukowski (who wrote the screenplay), whose sense of humor about the human condition runs second only to his capacity to imbibe. The bright sun of L.A. is used effectively to contrast with the film's wasteland tour of terminally seedy bars and backrooms.

Who's Afraid of Virginia Woolf? (1966, U.S., 129 mins., b/w) Dir: Mike Nichols; Cast: Elizabeth Taylor, Richard Burton, Sandy Dennis, George Segal.

This searing portrait of a marriage on the brink is said to be Bukowski's favorite. Not surprising. Dick and Liz use words (Edward Albee's, at his biting best) to rip each other's hearts out, and Sandy and George are dragged along for the ride. Talk about a bumpy night. Nichols's remarkable debut is further enhanced by Haskell Wexler's remarkable photography.

Arthur (1981, U.S., 97 mins.) Dir: Steve Gordon; Cast: Dudley Moore, Liza Minnelli, John Gielgud, Geraldine Fitzgerald, Jill Eikenberry, Stephen Elliott.

The warmest and most charming (next to William Powell, that is) drunk you'll ever meet. Semi-Cinderella tale has the outrageously wealthy Arthur forced to choose between the waitress he loves (an appealing Minnelli) and keeping his estate by marrying the deb his parents have chosen. Sir John lends a most witty and civilized hand as Arthur's faithful butler. Unfortunately, *Arthur 2: On the Rocks* doesn't even come close.

Under the Volcano (1984, U.S., 112 mins.) Dir: John Huston; Cast: Albert Finney, Jacqueline Bisset, Anthony Andrews, Katy Jurado.

Finney is excruciatingly well cast as the dissipated foreign consul in this evocative and atmospheric adaptation of Malcolm Lowry's brilliant novel that takes place during the Day of the Dead celebrations in Oaxaca, Mexico.

Harvey (1950, U.S., 104 mins.) Dir: Henry Koster; Cast: James Stewart, Josephine Hull, Peggy Dow, Jesse White, Cecil Kellaway.

Some drinkers see pink elephants; well, Jimmy sees bunnies. One in particular, that is. His name is Harvey and he's over six feet tall. Jimmy and Harvey are totally endearing and totally harmless, though certainly confusing to those around them in this charming and funny adaptation of a hit Broadway show.

GAMBLING

Playing cards or craps, in the back room, at the betting window, or somewhere over the roulette wheel, that's where you'll find them.

Atlantic City (1981, Canada-France, 104 mins.) Dir: Louis Malle; Cast: Burt Lancaster, Susan Sarandon, Robert Joy, Michel Piccoli, Kate Reid, Hollis Mc-Laren.

This is the seedy side of the Boardwalk during the days when Atlantic City was just beginning to make the transition to big-time gambling. The two-bit guys, like the hood played by the exceptional Lancaster, are still the main operators, but the big money's coming soon and the scene is well set with screenwriter John Guare's effec-

tive dialogue. A solid story told with humor and pathos, and notable performances, make this a must-see.

Honeymoon in Vegas (1992, U.S., 95 mins.) Dir: Andrew Bergman; Cast: James Caan, Nicholas Cage, Sarah Jessica Parker, Pat Morita, Johnny Williams, John Capodice, Anne Bancroft, Peter Boyle.

All right, another flimsy love story. But Cage always has a bit of unique charm and everyone seems to like Sarah Jessica. We like Caan the best here as the major bankroll gambler who tries to buy S. J. from Nick. Lots of Vegas scenery (with some Hawaii thrown in for good measure), and some cute bits—check out the flying Elvises. All in all pretty painless.

Eight Men Out (1988, U.S., 120 mins.) Dir: John Sayles; Cast: John Cusack, Clifton James, Christopher Lloyd, John Mahoney, Charlie Sheen, David Strathairn, D. B. Sweeney.

Not for Sayles fans only. Beautifully shot and acted baseball tragedy and period piece about Shoeless Joe Jackson and the games thrown by the Chicago "Black" Sox in the 1919 World Series. With especially superlative performances by Strathairn and Cusack, and Sayles himself showing up as writer Ring Lardner.

Guys and Dolls (1955, U.S., 138 mins.) Dir: Joseph L. Mankiewicz; Cast: Marlon Brando, Jean Simmons, Frank Sinatra, Vivian Blaine, Robert Keith, Stubby Kaye, Veda Ann Borg, Regis Toomey, Sheldon Leonard.

"Luck Be a Lady . . ." A pair of dice never had such a good time. So what if Marlon is more than a little odd in his role as the flamboyant Sky Masterson? The tunes (Frank Loesser) and dancing are swell in the Hollywood version of the Broadway adaptation of Damon Runyon's stories of the oldest established permanent floating crap game in New York.

Mr. Lucky (1943, U.S., 100 mins., b/w) Dir: H. C. Potter; Cast: Cary Grant, Laraine Day, Charles Bickford.

The ever-suave Cary plays the perennial con Mr. Lucky—until he falls for Mary (Day) and discovers he even has a conscience (not quite Bogey in *Casablanca,* but the same war and you get the idea). Not before we get to play some endearing Australian word games, however, and enjoy the gaming tables, have a little romance, and head off to sea.

The Music of Chance (1993, U.S., 98 mins.) Dir: Philip Haas; Cast: Mandy Patinkin, James Spader, Charles Durning, Joel Grey, M. Emmet Walsh.

Sort of *The Collector* of gambling movies. Spader is that sleazy character we're seeing just a little too often now, but he's just right as a poker player who convinces Patinkin to put up the cash for a high-stakes game in a very eccentric locale. Not for everyone, but memorable in a theatrical kind of way.

Bob le Flambeur (1955, France, 97 mins., b/w) Dir: Jean-Pierre Melville; Cast: Roger Duchesne, Isabel Corey, Daniel Cauchy.

Snazzy black-and-white photography and smart settings provide atmosphere for the story of the aging but always sleek and cool mastermind con Bob le Flambeur (Bob the Gambler, that is)— who can't resist a comeback heist. Loved and respected by the women and pals in his life, everyone tries to protect him. Charming and wry.

The Rocking Horse Winner (1949, Great Britain, 91 mins., b/w) Dir: Anthony Pelissier; Cast: Valerie Hobson, John Mills, John Howard Davies.

What a terrific movie! D. H. Lawrence's short story comes to devastating life

when a young boy, tortured by the money worries at home, finds he can pick winners at the track.

The Cincinnati Kid (1965, U.S., 113 mins.) Dir: Norman Jewison; Cast: Steve McQueen, Edward G. Robinson, Joan Blondell, Rip Torn, Ann-Margret, Tuesday Weld.

The young Steve McQueen plays poker against the likes of imposing Edward G. in this Depression-era New Orleans traveling poker game, with a provocative screenplay by Ring Lardner and Terry Southern.

CONS & SCAMS

The old hoodwink; charlatans, fakers, tricksters, and schemers; the survival of the cleverest—when they're very good, that is. But this is a world that's fodder for the fumbling likes of *The Honeymooners* as well. No matter what, to play this game you've got to know when your mark's at hand. And, sigh, there seems to be no shortage of suckers in this world. Here's a glimpse of the slick, and the not so.

Six Degrees of Separation (1993, U.S., 112 mins.) Dir: Fred Schepisi; Cast: Stockard Channing, Donald Sutherland, Will Smith, Ian McKellen, Bruce Davison, Richard Masur, Mary Beth Hurt, Anthony Michael Hall.

Here's a guy (an impressive Smith) who, capitalizing on his charm and wiles, cons his way into the liberal hearts and homes of N.Y.'s wealthy by posing as Sidney Poitier's son. Based on a true story, and in turn on John Guare's play, we are fascinated and repelled by this glimpse of the priviliged life.

Trading Places (1983, U.S., 106 mins.) Dir: John Landis; Cast: Dan Aykroyd,

Eddie Murphy, Ralph Bellamy, Don Ameche, Denholm Elliott, Jamie Lee Curtis, Paul Gleason.

Down-and-out hustler Eddie and high-toned stockbroker Dan are sharp and fast and will hold your attention as Murphy tests out his street smarts in the executive suite—and Aykroyd tests out life curbside. Plausible? No less so than what we read in the news every day.

F for Fake (1973, France, 85 mins.) Dir: Orson Welles.

Welles takes us on a semidocumentary tour of some of the great 20th-century cons and their victims. Art forgers (Elmyr de Hory) and Clifford Irving's ersatz Howard Hughes book contract are featured. More intriguing than fiction, though the research itself was considered somewhat questionable at the time.

House of Games (1987, U.S., 102 mins.) Dir: David Mamet; Cast: Lindsay Crouse, Joe Mantegna, Mike Nussbaum, Lilia Skala.

Initially almost unbearable in its stage-like pacing, this Mamet story of shrink Crouse's chance meeting with Mantegna and fascination with his almost voyeuristic evocation of the confidence racket is ultimately compelling and resonant. The starkness and simplicity of the sets and the dialogue combine to underscore this picture of deception.

Meet John Doe (1941, U.S., 132 mins., b/w) Dir: Frank Capra; Cast: Gary Cooper, Barbara Stanwyck, Walter Brennan, Edward Arnold, Spring Byington, James Gleason.

Media con, sentimental Capra style. Columnist Babs dreams up a voice-of-the-people publicity stunt for her ailing newspaper—then has to come up with his real-life impersonator. We end up somewhat manipulated and betrayed ourselves as her ballplayer-on-the-skids "John Doe" (the laconic Mr. Cooper at

his utter naïvest) comes to believe the bit himself. An interesting slice, just the same.

The Lady Eve (1941, U.S., 97 mins., b/w) Dir: Preston Sturges; Cast: Barbara Stanwyck, Henry Fonda, Charles Coburn, William Demarest, Eugene Pallette, Eric Blore.

Stanwyck is a lot more fun here as the ultrasophisticated schemer in this hysterical transoceanic floating con, and hayseed herpetologist Fonda's just swell as her innocent dupe. Fun, romance, sizzle, and style. Don't miss the opening credits.

Nothing Sacred (1937, U.S., 77 mins.) Dir: William Wellman; Cast: Carole Lombard, Fredric March, Walter Connolly, Charles Winninger, Sig Ruman, John Qualen, Maxie Rosenbloom, Hattie McDaniel.

We all get taken for a very smart and snappy ride with a Vermont girl (read: small-town, and Lombard's wickedly hilarious) whose "fatal" illness is revealed as a sham—but not before she takes those sharp N.Y. newsboys (and their readers) along for the sympathy. While the boys tumble for it, when they come to, it's ethics time. A grand movie for all you cynics out there, deftly served up.

The Sting (1973, U.S., 129 mins.) Dir: George Roy Hill; Cast: Paul Newman, Robert Redford, Robert Shaw.

You know about this one—it's charming, entertaining, and holds up quite well, though we're a little tired of the jazz-age score about now. But watch it for that Redford-Newman chemistry, and pick up a few pointers along the way.

Dead Heat on a Merry-Go-Round (1966, U.S., 104 mins.) Dir: Bernard Girard; Cast: James Coburn, Camilla Sparv.

Hey hey it's the sixties, and Harrison

Ford is here in his first role—a brief bit as a bellboy. A curious mix of topical references with Coburn cast in his consummate smooth but somehow suspect way. The fuzzy false-identity money-swindle plot twists and turns, but no matter, it's kind of fun in a pseudo-Bond sort of way.

The Grifters (1990, U.S., 119 mins.) Dir: Stephen Frears; Cast: Anjelica Huston, John Cusack, Annette Bening, Pat Hingle.

Who's conning who? Very tantalizing tension-builder with slithery Annette, sleek and shadowy Anjelica, and con-wannabe Cusack. Drug scheme gone awry is as much about the characters and their enigmatic relationships, put together with a noiry, street-life atmosphere.

A Fish Called Wanda (1988, U.S., 105 mins.) Dir: Charles Crichton; Cast: John Cleese, Jamie Lee Curtis, Kevin Kline, Michael Palin.

Funny, appealing, and occasionally quirked over-the-top amusement about an unusual bunch of bungling scam artists. The cast is having a good time and it shows. Nice fish, too.

Paper Moon (1973, U.S., 101 mins.) Dir: Peter Bogdanovich; Cast: Ryan O'Neal, Tatum O'Neal, Madeline Kahn, John Hillerman.

Young Tatum is spunky and tough as streetwise Addie Pray, who seems to know the swindle ropes even better than her veteran dad (Ryan O'). The Bible's their game, the corn belt's their turf, and satisfaction's guaranteed.

UFOria (1981, U.S., 100 mins.) Dir: John Binder; Cast: Cindy Williams, Harry Dean Stanton, Fred Ward, Robert Gray, Darrell Larson.

The evangelical scam still deserves a great movie (unless you count Lancaster in *The Rainmaker*, but that's not quite the same thing), which unfortunately this isn't. It'll do, however, until one comes along. Here, you get aliens and Harry Dean thrown in. That's not a bad deal, but we'll wait for the Tammy Faye and Jim story.

DRUGS

Drug movies are an especially tough lot—not much upbeat drug use in moralistic Hollywood. So while you'll find happy dopers in sixties reminiscences like *The Big Chill* and *Return of the Secaucus Seven*, not to mention the absolutely awful *I Love You Alice B. Toklas*, here are some of the best of the rest in substance abuse.

Rush (1991, U.S., 120 mins.) Dir: Lili Fini Zanuck; Cast: Jason Patric, Jennifer Jason Leigh, Sam Elliott, Max Perlich, Gregg Allman.

Long but driving action sizzler with old-hand narc Patric introducing his new partner (and love interest) to the risks of their trade in mid-seventies Texas. Compellingly portrayed story of their inevitable addiction is accompanied with a bit of police corruption subtext, a low-key bluesy background score by Eric Clapton, and believably hyped-up performances by Patric and Leigh; and a super Perlich, in a more educated variation of his *Drugstore Cowboy* character, as the regretful sell-out Walker. Check out *Deep Cover* for more.

One False Move (1992, U.S., 105 mins.) Dir: Carl Franklin; Cast: Bill Paxton, Cynda Williams, Billy Bob Thornton, Michael Beach, Jim Metzler, Earl Billings, Natalie Canerday.

Carl Franklin's striking and difficult first feature is absolutely riveting. Cold mastermind Pluto (Beach) and his dissipated junkie cohorts (Williams and

Thornton) follow a major cocaine heist and brutal murders in L.A. with a road trip that ends up in Dirt Road, Arkansas. There the drama mixes it up with the local sheriff's past and his misguided shot at stardom as he competes with the big-city L.A. detectives to make the capture.

Burroughs: The Movie (1983, U.S., 87 mins.) Dir: Howard Brookner; Cast: William S. Burroughs, Allen Ginsberg, Terry Southern, John Giorno, Herbert Huncke, Gregory Corso, Jackie Curtis, Brion Gysin, William Burroughs, Jr., Patti Smith, Francis Bacon.

A documentary about writer William S. Burroughs, the king of toxicity. Well-edited reminiscences feature interviews with Ginsberg, Corso, Huncke, and Southern, and clips with others from the *On the Road* gang. Firsthand telling of how Burroughs came to shoot his wife, how he came to write in his 40s, and the poignant yet objective story of his son Billy's brief life. Throughout, Burroughs appears matter-of-fact and straight although you wonder about the odd fact of his survival given the extent of his drug (and alcohol) use. Fascinating stuff.

Drugstore Cowboy (1989, U.S., 100 mins.) Dir: Gus Van Sant, Jr.; Cast: Matt Dillon, Kelly Lynch, William S. Burroughs, Heather Graham, James Remar, James Le Gros, Max Perlich, Beah Richards, Grace Zabriskie.

And Burroughs shows up here amusingly cast as (literally) a junkie priest. Kelly Lynch and Heather Graham are the film's stars, though Dillon is the mastermind of this small-beans, pill-popping, skin-popping, drugstore-robbing little gang, based in Portland in the early seventies. Van Sant mixes it up with some visual dream tricks loaded with portents, but the nicely unmoralistic story of these somehow vulnerable—yet tough—young junkies holds up pretty well by itself.

The Panic in Needle Park (1971, U.S., 110 mins.) Dir: Jerry Schatzberg; Cast: Al Pacino, Kitty Winn, Alan Vint.

Feels like the real thing, though you won't recognize that little patch of park at 72nd and Broadway anymore. Kitty Winn is so believable, and her and Pacino's deterioration from skin-poppers to full-blown "we'll do absolutely anything to get it" mainliners is so realistic, you'll walk away certain they had real habits. Tough, noirish script is brought to you by Joan Didion and John Gregory Dunne.

Lenny (1974, U.S., 111 mins.) Dir: Bob Fosse; Cast: Dustin Hoffman, Valerie Perrine, Jan Miner.

Lenny would get on stage and abuse everything, and everyone, but no one more than himself. Hoffman is scathing in his portrayal of the man who dared to use his stand-up act as a test case for First Amendment rights, vigorously challenging the obscenity laws, only to watch his own life go down the toilet. A brilliant portrait of a man who could be nothing different than who he was, with Perrine doing a zingy turn as his wife, Honey.

Wild in the Streets (1968, U.S., 97 mins.) Dir: Barry Shear; Cast: Shelley Winters, Christopher Jones, Diane Varsi, Hal Holbrook, Bert Freed, Millie Perkins, Richard Pryor.

Remember "You can't trust anyone over 30"? Well this is Hollywood's completely useless—LSD in the drinking water, "old folks" in internment camps, the vote at 14—exploitation of sixties youth culture. Stick with the *Woodstock* version.

A Hatful of Rain (1957, U.S., 109 mins.) Dir: Fred Zinnemann; Cast: Eva Marie Saint, Anthony Franciosa, Don Murray, Lloyd Nolan.

A junkie and those who love him. Zinnemann does an excellent job with this adaptation of Michael Gazzo's Broadway play, commanding striking performances from all the leads.

Go Tell the Spartans (1978, U.S., 114 mins.) Dir: Ted Post; Cast: Burt Lancaster, Craig Wasson, Marc Singer.

The Vietnam movie to see. By now you know our troops were continually exposed to drug opportunities in the Asian jungle. You've seen it in *Apocalypse Now,* in *Platoon,* in *Full Metal Jacket,* and in *Good Morning, Vietnam.* This one takes place early in the war, in 1964, when we just had "advisers" there—and even then officer Burt Lancaster was having his doubts.

Bird (1988, U.S., 160 mins.) Dir: Clint Eastwood; Cast: Forest Whitaker, Diane Venora, Michael Zelniker, Samuel E. Wright, Keith David.

It's heroin and it's reefer, and it goes on a bit too long, but it's Charlie Parker: alto sax jazzman extraordinaire. The music is an interesting assemblage of Bird's original sax tracks re-mixed with newly recorded backups. And it works.

Blue Velvet (1986, U.S., 120 mins.) Dir: David Lynch; Cast: Kyle MacLachlan, Isabella Rossellini, Laura Dern, Dennis Hopper, Dean Stockwell.

Nitrous and excess in small-town America, brought to you with Lynch's signature style, saturating the most mundane people and events with a Kodachrome edge—often of horror. Innocents MacLachlan and Dern look into the singer Rossellini's troubling life and encounter wacko Stockwell and full-blown psycho Hopper along the way. Makes for a terrific movie. Rossellini gets the modeling-world medal of bravery for allowing herself to be photographed so realistically.

Heroes for Sale (1933, U.S., 73 mins., b/w) Dir: William Wellman; Cast: Richard Barthelmess, Loretta Young, Aline MacMahon, Gordon Bennett, Robert Barrat, Grant Mitchell, Charlie Grapewin, Margaret Seddon, Douglas Dunbrille, Ward Bond.

This is a remarkable film covering the fate of WWI survivors and the adjustments they faced on their return to an industrializing America. The first third deals with the horror of morphine addiction. The rest is a moving, well-drawn parable about the true meaning of heroism, wrapped around a growing Depression.

OLDEST PROFESSION

When you think about it, it's not surprising that street life is a pretty acceptable theme in male-run Hollywood (and elsewhere in filmland). You even have happy hookers (and gigolos) tucked among the grittier portrayals.

Midnight Cowboy (1969, U.S., 113 mins.) Dir: John Schlesinger; Cast: Dustin Hoffman, Jon Voight, Sylvia Miles.

Voight is a down-in-the-teeth stud who watches his hopes drift away in this bus-terminal view of N.Y.C. He finds a glimmer of humanity in his relationship with Hoffman's wholly lowlife Ratso Rizzo, whose humanity also gets its moment. Not erotic, but terrifically poignant and well done.

Saint Jack (1979, U.S., 112 mins.) Dir: Peter Bogdanovich; Cast: Ben Gazzara, Denholm Elliott, James Villiers, Joss Ackland, George Lazenby, Lisa Lu, Peter Bogdanovich.

Another view of southeast Asia you might have missed, Singapore this time. Gazzara is well cast in this small film as a pimp with a heart. Set during the Vietnam War years.

Working Girls (1987, U.S., 90 mins.) Dir: Lizzie Borden.

A day in the life—of a N.Y.C. brothel, that is. Super documentary uses perspective and humor to portray this business as a reasonable economic alternative to more conventional professions.

Mona Lisa (1986, Great Britain, 104 mins.) Dir: Neil Jordan; Cast: Bob Hoskins, Cathy Tyson, Michael Caine, Robbie Coltrane, Clarke Peters.

Hoskins and Tyson are exceptional in this superbly realized Jordan (who co-wrote with David Leland) drama of intrigue about a naïve minor criminal with a heart (and conscience) hired to chauffeur a high-class call girl. Caine plays pure slime to the hilt. A must-see, whether or not you liked Jordan's *The Crying Game*.

Pretty Woman (1990, U.S., 117 mins.) Dir: Garry Marshall; Cast: Richard Gere, Julia Roberts, Ralph Bellamy, Jason Alexander, Laura San Giacomo, Hector Elizondo, Alex Hyde-White, Larry Miller.

So what if it's a stretch. Julia and Richard have oodles of chemistry, and this slight but charming streetwalker-turned-Cinderella tale should translate very well to the little screen.

The Roman Spring of Mrs. Stone (1961, Great Britain, 104 mins.) Dir: José Quintero; Cast: Vivien Leigh, Warren Beatty, Jill St. John, Lotte Lenya, Coral Browne.

You'll be surprised to hear young Beatty holding forth in an Italian accent as he plays a gigolo to the wealthy American matrons of Rome. This is a weird and dark—but not great—Tennessee Williams story, and things get nasty as we watch the ever-lovely Leigh fall for him, only to have him turn on her. Lotte Lenya is just swell as the pimpette.

Pretty Baby (1978, U.S., 109 mins.) Dir: Louis Malle; Cast: Keith Carradine, Brooke Shields, Susan Sarandon, Antonio Fargas.

Brooke's preteen WWI-era New Orleans prostitute is a compelling creation as directed by Malle (in his first American film), giving us a way to imagine what it might be like to grow up in an atmosphere where a brothel is a "normal" point of reference. Carradine, however, sort of fades as the impassioned photographer who pursues young Violet. Evocatively photographed by Sven Nykvist.

Taxi Driver (1976, U.S., 112 mins.) Dir: Martin Scorsese; Cast: Robert De Niro, Cybill Shepherd, Jodie Foster, Peter Boyle, Albert Brooks, Harvey Keitel, Martin Scorsese, Leonard Harris.

Jodie Foster is also a baby hooker named after a flower (Iris), but her bloom is of an unforgettably tougher—yet clearly vulnerable—N.Y.C. street variety. De Niro's utterly harrowing psycho Vietnam vet entangles her in his life, and ultimately both she and her pimp become victims of his gory rage against a life gone wrong. Difficult, compelling—you'll love it or hate it.

McCabe and Mrs. Miller (1971, U.S., 121 mins.) Dir: Robert Altman; Cast: Warren Beatty, Julie Christie, Shelley Duvall, Keith Carradine, René Auberjonois, William Devane, Michael Murphy.

Leonard Cohen's music is the perfect haunting refrain in this baldly human story of the frontier, when a woman with a head for business had her greatest opportunity by running the local bordello.

American Gigolo (1980, U.S., 117 mins.) Dir: Paul Schrader; Cast: Richard Gere, Lauren Hutton, Hector Elizondo.

Lots of Gere here, with and without clothes, but we wish the movie stuck with the story of the male side of prostitution. Instead, there's an unsatisfactory murder-framing plot tied up with political intrigue. Some good driving music (Giorgio Moroder), pretty L.A. beach scenes, sleek settings, and an OK Hutton keep this glued together.

Sweet Charity (1969, U.S., 148 mins.) Dir: Bob Fosse; Cast: Shirley MacLaine, Ricardo Montalban, Chita Rivera, Paula Kelly, John McMartin, Stubby Kaye, Sammy Davis, Jr.

Shirley and Fosse—a swell combo. Shirley is just perfect as the hoofer-hooker with that proverbial heart of gold—she just can't get herself to reveal her career to her innocent suitor. While we've seen her do this character before, in the dated *Irma la Douce,* this movie is a skedillion times better. Great tunes, great dancing, and it will break your heart. You should also check out *Nights of Cabiria,* the Fellini movie *Sweet Charity* is based on. Giulietta Masina will break your heart. Did we already say that? Well, she will, too.

Streetwise (1985, U.S., 92 mins.) Dir: Martin Bell.

Forget *My Own Private Idaho.* This documentary of teenage street life and prostitution in the Northwest strips that life to its grim bare reality. No fluff here, just important viewing.

WONDERFUL WORLD OF FASHION

DOES MACY'S TELL GIMBELS?

Some people were born to a higher calling. Some might say shopping *is* the higher calling. However you feel about it, these scenes from malls, department stores, and little shops around the corner often have that feel of the frenzy and seduction we find in the real-life version. So switch off QVC and try one of these.

The Big Store (1941, U.S., 80 mins., b/w) Dir: Charles Riesner; Cast: Groucho, Chico, and Harpo Marx, Tony Martin, Virginia Grey, Margaret Dumont, Douglass Dumbrille.

This lesser-known Marx Brothers comedy has its moments when they're called in to investigate something fishy at Dumbrille's department store. Yep, that's Tony Martin, the singer.

Employees Entrance (1933, U.S., 75 mins., b/w) Dir: Roy Del Ruth; Cast: Warren William, Loretta Young, Wallace Ford, Alice White, Allen Jenkins.

Now this is a real find, pre-code style. William is perfect as the driven manager of an old-style grand department store who wreaks havoc on the lives of loyal employees. Racy, real, true characters, and everything you'd like to know about style and the shopping biz, circa the 1930s.

The Store (1983, U.S., 120 mins.) Dir: Frederick Wiseman.

And while we're in department stores, you'll want to check out this PBS doc about the famed Neiman-Marcus chain. Started as the most exclusive store in oil-driven Dallas—it's their Christmas catalog that offers those lux exotic gifts like your own personal, fully outfitted, life-size elephant—they've since branched out. How they do what they do, and where they're headed—it's a pretty interesting story.

The Devil and Miss Jones (1941, U.S., 92 mins., b/w) Dir: Sam Wood; Cast: Jean Arthur, Robert Cummings, Charles Coburn, S. Z. Sakall, William Demarest.

No, NOT *The Devil in* . . . But you'd think this store's union organizers were the devil incarnate, in this bewitching story about the humanizing of the store's fabulously wealthy owner. Who could resist Arthur? Certainly not the curmudgeonly—yet lovable—grump Coburn as the owner, nor love-interest Cummings as the rabid union man.

The Shop Around the Corner (1940, U.S., 97 mins., b/w) Dir: Ernst Lubitsch; Cast: Margaret Sullavan, James Stewart, Frank Morgan, Joseph Schildkraut.

As light and appealing as a properly made strudel. This is a quaint and delightful story that, while Stewart seems a bit miscast, tells us about an almost star-crossed love, all the while charming us with the old-world manners and style befitting the Hungarian specialty shop where the protagonists work. The musical remake, *In the Good Old Summertime,* doesn't fare as well, but it does have Judy Judy Judy.

It (1927, U.S., 72 mins., silent, b/w) Dir: Clarence Badger; Cast: Clara Bow, Antonio Moreno, William Austin, Jacqueline Gadsdon (Jane Daly).

The original "It" girl gets discovered— where else?—working behind the hosiery counter of a department store. She's a bit of a gold digger, but she's got It and, apparently, the boss's heart. Check out Gary Cooper in a very little bit as a reporter.

Christmas in July (1940, U.S. 67 mins., b/w) Dir: Preston Sturges; Cast: Dick Powell, Ellen Drew, Raymond Walburn, Ernest Truex, Franklin Pangborn.

Bright young depression-era lovers fantasize about winning the lottery—and the shopping spree that would go with it. A couple of twists and turns later, voilà! We have a winner. While not Sturges's strongest, the warmth, compassion, and humor that he does so well are all here.

Bluebeard's Eighth Wife (1938, U.S., 85 mins., b/w) Dir: Ernst Lubitsch; Cast:

David Niven, Gary Cooper, Claudette Colbert.

We hate this movie but it has one of the all-time best shopping scenes. Watch it for Colbert and Cooper discovering how to share a pair of pajamas. That's all for this otherwise misogynist mess.

Scenes From a Mall (1991, U.S., 87 mins.) Dir: Paul Mazursky; Cast: Bette Midler, Woody Allen, Bill Irwin, Daren Firestone, Rebecca Nickels, Paul Mazursky.

The mall as metaphor. Of course, no teen film would be complete without its mall scene. Just look at the not bad *Fast Times at Ridgemont High.* And, for adults as well, you have the seminal "the mall is where they wanted to be before they died" *Dawn of the Dead.* You even have the driven-to-the-edge mall ramble in the truly powerful *Fearless.* And, while in the end *Scenes* doesn't work all that well, what better location to watch a marriage fall apart? Bette and Woody try their best, but the script isn't much help to them.

Moscow on the Hudson (1984, U.S., 115 mins.) Dir: Paul Mazursky; Cast: Robin Williams, Maria Conchita Alonso, Cleavant Derricks.

No shopping list would be complete without a trip to Bloomingdales. Where else would be a better place for a Moscow circus musician to defect? All those mirrors, all those perfume spritzers, all those endless counters to crawl around in. But this is really a very poignant movie, with Williams keeping his over-the-top under control, offering a nice slice of the immigrant experience from Brighton to Bloomies. And while we're there, we'll remind you to see *Starting Over* for the neurotic's delight, the Valium-in-the-bedding-department scene.

Pretty Woman (1990, U.S., 117 mins.) Dir: Garry Marshall; Cast: Richard Gere,

Julia Roberts, Ralph Bellamy, Jason Alexander, Laura San Giacomo, Hector Elizondo, Alex Hyde-White, Larry Miller.

Cinderella shops. Sort of Rodeo Drive supermarket bingo. Well who wouldn't, given the bucks, the looks, the inspiration, the stamina. And a charming modern-day fairy tale besides. Leave your p.c. defenses at the door.

DOWN THE RUNWAY

What makes fashion? It could be something as simple as Gable leaving off his undershirt in *It Happened One Night* . . . or Diane Keaton in *Annie Hall* . . . or even those '70s Travolta moments in *Saturday Night Fever* and *Urban Cowboy*. Here are a few that focus on the industry behind the seeming glamour of it all.

Darling (1965, Great Britain, 122 mins., b/w) Dir: John Schlesinger; Cast: Julie Christie, Dirk Bogarde, Laurence Harvey, Roland Curram, José Luis de Villalonga, Alex Scott, Basil Henson.

London: 1965. Christie is luminous as a bored supermodel ricocheting through the beds of London searching for something her vapid career can't provide. Hey, if it were the '90s she'd be getting tattoos . . . or navel rings. Instead, she finds an Italian count and lives unhappily ever after. Schlesinger delivers a very thoughtful, if a bit long, reflection on the European *mise en scène*.

Blow-Up (1966, Great Britain-Italy, 111 mins.) Dir: Michelangelo Antonioni; Cast: David Hemmings, Vanessa Redgrave, Sarah Miles, Verushka.

London: 1966. Antonioni captures the scene, the mystique, the high-fashion whirl. Really, the blur. Photographer's obsession with what may or may not be the scene behind the scene. Vague?

Yes. Fascinating? Yes. See it on a large screen.

A Life of Her Own (1950, U.S., 108 mins., b/w) Dir: George Cukor; Cast: Lana Turner, Ray Milland, Tom Ewell, Louis Calhern, Ann Dvorak, Margaret Phillips, Jean Hagen, Barry Sullivan, Phyllis Kirk.

Sudsy romance gains ballast from Dvorak's solid portrayal of an aging N.Y.C. model—and Lana's not bad either as an upstart fresh off the farm.

The Women (1939, U.S., 132 mins., c & b/w) Dir: George Cukor; Cast: Joan Crawford, Norma Shearer, Rosalind Russell, Mary Boland, Joan Fontaine, Paulette Goddard, Lucile Watson, Marjorie Main, Virginia Weidler, Phyllis Povah, Ruth Hussey, Mary Beth Hughes, Virginia Grey, Hedda Hopper, Butterfly McQueen.

We recommend this one for the hats. Just when you think you've seen the best, why, there's yet another confection beckoning to you. Otherwise, this is a soppy, occasionally witty, ladies who lunch, and shop, and watch fashion shows, and gossip, gossip, gossip time capsule that travels between N.Y. and a divorce farm in Reno, with just a little extra bit of class thanks to the glamorous cast.

Paris Is Burning (1990, U.S., 78 mins.) Dir: Jennie Livingston.

AIDS is doing its part to keep Andy Warhol's prediction to its limit of 15 minutes of fame. Good thing Livingston captured the voguing scene when she did. We've since lost many of its stars, vividly and respectfully shown in this documentary tracing the start of the drag "houses" and the fierce allegiance and identity associated with them. Sharp, clear-eyed, and moving.

Mahogany (1975, U.S., 109 mins.) Dir: Berry Gordy; Cast: Diana Ross, Billy Dee Williams, Anthony Perkins, Jean-

Pierre Aumont, Beah Richards, Nina Foch.

Wardrobe! Not much else happens in this cop-out tale of a model (Ross) turned wildly successful fashion designer who finds she misses the love and warmth of her early days. Perkins is always worth a look, though.

Star 80 (1983, U.S., 102 mins.) Dir: Bob Fosse; Cast: Mariel Hemingway, Eric Roberts, Cliff Robertson, Carroll Baker, Roger Rees, David Clennon, Josh Mostel, Keenen Ivory Wayans.

The Dorothy Stratten story. Brutal, unpleasant, and just plain sad. Fosse's last could have been better, but then maybe he's just the right cynic to have made this true-life version of the *Playboy* centerfold's murder by her pathetically jealous husband.

Funny Face (1957, U.S., 103 mins.) Dir: Stanley Donen; Cast: Fred Astaire, Audrey Hepburn, Kay Thompson, Suzy Parker, Michel Auclair.

Greenwich Village shop girl is discovered and becomes the toast of Paris. A lovely bauble of fashions, Fred (as a photographer modeled on Richard Avedon), Gershwin, and fun. Hepburn even gets to play a beatnik for a bit. This is all very stagy (they used Paris as a stand-in for N.Y.), but it's got its charm, and Thompson as a hot fashion-magazine soothsayer is just right. Think pink!

Designing Woman (1957, U.S., 117 mins.) Dir: Vincente Minnelli; Cast: Gregory Peck, Lauren Bacall, Dolores Gray, Sam Levene, Chuck Connors, Mickey Shaughnessy, Ed Platt, Jack Cole.

Another bauble from the same year, but not so fresh. We should be more excited about Bacall and her swell Helen Rose wardrobe, her swank N.Y. apartment, and her artsy theater pals. It is nicely shot (thanks to John Alton),

but we get bogged down in the non-chemical relationship with Peck and his sportswriter-world pals. The clothes here are the thing. This is the one where fighter Maxie Stoltz (Shaughnessy) sleeps with his eyes open.

The Thrill of It All (1963, U.S., 108 mins.) Dir: Norman Jewison; Cast: Doris Day, James Garner, Arlene Francis, ZaSu Pitts, Edward Andrews.

Housewife Day clevers herself into becoming a soap company spokesperson-model, and all hell breaks out on the home front. Well, not quite, but this jape at TV hucksterdom is a lot of fun. And Doris in the tub as the "Happy Soap" lady is a case of essential casting.

Cover Girl (1944, U.S., 107 mins.) Dir: Charles Vidor; Cast: Rita Hayworth, Gene Kelly, Phil Silvers, Eve Arden, Otto Kruger.

Not *The Red Shoes* of fashion-land, but respectable nevertheless. Hayworth's gorgeous model must choose between a Brooklyn boy and Mr. Manhattan—all to swell Jerome Kern/Ira Gershwin tunes and Kelly's distinctive choreography. And you get Arden at her crackling best in the bargain.

IF THE SHOE FITS

Shoes glorious shoes. Yeah, it was a tough call whether to put our shoe list in the vice section or here in fashion. Here are a few not for the obsessed only.

My Left Foot (1989, Ireland, 103 mins.) Dir: Jim Sheridan; Cast: Daniel Day-Lewis, Brenda Fricker, Ray McAnally, Hugh O'Conor, Fiona Shaw.

OK, this one is really about no shoes. Day-Lewis pulls off a remarkable performance as artist and author Christy

Brown; afflicted with cerebral palsy, he learns to write using the toes of his left foot to hold a pencil. Brilliant acting further illuminates this totally unsentimental, wildly creative, moving script ranging from the gritty to the celebrated sides of Ireland.

The Red Shoes (1948, Great Britain, 133 mins.) Dirs: Michael Powell, Emeric Pressburger; Cast: Moira Shearer, Anton Walbrook.

Now here's a pair of shoes that's possessed. Prima ballerina Vicky Page (Shearer) is maddened by conflict between her love for dance and her love for her husband. The buildup to the pivotal ballet scene is more than a bit dragged out, but it is quite beautiful and worth waiting for.

Shoeshine (1946, Italy, 93 mins., b/w) Dir: Vittorio De Sica; Cast: Rinaldo Smerdoni, Franco Interlenghi.

These shoes were made for heartbreak. Superb neo-realist look at postwar Italy through the distressing lives of two young boys struggling to survive—and realize their dream of owning a horse—with meager earnings from shining shoes for leftover American soldiers.

Morocco (1930, U.S., 92 mins., b/w) Dir: Josef von Sternberg; Cast: Marlene Dietrich, Gary Cooper, Adolphe Menjou, Francis McDonald, Eve Southern.

Well, Marlene + high heels are always worth a look. Both she, in her Hollywood first, and young Foreign Legionnaire Cooper are luscious. She must decide between staying with wealthy Menjou and her cabaret life in a twilight Morocco, or following the troops. The payoff is that last scene and the fade-off into the desert.

The Tall Blond Man With One Black Shoe (1972, France, 90 mins.) Dir: Yves Robert; Cast: Pierre Richard, Bernard Blier, Jean Rochefort, Mirielle Darc, Jean Carmet.

A spy spoof involving a musician tangled up in a case of mistaken identity. The title tells you most of what you need to know about this enjoyable romp that takes potshots at all sides of Cold War espionage.

The Wizard of Oz (1939, U.S., 102 mins., c & b/w) Dir: Victor Fleming; Cast: Judy Garland, Frank Morgan, Ray Bolger, Bert Lahr, Margaret Hamilton, Billie Burke, Jack Haley.

The most famous shoes of all, those ruby slippers. Heh, heh, heh, my pretty. Click them, just click them, you can do that, can't you? What can we say—without the Wiz, the world would be a far lesser place.

Cinderella (1950, U.S., 74 mins.) Dirs: Wilfred Jackson, Hamilton Luske, Clyde Geronimi; Cast: Voices of Ilene Woods, William Phipps, Eleanor Audley, Rhoda Williams, Lucille Bliss, Verna Felton.

This one runs a close second in famous-slipper fame, and the footwear in question is certainly the most fragile of the lot. So what if Cinderella shouldn't have been waiting around for the Prince to rescue her, the lovely animation should still warm a heart or two, and hopefully not instill one more drop of wasteful longing than necessary.

High Heels (1991, Spain, 115 mins.) Dir: Pedro Almodovar; Cast: Victoria Abril, Marisa Paredes, Miguel Bosé, Feodor Atkine, Bibi Andersson.

A freewheeling Almodovar wrapped around aging star's feelings for newscaster daughter's lover. Wild and stylish as always, uneven regardless, at best. You could also look into Claude Chabrol's 1972 movie with the same title about a doctor who marries an "ugly duckling."

Werner Herzog Eats His Shoe (1980, U.S., 20 mins.) Dir: Les Blank.

Twenty minutes of pure odd documentary delight. Filmmaker Herzog *(Fitz-carraldo)* told Errol Morris *(The Thin Blue Line)* he would eat his shoe if Morris ever got around to making his first feature, *Gates of Heaven* (a memorable ode to southern California's pet cemetery culture). Well he did, so he does—with Chez Panisse's illustrious founder Alice Waters along to help boil the boot and adjust the seasonings, heavy on the garlic, please. Cleverly intercut with clips of the famous (and desperate) boot-eating scene from Charlie Chaplin's *The Gold Rush,* Blank uses the dining event as an opportunity to present Herzog's intriguing theories on filmmaking and life.

■

NOTE: So many shoes, so little time. *They Died With Their Boots On, The Tree of Wooden Clogs, Sneakers* . . . and what about those establishing foot/shoe shots in *The Third Man* and *Strangers on a Train* . . . and those opening credits in *My Three Sons.*

SPORTS

COOPERSTOWN CLASSICS

Baseball may be the national pastime, but until recently it was considered major league box-office death in Hollywood. That's why there have been so few baseball films relative to the game's influence, and even fewer good ones. Here are the home runs.

Bang the Drum Slowly (1973, U.S., 98 mins.) Dir: John Hancock; Cast: Robert De Niro, Michael Moriarty, Vincent Gardenia, Heather MacRae, Phil Foster.

Mark Harris's story of an ambitious pitcher (Moriarty) and his roommate (De Niro), a catcher dying of cancer. Thankfully free of the worshipful attitude many baseball films have for the game. Danny Aiello's first movie. If you don't get a lump in your throat as De Niro bounces the ball back to the mound, you're a hard case.

Eight Men Out (1988, U.S., 120 mins.) Dir: John Sayles; Cast: John Cusack, Clifton James, Christopher Lloyd, John Mahoney, Charlie Sheen, David Strathairn, D. B. Sweeney.

Very realistic depiction of the Black Sox scandal of 1919. A rich and detailed re-creation of baseball's early days. The game action is superior because Sweeney and the others were cast in part for their playing abilities and they use them in the movie. Look for lifelong White Sox fan Studs Turkel in a cameo.

Field of Dreams (1989, U.S., 106 mins.) Dir: Phil Alden Robinson; Cast: Kevin Costner, James Earl Jones, Amy Madigan, Burt Lancaster, Ray Liotta, Timothy Busfield.

Based on W. P. Kinsella's *Shoeless Joe.* Ghostly voices impel Costner to build a baseball diamond in his cornfield. The most poetic baseball movie, heavy with the mythos of the game and all that fathers-playing-catch-with-their-sons baggage, but absolutely worth a lot of goose bumps for fans.

The Bingo Long Traveling All-Stars and Motor Kings (1976, U.S., 111 mins.) Dir: John Badham; Cast: Billy Dee Williams, James Earl Jones, Richard Pryor, Ted Ross.

Williams puts together a barnstorming team of black all-stars in the late 1930s. The only film that focuses on the Negro Leagues.

Bull Durham (1988, U.S., 108 mins.) Dir: Ron Shelton; Cast: Kevin Costner, Susan Sarandon, Tim Robbins, Trey Wilson, Robert Wuhl.

Romantic comedy featuring Costner as the veteran catcher of a North Carolina minor league team and Sarandon as the team groupie. A view of life in the minors and maybe the film that best captures the spirit of the game. Costner has been in three baseball movies; the third is *Chasing Dreams,* which we will spare you any further mention of.

Damn Yankees (1958, U.S., 110 mins.) Dirs: George Abbott, Stanley Donen; Cast: Gwen Verdon, Tab Hunter, Ray Walston, Jean Stapleton, Russ Brown, Rae Allen, Shannon Bolin.

Musical about a Washington Senators fan who sells his soul to the devil to become the star of the team. You know the songs—"You Gotta Have Heart," "Whatever Lola Wants." Good, clean (except for Gwen Verdon in those fishnets) fun from the more innocent days of baseball.

The Pride of the Yankees (1942, U.S., 127 mins., b/w) Dir: Sam Wood; Cast: Gary Cooper, Teresa Wright, Walter Brennan, Babe Ruth, Dan Duryea.

The Lou Gehrig story. Cooper is great as the Iron Horse in this, the best of all the baseball bio movies. Babe plays himself.

Fear Strikes Out (1957, U.S., 100 mins., b/w) Dir: Robert Mulligan; Cast: Anthony Perkins, Karl Malden, Norma Moore.

The other good bio. Tony Perkins warmed up for his more famous turn as a mentally disturbed person three years later with this portrayal of Jimmy Piersall, who battled mental illness throughout his playing career.

The Bad News Bears (1976, U.S., 105 mins.) Dir: Michael Ritchie; Cast: Walter Matthau, Tatum O'Neal, Vic Morrow, Joyce Van Patten, Brandon Cruz, Jackie Earle Haley.

Last, but not least. A shabby Matthau assembles a Little League team of loser kids. Somehow, this has improved with age, as long as you know what you're getting—vintage Kool-Aid. Maybe it's how truly shabby Matthau's character is; maybe it's the better-than-average bunch of kids that generally avoids sappiness. Plus, your kids might actually understand this, because they sure won't care about Costner playing catch with his dead father in the middle of Iowa. Warning—this is the only *Bad News Bears* movie you should remotely consider.

■

NOTE: *The Natural* is specifically excluded for, among other things, trying to fob off a fake Wrigley Field that bears no resemblance to the real thing.

SLAM DUNK

Even with all the domed stadiums, artificial turf, and new equipment, baseball and football players still play their games pretty much the same way they always have. But basketball has come a long way from Dr. Naismith and his peach baskets. Watch these five films in this order and you'll get a sense of how set shots turned into slam dunks.

The Bachelor and the Bobby Soxer (1947, U.S., 95 mins., b/w) Dir: Irving Reis; Cast: Cary Grant, Myrna Loy, Shirley Temple, Rudy Vallee.

Playboy Grant is forced by judge Myrna Loy to date her younger sister Shirley Temple, so Temple will lose her infatuation with him. One of their "dates" is to a high school basketball game from the days when the game was played by 10 white guys in shorts so small you'd be embarrassed to wear them to the beach. An amusing sequence that's even more amusing now for the touch of sports history.

The Absent-Minded Professor (1961, U.S., 104 mins., b/w) Dir: Robert

Stevenson; Cast: Fred MacMurray, Nancy Olson, Tommy Kirk, Ed Wynn, Keenan Wynn.

College prof Fred MacMurray invents flubber—flying rubber—and bad-guy Keenan Wynn tries to steal the formula. The climax comes when MacMurray outfits young Kirk's basketball team with flubber-bottomed shoes (sort of proto-Nikes), which let them get almost as high as Michael Jordan. At this point, white men absolutely could not jump.

Hoosiers (1986, U.S., 114 mins.) Dir: David Anspaugh; Cast: Gene Hackman, Barbara Hershey, Dennis Hopper, Sheb Wooley, Fern Parsons.

Gene Hackman, a man with a past, tries to coach an early sixties rural Indiana high school team to the state championship and save himself. Based on the true story of Milan High's championship season, one of the most famous Cinderella teams ever, from the state that brought you Bobby Knight and Larry Bird. Wonderful, true atmosphere, strong game action, and a great supporting role for Dennis Hopper.

Fast Break (1979, U.S., 107 mins.) Dir: Jack Smight; Cast: Gabe Kaplan, Harold Sylvester, Michael Warren, Bernard King.

Gabe Kaplan, a seventies guy if ever there was one, stars in this sleeper about 1970s basketball. Kaplan takes his last chance at making a living in the game by putting together and coaching a team for a small college in Nevada. The shorts are longer, the play is flashier, and style matters. Featuring Michael Warren, alumnus of UCLA and *Hill Street Blues,* and former NBA star Bernard King. Larry Fishburne has a bit part, too.

The Air Up There (1993, U.S., 108 mins.) Dir: Paul M. Glaser; Cast: Kevin Bacon, Sean McCann, Charles Gitonga Maina.

A young college coach with lots to learn goes to Africa to recruit a warrior-prince for his basketball team. All sorts of rites of passage/manhood stuff gets rolled in here, most of which would work better if it weren't so earnest. By the way, when will we see a film about a black man who teaches a bunch of loveable, but rather simple, white men how to play a game?

White Men Can't Jump (1992, U.S., 115 mins.) Dir: Ron Shelton; Cast: Wesley Snipes, Woody Harrelson, Rosie Perez.

L.A. basketball hustlers Snipes and Harrelson let their con games get out of hand. Shelton does a good job of capturing the grace, speed, and brilliance of the game as we know it now. Full of men wulfing and talking trash, but how they play the game becomes their real form of self-expression. One of the best sports movies because of how well it understands its subject's essence.

THE POPCORN BOWL

Football seems made for the screen. The action is faster than baseball, so you can plug an entire game into a movie without eyes glazing over. There are cheerleaders. And, most important, it's violent. People getting hauled off the field on stretchers or coming back from devastating injuries makes for good drama. The following might not be as classy as the baseball films, but the games that are played in them are certainly more fun to watch.

M*A*S*H (1970, U.S., 116 mins.) Dir: Robert Altman; Cast: Donald Sutherland, Elliott Gould, Robert Duvall, Sally Kellerman.

The story of a surgical unit during the Korean War. See it again for the football game at the end of the film—definitely one of the funniest sections.

Paper Lion (1968, U.S., 107 mins.) Dir: Alix March; Cast: Alan Alda, Alex Karras, Lauren Hutton, Sugar Ray Robinson.

Alan Alda is a journalist who becomes an honorary member of the Detroit Lions. Based on George Plimpton's book. Alda is very believable as Plimpton, which means he is not at all believable as a football player. Alex Karras was still an active player then—try to picture him in *Webster* as you watch.

North Dallas Forty (1979, U.S., 120 mins.) Dir: Ted Kotcheff; Cast: Nick Nolte, Mac Davis, Dayle Haddon, Bo Svenson, John Matuszak, Steve Forrest, Dabney Coleman.

Another look inside the real lives of football players, this one centers on their treatment by management. One of the top sports films—hard-hitting, realistic, and a good performance by Nolte. Look for the late John Matuszak.

Semi-Tough (1977, U.S., 108 mins.) Dir: Michael Ritchie; Cast: Burt Reynolds, Kris Kristofferson, Jill Clayburgh, Robert Preston, Lotte Lenya, Bert Convy, Roger Mosley, Carl Weathers.

A lighter take on football players, with Kristofferson, Reynolds, and Clayburgh as the three corners of a love triangle. Interesting casting (Lotte Lenya!).

The Longest Yard (1974, U.S., 123 mins.) Dir: Robert Aldrich; Cast: Burt Reynolds, Eddie Albert, Jim Hampton, Ed Lauter, Bernadette Peters.

The really good Burt Reynolds football movie. Burt is in the pen for fixing games and the warden has him arrange a cons vs. guards match. TBS has this on an endless loop, but it's worth a watch once a year. The game is great, even though the cheerleaders are men.

Everybody's All-American (1988, U.S., 127 mins.) Dir: Taylor Hackford; Cast:

Dennis Quaid, Jessica Lange, Timothy Hutton, John Goodman.

Quaid goes from college star to washed-up ex-jock. Football players like this one for how well it portrays one of their greatest fears—becoming a former football player.

All the Right Moves (1983, U.S., 113 mins.) Dir: Michael Chapman; Cast: Tom Cruise, Craig Nelson, Lea Thompson, Charles Cioffi.

Cruise is a high school football star in a Pennsylvania mining town. A good, gritty little film about growing up on and off the field.

Brian's Song (1971, U.S./MTV, 71 mins.) Dir: Buzz Kulik; Cast: James Caan, Billy Dee Williams, Jack Warden.

The story of the friendship between Chicago Bears stars Gale Sayers and Brian Piccolo and their battle against Piccolo's cancer. The original male tearjerker. Williams and Caan are perfect and there's lots of real footage of Sayers. A must even if you don't care about football.

Two-Minute Warning (1976, U.S., 112 mins.) Dir: Larry Peerce; Cast: Charlton Heston, John Cassavetes, Martin Balsam, Gena Rowlands.

A sniper at the Super Bowl. Based on a novel by Thomas Harris (*Silence of the Lambs*). Not a fabulous movie, but it has more action and excitement than most real Super Bowls.

Diner (1982, U.S., 110 mins.) Dir: Barry Levinson; Cast: Steve Guttenberg, Daniel Stern, Mickey Rourke, Kevin Bacon, Timothy Daly, Ellen Barkin.

A group of guys in 1950s Baltimore face up to adulthood. Guttenberg's fiancée must pass a football trivia test before he'll marry her.

The Fortune Cookie (1966, U.S., 125 mins., b/w) Dir: Billy Wilder; Cast: Jack

Lemmon, Walter Matthau, Ron Rich, Cliff Osmond, Lurene Tuttle.

A football player accidentally injures cameraman Lemmon, who tries to scam his insurance company at the urging of his sleazy lawyer, Matthau. A classic Billy Wilder film: cynical, dark, and funny. On the football side, no other movie captures the feel of the game at the time so well.

■

NOTE: Here are two more gridiron curiosities for you.

Number One (1969, U.S., 105 mins.) Dir: Tom Gries; Cast: Charlton Heston, Jessica Walter, Diana Muldaur, Al Hirt.
■
Charlton Heston plays an aging quarterback as if he were still marching through the Sinai and smashing false gods. Good for a laugh.

Knute Rockne—All American (1940, U.S., 98 mins., b/w) Dir: Lloyd Bacon; Cast: Pat O'Brien, Ronald Reagan, Gale Page, Donald Crisp.

Yes, the Gipper was indeed your president for eight years.

KO's

Say what you want about boxing, but no other sport works on the same level. Boxing doesn't represent conflict—it *is* conflict, the most primeval conflict possible. That makes for great drama and lots of great movies. The 10 films that follow are a selection of the best, but there's easily another 10 or 15 worth your time.

Raging Bull (1980, U.S., 128 mins., b/w) Dir: Martin Scorsese; Cast: Robert De Niro, Cathy Moriarty, Joe Pesci, Frank Vincent.

This biography of middleweight Jake LaMotta is Scorsese's best film and maybe De Niro's too. Filmed in black and white as all good boxing films should be, it hits and hits like LaMotta himself. Perfect supporting cast includes debuts by Pesci and Moriarty and the boxing action is as close to the real thing as a movie can get.

Fat City (1972, U.S., 100 mins.) Dir: John Huston; Cast: Stacy Keach, Jeff Bridges, Susan Tyrrell, Candy Clark.

John Huston's adaptation of Leonard Gardner's novel about a boxed-out pugilist who takes a young fighter under his wing. As bleak and understated as the book and certainly free of any romantic notions about boxing.

Kid Galahad (aka: *The Battling Bellhop,* 1937, U.S., 101 mins., b/w) Dir: Michael Curtiz; Cast: Edward G. Robinson, Bette Davis, Humphrey Bogart, Wayne Morris.

Robinson turns Morris into a champ, but loses his dame, Fluff, played by a young and surprisingly attractive Bette Davis. You can rent the film under this title, but on TV it's usually *The Battling Bellhop* because Elvis made a clunker called *Kid Galahad* that won the title, so to speak.

Gentleman Jim (1942, U.S., 104 mins., b/w) Dir: Raoul Walsh; Cast: Errol Flynn, Alexis Smith, Jack Carson, Alan Hale, Ward Bond, John Loder, William Frawley.

Sturdy period film starring Errol Flynn as Gentleman Jim Corbett. This lighthearted look at the early days of boxing comes as a very pleasant change after all the smoky, down-and-out dinge of most boxing films. Ward Bond's John L. Sullivan steals the show.

Body and Soul (1947, U.S., 104 mins.) Dir: Robert Rossen; Cast: John Garfield, Lilli Palmer, Anne Revere, Hazel Brooks, William Conrad, Joseph Penny.

The granddaddy of them all. John

Garfield does anything he has to in order to become champ. Nothing to say here except that it's up there with *Raging Bull* for best boxing movie ever.

The Set-Up (1949, U.S., 72 mins., b/w) Dir: Robert Wise; Cast: Robert Ryan, Audrey Totter, George Tobias.

A short, tough little film played out in real time about a washed-up boxer whose manager has fixed his fight without telling him. Wise doesn't play around. There's no sentiment, no easy ways out, just a stripped-down story about courage and integrity, Ryan's coal-dark eyes and boxing action that for once makes you feel the pain and fatigue of the sport. It'll make you ache.

Somebody Up There Likes Me (1956, U.S., 113 mins., b/w) Dir: Robert Wise; Cast: Paul Newman, Pier Angeli, Everett Sloane, Eileen Heckart, Sal Mineo, Robert Loggia, Steve McQueen.

Another boxing classic from Wise, this time a biography of Rocky Graziano, played by Newman. Wise's mastery of the game comes not only from his no-nonsense approach to its drama, but also from his appreciation of its visual strength. The gritty, back-alley look here and in *The Set-Up* was re-created by Scorsese in *Raging Bull*.

Broken Noses (1992, U.S., 77 mins., c & b/w) Dir: Bruce Weber.

For pure visuals, this could be the best. Bruce Weber, the man who brought you all those writhing bodies in Calvin Klein underwear, directed this documentary about a young fighter and the boxing club he runs for kids. Backed by songs from Chet Baker, Julie London, and others, Weber lingers—often too long—on the fighters in luscious black and white. Think of it as Joyce Carol Oates meets Calvin.

Champion (1949, U.S., 99 mins., b/w) Dir: Mark Robson; Cast: Kirk Douglas, Marilyn Maxwell, Arthur Kennedy, Ruth Roman.

Douglas stars in this tale of greed, ambition, and treachery in the fight game, based on a story by Ring Lardner.

Requiem for a Heavyweight (1962, U.S., 100 mins., b/w) Dir: Ralph Nelson; Cast: Anthony Quinn, Jackie Gleason, Mickey Rooney, Julie Harris, Muhammad Ali.

Classic movie about ex-fighter hitting bottom, adapted by Rod Serling from his *Playhouse 90* teleplay. The television version stars Jack Palance as the boxer. Given the quality of work Serling produced, it's about time somebody gave him credit as a great American writer. The public never had to come to Serling; he came to them and told their stories in ways they could appreciate, using the media of the age. Arch a brow in memory of one of the best.

THE CHECKERED FLAG

Car racing draws the largest number of fans to its events of any U.S. spectator sport; more proof—as if we needed it—that Americans love cars and driving. These 10 films about racers and racing should give you something to daydream about during your morning commute.

The Last American Hero (1973, U.S., 100 mins.) Dir: Lamont Johnson; Cast: Jeff Bridges, Valerie Perrine, Geraldine Fitzgerald, Art Lund, Gary Busey, Ed Lauter.

True story of Junior Jackson's rise from moonshine runner in the backwaters of North Carolina to stockcar champion. Based on articles by Tom Wolfe and buoyed by Bridges, Busey, and Perrine, this one's a lap ahead of the others on character development and story. Plus, there's a good demolition derby scene.

Le Mans (1971, U.S., 106 mins.) Dir: Lee H. Katzin; Cast: Steve McQueen.

Basically a documentary about Le Mans with some Steve McQueen edited in. It's the kind of bland, international film that popped up in the seventies, with five stars no one had ever heard of and one American who was the real draw. The good news is that you hardly see any acting because three-quarters of the film is great racing footage.

A Man and a Woman (1966, France, 102 mins., b/w) Dir: Claude Lelouch; Cast: Anouk Aimee, Jean-Louis Trintignant.

Classic French romance centered around the 24 hours of Le Mans has some nifty driving scenes and the added benefits of Anouk Aimee and a love story that will engage the nonracers among you. Two problems—French drivers who make you wish A. J. Foyt was around and a theme song that will tattoo itself onto your brain.

Corky (aka: *Lookin' Good,* 1971, U.S., 88 mins., b/w) Dir: Leonard Horn; Cast: Charlotte Rampling, Robert Blake, Patrick O'Neal.
■
Racing version of popular boxing theme—young man obsessed with sport alienates everyone around him to reach the top. Still, strong racing action.

The Crowd Roars (1932, U.S., 85 mins., b/w) Dir: Howard Hawks; Cast: James Cagney, Joan Blondell, Frank McHugh, Eric Linden, Ann Dvorak, Guy Kibbee.
■
Cagney's a race-car driver, see? You don't need more than that, do you? Standard, solid plot and cast and a fun look at racing in the thirties. Be sure you get the film made in 1932; the 1938 *The Crowd Roars* is a boxing flick.

Genevieve (1953, Great Britain, 86 mins.) Dir: Henry Cornelius; Cast: John Gregson, Kenneth More, Dinah Sheridan, Kay Kendall.

Two married couples take their vintage cars on an annual rally from London to Brighton. A charming, low-key British comedy, probably not for the Richard Petty fans in the house. By the way, "Genevieve" is a 1904 roadster belonging to one of the couples.

Smash Palace (1981, New Zealand, 100 mins.) Dir: Roger Donaldson; Cast: Bruno Lawrence, Anna Jemison, Greer Robson.

A wrenching Australian drama about a driver pushed to the edge by the dissolution of his marriage. More about a racer than about racing, the passion of Lawrence's character makes the melodramatic ending credible. Definitely worth seeing.

Winning (1969, U.S., 123 mins.) Dir: James Goldstone; Cast: Paul Newman, Joanne Woodward, Robert Wagner, Richard Thomas.

Newman plays an Indy car driver obsessed with taking the 500. Better than most, if only because Newman really races and does his own driving here.

Grand Prix (1966, U.S., 179 mins.) Dir: John Frankenheimer; Cast: James Garner, Eva Marie Saint, Yves Montand, Toshiro Mifune, Brian Bedford.

Lots and lots of Formula One racing, as we follow four drivers around the circuit. One thing you have to say about racing movies is that you get a lot of guy's guys in them—McQueen, Newman, Cagney, and here, Garner and Montand, a French guy's guy.

The Road Warrior (1982, Australia, 94 mins.) Dir: George Miller; Cast: Mel Gibson, Emile Minty, Virginia Hay, Bruce Spence.

So there's no race. So what? Anybody

who's ever gone over 55 mph enjoys the bizarre cars and driving in this futuristic story of an ex-cop trying to protect a town from fuel-hungry villains. Minute for minute, one of the best action movies ever made.

THE WIDE WORLD OF SPORTS

Not all sports involve Americans batting, bouncing, or passing balls. Hollywood has managed to capture enough different sports played by enough different kinds of people to create a moviegoer's Olympics.

This Sporting Life (1963, Great Britain, 134 mins., b/w) Dir: Lindsay Anderson; Cast: Richard Harris, Rachel Roberts, Alan Badel.

Rough-edged Welsh coal-miner Harris becomes a professional rugby player. Compelling rugby action adds to the interest of this fine example of the English "angry young man" films of the sixties.

Breaking Away (1979, U.S., 99 mins.) Dir: Peter Yates; Cast: Dennis Christopher, Dennis Quaid, Barbara Barrie, Paul Dooley, Daniel Stern, Jackie Earl Haley.

A bike race setting Gowns of Indiana University against Towns of Bloomington climaxes this sweet and intelligent film. It's *Rocky* on bicycles.

Slap Shot (1977, U.S., 122 mins.) Dir: George Roy Hill; Cast: Paul Newman, Strother Martin, Jennifer Warren, Michael Ontkean, Lindsay Crouse, Melinda Dillon.

You don't have to be a fan to enjoy this story of a crummy hockey team that tries to save the franchise by playing dirty. Paul Newman is, as always, pretty darn cool, and while Canadian Michael Ontkean seems to be there more for his skating ability than for anything else, the supporting performances are memorable.

Chariots of Fire (1981, Great Britain, 123 mins.) Dir: Hugh Hudson; Cast: Ben Cross, Ian Charleson, Nigel Havers, Nick Farrell, Alice Krige, Ian Holm, John Gielgud, Lindsay Anderson, Patrick Magee.

Classy British film about two runners in the 1924 Olympics. Somewhat dry for some tastes and the music, which you've been listening to during every televised sporting event for more than a decade, may drive you insane. Still, one of the few sports films for the *Masterpiece Theatre* crowd.

Kansas City Bomber (1972, U.S., 99 mins.) Dir: Jerrold Freedman; Cast: Raquel Welch, Helena Kallianiotes, Kevin McCarthy.
■
From the sublime to Raquel Welch. Here Raquel plays the toughest rollerderby mama on the banked-track circuit. Sadly, roller derby has faded away, so this now ranks as a historical document as well as a good opportunity to see Raquel in any number of catfights.

Monsieur Hulot's Holiday (1953, France, 91 mins., b/w) Dir: Jacques Tati; Cast: Jacques Tati, Michele Rolla, Valentine Camax, Nathalie Pascaud.

Tati, the ultimate Frenchman, goes on a vacation full of physical humor and sight gags. And before you mention Jerry Lewis, rest assured that this movie is actually funny. The best scene takes place on the tennis court, as M. Hulot, with a serve strangely resembling Boris Becker's, finds a talent at the game he didn't know he had.

The Odd Couple (1968, U.S., 105 mins.) Dir: Gene Saks; Cast: Jack Lemmon, Walter Matthau, Herb Edelman, Carole Shelley.

Newly divorced Felix moves in with

sports reporter Oscar. Like the movie *M*A*S*H,* this is the distillate form of the story, the very essence from which a few drops were taken and added to gallons of water to create the TV show.

Wee Geordie (1955, Great Britain, 93 mins., b/w) Dir: Frank Launder; Cast: Bill Travers, Alastair Sim.

■
A sweet Scottish comedy about a lumbering Highlander who goes to the Olympics to throw hammer for the United Kingdom. The romance is nothing new, but you probably don't know much about hammer throwing and the whole thing is completely endearing.

Olympia (*Olympische Spiele,* 1936, Germany, 225 mins., b/w) Dir: Leni Riefenstahl.

Leni Riefenstahl's majestic documentary of the 1936 Olympics. See if you can get the version with all the Hitler footage restored so you can keep all of this in perspective. Otherwise you might start thinking she was just a brilliant director and not a brilliant Nazi director. To add to the controversy you might also want to see the new doc that covers her story to the present, *The Wonderful, Horrible Life of Leni Riefenstahl.*

Downhill Racer (1969, U.S., 101 mins.) Dir: Michael Ritchie; Cast: Robert Redford, Gene Hackman, Camilla Sparv.

Ski scenes bring the charge to this sometimes slow story of U.S. skier Redford schussing his way to stardom. For fans of skiing and Redford only, and in that order.

Rollerball (1975, U.S., 123 mins.) Dir: Norman Jewison; Cast: James Caan, Ralph Richardson, John Houseman.

Sci-fi tale about globe-controlling corporation that pacifies the world with an ultraviolent sport. Caan plays the superstar who tries to buck the system. Who'd have thought that this film, out

of all sci-fi films, would come closest to predicting life at the end of the century? By the way, some folks actually tried to get a rollerball league off the ground. Too bad it didn't catch on; instead of Air Jordan, we could have had Roll Jordan.

██████████████████████

ANIMALS

██████████████████████

CELLULOID KITTIES

The best thing about movie cats is that precious few of them belong to sensitive tykes with no friends. These cats have sex, work for the FBI, come from outer space, even rise from the dead, and the last thing they'd ever do is wander cross-country to find a beloved owner. Apparently those inert lumps of fur can be interesting when they want to be.

Breakfast at Tiffany's (1961, U.S., 115 mins.) Dir: Blake Edwards; Cast: Audrey Hepburn, George Peppard, Patricia Neal, Buddy Ebsen, Mickey Rooney.

Not a starring role for "Cat," but certainly a vital one as Holly Golightly chucks her pet out into the street en route to a plane that will take her to her Brazilian paramour. George Peppard follows soon after. Will Holly make it to the airport in time? Or will she come back for Cat and true love Peppard, not necessarily in that order? If you want the realistic, unhappy ending, read the book.

Cat People (1942, U.S., 73 mins., b/w) Dir: Jacques Tourneur; Cast: Simone Simon, Kent Smith, Tom Conway, Jack Holt, Jane Randolph.

Classic Val Lewton thriller about a

woman who fears that she carries a family curse that turns her into a panther. Is it true? Does she become a wild cat, or is she just wacko? If you're expecting lots of gore, move on. The chills are all in suggestion and shadow.

The Three Lives of Thomasina (1963, U.S.-Great Britain, 97 mins.) Dir: Don Chaffey; Cast: Patrick McGoohan, Susan Hampshire, Karen Dotrice.

Better than average Disney flick with a strange hook. When a little Scottish girl's cat is diagnosed with tetanus, her nasty veterinarian father puts the kitty to sleep. Enter a mystical woman out of the woods, who then brings the cat back to life and returns it to the little girl. A charming fairy tale.

Pet Sematary (1989, U.S., 102 mins.) Dir: Mary Lambert; Cast: Dale Midkiff, Fred Gwynne, Denise Crosby, Brad Greenquist.

Let's say Stephen King retold the *Thomasina* story. The kitty would not look too good and it would not be in a particularly friendly mood having just been plucked out of wherever it is that dead cats go. And then, of course, he'd have to resurrect something else like, oh, a child. Based on the book King said he was too scared to write. What a chicken.

Fritz the Cat (1972, U.S., 77 mins.) Dir: Ralph Bakshi.

The movie that Ralph Bakshi's been dining out on for two decades. An animated celebration of the sixties, loosely based on the comics of R. Crumb, featuring a cat that gets around more than Warren Beatty. Given its X rating and use of certain synonyms for "kitty," you're advised not to rent *Felix the Cat* and *Fritz the Cat* on the same night if there are children in the house.

That Darn Cat! (1965, U.S., 116 mins.) Dir: Robert Stevenson; Cast: Dean Jones, Hayley Mills, Dorothy Provine, Elsa Lanchester, Roddy McDowall, William Demarest.

It wasn't enough for Hoover to wear dresses and shop at Filene's Basement for women's shoes in large sizes. Now we find out he complained that this film—about a cat helping an FBI agent find a kidnapped woman—showed the Bureau in a poor light because the cat rummaged through garbage cans. And we always thought the problem was Dean Jones.

The Late Show (1977, U.S., 94 mins.) Dir: Robert Benton; Cast: Art Carney, Lily Tomlin, Howard Duff, Bill Macy.

Again, not a lot of actual cat scenes, but the fact that Lily Tomlin's cat is missing is what brings her to see aging private eye Art Carney and get tangled up in his search for the people who killed his partner. A wonderful movie, highlighted by the energy between Tomlin and Carney.

The Cat From Outer Space (1978, U.S., 103 mins.) Dir: Norman Tokar; Cast: Ken Berry, Sandy Duncan, Harry Morgan, Roddy McDowall.

As far as we know, NASA did not get a chance to vet this Disney film about an alien feline who needs help fixing his spaceship after it crashes. Good for the kids, unless you just can't get enough of that Sandy Duncan.

Gay Purr-ee (1962, U.S., 86 mins.) Dir: Abe Levitow; Cast: Voices of Judy Garland, Robert Goulet.

Judy Garland and Robert Goulet lend their voices to this animated flick about cats in Paris. Enough to keep you and the kids interested. Disney's *The Aristocats* covers much of the same turf and is fine too.

Le Chat (1975, France, 88 mins.) Dir: Pierre Granier-Deferre; Cast: Jean Gabin, Simone Signoret.

Gabin and Signoret play a pair of elderly Parisians whose marriage has utterly deteriorated and Gabin's cat becomes the focal point of the conflict. A depressing film, but these two great actors near the end of their careers both give tremendous performances.

MOVIE MUTTS

The major difference between cat movies and dog movies is that dog movies almost always make you cry. Maybe it's the loyalty thing; maybe Hollywood figures that cats have so many lives that losing one isn't particularly dramatic. One way or the other, the canine mortality rate in film warrants looking into.

The Adventures of Milo and Otis (1986, Japan, 76 mins.) Dirs: Masanori Hata, Kon Ichikawa; Cast: Voice of Dudley Moore.

Dudley Moore narrates these little stories of a pug puppy and his kitten friend. It's sooooo cute in a Japanese, "Hello Kitty" way that it works. Besides, there aren't any other movies that we know of that star pug dogs.

Baxter (1991, France, 82 mins.) Dir: Jerome Boivin; Cast: Lise Delamore, Jean Mencure, Jacques Spiesser.

Here's the answer to every cute animal movie ever made. Baxter, a pit bull, pairs up with a nasty, Nazi-worshipping French kid, resulting in awful consequences. Beware the packaging, which tries to make it seem like a black comedy. This film will upset any child within a mile and it'll disturb most adults too.

Lassie Come Home (1943, U.S., 88 mins.) Dir: Fred M. Wilcox; Cast: Lassie, Roddy McDowall, Donald Crisp, Elizabeth Taylor, Nigel Bruce.

The film that launched a thousand collies, based on Eric Knight's novel about a dog traveling across England to find her young master. A classic among dog movies, sure to draw a few sniffles out of you. FYI: the Lassie of this movie was actually a male named Pal.

Old Yeller (1957, U.S., 83 mins.) Dir: Robert Stevenson; Cast: Dorothy McGuire, Fess Parker, Tommy Kirk, Kevin Corcoran, Chuck Connors.

No one can get through this story of a Texas boy and his dog without grabbing a hankie. Disney heartstring tugging at its best. Tell the kids you have something in your eye.

Greyfriars Bobby (1961, U.S.-Great Britain, 91 mins.) Dir: Don Chaffey; Cast: Donald Crisp, Laurence Naismith.

Another solid Disney dog weeper, this time the true story of a Skye terrier who would not abandon his master, even in death. Bobby kept watch over his owner's grave in Edinburgh's Greyfriars Cemetery and in time became a national hero. MGM bought the rights to a novel based on this story in the forties and made it as *Challenge to Lassie*, with Pal/Lassie as the star. Go with the real thing.

We Think the World of You (1988, Great Britain, 94 mins.) Dir: Colin Gregg; Cast: Alan Bates, Gary Oldman, Liz Smith.

A dog movie for grown-ups. When his lover Oldman goes to prison, Bates becomes a virtual member of his family and takes a special interest in Oldman's German shepherd. Based on J. R. Ackerley's novel, it stays witty and charming up until the last half hour or so when it loses control.

Antarctica (1983, Japan, 112 mins.) Dir: Koreyoshi Kurahara; Cast: Ken Takakura, Masako Natsume.

Japanese film about a group of sled dogs abandoned during an Antarctic expedition. Unusually close focus on the dogs amid the frozen wasteland lets them become characters for their own qualities as dogs and not as man's best friend. It's one of the weepers, though.

White Fang (1991, U.S., 107 mins.) Dir: Randal Kleiser; Cast: Ethan Hawke, Klaus Maria Brandauer, Seymour Cassel, Susan Hogan, James Remar.

Choose this version of Jack London's childhood favorite about a wolf dog in Alaska over the two earlier ones. The story isn't any different here, but the cinematography is tremendous.

Dog-Pound Shuffle (aka: *Spot,* 1975, Canada, 95 mins.) Dir: Jeffrey Bloom; Cast: Ron Moody, David Soul, Raymond Sutton, Ray Stricklyn, Pamela McMyler.

Amusing Canadian film about a down-on-his-luck ex-vaudevillian who puts together a new act so he can raise the money he needs to get his dog out of the pound. A sweet little sleeper.

Frankenweenie (1984, U.S., 27 mins.) Dir: Tim Burton; Cast: Shelley Duvall, Daniel Stern, Barret Oliver, Paul Bartel.

Tim Burton of *Batman* fame made his first strange noises with this short film. Victor Frankenstein's dog Sparky is killed, then brought back to life as a canine Boris Karloff. The kind of disgusting thing that you think will irreparably harm your children, but which they love.

Umberto D (1955, Italy, 89 mins., b/w) Dir: Vittorio De Sica; Cast: Carlo Battisti, Maria Pia Casilio.

The greatest film involving a dog ever made. Pensioner Umberto Ferrari and his dog Flag are about to be put out of their apartment. What will happen to Umberto D? And what will happen to Flag? A basic tale imbued with immense feeling that will send you straight to the pound to adopt a dog.

FILM FISH

A dozen films featuring fish and fishermen.

A Fish Called Wanda (1988, U.S., 108 mins.) Dir: Charles Crichton; Cast: John Cleese, Jamie Lee Curtis, Kevin Kline, Michael Palin.

Comedy starring Cleese as a lawyer involved with Curtis, who is part of a clumsy gang of bank robbers. The fish here are goldfish and while they're not central to the plot, they make the ultimate sacrifice for one of the best laughs in the film.

Man's Favorite Sport? (1964, U.S., 120 mins.) Dir: Howard Hawks; Cast: Rock Hudson, Paula Prentiss, Maria Perschy.

Prentiss pushes Hudson, a famous sportsman who has actually never fished, into entering a fishing tournament. Lots of splashing around in waders and lures stuck in hatbands, if you're interested in those sorts of things.

The Old Man and the Sea (1958, U.S., 86 mins.) Dir: John Sturges; Cast: Spencer Tracy, Felipe Pazos, Harry Bellaver.

Spencer Tracy plays the fisherman in this adaptation of Hemingway's Nobel Prize-winning novel. This isn't pleasure fishing; this is life-and-death, grace-under-pressure, fishing-as-metaphor fishing.

Jaws (1975, U.S., 124 mins.) Dir: Steven Spielberg; Cast: Roy Scheider, Robert Shaw, Richard Dreyfuss, Lorraine Gary, Murray Hamilton.

The biggest fish of them all. An enormous great white shark terrorizes a Long Island beach town. Robert Shaw is the ultimate barnacled fisherman and Bruce the Shark is the ultimate fish. Remember, hardcore fish fans—

not many other films have an ichthyologist as a major character.

Piranha (1978, U.S., 92 mins.) Dir: Joe Dante; Cast: Bradford Dillman, Heather Menzies, Keenan Wynn, Kevin McCarthy, Barbara Steele.

Campy takeoff on *Jaws,* with piranhas as the killer fish(es) this time. Script by John Sayles and directed by Joe Dante, later known for *Gremlins.*

The Incredible Mr. Limpet (1964, U.S., 102 mins.) Dir: Arthur Lubin; Cast: Don Knotts, Carole Cook, Jack Weston.

A sentimental favorite. Wimpy Don Knotts gets his wish and becomes a fish, albeit an animated one. Knotts's best work outside of *The Andy Griffith Show.* Robert Zemeckis has never admitted the influence its combination of live action and animation had on *Who Framed Roger Rabbit,* but we know the truth.

20,000 Leagues Under the Sea (1954, U.S., 127 mins.) Dir: Richard Fleischer; Cast: Kirk Douglas, Paul Lukas, James Mason, Peter Lorre.

Disney version of the Jules Verne classic. Another children's movie, but the battle with the giant squid is prime exposure for this most underrated fish.

Shark! (1969, U.S., 92 mins.) Dir: Sam Fuller; Cast: Burt Reynolds, Barry Sullivan, Arthur Kennedy, Silvia Pinal.

Undersea treasure hunters battle sharks. Fuller, king of the B movies, liked this film so much that he wanted his name taken off it. A minor fish film.

Moby Dick (1956, U.S., 116 mins.) Dir: John Huston; Cast: Gregory Peck, Orson Welles, Harry Andrews, Richard Basehart, James Robertson-Justice.

A major fish film, though in this case it's a whale. And like a whale, it's big,

blubbery, and awe-inspiring. A perfect match of director and source material.

Flipper (1963, U.S., 90 mins.) Dir: James Clark; Cast: Flipper, Chuck Connors, Luke Halpin.

The story of a boy and his dolphin. Yes, another marine mammal, but made in the days when we thought dolphins were just very smart fish.

Mr. Peabody and the Mermaid (1948, U.S., 89 mins., b/w) Dir: Irving Pichel; Cast: William Powell, Ann Blyth, Irene Hervey, Andrea King.

The story of a guy and his mermaid. The ultimate midlife-crisis fish story has hubby Powell drifting off to the siren call of fish-on-the-half-shell Blyth. It's all too weird, but worth a look because of it.

A River Runs Through It (1992, U.S., 123 mins.) Dir: Robert Redford; Cast: Craig Sheffer, Brad Pitt, Tom Skerritt, Emily Lloyd.

The fish movie to end all fish movies. Redford does a creditable job in turning Norman Maclean's paean to fly-fishing into an achingly beautiful and reasonably dramatic movie. After seeing this, you'll begin to understand why people stand up to their waists in cold running water to catch trout.

HOLLYWOOD HORSES

The horse is probably the one animal Hollywood couldn't do without. Can you picture Roy Rogers riding off into the sunset on a mule? Cavalry charges on bicycles? Pig rustling? While most equines are known for their work as extras, here are some films where horses were the whole point.

National Velvet (1944, U.S., 123 mins.) Dir: Clarence Brown; Cast: Mickey

Rooney, Elizabeth Taylor, Donald Crisp, Ann Revere, Angela Lansbury, Reginald Owen.

The classic film of a girl and her horse. Though Elizabeth Taylor had been in other movies, her performance as a girl who trains her horse to run in the Grand National steeplechase turned her into a star. Mickey Rooney is fine too. A good place to start. The sequel, *International Velvet,* stands up well against it.

Run Wild, Run Free (1969, Great Britain, 100 mins.) Dir: Richard C. Sarafian; Cast: John Mills, Mark Lester, Gordon Jackson, Sylvia Syms.
■
Good children's film (as most of these are) about a mute boy and the white horse he falls in love with. Your appreciation will depend on how much you can stand of the shaggy, fey English boy Mark Lester, who needs a haircut more than he needs a horse.

The Charge of the Light Brigade (1936, U.S., 115 mins., b/w) Dir: Michael Curtiz; Cast: Errol Flynn, Olivia de Havilland, David Niven, Donald Crisp, Henry Stephenson, Patric Knowles.

Though not specifically about horses, they take over during the final scene when the 600 English cavalrymen charge into the Russian guns in the Crimea. Other movie cavalry scenes may have more color or realism, but this is by far the longest and most rousing. It's also famous as the scene when, as David Niven reports, director Curtiz ordered the crew to "Bring on the empty horses!"

Kentucky (1938, U.S., 94 mins.) Dir: David Butler; Cast: Loretta Young, Richard Greene, Walter Brennan.

The bluegrass country of Kentucky has given us some great horses, so it's only right that there be a film about it. Here, the son and daughter of two rival families fall in love despite nearly a century of antagonism between their clans. Surprisingly good and a love letter to Kentucky horse breeders. Brennan won the Oscar for Best Supporting Actor.

The Black Stallion (1979, U.S., 125 mins.) Dir: Carroll Ballard; Cast: Kelly Reno, Mickey Rooney, Teri Garr, Clarence Muse.

Mickey Rooney does another great job as a horse trainer, this time in a beautiful adaptation of Walter Farley's much-loved tale of a boy's adventures with his horse. Nice film, definitely for the kids, young or old.

Equus (1976, U.S., 137 mins.) Dir: Sidney Lumet; Cast: Richard Burton, Peter Firth, Colin Blakely, Joan Plowright, Harry Andrews, Eileen Atkins, Jenny Agutter.

Much of the power of Peter Schaeffer's play about a psychiatrist trying to learn why a boy has been blinding horses derived from its theatricality, which obviously disappears on screen. Still, the mystique of horses and what they can represent comes across, along with Oscar-nominated performances from Burton and Firth.

Mazeppa (1993, France, 111 mins.) Dir: Bartabas; Cast: Bartabas, Miguel Bosé, Brigitte Marty, Evan Schakmundes.

Another film about equine-obsession. This time the French painter Géricault has the insane love for horse flesh and his relationship with famed—and equally crazy—horse trainer Franconi doesn't help. None of this makes much sense and it's all so arty that one doubts whether it's supposed to, but if you want horses, this film's for you. A solid 95 percent of the shots have a horse in them, and the horses are doing all those, well, natural things they don't show in *The Black Stallion.* The soundtrack sounds like part Gypsy Kings and part Mysterious Voices of Bulgaria and is worth buying if you can find it.

The Red Pony (1949, U.S., 89 mins.) Dir: Lewis Milestone; Cast: Robert Mitchum, Myrna Loy, Peter Miles.

Grown-ups can enjoy the Loy-Mitchum interplay and Aaron Copland score while the kids can sniffle along with this timeless version of Steinbeck's story about a boy from a battling family who finds solace in his horse.

The Horse in the Gray Flannel Suit (1968, U.S., 113 mins.) Dir: Norman Tokar; Cast: Dean Jones, Diane Baker, Fred Clark, Kurt Russell.

Peppy late sixties Disney comedy stars—surprise!—Dean Jones as a—surprise!—ad executive whose daughter loves—you guessed it—horses. Here's the biggest surprise of all—it's actually pretty good.

Into the West (1993, Great Britain, 92 mins.) Dir: Mike Newell; Cast: Gabriel Byrne, Ellen Barkin, Craion Fitzgerald, Rory Conroy.

A magical white horse comes into the lives of two Irish boys whose father has sunk to the bottom of the bottle following their mother's death. The kids might have some trouble following this blend of fairy tale and harsh realism on their own, but the grown-ups will be interested enough to stick around. Jim Sheridan, director of *My Left Foot* and *In the Name of the Father,* wrote the screenplay.

The Misfits (1961, U.S., 124 mins.) Dir: John Huston; Cast: Clark Gable, Marilyn Monroe, Eli Wallach, Montgomery Clift.

Somehow we doubt that the kids will be quite as interested as you'll be in seeing Monroe and Gable in their last roles, along with Montgomery Clift, in this Arthur Miller screenplay about down-and-out cowboys hunting wild horses for dog food. Considering everything that was going on behind the scenes—Gable nearing death, Monroe gobbling drugs and on the verge of breakup with Miller—it's a wonder that it's as good as it is. Gable thought it was his best film.

WILD KINGDOM

Wild animals have had a very difficult time getting good jobs in Hollywood. With so many of the juicy roles written for humans, animals must make do with what work they can find as extras in adventure epics and nature documentaries. And, of course, some wait tables. Following are some examples of what wild animals can do if they're only given a chance.

The Bear (1989, France, 93 mins.) Dir: Jean-Jacques Annaud; Cast: Bart, Douce, Jack Wallace, Tcheky Karyo, Andre Lacombe.

Ursine tearjerker about an orphaned cub who takes up with an older bear. Definitely a classic for animal fans; expect some sniffles. The starring bear had a development deal for a while at Fox, but it lapsed after he found out *The Hotel New Hampshire* had already been made into a movie.

The Birds (1963, U.S., 120 mins.) Dir: Alfred Hitchcock; Cast: Tippi Hedren, Rod Taylor, Suzanne Pleshette, Veronica Cartwright, Jessica Tandy.

Fine ensemble acting by thousands of gulls, sparrows, and crows and a fine supporting cast of humans make this Hitchcock masterpiece about killer birds an animal favorite. The ending doesn't quite make sense, but it doesn't matter by that point. If you're in a bird mood, don't forget *The Birdman of Alcatraz,* either.

Elephant Boy (1937, Great Britain, 100 mins.) Dirs: Robert Flaherty, Zoltan Korda; Cast: Sabu, Walter Hudd.

Sabu stars as a young Indian boy who knows the whereabouts of a lost elephant herd. Interesting teamwork by groundbreaking documentary maker Flaherty and Zoltan Korda puts this somewhere between fact and fiction.

Jungle Book (1942, U.S., 109 mins.) Dir: Zoltan Korda; Cast: Sabu, Joseph Calleia, John Qualen, Frank Puglia, Rosemary De Camp.

Another Korda/Sabu vehicle, this time a colorful adaptation of Kipling's tale about a young boy raised by wolves in the Indian jungle. The Disney cartoon is fun, but the real animals and the Indian flavor give this one a charm that animation can't touch.

Born Free (1966, Great Britain, 96 mins.) Dir: James Hill; Cast: Bill Travers, Virginia McKenna.

If you haven't rented this with the kids by now, do it. When you were young you loved this story of Elsa the lioness and the couple that adopts her, so why shouldn't they? Besides, won't it be fun to have that song rattle around in your head for a few days?

Ring of Bright Water (1969, Great Britain, 107 mins.) Dir: Jack Couffer; Cast: Bill Travers, Virginia McKenna, Peter Jeffrey.

Otters are true sleepers in the animal world. They're darn cute, smart, and sleek. If they were cars, they'd be Mazda Miatas. Travers and McKenna trade in their lion for something more compact in this good little film about a man with a pet otter. You'll want an otter after seeing this, but you don't have the room so forget about it.

Never Cry Wolf (1983, U.S., 105 mins.) Dir: Carroll Ballard; Cast: Charles Martin Smith, Brian Dennehy.

Nice adaptation of Farley Mowat's book about wolves in the Arctic. A strong human presence keeps it free of the anthropomorphizing that usually happens to the animals in these films. One of the best nature-oriented movies.

Gorillas in the Mist (1988, U.S., 125 mins.) Dir: Michael Apted; Cast: Sigourney Weaver, Bryan Brown, Julie Harris, John Omirah Miluwi.

Long biopic about Dian Fossey, whose murder was thought to be linked to her campaign to save mountain gorillas in Africa. Lots of gorilla action, though some of the gorillas are clearly not the real thing.

Koko—A Talking Gorilla (1978, U.S., 85 mins.) Dir: Barbet Schroeder.

A fascinating film about the real thing. Barbet Schroeder directed this documentary about a gorilla taught sign language by Stanford researcher Penny Patterson. The absence of voiceover narration lets the people, and in this case the gorilla, tell their own stories without an editorial slant. You can make your own judgment about the methodology used and whether Koko really is using language. Nestor Almendros was the cinematographer.

Bringing Up Baby (1938, U.S., 102 mins., b/w) Dir: Howard Hawks; Cast: Katharine Hepburn, Cary Grant, Barry Fitzgerald, Charlie Ruggles, May Robson, Ward Bond.

Many say Grant and Hepburn are the attraction in this famous screwball comedy, but animal lovers know differently. There would be no movie if it weren't for Baby the leopard. Apparently Baby wasn't all that tame in real life, so some of the fear-stricken faces you see in the film have nothing to do with acting.

MAKING

MOVIES

AUTEUR

SCREENWRITERS
■
THE ALGONQUIN ROUND TABLE

The Algonquin Hotel in New York City is more than a little tatty now, and sitting around a table every afternoon tossing about bon mots would probably wear thin pretty quickly. But many of us still wish we could have spent a few days trying to keep up with the likes of Dorothy Parker, James Thurber, and Robert Benchley. Here are 10 of the best films the Algonquinites and their extended circle produced.

A Night at the Opera (1935, U.S., 90 mins., b/w) Dir: Sam Wood; Cast: Groucho, Chico, and Harpo Marx, Kitty Carlisle, Allan Jones, Margaret Dumont.

Playwright George S. Kaufman, along with Morrie Ryskind, wrote the script for this ultimate Marx Brothers romp. Though it seems as if Groucho is making it all up as he goes, the fact is, he's only making up some of it. Kaufman also wrote the Broadway plays *The Cocoanuts* and *Animal Crackers,* which later became Marx Brothers screen vehicles.

His Girl Friday (1940, U.S., 92 mins., b/w) Dir: Howard Hawks; Cast: Cary Grant, Rosalind Russell, Ralph Bellamy, Helen Mack, Gene Lockhart.

One of the few examples of a remake that surpasses the original. Ben Hecht took another shot at *The Front Page*'s story of love in the newsroom and with the help of Grant and Russell came up with a shining comedy that hasn't

dated and doesn't slip into the crusty reporter stereotypes of the first.

A Star Is Born (1937, U.S., 110 mins.) Dir: William Wellman; Cast: Fredric March, Janet Gaynor, Andy Devine, Adolphe Menjou, Lionel Stander.

The original and, arguably, best version of this story of a young actress whose career soars as her actor husband fades into oblivion. Co-written by Dorothy Parker, whose own star had slipped seriously by the time this was released.

Waterloo Bridge (1940, U.S., 103 mins., b/w) Dir: Mervyn LeRoy; Cast: Vivien Leigh, Robert Taylor, Lucile Watson, Virginia Field.

World War I melodrama, based on a play by Robert Sherwood. Ballet dancer Leigh and officer Taylor fall in love at first sight during a London air raid, but have trouble making it last when the "all clear" sounds. A definite tearjerker clearly toned down for the screen, but strengthened by good performances.

The Petrified Forest (1936, U.S., 83 mins., b/w) Dir: Archie Mayo; Cast: Bette Davis, Leslie Howard, Humphrey Bogart, Dick Foran.

Bogart's performance here as Duke Mantee, an escaped mobster who terrorizes the people at a roadside diner, was the one that really broke him out of playing character roles. Bogart and Leslie Howard also starred in the original Broadway play by Robert Sherwood.

Alibi Ike (1935, U.S., 73 mins., b/w) Dir: Ray Enright; Cast: Joe E. Brown, Olivia de Havilland, William Frawley, Ruth Donnelly.
■
Joe E. Brown is wonderful in this Ring Lardner tale of a young pitcher who has more talent in his tongue than he has in his arm. Especially fun for Chicago Cub fans, who can see what their team

looked like during the years they used to win.

The Battle of the Sexes (1960, Great Britain, 88 mins., b/w) Dir: Charles Crichton; Cast: Peter Sellers, Robert Morley, Constance Cummings, Jameson Clark.

Truly hilarious adaptation of James Thurber's story "The Catbird Seat." By moving the story to Scotland and featuring Sellers as the put-upon functionary driven to drastic acts by a female "efficiency expert," the movie manages to combine the best of both Thurber and the understated English comedies of its period.

Foreign Correspondent (1940, U.S., 119 mins., b/w) Dir: Alfred Hitchcock; Cast: Joel McCrea, Laraine Day, Herbert Marshall, George Sanders, Albert Basserman.

Robert Benchley co-wrote and also has a role in this Hitchcock classic about a reporter who gets caught up in a Nazi spy ring. A humorist and magazine writer, Benchley was most famous for his series of short comic films on topics like *How to Sleep* and *How to Start the Day*.

Wuthering Heights (1939, U.S., 103 mins., b/w) Dir: William Wyler; Cast: Merle Oberon, Laurence Olivier, David Niven, Flora Robson, Donald Crisp, Geraldine Fitzgerald, Leo G. Carroll.

Ben Hecht and Charles MacArthur were not hard-core members of the Round Table and some say that their lack of New York snobbery let them write brilliant films. This adaptation of the Emily Brontë classic probably drew more people to great art than any number of snippy Alexander Woollcott columns.

You Can't Take It With You (1938, U.S., 127 mins., b/w) Dir: Frank Capra; Cast: Jean Arthur, Lionel Barrymore, James Stewart, Edward Arnold, Mischa Auer, Ann Miller, Spring Byington, Samuel S. Hinds, Donald Meek, H. B. Warner.

George S. Kaufman and Moss Hart wrote the original play about a bizarre and extremely happy family, which Capra then turned into this sweet film. If it's too corny for your tastes, just think of it as *The Addams Family* without the costumes.

SCREENWRITERS
■
SCREENWRITING PLAYWRIGHTS

The phenomenon of the fresh out of college, wet behind the ears kid who's never had anything published or produced in his life, getting a couple of million for his first screenplay is relatively recent. Historically, screenwriters have come from most every other literary discipline. They've been novelists, journalists, lyricists, essayists, ad writers, gag writers, even a couple of poets. But the discipline that is closest to commercial screenwriting is writing for the stage. Each involves dialogue and dramatic action, aimed not at a reader but a viewer sitting in a darkened theater (video notwithstanding) for some two hours. And each requires a director to mount it, and actors to bring it to life. Considering all the similarities, it's surprising how many great modern playwrights had little to do with screenwriting, while some, like David Mamet, write regularly for the screen. The thread that binds the following films is the theater. Not that they are based on plays—none of these are—but each is penned by a writer who cut his teeth and carved his reputation by writing for the stage.

Sweet Smell of Success (1957, U.S., 96 mins., b/w) Dir: Alexander Mackendrick; Cast: Burt Lancaster, Tony Curtis, Martin Milner, Sam Levene, Barbara Nichols.

Scathing drama of slithering press agent Curtis and venomous columnist Lancaster striking a sordid deal in the snake pit known as New York City. Clifford Odets, America's dramatist laureate of the 1930s, wrote the screenplay from a story by Ernest Lehman. The script, like the best of Odets's plays, strikes a perfect balance between naturalism and symbolism. The characters are acutely alive. The atmosphere is charged with the real sights, sounds, and smells of life. But peel away the surface, and you find layers of metaphor, allegory, and psychological meaning. Acting, direction, and James Wong Howe's cinematography are brilliant as well.

The Misfits (1961, U.S., 124 mins., b/w) Dir: John Huston; Cast: Marilyn Monroe, Clark Gable, Montgomery Clift, Thelma Ritter, Eli Wallach.

Neurotic but sensitive divorcée Monroe leads wrangler Gable away from the senseless slaughter of wild mustangs to a deeper view of the meaning of life. Famed playwright Arthur Miller *(Death of a Salesman)* wrote the script (his only successful original screenplay) while his marriage to Marilyn was crumbling. But in the character of Roslyn he gave her one of the most delicate, noblest, and arguably the richest role of her career. It was also her last. As it was for Clark Gable. The specter of death hangs over the film like a shroud.

The Servant (1963, Great Britain, 115 mins., b/w) Dir: Joseph Losey; Cast: Dirk Bogarde, James Fox, Sarah Miles, Wendy Craig.

Emotionally crippled, metaphysically challenged Fox hires manservant Bogarde to tend to his needs, but roles reverse and the servant becomes the master, eventually bringing his twisted "sister" into the mix. The screenplay by Harold Pinter (adapted from a novel by Robin Maugham) is marked by a surface naturalism that barely conceals a deeply absurd, morally ambiguous view of the world. Director Losey completely penetrates and ultimately transcends the material. Stylish, sexy, and very strange.

Tom Jones (1963, Great Britain, 129 mins.) Dir: Tony Richardson; Cast: Albert Finney, Susannah York, Hugh Griffith, Edith Evans.

. . . in which we follow a young rake of dubious parentage on a lusty romp through a Hogarth-like landscape of 18th-century manners, morals, and appetites. It's the product of a most unlikely marriage—Henry Fielding's bawdy Restoration novel and the angry-young-man, kitchen-sink school of British drama, represented by Finney, director Tony Richardson, and writer John Osborne, one of the most explosive forces in British theater. And while in tone and subject matter this stands quite apart from the rest of Osborne's work, it reflects the humanism, hopefulness, and idealism that bubbles under the anger and despair of his plays.

The Untouchables (1987, U.S., 118 mins.) Dir: Brian DePalma; Cast: Kevin Costner, Sean Connery, Robert De Niro, Charles Martin Smith, Andy Garcia.

David Mamet's screenplay relies less on the classic TV series than his own imagination in telling the story of innocent, idealistic lawman Eliot Ness and his battle against gangland crime in 1920s Chicago. The characters have a comic-book quality—Mamet's painting with broader strokes here than in any of his plays or other movies. His trademark clipped dialogue is hardly in evidence. Yet he seems to be having a wonderful time and he gives director DePalma the blueprint for one of his most successful films. Connery (Oscar for Best Supporting Actor) and De Niro have a field day.

The Romantic Englishwoman (1975, Great Britain, 115 mins.) Dir: Joseph Losey; Cast: Michael Caine, Glenda Jackson, Helmut Berger, Kate Nelligan.

Glenda Jackson is the woman of the title who decides that if her pulp-writer husband Caine won't satisfy her romantic longings, she might find fulfillment in houseguest Berger. Playwright Tom Stoppard rewrote Thomas Wiseman's adaptation of his own novel at the request of director Losey. The script lacks the verbal pyrotechnics of Stoppard's stage plays, but the characters, especially Berger, get off some stinging bon mots. More firecrackers than fireworks, but well worth the effort.

Atlantic City (1981, Canada-France, 104 mins.) Dir: Louis Malle; Cast: Burt Lancaster, Susan Sarandon, Kate Reid, Michel Piccoli, Hollis McLaren, Robert Joy.

John Guare (House of Blue Leaves, Six Degrees of Separation) takes a dozen or so small-time hustlers, dreamers, and schemers and deftly weaves their lives together against the backdrop of the Jersey shore town that wants to be Las Vegas. French director Malle takes full charge of the material. It's like a French chef forsaking nouvelle cuisine in favor of American fare. The result is less self-consciously stylish but much more filling than most of Malle's other work. Lancaster gives what may be the best performance of his career.

Five Corners (1988, U.S., 92 mins.) Dir: Tony Bill; Cast: Jodie Foster, Tim Robbins, Todd Graff, John Turturro.

Highly regarded off-Broadway playwright John Patrick Shanley, who went on to win a Best Screenplay Oscar for *Moonstruck*, wrote this neglected jewel about life in the Bronx circa 1964. Foster seems right at home with her Fordham Road accent and Turturro is suitably psychotic as the wacko ex-con who returns to the nabe hell-bent on inflicting misery. It's funny and engrossing. Shanley's characters are superbly drawn, the dialogue cracks like a Spaldeen against a schoolyard wall, and the plot takes a couple of outrageous turns. Definitely.

Paris, Texas (1984, U.S., 150 mins.) Dir: Wim Wenders; Cast: Harry Dean Stanton, Nastassja Kinski, Dean Stockwell, Aurore Clement, Hunter Carson, Bernhard Wicki.

Writer Sam Shepard (True West, Fool for Love) doesn't go as far out on the edge or as high over the top as he does in most of his plays, but this story of a man (Stanton) who's been missing for years, trying to reunite with his wife and young son, is definitely stamped by the Shepard style—it's odd and elliptical, featuring characters looking for answers without being clear on the questions. In collaboration with director Wim Wenders, Shepard establishes the film's locale as some strange time zone that seems to exist, as the title implies, suspended between Europe and the American West.

CINEMATOGRAPHERS
■
JAMES WONG HOWE

This Chinese cinematographer arrived in Hollywood in 1917 and his career spans more than 50 years of movie history. His work includes images of extraordinary beauty, shimmering sensuality, and graphic violence. His modus operandi was simple: do whatever it takes to capture what a director sees in his mind's eye and put it on film . . . then, if possible, make it better.

The Thin Man (1934, U.S., 93 mins., b/w) Dir: W. S. Van Dyke; Cast: William Powell, Myrna Loy, Maureen O'Sullivan, Nat Pendleton, Minna Gombell, Porter Hall.

Dashiell Hammett's Nick and Nora Charles (Powell and Loy) do their breezy, sophisticated crime-solving thing vs. a formidable gallery of suspects. Howe's well-knit cinematography gives the picture the sharp edge needed for a gripping thriller and the warmth and charm of the best romantic comedies. Lovely fun.

The Prisoner of Zenda (1937, U.S., 120 mins., b/w) Dir: John Cromwell; Cast: Ronald Colman, Madeleine Carroll, Douglas Fairbanks, Jr., David Niven, C. Aubrey Smith, Mary Astor, Raymond Massey.

Exhilarating swashbuckler stars Colman in dual role of devil-may-care Brit on holiday in Ruritania and his look-alike, the about-to-be-crowned Ruritanian king. Howe's photography not only captures the epic sweep and visual splendor of the story, it features some dazzling optical trickery—the scene in which one Ronald Colman shakes hands with the other is a wonderful example of cinematic problem solving and an important innovation in the history of special effects.

King's Row (1941, U.S., 127 mins., b/w) Dir: Sam Wood; Cast: Robert Cummings, Ronald Reagan, Ann Sheridan, Betty Field, Claude Rains, Judith Anderson, Charles Coburn, Maria Ouspenskaya, Nancy Coleman.

Big, pulsating melodrama about life in a midwestern town on the eve of WWI whips up the suds and gives Ron a chance to prove that the presidency was not his only effective acting performance. Much of the film's stature comes from the cinematography, and even if the soap-operatic storyline gets on your nerves, fast-forward to the thunderstorm climax, sit back and enjoy a kaleidoscopic black-and-white light show courtesy of Mr. Howe, set to the Wagnerian strains of Eric Wolfgang Korngold's score.

Hangmen Also Die (1943, U.S., 131 mins., b/w) Dir: Fritz Lang; Cast: Brian Donlevy, Walter Brennan, Dennis O'Keefe, Anna Lee.

Director Lang collaborated with fellow German émigré Bertolt Brecht on this story of Czech resistance fighters plotting the termination of Gestapo "hangman" Reinhard Heydrich, an architect of Hitler's final solution. Photographically designed by Howe to complement Lang's bleak Expressionist vision, the closed, geometric patterns visually entrap the characters inside the brutal reality of history's darkest nightmare.

Body and Soul (1947, U.S., 104 mins., b/w) Dir: Robert Rossen; Cast: John Garfield, Lilli Palmer, Anne Revere, Hazel Brooks, William Conrad, Joseph Penny.

Staggering drama of slum-kid Garfield selling his soul for material wealth and the middleweight crown clearly reflects the social idealism of director Rossen and screenwriter Abe Polonsky. Howe's artistry set the cinematographic standards against which all boxing films must be measured. For the fight sequences he actually strapped on roller skates and used a hand-held camera to intensify the action. A knockout all the way.

He Ran All the Way (1951, U.S., 77 mins., b/w) Dir: John Berry; Cast: John Garfield, Shelley Winters.

Garfield plays a paranoid but sympathetic thief wanted for murder who falls for small-town girl Winters (who, believe it or not, was a very effective ingenue) and winds up holding her entire family hostage. Howe brilliantly balances realism and Expressionism to set up the moral ambivalence of the protagonist, establishing a perfect visual motif for the Garfield persona. Tough, taut, absorbing little melodrama.

Pursued (1947, U.S., 101 mins., b/w) Dir: Raoul Walsh; Cast: Robert Mitchum, Teresa Wright, Judith Anderson, Dean Jagger.

Dark, brooding psychological western opens with hero Mitchum waiting in the shadows for a necktie party where he is to be the guest of honor, flashing back to thoughts of the mysterious stranger who has haunted him all his life. Character rich, structurally involved script via Aeschylus and Sigmund Freud is given a striking film noir treatment by director Walsh and cinematographer Howe, whom screenwriter Nevin Busch (thrilled with the final product) called "the best cameraman in the world."

Sweet Smell of Success (1957, U.S., 96 mins., b/w) Dir: Alexander Mackendrick; Cast: Burt Lancaster, Tony Curtis, Susan Harrison, Martin Milner, Sam Levene, Barbara Nichols.

Curtis gives his finest performance as oily press agent Sidney Falco (one of the great screen names!) going head to head with powerful Broadway columnist J. J. Hunsicker (Burt) in this cynical study of greed and decadence. The script by Clifford Odets spits venom and director Mackendrick never flinches. Neither does Howe. He perfectly captures the noirish underbelly of Manhattan—the city streets, the bars, the noisy nightclubs, and the quiet desperation. When we picture 1950s New York, these are the images.

The Rose Tattoo (1955, U.S., 117 mins., b/w) Dir: Daniel Mann; Cast: Anna Magnani, Burt Lancaster, Marisa Pavan, Ben Cooper, Virginia Grey, Jo Van Fleet.

Screen version of Tennessee Williams comedy/drama sporting Magnani's Oscar-winning work as a lusty Sicilian woman who pines for and whines about her dead philandering husband until studly Lancaster comes along and gets her juices flowing. Howe (who also won an Oscar) gives the film an earthy, sensual look, proving that a play does not have to be opened up real wide to be cinematic.

The Molly Maguires (1969, U.S., 124 mins.) Dir: Martin Ritt; Cast: Sean Connery, Richard Harris, Samantha Eggar.

Connery heads a secret society of 19th-century Pennsylvania coal miners; undercover cop Harris infiltrates. To obtain the authenticity Ritt wanted, Howe went with an unorthodox approach to lighting the film, often using no artificial light at all, and illuminating one particularly atmospheric scene exclusively by candlelight. The film's beauty more than makes up for its cumbersome script.

Seconds (1966, U.S., 106 mins., b/w) Dir: John Frankenheimer; Cast: Rock Hudson, Salome Jens, John Randolph, Jeff Corey, Murray Hamilton, Will Geer.
■
Superb sci-fi, about middle-aged guy (Randolph) who undergoes surgical rejuvenation procedure and emerges as Rock Hudson, builds to genuinely horrifying conclusion. Howe used the bizarre premise as an excuse to free-fall with the camera, experimenting with variable lighting, lenses, and hand-held techniques, keeping the viewer off balance at every turn. A touchstone in the art of cinematography.

CINEMATOGRAPHERS
■
GREGG TOLAND

Though best known for his work with Orson Welles on *Citizen Kane*, Gregg Toland was the man behind the camera on some of the most high-

ly regarded films ever made, and a couple that might surprise you. A true visual virtuoso, any movie he shot bears his unmistakable signature and is worth watching with a capital "W."

Citizen Kane (1941, U.S., 119 mins., b/w) Dir: Orson Welles; Cast: Orson Welles, Joseph Cotten, Dorothy Comingore, Ruth Warrick, Everett Sloane, Agnes Moorehead, George Coulouris.

While Welles was putting together the creative team, Toland, one of the most respected cameramen in Hollywood, asked in. Welles asked why. "It's your first film," Toland answered, "and you won't know what you can't do." The cinematography in *Kane,* with its startling combinations of deep focus, iconoclastic lighting, and complex camera movement, virtually reinvented film language. Toland's credit (on the same title card with Welles's) was an unprecedented, and well-deserved, tip of the hat from a director to a cinematographer.

Bulldog Drummond (1929, U.S., 80 mins., b/w) Dir: F. Richard Jones; Cast: Ronald Colman, Joan Bennett, Lilyan Tashman.

Much more than just a delightful detective story (which it is in spades), this film had a far-reaching effect on the future of the medium. Toland was listed as co-cinematographer (with George Barnes) and the camerawork in scene after scene, from its Germanic lighting and elaborate tracking shots to the use of deep focus, anticipates *Kane* by more than a decade.

We Live Again (1934, U.S., 82 mins., b/w) Dir: Rouben Mamoulian; Cast: Fredric March, Anna Sten, Sam Jaffe, Jane Baxter, C. Aubrey Smith.
▪
Producer Sam Goldwyn's big-budget attempt to turn "Russian Garbo" Sten into a star is built on a Tolstoy novel

adapted by Preston Sturges, Maxwell Anderson, and James Thurber (uncredited) among others. Toland's work on the film was hailed by one critic of the period as "some of the most breathtaking photography ever recorded by a motion-picture camera." Enough heavy hitters involved to recommend it no matter how slow it moves.

Les Miserables (1935, U.S., 108 mins., b/w) Dir: Richard Boleslawski; Cast: Fredric March, Charles Laughton, John Beal, Florence Eldridge, Rochelle Hudson, Cedric Hardwicke, John Carradine.

March's Valjean takes on Laughton's Javert in what is undoubtedly the best of many screen realizations of Victor Hugo's French literary classic. Toland's Academy Award-nominated cinematography, with its high-contrast lighting and visual density, was a clearcut influence on the lighting design for the musical *Les Miz.*

These Three (1936, U.S., 90 mins., b/w) Dir: William Wyler; Cast: Merle Oberon, Joel McCrea, Miriam Hopkins, Bonita Granville.

Thoughtful, emotional tale of two teachers (Oberon and Hopkins) done in by slanderous Granville is marred by mixing of messages. Lillian Hellman reworked her controversial play and eliminated lesbian theme for the sake of the censors. Toland, in his first of many films with William Wyler, gives the piece tremendous visual power, finding exciting ways of translating stage blocking into cinematic *mise en scène.*

Wuthering Heights (1939, U.S., 110 mins., b/w) Dir: William Wyler; Cast: Laurence Olivier, Merle Oberon, David Niven, Geraldine Fitzgerald.

Often overrated Hollywood handling of Emily Brontë's brooding, romantic novel. In attempting to establish the book's haunted locales, Wyler nixed location shooting in favor of studio sets hoping to create a "wilderness of the imagination" and Toland's cinematography, full of dense grays and blacks, renders it as "a chiaroscuro country of the mind." A visually stunning vacuum.

The Westerner (1940, U.S., 100 mins., b/w) Dir: William Wyler; Cast: Gary Cooper, Walter Brennan, Doris Davenport, Forrest Tucker, Dana Andrews.

First film installation of the life and times of Judge Roy Bean with Brennan copping his third Oscar as the wild and wooly western jurist. Neither Wyler's theatricality nor Toland's Expressionist sensibility jibes with the genre and the film lacks the genuine spirit of the best westerns. Still the performances are fun and the visual formality makes it interesting to look at.

The Little Foxes (1941, U.S., 116 mins., b/w) Dir: William Wyler; Cast: Bette Davis, Herbert Marshall, Teresa Wright, Dan Duryea, Richard Carlson, Charles Dingle, Carl Benton Reid.

Bette is Lillian Hellman's insidiously foxy lady in this powerful tale of a southern family crumbling under the weight of greed and corruption. First post-*Kane* pairing of Wyler and Toland is marked by Toland's work with Welles—use of deep focus, long takes, ominous angles, and odd framing is more pronounced (and dramatically effective) here than in any other Wyler film.

The Grapes of Wrath (1940, U.S., 128 mins., b/w) Dir: John Ford; Cast: Henry Fonda, Jane Darwell, John Carradine, Charley Grapewin, Dorris Bowden, John Qualen.

Dust-bowl journey of John Steinbeck's Joad family via route mapped out by John Ford with cinematographic direction courtesy of Toland. And while Ford replaces the novel's radical, so-cial-realist tone with a nostalgic yearning for the simplicities of the past, Toland bridges the gap. The use of available light and documentary technique makes the film much more realistic than the run of the Hollywood mill. At the same time, the visuals are dramatic, symbolic, and even romantic. A profoundly moving vision of Depression-era America.

The Long Voyage Home (1940, U.S., 105 mins., b/w) Dir: John Ford; Cast: John Wayne, Thomas Mitchell, Barry Fitzgerald, Mildred Natwick, Ian Hunter, Ward Bond, John Qualen, Wilfrid Lawson, Arthur Shields, Joe Sawyer.

Ford and screenwriter Dudley Nichols combined four one-act plays by Eugene O'Neill into this seagoing saga of a munitions ship trying to beat a U-boat blockade and reach London at the beginning of WWII. Toland's cinematography wraps the film in a sensual, ghostlike shroud—the air of death hovering over the sailors has a palpable presence. An eloquent, poetic, tragic work in which the lingering impression for the viewer comes less from the story and characters than from the visuals.

Ball of Fire (1941, U.S., 111 mins., b/w) Dir: Howard Hawks; Cast: Barbara Stanwyck, Gary Cooper, Oscar Homolka, Henry Travers, S. Z. Sakall, Dana Andrews, Dan Duryea, Richard Haydn, Gene Krupa, Tully Marshall.

Comic gem about hot tomato Stanwyck, on the lam from the D.A., falling in with pedantic professor Coop and his bookish buddies in the isolated mansion where they're toiling away on an encyclopedia. Incredibly inventive script is a Billy Wilder/Charles Brackett riff on Snow White, directed by Hawks with the assurance of a screwball master. Toland brings a visual depth to the project hitherto nonexistent in this kind of comedy, giving the wonderful cast of supporting characters plenty of room to play.

CINEMATOGRAPHERS

■

JOHN ALTON

Film noir generally refers to those films of the late 1940s and early 1950s, often made on B-level budgets, which plunge us into a world of blind alleys, dark, slick streets, and dimly lit hallways—a culture of crime and corruption where the lines between right and wrong, good and evil are often obscured by shadows. Expressive cinematography—customarily black and white—is an essential ingredient to success in the genre, and the work of John Alton stands out as the most consistently eloquent, distinctive, and exciting of any film noir cameraman.

T-Men (1947, U.S., 96 mins., b/w) Dir: Anthony Mann; Cast: Dennis O'Keefe, Alfred Ryder, June Lockhart.

Story of U.S. Treasury agents posing as hoods to infiltrate an L.A. counterfeit mob features a flat, matter-of-actual-fact voiceover narration countered by Alton's intensely Expressionistic photographic style. Frame after frame brings us deeper into a visual maelstrom, and the death by steamroom scene is a doozy. This film, director Mann and cinematographer Alton's first together, established the pair as one of the most formidable collaborative forces in all of film noir.

Border Incident (1949, U.S., 92 mins., b/w) Dir: Anthony Mann; Cast: Ricardo Montalban, George Murphy, Howard da Silva, Teresa Celli, Charles McGraw.

Close cousin to *T-Men*—the agents in this one are immigration officials who go undercover to stop criminal exploitation of wannabe Americans by a gang of murderous thugs hell-bent on undermining the sanctity of the U.S.-Mexican border. Brutally violent sequences are intensified by Alton's use of deep focus and night lighting, rendering the southwestern landscape in the same noirish terms as urban L.A.

Raw Deal (1948, U.S., 79 mins., b/w) Dir: Anthony Mann; Cast: Dennis O'Keefe, Claire Trevor, Marsha Hunt, Raymond Burr.
■
Extremely brutal thriller about an escaped con (O'Keefe) who gets caught between two dames while going after the rotten, sadistic piece of subhuman excrement (Burr) who framed him. Sexy, violent, richly textured, and atmospheric. A hard-boiled home run.

Reign of Terror (1949, U.S., 89 mins., b/w) Dir: Anthony Mann; Cast: Robert Cummings, Arlene Dahl, Richard Hart, Richard Basehart, Arnold Moss, Beulah Bondi.

French Revolution period piece about rival political factions fighting it out in a manner befitting gangsters in an urban melodrama, and Alton shoots it as if it were exactly that. An intriguing, original work that moves ever so much faster than conventional, overdressed costumers usually do.

He Walked by Night (1948, U.S., 79 mins., b/w) Dir: Alfred L. Werker; Cast: Richard Basehart, Scott Brady, Jack Webb.

Based on true story of crazed cop killer on the loose in L.A., this docu-noir police procedural was co-directed by an uncredited Anthony Mann. Basehart as the killer does an excellent job in a woefully underwritten role. And Alton's camerawork takes us deep down into the character's dark night of the soul, bottoming out in an exquisitely photographed chase through the L.A. sewer system—a scene that predates (and rivals) the strikingly similar conclusion to *The Third Man* by a full year.

The Big Combo (1955, U.S., 89 mins., b/w) Dir: Joseph Lewis; Cast: Cornel Wilde, Richard Conte, Jean Wallace.

Solid hard-boiled script by Philip Yordan about tough cop Wilde's determination to bring down Conte and his crime combo attains masterpiece status courtesy of dazzling direction by Joseph *(Gun Crazy)* Lewis and the daring abstractions in light and shadow by cinematographer Alton. In the fog-drenched airplane hangar finale, a scene fraught with B-graded shades of *Casablanca,* sudden shafts of illumination prove as deadly as bullets, and the eternal romanticism of Rick and Ilsa is replaced by the unremitting fatalism of classic film noir. A must.

I, the Jury (1953, U.S., 87 mins., b/w) Dir: Harry Essex; Cast: Biff Elliot, Preston Foster, Peggie Castle, Elisha Cook, Jr., John Qualen.

This Mike Hammer murder mystery is basically faithful to the novel, with the hard-boiled detective hunting down his buddy's killer, but most of the brutality we associate with Mickey Spillane's hero is gone. Still, it's a good, tough, rarely seen noir—the only film in the genre to be shot in 3-D and the one time Alton worked with the process. If you come across a 3-D print, let us know. But any way you look at it, Alton's high-contrast, high-angle, forced-focus photography captures the specter of paranoia that hangs over all of Spillane's work.

Slightly Scarlet (1956, U.S., 99 mins.) Dir: Allan Dwan; Cast: John Payne, Arlene Dahl, Rhonda Fleming.

Effective potboiler, loosely based on James M. Cain novel *Love's Lovely Counterfeit,* finds hood-with-a-heart Payne walking the dangerous line between a political reformer and the mob, his situation complicated by two sisters, one good, one not-so-good, both with the hots for him. Rare example of 1950s noir shot in color and Alton mixes his palette well, finding just the right combination of gaudiness and

Expressionist lighting to enhance the deliberately sordid and violent mood.

An American in Paris (1951, U.S., 113 mins., b/w) Dir: Vincente Minnelli; Cast: Gene Kelly, Leslie Caron, Oscar Levant, Nina Foch, Georges Guetary.

His most notable achievement outside film noir, Alton's mellifluous camerawork on this Minnelli-Kelly-Gershwin musical won him an Oscar, and it has much to do with the overall impression left by the film. From the opening shot, the camera movement is as elaborately "choreographed" as the dancing, and the interplay of color and light is magnificent, conjuring up the Impressionist masters who provided the inspiration. Eye-popping.

WRITERS
■
WRITTEN, BUT NOT DIRECTED, BY PRESTON STURGES

In the early 1940s Preston Sturges set a new standard for artistry in Hollywood, writing and directing a remarkable string of vibrant, original, razor-sharp screwball comedies. Films like *The Great McGinty, The Lady Eve, The Miracle of Morgan's Creek,* and *Sullivan's Travels* offered a satiric, bitterly funny vision at a time when movies tended to be soaked in corn syrup. And while his work in the dual role of writer/director is what he's best known for, you might enjoy a little archaeological dig into the films that Sturges wrote before he got a chance to call the shots. Here are the most notable movies written by Preston Sturges, directed by somebody else.

Fast and Loose (1930, U.S., 75 mins., b/w) Dir: Fred Newmeyer; Cast: Miriam Hopkins, Frank Morgan, Carole Lombard.

Rather stagy adaptation of Broadway play features some very witty, sophisticated dialogue written for the screen by Sturges. Hopkins is excellent in her film debut.

Strictly Dishonorable (1931, U.S., 91 mins., b/w) Dir: John M. Stahl; Cast: Paul Lukas, Sidney Fox, Lewis Stone, Sidney Toler.

A womanizing opera star living above a speakeasy in Prohibition-era New York gets a very innocent girl into an extremely compromising position. Sturges did not write the script, but it's an extremely faithful adaptation of his 1926 Tony-winning play. Sturges loved the film. The 1951 remake, with Ezio Pinza (Humphrey Bogart almost played the opera singer), bore almost no resemblance to the original and Sturges had nothing to do with it.

The Power and the Glory (1933, U.S., 76 mins., b/w) Dir: William K. Howard; Cast: Spencer Tracy, Colleen Moore, Ralph Morgan, Helen Vinson.
∎
This film about a wealthy industrialist marked a major step for the American cinema. It embodies a serious theme, a realistic voice, storytelling complexity, and rich characterization in a way that no film did before. In structure and subject matter it was a clear forerunner of *Citizen Kane*. While the studio had high hopes for its success, the movie was a box-office failure. The original negative was destroyed in a fire and for years it was considered lost. A recently discovered print has been restored and put in circulation.

We Live Again (1934, U.S., 82 mins., b/w) Dir: Rouben Mamoulian; Cast: Fredric March, Anna Sten, Sam Jaffe, Jane Baxter, C. Aubrey Smith.
∎
Not your typical Preston Sturges picture, this is actually an adaptation of Tolstoy's novel *Resurrection*. MGM hated the first-draft screenplay by Maxwell Anderson, and director Mamoulian prevailed upon Sam Goldwyn to hire Sturges for a rewrite. Thornton Wilder did some touching up. Extremely awkward costume drama, notable principally for the succession of superstar scribblers on the script.

Twentieth Century (1934, U.S., 91 mins., b/w) Dir: Howard Hawks; Cast: John Barrymore, Carole Lombard, Walter Connolly, Roscoe Karns.

One of the all-time great screwball comedies is the story of an egomaniacal producer, a headstrong actress, and a train ride from New York to Chicago. Sturges worked on the first draft but was fired from the project when Columbia boss Harry Cohn decided that he had no real flair for comedy. But Cohn, foolish though he was, lucked out. The script that Ben Hecht and Charles MacArthur eventually wrote from their own play is a model in the genre. Sturges would later use the comic possibilities of train travel to great advantage in *The Lady Eve* and *The Palm Beach Story*.

Diamond Jim (1935, U.S., 100 mins., b/w) Dir: A. Edward Sutherland; Cast: Edward Arnold, Binnie Barnes, Jean Arthur.
∎
Splashy bio of 19th-century railroad magnate Jim Brady. Sturges was originally hired to rewrite a sour script adapted from a best-selling nonfiction book, but wound up throwing it all out and starting from scratch, making most of it up as he went along. Arnold and Arthur are both quite good.

Easy Living (1937, U.S., 90 mins., b/w) Dir: Mitchell Leisen; Cast: Jean Arthur, Edward Arnold, Ray Milland.
∎
Sturges's first important screwball comedy script. Arnold is B. B. Ball, the "Bull of Broad Street," a gruff 'n' tumble millionaire who tosses his spoiled wife's mink out the window only to

have it land on a hardworking secretary (Arthur). Milland is the son who falls in love with her. Very fast and funny but Sturges despised how director Leisen softened the frantic screenplay. Sturges, tired of seeing his material butchered, had a burning desire to direct his own projects.

Remember the Night (1940, U.S., 86 mins., b/w) Dir: Mitchell Leisen; Cast: Fred MacMurray, Barbara Stanwyck, Beulah Bondi.
■
Charming, sentimental romantic comedy about a nice-guy prosecuting attorney (MacMurray) who takes pity on a poor shoplifter (Stanwyck). Rather than let her spend Christmas in jail, he takes her home to meet the family. A lovely film but once again Sturges hated what Leisen did with his material. The director evidently made numerous indiscriminate cuts in the script. Sturges was so incensed that the only thing Paramount could do to appease him was to let him direct his next script himself. The rest, as they say, is history.

WRITERS
■
WRITTEN, BUT NOT DIRECTED, BY BILLY WILDER

From *The Major and the Minor* in 1942 through *Buddy, Buddy* 40 years later, Billy Wilder exercised enormous control over his films. He coauthored the screenplay of every movie he directed and while his two main writing partners, Charles Brackett and I. A. L. Diamond (and one-shots like Raymond Chandler), obviously made creative contributions, they were there primarily because Wilder was an immigrant who never gained a complete command of English. Certain themes run through his work no matter what the genre or who collaborated on the script. That life is a masquerade to Billy Wilder is equally evident in *Five Graves to Cairo* and *Some Like It Hot;* his characters are constantly conning each other by donning disguises or saving their skins by slipping into new ones. He turns sexual convention upside down, tickles and pricks it with his rapierlike wit, his cynical, often savagely funny, vision of human relations working as an antidote to the sanctimony so many other filmmakers force us to swallow. The seeds of this vision—a unified, personal vision that makes him a true auteur—were sown in Berlin (he wrote nearly 200 silent film scenarios, generally without credit, for Germany's UFA studios during the 1920s) and began to blossom during the 1930s in Hollywood. These are the fruits of his early labor, when Wilder concocted the stories or fashioned the dialogue, but somebody else directed.

Emil and the Detectives (*Emil und die Detektive,* 1931, Germany, 73 mins., b/w) Dir: Gerhard Lamprecht; Cast: Rolf Wenkhaus, Fritz Rasp, Kaethe Haack, Olga Engl.
■
One of the few films that Wilder received credit for in Germany, this charming comedy, adapted from a best-selling children's book, tells the story of a kid who gets robbed and enlists his pals to help him pursue the thief. The boys, all avid mystery buffs, get caught up in playing detective, and find ingenious ways to outfox their prey. Unavailable for years, the film has shown up at recent Wilder retrospectives. Remade numerous times, including a Disney version in 1964.

Adorable (1933, U.S., 83 mins., b/w) Dir: William Dieterle; Cast: Janet Gaynor.

Janet Gaynor stars as a Ruritanian princess who poses as a peasant girl and falls in love with a handsome sailor. Wilder gets a story credit on this little linzer torte of a musical based on a German film for which he wrote the original script. The fairy tale premise is a harbinger of plots to come.

Music in the Air (1934, U.S., 85 mins., b/w) Dir: Joe May; Cast: Gloria Swanson, John Boles, Douglass Montgomery, June Lang, Reginald Owen.
•
This adaptation of a rather innocuous Broadway musical boasts a couple of catchy tunes by Jerome Kern and Oscar Hammerstein II as well as Billy Wilder's first American screenwriting credit. The film's dismal showing at the box office was indicative of Swanson's inability to find an audience during the sound era—an interesting sidebar in light of Wilder's use of Dame Gloria two decades later in *Sunset Boulevard*.

Champagne Waltz (1937, U.S., 100 mins., b/w) Dir: A. Edward Sutherland; Cast: Fred MacMurray, Gladys Swarthout.
•
MacMurray is a gum-chewing press agent who takes a group of swing musicians to Vienna where they wind up in a battle of the bands and cultures with the boys from the waltz palace next door. Wilder's script was rewritten a number of times and all that's left of his work in this decidedly second-rate musical schnitzel is the basic story.

Bluebeard's Eighth Wife (1938, U.S., 85 mins., b/w) Dir: Ernst Lubitsch; Cast: David Niven, Gary Cooper, Claudette Colbert.
•
Colbert and Cooper have one of Hollywood's classic "meet cute" scenes—in a men's haberdashery, she wants to purchase a pair of pajama tops and he wants only the bottoms. It's pretty much downhill from there. The film is significant in that it teamed Wilder with Charles Brackett, in what proved to be the beginning of a beautiful writing partnership, and director Ernst Lubitsch, who had more than a passing influence on Wilder's career. But beyond some clever innuendo designed to slip sex jokes past the censor, they all come up empty.

Ninotchka (1939, U.S., 120 mins., b/w) Dir: Ernst Lubitsch; Cast: Greta Garbo, Melvyn Douglas, Bela Lugosi, Ina Claire.

Humorless Russian comradette Garbo comes to Paris, falls for bon vivant Douglas, trades in her Marxist ideology for love, kisses, and French champagne, and swaps the party line for the slogan "Lovers of the world unite!" Brackett and Wilder, completely rewriting what Lubitsch considered an unusable script, deftly juggle romance, politics, and wisecracks, and their sensibility, more than that of the director, shapes the film. The celebrated Lubitsch touch is certainly in evidence, but it plays second fiddle to the Wilder wit. This is the film in which Garbo laughs! She, the picture, the script, and story were all nominated for Oscars.

Midnight (1939, U.S. 94 mins., b/w) Dir: Mitchell Leisen; Cast: Claudette Colbert, Don Ameche, John Barrymore, Mary Astor, Francis Lederer.
•
Brackett and Wilder take the art of fracturing fairy tales to delicious extremes in this Cinderella story of American golddigger Colbert masquerading as a Hungarian countess and crashing Paris society with the help of improbable "fairy godmother" Barrymore. But taxi driver Ameche, her coachman and proletarian Prince Charming rolled into one, points out the real way to happily ever after. Wilder knew he had crafted a gem and fought constantly with Mitchell Leisen over the director's mishandling of what the writer felt was inviolate—the script.

Arise, My Love (1940, U.S., 113 mins., b/w) Dir: Mitchell Leisen; Cast: Clau-

dette Colbert, Ray Milland, Walter Abel, Dennis O'Keefe, Dick Durcell.
■

During the Spanish Civil War flyer-of-fortune Milland, fighting for the Loyalists, kills time between bombing runs by romancing foreign correspondent Colbert (inspired by Hemingway's wife, Martha Gelhorn). Like *Ninotchka*, but with far less wit, the Brackett/Wilder screenplay effectively blends love and politics, openly calling for an end to U.S. isolationism during the early days of WWII. Feud between Wilder and Leisen escalated during filming, with the two men actually coming to blows.

Hold Back the Dawn (1941, U.S., 115 mins., b/w) Dir: Mitchell Leisen; Cast: Charles Boyer, Olivia de Havilland, Paulette Goddard.
■

Brackett and Wilder drastically altered the plot of Ketti Frings's novel in constructing one of their most intricate, innovative screenplays, which begins with the Boyer character arriving at Paramount Studios, where he regales Mitchell Leisen (playing himself) with his "true" story—a *Casablanca*-like tale of romance and intrigue set in Mexico. Eminently watchable film received six Oscar nominations including Best Screenplay and Best Picture, but still Wilder was incensed by the cutting of scenes and alteration of his dialogue. So Billy, like Preston Sturges before him, fed up with Leisen's lack of respect for the script, decided to try his hand at directing.

Ball of Fire (1941, U.S., 111 mins., b/w) Dir: Howard Hawks; Cast: Barbara Stanwyck, Gary Cooper, Oscar Homolka, Henry Travers, S. Z. Sakall.

Brackett and Wilder return to the land of fairy tales, turning Snow White into stripper/lounge singer Sugarpuss O'Shea and the seven dwarfs into a houseful of nutty professors, one of whom happens to be high, wide, and handsome Cooper. Written after Wilder had directed his first feature, he gave the script to Hawks in exchange for a chance to sit at the master's feet and learn about directing—a trade-off that yielded multiple dividends, not the least of which is this peppery, slang-filled screwball classic. A fortuitous collaboration in every respect.

WRITERS
■
WRITTEN, BUT NOT DIRECTED, BY JOHN HUSTON

John Huston's output as a director, generally working from scripts he wrote himself, includes some of the best-loved films of all time. He drove what are arguably Bogie's top three vehicles—*The Maltese Falcon*, *The Treasure of the Sierra Madre*, and *The African Queen*. His style—rough-hewn, full of the spirit of adventure, and charged with a healthy dose of cynicism—is the cinematic equivalent of Hemingway, Hammett, and the hard-boiled writers of the 1930s and 1940s. But his literary tastes were expansive—he filmed adaptations of Melville, Joyce, and Flannery O'Connor. In every movie he made, he reached for something beyond mere entertainment. Considering John Huston's place in the history of the American cinema, we thought it would be fun as well as instructive to look at some contributions he made from behind the typewriter, even when he wasn't behind the camera.

A House Divided (1931, U.S., 70 mins., b/w) Dir: William Wyler; Cast: Walter Huston, Kent Douglass, Helen Chandler, Vivian Oakland, Mary Foy.
■
Clearly inspired by Eugene O'Neill's *Desire Under the Elms*, with the au-

thor's farmer changed to a fisherman—a geezer who gets himself a mail-order bride only to have her fall in love with his son. Huston got his first writing credit for revising (at the behest of his father, who starred) an overly wordy and melodramatic screenplay, paring it down to its bare essentials, making the characters inarticulate. Grandiloquence, he felt, was best left for the stage and writers like Eugene O'Neill.

Law and Order (1932, U.S., 70 mins., b/w) Dir: Edward L. Cahn; Cast: Walter Huston, Harry Carey, Raymond Hatton, Russell Hopton, Ralph Ince, Andy Devine.
▪
Early screen version of the Wyatt Earp legend, with dad Walter as the marshal who cleans up Tombstone. Adapted from a novel by W. R. Burnett, this lean, hard little western, well-directed by the largely forgotten Eddie Cahn, marks Huston's first solo screenwriting effort. Burnett (*Little Caesar*) and Huston would later work together on such landmark gangster films as *High Sierra* and *The Asphalt Jungle*.

High Sierra (1941, U.S., 100 mins., b/w) Dir: Raoul Walsh; Cast: Humphrey Bogart, Ida Lupino, Arthur Kennedy.

Bogart jumped from Warner Bros. second string into the starring line-up with his portrayal of "Mad Dog" Roy Earle, a hardened criminal with a soft underside, an outlaw struggling to "crash out," more a tragic victim than a figure of menace and malignity. W. R. Burnett wrote the novel that he and Huston turned into a screenplay, and the narrative perfectly balances action with human relationships. Walsh's direction is, as always, pictorially rich with no ostentation. Remade as the western *Colorado Territory* and again as *I Died a Thousand Times*. The film was adored by François Truffaut, who paid tribute in *Shoot the Piano Player*.

Murders in the Rue Morgue (1932, U.S., 62 mins., b/w) Dir: Robert Florey; Cast: Bela Lugosi, Sidney Fox.

Huston, one of three writers to work on this adaptation of the Edgar Allan Poe tale of terror, tried to infuse the script with Poe's linguistic style, but much of his dialogue was rewritten on the set by director Robert Florey. The film, exquisitely shot by the great German Expressionist cinematographer Karl Freund, owes a lot more to *The Cabinet of Dr. Caligari* than it does to Poe or John Huston and is quite successful on its own terms. Lugosi's Transylvanian-in-Paris performance is grand.

Jezebel (1938, U.S., 103 mins., b/w) Dir: William Wyler; Cast: Bette Davis, Henry Fonda, Fay Bainter, George Brent, Margaret Lindsay, Richard Cromwell, Donald Crisp, Spring Byington, Henry O'Neill.

Davis grabbed her second Oscar as the vain, tempestuous southern belle who out-scarletts Scarlett O'Hara, flouting convention and losing the man she loves in the process. The original script, hurriedly prepared so Warners could beat MGM's *Gone With the Wind* into theaters, was quite problematic and director William Wyler brought Huston in to fix it. What wound up on screen is a sumptuous, evocative melodrama that is far more literate and profound artistically than its famous counterpart at Metro.

The Amazing Dr. Clitterhouse (1938, U.S., 90 mins., b/w) Dir: Anatole Litvak; Cast: Edward G. Robinson, Claire Trevor, Humphrey Bogart.
▪
Amusing comedy melodrama in which bookish criminologist Robinson joins Bogie's mob in order to get closer to the real deal and finds himself addicted to crime. Huston collaborated with tough-guy screenwriter John (*Angels With Dirty Faces*) Wexley on the extremely clever script.

Juarez (1939, U.S., 132 mins., b/w) Dir: William Dieterle; Cast: Bette Davis, Paul Muni, Brian Aherne, John Garfield, Claude Rains, Donald Crisp, Gale Sondergaard, Joseph Calleia, Gilbert Roland.

Biggest in scope of the old Warners biopics. Script by Huston, Wolfgang Reinhardt, and Scot historian Aeneas MacKenzie chronicles and builds a political dialectic out of the conflict between Mexican revolutionary leader Benito Juarez (Muni)—the founder of the republic—and French puppet Emperor Maximilian. Huston complained that Muni demanded changes that did irreparable harm to the material, but the finished film is beautifully mounted, featuring excellent performances by Davis and Aherne as well as Muni.

Sergeant York (1941, U.S., 134 mins., b/w Dir: Howard Hawks; Cast: Gary Cooper, Walter Brennan, Joan Leslie, George Tobias, Stanley Ridges, Margaret Wycherly, Ward Bond, Noah Beery, Jr., June Lockhart.

True story cum moral-political-spiritual allegory based on the legendary exploits of a God-fearing yokel (Cooper) who gets drafted in spite of his pacifist beliefs, kills or captures half the German army single-handedly, and becomes the most decorated American hero of World War I. Hawks was handed a script that he hated and agreed to do the picture under the condition that the studio bring Huston in to rewrite. Huston gave Hawks exactly what he wanted—the film earned Hawks his only Oscar nomination and he recommended that Huston be given a chance to direct, whereupon the writer turned his attention to *The Maltese Falcon*.

Three Strangers (1946, U.S., 92 mins., b/w) Dir: Jean Negulesco; Cast: Sydney Greenstreet, Geraldine Fitzgerald, Peter Lorre.
■

Three people who don't know each other go partners on a lottery ticket and their fortunes become hopelessly intertwined—one of them may be a killer. Great performances by Greenstreet, Lorre, and Fitzgerald get bogged down by Negulesco's sluggish handling of the material—Huston and Howard *(Casablanca)* Koch's rather bizarre story of destiny, greed, and guilt. At one point Alfred Hitchcock was interested in the project. Too bad he (or Huston himself) didn't direct.

WRITERS
■
BY HECHT

Between 1915 when he did an uncredited rewrite of a D. W. Griffith script and 1967 when he worked on the James Bond spoof *Casino Royale*, Ben Hecht wrote, co-wrote, or made significant contributions to nearly 150 films. Coming to Hollywood from the newsrooms of Chicago, Hecht's way with words and a story had an enormous impact on the transition of movies from the silent era to sound and the evolution of screen language. He was the highest paid, most sought after screenwriter of the 1930s. Here are 11 films on which Ben Hecht received credit for his writing, followed by seven on which he didn't.

Underworld (1927, U.S., 73 mins., b/w) Dir: Josef von Sternberg; Cast: George Bancroft, Evelyn Brent, Clive Brook.

Hecht wrote the Academy Award-winning story and created the characters—with names like Bull Weed, Feathers McCoy, Rolls Royce, and Slippy Lewis—for this silent classic, precursor of the great gangster films of the 1930s. Loosely based on Chicago mobsters Tommy O'Connor and Al Capone, this crisp crime drama is clearly marked by director Sternberg's personal style, and Hecht's sordid, savage underworld is rendered as a shadowy hell of smoking guns, filtered lights, and false illusions.

Scarface: The Shame of the Nation (aka: *The Shame of the Nation*, 1932, U.S., 99 mins.) Dir: Howard Hawks; Cast: Paul Muni, Ann Dvorak, Boris Karloff.

If *Underworld* is the precursor of the Hollywood gangster film, *Scarface* is the prototype. And while the genesis of this Hecht/Howard Hawks masterpiece may be found in the earlier film, Tony Camonte (Muni) is much closer to the real Al Capone, with his family portrayed as Chicago's answer to the Borgias. Brutally violent, filled with strange sexual and religious implications, crackling with Hecht's hard-boiled dialogue, and masterfully realized on screen, it stands as a poetic landmark in cinema history; and besides, it's fun to watch.

Where the Sidewalk Ends (1950, U.S., 95 mins., b/w) Dir: Otto Preminger; Cast: Dana Andrews, Gene Tierney, Gary Merrill, Karl Malden.
■
While *Scarface* and *Underworld* were painted on a broad social canvas, Hecht's later crime dramas turn down and in. The hero here, a cynical cop (Andrews) who beats a suspect to death and falls in love with the dead guy's girlfriend (Tierney), is a morally ambiguous figure, reacting in kind to the dark forces of the violent, indifferent world that made him. The script is Hecht at his hard-boiled best—a prime example of film noir screenwriting.

Kiss of Death (1947, U.S., 98 mins., b/w) Dir: Henry Hathaway; Cast: Victor Mature, Brian Donlevy, Richard Widmark, Mildred Dunnock, Coleen Gray.

Nick Bianco (Mature) is a tough con who knows how to keep his mouth shut but for the sake of his family turns state's evidence in exchange for release from prison. Hecht and co-writer Charles Lederer created in Nick a genuinely tragic noir figure. His nemesis Tommy Udo, brought vividly to life by Widmark, is one of the most famous of all screen villains—a gleeful gargoyle who kills for kicks. The script takes the original tack of having a woman, Nick's wife, provide voiceover narration.

Twentieth Century (1934, U.S., 91 mins., b/w) Dir: Howard Hawks; Cast: John Barrymore, Carole Lombard, Walter Connolly, Roscoe Karns.

Ben Hecht and Charles MacArthur stage play, adapted by the writers and filmed by Howard Hawks, considered the "first" screwball comedy since it was the first time that established dramatic movie stars did their own slapstick instead of assigning it to second bananas. Barrymore as the crazed theatrical producer/director and Lombard as the star he created battle it out on the New York-Chicago express, having a field day with dialogue that moves faster than the train. All aboard!

Design for Living (1933, U.S., 90 mins., b/w) Dir: Ernst Lubitsch; Cast: Gary Cooper, Fredric March, Miriam Hopkins.
■
Best buddies Cooper and March move in with the woman both of them love (Hopkins) . . . who happens to love them both right back. Hecht reworked Noel Coward's scandalous play for Ernst Lubitsch, scrapping practically all of Coward's dialogue (too racy by Hays code standards), replacing it with bits and pieces from other Coward plays and material he wrote himself. Hecht's handiwork, tempered and molded by the Lubitsch touch, makes this madcap ménage à trois into one of the enduring comedies of the period.

Nothing Sacred (1937, U.S., 77 mins., b/w) Dir: William Wellman; Cast: Carole

Lombard, Fredric March, Walter Connolly, Charles Winninger, Sig Ruman, John Qualen, Maxie Rosenbloom, Hattie McDaniel.

Vermont girl (Lombard), apparently dying of a rare disease, is exploited for her human-interest value by New York reporter March. Using a fictional magazine piece called "Letter to the Editor" as a springboard, Hecht built a cynical, scathingly funny attack on tabloid sensationalism, filled it with wisecracks and mixed in just enough romance to give it an emotional hook. That Wellman's direction is uninspired hurts a little . . . but not too much. Remade as *Living It Up* with Martin and Lewis, putting Jerry in the Lombard role.

Gunga Din (1939, U.S., 117 mins., b/w) Dir: George Stevens; Cast: Cary Grant, Douglas Fairbanks, Jr., Victor McLaglen, Sam Jaffe, Eduardo Ciannelli, Montagu Love, Robert Coote, Abner Biberman, Joan Fontaine.

Hecht and MacArthur turn Rudyard Kipling's poem about British imperialism and the white man's burden into one of the most enjoyable adventure yarns ever put on screen. The script, chock-full of clever asides, is closer to the spirit of screwball comedy than to Kipling, but that hardly matters; the characters are marvelously drawn, the action scenes well conceived, the ensemble playing terrific, and Stevens does a fine job in mounting the production. Splendid.

The Scoundrel (1935, U.S., 78 mins., b/w) Dirs: Ben Hecht, Charles MacArthur; Cast: Noel Coward, Stanley Ridges, Julie Haydon, Martha Sleeper, Eduardo Ciannelli, Alexander Woollcott, Lionel Stander.

■
Hecht and MacArthur collaborated on the script as well as direction of this screen adaptation of a play written by Hecht and his wife Rose. The story involves a heartless publisher killed in a plane crash who will be spared from eternal damnation if he can find someone on earth willing to cry for him. Arty, self-conscious, and wonderfully witty in the best Algonquin tradition, this existential screwball film noir stands quite apart from the mainstream.

Angels Over Broadway (1940, U.S., 80 mins., b/w) Dirs: Lee Garmes, Ben Hecht; Cast: Rita Hayworth, Douglas Fairbanks, Jr., Thomas Mitchell, John Qualen.

Fast-talking Fairbanks, hooker Hayworth, and booze-hound Mitchell get stung by do-gooder spirit and attempt to save embezzler Qualen from suicide. While it earns high marks for originality and wit, the whole thing has trouble holding together. Hecht, who wrote, produced, and shared directing chores with his cameraman Lee Garmes, put out a press release slamming Columbia prexy Harry Cohn for butchering the film in the editing room.

Notorious (1946, U.S., 102 mins., b/w) Dir: Alfred Hitchcock; Cast: Ingrid Bergman, Cary Grant, Claude Rains, Louis Calhern, Leopoldine Konstantin.

Bergman is at her most ravishing as the debauched daughter of a convicted German spy, romanced by American agent Grant and talked into seducing her father's old friend (Rains) so she can insinuate herself into a nest of Nazi vipers. A magnificent and complex expression of love, anguish, and redemption that many Hitchcockians regard as the master's finest film of the 1940s. We heartily agree, but must insist that a reasonable share of the credit for the film's greatness belongs to Hecht for his brilliantly crafted screenplay.

■

NOTE: Here are some films on which Ben Hecht worked but received no screen credit.

Monkey Business (1931, U.S., 77 mins., b/w) Dir: Norman McLeod; Cast: Groucho, Harpo, Chico, and Zeppo Marx, Thelma Todd.

First Marx Brothers comedy written directly for the screen (*The Cocoanuts* and *Animal Crackers* came from stage plays) casts the boys as stowaways on a luxury liner. Hecht sketched out the original story; S. J. Perelman wrote the screenplay, which was revised by a couple of other writers and wildly improvised upon by Groucho, Harpo, Chico, and Zeppo.

A Star Is Born (1937, U.S., 110 mins.) Dir: William Wellman; Cast: Fredric March, Janet Gaynor, Andy Devine, Adolphe Menjou, Lionel Stander.

First time around, sans songs, for story of woman (Gaynor) who makes it big in pictures while her husband (March) becomes a has-been. Hecht, hired to polish the script, added much beef to the March role and came up with the spectacular, genuinely disturbing ending. Dorothy Parker then did a major rewrite, but Ben's ideas were kept in the script. Lustrous Hollywood drama, remade twice with tunes.

Angels With Dirty Faces (1938, U.S., 97 mins., b/w) Dir: Michael Curtiz; Cast: James Cagney, Pat O'Brien, Humphrey Bogart, Ann Sheridan, Huntz Hall, Leo Gorcey, Billy Halop.

Curtiz, Cagney, and the Dead End Kids team up in archetypal good-guy/gangster flick, fertile with visual and narrative ideas. Hecht and MacArthur worked (as a favor to a struggling writer friend) on the original story, which was nominated for an Academy Award. John Wexley and Warren Duff wrote the screenplay. Great score by Max Steiner.

Stagecoach (1939, U.S., 100 mins., b/w) Dir: John Ford; Cast: Claire Trevor, John Wayne, Thomas Mitchell, Louise Platt, Andy Devine, John Carradine.

By no means the first, but perhaps the first really great American western, Ford's dusty classic, taken from a story called "Stage to Lordsburg," has been called "a *Grand Hotel* on wheels," with the titular vehicle making the perilous journey west under constant threat of Indian attack. Hecht had substantial input on the adaptation, hardening some of the soft edges by making Ringo (Wayne) a jailbird and Dallas (Claire Trevor) a prostitute. Dudley Nichols gets sole credit for the script.

His Girl Friday (1940, U.S., 92 mins., b/w) Dir: Howard Hawks; Cast: Cary Grant, Rosalind Russell, Ralph Bellamy, Helen Mack, Gene Lockhart.

When Howard Hawks came up with the idea of remaking Hecht and MacArthur's *The Front Page* (filmed first in 1931) with Hildy Johnson as a woman, Hecht's response to the sex change was "I wish we'd thought of that," and he proceeded to help the director restructure the material. Frequent Hecht writing partner Charles Lederer helped rework the dialogue—delivered in tommy-gun bursts by Grant and Russell—and received the only screenwriting credit on the film. So fast, furious, and perfectly put together that the movie improves on the source.

Foreign Correspondent (1940, U.S., 119 mins., b/w) Dir: Alfred Hitchcock; Cast: Joel McCrea, Laraine Day, Herbert Marshall, George Sanders, Albert Basserman.

Hecht adapted the autobiography of journalist Vincent Sheehan, converting it into a Nazi suspense saga set on the eve of World War II, but prior commitments kept him from completing the project. John Howard Lawson, Budd Schulberg, Harold Clurman, Robert Benchley, James Hilton, Charles Bennett, and Joan Harrison worked on the script, the last four receiving credit and an Oscar nomination. No matter who wrote the screenplay, the look, feel, thematic concerns, and style of story-telling are pure Hitchcock.

Roman Holiday (1953, U.S., 119 mins.) Dir: William Wyler; Cast: Gregory Peck, Audrey Hepburn, Eddie Albert.

This enchanting romantic comedy/ fairy tale about a European princess who ducks out on her royal duties and goes incognito in Rome where she falls in love with an American newspaper-man vaulted eternal gamine Hepburn to stardom. By the 1950s Hecht was the best-known script doctor in Hollywood and his surgical skills, deft screwball-comedy touch, and journalistic back-ground are all in evidence in the Oscar-nominated screenplay, credited to Ian McLellan Hunter and John Dighton; Hunter (a front for blacklisted writer Dalton Trumbo) won the Oscar for Best Story.

HOLLYWOOD COMPOSERS

■

The idea of using music as an accom-paniment to film first arose out of the practical need to mask the noise of silent-movie projectors. It wasn't long before clever musicians began match-ing melody to action and inevitably musical scores were commissioned specifically for the movies. With the coming of sound, music became an integral part of the film experience. In the 1930s a new breed of specialist established just how important the art of film scoring was; how, when prop-erly conceived, music not only sup-ported the script and the visuals but often dictated the mood, tone, and rhythm of a film, and more than that, determined how the audience would respond. Men like Max Steiner, Di-mitri Tiomkin, and Bernard Herr-mann came to Hollywood from the

world of the European conservatory and the concert hall, from vaudeville theater pits and Tin Pan Alley. Wher-ever they started, they built their rep-utations in Hollywood. We contend that the appearance of these names in the credits of almost any film indi-cates substantial musical rewards within. Here are some of the best from each.

MAX STEINER

King Kong (1933, U.S., 100 mins., b/w) Dirs: Merian C. Cooper, Ernest B. Schoedsack; Cast: Fay Wray, Bruce Cabot, Robert Armstrong, Noble John-son, Sam Hardy.

That this classic reworking of the beau-ty and the beast legend transcends fairy-tale notions and monster-movie melodramatics and approaches the realm of tragedy (with the big monkey as tragic hero!) is due in no small part to Steiner's music, built on Wagnerian leitmotiv principles. The descending three-note Kong motif creates a feeling of physical enormity as well as a deep sense of impending doom. The score was one of the first in film history to win acclaim on purely musical criteria.

The Informer (1935, U.S., 100 mins., b/w) Dir: John Ford; Cast: Victor McLa-glen, Preston Foster, Heather Angel.

While Ford aficionados are mixed on its merits, this Christian parable about an IRA Judas (McLaglen) in Dublin during the 1922 Sinn Fein rebellion remains one of the director's most honored films. Among its numerous Oscars was Steiner's first. His lush score beautifully complements the fog-drenched visuals and all of the themes have noticeable links with Irish folk song. McLaglen's inner tur-moil is brilliantly expressed in musical terms. All in all, a major step forward in the art of film music.

Angels With Dirty Faces (1938, U.S., 97 mins., b/w) Dir: Michael Curtiz; Cast: James Cagney, Pat O'Brien, Humphrey Bogart, Ann Sheridan, Huntz Hall, Leo Gorcey, Billy Halop.

Archetypal Warners melodrama about two young hoodlums who go different ways; one (O'Brien) becomes a priest, the other (Cagney) a criminal and hero to the new kids in the old neighborhood. Cagney's pugnacious performance and Curtiz's fluid direction are matched by Steiner's musical evocation of tenement life in two different eras and the sanctified spirit of the church in both. The use of music throughout is as brilliantly cinematic as the cutting and the camera movement.

Gone With the Wind (1939, U.S., 219 mins.) Dir: Victor Fleming; Cast: Clark Gable, Vivien Leigh, Leslie Howard, Olivia de Havilland, Hattie McDaniel, Butterfly McQueen, Thomas Mitchell, Ona Munson, Ann Rutherford, Evelyn Keyes, George Reeves, Laura Hope Crews.

One of the most beloved (and most overblown, bloated, and laborious) films of all time, the story of Rhett Butler and Scarlett O'Hara played out against the raging fires of the Civil War, presented Steiner with his most daunting assignment. His score is a full-blown symphonic work containing over three hours of music and 99 separate pieces, weaving patriotic tunes, military marches, regional folk songs, and his own sweeping original melodies into a rich musical tapestry. Tara's theme is unquestionably the most universally recognizable strain of movie music ever written.

The Letter (1940, U.S., 95 mins., b/w) Dir: William Wyler; Cast: Bette Davis, Herbert Marshall, James Stephenson, Gale Sondergaard.

Lurid tale of lust, murder, and courtroom melodramatics set in Singapore features a darkly poetic script by Howard Koch from a play by Somerset Maugham, suitably noirish direction by Wyler, one of Davis's most feverish performances, and an insidiously nerve-jangling score by Steiner, full of torment, sinister intrigue, and the music of tragic passion.

Dodge City (1939, U.S., 105 mins.) Dir: Michael Curtiz; Cast: Errol Flynn, Olivia de Havilland, Ann Sheridan, Bruce Cabot, Alan Hale.

First in a series of large-scale Warner Bros. westerns starring Flynn and de Havilland finds Errol cast as an Irish rogue plunked down in the Wild West, where he brings order to lawless Dodge. In scoring the film, Steiner proved conclusively that a Viennese composer schooled in the romantic tradition could capture the homespun simplicity and visual splendor of the American West. Westerns were not Warners strongest suit but the music is masterful.

Casablanca (1942, U.S., 102 mins., b/w) Dir: Michael Curtiz; Cast: Humphrey Bogart, Ingrid Bergman, Paul Henreid, Conrad Veidt, Claude Rains, Peter Lorre, Dooley Wilson, Sydney Greenstreet, S. Z. Sakall.

First and foremost a love story, the saga of Rick and Ilsa (Bogart and Bergman) grabs and holds from start to finish as it weaves back and forth through an atmospheric web of wartime intrigue. Steiner's dense, impressive score is perfectly in tune with every frame, dramatically quoting music from the body of the film. And while he didn't pen "As Time Goes By," the Tin Pan Alley chestnut played again and again by Sam, he brilliantly expands upon the melody as if to say, in this love story, a kiss is more than just a kiss.

The Treasure of the Sierra Madre (1948, U.S., 124 mins., b/w) Dir: John

Huston; Cast: Humphrey Bogart, Walter Huston, Tim Holt.

John Huston's blistering adaptation of B. Traven's tale of gold and greed in the mountains of Mexico gave Bogart (as Fred C. Dobbs) the most demanding role of his career and Steiner the opportunity to create some of his most memorable music. He works and reworks his magnificent main theme to convey the majesty of the mountains, the complex nature of this avaricious adventure, and Bogart's descent into madness. Huston copped Oscars for writing and directing; his dad, Walter, won as Best Supporting Actor.

The Searchers (1956, U.S., 119 mins.) Dir: John Ford; Cast: John Wayne, Jeffrey Hunter, Natalie Wood, Ward Bond, Vera Miles, John Qualen, Harry Carey, Jr., Olive Carey.

John Ford's glorious western, the story of Wayne and Hunter's five-year search for a young girl kidnapped by Indians, is given tremendous support by Steiner. From its celebrated opening shot through the very last frame, the film's visual and structural unity are amplified by the music. Although the great power of *The Searchers* comes from Ford's personal vision, it is rooted in American myth and history and Steiner utilizes the director's favorite folk themes and hymns (tunes that appear time and again in Ford's work) transforming them into an epic score that perfectly serves the Homeric sweep of the narrative.

HOLLYWOOD
COMPOSERS
■
BERNARD HERRMANN

Citizen Kane (1941, U.S., 119 mins., b/w) Dir: Orson Welles; Cast: Orson Welles, Joseph Cotten, Dorothy Comingore, Ruth Warrick, Everett Sloane, Agnes Moorehead, George Coulouris.

While working with Orson Welles in radio, Bernard Herrmann elevated the use of musical sound effects to an art. When Welles made *Kane* (his first film), he had Herrmann write the music (his first film score). For Susan Kane's disastrous singing debut, he composed a brilliant grand opera pastiche, *Salammbô*. Since Herrmann worked closely with Welles during shooting and editing, sound and music are deeply woven into the film's fabric and *Kane* demands as close a listening as it does a watching.

On Dangerous Ground (1951, U.S., 82 mins., b/w) Dir: Nicholas Ray; Cast: Robert Ryan, Ida Lupino, Ward Bond, Ed Begley.

Messed-up cop (Ryan) hunts down murderous teen and falls for kid's blind sister (Lupino) in this brooding melodrama superbly directed by Ray and scored by Herrmann to spectacular effect. Overture establishes N.Y.C. as treacherous territory, but the unrelenting ferocity of the horns and timpani blasting through the climactic chase across a wilderness landscape musically defines the frozen wasteland as the dangerous ground of the title.

The Day the Earth Stood Still (1951, U.S., 92 mins., b/w) Dir: Robert Wise; Cast: Patricia Neal, Michael Rennie, Hugh Marlowe, Sam Jaffe.

Michael Rennie is a humanistic, humanoid extra-terrestrial who lands in Washington, D.C., with an anti-nuclear warning. Literate, liberal, landmark sci-fi message pic gets modernistic treatment from Herrmann, trading in a traditional orchestra for an odd assortment of electronic instruments, creating a weightless otherworldly mass of sound.

Jason and the Argonauts (1963, Great Britain, 104 mins.) Dir: Don Chaffey; Cast: Todd Armstrong, Nancy Kovack, Gary Raymond.

Saturday matinee fave featuring special effects wizardry of Ray Harryhausen takes us on the mythological quest of Jason and his handpicked crew of hunky sailors in hot pursuit of the golden fleece. Harryhausen's process, called "dynamation," finds its aural equivalent in Herrmann's dynamic score, a fantastic musical voyage in its own right.

It's Alive (1974, U.S., 90 mins.) Dir: Larry Cohen; Cast: John P. Ryan, Sharon Farrell, Andrew Duggan, Guy Stockwell, Michael Ansara.

Schlockmeister/auteur Cohen actually takes the idea of a monstrous killer baby and transforms it into a poignant examination of fatherhood and family devotion. Bloodcurdling horror film that manages to be simultaneously silly and profound owes goodly percentage of its weight to Herrmann's score, a lilting lullaby wrapped in a screaming symphony of mutant terror.

North by Northwest (1959, U.S., 136 mins.) Dir: Alfred Hitchcock; Cast: Cary Grant, Eva Marie Saint, James Mason, Martin Landau, Leo G. Carroll.

Bernard Herrmann's work with Alfred Hitchcock on six films stands as a monument to artistic collaboration. This particular score, a kaleidoscopic fandango accompaniment to Cary Grant's plunge into the hair-raising adventure that takes him from New York to Mount Rushmore, is Herrmann's most energetic and most fun.

Vertigo (1958, U.S., 128 mins.) Dir: Alfred Hitchcock; Cast: Kim Novak, James Stewart, Tom Helmore, Barbara Bel Geddes, Ellen Corby, Raymond Bailey, Lee Patrick, Henry Jones.

One of the cinema's most profoundly beautiful films, Hitchcock's masterpiece about an ex-cop (Stewart) with a fear of falling who tumbles for the woman he's hired to follow (Novak) is a meditation on love and death. Since much of the film unfolds without dialogue, the music is of paramount importance. Herrmann's sublime vertiginous orchestral requiem blends harmoniously with the characters, color, and camera movement to help create a near perfect organism.

Psycho (1960, U.S., 109 mins., b/w) Dir: Alfred Hitchcock; Cast: Anthony Perkins, Janet Leigh, Simon Oakland, John Anderson, Vera Miles, Martin Balsam, John Gavin, John McIntire.

Bernard Herrmann's collaboration with Hitch reaches its apex here with some of the most violent, insistent, nightmarish music ever written. Using only strings, Herrmann penetrates every dramatic, emotional, and visual crevice of the film—the story of a woman (Leigh) who runs off with $40,000, stops at a creepy motel, and takes the most famous shower in movie history. If you have any doubts at all as to how important film music is, watch the shower scene without the sound.

Cape Fear (1991, U.S., 128 mins.) Dir: Martin Scorsese; Cast: Robert De Niro, Nick Nolte, Jessica Lange, Juliette Lewis, Joe Don Baker, Robert Mitchum, Gregory Peck.

Scorsese/De Niro remake of 1962 vengeance-is-mine-sayeth-the-psycho suspense shocker takes OK material, twists and tattoos it, sucks on it, and spits it out. Every character is reworked and deepened. Kept intact is Bernard Herrmann's score (reorchestrated by Elmer Bernstein) from the original, which bears more than a passing resemblance to his work for *Psycho* made the year before. The depth and darkness Scorsese wanted were already in the music.

Taxi Driver (1976, U.S., 112 mins.) Dir: Martin Scorsese; Cast: Robert De Niro, Cybill Shepherd, Jodie Foster, Peter Boyle, Albert Brooks, Leonard Harris.

Cabbie Travis Bickle (De Niro's most riveting role) describes the New York netherworld in which he plies his trade as "sick" and "venal," but Scorsese's savage vision of the city that never sleeps is tempered by sympathy (affection even) for his character and his environment. Herrmann's beautiful jazz-inflected score (his last), built around a sensuous melody for alto-sax, captures the many layers on which the film works, countering some of the harshest imagery with the most tender music imaginable.

HOLLYWOOD COMPOSERS
■
DIMITRI TIOMKIN

Lost Horizon (1937, U.S., 132 mins., b/w) Dir: Frank Capra; Cast: Ronald Colman, Sam Jaffe, Jane Wyatt, H. B. Warner, Edward Everett Horton, Margo, Thomas Mitchell, Isabel Jewell, John Howard.

Adaptation of James Hilton novel about five plane-crash survivors who stumble into the earthly paradise of Shangri-La. In making the film, director Capra's biggest worry was the musical scoring. Would Dimitri Tiomkin—a Russian-born pianist who'd never scored a film—capture the mystical mood of the story? Capra later wrote, "His music not only captured the mood, it darned near captured the film," and Tiomkin became one of the most sought-after composers in Hollywood.

Angel Face (1952, U.S., 90 mins., b/w) Dir: Otto Preminger; Cast: Jean Simmons, Robert Mitchum, Herbert Marshall.
■
Preminger is at his most bleak and oblique in this top-notch noir about lower-class ambulance driver Mitchum and his fatal attraction for upper-crust nut-job Simmons. While much of the film is understated, Tiomkin's music is charged with a neurotic electricity— the scoring of the ambulance ride at the beginning has a delirious, almost balletic quality, setting up the deadly pas de deux played out by the protagonists.

I Confess (1953, U.S., 95 mins., b/w) Dir: Alfred Hitchcock; Cast: Montgomery Clift, Anne Baxter, Karl Malden.

Story of a priest (Clift) who hears the confession of a killer and then finds himself falsely accused of the crime is the most overtly Catholic of Hitchcock's films. Tiomkin's haunting, fatalistic music lyrically sustains the fundamental moral dilemma of the protagonist, ultimately attaining a genuinely spiritual majesty. Of all the scores Tiomkin composed for Hitch (he also did *Shadow of a Doubt, Strangers on a Train,* and *Dial M for Murder*) this is the strongest.

Duel in the Sun (1946, U.S., 138 mins.) Dir: King Vidor; Cast: Jennifer Jones, Gregory Peck, Joseph Cotten, Lionel Barrymore, Walter Huston, Lillian Gish.

Massive, sprawling, colorful western about fiery half-breed Jones and her torrid romance with cattle-rancher Peck is as sensual as it is stupid; it's overwrought but it's wonderfully overwrought. Producer David Selznick's western *Gone With the Wind* has been called a "Wagnerian horse opera," and Tiomkin's daring operatic score, a sort of sagebrush *Tristan und Isolde,* is saturated with a passionate mystical eroticism that contributes mightily to the film's emotional impact. See it in a theater if you can.

Red River (1948, U.S., 133 mins., b/w) Dir: Howard Hawks; Cast: John Wayne, Montgomery Clift, Walter Brennan, Joanne Dru, John Ireland, Noah Beery, Jr., Coleen Gray, Paul Fix, Harry Carey, Sr., Harry Carey, Jr.

Powerful tale of the first cattle drive up the Chisholm Trail and the personal struggle between tyrannical Tom Dunson (Wayne) and his adopted son (Clift) is director Howard Hawks's favorite of all his westerns. Tiomkin's exhilarating and expansive score, as big and wide as the western sky, rides herd on the thundering longhorns along with the cowhands, capturing all the grit and determination of the epic journey and emotional resonance of the human conflict.

High Noon (1952, U.S., 85 mins., b/w) Dir: Fred Zinnemann; Cast: Gary Cooper, Grace Kelly, Lloyd Bridges.

It's Cooper's wedding day and the bad guy arriving on the noon train has sworn to gun him down. Innovative script unfolds in "real time" and Tiomkin's musical concept is just as bold. Dispensing with the usual western bigness, entire score is built on simple Tiomkin/Ned Washington ballad "Do Not Forsake Me, Oh My Darlin'," sung by Tex Ritter (Frankie Laine had the hit record). Trend-setting but self-important western is generally overrated; not so Tiomkin's score. Worth watching for the music alone.

The Alamo (1960, U.S., 192 mins., b/w) Dir: John Wayne; Cast: John Wayne, Richard Widmark, Laurence Harvey, Chill Wills, Richard Boone, Carlos Arruza, Frankie Avalon, Patrick Wayne, Linda Cristal.

Wayne does triple duty as producer, director, and Davy Crockett in this saga of the famed Texas standoff that sometimes seems as long as the siege itself. Don't let this prevent you from reaping the pleasures of the score. Tiomkin composed magnificent music for a host of westerns, and this (believe it or not) is his best, most vibrant work in the genre. Spectacular battle climax of both film and score is well worth waiting for.

The High and the Mighty (1954, U.S., 147 mins.) Dir: William Wellman; Cast: John Wayne, Claire Trevor, Robert Stack, Jan Sterling, Laraine Day, David Brian.
▪
Tiomkin was nominated for 24 Academy Awards, winning four times. The hilarious speech he made when he won (his third) for this score, thanking Brahms, Strauss, Wagner, Beethoven, and Rimsky-Korsakov is one of the most famous in Oscar history. The film, progenitor of all the high-flying disaster movies parodied hilariously in *Airplane!,* is actually a grand entertainment and we guarantee you'll be whistling the title theme for days.

The Guns of Navarone (1961, U.S., 159 mins.) Dir: J. Lee Thompson; Cast: Gregory Peck, David Niven, Anthony Quinn, Anthony Quayle, Irene Papas, James Darren, Gia Scala, Stanley Baker, Richard Harris.

Rip-roaring action yarn from book by Alistair MacLean about Allied commando mission to destroy heavy German artillery fortress in the Aegean during World War II uses its big budget to tremendous effect. The excitement, suspense, and pyrotechnics, as well as the breathtaking beauty of the settings, are incomparably enhanced by Tiomkin's rousing score, a splendid blend of martial themes and the lyrical folk rhythms of the Greek Islands.

36 Hours (1964, U.S., 115 mins.) Dir: George Seaton; Cast: James Garner, Rod Taylor, Eva Marie Saint.
▪
American officer (Garner), nabbed by Nazis just before D-Day, is doped up and tricked into thinking the war is over so he'll give away invasion plans. Absorbing, original intrigue from twisty Roald Dahl story works great until Garner figures out the plot; the rest is conventional. The lean, clean, piano-driven score by Tiomkin is anything but, indicating that even near the

end of his career, this extraordinary artist found new ways to stretch.

CREDIT WHERE CREDIT IS DUE

Ben Hecht wasn't the only creative force in Hollywood to render his services and receive no credit. It was, and is, a common practice. Over the years countless films, some attributed to the most famous names in the business, have been touched and retouched by other hands. A script is in trouble, the producer brings in a rewrite man. The action scenes are great but the love scenes need work, bring in a romantic specialist. The story is aces but the jokes don't cut it, bring in a gag man. Even once a film begins shooting, if the director is floundering on the set, he gets fired or gets help quick. Often guild regulations determine who gets credit and who doesn't for their work on a film. Sometimes it's stipulated in a contract. For whatever reason, the audience is often left in the dark. Here are some major films in which uncredited fingers have fiddled and diddled.

Three Comrades (1938, U.S., 98 mins., b/w) Dir: Frank Borzage; Cast: Robert Taylor, Robert Young, Margaret Sullavan, Franchot Tone, Lionel Atwill.

Taylor, Tone, and Young are the buddy-boy trio—three friends in Germany between WWI and the rise of the Third Reich—all in love with tubercular Sullavan. Erich Maria Remarque's novel was adapted by F. Scott Fitzgerald and he shares the writing credit with Edward Paramore, but Joe Mankiewicz completely overhauled the script. A moving but politically muddled tearjerker that can't quite make up its mind if it's attacking Nazism or Communism, it's nonetheless a beautifully made film, diving much deeper than the surface of suds—thanks more to director Borzage than either Fitzgerald or Mankiewicz.

Casablanca (1942, U.S., 102 mins., b/w) Dir: Michael Curtiz; Cast: Humphrey Bogart, Ingrid Bergman, Paul Henreid, Conrad Veidt, Claude Rains, Peter Lorre, Dooley Wilson, Sydney Greenstreet, S. Z. Sakall.

Volumes have been written around all that went into the making of this all-time classic romantic intrigue—we know who the usual suspects are, we're just not quite sure who did what. One of the more interesting claims is by writer Casey Robinson (*Dark Victory; Now, Voyager*), who asserts that he discovered the original unproduced play on which the movie is based and that he developed and wrote the Rick/Ilsa love story at Bogie's request, refusing a credit because he would not put his name on screen with another writer—a decision he lived to regret.

Gun Crazy (1949, U.S., 86 mins., b/w) Dir: Joseph H. Lewis; Cast: Peggy Cummins, John Dall, Morris Carnovsky.

Joseph H. Lewis's B-movie masterpiece, about a couple of hot-blooded kids whose passion is fueled by their mutual love of side arms, is based on a story by MacKinlay Kantor who gets credit for the screenplay along with Millard Kaufman—both names serving as a front for blacklisted Dalton Trumbo, who actually wrote the script.

Bonnie and Clyde (1967, U.S., 111 mins.) Dir: Arthur Penn; Cast: Warren Beatty, Faye Dunaway, Estelle Parsons, Gene Hackman, Michael J. Pollard.

The original script called for Bonnie to be romantically and sexually involved with W.D. (Pollard) as well as Clyde (Beatty) but Warren, Penn, and the studio wanted it changed. Robert Towne was called in, and he did extensive revisions, changing the structure, writing new scenes and lines of dialogue, working on the set during filming, but receiving no credit for his participation. It established his reputation as the pre-eminent script doctor in Hollywood before he gained public recognition with his own scripts for *Chinatown* and *Shampoo*.

The Godfather (1972, U.S., 175 mins.) Dir: Francis Ford Coppola; Cast: Marlon Brando, Al Pacino, James Caan, Sterling Hayden, Robert Duvall, Diane Keaton, John Cazale, Talia Shire, John Marley, Richard Conte.

When Coppola ran into trouble during filming he brought in Bob Towne, much in the way a baseball manager turns to an ace reliever in the late innings. The writer came up with a key scene in which Don Corleone, realizing he's close to death, passes the Godfather mantle to son Michael (Pacino). It's a beautifully crafted exchange that resolves the most important relationship in the film and Coppola acknowledged Towne's contribution during his Academy Award acceptance speech. Credit the writer with a save.

The Stranger (1946, U.S., 95 mins., b/w) Dir: Orson Welles; Cast: Edward G. Robinson, Orson Welles, Loretta Young.

Welles's most commercial studio project—the story of an escaped Nazi war criminal living in Connecticut teaching school and fixing clocks while he waits for the Reich to rise again—has always been underrated by critics because of its straightforward narrative style. The first draft of the script was written by Anthony Veiller and he gets sole screen credit, but Welles and John Huston completely rewrote it before shooting began.

He Walked by Night (1948, U.S., 79 mins., b/w) Dir: Alfred L. Werker; Cast: Richard Basehart, Scott Brady, Jack Webb.

Director Alfred Werker's career began during the early days of silent film and extends all the way into the 1950s, but nothing else he ever did approaches the rich visual textures and psychological intensity of this underappreciated film noir classic—possibly because the great Anthony Mann directed the film's most interesting sequences after Werker was taken off the project.

The Alamo (1960, U.S., 192 mins.) Dir: John Wayne; Cast: John Wayne, Richard Widmark, Laurence Harvey, Chill Wills, Richard Boone, Carlos Arruza, Frankie Avalon, Patrick Wayne, Linda Cristal.

The climactic battle scene in this historical epic about the heroic defense of the little Texas fort by Davy Crockett and company is just too good for a big lug like The Duke (whose only other directorial credit is *The Green Berets*) to have skippered himself. We're inclined to believe the rumors that Wayne's pal and mentor "Pappy" (otherwise known as John Ford) took the helm for the action sequences.

Macao (1952, U.S., 80 mins., b/w) Dir: Josef von Sternberg; Cast: Robert Mitchum, Jane Russell, William Bendix, Brad Dexter, Gloria Grahame.

Josef (*The Blue Angel, Morocco*) von Sternberg's heart clearly wasn't in this bit of foreign intrigue and he never got to finish the film. Nicholas Ray stepped in during production, though his name is not in the credits. A rare example of two darlings of auteurist critics having significant input on the same project.

Tootsie (1982, U.S., 110 mins.) Dir: Sydney Pollack; Cast: Dustin Hoffman, Teri Garr, Jessica Lange, Sydney Pollack, Bill Murray.

The first draft of this script about struggling actor Hoffman pretending to be a woman in order to get a part was written by relative unknown Don

McGuire (who wound up with story credit). The principal rewrites were done by Murray Schisgal and Larry Gelbart, who shared the screenplay credit. But numerous other writers worked on the project: Elaine May, for example, created the character played by Bill Murray (Hoffman's roommate), who has some of the cleverest dialogue and richest moments in the film.

The Last Action Hero (1993, U.S., 130 mins.) Dir: John McTiernan; Cast: Arnold Schwarzenegger, F. Murray Abraham, Art Carney, Charles Dance, Frank McRae, Tom Noonan, Robert Prosky, Anthony Quinn, Mercedes Ruehl, Ian McKellen, Tina Turner, Joan Plowright.

Neophyte scenarists Zak Penn and Adam Leff (credited with the story) wrote the original high-concept script in which an 11-year-old kid takes a magic-ticket ride into a movie starring his, and everyone's, favorite human superman, Arnold Schwarzenegger. The script was rewritten by Shane Black and David Arnott (credited with the screenplay), but a number of other writers made significant contributions, most notably William Goldman (*Butch Cassidy, All the President's Men*), who added flesh and heart to Arnold's character. When you see the finished product you'll understand why Goldman insisted on not getting any credit, even though he wrote a substantial portion of the film.

CUTTING ROOM FLOOR

HOLLYWOOD WOMEN (AND THEIR MEN): BEFORE THE CODE

These are the pre-screwball films—if you accept the screwball definition that all the high-rolling glitz and glam and innuendo are covers for SEX SEX SEX. So here they are telling it (and showing it—well, almost) like it was—at home, at work, in bed—before the Legion of Decency and Will Hays got their censoring paws on this still wide-open new medium.

Madam Satan (1930, U.S., 105 mins., b/w) Dir: Cecil B. DeMille; Cast: Kay Johnson, Reginald Denny, Lillian Roth, Roland Young.

Totally ridiculous, though DeMille comes through with that fabulous dress-ball-in-a-blimp scene. This one looks dated in a silent-film kind of way, but it is notable for its straightforward approach to adultery, though taken from the standard male point of view. The wifey seductress-to-win-him-back shenanigans are more notable for their hothouse costuming than for any sign of female independence.

Skyscraper Souls (1932, U.S., 80 mins., b/w) Dir: Edgar Selwyn; Cast: Warren William, Maureen O'Sullivan, Gregory Ratoff, Anita Page, Jean Hersholt, Wallace Ford, Hedda Hopper.

Building a skyscraper monument to himself, the letch at the top (William) shows us his priorities as he toys with his women and the stock market with equal charm and deceit. Interesting how those female execs abound (and how William's wife is also given uncensored room to adulter herself), but still it's clear the big boys are in charge. Well-developed plot about power, money, and modern architecture during the Depression. Good stuff.

Female (1933, U.S., 60 mins., b/w) Dir: Michael Curtiz; Cast: Ruth Chatterton, George Brent, Ferdinand Gottschalk, Philip Faversham, Ruth Donnelly, Johnny Mack Brown, Lois Wilson, Gavin Gordon.

A table-turner with ruthless car-factory boss Chatterton using her adorable hunky factory workers, then discarding them in boredom. No mere figurehead, she fights hard to save the company—even to the extreme of giving up the one "real" man who can't be bought. The portrayal of her ultimate change of heart is more than a little limp but the ride is unusual—for then and now. And Brent's sensitive-but-strong guy is also a nice surprise.

Possessed (1931, U.S., 72 mins., b/w) Dir: Clarence Brown; Cast: Clark Gable, Joan Crawford, Wallace Ford, Skeets Gallagher.

Crawford, clearly in it for the money, leaves small town and suitor to make it in the big city. She tangles with politico Gable and we have one of the firsts of filmland—she's clear-sighted and not manipulative. Another difference here is he's not married—and doesn't want to be, but she can still bring down his career. They're both tough cookies with hearts, and swell to watch.

Baby Face (1933, U.S., 70 mins., b/w) Dir: Alfred E. Green; Cast: Barbara Stanwyck, George Brent, Donald Cook, Douglass Dumbrille, Margaret Lindsay.

Stanwyck's plan is to get out of her steel-mill town and work her way up the ladder—or sleep her way to the top, whichever comes first. Her Lily Powers,

obviously a girl with major smarts, makes fast progress till lover-cum-bank-pres Brent faces ruin and it's soul-searching time.

She Done Him Wrong (1933, U.S., 66 mins., b/w) Dir: Lowell Sherman; Cast: Mae West, Cary Grant, Gilbert Roland.

C'mon up and see Mae at her bawdy best. She's tough, she's sharp, and she knows what she wants and how to get it, giving new meaning to the use of feminine wiles. You know she's never been anyone's fool; she didn't have to sleep her way to the top—she was already there. Oh, yeah, this is the one with that line . . . and Cary.

Ex-Lady (1933, U.S., 65 mins., b/w) Dir: Robert Florey; Cast: Bette Davis, Gene Raymond, Frank McHugh.

Bette's first above the title. Here's one of the early career women but, unlike post-code, the film doesn't shy away from sharing her domestic life as well, as successful *Cosmo* magazine cover illustrator resists pressure from her live-in boyfriend to tie the knot.

Red-Headed Woman (1932, U.S., 74 mins., b/w) Dir: Jack Conway; Cast: Jean Harlow, Chester Morris, Charles Boyer, Lewis Stone.

You may not agree with Harlow's m.o. of sleeping her way to the top, and while she doesn't get our sympathy, the sexpot homewrecker manages to do it and make it clear she's no fool either. Anita Loos's screenplay doesn't quite make up for a whiny Harlow, but a few elegant little twists keep this interesting.

Bombshell (aka: *Blonde Bombshell*, 1933, U.S., 90 mins., b/w) Dir: Victor Fleming; Cast: Jean Harlow, Lee Tracy, Franchot Tone, Frank Morgan, Pat O'Brien.

Here she is again, and she's nobody's fool. Tracy is distinctive as a PR man with all the angles. It takes a hot Harlow as megastar Lola Burns, helped with some sizzling fast dialogue, snappy sets, and a sharp look at thirties Hollywood, to get him to see beyond his own hype.

Our Modern Maidens (1929, U.S., 70 mins., silent, b/w) Dir: Jack Conway; Cast: Joan Crawford, Rod La Rocque, Douglas Fairbanks, Jr., Anita Page.

Sort of an Ivy League Plato's Retreat melodrama. Crawford does well as the friend who forfeits her hold on her lover when she recognizes he has a chance at true love with the object of his indiscretion.

Blonde Venus (1932, U.S., 97 mins., b/w) Dir: Josef von Sternberg; Cast: Marlene Dietrich, Cary Grant, Herbert Marshall.

Successful performer gives up career for traditional husband and motherhood, until life throws in one of its proverbial monkey wrenches. Once you get past dealing with Dietrich as the perfect mom and wifey, you've got major melodrama here. Terminal illness, rampant chauvinism, high glamour, destitution, adultery, N.Y.!, Paris!, somehow all that matters is that luminous Dietrich. By the way, this is the one in which she sings "Hot Voodoo" in a chimp suit, and offers us her unique brand of glittering androgyny in that white tux.

ENABLING KANE

What can we say about *Citizen Kane* that hasn't been said before? No film in the history of the cinema has been written about as comprehensively. Whole books are devoted to it, articles exploring its themes and techniques appear regularly in film magazines. College professors wax academic about its significance. In 1962, a survey of international film critics voted *Citizen Kane* as the greatest movie ever made. François Truffaut called it "the film of films." What follows is a list of movies that were precursors, influences, and stepping-stones to the making of *Kane.* These are the films (some obvious, some not so obvious) that paved the way for Orson Welles's audacious narrative style, the visual pyrotechnics he crafted with cinematographer Gregg Toland, and the stunning screenplay he co-wrote with Herman Mankiewicz.

The Power and the Glory (1933, U.S., 76 mins., b/w) Dir: William K. Howard; Cast: Spencer Tracy, Colleen Moore, Ralph Morgan, Helen Vinson.

Made eight years before *Kane*—and seven years before the remarkable Preston Sturges (who wrote the script) would direct his own first film—*The Power and the Glory* looks at an American dream that turns into a nightmare; it's about wealth and happiness as the prelude to tragedy. Its structure is strikingly similar to that of *Citizen Kane*. Written first as a play, this story of a callous industrialist (Tracy) begins with his funeral and flashes back to various vignettes of his life. Tracy is superb as this Depression-era victim of fate's fickle finger.

Mad Love (1935, U.S., 70 mins., b/w) Dir: Karl Freund; Cast: Peter Lorre, Frances Drake, Colin Clive.

Reworking of the classic horror story "The Hands of Orlac" casts Lorre as a doctor who operates on the mutilated hands of a famous pianist whose wife he is madly in love with. *Kane* and *Mad Love* share Expressionist roots (director Freund was one of the great German Expressionist cameramen), cinematographer (Toland), plot elements (obsessive love), makeup (Lorre's mad doctor bears an uncanny resemblance to the aging Kane), setting (Lorre's domain looks a lot like Xanadu), and a screeching white cockatoo. Enough in common to make this moody melodrama worth a serious look.

Stagecoach (1939, U.S., 100 mins., b/w) Dir: John Ford; Cast: Claire Trevor, John Wayne, Thomas Mitchell, Louise Platt, Andy Devine, John Carradine.

"Now, what on earth could this classic John Ford/John Wayne western have in common with *Citizen Kane*?" you might ask. Well, it so happens, when Welles first went out to Hollywood this is the movie he screened over and over for inspiration. Take a look at *Stagecoach* and you'll see that along with its breathtaking western vistas there's a surprisingly stylized, broodingly theatrical use of interiors. It's one of the first Hollywood films to utilize ceilings in its scenic design, a technique that Welles elaborated upon with great success.

The Long Voyage Home (1940, U.S., 105 mins., b/w) Dir: John Ford; Cast: John Wayne, Thomas Mitchell, Barry Fitzgerald, Mildred Natwick.

A saga of men at sea, this is a tribute to Britain in its darkest hour against the Nazi hordes. Also directed by John Ford, this adaptation of four one-act plays by Eugene O'Neill is moody, shadowy, and romantically fatalistic— its deep, dark look is much more directly related to *Citizen Kane* than *Stagecoach*. And who was the cinematographer? Gregg Toland. Particularly poetic, stunning visually.

The Cabinet of Dr. Caligari (1919, Germany, 69 mins., silent, b/w) Dir: Robert Wiene; Cast: Werner Krauss, Conrad Veidt, Lil Dagover, Friedrich Feher.

Silent German Expressionist masterpiece. This is the other film that Welles said he watched repeatedly before making *Kane*. With its highly stylized sets and acting, it's one of the first great works of cinema. The idea of film as Art with a capital "A" obviously appealed to Welles. A must-see for anyone remotely interested in the history of the medium.

The Rules of the Game (1939, France, 110 mins., b/w) Dir: Jean Renoir; Cast: Marcel Dalio, Nora Gregor, Roland Toutain, Gaston Modet, Julien Carette, Jean Renoir.

Almost always included on the lists of the greatest films of all time. While *Citizen Kane* is often given credit for inventing deep-focus photography (a visual style that has background and foreground in focus at the same time), Renoir employed the technique here two years earlier. The film is also about the lifestyles of the rich and famous, but much different in tone from *Kane*. A social-realist comic masterpiece.

A Night at the Opera (1935, U.S., 90 mins., b/w) Dir: Sam Wood; Cast: Groucho, Chico, and Harpo Marx, Kitty Carlisle, Allan Jones, Margaret Dumont.

Oh really? In the same breath as *Citizen Kane?* What could they possibly have in common? Fact is, Herman Mankiewicz was one of the original writers . . . until he was thrown off the project by Irving Thalberg. And don't forget, the send-up of opera in *Citizen Kane* is wicked and very, very funny. Just another link in the chain.

John Meade's Woman (1937, U.S., 87 mins., b/w) Dir: Richard Wallace; Cast: Edward Arnold, Francine Larrimore, Gail Patrick, George Bancroft, Sidney Blackmer.
■
A veritable study for his later, much greater work, this story of a tycoon who suffers personal isolation and loneliness in the pursuit of power and money was written by Herman Mankiewicz. A mediocre movie on its own, but a very interesting glimpse into the social and political leanings of the man who

wrote, at the very least, half of *Citizen Kane*.

The Front Page (1931, U.S., 101 mins., b/w) Dir: Lewis Milestone; Cast: Pat O'Brien, Adolphe Menjou, Frank McHugh, Edward Everett Horton, Mary Brian.

First and most faithful film adaptation of stage stalwart about life in the newspaper game. Written by Ben Hecht and Charles MacArthur, it was a definite influence on Mankiewicz. Hecht and Mankiewicz were friends. The character of Walter Burns is based on Walter Howey, city editor of the *Chicago Tribune* until William Randolph Hearst lured him away by offering him more money. This real-life event, though not used in *The Front Page,* shows up in *Kane,* a thinly veiled film à clef about Hearst. Both *Citizen Kane* and *The Front Page* share a similar cynicism regarding the fourth estate.

■

NOTE: If *Citizen Kane* borrowed a bit from all of the above films, that's nothing compared to the films that borrowed from it. Here are a few you might not have thought of.

Caught (1949, U.S., 88 mins., b/w) Dir: Max Ophuls; Cast: James Mason, Barbara Bel Geddes, Robert Ryan.

The masterful Max Ophuls takes this rather soap-operaish story of a dress-shop model who marries a millionaire, and turns it into something quite compelling. Ryan's powerful, obsessive tycoon is a sort of film noir variation on Welles's Charles Foster Kane. The script is by Arthur Laurents (he wrote *Gypsy*). The camera movement alone makes the film well worth watching.

Lenny (1974, U.S., 111 mins., b/w) Dir: Bob Fosse; Cast: Dustin Hoffman, Valerie Perrine, Jan Miner.

Julian Barry adapted his Broadway play for the screen, but Fosse hangs this Lenny Bruce bio on a *Kane*-like hook. After Lenny's death, a journalist interviews the people who knew him best. The story is told, in flashbacks, through their eyes. Sound familiar? A terrific performance by Hoffman as the foul-mouthed comic is matched by Valerie Perrine in the Oscar-nominated role of his wife. The stark documentary-like b&w cinematography by Bruce Surtees is an added treat.

Eddie and the Cruisers (1983, U.S., 92 mins.) Dir: Martin Davidson; Cast: Tom Berenger, Ellen Barkin, Michael Pare.

Surprisingly entertaining rock 'n' roll rip-off of *Citizen Kane*. Barkin is a TV journalist piecing together a documentary about a dead rock star by interviewing the members of his band. There's even a mystery revolving around missing tapes that gives the story its very own rock 'n' roll Rosebud. The Springsteen-like score by John Cafferty and the Beaver Brown Band spawned a very successful soundtrack album and a couple of hit records.

HOWARD HUGHES

Was he a billionaire lunatic or crazy like a fox? A genius ahead of his time or a nasty manipulative so and so? All we do know for sure is that Ted Turner's role model had a finger in every pot and, hopefully for Jane, Ted won't end up the same way and refuse to touch her without a tissue at hand.

Tucker: The Man and His Dream (1988, U.S., 110 mins.) Dir: Francis Ford Coppola; Cast: Jeff Bridges, Joan Allen, Martin Landau, Frederic Forrest, Mako, Dean Stockwell, Lloyd Bridges.

Dean Stockwell's few scenes as Hughes are some of the best in a movie with lots of great scenes. Visionary automaker Tucker meets Hughes for help in launching his new car and gets to meet an enormous, looming Spruce Goose, too. A perfect little cameo that adds richness to a fine film.

Caught (1949, U.S., 88 mins., b/w) Dir: Max Ophuls; Cast: James Mason, Barbara Bel Geddes, Robert Ryan.

Robert Ryan plays a decidedly evil magnate based on Hughes in this Ophuls melodrama about a young woman who finds herself caught in a loveless marriage to a millionaire. Out of all the film Hugheses, Ryan best captures his look and his slightly scary unpredictability.

The Carpetbaggers (1964, U.S., 150 mins.) Dir: Edward Dmytryk; Cast: George Peppard, Alan Ladd, Carroll Baker, Bob Cummings, Martha Hyer, Elizabeth Ashley.

Peppard dons the goggles in this adaptation of Harold Robbins's overblown novel about Hughes and his forays into Hollywood. Peppard is no Robert Ryan, but the movie is what it is—big, mindless entertainment that's pretty sanitary considering what you see nowadays.

Hell's Angels (1930, U.S., 135 mins., b/w) Dir: Howard Hughes; Cast: Ben Lyon, Jean Harlow, James Hall, John Darrow.

The proof that Hughes was a success at almost everything he tried is right here in this World War I flying epic. Though much of the acting has that stagy, early-talkie jerkiness, Harlow raises all boats with her performance as a slut beloved by two opposite-minded RAF brothers. The flying scenes haven't been matched yet for detail and excitement and, given Hughes's interest, there's a lot of them. He also colorized some sequences. All in all, diverting, engaging filmmaking and well worth seeing.

The Outlaw (1943, U.S., 123 mins., b/w) Dir: Howard Hughes; Cast: Walter Huston, Thomas Mitchell, Jane Russell, Jack Beutel.

Not enough steam to fog up a Chevette, but this Hughes-directed western boasts enough cleavage to have sparked quite a scandal in its day. Though the Billy the Kid story takes a backseat to Russell's obvious assets, the film remains eminently watchable as long as you know you're getting more romance than rustling.

Melvin and Howard (1980, U.S., 95 mins.) Dir: Jonathan Demme; Cast: Paul LeMat, Jason Robards, Jr., Mary Steenburgen, Elizabeth Cheshire, Michael J. Pollard, Pamela Reed.

The true story of Melvin Dummar, who once gave a lift to Howard Hughes and later claimed that he was the heir to the Hughes fortune. Bo Goldman's script tells the tale with great wit and humanity and won an Oscar, as did Steenburgen for Best Supporting Actress. Robards makes for a good, shaggy Hughes.

Ice Station Zebra (1968, U.S., 148 mins.) Dir: John Sturges; Cast: Rock Hudson, Ernest Borgnine, Patrick McGoohan, Jim Brown.

It's not hard to see why Hughes watched this again and again in his last years—good action scenes; fine cast; a big shoot-out at the end. If you're going to watch a movie a few hundred times it might as well be fun, and this submarine thriller is definitely fun.

THE AESTHETICS OF ELVIS

Are you an Elvis maniac? Did every twitch of his lip and dip of his hip make you quiver? Did every breathy hum, low-down growl, and dragged out vowel make you all warm and

runny every time he sang? Did you love equally the fat Elvis and the thin Elvis? Do you have a velvet painting of him over your couch? Tell the truth, do you totally adore every single one of his cinematic stinkeroos? Well, if that describes you, you might as well turn the page; this list does not pertain. But for the more objective rest of you, we have a few interesting observations to make. Now, we admit that most of his films were strenuous, tuneless, antiseptic, and juvenile, stressing a wholesomeness that made his movie career the Hollywood equivalent of overly sweetened orange marmalade. But we contend that there are jewels in the jelly jar—a number of Presley vehicles directed by filmmakers of note, who actually put some artistry into the effort. Plus, there have been numerous sightings since his death that warrant discussion.

King Creole (1958, U.S., 116 mins., b/w) Dir: Michael Curtiz; Cast: Elvis Presley, Dolores Hart, Walter Matthau, Carolyn Jones, Dean Jagger.

Not only is this the most interesting cast of any Elvis movie, it's directed by the guy who did Casablanca, Mildred Pierce, Yankee Doodle Dandy, and Angels With Dirty Faces. And it's directed with style. Loose adaptation of Harold Robbins's A Stone for Danny Fisher features Elvis as a New Orleans nightclub singer sucked into a life of crime. The good collection of lesser-known Elvis tunes is matched by Curtiz's soulful cinematic style.

Flaming Star (1960, U.S., 101 mins.) Dir: Don Siegel; Cast: Elvis Presley, Steve Forrest, Barbara Eden, Dolores Del Rio, John McIntire.

The King sings at the beginning, but this is the only Elvis film that is not a musical; it's a legitimate western. Elvis shows some serious acting ability as a half-breed who has to choose sides when his mom's tribe goes on the warpath. Action director Siegel (Invasion of the Body Snatchers, Dirty Harry) is known for a film career that expresses the individuality of the antisocial outcast. Flaming Star finds Elvis fitting very effectively into the Siegel mold.

Wild in the Country (1961, U.S., 114 mins.) Dir: Philip Dunne; Cast: Elvis Presley, Hope Lange, Tuesday Weld, Millie Perkins, John Ireland, Gary Lockwood.

Big E's a wannabe wordsmith with some heavyweight literary support here. The rather sober, but interesting screenplay was written by Clifford Odets. The source was a respectable novel by J.R. Salamanca. Director Dunne was a major-league Hollywood screenwriter whose credits include the Oscar-nominated script for How Green Was My Valley. And if that's not enough to recommend it, you've got 17-year-old Tuesday Weld, cream-dreamiest of '60s screen nymphets, giving a first-rate performance.

Kid Galahad (1962, U.S., 95 mins.) Dir: Phil Karlson; Cast: Elvis Presley, Gig Young, Charles Bronson, Lola Albright.

Remake of classic Warner Bros. boxing pic that starred Bogey, Bette Davis, Edward G. Robinson, and Wayne Morris as the boxer. This update finds Elvis as a garage mechanic with a flair for fisticuffs, but no real desire to fight. Director Karlson has a solid reputation as one of the kings of 1950s B movies (The Phoenix City Story, Kansas City Confidential), and he gives what could have been just another saccharine scenario a suitably sordid underside. The movie is much more memorable than the throwaway songs.

Viva Las Vegas (1964, U.S., 86 mins.) Dir: George Sidney; Cast: Elvis Presley, Ann-Margret, Cesare Danova, William Demarest, Jack Carter.

If the coupling of Elvis and Ann-Margret set against a background of race cars and roulette isn't enough to send you into paroxysms of joy, keep in mind that this baby was directed by one of the mainstays of the Hollywood musical. Sidney was no Vincente Minnelli but he did pilot *Annie Get Your Gun, Kiss Me Kate,* and *Bye Bye Birdie* (starring Ms. Margret). *Viva Las Vegas* is fun, colorful, and features some pretty fair rock 'n' roll. Matter of fact, Springsteen did a cover of the title tune.

Change of Habit (1969, U.S., 93 mins.) Dir: William Graham; Cast: Elvis Presley, Mary Tyler Moore, Barbara McNair, Edward Asner, Regis Toomey.

Though not notable for its director, this final film vessel for the real-life Elvis marked a change of direction for its star. The holier-than-thou plot in which E.P. plays a ghetto doctor backed by a chorus of nuns is more ambitious than the usual clambake. With MTM as a soon-to-be Sister of Mercy who must choose between the King of Kings and the King of Rock and Roll (a theme that is emphasized in the editing) this one gives new meaning to the term "cross-cutting." Lord Almighty!

Elvis (1979, U.S./MTV, 150 mins.) Dir: John Carpenter; Cast: Kurt Russell, Shelley Winters, Pat Hingle, Season Hubley, Joe Mantegna.

Chronicle of the King's rise from his rockabilly roots to his Pillsbury dough-boy days in Vegas is a first-rate made-for-TV Elvis biopic thanks to quality direction by Carpenter and a canny performance by Russell that neatly avoids impersonation. The well-chosen songs were dubbed by country and western warbler Ronnie McDowell. And what better choice for E.P.'s mama than Shelley Winters?!?

Heartbreak Hotel (1988, U.S., 93 mins.) Dir: Chris Columbus; Cast: David Keith,

Tuesday Weld, Charlie Schlatter, Chris Mulkey, Jacque Lynn Colton.

Fanciful fiction in which the King circa 1972 is kidnapped by a midwestern teen in search of a surrogate father. Connecting it sweetly to E.P.'s real-life career is the use of *Wild in the Country* co-star Weld as the kid's mom who's been steaming her jeans over Elvis since the days of her youth. Writer/director Columbus shows an obvious affection for the material but an unfortunate lack of depth and ability.

Honeymoon in Vegas (1992, U.S, 95 mins.) Dir: Andrew Bergman; Cast: James Caan, Nicolas Cage, Sarah Jessica Parker, Pat Morita, Anne Bancroft, Peter Boyle.

Marriage phobic Cage uses bride-to-be Parker as table stakes in a Las Vegas card game with gambling man Caan and loses. The solid screwball set-up goes over the edge as Vegas is besieged by Elvis impersonators. There's Elvis the fat and Elvis the skinny, there's a little boy Elvis, an Oriental Elvis, a black Elvis, a female Elvis, and a troop of flying Elvises. Bergman's direction is not quite up to the cleverness of his script, but the wonderful soundtrack is wall-to-wall Presley covers by the likes of Springsteen, Billy Joel, Bruce Hornsby, and others.

True Romance (1993, U.S., 121 mins.) Dir: Tony Scott; Cast: Christian Slater, Patricia Arquette, Dennis Hopper, Val Kilmer, Gary Oldman, Brad Pitt, Christopher Walken.

Most interesting of the recent Elvis homages, this *Bonnie and Clyde/Badlands* pastiche written by Quentin Tarantino (*Reservoir Dogs*) opens with comic book maven, Kung Fu freak Slater delivering a tribute to Presley and "Jailhouse Rock" that includes the declaration that he's no fag . . . but he'd do Elvis. As for the King himself, he appears as a spirit-figure (played by Val Kilmer) in a gold lamé jacket, counseling the hero throughout the film—much like Woody Allen's use of Bogart in *Play It Again, Sam.*

THE RAT PACK

In the early 1950s Humphrey Bogart and Betty Bacall formed friends and admirers into an exclusive and much envied Hollywood social club known as the Rat Pack. They were dedicated to drinking a lot of bourbon, living the high life, and protecting each other from adverse publicity. Members actually paid dues and Frank Sinatra was elected president. When Bogie died, Sinatra was promoted to King Rat. The pack, or clan as they were also called, consisted of Frank, Dean Martin, Sammy Davis, Jr., Peter Lawford, Joey Bishop, and songwriters James Van Heusen and Sammy Cahn, among others. Shirley MacLaine was the unofficial official "mascot." While most of the members had distinguished film careers by themselves, they also had ample opportunity to work with each other. The following list includes films in which members of Sinatra's Rat Pack rode together, and they comprise, depending on your perspective, some of the high points or low points of fifties and sixties popular culture.

Ocean's Eleven (1960, U.S., 127 mins.) Dir: Lewis Milestone; Cast: Frank Sinatra, Dean Martin, Sammy Davis, Jr., Joey Bishop, Peter Lawford, Angie Dickinson, Richard Conte, Cesar Romero, Akim Tamiroff.

Quintessential clan-bake plunks the pack in Vegas with plot to rip off five casinos. Smug (what'd you expect?), breezy caper flick incorporates the different personalities quite smoothly. Tamiroff, Romero, and Conte add spice. Director Milestone comes aboard with

hefty credentials *(The Front Page, All Quiet on the Western Front)* and manages to give the project a melancholy undertow. There's a neat little twist at the end, and we definitely dig that theme song.

Robin and the Seven Hoods (1964, U.S., 103 mins.) Dir: Gordon Douglas; Cast: Frank Sinatra, Dean Martin, Bing Crosby, Sammy Davis, Jr., Barbara Rush, Peter Falk.

Guys and Dolls meets *Robin Hood* in roaring twenties Chicago. Frank, Dean, Sammy, Peter, and company make merry to tunes by Jimmy Van Heusen and Sammy Cahn ("My Kind of Town" and "Style"). Der Bingle lends a very helpful hand as Alan A. Dale.

Sergeants 3 (1962, U.S., 112 mins.) Dir: John Sturges; Cast: Frank Sinatra, Dean Martin, Sammy Davis, Jr., Peter Lawford, Joey Bishop.

Sinatra came up with this Gunga Din goes west remake, casting Martin, Lawford, and himself in roles originated by Cary Grant, Victor McLaglen, and Douglas Fairbanks, Jr. Sammy, of course, is the swingin' little bugle cat. Screenwriter W. R. Burnett considers finished film one of the best ever made from his work, and while it is good, irreverent satire . . . to Burnett, who wrote *Little Caesar, High Sierra, Asphalt Jungle,* and *The Great Escape,* all we can say is, "Really?"

Four for Texas (1963, U.S., 124 mins.) Dir: Robert Aldrich; Cast: Dean Martin, Frank Sinatra, Anita Ekberg, Ursula Andress, Charles Bronson, The Three Stooges.

Double-barrel opening directed with explosive action/comic style by vet auteur Aldrich raises expectations for this rats-on-the-range saga starring Frank and Dino as gun-totin' sidewinders who chew dirt, talk tough, and swindle each other constantly, but things don't exactly pan out. Maybe they'd have been better off with Sammy, Peter, and Joey Bishop instead of the Three Stooges.

Artists and Models (1955, U.S., 109 mins.) Dir: Frank Tashlin; Cast: Dean Martin, Jerry Lewis, Shirley MacLaine, Dorothy Malone.

Martin and Lewis comedy makes the list because it brought Shirley Mac-Laine (her second film) into the fold. Co-written and directed by Tashlin with wonderful comic invention, story of a womanizing cartoonist who gets his ideas from the loony-toon dreams of his daffy pal is one of Dean and Jerry's best.

Some Came Running (1958, U.S., 127 mins.) Dir: Vincente Minnelli; Cast: Frank Sinatra, Shirley MacLaine, Dean Martin, Martha Hyer, Arthur Kennedy.

Minnelli potboiler gives rodents Sinatra and Martin and little mouse MacLaine (Frank insisted she get the part) a vehicle of distinction and the opportunity to work with a quality director going full tilt. Adapted from James Jones novel about a soldier boy's return home after WWII, the film has a great look and terrific performances. Godard paid his compliments in *Breathless* by having Belmondo wear his hat in the bathtub à la Dino in this picture. Cahn and Van Heusen wrote Oscar-nominated song "To Love and Be Loved," which became a Sinatra hit.

Can-Can (1960, U.S., 131 mins.) Dir: Walter Lang; Cast: Frank Sinatra, Shirley MacLaine, Maurice Chevalier, Juliet Prowse, Louis Jourdan.

So-so film version of Cole Porter's Broadway triumph features Frank as lawyer who defends Shirley's right to dance the can-can in Belle Epoque Paris. Saved by songs such as "I Love Paris" and other Porter plums added for the film.

Road to Hong Kong (1962, U.S., 91 mins., b/w) Dir: Norman Panama; Cast: Bing Crosby, Bob Hope, Joan Collins, Dorothy Lamour.

This road pic deserves a footnote because Hope and Crosby's zany travels lead them not only to China but to outer space where they encounter a couple of swingin' spacemen played by Frank and Dino.

Marriage on the Rocks (1965, U.S., 109 mins.) Dir: Jack Donohue; Cast: Frank Sinatra, Dean Martin, Deborah Kerr.
■
Frank and Dean try their hands at screwball comedy in this marriage-go-round that goes very wrong. Meant to be fast and furious laugh-a-minute fun, it falls flat. Dean is obviously much more comfortable with this kind of nonsense than Frank, who seems surprisingly lost.

Never So Few (1959, U.S., 124 mins.) Dir: John Sturges; Cast: Frank Sinatra, Gina Lollobrigida, Peter Lawford, Steve McQueen.

Sinatra and Lawford find themselves fighting in the Burmese jungle during WWII. Gina heats up the proceedings quite well, thank you, and young McQueen shows why he became a star. Director Sturges (*Sergeants 3*) does a good job blending action and romance, but story is slowed by philosophical posturing, not surprising since script is credited to Millard Kaufman, front for blacklisted writer Dalton Trumbo.

Salt and Pepper (1968, Great Britain, 101 mins.) Dir: Richard Donner; Cast: Peter Lawford, Sammy Davis, Jr., Michael Bates, Ilona Rodgers.
■
Lawford and Davis tried to spice up flagging (almost nonexistent) film careers as nightclub owners embroiled in spy vs. spy in swinging London silliness. A good example of what happens when second-string rats try to make a

go of it without big cheese-eaters Frank and Dean. In the event that you just can't get enough of this kind of tomfoolery, Peter and Sammy do it again in sequel, *One More Time*.

PRE-*STAR WARS* SPECIAL EFFECTS

Long ago, in a galaxy far, far away, before computers and morphing and Industrial Light and Magic, special effects were done with the same pipe cleaners, clay, and HO scale models you had in your basement. They never seemed quite real, but weren't they that much more fun because of it?

King Kong (1933, U.S., 100 mins., b/w) Dirs: Merian C. Cooper, Ernest B. Schoedsack; Cast: Fay Wray, Bruce Cabot, Robert Armstrong, Noble Johnson, Sam Hardy.

That big crazy old monkey looks more like a stuffed animal than an enormous simian killer, but the seventies remake wasn't able to improve much on these effects, so just enjoy. A classic.

The Thief of Bagdad (1940, Great Britain, 106 mins.) Dirs: Michael Powell, Tim Whelan, Ludwig Berger; Cast: Sabu, John Justin, Rex Ingram, June Duprez, Conrad Veidt.

There are four films with this title, so make sure you get the one starring Sabu and produced by Korda because it's a delight in every way, especially its effects. Flying carpets, genies in and out of bottles; it goes on and on with color, magic, and wonderful music. Treat yourself and slip this in the VCR instead of *Aladdin* sometime—the kids won't mind.

When Worlds Collide (1951, U.S., 81 mins.) Dir: Rudolph Mate; Cast: Richard Derr, Barbara Rush, Peter Hanson, Larry Keating.

Aside from its compelling story about a selected group of humans racing the clock to get off the planet before it smacks into another planet, this film has some terrific effects, like tidal waves in New York. Who cares if the acting stinks?

The Lost World (1925, U.S., 71 mins., silent, b/w) Dir: Harry O. Hoyt; Cast: Bessie Love, Wallace Beery, Lewis Stone, Lloyd Hughes.

Get the silent version for the good special effects; they were done by Willis O'Brien, who also did *King Kong* and taught Ray Harryhausen. *Jurassic Park* may reflect all the latest paleontological research, but admit it, those big lumbering dinosaurs of *The Lost World* were a lot scarier and neater than the new speedy versions. It's like comparing a '70 Cutlass with a '94 Lexus—which sounds like more fun?

The Invisible Man (1933, U.S., 80 mins., b/w) Dir: James Whale; Cast: Claude Rains, Henry Travers, Gloria Stuart, Una O'Connor.

Brilliant special effects turn a good story about a nutsy doctor who makes himself invisible into a great movie. Seamless visuals and fine voice matchup with Rains. The recent Chevy Chase film *Memoirs of an Invisible Man* plays some of the same tricks and even goes it one better in a few spots, but the magic isn't there.

The Incredible Shrinking Man (1957, U.S., 81 mins.) Dir: Jack Arnold; Cast: Grant Williams, Randy Stuart.

Williams gets sprayed with some radioactive material while he's out boating one day, and he begins to shrink into nothingness. Sounds like another goofy horror flick, but the effects are stunning and the story treats the psychological traumas as well as the physical ones. *Dr. Cyclops* has similar effects done well, but it's a more standard mad-doctor plot.

Fantastic Voyage (1966, U.S., 100 mins.) Dir: Richard Fleischer; Cast: Stephen Boyd, Arthur Kennedy, Raquel Welch, Donald Pleasence.

Is this what we look like inside? Even if we're not full of Peter Max colors and scary bacteria, we'd be pretty entertaining if half of this was fact. Of course laser surgery makes the idea of shrinking doctors down to microscopic size moot now. Still, it's good, tiny fun.

The Birds (1963, U.S., 120 mins.) Dir: Alfred Hitchcock; Cast: Tippi Hedren, Rod Taylor, Suzanne Pleshette, Veronica Cartwright, Jessica Tandy.

The best evidence for the strength of the special effects here is that you don't really think of them as special effects. But how do you think all those birds got down the chimney? This Hitchcock thriller about birds taking over a northern California town makes no sense, which takes nothing away from it.

2001: A Space Odyssey (1968, U.S.-Great Britain, 138 mins.) Dir: Stanley Kubrick; Cast: Keir Dullea, Gary Lockwood, William Sylvester.

This adaptation of Arthur C. Clarke's futuristic novel makes no sense, which does take away from it. The outer-space effects are tremendous and certainly rival the Spielberg/Lucas effects that came afterward. A visual triumph, if not a particularly coherent film, and you can't blame them for thinking Pan Am would be around forever.

■

NOTE: We haven't forgotten the glory days of disaster movies. *The Poseidon Adventure, Earthquake,* and *The Towering Inferno* all exist for their great special effects.

UNCREDITED REMAKES

Originality is tough to come by and there's an old Hollywood saw claiming there are only seven original stories. Our answer to that is, "Maybe —it depends on how you look at it." At any rate, it's obvious that movies, Hollywood in particular, have always shown a fondness for cashing in on the tried and true, often replaying familiar tunes without repaying the piper. Some of these films are uncredited remakes and shameless rip-offs, others are loving homages; we're not here to judge or defend. We just thought it'd be fun to look at a handful (some obvious, some not so obvious) that beg, borrow, or steal inspiration—setups, plot twists, pay-offs, and characters—from films that came before.

Star Wars (1977, U.S., 121 mins.) Dir: George Lucas; Cast: Mark Hamill, Harrison Ford, Alec Guinness, Carrie Fisher, Peter Cushing, Anthony Daniels, David Prowse, voice of James Earl Jones.

Luke Skywalker, finding his village destroyed by the Empire, joins with Han Solo to search the galaxy for a kidnapped princess. Epic plotline is lifted from John Ford's *The Searchers* (Lucas also acknowledges debt to Akira Kurosawa's *Hidden Fortress*), where John Wayne and Jeffrey Hunter, after similar devastation, spend years hunting for Natalie Wood. *Star Wars* is an extraordinary blend of myth, starlight, and magic; *The Searchers* remains one of the cinema's profound experiences.

Taxi Driver (1976, U.S., 112 mins.) Dir: Martin Scorsese; Cast: Robert De Niro, Cybill Shepherd, Jodie Foster, Peter Boyle, Albert Brooks, Leonard Harris, Harvey Keitel.

Scorsese and screenwriter Paul Schrader acknowledge *The Searchers* inspiration in subplot involving cab driver

Travis Bickle (De Niro) liberating child hooker Foster from clutches of pimp Keitel. Schrader says scene where Foster and Keitel dance reveals what Ford never showed—depth of psychological hold Comanche Chief Scar had on Debbie (Natalie Wood) in *The Searchers*.

Hardcore (1979, U.S., 105 mins.) Dir: Paul Schrader; Cast: George C. Scott, Season Hubley, Peter Boyle, Dick Sargent.

Here serving as writer and director, Schrader (who started as a film critic/scholar) builds entire main frame of his plot on *The Searchers*—Calvinist dad (Scott) hunts for runaway daughter in the world of underground porn. Enlightening and repugnant, this unflinching look at subculture of perversion leaves a feeling of emptiness, hitting far less responsive chord than its prototype. Still, very interesting.

Obsession (1976, U.S., 98 mins.) Dir: Brian DePalma; Cast: Genevieve Bujold, Cliff Robertson, John Lithgow.

Hitchcock copycat DePalma has never been more blatant than with this *Vertigo* retread written by Schrader. Consider similarities: Each has a haunting score by Bernard Herrmann; in each, a man (Robertson/Jimmy Stewart), guilt-ridden over the death of his lover (Bujold/Kim Novak), finds her exact double and reenacts her death. *Vertigo* stands as a masterpiece; *Obsession* builds promise on borrowed premise, but blows it big-time in the end.

Terror in a Texas Town (1958, U.S., 80 mins., b/w) Dir: Joseph H. Lewis; Cast: Sterling Hayden, Sebastian Cabot, Carol Kelly, Eugene Martin, Ned Young.
■
Soft-spoken Swede Hayden avenges father's death and defends town from greedy oil baron. Unbelievably strange, brooding western shot in stark b&w has (of all films) *The Seventh Seal* stamped all over it. "Death" is a gunslinger dressed in black and the chess game becomes (what else?) a shoot-out—with an unusual angle. Last film by director Lewis (made in 10 days on $80,000!) who was, in his way, the Bergman of B (and C and D) movies.

The Magnificent Seven (1960, U.S., 126 mins.) Dir: John Sturges; Cast: Yul Brynner, Steve McQueen, James Coburn, Charles Bronson, Robert Vaughn, Eli Wallach.

One of movie history's most successful and famous transmutations turns Akira Kurosawa's *The Seven Samurai* into archetypal western gunfighters, hired for coolie wages to protect a peasant village from murderous bandits. McQueen, Coburn, and Bronson are the best of the bunch and Wallach is terrific as the big bandito. Elmer Bernstein's rousing score has an unfortunate side effect, causing people who've quit smoking to light up a Marlboro.

A Fistful of Dollars (1964, Italy-Spain-West Germany, 96 mins.) Dir: Sergio Leone; Cast: Clint Eastwood, Marianne Koch, Gian Maria Volonte.

Sergio Leone's response to world appetite for American westerns was to serve 'em up spaghetti-style. This is the first of its kind and its source, like pasta itself, comes from the Orient— here, Kurosawa's *Yojimbo*. Samurai warriors are relocated in American West as reinvented by Leone in European locales. Enigmatic "Man With No Name" character made Eastwood a star.

Pale Rider (1985, U.S., 113 mins.) Dir: Clint Eastwood; Cast: Clint Eastwood, Michael Moriarty, Carrie Snodgress, Richard Dysart, Christopher Penn.

Visually beautiful *Shane* clone has mysterious good guy (Clint) riding into town and standing up for humble miners against wicked land-grabbers, becoming mythic hero to little boy in the process. Pretentious rip-off is now required viewing in light of leaps and bounds Eastwood *(Unforgiven)* has made as a director.

Unlawful Entry (1992, U.S., 111 mins.) Dir: Jonathan Kaplan; Cast: Kurt Russell, Ray Liotta, Madeline Stowe, Roger E. Mosley, Ken Lerner, Deborah Offner.

Contemporary thriller begins with yuppie couple calling police when a prowler breaks into their home. Cops scare away intruder but one of them (Liotta) insinuates himself into the couple's lives, becoming their worst nightmare. Intriguing setup covers identical territory found in Joseph Losey's little-known, but first-rate noir, *The Prowler*. Too bad it veers off in a different direction, becoming its own worst enemy.

What's Up Doc? (1972, U.S., 90 mins.) Dir: Peter Bogdanovich; Cast: Barbra Streisand, Ryan O'Neal, Madeline Kahn, Austin Pendleton.

Bogdanovich and screenwriters Robert Benton and David Newman, all (like Paul Schrader) former film critics, bow at the altar of *Bringing Up Baby* for this loving tribute to screwball comedy. Cary Grant's professorial obsession with dinosaur bones is replaced by Ryan O'Neal's passion for rocks; Hepburn's bubbling nincompoop becomes an incredibly smart-mouthed Barbra Streisand; and the mixed-up leopards change spots, becoming five identical suitcases. The filmmakers get what they're after, in spades!

The Sure Thing (1985, U.S., 94 mins.) Dir: Rob Reiner; Cast: John Cusack, Daphne Zuniga, Anthony Edwards, Viveca Lindfors.

Setup is different, but the heart of this well-made battle-of-the-sexes comedy with mismatched pair (Cusack/Zuniga) making their way cross-country bears more than a passing resemblance to *It Happened One Night*. Director Reiner claims never to have seen Capra's screwball classic, and who are we to call him a liar?

Sister Act (1992, U.S., 100 mins.) Dir: Emile Ardolino; Cast: Whoopi Goldberg, Maggie Smith, Harvey Keitel, Bill Nunn, Kathy Najimy, Wendy Makkena, Mary Wickes.

Clever conversion of Barbara Stanwyck comedy *Ball of Fire* has Whoopi in similar situation with interesting twist. Nightclub singer (Whoopi sings Motown, Stanwyck boogie-woogie) with mobster boyfriend is forced into hiding (Stanwyck in an isolated mansion with a monastic group of nutty professors, Whoopi in a convent with a bunch of singing nuns). Way in which plots unravel is too close to call coincidence, but Whoopi's sister act has enough soul of its own to make believers out of us.

Ali—Fear Eats the Soul (1974, Germany, 94 mins.) Dir: Rainer Werner Fassbinder; Cast: Brigitte Mira, El Hedi Ben Salem, Barbara Valentin, Irm Hermann.

A 60-year-old German charwoman marries a young Moroccan immigrant and their union brings out fear, prejudice, and snobbery all around them. Fassbinder's angst-ridden melodrama, one of his most moving and accessible films, is a conscious reworking of Douglas Sirk's 1950s Hollywood fable, *All That Heaven Allows*. Watch both films back to back for a clear-eyed view of two similar sensibilities working in vastly different artistic environments.

KID STUFF

Every generation of moviegoers has its share of child stars—prepubescent pip-squeaks and pint-sized charmers—kids who light up the screen with their fresh-faced inno-

cence, shining down on us even when the visage in question is in serious need of a scrubbing. Here are some of the vehicles that kids from Jackie Coogan to Macauley Culkin rode to fame.

The Kid (1921, U.S., 90 mins., silent, b/w) Dir: Charles Chaplin; Cast: Charles Chaplin, Jackie Coogan, Lita Grey, Edna Purviance.

Chaplin stepped out of the realm of two-reelers, extending and expanding his comic genius, injecting his first full-length feature with a large dose of pure sentiment as the little tramp becomes surrogate father to a child of the streets. Coogan (sensational as the kid) and Charlie form such a profound emotional connection, and the film elicits such a deep response, that the word comedy doesn't seem to do it justice. Beyond enchantment.

The Devil Is a Sissy (1936, U.S., 92 mins., b/w) Dir: W. S. Van Dyke; Cast: Mickey Rooney, Jackie Cooper, Freddie Bartholomew.

Moldy but goody kiddie melodrama stars Freddie Bartholomew as the sissified son of divorced parents—mom's a cafe-society snob, dad's a denizen of the slums, and each gets the boy for half the year. Rooney is a wonderful blend of sweet-faced sentimentality and back-alley belligerence as the tough little angel who knocks the starch out of Freddie. Roland Brown, Oscar winner for the like-minded *Angels With Dirty Faces,* was one of the screenwriters. Nicely directed by Van Dyke; superbly shot by Harold Rosson.

A Midsummer Night's Dream (1935, U.S., 117 mins., b/w) Dirs: Max Reinhardt, William Dieterle; Cast: James Cagney, Dick Powell, Olivia de Havilland, Joe E. Brown, Mickey Rooney.

The Bard's moonlit midnight wood-

land, magically brought to life on the Warners back lot by German theater-meister Reinhardt and studio stalwart Dieterle, features a delightfully unlikely assortment of contract players having tons of fun with iambic pentameter. But it's young Mickey Rooney's giddy sprite-elf-urchin-Pan of a Puck that lingers in the mind and stands alongside his bad-boy at Boys Town as his most impressive juvenile work.

The Wizard of Oz (1939, U.S., 93 mins., c & b/w) Dir: Victor Fleming; Cast: Judy Garland, Frank Morgan, Ray Bolger, Bert Lahr, Margaret Hamilton, Billie Burke, Jack Haley.

Garland made her screen debut at 13 in *Every Sunday* and hit pay dirt that same year in *Pigskin Parade.* She had a string of teenage teamings with Mickey Rooney, including *Love Finds Andy Hardy* and *Babes in Arms,* but it was this little trip down the yellow brick road that sent her star flying over the rainbow and made her an absolute icon for children (and the child that lives in all of us) in every generation since.

Wee Willie Winkie (1937, U.S., 75 mins., b/w) Dir: John Ford; Cast: Shirley Temple, Victor McLaglen, June Lang, Cesar Romero.

During the heyday of the Raj, an adorable little girl becomes the heroine of a British regiment when she musters all of her impish charm, goodwill, and faith to persuade an Indian rebel to give himself up. The highly improbable combo of Hollywood's ultimate macho Irish patriot (Ford) directing America's ultimate cutie pie (Temple) in a glorification of the British Empire adds up to an enigmatic, but surprisingly effective, retelling of Rudyard Kipling's tale.

Meet Me in St. Louis (1944, U.S., 113 mins.) Dir: Vincente Minnelli; Cast: Judy Garland, Tom Drake, Margaret O'Brien, Lucille Bremer, Mary Astor.

Judy plays the big sister and sings a number of classic tunes—including "The Trolley Song" and "The Boy Next Door"—in this turn-of-the-century slice of American pie. But when little Tootie, played by seven-year-old Margaret O'Brien, sneaks downstairs to crash a teenage party and duets with sis on "Under the Bamboo Tree," she just about steals the show. And, as the Halloween and Christmas Eve scenes prove, the kid could act.

How Green Was My Valley (1941, U.S., 118 mins., b/w) Dir: John Ford; Cast: Walter Pidgeon, Maureen O'Hara, Donald Crisp, Anna Lee, Roddy McDowall, Sara Allgood, Barry Fitzgerald, John Loder, Patric Knowles.

John Ford's exquisite manifestation of hearth and home in a Welsh mining town, steeped in pathos and the poetry of the past, begins with an adult narrator wistfully remembering the days of his youth. The character appears on screen as a boy in the person of Roddy McDowall, his performance resonant with wide-eyed wonder and keen awareness, the window through which we enter the world of his family. It's a hard-hearted thing you are if you don't shed a tear or two for this one. Oscars for Picture, Director, Art Direction, Actor (Crisp), and Cinematography.

National Velvet (1944, U.S., 123 mins.) Dir: Clarence Brown; Cast: Mickey Rooney, Elizabeth Taylor, Donald Crisp, Ann Revere, Angela Lansbury, Reginald Owen.

Little Lizzie is irresistible as a young equestrian determined to enter her horse in the Grand National Steeplechase. Rooney is in top form as her cohort, and solid support is provided by Crisp, Revere (Best Supporting Actress Oscar), and Angela Lansbury. But it's Taylor's rapturous face, as radiant in the child as it would later become in the woman, that keeps your eyes riveted to the screen. The horse is good too.

Miracle on 34th Street (1947, U.S., 96 mins., b/w) Dir: George Seaton; Cast: Edmund Gwenn, John Payne, Maureen O'Hara, Natalie Wood.

Natalie Wood is all unadulterated charm as a no-nonsense child with her feet planted firmly on the ground who gets her non-belief system shaken by Kris Kringle (Gwenn), the man hired by Macy's to play Santa. Kris, you see, claims that he really *is* Santa Claus. Writer/director Seaton has much to say about the Yuletide spirit and the meaning of imagination—plus, the film has a hidden message or two (see *The Red Menace*).

The 400 Blows (1959, France, 99 mins., b/w) Dir: François Truffaut; Cast: Jean-Pierre Léaud, Patrick Auffay, Claire Maurier.

Truffaut's first feature, and the first in his semiautobiographical Antoine Doinel cycle, stars Jean-Pierre Léaud as an 11-year-old loner—an angry pre-adolescent, filled with intoxication, pride, and regret at feeling himself apart from society. Léaud's cocky, vivid, aggressive performance gives extra resonance and dimension to the director's compelling mosaic, one of the most vital and honest visions of childhood ever put on a movie screen.

Paper Moon (1973, U.S., 101 mins., b/w) Dir: Peter Bogdanovich; Cast: Ryan O'Neal, Tatum O'Neal, Madeline Kahn, John Hillerman, Randy Quaid.

Tatum O'Neal became the youngest actress ever to cop an Oscar (Best Supporting Actress) for her portrayal of Addie Pray, a sharp-as-a-tack and cute-to-boot kid who lands in the lap of ersatz Bible salesman (and real-life dad) Ryan. The two together take the art of the con to impressive heights, bilking their way through the Depression-era dust bowl, forging a bond as they go. Bogdanovich directs with tremendous affection for films of the thirties, and it works wonderfully.

Alice Doesn't Live Here Anymore (1974, U.S., 112 mins.) Dir: Martin Scorsese; Cast: Ellen Burstyn, Kris Kristofferson, Alfred Lutter, Jodie Foster, Diane Ladd, Harvey Keitel, Vic Tayback, Billy Green Bush, Valerie Curtin, Lane Bradbury, Mia Bendixsen.

In the main plot of Martin Scorsese's odd, dark, feminist, pseudo-screwball comedy, Alice is a woman who loses her husband and takes off (in true early seventies fashion) in search of herself. The subplot revolves around the relationship between her young son (Lutter) and a streetwise, butt-smoking 10-year-old tomboy, played by Jodie Foster. As one might expect from Scorsese, the film is marked by the absence of anything resembling cornball sentiment in its approach to the problems of childhood.

Home Alone (1990, U.S., 102 mins.) Dir: Chris Columbus; Cast: Macaulay Culkin, Joe Pesci, Daniel Stern, John Heard, Catherine O'Hara.

Kid-flick mogul John Hughes wrote and produced this exuberant but uneven romp about an eight-year-old boy accidentally left behind when his family goes to Europe on Christmas vacation. So popular when first released that kids went to see it over and over, making it one of the screen's all-time big moneymakers. While much of the film's appeal comes from Hughes's clever premise, the real pull is from the "everykid" charisma of then eight-year-old Culkin, a force field strong enough to land him on equal footing with the serious Hollywood power brokers. Though by the time Mac hit 11, he was well on his way to over-the-hill.

CULTURE

LITERARY ADAPTATIONS

THE BARD

Generations of soporific high school English teachers and pretentious Brits more interested in enunciation than expression have done serious disservice to the greatest master of the English language. Though Hollywood catches a lot of flack for dishing out mounds of movie garbage, the movies have also brought Shakespeare back from the dusty shelves and shown us how vital and relevant his work still is.

Henry V (1944, Great Britain, 137 mins.) Dir: Laurence Olivier; Cast: Laurence Olivier, Robert Newton, Leslie Banks, Leo Genn.

Simply a wonder of a film. Olivier turns King Henry's incursion into France and the battle of Agincourt into a gripping storybook adventure. The rich colors and pageantry hearken back to your favorite tales of knights and kings, and Olivier goes to great lengths to make it all comprehensible. On another level, it's a final, post-World War II tribute to a fading England. Just see it.

Henry V (1989, Great Britain, 135 mins.) Dir: Kenneth Branagh; Cast: Kenneth Branagh, Paul Scofield, Derek Jacobi, Ian Holm, Alec McGowen, Judi Dench, Brian Blessed, Emma Thompson, Robbie Coltrane.

If Olivier's is the storybook version, Branagh's gives us the time as it really was and characters who live and breathe. It's hard to believe the man who wrote this is the same man artists have depicted with a little goatee and a frilly collar. Agincourt here is more about mud and blood than shining armor. Each version is superior in its own way and even though they tell the same story in virtually the same words, they create two very different viewing experiences.

A Midsummer Night's Dream (1935, U.S., 117 mins., b/w) Dirs: Max Reinhardt, William Dieterle; Cast: James Cagney, Dick Powell, Olivia de Havilland, Joe E. Brown, Mickey Rooney.

An enchanting, gossamer Hollywood presentation of this comedy of romance and magic. Rooney as Puck leads the parade of Warner Bros. stars through the woods of Athens. Yes, it tends to be cloying at times, but so does the play. If you want depressing, watch *Titus Andronicus.*

Chimes at Midnight (aka: *Falstaff,* 1966, Spain-Switzerland, 115 mins., b/w) Dir: Orson Welles; Cast: Orson Welles, Jeanne Moreau, Margaret Rutherford.

Orson Welles stitched together all the sections from the Histories regarding the morally ambiguous Falstaff into one stunning movie. No fool, Welles cast himself as Falstaff and his performance here may be his best as he captures all the tragedy of this beloved, and ultimately rejected, mentor to King Henry V. Stylized in certain ways, and enormously powerful. The battle scene is terrific.

Othello (1951, France-U.S., 91 mins., b/w) Dir: Orson Welles; Cast: Orson Welles, Michael MacLiammoir, Fay Compton, Robert Cook, Suzanne Cloutier.

Over the course of many years, whenever Welles amassed enough money he'd scramble and shoot a few hundred feet more of this tale of jealousy and deceit. Every frame is a composed work of art in itself. If there are any doubts that Welles had a strong involvement in the making of *The Third Man,* they should be dispelled by scenes from this film made during the same period. Movie-making of the highest order.

Macbeth (1948, U.S., 112 mins., b/w) Dir: Orson Welles; Cast: Orson Welles, Roddy McDowall, Jeanette Nolan, Dan O'Herlihy, Edgar Barrier.

Probably the one Welles Shakespeare film that, because of the intentionally murky production and the heavy Scottish accents, is a little hard to get into. Still, a classic interpretation of the play. All in all, the greatest filmmaker ever did well by history's greatest playwright.

Julius Caesar (1953, U.S., 120 mins., b/w) Dir: Joseph L. Mankiewicz; Cast: John Gielgud, Marlon Brando, James Mason, Deborah Kerr, Greer Garson, Edmond O'Brien, Louis Calhern.

When Brando ascends the steps of the Forum and delivers Marc Antony's eulogy of Caesar, you know you're seeing a new kind of Shakespeare, a production that cares more about the characters than it does about histrionics and delivery. This is Shakespeare treated as new material and really *acted,* instead of declaimed. John Houseman produced this all-star film and both Brando and Gielgud were nominated for Oscars.

Hamlet (1948, Great Britain, 153 mins., b/w) Dir: Laurence Olivier; Cast: Laurence Olivier, Jean Simmons, Basil Sydney, Eileen Herlie, Stanley Holloway, Anthony Quayle, Peter Cushing.

Do you want Hamlet, or Mel Gibson? If you want Mel, may we suggest *Lethal Weapon, Gallipoli,* or *Mad Max,* all of which are fine films. If you want Hamlet, you have to go with the pro and that means Olivier. Gibson's Hamlet was a surprisingly successful curiosi-ty and an indulgence for a big star; Olivier's Hamlet won Best Picture and he won Best Actor. Enough said.

Romeo and Juliet (1936, U.S., 140 mins., b/w) Dir: George Cukor; Cast: Norma Shearer, Leslie Howard, John Barrymore, Basil Rathbone, Edna May Oliver, C. Aubrey Smith, Violet Kemble Cooper, Ralph Forbes, Andy Devine.

Coin-flip here. On the one hand you've got the cool sixties version with teenagers Olivia Hussey and Leonard Whiting, directed by Zeffirelli. On the other, there's the big MGM version with a much too old Norma Shearer leading a fabulous cast directed by George Cukor. The Zeffirelli is great to look at, but at the end of the day it's all about acting and the 1936 film takes it on that score.

Much Ado About Nothing (1993, Great Britain-U.S., 111 mins.) Dir: Kenneth Branagh; Cast: Kenneth Branagh, Emma Thompson, Denzel Washington, Michael Keaton, Keanu Reeves, Robert Sean Leonard, Richard Briers, Ben Elton.

Branagh extends his claim to our generation's version of Olivier or Welles with this charming, colorful rendition of love gone awry. If you have even the least interest in Shakespeare, you'll enjoy it. The only question is Reeves, who seems to be sleepwalking here, but don't let him spoil your fun.

THE BARD BOWDLERIZED

If Shakespeare had a good copyright attorney, there'd be hell to pay around Hollywood. Of course the Bard wasn't too scrupulous about acknowledging all the ideas that he lifted, so all's well that ends well.

My Own Private Idaho (1991, U.S., 102 mins.) Dir: Gus Van Sant; Cast: River Phoenix, Keanu Reeves, James Russo, William Richert, Rodney Harvey.

Henry IV, Parts 1 and *2* get a loose updating from Gus Van Sant, as disinherited rich-kid Reeves helps narcoleptic punk Phoenix track down his mother. Though the plot wanders all over the place, many elements are directly out of Shakespeare and some of the scenes feature the Bard's actual dialogue. A good film and even more interesting if you know the *Henry IV* tie.

Forbidden Planet (1956, U.S., 98 mins.) Dir: Fred McLeod Wilcox; Cast: Walter Pidgeon, Anne Francis, Leslie Nielsen, Earl Holliman, James Drury.

One of the all-time best science fiction movies and a respectful interpretation of *The Tempest.* An American spaceship goes to a planet to learn what happened to a failed space colony and finds a strange genius living there with his daughter. Great set designs, special effects, and an intelligent script. We won't give you that "See it in the theater" stuff, but try to get the letterboxed version. It makes a big difference.

West Side Story (1961, U.S., 155 mins.) Dirs: Robert Wise, Jerome Robbins; Cast: Natalie Wood, Rita Moreno, Richard Beymer, George Chakiris, Russ Tamblyn.

Polish boy Tony and Puerto Rican girl Maria fall in love, much to the dismay of their respective gangs. Though in these days of Bloods and Crips and drive-by shootings, this doesn't have the same cutting-edge feel it once had. The Bernstein music is wonderful, Natalie Wood is lovely and it probably has more of *Romeo and Juliet's* romance and tragedy than any straight version on film.

Throne of Blood (1957, Japan, 109 mins., b/w) Dir: Akira Kurosawa; Cast: Toshiro Mifune, Isuzu Yamada, Takashi Shimura, Minoru Chiaki.

Kurosawa moves *Macbeth* to medieval Japan and the world of samurai warriors, proving that he is the greatest liaison between Japanese and Western cultures. More than a personal interpretation, it gives the play a Japanese sensibility. Not the easiest film to watch, but a powerful experience.

Ran (1985, Japan-France, 160 mins.) Dir: Akira Kurosawa; Cast: Tasuya Nakadai, Satoshi Terao, Jinpachi Nezu, Daisuke Ryu.

Kurosawa has made too many masterpieces to say that any one film is his greatest, but some claim that this adaptation of *King Lear* deserves that title. An enormous epic with fabulous costumes and art direction, it's slow going at times—especially at the beginning—but the story of family infighting and filial piety is totally gripping.

Joe Macbeth (1955, Great Britain, 90 mins., b/w) Dir: Ken Hughes; Cast: Paul Douglas, Ruth Roman, Bonar Colleano.

English interpretation of *Macbeth* turns the master of Glamis Castle into a Depression-era mobster whose nagging wife pushes him to the top. The recent *Men of Respect* is a similar gangster take on *Macbeth,* with fairly dismal results.

Kiss Me Kate (1953, U.S., 109 mins.) Dir: George Sidney; Cast: Kathryn Grayson, Howard Keel, Ann Miller, Bobby Van, Keenan Wynn, James Whitmore, Bob Fosse.

Cole Porter's music is the highest point among many in this meta-musical adaptation of *The Taming of the Shrew,* which turns Petruchio and Katherine into quarreling performers starring in a musical version of *The Taming of the Shrew.* Grayson and Keel are their usual sturdy selves, Ann

Miller, Bobby Van, and Bob Fosse do some major hoofing and the "Brush Up Your Shakespeare" number is a classic.

Tempest (1982, U.S., 140 mins.) Dir: Paul Mazursky; Cast: John Cassavetes, Gena Rowlands, Susan Sarandon, Vittorio Gassman, Raul Julia, Molly Ringwald.

Paul Mazursky waters down *The Tempest* into the story of an architect, fed up with life in New York, who runs away with his daughter to a Greek island. Shakespeare contemplated middle age; Mazursky whines about it.

Jubal (1956, U.S., 101 mins.) Dir: Delmer Daves; Cast: Glenn Ford, Ernest Borgnine, Rod Steiger, Felicia Farr.

Ernest Borgnine IS Othello! If that isn't enough to intrigue you, maybe Rod Steiger as Iago will do it. *Othello* goes western here, as rancher Borgnine suspects his wife of dallying with cowpuncher Glenn Ford. More successful as a western for Shakespeare fans than as Shakespeare for western fans.

Smiles of a Summer Night (1955, Sweden, 108 mins., b/w) Dir: Ingmar Bergman; Cast: Ulla Jacobsson, Eva Dahlbeck, Harriet Anderson, Margit Carlquist, Jarl Kulle.

Hard as it is to believe, this is a comedy by Bergman, though he needed to riff off of *A Midsummer's Night Dream* to do it. The film is a silvery, lovely tale of Swedish aristocrats pairing off during a weekend in the country. This, in turn, became the basis for Stephen Sondheim's *A Little Night Music* and Woody Allen's *A Midsummer Night's Sex Comedy*.

Theatre of Blood (1973, Great Britain, 104 mins.) Dir: Douglas Hickox; Cast: Vincent Price, Diana Rigg, Robert Morley, Ian Hendry, Harry Andrews, Diana Dors.

A gory romp that features Vincent Price as a Shakespearean actor, presumed dead, who murders unfavorable critics by restaging death scenes from the Bard's plays. Silly, hammy, cheesy, and definitely fun.

ENGLISH LIT
■
18TH & 19TH CENTURIES

Cervantes and Rabelais notwithstanding, this is where the novel as we know it began and was perfected. Though these centuries of powdered wigs and Industrial Revolution seem deep in the past as you flip on your VCR, Tom Jones, Becky Sharp, and Pip are all struggling, like you, with life, death, love, and success. The strength of these films lies in their ability to convey the same human immediacy that makes the books they're based on live today.

Adventures of Robinson Crusoe (1954, Mexico, 90 mins.) Dir: Luis Buñuel; Cast: Dan O'Herlihy, Jaime Fernandez.
■
Luis Buñuel is maybe the last person one would imagine making a straightforward version of Defoe's classic tale about a shipwrecked man creating his world. But then again, maybe not. Without engaging in the excessive polemics of later adaptations, Buñuel still scores his points about colonialism and the progress of western civilization. The film even won a prize from *Parents* magazine!

Tom Jones (1963, Great Britain, 131 mins.) Dir: Tony Richardson; Cast: Albert Finney, Susannah York, Diane Cilento, Joan Greenwood, Hugh Griffith, Joyce Redman, Edith Evans.

A fabulous romp that follows our young hero, played by Finney at his finest, as he drinks, eats, and bawds his way through England. As funny, racy, and sly as Fielding's book, yet Richardson is never reverent. Instead, he made the film that Fielding would have made if he had been born two centuries later. By the way, the famous dinner scene is far from the film's best or sexiest.

Pride and Prejudice (1940, U.S., 116 mins., b/w) Dir: Robert Z. Leonard; Cast: Greer Garson, Laurence Olivier, Edmund Gwenn, Mary Boland, Edna Mae Oliver, Maureen O'Sullivan.

Director Robert Leonard turned Jane Austen's timeless novel about the battle of the sexes into something very much like a screwball comedy, and a brilliant one at that. Pre-*Mrs. Miniver* Garson is surprisingly sassy as Liza, and Olivier plays Darcy perfectly. Aldous Huxley worked on the script.

Becky Sharp (1935, U.S., 83 mins.) Dir: Rouben Mamoulian; Cast: Miriam Hopkins, Cedric Hardwicke, Frances Dee, Billie Burke, Alison Skipworth.

Thackeray's *Vanity Fair* defies conventional adaptation, so Mamoulian pulled out Becky Sharp's story and delivered much of the original's wit. Though stagy at times, Miriam Hopkins—an absolute dead ringer for Ann Magnuson—bounces off the walls in an endearing way. Best known as the first movie filmed in Technicolor, *Becky Sharp* is one of Martin Scorsese's favorite movies. Go figure.

Jane Eyre (1944, U.S., 96 mins., b/w) Dir: Robert Stevenson; Cast: Orson Welles, Joan Fontaine, Elizabeth Taylor, Margaret O'Brien, Peggy Ann Garner.

Orson Welles leads the way in this moody version of Charlotte Brontë's novel of a governess working for a family with many dark secrets. A solid film, but like the book, it seems controlled, almost repressed, when compared to *Wuthering Heights*. Then again, Charlotte *was* the older sister.

Tom Brown's School Days (1951, Great Britain, 93 mins., b/w) Dir: Gordon Parry; Cast: Robert Newton, Diana Wynyard.

Take this version over the earlier one with Freddie Bartholomew. Thomas Hughes's book played a large part in immortalizing the English public school and, consequently, affected the spread of Victoria's empire. The same claim can't be made for the movie, but it's a fine film all the same.

Great Expectations (1946, Great Britain, 115 mins., b/w) Dir: David Lean; Cast: John Mills, Valerie Hobson, Finlay Currie, Alec Guinness, Bernard Miles, Francis L. Sullivan, Jean Simmons, Martita Hunt.

There have been scores of films made of Dickens's books, but none this well. The perfect casting and crisp pace capture two of Dickens's greatest strengths; a happy ending to Pip's journey toward success, in place of the book's more ambiguous finish, is the only problem. A small point, though, compared to all that is memorable about this masterpiece. Argue all you want for *David Copperfield*—this is the best Dickens on film.

Oliver Twist (1948, Great Britain, 105 mins., b/w) Dir: David Lean; Cast: Alec Guinness, John Howard Davies.

David Lean made the second-best Dickens film, too. Blessed with the same virtues as *Great Expectations*, but with more action, this would make a very nice introduction to Dickens for a young person. The musical *Oliver!* is worth another viewing as well.

The Picture of Dorian Gray (1945, U.S., 110 mins., c & b/w) Dir: Albert Lewin; Cast: George Sanders, Hurd Hatfield, Donna Reed, Angela Lansbury.

Scary telling of Oscar Wilde's story of a seemingly ageless man whose portrait reveals his many sins. One of the best

Hollywood adaptations of an English novel. The actual painting was done by the artist Ivan Albright.

ENGLISH LIT
■
20TH CENTURY

England has really taken it on the chops this century. First, they lose the empire. Then they send an entire generation to get wiped out in the trenches in the First World War. The Germans blitz them in the Second and now the Queen is one more affair away from calling it quits. At least their writers have been able to keep in top form by chronicling all this bad news, and the movie business has kept busy turning the resulting classics into films.

Howards End (1992, Great Britain, 140 mins.) Dir: James Ivory; Cast: Anthony Hopkins, Emma Thompson, Vanessa Redgrave, Helena Bonham Carter.

The lovingly detailed interpretations of E. M. Forster's work by Ismail Merchant and James Ivory have clearly been instrumental in the author's recent emergence from behind the shadows of D. H. Lawrence and Virginia Woolf. As much as this rumination on the future of England is Forster's most mature work, so is this Merchant-Ivory's finest film. An intense, artful movie that never wallows in artiness.

Sons and Lovers (1960, U.S.-Great Britain, 103 mins., b/w) Dir: Jack Cardiff; Cast: Trevor Howard, Dean Stockwell, Mary Ure, Wendy Hiller.
■
Stockwell may star as Paul Morel, Lawrence's aspiring artist who wants to leave his Welsh mining village for a better life, but Wendy Hiller and Trevor Howard as his parents are the real reasons to watch this film. They bring a

kind of volcanic energy that compensates for Stockwell's near miss of a performance and of which Lawrence would certainly have approved.

The Rocking Horse Winner (1949, Great Britain, 91 mins., b/w) Dir: Anthony Pelissier; Cast: Valerie Hobson, John Mills, John Howard Davies.

This focused and most satisfying film adaptation of Lawrence's work centers on Lawrence's story of a boy who can predict racetrack winners. Instead of getting all tangled up in sexual politics, fecund dirt, and the rest of the usual blather, this sad and eerie movie drives ahead on emotion and the strength of its plot. An unheralded classic.

Orlando (1993, Great Britain-Russia-France-Holland, 93 mins.) Dir: Sally Potter; Cast: Tilda Swinton, Billy Zane, Lothaire Bluteau, Quentin Crisp.

Virginia Woolf's novel of a woman who transcends time and gender receives a careful and exuberant treatment here. Quentin Crisp plays the Queen of England, a role that he has been playing most of his life.

The Horse's Mouth (1958, Great Britain, 93 mins.) Dir: Ronald Neame; Cast: Alec Guinness, Kay Walsh, Ernest Thesiger, Renée Houston, Michael Gough, Robert Coote.

Alec Guinness wrote the screenplay for this version of Joyce Cary's comic novel about an impoverished London painter trying to satisfy both his stomach and his muse. Though Cary is usually placed on the second tier of English writers, Guinness's performance sets this charming film on the first tier of English films.

1984 (1984, Great Britain, 123 mins.) Dir: Michael Radford; Cast: John Hurt, Richard Burton.

Well, thank God it didn't turn out like this. The brilliant art direction creates all that George Orwell could have imagined for his suffocating view of a totalitarian future. The passing of 1984, though, has somehow drained some of the mythic power of the title and, hence, the story. If only Orwell had requested in his will that every once in a while they add another 50 years to the name, maybe we'd remember that we're not out of the woods yet.

Lord of the Flies (1963, Great Britain, 90 mins., b/w) Dir: Peter Brook; Cast: James Aubrey, Tom Chapin, Hugh Edwards, Roger Elwin.

Whether or not William Golding deserved a Nobel Prize (he won for Literature in 1983) is debatable, but both his story of boys reverting to primitives and this film based on it are undoubtedly classics. For some dreadful reason this was remade in 1990 with your typically polished American child actors. You deserve a Piggy-like fate if you choose that one over Brook's.

The Loved One (1965, U.S., 116 mins., b/w) Dir: Tony Richardson; Cast: Robert Morse, Jonathan Winters, Anjanette Comer, Milton Berle, John Gielgud, Rod Steiger, Liberace.

This grotesque, rollicking satire on the business of death in America may come as quite a shock to those who sipped tea and hugged their teddies through the endless hours of *Brideshead Revisited*. What else can you say about a movie that features John Gielgud, Liberace, and Milton Berle? Terry Southern and Christopher Isherwood adapted Evelyn Waugh's novel with brio and bad taste equal to the original.

Saturday Night and Sunday Morning (1960, Great Britain, 98 mins., b/w) Dir: Karel Reisz; Cast: Albert Finney, Shirley Anne Field.
■
An early and prime example of England's angry young man films of the sixties, based on the angry young novel by Alan Sillitoe. Finney's first starring role as the boozing, whoring, but still redeemable yobbo Arthur Seaton propels this marvelous movie.

A Clockwork Orange (1971, Great Britain, 135 mins.) Dir: Stanley Kubrick; Cast: Malcolm McDowell, Patrick Magee, Adrienne Corri.

Usually novels and movies loaded with warnings of imminent demise and degeneration become dated about two months after their release. Not here. Oh no, dear reader. Anthony Burgess's novel and Kubrick's film about gangs of murderous punks and the brutal methods used to rehabilitate them are even more powerful now than they were in the seventies. A horrifying movie, and required viewing in a world that glorifies youth violence.

AMERICAN LIT
■
19TH CENTURY

Unlike the movies, where English films have always been overshadowed by those made in Hollywood, the literary world for centuries looked to England for its lead and considered American literature a sort of tag-along little brother. The irony, of course, is that English films are often superior to the big-budget studio jobs and American writers of the 19th century match up quite well to the vaunted Brits of their time, thank you very much. In the following, early American literature gets its full due on film. Now someone has to write a great novel about English movies.

House of Usher (1960, U.S., 79 mins.) Dir: Roger Corman; Cast: Vincent Price, Myrna Fahey, Harry Ellerbe, Mark Damon.

Accept no imitations. You want the Roger Corman/Vincent Price adaptation of Edgar Allan Poe's great story about a family bringing its line to a horrific end. Macabre, scary, and entertaining, as befits the Jerry Lee Lewis of American letters.

The Scarlet Letter (1973, West Germany-Spain, 94 mins.) Dir: Wim Wenders; Cast: Senta Berger, Lou Castel, Hans Christian Blech, Yella Rottlander, Yelina Samarina, William Layton.

German Wim Wenders makes a credible attempt at Hawthorne's novel about the stigmatized adulteress, Hester Prynne, but he left out the redemption. Senta Berger plays Hester as something of a slut, which is certainly a spin. Modernizing the sensibility to say that it shouldn't matter what she's done misses the point, though the film does have its moments. The PBS version from the late 1970s is better.

Moby Dick (1956, U.S., 116 mins.) Dir: John Huston; Cast: Gregory Peck, Orson Welles, Harry Andrews, Richard Basehart, James Robertson-Justice.

Not quite up to the grandeur and sweep of Melville's tome on obsessed Captain Ahab's suicidal pursuit of the Great White Whale; it would be a miracle if it was. Peck does well by Ahab, and Huston does as well as possible by a writer whose work almost defies screen adaptation.

Huckleberry Finn (1939, U.S., 90 mins., b/w) Dir: Richard Thorpe; Cast: Mickey Rooney, Rex Ingram, Walter Connolly, William Frawley, Victor Kilian.

Out of all the versions of both *Huckleberry Finn* and *Tom Sawyer,* this version with Mickey Rooney is the best, with—surprise—the 1973 musical *Tom Sawyer* starring Johnny *"Family Affair"* Whitaker finishing second. A good film that never gets as pungent and true as

Twain's writing, but it's hard to blame director Thorpe; he probably read the book in seventh grade, too.

The Red Badge of Courage (1951, U.S., 69 mins., b/w) Dir: John Huston; Cast: Audie Murphy, Bill Mauldin, Douglas Dick, Royal Dano, John Dierkes, Arthur Hunnicutt.

John Huston's masterful adaptation of Stephen Crane's classic Civil War meditation on cowardice and bravery ironically stars World War II hero Audie Murphy. It's at least as powerful as Crane's book and further evidence that Huston, out of all American directors, had the most success with turning books into movies.

The Innocents (1961, U.S.-Great Britain, 100 mins., b/w) Dir: Jack Clayton; Cast: Deborah Kerr, Martin Stephens, Pamela Franklin.

The positively baroque prose style of Henry James often overshadows his fabulous plots; you're so happy to finish a sentence that you forget what the hell just happened. This moody, brilliant version of his ghost story *The Turn of the Screw,* co-scripted by Truman Capote, makes it clear that James could have been the 19th century's Stephen King if he had wanted to.

The Heiress (1949, U.S., 115 mins., b/w) Dir: William Wyler; Cast: Olivia de Havilland, Montgomery Clift, Ralph Richardson, Miriam Hopkins.

William Wyler's version of James's *Washington Square* deserves mention in any discussion of the finest American films, but for some reason it's usually overlooked. De Havilland won an Oscar for her portrayal of a plain, wealthy woman on the brink of spinsterhood, who is courted by a man her father suspects is a fortune hunter. Richardson and Clift are also superior and the Aaron Copland score unites the whole heartbreaking film.

The Age of Innocence (1993, U.S., 137 mins.) Dir: Martin Scorsese; Cast: Daniel Day-Lewis, Michelle Pfeiffer, Winona Ryder.

Overall an intelligent adaptation of Edith Wharton's novel about a socialite in 1890s New York who is torn between two women and the different worlds they represent. Scorsese gets credit for some inventive direction and a clear love of the material, but his major mistake is to include bits of narration from the book; nothing in the film matches the sharp wit and insight of Wharton's prose. On its own terms the film works, but it fades in the comparison Scorsese invites.

Carrie (1952, U.S., 118 mins., b/w) Dir: William Wyler; Cast: Jennifer Jones, Laurence Olivier, Miriam Hopkins, Eddie Albert, Mary Murphy.

Another fine Wyler adaptation of an American classic, here Theodore Dreiser's realist tale of a farm girl who comes to Chicago and eventually becomes an actress. If you've ever had any doubts about Olivier—too snooty and British, overrated—this film proves that he earned every superlative. Jennifer Jones just barely keeps up with him and, to be honest, Eddie Albert shows her up too.

Kwaidan (1964, Japan, 164 mins.) Dir: Masaki Kobayashi; Cast: Michiko Aratama, Keiko Kishi, Tasuyai Nakadai.

Lafcadio Hearn was an American writer who moved to Japan and if expatriate Henry James belong on this list, Hearn does too. A stately and scary retelling of four ghost stories, deeply imbued with Japanese culture. In fact, though they are presented with a Japanese restraint and aesthetic, the stories themselves are good old late-at-night-with-the-lights-out ghost stories. Who says Americans can never understand the Japanese?

AMERICAN LIT
■
20TH CENTURY

When we think of American writers of this century, the names that most often come to mind are Hemingway, Faulkner, and Fitzgerald. But American men and women of letters have also shown us aspects of this nation's experience that do not take place in either Paris, Mississippi or East Egg, Long Island. And where literature goes, Hollywood follows.

All the King's Men (1949, U.S., 109 mins., b/w) Dir: Robert Rossen; Cast: Broderick Crawford, Joanne Dru, John Ireland, Mercedes McCambridge, John Derek, Shepherd Strudwick, Anne Seymour.

Powerful version of Robert Penn Warren's novel, loosely based on the life of Louisiana governor Huey Long. Broderick Crawford and Mercedes McCambridge both won Oscars, as did the film for Best Picture. A classic study of corruption and politics.

Naked Lunch (1991, Great Britain-Canada, 115 mins.) Dir: David Cronenberg; Cast: Peter Weller, Judy Davis, Ian Holm, Julian Sands, Roy Scheider.

A disgusting film about one of America's most disgusting writers, which doesn't mean that it's not worth seeing. This is really more of a pastiche of William S. Burroughs's life than it is an adaptation of his novel. The plot, as it is, follows an exterminator's descent into a world of drugs, hallucinations, omnisexual behavior, and enormous, scary, gross bugs. As compelling as Burroughs can often be, and certainly not for the kids. But since when was Burroughs ever for the kids?

The Naked and the Dead (1958, U.S., 131 mins.) Dir: Raoul Walsh; Cast: Aldo Ray, Cliff Robertson, Raymond Massey, Joey Bishop, Lili St. Cyr.

Norman Mailer bulled his way into American literary history with this novel about enlisted men clashing with officers during World War II and while the film doesn't pack the same punch, it works pretty well on its own terms. Joseph Heller's *Catch-22* was a strong literary counterpoint to Mailer, and Mike Nichols's 1990 film version of that book balances this film in much the same way.

The Swimmer (1968, U.S., 94 mins.) Dirs: Frank Perry, Sydney Pollack; Cast: Burt Lancaster, Janice Rule, Janet Landgard, Diana Muldaur, Kim Hunter.

Burt Lancaster is perfect as a troubled, upper-middle-class suburbanite swimming home through his neighbors' backyard pools. Based on a short story by John Cheever, the master of upper-middle-class troubles, it captures the frightening blankness of a man facing an unexamined life led in an unexamined place.

Mr. and Mrs. Bridge (1990, U.S., 124 mins.) Dir: James Ivory; Cast: Paul Newman, Joanne Woodward, Blythe Danner, Simon Callow, Kyra Sedgwick, Robert Dean Leonard, Austin Pendleton, Margaret Welsh, Saundra McClain.

More troubled upper-middle-class types, this time in Depression-era Kansas City. Evan Connell originally wrote this as two books, one that told the story from Mr. Bridge's point of view and the other from Mrs. Bridge's. Rather than trying some dreadful *Rashomon* conceit, Ivory and producer Ismail Merchant play it straight as one story and let Woodward and Newman carry the film to its emotional heights.

Lolita (1962, U.S.-Great Britain, 152 mins., b/w) Dir: Stanley Kubrick; Cast: James Mason, Peter Sellers, Shelley Winters, Sue Lyon.

Doesn't hold a candle to Vladimir Nabokov's tale of a decadent European

seducing an underage American girl, but the script helps this version by Kubrick go over the top in enough ways to become a work of art on its own terms. Mason, Sellers, Winters, and Sue Lyon are all wonderful, and the film wisely stops short of trying to replicate the novel's examination into voyeurism. What works in the book would have been awful on the screen.

Breakfast at Tiffany's (1961, U.S., 115 mins.) Dir: Blake Edwards; Cast: Audrey Hepburn, George Peppard, Patricia Neal, Buddy Ebsen, Mickey Rooney.

Sometimes all the pieces come together and a moment in time is perfectly preserved. Here, Blake Edwards's direction, Truman Capote's novel (though sugarcoated), Henry Mancini's music, and Audrey Hepburn's performance as party-girl Holly Golightly combine to save late fifties New York for the ages. A charming film that is almost as knowing as its source.

Slaughterhouse-Five (1972, U.S., 104 mins.) Dir: George Roy Hill; Cast: Michael Sacks, Ron Liebman, Sharon Gans, Valerie Perrine.

There may be greater writers than Kurt Vonnegut, but his openness, humor, and love of truth brought a generation of Americans to books and a humanistic view of life. This version of Vonnegut's novel about a man who becomes "unstuck" in time (sound familiar, *Quantum Leap* fans?) doesn't make a lot of sense unless you've read the book and, well, the book doesn't make much sense either. The images and the sensibility are really all that matter anyway.

Short Cuts (1993, U.S., 189 mins.) Dir: Robert Altman; Cast: Lily Tomlin, Tom Waits, Andie MacDowell, Fred Ward, Anne Archer, Tim Robbins, Lyle Lovett, Jennifer Jason Leigh.

Altman cut and pasted a group of Raymond Carver's short stories into this fascinating, immensely watchable film that lacks the depth, the humor, and the pain of Carver's work. However much we now like to think of Altman as a rebel, he proves here with this high-gloss treatment that he is more Hollywood than he's been letting on recently.

A River Runs Through It (1992, U.S., 123 mins.) Dir: Robert Redford; Cast: Craig Sheffer, Brad Pitt, Tom Skerritt, Emily Lloyd.

A dense book about fly-fishing and a prickly Montana family isn't a natural for film adaptation, but Redford gets points for turning Norman Maclean's novel into an effective movie. The visual beauty of the film buoys the less-than-compelling story, just as Maclean's brilliant prose keeps the reader turning the pages.

The Witches of Eastwick (1987, U.S., 122 mins.) Dir: George Miller; Cast: Jack Nicholson, Cher, Susan Sarandon, Michelle Pfeiffer, Veronica Cartwright.

There's overacting, and then there's Jack Nicholson overacting. Following the cue of John Updike, who didn't take this story of Satan coming to modern-day New England too seriously, director Miller lets everyone have fun, especially Jack. If you don't take it too seriously, you'll have fun too.

LIT FRANÇAISE

Maybe the French love for film comes from the parallels between their literature and their cinema. Literary giants like Hugo, Flaubert, and Proust have their equivalents in Renoir, Ophuls, and Truffaut, and avant-garde writers like Queneau and Robbe-Grillet are matched with Godard and Malle. No matter who **has adapted them, though, the French classics have been well-served by film.**

Dangerous Liaisons (1988, U.S., 120 mins.) Dir: Stephen Frears; Cast: Glenn Close, John Malkovich, Michelle Pfeiffer, Swoozie Kurtz, Keanu Reeves, Mildred Natwick.

There have been three adaptations of Pierre Laclos's novel of manipulation and love in 18th-century France. Even though this one is based on a theatrical adaptation by Christopher Hampton, it's probably most in keeping with the original. As chilling as it is visually beautiful. Roger Vadim's 1959 modern-dress version might be a fun follow-up.

The Hunchback of Notre Dame (1939, U.S., 115 mins.) Dir: William Dieterle; Cast: Charles Laughton, Maureen O'Hara, Edmond O'Brien, Sir Cedric Hardwicke, Thomas Mitchell, George Zucco, Walter Hampden, Alan Marshal, Rod La Rocque, George Tobias.

Victor Hugo is the greatest pillar in French literature and both this book and *Les Miserables* have been put on film many times. Though the Lon Chaney version of *Hunchback* is fine, you can't beat Charles Laughton as the deformed bell-ringer or Maureen O'Hara as the object of his sad desire.

Les Miserables (1935, U.S., 108 mins., b/w) Dir: Richard Boleslawski; Cast: Fredric March, Charles Laughton, John Beal, Florence Eldridge, Rochelle Hudson, Cedric Hardwicke, John Carradine.

Another triumph for Laughton, who plays Javert, the soldier who hunts the petty criminal Jean Valjean. It's one thing to pile on makeup and play to the cheap seats as a hunchback, but here Laughton expresses the subtleties of his character with his eyes and lips and overall carriage. Sorry, no cast album or

T-shirts; just superior acting by everyone involved.

Madame Bovary (1991, France, 130 mins.) Dir: Claude Chabrol; Cast: Isabelle Huppert, Jean-Francois Balmer, Christopher Malavoy, Jean Yanne, Lucas Belvaux.

Though this lavish version of Flaubert's masterpiece drifts toward *Masterpiece Theatre* at times, Chabrol and Huppert make it special by emphasizing the feminist underpinnings of the story. Huppert's Emma Bovary appears caught in the headlights of her inevitable doom. Another interesting Flaubert/film combination is *Sentimental Education* and *Children of Paradise*. Both take place at the same time, so whichever you put first will definitely heighten your enjoyment of the other.

Cyrano de Bergerac (1950, U.S., 112 mins., b/w) Dir: Michael Gordon; Cast: José Ferrer, Mala Powers, William Prince, Morris Carnovsky, Elena Verdugo.

Some will claim that the 1990 version is definitive, but once in a while it's nice to see a movie about France that doesn't star Gerard Depardieu. Nostalgia also gives the nod to José Ferrer's interpretation of Edmond Rostand's nasally overendowed hero. Yes, Steve Martin *would* have made a great Cyrano, but unless he's willing to try it again with a new director and without Daryl Hannah, we'll never know.

La Bête Humaine (1938, France, 105 mins., b/w) Dir: Jean Renoir; Cast: Jean Gabin, Simone Simon, Julien Carette.

Renoir himself makes an appearance in this stunning version of Emile Zola's realist landmark. Jean Gabin, who deserves more recognition than he gets, plays the imbalanced train engineer ensnared in a murder plot. A tough, honest film that's never self-conscious of its toughness or its honesty.

Le Plaisir (1951, France, 97 mins., b/w) Dir: Max Ophuls; Cast: Jean Gabin, Danielle Darrieux, Simone Simon, Claude Dauphin, Gaby Morlay.

Guy de Maupassant was the first true master of the short story as we know it and here Max Ophuls, a master of the short form himself, brings three of them to film. Ophuls's taste for the sensual pleasures of the Belle Epoque puts him so in sync with de Maupassant that it's easy to believe that it's the author himself narrating, and not Peter Ustinov. The final story about a madame who takes her employees to the country for her niece's communion is just perfect.

Swann in Love (1984, France-West Germany, 110 mins.) Dir: Volker Schlondorff; Cast: Jeremy Irons, Ornella Muti, Alain Delon, Fanny Ardant, Marie-Christine Barrault.

Why didn't Max Ophuls ever adapt Proust? There must be a reason. It's a shame he didn't, because Volker Schlondorff certainly wasn't the right person to do it. In typical teutonic fashion, Schlondorff gets the details right but misses all the passion, romance, and complexity that Proust goes to unmatched lengths to express. Proust fans may also be interested in *Céleste*, an intriguing film about the relationship between the author and his housekeeper.

Last Year at Marienbad (1961, France-Italy, 93 mins., b/w) Dir: Alain Resnais; Cast: Delphine Seyrig, Giorgio Albertazzi, Sacha Pitoeff.

Alain Robbe-Grillet's repetitive, rather perverse writing is an acquired taste to be sure, and so is this film for which he wrote the screenplay. The story is much less important than the repetitive, rather perverse way it is told. Just think of it as an artsy *Groundhog Day*.

Zazie dans le Métro (1960, France, 92 mins.) Dir: Louis Malle; Cast: Catherine

Demonget, Philippe Noiret, Carla Marlier, Hubert Deschamps.

Louis Malle did an amazing thing—he made a movie with exactly the same pluses and minuses as the book it's based on. Like Raymond Queneau's novel, it's sprightly, comic, and endearing, and Malle's jump cuts and time compressions are cinematic equivalents of the author's formal conceits. Now for the bad news. Just as you get your fill around the halfway point of the book, you get the idea in the film pretty quickly. Even though their hearts are in the right place, neither the book nor the movie has much substance and neither one knows when to stop. But you will.

STEPPE CLASS

Russian writers don't like to do things small. If they're exploring the psyche, they go all the way to the soul. If it's history, they give you decades of time, battlefields, and the entire sweep of the world's largest nation. Since this all-or-nothing attitude is attractive in a business that gave us *Heaven's Gate* and Cecil B. DeMille, there's a wide choice of Russian novels and stories on film.

The Queen of Spades (1948, Great Britain, 96 mins., b/w) Dir: Thorold Dickinson; Cast: Anton Walbrook, Edith Evans, Ronald Howard, Mary Jerrold, Yvonne Mitchell, Anthony Dawson.

An atmospheric, spooky retelling of Alexander Pushkin's tale of an army officer in the early 19th century whose obsession with card playing leads him to the occult. Anton Walbrook plays the officer with that vaguely mysterious pan-European sophistication and élan Americans tend to find both enormously attractive and deeply annoying. But that's our problem, not Anton's.

Oblomov (1981, U.S.S.R., 146 mins.) Dir: Nikita Mikhalkov; Cast: Oleg Tabakov, Yuri Bogatryev, Elena Soloyei, Andrei Popov.

Considering that Ivan Goncharov's mid-19th-century novel is about a man who never leaves his bed, one should not expect a great deal of action in this faithful adaptation. What you should expect is a careful and amusing character study of an average, though rather indolent, noble of the period, built, like the novel, on details and subtlety. Plus, you get some sumptuous photography, which those of us who had to read this in college were unfortunately not favored with.

Anna Karenina (1935, U.S., 95 mins., b/w) Dir: Clarence Brown; Cast: Greta Garbo, Fredric March, Basil Rathbone, Maureen O'Sullivan, Freddie Bartholomew.

Though Vivien Leigh gives as good a performance in the 1948 British version as her limited abilities allow, Garbo rushes past her like a train bound for St. Petersburg in this one. The same goes with just about every other aspect of the film, from script to set design. This *Karenina* sparkles with all the romantic vitality and Fabergé excess of tsarist Russia.

War and Peace (1956, U.S.-Italy, 208 mins.) Dir: King Vidor; Cast: Audrey Hepburn, Henry Fonda, Mel Ferrer, Vittorio Gassman, John Mills.

It all depends on how much time you have. A great cast and King Vidor at the helm give this Hollywood version its share of memorable moments, but Sergei Bondarchuk's Russian adaptation stays closer to Tolstoy and most agree that it's the better of the two. Still, it's 373 minutes long. Given the kind of commitment you have to make, you might consider reading the book instead.

The Idiot (1951, Japan, 166 mins., b/w) Dir: Akira Kurosawa; Cast: Masayuki Mori, Setsuko Hara, Toshiro Mifune, Takashi Shimura.

Kurosawa updates Dostoyevsky's novel to post-World War II Japan. His Myshkin, a man with a perfect soul, is portrayed as a dewy-eyed victim of battle fatigue. Despite the length of the scenes and their talkiness, Kurosawa keeps a low, hot fire burning beneath it all so you stay glued to the screen.

The Brothers Karamazov (1958, U.S., 146 mins.) Dir: Richard Brooks; Cast: Yul Brynner, Maria Schell, Lee J. Cobb, Claire Bloom, Richard Basehart, William Shatner, Albert Salmi.

Hollywood takes a stab at Dostoyevsky, with surprisingly good results. Brynner, Basehart, Salmi, and, in his first movie role, William Shatner play the brothers whose lives are changed by the death of their father. The film goes for the full Technicolor treatment, but Richard Brooks, who also wrote the script, never lets the style get too far ahead of the substance.

The Three Sisters (1970, Great Britain, 165 mins.) Dir: Laurence Olivier (with John Sichel); Cast: Laurence Olivier, Joan Plowright, Alan Bates, Jeanne Watts, Louise Purnell.

Olivier shows his directorial talents as well as his more famous skills as an actor in this rendering of Chekhov's classic play about three sisters in turn-of-the-century Russia. As in the other films he based on plays, Olivier knows when to be theatrical and when to be cinematic, a discernment rare in most adaptations from the stage.

The Lower Depths (1936, France, 92 mins., b/w) Dir: Jean Renoir; Cast: Jean Gabin, Vladimir Sokoloff, Louis Jouvet, Robert Le Vigan, Suzy Prim, Jany Holt.

Renoir and Kurosawa both did versions of this 1902 Maxim Gorky play about lowlifes in tsarist Russia. As usual, Kurosawa went in for lots of dialogue and while his film is probably superior overall, Renoir keeps things moving along better. Renoir isn't afraid to get sordid, and this is a most sordid affair of love, treachery, and murder.

Doctor Zhivago (1965, Great Britain, 200 mins.) Dir: David Lean; Cast: Julie Christie, Omar Sharif, Rod Steiger, Alec Guinness, Geraldine Chaplin, Tom Courtenay.

Critics may think this is too long and extravagant, but that's the point. This is Russia, remember? The novel by Boris Pasternak about a doctor and the two loves of his life is by no means free of excess either. If you want a movie with just a little too much of everything, a movie you can completely sink into and forget the world with, this is your baby.

One Day in the Life of Ivan Denisovich (1971, Great Britain-Norway-U.S., 100 mins.) Dir: Casper Wrede; Cast: Tom Courtenay, Alfred Burke.

It's extremely hard to do justice by the works of Russia's greatest living author, and this bleak, by-the-numbers adaptation of Alexander Solzhenitsyn's novel about life in the gulag is as close as anyone has come. The book could have been better served by someone with their own creative vision, though. Just imagine what Welles would have done in black and white with the snowy wastes of Siberia and scores of forgotten men trying to survive in a place designed to drive them mad.

THE LOST GENERATION

Then Brett and I went to a little video shop owned by the Spaniard with a scar from the bulls. We opened a bottle of good red wine and

the Spaniard told us about the new arrivals. Brett had seen them all, so we rented some of these films based on books by Hemingway, Fitzgerald, and their circle.

They were good.

A Farewell to Arms (1932, U.S., 78 mins.) Dir: Frank Borzage; Cast: Helen Hayes, Gary Cooper, Adolphe Menjou.

Don't go for the Rock Hudson version, despite his Hemingwayesque name. Gary Cooper was Papa's kind of guy and he proves it with a fine performance as an injured American ambulance driver who falls in love with his nurse.

For Whom the Bell Tolls (1943, U.S., 170 mins.) Dir: Sam Wood; Cast: Gary Cooper, Ingrid Bergman, Akim Tamiroff.
■
In case you're one of the many people who always gets this confused with *A Farewell to Arms,* remember that this is the one with Ingrid Bergman. Somehow, despite Cooper, the great story about an American mercenary in the Spanish Civil War, and the solid action scenes, Bergman is still the most memorable aspect of this wonderful film.

The Snows of Kilimanjaro (1952, U.S., 117 mins.) Dir: Henry King; Cast: Gregory Peck, Susan Hayward, Ava Gardner, Hildegarde Neff.

Sort of a Hemingway scrapbook. Peck plays a writer (hmm, whom could he be based on?) reviewing his life as he nears his end in Africa, and his reminiscences just happen to be Hemingway stories. Peck isn't Cooper, but his steely, laconic style works well here on its own terms.

To Have and Have Not (1944, U.S., 100 mins., b/w) Dir: Howard Hawks; Cast: Humphrey Bogart, Lauren Bacall, Walter Brennan, Marcel Dalio, Dan Seymour, Hoagy Carmichael.

A must-see thriller based on a Hemingway story about a French Resistance fighter and the woman he falls in love with. William Faulkner worked on the great dialogue Bogey and Bacall (her film debut) deliver in their fiery love scenes.

The Old Man and the Sea (1958, U.S., 86 mins.) Dir: John Sturges; Cast: Spencer Tracy, Felipe Pazos, Harry Bellaver.
■
This story of an old fisherman and his final epic battle with a fish was Hemingway's swan song. Tracy and the film aren't quite up to the simple mastery of the book, but it's still worth seeing.

The Killers (1946, U.S., 105 mins.) Dir: Robert Siodmak; Cast: Burt Lancaster, Ava Gardner, Edmond O'Brien, Albert Dekker, Sam Levene.

Hemingway's story of the investigation following the murder of a boxer gets a fine treatment in this film, which was also Lancaster's first. A 1964 film with the same name is a quirky remake of sorts starring Lee Marvin as a hit man who knocks off a race-car driver and then discovers that he is part of a bigger plot. The first is the better movie, but the second definitely has its moments.

The Great Gatsby (1974, U.S., 144 mins.) Dir: Jack Clayton; Cast: Robert Redford, Mia Farrow, Karen Black, Sam Waterston, Bruce Dern, Scott Wilson, Howard Da Silva, Edward Herrmann, Patsy Kensit.

Some say this Fitzgerald story of a nouveau riche Long Island man who falls in love with an empty woman with old money is the Great American Novel. Agree or disagree. Compare the performances by Farrow and Redford to grass growing. Which is more interesting? Defend your choice. Extra credit: With all the attention paid to the costumes and art design, do you think anyone thought about anything else during the making of this film?

The Last Tycoon (1976, U.S., 125 mins.) Dir: Elia Kazan; Cast: Robert De Niro, Tony Curtis, Ingrid Boulting, Robert Mitchum, Jeanne Moreau.

Fitzgerald never finished this novel about Hollywood and the early moguls of the film industry, but director Kazan and screenwriter Harold Pinter assembled a fine cast and did the job for him. Intriguing viewing, especially for De Niro's performance as a studio head on his way down.

The Day of the Locust (1975, U.S., 140 mins.) Dir: John Schlesinger; Cast: Donald Sutherland, Karen Black, Burgess Meredith, William Atherton, Geraldine Page.

Nathanael West wasn't an expatriate or a poseur like Hemingway and Fitzgerald, but his one great book is as bleak, compelling, and indulgent as the masters' best. The film—which is quite good, too, and more than a little scary—features Karen Black as a pathetic would-be movie actress whose affair with an accountant has tragic results.

The Moderns (1988, U.S., 126 mins.) Dir: Alan Rudolph; Cast: Keith Carradine, Linda Fiorentino, Wallace Shawn, John Lone, Genevieve Bujold, Geraldine Chaplin.

Though the whole Lost Generation bit is certainly overrated, romantic hooey, it could never have been as awful as this. Pretentious and at times painful to watch, the film features brief portraits of Hemingway, Gertrude Stein, et al. Carradine plays an artist trying to make it in Paris during the Crazy Years. In truth, some loved this movie. Your affinity for the myth of Paris in the twenties may determine how much you like this film.

THE WOMEN'S ROOM

The movie world has had no problem with turning books by women writers into films, but don't strain yourself looking for women in the credits. While the world of letters has been relatively open to women, women filmmakers have had to struggle for recognition in Hollywood. It's not an idle thought to ask what any of these films would have been like if they had been made by women.

The Color Purple (1985, U.S., 155 mins.) Dir: Steven Spielberg; Cast: Whoopi Goldberg, Danny Glover, Rae Dawn Chong, Margaret Avery, Oprah Winfrey.

Though Spielberg gets all the visuals and details right, you have to wonder just how well he captures the essence of living as a poor black woman in the first half of the 20th century. Strong feelings pro and con on this one, but no one faults the performances by Whoopi and Oprah, or Alice Walker's novel.

Wise Blood (1979, U.S., 108 mins.) Dir: John Huston; Cast: Brad Dourif, Amy Wright, Harry Dean Stanton, Ned Beatty.

Flannery O'Connor was lucky to have John Huston bring her world of southern grotesques to the screen. As he always did when adapting books, Huston found the aspect of himself through which he could filter the author's work, and here it was the place where humor and damnation meet. At once strange, bleak, and funny, and a true representation of O'Connor's book.

The Group (1966, U.S., 150 mins.) Dir: Sidney Lumet; Cast: Joan Hackett, Jessica Walter, Joanna Pettet, Kathleen Widdoes, Candice Bergen, Shirley Knight, Elizabeth Hartman, Larry Hagman, Hal Holbrook, Richard Mulligan.

Mary McCarthy's novel about the lives

of eight graduates of an exclusive women's college during the Depression raised eyebrows when it came out, and this adaptation managed to raise a few too. While not a masterpiece, it's solid Lumet and Candice Bergen's first film.

Fried Green Tomatoes (1991, U.S., 130 mins.) Dir: Jon Avnet; Cast: Kathy Bates, Jessica Tandy, Mary Stuart Masterson, Mary-Louise Parker, Cicely Tyson, Chris O'Donnell.

A movie full of good intentions and manipulating situations that you want to hate, but by the end you're won over. Fannie Flagg of *Candid Camera* fame wrote the screenplay, based on her own novel about an unhappy woman who finds the strength to change her own life after she hears the stories of two brave Depression-era women.

Chilly Scenes of Winter (1982, U.S., 99 mins.) Dir: Joan Micklin Silver; Cast: John Heard, Mary Beth Hurt, Gloria Grahame, Peter Riegert, Kenneth McMillan.

Finally, a woman director giving screen life to a book written by a woman (Ann Beattie). The result is an odd film about a man trying to win back an old flame who's now married. *Head Over Heels* is the same movie cut with a different ending. Beattie herself appears as a waitress.

The Heart Is a Lonely Hunter (1968, U.S., 125 mins.) Dir: Robert Ellis Miller; Cast: Alan Arkin, Sondra Locke, Stacy Keach, Cicely Tyson.

Southern gothic about a deaf mute and his effects on the people around him profits from strong performances by Arkin and Locke. It does drag some, but at least you know that Carson McCullers didn't twirl in her grave the way she did when the film version of her novella *The Ballad of the Sad Cafe* came out.

To Kill a Mockingbird (1962, U.S., 129 mins., b/w) Dir: Robert Mulligan; Cast: Gregory Peck, Mary Badham, Philip Alford, Brock Peters.

The last southern story on the list is maybe the most memorable. (See "The Civil War" list if you have any thoughts about mentioning Margaret Mitchell here.) You probably read Harper Lee's book in school, but if you haven't, it's the story of a lawyer (Peck) in a southern town defending a black man accused of raping a white woman. Horton Foote's screenplay won an Oscar.

The Fountainhead (1949, U.S., 114 mins., b/w) Dir: King Vidor; Cast: Gary Cooper, Patricia Neal, Raymond Massey, Kent Smith, Robert Douglas.

The book that launched a thousand neo-cons and libertarians. Cooper stars as Ayn Rand's idealist architect who blows up one of his own buildings because the structure's design had been altered. So much for the architect-client dialogue.

The Accidental Tourist (1988, U.S., 120 mins.) Dir: Lawrence Kasdan; Cast: William Hurt, Geena Davis, Kathleen Turner, Amy Wright, Bill Pullman, David Ogden Stiers, Ed Begley, Jr.

Extravagant dog-trainer Davis helps pull reclusive Hurt back into the world after the death of his son. A faithful, leisurely paced screen translation of Anne Tyler's bestseller and a big film for corgi fans.

FINE ARTS

ART HISTORY

Watching movies about famous artists will tell you as much about art history as a trip to Epcot Center will tell you about Europe. There are other similarities, too—everything you see is a set, all the natives are actors, and everyone speaks English. On the other hand, you can definitely have some guilty fun if you don't take it too seriously.

The Agony and the Ecstasy (1965, U.S., 140 mins.) Dir: Carol Reed; Cast: Charlton Heston, Rex Harrison.

A disappointing outing by the underrated Carol Reed, based on Irving Stone's novel about Michelangelo and the Sistine Chapel. As you'd expect from an epic starring Charlton Heston, the film is sweeping and visually grand, but never as inspired as the paintings it depicts.

Caravaggio (1986, Great Britain, 93 mins.) Dir: Derek Jarman; Cast: Nigel Terry, Sean Bean, Garry Cooper, Tilda Swinton.

Stylized, arty film about a stylized, arty painter. Jarman plays with time and detail as he tries to plumb the depths of Caravaggio's soul and our patience. You'd better like Caravaggio if you're thinking about this one.

Rembrandt (1936, Great Britain, 84 mins., b/w) Dir: Alexander Korda; Cast: Charles Laughton, Gertrude Lawrence, Elsa Lanchester.

A real find. Korda lovingly re-creates the world of 17th-century Holland and Laughton re-creates Rembrandt at different phases of his life with even more love, care, and verisimilitude. Even with a tremendous cast that includes Lanchester and Lawrence, Laughton seems to be acting a few levels beyond anyone around him. It's as close as we'll get to seeing Rembrandt in the flesh.

Impromptu (1990, U.S., 109 mins.) Dir: James Lapine; Cast: Judy Davis, Hugh Grant, Mandy Patinkin, Bernadette Peters, Julian Sands, Emma Thompson, Anna Massey.

A charming film primarily about the romance between George Sand and Frédéric Chopin. Director James Lapine blends just enough period realism with a pinch of modern sensibility to create a colorful, diverting comedy for adults. Mandy Patinkin plays a very affable Eugène Delacroix.

Lust for Life (1956, U.S., 122 mins.) Dir: Vincente Minnelli; Cast: Kirk Douglas, Anthony Quinn, James Donald, Pamela Brown.

Down this hall, we begin the post-Impressionists, of which there are many. Take, for instance, this film starring Kirk Douglas as Vincent Van Gogh. Notice the violent color and emotion, the piling on of effects, called "overacting." Some critics feel this is a brilliant film; others think it is Hollywood kitsch.

Vincent and Theo (1990, Great Britain-France, 138 mins.) Dir: Robert Altman; Cast: Tim Roth, Paul Rhys, Jip Wijngaarden, Johanna Ter Steege, Wladimir Yordanoff, Jean-Pierre Cassel.

As we move along, we see another Van Gogh, this time directed by the master Robert Altman. *Lust for Life* is the old classic, but this dual biography of Vincent and his art-dealer brother Theo is better history and better drama. Tim Roth sympathetically conveys Vincent's creative drive and consuming insanity. He gives us a flesh and blood

Van Gogh who we like and understand, instead of the usual romantic Van Gogh myth.

The Wolf at the Door (1987, Denmark-France, 90 mins.) Dir: Henning Carlsen; Cast: Donald Sutherland, Max von Sydow, Fanny Bastien.

If you've seen all the Van Goghs, you've seen a lot of Gauguins, too. Odd, though, that a man who spent years painting scantily clad Tahitian women is usually only depicted in films hanging around with Van Gogh. Then, when someone finally makes a film about him, it's about his years in Paris, between trips to the South Pacific. Sutherland matches up well against Quinn (*Lust for Life*) and Yordanoff (*Vincent and Theo*) in the Gauguin competition.

Moulin Rouge (1952, Great Britain, 119 mins.) Dir: John Huston; Cast: José Ferrer, Colette Marchand, Zsa Zsa Gabor, Eric Pohlman, Suzanne Flon, Christopher Lee.

Somehow cinematic excess seems more appropriate to Toulouse-Lautrec than Van Gogh. John Huston goes over the top creating Toulouse-Lautrec's seamy Parisian world and José Ferrer goes underneath it creating the stunted Toulouse-Lautrec. Garish, sentimental fun that the artist would have liked. Face it, if Henri was around today, he'd probably be a television producer.

Camille Claudel (1989, France, 149 mins.) Dir: Bruno Nuytten; Cast: Isabelle Adjani, Gerard Depardieu, Laurent Crevill, Alain Cluny.

Overlong French film about the titled sculptress, who sacrificed her own career and sanity to help her lover Rodin. An interesting look at the art world of the time, but Adjani did a better job as a woman obsessed in *The Story of Adele H.*

Frida (1984, Mexico, 108 mins.) Dir: Paul Leduc; Cast: Ofelia Medina, Juan José Gurrola, Max Kerlow.

On her deathbed, Mexican artist Frida Kahlo recalls fragments of her life. Very strong on atmospherics and the look of Kahlo's work. Slow going if you're not a fan, but if you are you'll be fascinated.

The Adventures of Picasso (1978, Sweden, 88 mins.) Dir: Tage Danielsson; Cast: Gosta Ekman, Hans Alfredson, Margaretha Krook, Per Oscarsson, Bernard Cribbins, Wilfred Brambell.

A second-rate Pythonesque version of Picasso's life. Mostly a brave and failed attempt to make a Swedish comedy, the film does have its moments, especially Gertrude Stein and Alice B. Toklas as drag queens. A chuckle here and there, but don't make it the centerpiece of the evening. For a look at the real Picasso at work, see Henri-Georges Clouzot's *The Mystery of Picasso,* a documentary in which Clouzot captures the artist creating a painting.

PHOTOGRAPHY

Since motion pictures are essentially thousands of photographs shown at the rate of 24 per second, Hollywood has paid tribute to its older brother with some fine films by and about photographers and photography.

Rear Window (1954, U.S., 112 mins.) Dir: Alfred Hitchcock; Cast: James Stewart, Grace Kelly, Raymond Burr, Wendell Corey, Thelma Ritter.

Consummate Hitchcock thriller features Stewart as a photojournalist laid up with a broken leg who witnesses a murder out his rear window. Or did he? The fascinating, and frustrating, question is why doesn't he just shut the damn drapes and concentrate on Grace Kelly? Stewart's voyeurism is as much at issue here as Raymond Burr's guilt.

The Learning Tree (1969, U.S., 107 mins.) Dir: Gordon Parks; Cast: Kyle Johnson, Alex Clarke, Estelle Evans.

Legendary photographer Gordon Parks directed this adaptation of his own autobiographical novel about growing up black in the South during the twenties. Also worth seeing again if you're a Parks fan is his best movie, the one and only *Shaft*.

Funny Face (1957, U.S., 103 mins.) Dir: Stanley Donen; Cast: Fred Astaire, Audrey Hepburn, Kay Thompson, Suzy Parker, Michel Auclair.

Richard Avedon got credit as visual consultant on this musical about bookseller Hepburn's transformation into a model by fashion photog Astaire. Not surprisingly, the Astaire character is a lot like Avedon. The Gershwin music sounds as good as the movie looks.

The Eyes of Laura Mars (1978, U.S., 104 mins.) Dir: Irvin Kershner; Cast: Faye Dunaway, Tommy Lee Jones, Brad Dourif, René Auberjonois, Raul Julia, Frank Adonis, Lisa Taylor.

Faye Dunaway, another fashion photographer, begins to foresee murders in her shots. Not the greatest thriller ever made, but it has its moments and the fashion shoots are a hoot.

Margaret Bourke-White (1989, U.S./ MTV, 105 mins.) Dir: Lawrence Schiller; Cast: Farrah Fawcett, Frederic Forrest, Mitchell Ryan, David Huddleston.

We found out in *Extremities* and *The Burning Bed* that Farrah really can act. She's not Meryl Streep, but she does a good job here in this made-for-cable biography of the famous *Life* photographer. Though connections between what happened in her life and Bourke-White's photographs are contrived beyond credibility, which also drains some of the drama, at least give the filmmakers credit for making the connections.

The Unbearable Lightness of Being (1988, U.S., 171 mins.) Dir: Philip Kaufman; Cast: Daniel Day-Lewis, Juliette Binoche, Lena Olin, Derek de Lint.

Kaufman adapts Milan Kundera's book with grace and intelligence, moving things along at the same leisurely pace as Kundera does in telling the story of a Czech doctor torn between two women and two ways of living. His wife, played by Binoche, is a photographer and a pivotal scene involves a photo session with Olin, her husband's lover.

Proof (1992, Australia, 91 mins.) Dir: Jocelyn Moorhouse; Cast: Hugo Weaving, Genevieve Picot, Russell Crowe, Heather Mitchell.

A strange and affecting little Australian film about a blind man who takes photographs and asks others to describe what's in them. A fascinating study of trust and truth with great, low-key performances from everyone involved. A real sleeper.

The Cameraman (1928, U.S., 69 mins., b/w) Dir: Edward Sedgwick; Cast: Buster Keaton, Marceline Day, Harold Goodwin, Sidney Bracy.

Silent starring Keaton as a photographer who becomes a gloriously inept newsreel cameraman in order to impress the girl he loves. Minor Keaton, but still full of laughs and an entertaining look at the world before satellite remotes.

The Public Eye (1992, U.S., 99 mins.) Dir: Howard Franklin; Cast: Joe Pesci, Barbara Hershey, Stanley Tucci, Jerry Adler.

Pesci plays a street-wise '40s newsphotographer based on real-life great Weegee (whose photos are appropriated here). Interesting, but overly serious and the chemistry between Pesci and Hershey is so unconvincing that you'll suspect she's leading him on way beyond the point that you're supposed to believe they're in love.

Blow-Up (1966, Great Britain-Italy, 111 mins.) Dir: Michelangelo Antonioni; Cast: David Hemmings, Vanessa Redgrave, Sarah Miles, Verushka.

One weird movie that you have to see. Did photographer Hemmings catch a murder in one of his photos or not? Does it matter? The mod London atmosphere, the decadence, the rhythm of it all draws you in and turns you around in circles. As good as director Antonioni ever got.

THE ART SCENE

Movies about the art world seem to be about: 1) painting; and 2) N.Y.C. So while we've dutifully covered some of these, we also try to broaden the perspective a bit.

3 Women (1977, U.S., 125 mins.) Dir: Robert Altman; Cast: Shelley Duvall, Sissy Spacek, Janice Rule, John Cromwell, Robert Fortier.
■
A mysterious shimmering siren call from the desert. Millie (Duvall), Willie (Rule), and Pinky (Spacek) have lives that seem as vague and unbounded as the desert itself. While the film focuses on the seeming melding and transmutation of the personalities of Millie (a self-involved physical therapist at the local spa), Pinky (a recent hire), and Spacek (at her most ephemeral), the murals the mute Willie paints on the bottom of the swimming pool at their Southern California motel residence provide a most unsettling, yet pervasive and visionary counterpoint.

Utz (1992, Great Britain-Germany-Italy, 95 mins.) Dir: George Sluizer; Cast: Armin Mueller-Stahl, Brenda Fricker, Peter Riegert, Paul Scofield.

Interesting tale of collection and obsession from Dutch director Sluizer *(The Vanishing)*, and based on Bruce Chatwin's last novel. Mueller-Stahl inhabits the eccentric character of Czech nobleman Baron von Utz, known for his fantastic collection of Meissen porcelains and *zaftig* opera singers. The mystery of his Meissen obsession is pursued by covetous N.Y. gallery owner Riegert. Keeping track of the Baron's singers is more the domain of his housekeeper, Fricker.

Three Cases of Murder (1954, Great Britain, 99 mins., b/w) Dirs: Wendy Toye, George More O'Ferrall, David Eady; Cast: Alan Badel, Hugh Pryse, John Gregson, Elizabeth Sellars, Emrys Jones, Orson Welles.

Weirdly satisfying *Twilight Zone*ish episodic venture. The first section, "In the Picture," has our hero sucked into the odd inner life of a seemingly innocent museum landscape as he stands fixated by the painting detail. Stick with it for the Orson Welles-Somerset Maugham teaming in the "Lord Mountdrago" segment.

After Hours (1985, U.S., 97 mins.) Dir: Martin Scorsese; Cast: Griffin Dunne, Rosanna Arquette, Teri Garr, Linda Fiorentino, John Heard.

A neurotically manic jaunt into the lofts of SoHo. Dunne's computer tech is suitably bewildered by his bad-dream encounters with the colorful (though dressed appropriately in black, of course) keepers of the nethernight artworld scene. You can blow off the hopeless adaptation of Tama Janowitz's *Slaves of New York* covering the same territory. If you're just searching for a certain breed of egotistical tortured artist, have a look-see at Scorsese's segment of his own *New York Stories,* Woody Allen's great *Hannah and Her Sisters,* or Paul Mazursky's *An Unmarried Woman.*

Six Degrees of Separation (1993, U.S., 112 mins.) Dir: Fred Schepisi; Cast: Stockard Channing, Donald Sutherland, Will Smith, Ian McKellen, Bruce Davison, Mary Beth Hurt, Anthony Michael Hall.

John Guare's theatrical play (he wrote the screenplay also) remains just a little too stagy to cut it as great cinema. Members of that 1980s N.Y. wealthy and mighty Upper East Side community, "Flan" (Sutherland), an art dealer, and "Oisa" (a strong Channing), whose pride and joy is an unusual two-sided Kandinsky, are prime to be scammed by a pretender son of Sidney Poitier (portrayed by Smith with a well-honed blend of charm and deceit). An absorbing look at the emptiness still possible in having it all.

Bagdad Cafe (1988, West Germany, 91 mins.) Dir: Percy Adlon; Cast: Marianne Sägebrecht, CCH Pounder, Jack Palance.

Palance has a rollicking time (in his twisted way) with this role as a dissipated Hollywood set painter living in a Mojave roadside motel attached to a rundown eatery where the ensemble of characters is as charming as it is eccentric.

The Belly of an Architect (1987, Great Britain-Italy, 108 mins.) Dir: Peter Greenaway; Cast: Brian Dennehy, Chloe Webb, Sergio Fantoni, Lambert Wilson.

Skyscraper Souls (1932, U.S., 80 mins., b/w) Dir: Edgar Selwyn; Cast: Warren William, Maureen O'Sullivan, Gregory Ratoff, Anita Page, Jean Hersholt, Wallace Ford, Hedda Hopper.

Gorgeous cinematography balances some heavy slogging in *Belly of an Architect*, but Greenaway and Dennehy fans should check out this symbolism-fraught story of an American architect questioning his life and his art during an assignment in bella Roma. But we recommend the more straightforward, delightfully pre-code *Skyscraper Souls* about the rapacious monument builders in 20th-century

N.Y. who catch a slice of the "spirit of an age crystallized in steel and stone."

Portrait of Jennie (1948, U.S., 86 mins., c & b/w) Dir: William Dieterle; Cast: Jennifer Jones, Joseph Cotten, Ethel Barrymore, David Wayne.

Down and out painter-in-search-of-a-muse Cotten is mesmerized by a mysterious young woman (a luminous Jones) he encounters in Central Park. Truly a lovely and moving movie, enhanced by the artful use of color in the last reel.

Laura (1944, U.S., 88 mins., b/w) Dir: Rouben Mamoulian; replaced by Otto Preminger; Cast: Gene Tierney, Dana Andrews, Clifton Webb, Vincent Price, Judith Anderson, Grant Mitchell, Lane Chandler, Dorothy Adams.

Another case of mesmerization. This time a detective involved in the search for the presumed missing (and quite breathtaking) Tierney becomes enthralled with her portrait. A superb mystery and a must-see.

The Picture of Dorian Gray (1945, U.S., 110 mins., c & b/w) Dir: Albert Lewin; Cast: George Sanders, Hurd Hatfield, Donna Reed, Angela Lansbury, Peter Lawford.

The classically spooky Oscar Wilde story about a man's portrait aging while he remains forever young. Sanders plays the heavy with his inimitable style. The Harry Stradling cinematography won an Oscar. All in all, well done.

The Ghost and Mrs. Muir (1947, U.S., 104 mins.) Dir: Joseph L. Mankiewicz; Cast: Rex Harrison, Gene Tierney, George Sanders, Edna Best.

Ghost of a sea captain pops out of a painting and captivates Tierney. Maybe a little too romantic and over-long, but hey, what's wrong with some sentimentality every so often? And you can count on Sanders (again) to add his quotient of slither as counterpoint.

The Horse's Mouth (1958, Great Britain, 93 mins.) Dir: Ronald Neame; Cast: Alec Guinness, Kay Walsh, Ernest Thesiger, Renée Houston, Michael Gough, Robert Coote.

Guinness is his rambunctious best as spirited painter Gully Johnson, who spends much of his time searching for big white spaces to cover with, among other things, detailed renderings of feet. He just loves feet. Based on Joyce Cary's novel, this is an enjoyable romp with a whirl of the bowler at stuffy London society.

Legal Eagles (1986, U.S., 114 mins.) Dir: Ivan Reitman; Cast: Robert Redford, Debra Winger, Daryl Hannah, Terence Stamp, Brian Dennehy, John McMartin.

Redford and Winger investigate the enigmatic performance artist Hannah's claim on a painting by her famous father. While, surprise, Hannah doesn't quite come across, you will get some gen-u-ine performance art mixed in with the art-world scene (yes, N.Y.). Entertaining, though plot doesn't always connect.

M U S I C

TIN PAN ALLEY TUNESMITHS

After Jolson sang in *The Jazz Singer,* movie moguls knew that as surely as they needed stories, scripts, stars, and directors, they had to have songs. So they bought the rights to Broadway musicals, they bought tunes from Tin Pan Alley, and they brought the song pluggers out to Hollywood to write for the new "all talking, all singing, all dancing" motion pictures they were making. The following lists focus on the romance between Hollywood and the tunesmiths of Tin Pan Alley. We open wide and move in for a couple of close-ups.

Love Me Tonight (1932, U.S., 100 mins., b/w) Dir: Rouben Mamoulian; Cast: Maurice Chevalier, Jeanette MacDonald, Myrna Loy, Charlie Ruggles.
■
There aren't enough superlatives to describe this enchanting fairy-tale musical about a Parisian tailor who falls in love with a princess. Score by Rodgers and Hart is one of the best written expressly for film and Mamoulian's (he directed original Broadway *Porgy and Bess*) ingenious use of cinematic form makes the musical magical. We are swept along on the songs, including the classic "Isn't It Romantic?," which worked its way onto most every Paramount soundtrack for the next 30 years.

Show Boat (1936, U.S., 113 mins., b/w) Dir: James Whale; Cast: Irene Dunne, Allan Jones, Helen Morgan, Paul Robeson, Charles Winninger, Hattie McDaniel.

This 1936 Universal adaptation (primitive version made in 1929 is lost) of the Jerome Kern/Oscar Hammerstein II landmark musical is far more interesting than its 1951 MGM remake, due in part to exceptional cast, but also to fluid style of director Whale (*Frankenstein*). Hammerstein's lyrics and overly wordy script (based on Edna Ferber novel) raise more than a few racial issues, while Kern's dignified, soulful melodies attempt to transcend them. With "Can't Help Lovin' Dat Man" (sung by Kern's favorite singer, Irene Dunne, as well as Helen Morgan) and Robeson's definitive rendition of "Ol' Man River," he comes mighty close.

Top Hat (1935, U.S., 99 mins., b/w) Dir: Mark Sandrich; Cast: Fred Astaire, Ginger Rogers, Edward Everett Horton, Eric Blore, Erik Rhodes, Helen Broderick, Lucille Ball.

Delightfully fulfills every element of the Fred & Ginger formula: a mistaken-identity plot played out in elegantly fabricated surroundings, with fussbudgets Horton and Blore harrumphing around, and dancing that epitomizes grace, style, and sophistication. All perfectly matched by Irving Berlin's scintillating score, including "Cheek to Cheek," "Isn't This a Lovely Day?," and "Top Hat, White Tie and Tails," which more than any other is Fred Astaire's signature song.

Swing Time (1936, U.S., 103 mins.) Dir: George Stevens; Cast: Fred Astaire, Ginger Rogers, Victor Moore, Eric Blore, Helen Broderick, Betty Furness.

Best-directed Astaire/Rogers musical; dance, decor, and cinematic style reach complete harmony under Stevens's watchful eye. Jerome Kern's "popular" song score (lyrics by Dorothy Field) here, contrasted with his almost operatic stylings in *Show Boat,* reveals his versatility as a composer. Astaire's vocals on the Oscar-winning "The Way You Look Tonight" and "A Fine Romance" firmly establish just how brilliant a singer he was. The tribute to Bill "Bojangles" Robinson is a knockout.

The Band Wagon (1953, U.S., 112 mins.) Dir: Vincente Minnelli; Cast: Fred Astaire, Cyd Charisse, Jack Buchanan, Nanette Fabray, Oscar Levant.

Minnelli and Astaire are both working on many levels, striving for, and reaching, artistic heights, while poking fun at their efforts along the way. The songs by Howard Dietz and Arthur Schwartz (most from the 1931 *Band Wagon* stage review, some from other shows) are brilliantly brought to life. "Dancing in the Dark" is one of

Astaire's loveliest numbers and "Shine on Your Shoes" his most fun. "That's Entertainment" is the eternal anthem to the spirit of the Hollywood musical.

The Sky's the Limit (1943, U.S., 89 mins., b/w) Dir: Edward H. Griffith; Cast: Fred Astaire, Joan Leslie, Robert Ryan, Robert Benchley.

Patriotic WWII musical puts Fred in an Air Force pilot's uniform, but more important, fits him up with some terrific tunes by Harold Arlen and Johnny Mercer, including "My Shining Hour" and the ultimate bluesy, boozy late-night bar ballad, "One for My Baby."

Summer Stock (1950, U.S., 100 mins.) Dir: Charles Walters; Cast: Judy Garland, Gene Kelly, Eddie Bracken, Gloria De Haven.

Model of the MGM barnyard musical is relatively unexciting considering the star power of Kelly and Garland, but Harold Arlen's thumpingly rhythmic "Get Happy" kicks out all the stops and serves as the source for one of Judy's most exhilarating performances—Liza thinks it's her mom's best number in any movie.

A Star Is Born (1954, U.S., 176 mins., b/w) Dir: George Cukor; Cast: Judy Garland, James Mason, Charles Bickford, Jack Carson.

As written by Moss Hart and directed by George Cukor, this is one of the most dramatically powerful movie musicals of the 1950s, the dark side of *Singin' in the Rain.* The depth of emotion is overwhelming. And nowhere is that emotion more evident than in Garland's performance of "The Man That Got Away," another Harold Arlen song. And while Judy Garland could undoubtedly have sung the phone book and made it music, it is in the songs of Harold Arlen (from "Somewhere Over the Rainbow" to here) that she finds the material that seems to best define her career.

42nd Street (1933, U.S., 98 mins., b/w) Dir: Lloyd Bacon; Cast: Dick Powell, Ruby Keeler, Ginger Rogers, Warner Baxter, Una Merkel.

First of the famous Busby Berkeley behind-the-footlights musicals made at Warners in the 1930s, this is the most honest in its depiction of the backstage battles, bitchiness, rigor, and romance. But the real reason to watch it (or the Gold Diggers movies, or *Footlight Parade*) is Berkeley's kaleidoscopic conception of the musical sequences. The songs (in all these films) by composer Harry Warren with lyrics by Al Dubin capture the essence of Depression-era America—they are songs of the common people, songs of despair washed away by waterfalls of wishful thinking.

Casablanca (1942, U.S., 102 mins., b/w) Dir: Michael Curtiz; Cast: Humphrey Bogart, Ingrid Bergman, Paul Henreid, Conrad Veidt, Claude Rains, Peter Lorre, Dooley Wilson, Sydney Greenstreet, S. Z. Sakall.

The enduring appeal of this movie has to do with a near perfect blend of cast, characters, romance, intrigue, setting, dialogue, and direction. It also features a wonderful selection of songs, including a relatively obscure 1931 Tin Pan Alley tune by an equally obscure composer (Herman Hupfeld) recycled specifically for the film. But the first time Bergman's Ilsa asked Sam (Dooley Wilson) to play it, "As Time Goes By" entered into the popular culture as a love song for the ages.

S'WONDERFUL

George Gershwin did more to create, establish, and popularize a distinctive American musical art form than any other composer. His mastery of both popular and classical music and his ability to fuse them together make his body of work stand high among the great cultural achievements of the 20th century. The Gershwin touch (which brother Ira had a hand in with his wonderful lyrics) can be felt and heard as one long and lingering melody that runs through movie history. Here are some of the high notes.

Delicious (1931, U.S., 106 mins., b/w) Dir: David Butler; Cast: Janet Gaynor, Charles Farrell, El Brendel, Virginia Cherrill, Mischa Auer.

Mundane movie made meaningful by virtue of Gershwin score—the brothers' first for motion pictures. Though songs are forgettable, George devised a six-minute orchestral sequence describing the sounds and movements of the city, highlighted by the rhythm of riveting, that did much to advance the art of film composing.

Shall We Dance (1937, U.S., 120 mins., b/w) Dir: Mark Sandrich; Cast: Fred Astaire, Ginger Rogers, Eric Blore, Edward Everett Horton.

George and Ira's first film triumph is not the best directed or written of the Astaire-Rogers musicals (that honor belongs to *Swingtime*), but with this score, who cares? Songs include "They All Laughed," "They Can't Take That Away From Me," and that masterpiece of phonetic incompatibility, "Let's Call the Whole Thing Off."

A Damsel in Distress (1937, U.S., 101 mins., b/w) Dir: George Stevens; Cast: Fred Astaire, George Burns, Gracie Allen, Joan Fontaine, Ray Noble.

More Gershwin classics (including "A Foggy Day") highlight this strange example of Hollywood thinking. Strange in that RKO, in deciding to pair Fred with someone other than Ginger, chose Joan Fontaine, who had the curious qualification of neither singing nor dancing—nice work if you can get it!

Rhapsody in Blue (1945, U.S., 139 mins., b/w) Dir: Irving Rapper; Cast: Robert Alda, Oscar Levant, Charles Coburn, Alexis Smith, Joan Leslie, Morris Carnovsky.

Gershwin biopic is typical Hollywood blend of fact and fancy focusing on George's struggle between writing jazz tunes and classical music (early script by Clifford Odets was rejected by Warners). Alda makes an agreeable Gershwin, and Carnovsky is fun as his dad. Highlight of the film is Gershwin buddy Oscar Levant (appearing as himself) performing title piece.

The Man I Love (1946, U.S., 96 mins., b/w) Dir: Raoul Walsh; Cast: Ida Lupino, Robert Alda, Alan Hale, Bruce Bennett, Dolores Moran.

Tough, atmospheric Raoul Walsh melodrama-with-music about nightclub singer Lupino who gets mixed up with a mobster (Alda) echoes with the haunting, moody feel of the Gershwin ballad that inspired it. Martin Scorsese cites film as an influence on *New York, New York*. Songs (Lupino's singing was dubbed) include the title tune, "Liza," and some terrific standards by other composers. Score is by the great Max Steiner.

The Shocking Miss Pilgrim (1947, U.S., 85 mins.) Dir: George Seaton; Cast: Betty Grable, Dick Haymes.
■
Of interest only to ardent Gershwin fans, this posthumously produced musical was put together from previously unpublished Gershwin manuscripts and the score is almost as pedestrian as everything else in the film—but not quite.

An American in Paris (1951, U.S., 113 mins.) Dir: Vincente Minnelli; Cast: Gene Kelly, Leslie Caron, Oscar Levant, Nina Foch, Georges Guetary.

From the graceful opening movements of Minnelli's camera and Kelly's body to the closing balletic interpretation of Gershwin's symphonic poem to the city of lights, this movie is a joy. Most sumptuous of all MGM musicals, the color is exquisite. Caron is perfect gaminlike object of Kelly's affections, and Levant gives his best performance as screen variation of his real neurotic self. Gershwin songs include "I've Got Rhythm" and "Our Love Is Here to Stay." Oscar winner for Best Picture, Art Direction, Musical Arrangements, and Screenplay by Alan J. Lerner (*My Fair Lady*).

Funny Face (1957, U.S., 103 mins.) Dir: Stanley Donen; Cast: Fred Astaire, Audrey Hepburn, Kay Thompson, Suzy Parker, Michel Auclair.

Speaking of gamins, Hepburn is at her most ephemeral and radiant as the bookshop clerk turned supermodel in this lovely, lyrical reworking of Gershwin's 1927 Broadway musical superbly directed by Donen. Astaire (who also starred in original stage production) plays the fashion photographer (based on Richard Avedon) who discovers her. The Donen/Astaire interpretation of Gershwin is softer, subtler, more elegant than the Minnelli/Kelly approach, and frankly, we like it better.

Porgy and Bess (1959, U.S., 116 mins.) Dir: Otto Preminger; Cast: Sidney Poitier, Dorothy Dandridge, Sammy Davis, Jr., Pearl Bailey, Diahann Carroll.
■
Whether or not purists consider *Porgy and Bess* to be The Great American Opera, for Gershwin it represented the ultimate meeting of serious and popular music he pursued all his life. Its collection of glorious songs woven together by sustained symphonic music remains a soaring achievement. Unfortunately, this stagy, ponderous film never takes off. Nonsinging Poitier and Dandridge as P&B (their vocals were dubbed) never catch fire dramatically and the opera is watered down considerably. Still, the Technicolor is

gorgeous, Sammy is good as Sportin' Life, and oh those songs!

Kiss Me Stupid (1964, U.S., 124 mins., b/w) Dir: Billy Wilder; Cast: Dean Martin, Ray Walston, Kim Novak, Felicia Farr, Cliff Osmond, Barbara Pepper, Doro Merande, Henry Gibson.

Oddball rarity that is (surprise!) a must-see, less for Gershwin fans than for devotees of Billy Wilder. Story of schnook composer Walston attempting to sell songs to a well-known singer/lothario named Dino (played by guess who?) by dangling his wife as bait is borderline perversity, but very funny stuff. Silly songs, including "I'm a Poached Egg," from unused Gershwin manuscripts, are perfectly suited to Wilder's strangest, most cynical film.

Manhattan (1979, U.S., 93 mins., b/w) Dir: Woody Allen; Cast: Woody Allen, Diane Keaton, Mariel Hemingway, Michael Murphy, Meryl Streep.

One of Woody's most romantic films, this valentine to life and love in the Big Apple finds its soul in the music of Gershwin. Rarely has song been more smoothly integrated into a soundtrack—the score shimmers beneath Gordon Willis's radiant black-and-white images, it caresses the characters and contributes mightily to what we feel, the melodies almost literally lifting us up. It is, in many ways, the most perfect use the movies ever made of Gershwin's remarkable talent.

HE'S THE TOP

When we think of Cole Porter the words urbane, elegant, and debonair float through the mind like so many champagne bubbles. His music is, to use his own phrase, the essence and quintessence of sophistication and chic. Compared to the soulful ethnicity of Gershwin, Porter's songs are engagingly aristocratic and Waspish. But he differed from Gershwin and other of his predominantly Jewish contemporaries as much for being gay, as for being a goy; he was the Oscar Wilde of the American musical. For anyone remotely concerned with cultured individualism, verbal virtuosity, and musical style, the films that contain music and lyrics by Cole Porter form a delightful, delicious, and delectable list.

Night and Day (1946, U.S., 128 mins.) Dir: Michael Curtiz; Cast: Cary Grant, Alexis Smith, Monty Woolley, Jane Wyman, Eve Arden.

Warners biopic is a lavish package of fabrication wrapped in Technicolor gloss and tied together by a ribbon of Porter pearls. The composer publicly praised the film while privately ridiculing its silliness. Scene where Grant as Porter is inspired to write the title tune is borderline absurd and unintentionally funny. Still, director Curtiz loads it up with enough cinematic invention to keep things interesting, and there is that Cole Porter Songbook.

The Gay Divorcee (1934, U.S., 107 mins., b/w) Dir: Mark Sandrich; Cast: Ginger Rogers, Fred Astaire, Edward Everett Horton, Alice Brady.

First of the seven Astaire-Rogers classics made at RKO in the thirties adapted from the Broadway musical *The Gay Divorce,* for which Porter wrote the score. Although the film uses only one of his original songs "Night and Day," given a wonderfully romantic treatment on screen, this already popular tune became an instant classic.

Broadway Melody of 1940 (1940, U.S., 101 mins., b/w) Dir: Norman Taurog; Cast: Fred Astaire, Eleanor Powell, George Murphy, Frank Morgan, Ian Hunter.

Astaire and Murphy are a couple of

hoofers vying for the attention of Eleanor Powell. Guess which one dances his way into her heart? Only film in which Fred and Eleanor worked together has a lame plot but great choreography and Porter score that introduced "Begin the Beguine."

Born to Dance (1936, U.S., 105 mins.) Dir: Roy Del Ruth; Cast: Eleanor Powell, James Stewart, Buddy Ebsen, Reginald Gardiner, Virginia Bruce.

Less remembered by film buffs for Porter score than for Jimmy Stewart's valiant attempt at singing and dancing, this blatant *42nd Street* knock off has second-stringer Powell getting big break, going out there a chorus girl, and coming back a star! Production values reflect MGM's no-holds-barred approach to movie musicals, and two of the songs introduced—"Easy to Love" and "I've Got You Under My Skin"—are Porter classics.

Break the News (1937, U.S.-Great Britain, 83 mins., b/w) Dir: René Clair; Cast: Maurice Chevalier, Jack Buchanan, June Knight.

Extremely rare Porter musical mystery featuring Chevalier and Buchanan as a couple of song-and-dance men who pull a phony publicity stunt and wind up in extremely hot water. Director René Clair applied his Dadaist roots to some interesting and unusual projects. This is one of them.

The Pirate (1948, U.S., 102 mins.) Dir: Vincente Minnelli; Cast: Judy Garland, Gene Kelly, Walter Slezak, Gladys Cooper.

Consciously self-conscious pastiche about a traveling player (Kelly) who masquerades as a notorious pirate in order to win the heart of well-to-do but hopelessly naive Manuela (Garland). Stars punctuate every line and gesture with exclamation points, Minnelli's direction is over the top, sets and cos-

tumes are so loud they almost drown out the Cole Porter score, but somehow it all adds up to a grand experience. "Be a Clown," Porter's bouncy tribute to vaudeville, is the springboard for one of Kelly's most memorable dance routines, and the "Nina" ballet is exquisite.

Kiss Me Kate (1953, U.S., 109 mins.) Dir: George Sidney; Cast: Kathryn Grayson, Howard Keel, Ann Miller, Keenan Wynn, Bob Fosse.

Porter's most ambitious theatrical undertaking—the transformation of Shakespeare's *Taming of the Shrew* into a Broadway musical—was also his most successful. Director Sidney brings it smoothly to the screen, with spirited performances by Keel and Grayson. Staggering score includes the rousing "Another Op'ning, Another Show," the cynical "Always True to You in My Fashion," and the Shakespearian "I've Come to Wife it Wealthily in Padua." "From This Moment On" (not in the original show) spotlights a young dancer named Bob Fosse.

High Society (1956, U.S., 107 mins.) Dir: Charles Walters; Cast: Bing Crosby, Grace Kelly, Frank Sinatra, Celeste Holm, Louis Armstrong.

Musical treatment of *The Philadelphia Story,* Philip Barry's sophisticated play and nonmusical screen classic. It's difficult to imagine material more perfectly suited to the Porter style. Location is switched from Philly to Newport, but plot of socialite's wedding complicated by arrival of her first husband and a couple of pesky reporters is basically intact. Crosby pairs up with Sinatra for delightful "Did You Evah?" and with Kelly (hardly known for her singing) on "True Love," one of Porter's simplest, most tender, and beautiful songs.

Les Girls (1957, U.S., 114 mins.) Dir: George Cukor; Cast: Gene Kelly, Kay Kendall, Mitzi Gaynor, Taina Elg.

Rashomon-like fable written by John Patrick (he also wrote *High Society*) has members of a Parisian song-and-dance troupe—Kelly, Gaynor, Kendall, and Elg—telling conflicting tales in court after one of them writes a memoir the the others consider libelous. Director Cukor works five amiable Porter songs into one of the most stylish, witty, and original musical films of the period.

Silk Stockings (1957, U.S., 117 mins.) Dir: Rouben Mamoulian; Cast: Fred Astaire, Cyd Charisse, Janis Paige, Peter Lorre.

Broadway musical, adapted from the 1939 Lubitsch film *Ninotchka*, comes back to the screen with Charisse in the Garbo role of cold Russian commissar warmed up and swept off her feet by a Hollywood producer (Astaire). Porter's score is far from his best, but contains some clever political barbs. The dancing (natch!) is divine.

Can-Can (1960, U.S., 131 mins.) Dir: Walter Lang; Cast: Frank Sinatra, Shirley MacLaine, Maurice Chevalier, Juliet Prowse, Louis Jourdan.

One of Porter's most successful Broadway shows loses much of its kick in this screen adaptation. Sinatra doesn't seem to care, Shirley is annoying, Chevalier and Jourdan try hard but come up short. The score, which features most of the original songs as well as some transplanted material, makes the film much more fun to listen to than to watch.

Adam's Rib (1949, U.S., 101 mins., b/w) Dir: George Cukor; Cast: Spencer Tracy, Katharine Hepburn, Judy Holliday, Jean Hagen, Tom Ewell, David Wayne.

Arguably Tracy and Hepburn's best work together, this battle of the sexes courtroom comedy written by Garson Kanin and Ruth Gordon, flawlessly directed by Cukor, gets much mileage

out of Porter's "Farewell Amanda," neatly integrating song and plot. The tune may not be a gem, but the film is a treasure.

Let's Make Love (1960, U.S., 118 mins.) Dir: George Cukor; Cast: Marilyn Monroe, Yves Montand, Tony Randall.

Most of the tunes in this comedy about a millionaire (Montand) who takes a stab at show biz are by Sammy Cahn and Jimmy Van Heusen, but the high point is Monroe's sizzling double- and triple-entendre version of Porter's "My Heart Belongs to Daddy."

At Long Last Love (1975, U.S., 115 mins.) Dir: Peter Bogdanovich; Cast: Burt Reynolds, Cybill Shepherd, Madeline Kahn, Eileen Brennan, Duilio Del Prete, John Hillerman.

Bogdanovich's bouquet to Hollywood musicals of days gone by seems, on one level, to be a genuine attempt to express his love for the form. We can't help but wonder why, then, he would sabotage the project by using a cast that can't sing or dance. Great Porter material is positively brutalized. Stay away!

ALL THAT JAZZ

Jazz and the movies are this country's two great contributions to the world of art, so it's fitting that Hollywood has made some entertaining films about the most uniquely American form of music.

Round Midnight (1986, U.S.-France, 130 mins.) Dir: Bertrand Tavernier; Cast: Dexter Gordon, François Cluyet, Gabrielle Haker, Lonette McKee, Sandra Reaves-Phillips, Christine Pascal, Herbie Hancock, Martin Scorsese.

A fifties jazzman with a drinking problem, based on Bud Powell, plays a Paris club and makes friends with a French fan who has some problems of his own. Dexter Gordon stars and is so convincing that you have to remind yourself that he's acting. Herbie Hancock directed the music, and you can see him behind Gordon along with Bobby Hutcherson and Wayne Shorter.

Let's Get Lost (1989, U.S., 119 mins., b/w) Dir: Bruce Weber.

A long but fascinating documentary about trumpeter Chet Baker, one of the pioneers of West Coast jazz and a man who loved trouble as much as he did music. Director Bruce Weber tries to make a valentine to Baker, but the facts of the musician's life balance out the tribute. If you check out on the story, the look of the film and its music will keep you watching to the end.

The Gig (1985, U.S., 92 mins.) Dir: Frank Gilroy; Cast: Wayne Rogers, Cleavon Little, Andrew Duncan, Jerry Matz, Joe Silver.

Though a bunch of white guys playing Dixieland jazz in the Catskills sounds more like a reason to jump out a window than like a plot line, this unpretentious little film knows exactly what it's about—middle age, commitment, race, and friendship. A sleeper.

Mo' Better Blues (1990, U.S., 129 mins.) Dir: Spike Lee; Cast: Denzel Washington, Joie Lee, Wesley Snipes, Spike Lee, Cynda Williams, Rubén Blades, John Turturro, Giancarlo Esposito.

Not Spike Lee's best outing by far, but Denzel has his moments as a trumpeter who connects with his music and little else. Music from the Branford Marsalis Quartet gives this more life than the script does.

Lady Sings the Blues (1972, U.S., 144 mins.) Dir: Sidney J. Furie; Cast: Diana Ross, Billy Dee Williams, Richard Pryor.

Diana Ross in an over-the-top, Streisand-like performance as the leg-

endary jazz singer Billie Holliday. Williams and Pryor keep up their end of things, but Ross provides more energy than realism to her role. Pick up a copy of Lady Day's autobiography of the same title and you'll see that her life was even more interesting than this movie. She was a better singer than Ross, too.

Thelonious Monk: Straight, No Chaser (1988, U.S., 90 mins., c & b/w) Dir: Charlotte Zwerin.

A tremendous documentary about the groundbreaking composer and pianist Thelonious Monk. Though the music is first-rate, it's the vision of Monk's long battle with depression that makes this film so compelling and sad. The scene of him doing his aimless, out-of-it "Monk dance" in a crowded airport will haunt you.

Paris Blues (1961, U.S., 98 mins., b/w) Dir: Martin Ritt; Cast: Paul Newman, Joanne Woodward, Sidney Poitier, Diahann Carroll, Louis Armstrong.

Newman and Poitier play a couple of Americans playing *le jazz hot* on the *rive gauche* who court two tourists from the States. Louis Armstrong makes a guest appearance and the music is wall-to-wall Duke Ellington. A sleeper. The rough edges only make it more likable.

Jazz on a Summer's Day (1959, U.S., 85 mins.) Dir: Bert Stern; Cast: Louis Armstrong, Dinah Washington, Thelonious Monk, Gerry Mulligan, Chuck Berry, Big Maybelle, Anita O'Day, Mahalia Jackson.

The lineup for this film about the 1958 Newport Jazz Festival tells you all you need to know.

Bird (1988, U.S., 160 mins.) Dir: Clint Eastwood; Cast: Forest Whitaker, Diane Venora, Michael Zelniker, Keith David.

A downbeat film about brilliant saxo-phonist Charlie Parker, but what did you expect? Parker's own playing makes up the soundtrack and Forest Whitaker as Bird captures the sadness of a life sacrificed to heroin. Eastwood does let this go on a bit longer than it has to; still, definitely worth a watch for jazz buffs.

The Fabulous Baker Boys (1989, U.S., 113 mins.) Dir: Steve Kloves; Cast: Jeff Bridges, Michelle Pfeiffer, Beau Brid-ges, Ellis Raab, Jennifer Tilly.

A sexy, stylish, understated film about two brothers who must reevaluate their nightclub act and their relationship when they add a singer. Kloves wisely never clubs us over the head with plot and detail; he lets the simple story and fine performances pull us along through the smoky atmosphere. Michelle Pfeif-fer singing "Makin' Whoopee" is a scene beyond words. Rita Hayworth would be jealous.

Alfie (1966, Great Britain, 114 mins.) Dir: Lewis Gilbert; Cast: Michael Caine, Shelley Winters, Millicent Martin, Vivien Merchant, Shirley Anne Field, Denholm Elliott, Julia Foster.

This sophisticated story of a playboy learning that it's time to stop playing boasts a terrific Sonny Rollins score that's worth listening to even if you hate the movie. Which you won't.

ROCK AROUND
THE CLOCK:
1950s ROCK 'N' ROLL

In the beginning, there was scandal. The critics called it "lewd, immoral, disgusting." Parents were horrified by the signs of pagan lust it stimulat-ed in their children . . . and they hated the noise. They hoped, more than anything, that it would go away and never come back, but DJs like Alan Freed, record company execs, and Hollywood honchos all had the sneaking suspicion that rock and roll was here to stay. Here's how the big beat looked and sounded on the sil-ver screen from the mid-fifties to the early sixties, with a couple of latter-day retro glances thrown in for good measure.

The Blackboard Jungle (1955, U.S., 101 mins.) Dir: Richard Brooks; Cast: Glenn Ford, Anne Francis, Vic Morrow, Louis Calhern, Sidney Poitier, Richard Kiley, Warner Anderson, Paul Mazursky, John Hoyt, Jamie Farr.

It starts here. Bill Haley's "Rock Around the Clock" on the soundtrack under the opening credits, the first use of rock and roll in a movie, sets the kick-ass tone for this seminal, tough, well-made, surprisingly balanced youth-in-rebel-lion, school-system-sucks melodrama. Ford, Poitier, and Morrow are excellent. Jamie Farr of *M*A*S*H* fame is one of the kids.

Rock Around the Clock (1956, U.S., 77 mins., b/w) Dir: Fred F. Sears; Cast: Bill Haley and His Comets, Johnny John-ston.

Song became so big Columbia built a whole film around it. Minimal plot has Freed (as himself) flying in the face of convention to blast rock and roll into the stratosphere. Bill Haley and His Comets do an album's worth of materi-al and the Platters mellow out with "The Great Pretender" and "Only You." Huge international hit caused riots everywhere. Egyptian government thought the film was part of an "Eisen-hower-led plot" to undermine moral stability in the Middle East.

Don't Knock the Rock (1956, U.S., 84 mins.) Dir: Fred F. Sears; Cast: Bill Haley and His Comets, Alan Dale, Alan Freed, Little Richard.
■
More Freed as Freed, more antiestab-

lishment editorializing. This sequel (better than the original) tackles the subjects of rock-induced rioting, dirty dancing, heavy petting, and payola. Little Richard's blood-boiling renditions of "Tutti Frutti" and "Long Tall Sally" make the white boys like Haley look positively anemic.

Rock, Rock, Rock (1957, U.S., 83 mins., b/w) Dir: Will Price; Cast: Tuesday Weld, Alan Freed, Frankie Lymon and the Teenagers, Chuck Berry, The Moonglows, The Flamingos, LaVern Baker.

Chief musical interest in this next installment of Freed on film is Frankie Lymon and the Teenagers doing "I'm Not a Juvenile Delinquent." But the real reason to watch it is for 16-year-old Tuesday Weld (Connie Francis dubs her singing) looking ever so sex-kittenish in her film debut.

The Girl Can't Help It (1956, U.S., 99 mins.) Dir: Frank Tashlin; Cast: Tom Ewell, Jayne Mansfield, Edmond O'Brien, Julie London.

Auteurist darling Tashlin (who began his career directing Porky Pig and Daffy Duck) applies his Looney Tune touch to this Garson Kanin story of a sleazy press agent's attempt to turn a gangster's talentless girlfriend into a singing star. Mansfield is the quintessential fifties bombshell and rock 'n' roll lights her fuse. Fats Domino, Little Richard, Gene Vincent, and Eddie Cochran do the detonating in this classic parody of the Alan Freed genre. As close to a masterpiece as Tashlin ever got.

American Hot Wax (1978, U.S., 91 mins.) Dir: Floyd Mutrux; Cast: Tim McIntire, Fran Drescher, Laraine Newman, Chuck Berry, Jerry Lee Lewis.

Generally dismissed as Hollywood fluffola, this Alan Freed biopic is one of the best rock and roll movies ever made. McIntire is brilliant in the lead and

Mutrux's direction is nonstop invention. Plot is ripped right out of Freed flicks of the fifties and a couple of generic oldies retread groups do most of the songs, but the feel for the era and the music are dead-on. The real Jerry Lee Lewis, Chuck Berry, and Screamin' Jay Hawkins appear at the end and the soundtrack sparkles with hits by Jackie Wilson, Buddy Holly, The Drifters, The Moonglows, and more.

The Buddy Holly Story (1978, U.S., 114 mins.) Dir: Steve Rash; Cast: Gary Busey, Don Stroud, Charles Martin Smith, Bill Jordan, Maria Richwine, Conrad Janis, Dick O'Neill.

Gary Busey's riveting performance earned an Oscar nomination in this neatly directed enterprise chronicling the life and times of the legendary rock and roller from his garage-band beginnings to the day the music died in an Iowa snowstorm. That Busey does his own singing gives the film an honest edge in spite of the hooey in the script.

La Bamba (1987, U.S., 106 mins.) Dir: Luis Valdez; Cast: Lou Diamond Phillips, Esai Morales, Rosana De Soto, Elizabeth Peña, Marshall Crenshaw, Brian Setzer.

Story of Richie Valens, killed in the same plane crash as Holly, is another massive load of hokum, but if you can avoid stepping in la bamba laid by the script, there's a whole lotta rockin' goin' on. Los Lobos dubs in the Valens tunes and cranks them up a notch or two, Setzer (the former Stray Cat) does an excellent Eddie Cochran, and underappreciated contemporary rocker Crenshaw's conception of Buddy Holly as a fifties hipster is extremely cool.

Who's That Knocking at My Door? (1968, U.S., 90 mins., b/w) Dir: Martin Scorsese; Cast: Harvey Keitel, Zina Bethune, Anne Collette.

Scorsese's first commercial film—a

new-wavey, hand-held, jump-cut, neo-realist, pseudo-documentary finger exercise for *Mean Streets*—leaps off the screen to a rock-and-roll beat. Creative integration of title tune by the Genies, "I've Had It" by the Bellnotes, and especially Ray Barretto's "El Watusi" set new standards for use of oldies on a movie soundtrack.

American Graffiti (1973, U.S., 110 mins.) Dir: George Lucas; Cast: Ronny Howard, Cindy Williams, Charlie Martin Smith, Richard Dreyfuss, Mackenzie Phillips, Candy Clark, Harrison Ford, Suzanne Somers.

A wonderful, nostalgic cruise through a day in the life of America's teen car culture scene, this little baby launched the careers of half of its stars and put George Lucas into orbit. The wall-to-wall fifties and sixties hit-record soundtrack blaring forth from car radios, jukeboxes, and sock-hop bands remind us that the dreams of our youth had a rock-and-roll beat.

THE BRITISH ARE COMING

From the mid-fifties to the early sixties, rock and roll was a particularly American graffiti, but by 1963 it was losing its edge. The rip-it-up rebels were being replaced by pre-fab pretty boys, media-manufactured teen idols like Fabian and Frankie Avalon who were soft, safe, and decidedly all-American. Rock and roll needed help . . . and the liberating forces came from England. The Beatles exploded in the U.S. in 1964, spearheading a full-scale British invasion. Within a few months English groups were all over the pop charts, TV, and, of course, the movies.

Ring-a-Ding Rhythm (1962, Great Britain, 78 mins., b/w) Dir: Richard Lester; Cast: Helen Shapiro, Craig Douglas, Felix Felton, Arthur Mullard, John Leyton.

A prelude to the deluge, this British variation on the Alan Freed "teenagers-versus-old-farts" flick is distinguished by directorial presence of Richard Lester two years before he and the Beatles shattered the movie musical form with *A Hard Day's Night*. Some of the innovations he later used with the Fab Four are in evidence here, but the oldies by Del Shannon, Gary "U.S." Bonds, Chubby Checker, and Gene Vincent are hardly the goodies.

A Hard Day's Night (1964, Great Britain, 85 mins., b/w) Dir: Richard Lester; Cast: John Lennon, Paul McCartney, George Harrison, Ringo Starr, Wilfrid Brambell, Victor Spinetti.

Andrew Sarris called it "the *Citizen Kane* of the Jukebox musical" and he was right. Not only did Lester's antic mix of fiction and cinema verité capture Beatlemania and the distinctive personalities of John, Paul, George, and Ringo, it caught the pop of pop art and redefined it in terms of movies, music, and mass culture. The wonderful Beatles tunes are given a visual life that makes this the wellspring from which all rock video comes.

Help! (1965, Great Britain, 90 mins.) Dir: Richard Lester; Cast: John Lennon, Paul McCartney, George Harrison, Ringo Starr, Leo McKern, Eleanor Bron, Victor Spinetti.

While "Fab Four, Part II" is not as fresh and pure as "Part I," it has enough energy, color, originality, and outrageous invention to stand up just fine on its own. Improbable blend of Beatlemania, Marx Brothers movies, and political satire all tossed into a plot lifted from a Wilkie Collins murder mystery *(The Moonstone)* is perfectly handled by Lester. The visual wizardry around the Beatles' musical numbers goes beyond *A Hard Day's Night.*

Having a Wild Weekend (aka: *Catch Us If You Can,* 1965, Great Britain, 91 mins., b/w) Dir: John Boorman; Cast: Dave Clark Five.
■
Obvious attempt by the DC 5 to cash in on Beatles' success formula has its moments but comes up short. While the Five had their share of hit records and were cute and mop-toppy, they never created a mania. Director Boorman *(Deliverance, Excalibur)* apes the Lester style, adding some clever touches, but his sensibility is better suited to weightier material. Solid songs include title track and "Catch Us If You Can," film's original British title.

Hold On! (1966, U.S., 85 mins., b/w) Dir: Arthur Lubin; Cast: Peter Noone, Shelley Fabares, Herman's Hermits.
■
Another variation on the *Hard Day's Night* formula follows Herman's Hermits on their first American tour. The script would have us believe that these guys create such a sensation that they actually have a Gemini spaceship named after them. Fact is, they were a sweet-faced group that produced a few modest hit records, then faded into relative obscurity. The movie, like their music, is likable and confectionery.

Bunny Lake Is Missing (1965, U.S., 107 mins., b/w) Dir: Otto Preminger; Cast: Laurence Olivier, Keir Dullea, Carol Lynley, Noel Coward.
■
Craze around British invasion groups had Columbia hyping the hell out of the Zombies' appearance in this film—they were prominently featured in posters and trailers. Given the plot, which revolves around disappearance of a young child in swinging London, we keep expecting to hear "She's Not There" (the Zombies' biggest hit), but we don't. Alas, the group only shows up briefly on a pub TV performing a couple of barely audible nonhits. None of which should stop you from catching this masterpiece of moral ambiguity

brilliantly directed by Preminger, featuring wonderfully wily old-pro turns by Coward and Olivier.

The Kids Are Alright (1979, U.S., 108 mins., c & b/w) Dir: Jeff Stein; Cast: Peter Townshend, Roger Daltrey, John Entwhistle, Keith Moon.

First-rate compilation film chronicles career of The Who from early 1960s through late 1970s. Television appearances, rare promo films, concert footage, interviews, and an oddball narration by Ringo Starr are splashed on a broad canvas to paint a compelling portrait of the group, capturing their particular brand of destructo-art-rock energy in action. Excellent greatest-hits package should delight old Who fans and create new ones.

Quadrophenia (1979, Great Britain, 115 mins.) Dir: Franc Roddam; Cast: Phil Daniels, Mark Wingett, Leslie Ash, Philip Davis, Sting.

Dramatic look back at what was going on in England while Brit bands were invading America. Interesting adaptation of rock opera by The Who plunges headlong into the violent world of the "mods" and the "rockers," rival teen gangs and representatives of stylistic extremes. With one alienated teen (Daniels) as the focal point, the story digs beneath the squeaky clean surface we tend to associate with the music of the era. The Who's soundtrack rides on a bed of period American rock-and-roll hits. Warning: the cockney accents are so thick, we wanted subtitles. Sting is featured in a small role.

Blow-Up (1966, Great Britain-Italy, 111 mins.) Dir: Michelangelo Antonioni; Cast: David Hemmings, Vanessa Redgrave, Sarah Miles, Verushka.

Italian master Antonioni's first English-language film centers around a British fashion photographer (Hemmings) who may or may not have photographed a murder. Dazzling, puzzling parable of pop-culture trends, artistic obsession, and human isolation set in the swinging world of mod London. The madness and dazzle of the scene are best captured during famous party sequence where the Yardbirds do some Who-style on-stage damage after performing the song "Stroll On."

One Plus One (aka: *Sympathy for the Devil,* 1969, Great Britain, 99 mins.) Dir: Jean-Luc Godard; Cast: Mick Jagger, Keith Richards, Brian Jones, Charlie Watts, Bill Wyman, Nicky Hopkins.

With the exception of *The Rolling Stones Rock and Roll Circus,* an unreleased bit of psychedelia, and a dynamic appearance in *The T.A.M.I. Show* film (well worth a look), the Stones never entered the same self-promoting movie market sweepstakes as their British brethren. They obviously saw themselves in a different, darker light. Here, the rehearsal and recording of "Sympathy for the Devil" is documented by Godard and used as a point/counterpoint commentary for his cinematic stream of revolutionary rhetoric. Beware of bastardized version distributed as *Sympathy for the Devil. One Plus One,* the original cut, is available.

A BOX AT THE OPRY

If you drive anywhere outside any big U.S. city, be it in Georgia, Vermont, Ohio, or Montana, you'll hear country music. Jazz may be America's greatest contribution to music, but country is by far the most popular. Dolly Parton and Johnny Paycheck aside, here are some films that may be of interest if you're an Opry buff.

Tender Mercies (1983, U.S., 90 mins.) Dir: Bruce Beresford; Cast: Robert Duvall, Tess Harper, Ellen Barkin.

Robert Duvall gives a brilliant, low-key performance as an alcoholic songwriter who comes to terms with his past and starts a new life. A sensitive, honest film that doesn't manipulate or contrive. Duvall and screenwriter Horton Foote both won Oscars. The young Ellen Barkin plays Duvall's daughter.

Sweet Dreams (1985, U.S., 115 mins.) Dir: Karel Reisz; Cast: Jessica Lange, Ed Harris, Ann Wedgeworth, Dave Clennon.

Jessica Lange lip-synching to Patsy Cline's voice is one of the rewards of paradise that was accidentally shared with us. Patsy was the Aretha of country music, a goddess, but, unfortunately for the viewers of this film, her life wasn't too interesting. The romance whipped up with Ed Harris is too obviously just an excuse for a plot, and we end up without a real sense of who Patsy was. You can't beat the music, though.

Coal Miner's Daughter (1980, U.S., 125 mins.) Dir: Michael Apted; Cast: Sissy Spacek, Tommy Lee Jones, Beverly D'Angelo, Levon Helm, Phyllis Boyens, Ernest Tubb.

The best of the bunch. Spacek won an Oscar for her portrayal of singer Loretta Lynn and her rise from the piney woods of West Virginia to stardom. Everything about this is fresh and alive. Spacek and Tommy Lee Jones, who plays her husband, actually seem to be in love, the highs and lows hit you like a good country song, and D'Angelo proves that Patsy Cline is best treated as a supporting role. Look for Levon Helm and Ernest Tubb.

Honeysuckle Rose (aka: *On the Road Again,* 1980, U.S., 119 mins.) Dir: Jerry Schatzberg; Cast: Willie Nelson, Dyan Cannon, Amy Irving, Slim Pickens.

Willie Nelson gives us a look at what things were like in the days before the taxman got him, in this story of a singer/songwriter whose high life starts to come apart when he strays from his wife (Cannon). By no means a revelation, but Willie is so watchable that it's worth it.

Convoy (1978, U.S., 111 mins.) Dir: Sam Peckinpah; Cast: Kris Kristofferson, Ali MacGraw, Ernest Borgnine.

Breaker, breaker. You remember the C. W. McCall hit about truckers banding together to beat the Smokeys. Well, Sam Peckinpah rounded up some of his good buddies and turned it into a movie that's just about as goofy as the song. Pair this up with *Take This Job and Shove It.*

Nashville (1975, U.S., 159 mins.) Dir: Robert Altman; Cast: Lily Tomlin, Shelley Duvall, Henry Gibson, Ronee Blakley, Karen Black, Barbara Harris, Allen Garfield, Barbara Baxley, Geraldine Chaplin, Keenan Wynn, Keith Carradine.

Altman's incisive look at America through a political/music rally held in Nashville represents the high point of his unique, tightly woven style. Unfortunately, it isn't likely that your average country music fan is going to enjoy it all that much—this isn't light entertainment. By the way, whatever happened to Ronee Blakley?

Songwriter (1984, U.S., 94 mins.) Dir: Alan Rudolph; Cast: Willie Nelson, Kris Kristofferson, Lesley Ann Warren, Rip Torn.

This one's more about music than anything else. Willie and Kris team up to take on a greedy investor in Willie's company. But mostly they sing. A lot.

Falling From Grace (1992, U.S., 100 mins.) Dir: John Mellencamp; Cast: John Mellencamp, Mariel Hemingway, Kay Lenz, Claude Akins, Dub Taylor, Larry Crane.

It could be the Larry McMurtry script or it could be that John Mellencamp is more talented than you think. Whatever it is, this film about yet another singer at a crossroads in his life, though only a blip on the screen during its theatrical release, makes for a good rental.

Honkytonk Man (1983, U.S., 122 mins.) Dir: Clint Eastwood; Cast: Clint Eastwood, Kyle Eastwood, John McIntire, Verna Bloom, Alexa Kenin, Matt Clark.

Clint didn't exactly come out of the directorial gate full steam. This tale of a dying singer during the Depression trying to get to the Grand Ole Opry for one last shot ain't *Unforgiven*. It ain't even *Convoy*, but if you're a Clint fan you might find something to like here.

Urban Cowboy (1980, U.S., 135 mins.) Dir: James Bridges; Cast: John Travolta, Debra Winger, Scott Glenn, Madolyn Smith, Barry Corbin.

John Travolta works in the Texas oilfields by day, then shoves a Stetson on his head and rides the mechanical bull at Gilley's roadhouse at night. Somehow you know that Clint or Willie Nelson wouldn't be caught dead on a mechanical bull, and they'd still manage to rope in that little filly Debra Winger. What was once social commentary is now good for some laughs.

Pure Country (1992, U.S., 112 mins.) Dir: Christopher Cain; Cast: George Strait, Lesley Ann Warren, Isabel Glasser, Kyle Chandler.

In a real twist, C&W star George Strait plays an embarrassingly successful C&W star who tires of all the smoke and amplifiers and decides to drop out of his tour to wander incognito among his subjects. Lesley Ann Warren is his shrew of a manager and one can only hope that she's supposed to appear 20 years too old for the outfits she wears. For Strait fans only.

CLASSICAL MUSIC

The concert hall and the movie theater are usually more than a few blocks away from each other, but once in a while Hollywood brings culcha to da masses. Here are some of the better efforts.

Beethoven (1936, France, 116 mins., b/w) Dir: Abel Gance; Cast: Harry Baur, Jean-Louis Barrault, Marcel Dalio, Jany Holt, Annie Decaux, Jean Debucourt.

A magnificent telling of Beethoven's last years from the director of *Napoleon;* a true sleeper. Gance pulls out all the stops and lets this become not just romantic melodrama, but Romanticism. Baur is a living, breathing Beethoven for the ages. If you liked *Children of Paradise,* you must try this.

Humoresque (1947, U.S., 125 mins., b/w) Dir: Jean Negulesco; Cast: Joan Crawford, John Garfield, Oscar Levant.

Another terrific film, this time unabashed Hollywood melodrama. Garfield is a kid from the wrong side of the tracks who becomes a violin virtuoso and Crawford is the rich patroness he has an affair with. Tears galore, leavened by Oscar Levant's wisecracks, which are actually pretty funny.

Unfaithfully Yours (1948, U.S., 105 mins., b/w) Dir: Preston Sturges; Cast: Rex Harrison, Linda Darnell, Rudy Vallee, Lionel Stander.

Harrison plays a conductor who becomes convinced that his wife is having an affair, so during one night's concert he plots his revenge. A blend of sophisticated wit and physical comedy, backed by some classical favorites.

Basileus Quartet (1984, Italy, 118 mins.) Dir: Fabio Carpi; Cast: Pierre Malet, Hector Alterio, François Simon.

When a member of a chamber music quartet dies, his young replacement changes the emotional tone of the group. A film as studied, intricate, and beautiful as chamber music itself; your enjoyment of it depends on how much that description appeals to you.

Fantasia (1940, U.S., 120 mins.) Story Dirs: Joe Grant, Dick Huemer; Cast: Leopold Stokowski and the Philadelphia Orchestra; Narration: Deems Taylor.

The one film that has done more to spread classical music than any orchestra, conductor, or composer. When those hippos first came cruising out in their tutus, the purists may have scoffed, but we were finally told that this was music we could *enjoy.* So it's not the coolest thing in the world; neither was your favorite elementary school teacher and it would probably be nice to see her, too. *Allegro Non Troppo* is another imaginative animated interpretation of classical music, but it's just not the same.

Intermezzo (1939, U.S., 70 mins.) Dir: Gregory Ratoff; Cast: Leslie Howard, Ingrid Bergman, John Halliday, Edna Best.

Why did Leslie Howard always play such simps? The man was a great actor who spent much of his screen time mewling and puking over the likes of Bette Davis, Vivien Leigh, and, here, Ingrid Bergman. Howard plays a violinist who has an affair with his protégé, with tragic results. A big-time tearjerker that's hard to get all sniffly about—who would cry over losing this guy?

Amadeus (1984, U.S., 158 mins.) Dir: Milos Forman; Cast: Tom Hulce, F. Murray Abraham, Elizabeth Berridge, Roy Dotrice, Charles Kay, Jeffrey Jones.

Engaging film version of Peter Shaffer's middle-brow play about the consuming jealousy of mediocre court composer Salieri toward the bawdy genius Mozart. If you're looking for a more serious treatment of Wolfgang Amadeus, try *Mozart—A Childhood Chronicle*, a long, dark, and atmospheric view of Mozart that focuses more on his music than on his life and features his work played on period instruments.

Impromptu (1990, U.S., 109 mins.) Dir: James Lapine; Cast: Judy Davis, Hugh Grant, Mandy Patinkin, Bernadette Peters, Julian Sands, Emma Thompson.

A lively, sharp costumer about the romance between the sickly Chopin and the lusty George Sand, played by Judy Davis at her best. Chopin's contemporary, Franz Lizst, is featured prominently in this as well. A charming, entertaining film. *A Song to Remember* is the old Hollywood bio of Chopin that lays the schmaltz on as heavily as it does the music.

The Competition (1980, U.S., 129 mins.) Dir: Joel Oliansky; Cast: Lee Remick, Richard Dreyfuss, Amy Irving, Sam Wanamaker.

Pianists Amy Irving and Richard Dreyfuss fall in love during a competition and try to keep their relationship going while they're working to beat each other at the keys. This simple film, which doesn't try to be anything more than it is, has the finest example of finger-synching you'll ever see.

Wagner (1985, Great Britain/MTV, 208 mins.) Dir: Tony Palmer; Cast: Richard Burton, John Gielgud, Ralph Richardson, Laurence Olivier.

A numbingly long bio of the troubled, and troubling, composer that has the same soporific effect that *Das Rheingold* has in a warm, crowded opera hall. Richard Burton plays Wagner and a host of other greats show up too, but you won't be awake to see them. You've got to be hard core to enjoy this.

A Song of Love (1947, U.S., 119 mins., b/w) Dir: Clarence Brown; Cast:

Katharine Hepburn, Paul Henreid, Robert Walker, Henry Daniell, Leo G. Carroll.

Hepburn plays Clara Schumann, Henreid is her husband, Robert, and Walker is Brahms. Of mostly historical interest, as is the Liszt biopic *Song Without End*. Both are sturdy films with loads of music and costumes, but low on emotional impact.

Letter From an Unknown Woman (1948, U.S., 90 mins., b/w) Dir: Max Ophuls; Cast: Joan Fontaine, Louis Jourdan, Mady Christians, Marcel Journet, Art Smith.

A rich, romantic, almost overripe Ophuls film about a woman's lifelong infatuation with a pianist (Jourdan). A beautiful weeper that will take your heart away, if you like that sort of thing.

ONE OF A MUSICAL KIND

While most movie music over the years has been written by men who earned regular paychecks and built reputations as film composers, ever so often a musician will come from out of left field and create a noteworthy soundtrack. Here are some films scored by composers who made their mark in recording studios and concert halls, paid a tithe or two to the god of cinema, and then moved on.

Nothing Sacred (1937, U.S., 77 mins., b/w) Dir: William Wellman; Cast: Carole Lombard, Fredric March, Walter Connolly, Charles Winninger, Sig Ruman, John Qualen, Maxie Rosenbloom, Hattie McDaniel.

When producer David Selznick hired Algonquin round tabler, celebrated pianist, and well-known neurotic Oscar Levant to score this hilarious medical misdiagnosis comedy, Oscar came up with some very progressive musical ideas. But, as Levant later wrote, if he appeared at the studio with anything even faintly modern Selznick's invariable comment was, "It sounds Chinese." The producer prevailed. And the finished score, while straight as can be, more than suits this uniquely American screwball classic.

You and Me (1938, U.S., 90 mins., b/w) Dir: Fritz Lang; Cast: Sylvia Sidney, George Raft, Robert Cummings.
■
One of the most incontrovertibly strange movies of the thirties, this brooding Expressionist musical comedy about a department store owner taken to hiring ex-cons comes off as a Capraesque version of *The Threepenny Opera.* But with Lang directing, Bertolt Brecht working (uncredited) on the story, and Kurt Weill composing the score, what do you expect?

The Third Man (1949, Great Britain, 100 mins., b/w) Dir: Carol Reed; Cast: Joseph Cotten, Orson Welles, Alida Valli, Trevor Howard.

The exotic zither music by Anton Karas, with its famous "Harry Lime Theme" and "Cafe Mozart Waltz," provides an inspired counterpoint to Graham Greene's meaty tale of duplicity and disaffection in postwar Vienna. While adding an enormous amount of spice to one of the screen's most poetically conceived thrillers, it stands as a completely unique achievement in the art of motion-picture scoring. Unforgettable.

On the Waterfront (1954, U.S., 108 mins., b/w) Dir: Elia Kazan; Cast: Marlon Brando, Eva Marie Saint, Karl Malden, Lee J. Cobb, Rod Steiger.

Brando, Steiger, Cobb, Malden, Saint, Kazan, and screenwriter Budd Schulberg, contendah's all, score a major knockout with this brooding, brawling account of ex-boxer Terry Malloy and his bout with the longshoremen's union. The mood is more than enhanced by Leonard Bernstein's music, full of allusions to classical giants ranging from Mahler to Gershwin, but marked by a furious energy and emotional intensity of its own. Listen carefully and you hear the Jets and Sharks getting ready to rumble.

Elevator to the Gallows (aka: *Frantic,* 1957, France, 92 mins., b/w) Dir: Louis Malle; Cast: Jeanne Moreau, Maurice Ronet, Georges Poujouly.

Sullen, sultry Jeanne Moreau is left high, dry, and frantic waiting for her lover, who is stuck in an elevator after killing her husband. Malle's first feature film is cool, controlled, and velvet smooth . . . qualities complemented and expanded upon in the cool jazz score by Miles Davis. The director's *Murmur of the Heart,* made years later, makes extensive use of jazz recordings, particularly Charlie Parker's, on the soundtrack.

Anatomy of a Murder (1959, U.S., 160 mins., b/w) Dir: Otto Preminger; Cast: James Stewart, Lee Remick, Ben Gazzara, Joseph Welch, Arthur O'Connell, Eve Arden, George C. Scott, Murray Hamilton.

Totally engrossing courtroom drama, built on irony and paradox with attorney Stewart defending a man of dubious character, on trial for murdering the slug who allegedly raped his far from virtuous wife. Who's zoomin' who? Preminger effectively undercuts audience expectations at every turn and Duke Ellington's score darts brilliantly back and forth between smoky ballads and high-flying jazz excursions, threatening to blow the tight structure of the film to pieces at any moment. The Duke himself shows up in a cameo, playing piano in a roadside gin joint.

The Family Way (1967, Great Britain, 115 mins.) Dirs: John and Roy Boulting;

Cast: Hayley Mills, John Mills, Hywel Bennett.

■
Surprisingly thoughtful comedy/drama about an unconsummated marriage raised eyebrows for a couple of reasons—1) popular 1960s child star Mills, in her first adult role, boozed it up and bared her bod on screen, and 2) Paul McCartney, in the first solo work by a Beatle, ventured outside the realm of rock and roll to compose the score. Knowing Paulie's affinity for sugar, you might think the film is hazardous to the health of hypoglycemics, but the music, like the story, acting, and direction, is full of subtle textures. Extremely effective.

Trouble Man (1972, U.S., 99 mins.) Dir: Ivan Dixon; Cast: Robert Hooks, Paul Winfield, Ralph Waite, William Smithers, Paula Kelly, Julius W. Harris.

Blaxploitaion with T-man Hooks getting caught between rival gangs. Not bad if you like over-the-top drive-in style action—better if you get gooey over the music of Marvin Gaye. Soulmaster Marvin wrote the score and while most of the material is instrumental, there is one vocal and some of Gaye's patented soulful moaning is mixed in with the orchestrations. Not a major musical work, but some good funky stuff that anticipates the grinding sexuality of his "Let's Get It On" album made the following year.

Sleeper (1973, U.S., 88 mins.) Dir: Woody Allen; Cast: Woody Allen, Diane Keaton, John Beck, Don Keefer.

After a botched ulcer operation, Rip Van Woody gets wrapped in tinfoil and flash-frozen, only to wake up 200 years later in a state of total confusion. Though slow in spots, funny enough to provoke whoops of laughter. The improbable Dixieland score, which kicks things further out over the edge than they already are, is credited to Allen (on clarinet) with the Preservation Hall Jazz Band and the New Orleans Funeral Ragtime Orchestra. This is the only one of his films in which the writer-director-star added composer-musician to the hyphenated string.

Rush (1991, U.S., 120 mins.) Dir: Lili Fini Zanuck; Cast: Jason Patric, Jennifer Jason Leigh, Sam Elliott, Max Perlich, Gregg Allman, Tony Frank.

Two narcs go undercover to nail dealer Allman, get hooked on each other, and wind up consuming fistfuls of pharmaceuticals themselves. Patric and Leigh are excellent as the strung-out cops, but the real star of this incredibly downbeat melodrama is soundtrack composer Eric Clapton's guitar, which screams through the characters' pain and suffering, strokes them during sex, and wraps itself up in their tender embraces. The Grammy winning-song "Tears in Heaven," written by Clapton after the tragic death of his son, is featured under the closing credits.

■■■■■■■■■■■■■■■■

LIVELY ARTS

■■■■■■■■■■■■■■■■

ON YOUR RADIO DIAL

Radio turns out to be a field that inspires filmmakers. Although two major periods are not much available on video, yet: movies about radio's early years like *Big Broadcast* (Bing's big break), *Professional Sweetheart* (early Ginger, spoof on radio), *Twenty Million Sweethearts*, and a bio about Walter Winchell, *Wake Up and Live*, and a whole genre of God-speaks-via-transistor, including Ron Reagan's first, *Love Is on the Air*, plus *The Next Voice You Hear*, and

Red Planet Mars. **We're sure you'll want to catch some of these, so stay tuned.**

Play Misty for Me (1971, U.S., 102 mins.) Dir: Clint Eastwood; Cast: Clint Eastwood, Jessica Walter, Donna Mills.

Eastwood's propitious start as a director. In this taut suspense thriller, late-night radio DJ Eastwood is stalked by a psychotic, played by Walter. Effort is supported by a soundtrack that features Johnny Otis and the Cannonball Adderley Quintet.

Talk Radio (1988, U.S., 100 mins.) Dir: Oliver Stone; Cast: Eric Bogosian, Ellen Greene, Leslie Hope, Alec Baldwin.

Like the title says, Bogosian talks—vicious, vulgar, and nasty—in his portrayal of a master of the modern radio phenomenon of audience abuse via the airwaves. Details of the career of Alan Berg (a real-life Colorado DJ who was assassinated by white supremacists) are melded into the screenplay, which is based on Bogosian's original theatrical piece.

Handle With Care (aka: *Citizens Band,* 1977, U.S., 98 mins.) Dir: Jonathan Demme; Cast: Paul Le Mat, Candy Clark, Ann Wedgeworth, Charles Napier, Marcia Rodd.

This special movie à la Demme captures a moment of Americana during the height of the CB radio craze. The story is woven around the quirky characters who are busy talking back and forth as they roll down our highways.

Pump Up the Volume (1990, U.S., 105 mins.) Dir: Allan Moyle; Cast: Christian Slater, Scott Paulin, Ellen Greene, Samantha Mathis, Chris Jacobs, Annie Ross, Mimi Kennedy, Cheryl Pollak, Seth Green, Ahmet Zappa, Billy Morrissette, Lala.

Teen angst, pirate radio, and Christian Slater as the DJ providing words of wisdom and appropriate tunes, house music vintage, to help his friends get through the night.

American Graffiti (1973, U.S., 110 mins.) Dir: George Lucas; Cast: Ronny Howard, Cindy Williams, Charlie Martin Smith, Richard Dreyfuss, Mackenzie Phillips, Candy Clark.

Car-radio cruising, early 1960s style. Wolfman Jack DJs this entire movie with tunes that will take you back. The story—teen angst on wheels in middle America during a much more innocent time—is pretty swell.

American Hot Wax (1978, U.S., 91 mins.) Dir: Floyd Mutrux; Cast: Tim McIntire, Fran Drescher, Laraine Newman, Chuck Berry, Jerry Lee Lewis.

And now, back to the 1950s with the king of rock 'n' roll DJs, Brooklyn's Alan Freed. Movie features his radio schtick as well as some of the great acts he aired, live in concert.

Good Morning, Vietnam (1987, U.S., 121 mins.) Dir: Barry Levinson; Cast: Robin Williams, Forest Whitaker, Tung Thanh Tran, Bruno Kirby, Richard Edson.

Robin Williams does a virtuoso turn in a bio loosely based on the experiences of Adrian Cronauer, an Armed Forces radio DJ stationed in Saigon in 1965. Williams's wit brings him into conflict with the Army brass, but the greater part of the story is about his evolution from a man who uses humor to distance himself, to one who becomes increasingly sensitive to the concerns of a local population caught in a war nobody seems to want.

Orpheus (1949, France, 95 mins.) Dir: Jean Cocteau; Cast: Jean Marais, Maria Casares, François Perier, Juliette Greco, Roger Blin.

A magical allegory as concocted by Cocteau, where the poet Marais meets the Princess of Death, but not before he is besieged over his radio by voices from other worlds.

Christine (1983, U.S., 116 mins.) Dir: John Carpenter; Cast: Keith Gordon, John Stockwell, Harry Dean Stanton, Alexandra Paul.

Voices over the radio here also, but this time Stephen King style. This is Christine, the evil-talking car. You won't be too scared, but then you might not look at that heap of metal and fiberglass as quite the inanimate object you used to.

The King of Marvin Gardens (1972, U.S., 104 mins.) Dir: Bob Rafelson; Cast: Jack Nicholson, Bruce Dern, Ellen Burstyn, Julia Anne Robinson.

A complex movie about the relationship between two brothers. Nicholson is an all-night disc jockey who uses his monologues as a kind of therapy—and to mythologize his brother (Dern), who's really more like a low-rent scuzz, an Atlantic City dreamer. Compelling, uneven, worth seeing.

Comfort and Joy (1984, Scotland, 106 mins.) Dir: Bill Forsyth; Cast: Bill Peterson, Eleanor David, C. P. Grogan, Alex Norton.

Forsyth is a delight, and this is no exception, though it's somewhat weaker than his earlier work, like *Local Hero*. Here, a Scottish DJ gets involved in a territorial dispute between rival ice-cream truck owners.

Radio Days (1987, U.S., 85 mins.) Dir: Woody Allen; Cast: Mia Farrow, Seth Green, Julie Kavner, Diane Keaton, Tony Roberts, Danny Aiello, Jeff Daniels, Josh Mostel, Dianne Wiest.

A nostalgic montage of growing up in the 1940s, when glamor was defined by the music and the stars of radioland, and home was an overcrowded house in Brooklyn's Brighton Beach. Beauti-fully photographed time capsule lushly supported with the big-band music, original programs (including many actual old-time radio stars), and Santo Loquasto set designs of the era.

ON THE TUBE

From the beginning this invention was viewed with wonder. Movieland was of course afraid for its life, so with some notable exceptions, television was pretty much ignored until it had taken over our living rooms and could be ignored no longer. From boob tube to the not-so-subliminal effect it has on all our lives, here's how the box shows up on the silver screen.

International House (1933, U.S., 72 mins., b/w) Dir: A. Edward Sutherland; Cast: W. C. Fields, George Burns, Gracie Allen, Stuart Erwin, Bela Lugosi.

Charming comedy, notable for its cast (spotted with early radio entertainers); its plot, which centers on an inventor's early television experiment, "radioscope"; and, Cab Calloway singing "Reefer Man." Check out Lugosi again in the 1935 *Murder by Television* for another TV inventor, dated and dim, but also way ahead of its time.

Network (1976, U.S., 121 mins.) Dir: Sidney Lumet; Cast: Faye Dunaway, William Holden, Peter Finch, Robert Duvall, Beatrice Straight, Ned Beatty.

Riveting and explosive (even to us jaded media-watchers) view from inside the network machinery. The ferocity of competition to get maximum "share" is seen in the exploitation of Finch's snapped newsman who becomes a mad prophet of the airwaves. Paddy Chayefsky's Oscar-winning screenplay is an insider's gem. Oscars went to Dunaway, Finch, and Straight as well.

My Favorite Year (1982, U.S., 92 mins.) Dir: Richard Benjamin; Cast: Peter O'Toole, Bill Macy, Jessica Harper, Lainie Kazan, Lou Jacobi, Mark Linn-Baker, Joseph Bologna.

A young writer (Linn-Baker) is assigned to play nursemaid to O'Toole's debauched screen swashbuckler, the guest star on a zany 1950s comedy show styled on the incomparable Sid Caesar/Imogene Coca *Your Show of Shows*. Fun glimpse back at the days of live TV and lively performances. Lasted 10 minutes as a late 1992 Broadway musical.

The King of Comedy (1983, U.S., 109 mins.) Dir: Martin Scorsese; Cast: Jerry Lewis, Robert De Niro, Sandra Bernhard.

Rupert Pupkin (De Niro) is a pathetic, tightly wound everyman whose life centers on his belief that with the right break into national TV, he would be a great comedy star. Lewis is fascinating as the Johnny Carson-type late-night talk-show host on whom Rupert focuses his obsession. Bernhard also contributes a strong performance in this bleak and troubling black comedy.

Being There (1979, U.S., 107 mins.) Dir: Hal Ashby; Cast: Peter Sellers, Melvyn Douglas, Shirley MacLaine, Jack Warden, Richard Dysart, Richard Basehart.

We just like watching, and you will too. In this evocative interpretation of Jerzy Kosinski's novel, Sellers is just perfect as a very simple man who is mistaken for much more. A brilliantly satirical exploration of the foibles of the fashionable who are always eager to embrace the guru of the month.

The Thrill of It All (1963, U.S., 108 mins.) Dir: Norman Jewison; Cast: Doris Day, James Garner, Arlene Francis, ZaSu Pitts.

A nice little spoof of TV and those commercial breaks, highlighted by Carl Reiner's deft script and Doris's ideal housewife-turned-soap-peddler of the airwaves.

Stay Tuned (1992, U.S., 87 mins.) Dir: Peter Hyams; Cast: John Ritter, Pam Dawber, Jeffrey Jones, Eugene Levy, David Tom, Heather McComb, Bob Dishy.

Variation on a familiar movies-about-TV theme has Ritter and Dawber sucked through their satellite dish into videoland, popping in and out of shows and films from the past. Not enough of a satire of their couch-potato lifestyle, but the clips are fun.

Kentucky Fried Movie (1977, U.S., 78 mins.) Dir: John Landis; Cast: Evan Kim, Donald Sutherland, George Lazenby, Bill Bixby, Henry Gibson.

The pre-*Airplane!* writing crew lampoons TV shows from kung-fu to softcore, often being quite tasteless, though funny, along the way. Check out *Groove Tube* and *Tunnelvision* too (for trips to televisionland featuring Chevy Chase and other *Saturday Night Live* alumni).

Poltergeist (1982, U.S., 114 mins.) Dir: Tobe Hooper; Cast: JoBeth Williams, Craig T. Nelson, Beatrice Straight, Zelda Rubinstein, Dominique Dunne, Oliver Robins, Heather O'Rourke.

Then we have the message movies—that is movies that depict TV as the transmitter of messages from, uh, beyond. This movie is wonderful in how it combines humor with terror—it just makes perfect sense for the evil spirit to make its presence known through what could be *your* TV set. Rod Serling's classic television series *The Twilight Zone* had an episode that was the best of this genre, but that's another story. Back in movieland, David Cronenberg's *Videodrome* takes the same idea and pushes it even further, with questionable success.

Medium Cool (1969, U.S., 111 mins.) Dir: Haskell Wexler; Cast: Robert Forster, Verna Bloom, Peter Bonerz, Marianna Hill, Sid McCoy.

This brilliant film, ostensibly about the 1968 Chicago Democratic Convention riots from the cameraman's point of view, is most powerful in its perception of his detachment from the extreme events swirling around him.

Tanner 88 (1988, U.S., 11 episodes, 40 mins. each) Dir: Robert Altman; Cast: Michael Murphy, Pamela Reed, Cynthia Nixon, Kevin J. O'Connor.

Miss this on HBO? Well run out right now and catch any of the three compilation volumes now available on video. This most witty, acerbic view of media and the campaign trail set the ground work for everything the spin doctors have had to offer right on up to *The War Room*, a perfect night cap.

Deathwatch (1980, France-West Germany, 128 mins.) Dir: Bertrand Tavernier; Cast: Harvey Keitel, Romy Schneider, Harry Dean Stanton, Max von Sydow.

Interesting cast sparks this futuristic drama of media manipulation and abuse. Keitel has a camera embedded in his brain—a TV producer's (Stanton) idea of a great way to report on all the dying details of the terminally-ill Schneider's life.

Hero (1992, U.S., 112 mins.) Dir: Stephen Frears; Cast: Dustin Hoffman, Geena Davis, Andy Garcia, Joan Cusack, Kevin J. O'Connor, Maury Chaykin, Stephen Tobolowsky.

A Face in the Crowd (1957, U.S., 125 mins., b/w) Dir: Elia Kazan; Cast: Andy Griffith, Patricia Neal, Anthony Franciosa.

More media manipulation in *Hero*, a glitzed-up, marginal tale of the media inventing a hero when reporters wrong-ly identify Garcia as the man who rescued 54 people from a plane crash. The earlier *A Face in the Crowd*, a parable of a backwoods musician (Griffith—who's super) who is turned into a national star, is a compelling and powerful (and successful) mirror of *Hero*. Both deal with the victimization of those suddenly in the limelight.

■

NOTE: Honorable mention goes to: *Bye, Bye Birdie* for its tribute to the *Ed Sullivan Show*; *A Thousand Clowns*, for Jason Robards's poignant nonconformist TV kid's show host; *Bob Roberts* for its cutting-edge look at the influence of the media in political campaigns today; and *THX-1138*, which takes TV (and its *1984* implications) as far as we care to go.

MOVIES ABOUT THE MOVIES: BEHIND THE SCENES

The magic, the mystery, the mystique. (Interesting how many of the good ones are *about* screenwriters—guess they took their writing coaches' advice and wrote about what they know. . . .)

8½ (1963, Italy, 135 mins.) Dir: Federico Fellini; Cast: Marcello Mastroianni, Claudia Cardinale, Sandra Milo, Anouk Aimee.

Fellini's semiautobiographical extravaganza about the inseparability of his life, his women, and his art. Mastroianni is peak, and Aimee is perfectly cast as his alienated, intellectual wife. The plot's a swirl of cinematic atmosphere as Marcello, as a director who's supposed to be starting a new movie but has trouble finding his story, magically orchestrates the wisps of ideas into his cinematic vision, all accompanied by the wonderful Nino Rota score.

Contempt (1963, France-Italy, 103 mins.) Dir: Jean-Luc Godard; Cast: Brigitte Bardot, Jack Palance, Fritz Lang, Michel Piccoli, Georgia Moll.

American producer Palance offers writer Piccoli big bucks to pen a screenplay based on Homer's *The Odyssey*. An added inducement is the director, Fritz Lang, playing himself. An added complication is the writer's insatiable wife, Bardot. One of the aesthetic and commercial peaks of the first wave of Godard's career, this inside-out view of the biz balances a love of the medium with an abhorrence for the wheeling and dealing behind the scenes. A profound commentary on the art of cinema, the scourge of capitalism, and the deconstruction of storytelling tradition.

Day for Night (1973, France, 116 mins.) Dir: François Truffaut; Cast: François Truffaut, Jacqueline Bisset, Jean-Pierre Léaud, Valentina Cortese, Jean-Pierre Aumont, Alexandra Stewart.

8½ with the Truffaut touch—charming, lightly satirical—pervades this delightful film about the day-to-day problems with cast and production in making a film, all unfolding as we watch the film actually being shot. Truffaut is a man who loves film and it really comes across.

Hearts of Darkness: A Filmmaker's Apocalypse (1991, U.S., 97 mins.) Dirs: Fax Bahr, George Hickenlooper; Cast: Francis Ford Coppola, Marlon Brando, Dennis Hopper, Martin Sheen.

Burden of Dreams (1982, U.S., 95 mins.) Dir: Les Blank; Cast: Werner Herzog, Klaus Kinski, Claudia Cardinale, Mick Jagger, Jason Robards.

In *Hearts of Darkness*, Eleanor Coppola (working with directors Bahr and Hickenlooper) has put together a remarkable document tracing her husband's excesses, and brilliance, in the making of *Apocalypse Now*. Cinema and reality are the same for Mr. Coppola, and eventually the actors and crew as well, as we observe the absolutely surreal atmosphere and logistical nightmare of filming in the jungles and monsoon-hit terrain of Thailand. Lots of superb footage of the actual shooting and fascinating commentary by the participants. Les Blank's *Burden of Dreams*, tracking the shooting of Werner Herzog's *Fitzcarraldo* in the Peruvian Amazon, is also a hugely compelling—and somehow even more mesmerizing—look at against-all-odds movie-making by a determined (and completely obsessed) director who, like Coppola, is ready to tangle with the forces of nature and culture that challenge him.

Inserts (1975, Great Britain, 99 mins.) Dir: John Byrum; Cast: Richard Dreyfuss, Veronica Cartwright, Jessica Harper, Bob Hoskins.

Good cast in quirky and at best uneven little film about 1930s "boy-wonder" director (Dreyfuss) who no longer has it and turns to shooting porno. Dividend: a hummable background rendition of "Moonglow."

The Day of the Locust (1975, U.S., 140 mins.) Dir: John Schlesinger; Cast: Donald Sutherland, Karen Black, Burgess Meredith, William Atherton, Geraldine Page.

Nathanael West's novel is searingly interpreted in this view of the characters that inhabited Hollywood's underside during the 1930s. Atherton is well cast as the fresh screenwriter through whose eyes we see the proverbial tarnish on Tinseltown.

The Bad and the Beautiful (1952, U.S., 118 mins.) Dir: Vincente Minnelli; Cast: Kirk Douglas, Lana Turner, Dick Powell, Gloria Grahame, Walter Pidgeon, Barry Sullivan.

Highly entertaining five-Oscar potboiler about power and glory in Hollywood studioland, as revealed through the relationships between ruthless producer Douglas and the minions around him. Ten years later clips from this were used in another Minnelli film, *Two Weeks in Another Town,* a less successful look at making a film, this time in Rome, with Douglas playing an actor.

Sullivan's Travels (1942, U.S., 91 mins.) Dir: Preston Sturges; Cast: Joel McCrea, William Demarest, Eric Blore, Veronica Lake.

Sturges and McCrea are in top form in this classic jape at Hollywood. To prepare for shooting his next film, director McCrea sets off into the "real world" with barely a dime in his pocket and picks up Veronica Lake along the way.

The Player (1992, U.S., 123 mins.) Dir: Robert Altman; Cast: Tim Robbins, Greta Scacchi, Fred Ward, Whoopi Goldberg, Peter Gallagher, Brian James.

The ultimate insider's guide to modern Hollywood. Perfectly cast Tim Robbins's hot-shot producer is under suspicion for murder. Lots of insider bits about Hollywood royalty, and once again the theme that, for this crowd, the line between movies and reality is pretty fuzzy.

Sunset Boulevard (1950, U.S., 110 mins.) Dir: Billy Wilder; Cast: Gloria Swanson, William Holden, Erich von Stroheim, Nancy Olson, Jack Webb, Cecil B. DeMille, Hedda Hopper, Buster Keaton, Fred Clark.

Oh Gloria. Totally over-the-top performance in this not-to-be-missed swan dance of fading star kept up by the ever-strange "housekeeper" von Stroheim and her parasitic relationship with the young(er), washed-up screenwriter Holden.

The Stunt Man (1980, U.S., 129 mins.) Dir: Richard Rush; Cast: Peter O'Toole,

Steve Railsback, Chuck Bail, Allen Goorwitz (Garfield), Barbara Hershey.

This small, quite unusual film plays with that venerable "Is It Real?" theme once again, while we learn about the wonder of stunts and makeup from behind the scenes of a shoot directed by a dictatorial yet charismatic O'Toole. Is the stunt man psycho? Worth watching to find out. Shot in 1978. If you're still in the mood there are also the not-bad thrillers *Stunts* and *F/X.*

In a Lonely Place (1950, U.S., 91 mins., b/w) Dir: Nicholas Ray; Cast: Humphrey Bogart, Gloria Grahame, Frank Lovejoy, Carl Benton Reid, Billy Gray.

The noirest of the 1950s looks at the dark side of Hollywood success. Plot tackles the effect a murder charge has on driven, hot-headed screenwriter (Bogart) and his lover, the enigmatic Gloria Grahame. Moody and moving in gorgeous black and white.

What Price Hollywood? (1932, U.S., 88 mins., b/w) Dir: George Cukor; Cast: Constance Bennett, Lowell Sherman, Neil Hamilton, Gregory Ratoff.

The grand grandparent of *A Star Is Born* (all three: 1937, 1954, and the 1976 rock 'n' roll version). The title says it all in this now-familiar but vibrantly hard-edged and insightful story of (this time) a famous director whose career and life give way to alcohol as he watches his young protégé become a huge star.

Barton Fink (1991, U.S., 117 mins.) Dir: Joel Coen; Cast: John Turturro, John Goodman, Judy Davis, Michael Lerner, John Mahoney, Tony Shalhoub.

A noir after the fact, with a special nod to Welles's *A Touch of Evil* among other works. The fabulous Coen brothers immerse us in the mind of a 1930s Hollywood screenwriter, freshly brought in from the literary world of the East Coast, and staying at a very strange hotel. There may or may not have been a murder; the Goodman character may or may not be involved. However you interpret it, the tension, the art direction, the effects, and Turturro and Goodman's performances are stunning.

The Front (1976, U.S., 94 mins.) Dir: Martin Ritt; Cast: Woody Allen, Zero Mostel, Andrea Marcovicci, Joshua Shelley, Georgann Johnson.

Written by and cast with a number of the victims themselves, this Hollywood blacklist story, ably and painfully—yet not without a sense of humor—evokes a period when the careers of some of America's most talented people were derailed by the McCarthy communist witch-hunts. Allen is fine in a straight role as the "front" who gives his name to scripts as a cover for blacklisted authors. Mostel is even better as a comic fighting to survive.

THE MOVIEGOERS

The view from the other side of the silver screen. You and me, sitting out there with our popcorn, in it for a bit of escape, a bit of fantasy, a bit of magic, or, just a good time at the old Bijou. What the movies mean to us.

Spirit of the Beehive (1973, Spain, 98 mins.) Dir: Victor Erice; Cast: Fernando Fernan Gomez, Teresa Gimpera, Ana Torrent.

Frankenstein is shown in a small rural village in post-Civil War Spain and a young child is disturbingly affected, imagining Frankenstein's monster is actually there. Child actress Torrent's performance is mesmerizing and makes the story all the more upsetting in its beauty and gravity.

The Purple Rose of Cairo (1985, U.S., 84 mins.) Dir: Woody Allen; Cast: Mia Farrow, Jeff Daniels, Danny Aiello, Dianne Wiest, Edward Herrmann.

Farrow finds solace at the movies when she desperately needs an escape from her miserable Depression-era home. Her fantasies seem to come true as the glamorous male lead (Daniels, who is perfectly charming, but sort of one-dimensional, as you might expect) steps off the screen and into her life. It's an Allen movie and that means a great sense of authenticity in characters, sets, and setting, yet somehow we wish he could have let go of his cynicism a little more.

The Last Picture Show (1971, U.S., 118 mins., b/w) Dir: Peter Bogdanovich; Cast: Timothy Bottoms, Jeff Bridges, Cybill Shepherd, Ben Johnson, Cloris Leachman, Ellen Burstyn, Eileen Brennan, Clu Gulager, Randy Quaid, Sam Bottoms.

A finely detailed study of survival in a small, dying 1950s Texas town where there's not much to do but cruise, drink beers, shoot pool, and go to the local movie theater. First Shepherd and early Timothy Bottoms; Johnson's and Leachman's Oscars were well deserved. Haunting black-and-white photography by Robert Surtees. A special, re-edited (1990, by Bogdanovich) laser-disc version is available of this superb adaptation of a Larry McMurtry novel.

Those Wonderful Men With a Crank (1978, Czechoslovakia, 90 mins.) Dir: Jiri Menzel; Cast: Rudolf Hrusinsky, Jiri Menzel, Blazena Holisova, Vlasta Fabianova, Vladimir Mensik.

Menzel (*Closely Watched Trains),* with his sly and charming sense of humor, brings us the story of a man who shows one-reelers throughout the countryside to raise money to fulfill his dream of opening the first movie house in 1907 Prague.

The Smallest Show on Earth (1957, Great Britain, 81 mins., b/w) Dir: Basil Dearden; Cast: Peter Sellers, Margaret

Rutherford, Bill Travers, Virginia McKenna.

A British tea cake. In other words, a typically charming and eccentric story with a very understated, but absolutely right, Sellers in a supporting role. Young couple think they've come into a major inheritance until they discover it's the decrepit, long-closed Bijou, replete with former employees. Their idea is to revive it, then take the money and run, but they also have a heart.

Coming Up Roses (1986, Great Britain, 90 mins.) Dir: Stephen Bayly; Cast: Dafydd Hywel, Iola Gregory, W.J. Phillips, Glan Davies.

Another British attempt to save a dying movie house, this time involving a clandestine plot to raise money by growing mushrooms in the dark cinema. The story requires movement of the illicit crop only at night—using miners hats, of course—making for some very odd and amusing scenes.

Cinema Paradiso (1989, Italy-France, 123 mins.) Dir: Giuseppe Tornatore; Cast: Philippe Noiret, Jacques Perrin, Salvatore Cascio, Agnese Nano.

Anyone who has experienced wonder and magic in a movie theater will be taken with this delightful and poignant tale of a boy growing up in post-WWII Italy, whose life seems to take place entirely within and around the theater, its movies, and its projectionist (a character whose life is similarly defined, and wonderfully captured, by Noiret). Best Foreign Film Oscar; Cannes Special Jury Prize.

Edison the Man (1940, U.S., 107 mins.) Dir: Clarence Brown; Cast: Spencer Tracy, Charles Coburn.

So what if Thomas A. didn't really invent the motion-picture projector — he knew a good thing when he heard about it. Tracy is fine as the American entrepreneur/inventor, who brought us telephone transmitters, electric lights, the phonograph—and, oh yes, film sprockets. Good sequel to *Young Tom Edison.*

Kiss of the Spider Woman (1985, Brazil-U.S., 119 mins., c & b/w) Dir: Hector Babenco; Cast: William Hurt, Raul Julia, Sonia Braga, José Lewgoy.

There are those who go to movies to live their lives vicariously through the action on the screen. Then there's this case, where doing so is a matter of survival. Hurt's conjuration of a nocturnal Hollywood melodrama for himself and cellmate Julia is the thread binding this story of political oppression in a Latin American country. As resonant and compelling as Manuel Puig's novel.

■

NOTE: We wouldn't want to forget Tab Hunter's role as the drive-in movie manager in that smell-o-vision sensation *Polyester,* by John Waters; or that the main character in Hitchcock's *Sabotage* was a movie theater manager; *or,* that a primary center of action in the Steve McQueen version of *The Blob* was, indeed, the local movie theater.

STAND-UP COMEDY

Take this list.
Please.

Punchline (1988, U.S., 123 mins.) Dir: David Seltzer; Cast: Sally Field, Tom Hanks, John Goodman, Mark Rydell, Kim Greist, Paul Mazursky, Taylor Negron.

Sally Field plays a Roseanne Arnold-ish housewife who pursues her secret ambition to be a stand-up comedian and Tom Hanks is the talented, yet self-destructive, comic she looks to for help and respect. As serious a look as you'll ever want, or need, at the comedy explosion of recent years. Funny at times, drippy at others, but the jokes do keep coming.

Lenny (1974, U.S., 111 mins., b/w) Dir: Bob Fosse; Cast: Dustin Hoffman, Valerie Perrine, Jan Miner.

A gritty, beautifully shot film about the rise and fall of groundbreaking comedian Lenny Bruce. Dustin Hoffman, who hadn't yet become DUSTIN HOFFMAN, gives a fine performance as Bruce, whose blue comedy got him blacklisted in the fifties, but would seem tame now on "Comedy from Caroline's." It's hard to see why so many critics hated this movie when it came out. Fosse's black-and-white, quasi-documentary style predates *Raging Bull* by six years and looks better all the time.

This Is My Life (1992, U.S., 105 mins.) Dir: Nora Ephron; Cast: Julie Kavner, Samantha Mathis, Gaby Hoffmann, Carrie Fisher, Dan Aykroyd.

Julie Kavner stars as a working-class single mom making her way up in the world of stand-up, almost leaving her children behind as she goes. Slickly directed by Nora Ephron, the movie has good intentions that don't exactly lead to hell, but you won't find heaven, either. At best, it's movie purgatory.

Let's Make Love (1960, U.S., 118 mins.) Dir: George Cukor; Cast: Marilyn Monroe, Yves Montand, Tony Randall.

A silly, star-studded excuse for Marilyn to wear leotards and curl around Yves Montand, which is not to say it's not immensely entertaining. Montand is a shy, stupidly wealthy man who infiltrates a small theater company when he hears that they're lampooning him. In order to develop his performing talents, he hires famous entertainers to teach him the tricks, including Milton Berle, who steals his scene as he tries to make Montand funny. Don't think about this film; just enjoy it.

Mickey One (1965, U.S., 93 mins., b/w) Dir: Arthur Penn; Cast: Warren Beatty, Alexandra Stewart, Hurd Hatfield.

Warren Beatty as a stand-up comedian. Hard to believe that it would work, but it does in this tale of a performer's search for meaning in his life. A solid, engrossing film.

The King of Comedy (1983, U.S., 109 mins.) Dir: Martin Scorsese; Cast: Jerry Lewis, Robert De Niro, Sandra Bernhard.

A brilliant film that now seems all too prescient. De Niro plays Rupert Pupkin, a would-be comedian who stalks and finally kidnaps a famous talk-show host so he can have his chance at fame. The young Sandra Bernhard is terrific and Jerry Lewis should have won an Oscar as the host. A realistic and frightening look at our obsession with fame. Scorsese's master stroke is to make Pupkin a relatively funny performer.

Mr. Saturday Night (1992, U.S., 119 mins.) Dir: Billy Crystal; Cast: Billy Crystal, David Paymer, Julie Warner, Helen Hunt, Mary Mara, Jerry Orbach.

Billy Crystal has the unfortunate job of playing a comedian much less talented and likable than he is. The result is an interesting look at Jewish comics of the last few decades that plays behind the middling story of a nasty comic who's finally learning about the kind of person he's been all these years.

BIG TOPS & MIDWAYS

Even if weepy clowns and besequined German lion tamers set your teeth on edge, the circus still manages to awaken some sleepy bit of juvenile wonder in all of us. Carnivals, on the other hand, are not always so innocent. The pressure to win a three-foot-high stuffed animal on a hot summer night can arouse

very adult emotions. Here are 10 trips to the big top and the midway to satisfy any mood.

The Greatest Show on Earth (1952, U.S., 153 mins.) Dir: Cecil B. DeMille; Cast: James Stewart, Charlton Heston, Betty Hutton, Cornel Wilde, Gloria Grahame, Henry Wilcoxon, Lyle Bettger, Lawrence Tierney, Dorothy Lamour.

Cecil B. DeMille presents the great American circus as you remember it— or think you do. Certainly the number-one pick for a straightforward circus film and proof that you can make a classic by putting every imaginable cliché about a particular subject into one overwhelming package. It's bigger than any big top you've ever seen, and with no bratty kids screaming for more popcorn.

Freaks (1932, U.S., 64 mins., b/w) Dir: Tod Browning; Cast: Leila Hyams, Olga Baclanova, Harry Earles, Wallace Ford.

Sideshow freaks plot revenge when a beautiful acrobat takes advantage of a wealthy midget. Browning's dark, frightening, and unforgettable film was a huge influence on David Lynch; *The Elephant Man* feels like a total lift after you see this. The brilliant performances by real freaks inspire respect, not pity. There's no exploitation here, which is more than one can say about most of Lynch's work.

The Circus (1928, U.S., 60 mins.) Dir: Charles Chaplin; Cast: Charles Chaplin, Merna Kennedy, Betty Morrissey.

A perfect marriage. Charlie Chaplin toddles into the ring and shows how his brand of physical comedy is the true descendant of the great clowning traditions. The trapeze scene, with Chaplin set upon by a pack of monkeys, is an unheralded gem.

7 Faces of Dr. Lao (1964, U.S., 100 mins.) Dir: George Pal; Cast: Tony Randall, Barbara Eden, Arthur O'Connell.

Strangely engrossing film about a mysterious Chinese man and the circus he puts on in a troubled rural town. The edgy undertones, special effects that are just this side of cheesy, and more Tony Randall than you thought possible in one movie—all seven faces are his—make this solid fun.

Lola Montes (1955, France-West Germany, 140 mins.) Dir: Max Ophuls; Cast: Martine Carol, Peter Ustinov, Oskar Werner, Anton Walbrook.

Amazing Max Ophuls film that suffers on the small screen, but who cares? A spoonful of chocolate mousse can taste as good as a cup. Famed courtesan Montes, now down on her luck, is forced by poverty to tell her tragic story as a circus entertainment. The costumes and staging of the performance scenes presage Bob Fosse's style and like all Ophuls, it's Romantic with a capital "R," so don't expect any clown cars or seal acts.

The Clowns (1971, Italy-France, 90 mins.) Dir: Federico Fellini; Cast: Mayo Morin, Lima Alberti, Alvaro Vitali, Gasparmo.

A mock documentary by Fellini that lets the circus completely entertain us while asking the question, why are we no longer entertained by the circus? A guaranteed cure for the clown-averse and circusphobic, as well as the only good look at circus history. *La Strada,* Fellini's masterpiece about a brutal strongman and his sweet companion, is an absolute must, too.

Carny (1980, U.S., 107 mins.) Dir: Robert Kaylor; Cast: Gary Busey, Jodie Foster, Robbie Robertson, Meg Foster, Bert Remsen, John Lehne.

Jodie Foster was doing some very good work before people finally decided she was a star. Here she plays a runaway who falls in with carnies Busey and Robertson and goes along with them on the road. A gritty view of carnival life, co-written by Band member Robertson.

Nightmare Alley (1947, U.S., 111 mins., b/w) Dir: Edmund Goulding; Cast: Tyrone Power, Joan Blondell, Coleen Gray, Helen Walker, Mike Mazurki.
∎
Power is a small-time con man who, along with a phony fortune teller and semi-legitimate shrink, sets up an elaborate scam to rip off the rich and gullible. Exposed as a fraud, he sinks into the lower depths of carnival life, surrounded by a moribund cast of sideshow freaks and sub-human aberrations. With a script by Jules Furthman from the wildly popular novel by William Gresham this descent into the maelstrom is given Expressionist weight by Lee Garmes's extraordinary cinematography and a suitably macabre score by Cyril Mockridge. For director Goulding, a notorious sybarite, it stands as his most personal and revealing work.

Carousel (1956, U.S., 128 mins.) Dir: Henry King; Cast: Gordon MacRae, Shirley Jones, Cameron Mitchell, Barbara Ruick.
∎
Rodgers and Hammerstein musical about the reforming effects of love on a free-living carnival barker. More romance than realism here, but it's first-class romance and the Hollywood carnival is colorful enough to make you forget how tatty the real thing usually is.

Lili (1953, U.S., 81 mins.) Dir: Charles Walters; Cast: Leslie Caron, Mel Ferrer, Jean-Pierre Aumont, Zsa Zsa Gabor.

Another musical carnival (perhaps you remember "Hi Lili, Hi Lo," the hit song from the Oscar-winning score), this time with Leslie Caron as a young orphan who gets involved with a crippled puppeteer. Awfully sweet, but so's cotton candy. After the seaminess and slime of *Carny* and *Nightmare Alley,* it would probably be a relief.

DANCE CARD
∎
FRED, GINGER & GENE

. . . and Cyd, and Donald, and Debbie, Leslie, Ruby, and Jane. What does it spell? SUBLIME. You can argue all you want whether Cyd was better than Ginger. We're talking about more here—grace, charm, sophistication, romance, fabulous music, and of course that without which everything else would be meaningless, their angel feet.

Shall We Dance (1937, U.S., 120 mins., b/w) Dir: Mark Sandrich; Cast: Fred Astaire, Ginger Rogers, Eric Blore, Edward Everett Horton.

Fred's a ballet dancer, Ginger's a musical comedy star. Third of the trio of F&G's super-luxury films (along with *The Gay Divorcee* and *Top Hat*). Usual flimsy plot, but who cares when you have Gershwin tunes and their famous roller-skating dance ("Let's Call the Whole Thing Off")?

Top Hat (1935, U.S., 99 mins., b/w) Dir: Mark Sandrich; Cast: Fred Astaire, Ginger Rogers, Edward Everett Horton, Eric Blore, Erik Rhodes, Helen Broderick, Lucille Ball.

Quintessential F&G, tunes by Berlin in his first major Hollywood musical. Romantic and dazzling white art-deco sets provide the atmosphere for this romantic love-at-first-sight plot, which moves from London to carnival in Venice. Also to be remembered for the introduction of a new dance, the Piccolino, and Ginger's famous molting-feather dress ("Cheek to Cheek"), Fred's wild hotel room tap-dance scene, the charm of "Isn't This a Lovely Day?" and the title song, "Top Hat, White Tie and Tails," as performed by Fred with a suave male chorus.

Cover Girl (1944, U.S., 107 mins.) Dir: Charles Vidor; Cast: Rita Hayworth,

Gene Kelly, Phil Silvers, Eve Arden, Otto Kruger.

Kelly's full range is revealed in glorious Technicolor, fulfilling the promise of his 1942 film debut, *For Me and My Gal.* Lovely Rita must either take her big Broadway break or stick with Brooklyn nightclub performer Gene. While she decides, we're entertained with "Alter Ego"—Gene dancing with his shadow (shades of Fred and *Swing Time*), and the exuberant "Make Way for Tomorrow" with Phil and Rita.

Silk Stockings (1957, U.S., 117 mins.) Dir: Rouben Mamoulian; Cast: Fred Astaire, Cyd Charisse, Janis Paige, Peter Lorre.

Successful remake of Garbo's *Ninotchka* (movie capitalist Astaire woos Cyd the Red agent) with Cole Porter on board following his Broadway version. Catch Fred in full white-tie mufti in "The Ritz Rock 'n' Roll" and "All of You."

Swing Time (1936, U.S., 103 mins., b/w) Dir: George Stevens; Cast: Fred Astaire, Ginger Rogers, Victor Moore, Eric Blore, Helen Broderick, Betty Furness.

Fred is a gambling hoofer who teams up with Ginger in a film that, despite the title, has nothing to do with big bands or the jitterbug. Swell tunes by Jerome Kern and Dorothy Fields give us some other dance oddities: Fred in blackface for "Bojangles of Harlem" (this is the one where he dances with silhouettes of himself), and Fred does not win Ginger in their "Never Gonna Dance" number. But they are sublime in it, and in "A Fine Romance" as well.

Singin' in the Rain (1952, U.S., 103 mins.) Dirs: Gene Kelly, Stanley Donen; Cast: Gene Kelly, Debbie Reynolds, Donald O'Connor, Jean Hagen, Cyd Charisse.

You all know about Gene's tour-de-force title number in this story about the transition from silent to sound films, but other showstoppers include O'Connor's "Make 'Em Laugh" and Cyd and Gene's "Broadway Ballet." In Debbie's first major Hollywood outing she plays the dubber for Jean Hagen's silent star, but guess what—Debbie sounded too Dallas so Hagen dubbed for Debbie's speaking parts and Betty Noyes covered her singing! Music: Nacio Herb Brown; lyrics: Arthur Freed.

An American in Paris (1951, U.S., 113 mins.) Dir: Vincente Minnelli; Cast: Gene Kelly, Leslie Caron, Oscar Levant, Nina Foch, Georges Guetary.

Shot entirely in Culver City, but still makes Paris seem like the most romantic place in the world when Gene and Leslie are dancing together (and they have a little help from Gershwin). Gene is an ex-pat artist in Paris on the GI Bill who meets Leslie but must win her from another. Fantastic impressionistic ballet uses locales from famous paintings for the sets.

Follow the Fleet (1936, U.S., 110 mins., b/w) Dir: Mark Sandrich; Cast: Fred Astaire, Ginger Rogers, Lucille Ball, Randolph Scott, Harriet Hilliard.

White tie and tails and breathtaking "Let's Face the Music and Dance." Plenty opulent even though Fred's casting as a sailor keeps his wardrobe and social standing below par in this Berlin-penned seagoing story of a reunited vaudeville team.

Flying Down to Rio (1933, U.S., 72 mins., b/w) Dir: Thornton Freeland; Cast: Dolores Del Rio, Gene Raymond, Fred Astaire, Ginger Rogers, Raul Roulien, Franklin Pangborn.

Everyone knew Fred and Ginger had "it" after this one, their first screen pairing movie. Even in supporting roles, they'll whisk you away as they do the "Carioca" tête-à-tête atop seven white grand pianos. Memorable Vincent Youmans score with a Latin beat. Samba!

The Gay Divorcee (1934, U.S., 107 mins., b/w) Dir: Mark Sandrich; Cast: Ginger Rogers, Fred Astaire, Edward Everett Horton, Alice Brady.

Cole Porter's sublime "Night and Day" is the centerpiece of this first starring vehicle for Fred and Ginger. Plot involves ersatz adultery, mistaken identity, the invention of a new dance, "The Continental," and the discovery of true love, all in a gorgeous 24 hours at an English resort. Also an inspired bit of Fred business—his rendition of "Looking for a Needle in a Haystack." No one can dance and dress—at the same time—like Fred.

The Band Wagon (1953, U.S., 112 mins.) Dir: Vincente Minnelli; Cast: Fred Astaire, Cyd Charisse, Jack Buchanan, Nanette Fabray, Oscar Levant.

Loads of fun and the usual boffo dancing as Astaire's character makes a Broadway comeback to fabulous Arthur Schwartz and Howard Dietz tunes. Especially notable are Fred's amusement arcade tap-dance scene ("A Shine on Your Shoes") and "Dancing in the Dark" with Cyd.

On the Town (1950, U.S., 98 mins.) Dirs: Gene Kelly, Stanley Donen; Cast: Gene Kelly, Frank Sinatra, Betty Garrett, Ann Miller, Vera Ellen, Jules Munchin.

Exuberant (!) Bernstein (Leonard), Comden (Betty), and Green (Adolph) tunes, N.Y. location shots, and Kelly, Sinatra, and Munchin hoofing it all over town as three sailors on leave, with only 24 hours to do it all. "New York, New York" will feel like a wonderful town to you, too.

■

NOTE: Well, not all of these movies are great, but they all feature some spectacular dance scenes. Stanley Donen's *Royal Wedding,* (with Fred, Peter Lawford, and Jane Powell), has that incredible bit with Fred dancing his way up the walls and onto the ceiling. In *Carefree* (F&G; directed by Mark Sandrich) watch for Berlin's fabulous "Change Partners" and Fred's golf-playing scene. And don't miss *Roberta* (F&G again) for their "I Won't Dance" and "Smoke Gets in Your Eyes" numbers; *Ziegfeld Follies* (directed by Vincente Minnelli), the only time Fred Astaire and Gene Kelly dance together (except for *That's Entertainment, Part 2*), and they do it to Gershwin; and, Gene's odd no-talking, no-singing, all-dance musical, *Invitation to the Dance* with its "Gene Dances With Cartoons" section.

DANCE CARD
■
GOTTA DANCE

Just about all the Fred and Ginger (and Fred and whoever) films are plotted on backstage life in some way. We're making room here for other dance movies. What do they all have in common? Characters with seemingly unlimited drive, talent, and ambition, and they all just gotta dance.

Ginger and Fred (1985, Italy, 127 mins.) Dir: Federico Fellini; Cast: Giulietta Masina, Marcello Mastroianni, Franco Fabrizi, Frederick Ledebur.

Marcello and Giulietta, an aging dance team famous for their imitation of the real Fred and Ginger, are brought back together for one more performance. The charm of their partnership as friends and dancers is fully realized in this poignant backstage (Italian TV) drama with that Fellini stamp.

Roseland (1977, U.S., 103 mins.) Dir: James Ivory; Cast: Lou Jacobi, Teresa

Wright, Christopher Walken, Geraldine Chaplin.

Producer Ismail Merchant, director James Ivory, and writer Ruth Prawer Jhabvala do it again. A wistful, sad close-up of a very specific slice of life and time, with a sensitivity like no other. Here we are in N.Y.'s Roseland Ballroom; everyone's hopes and dreams are laid out on the dance floor. The ballroom, now seedy, is a relic, just like these aging, overpainted, and overdressed dancers. But how they dance.

Strictly Ballroom (1992, Australia, 94 min.) Dir: Baz Luhrmann; Cast: Paul Mercurio, Tara Morice, Bill Hunter, Barry Otto, Pat Thompson, Gia Carides.

A powerhouse of dancing determination. With great wit and charm, puts *Flashdance, Dirty Dancing,* and all the rest on the back burner. Terrific, eccentric characters like only non-American films seem to offer, populate this story of fierce dancing competitions and the young guy who just has to dance to his own tune. Love, sex, and viva la Paso Doble!

All That Jazz (1979, U.S., 119 mins.) Dir: Bob Fosse; Cast: Roy Scheider, Jessica Lange, Ann Reinking, Ben Vereen, Cliff Gorman.

Meanwhile back in America, we did have one of the fiercest all-time great theatrical choreographers. This is the not-too-fictionalized story of Bob Fosse—he just HAD to dance, and the electricity and drive come right off the screen, through him and the dancers, especially the super Ann Reinking. Some of the treatment of his personal life (and death) may seem excessive, but hey, this guy was legitimately over the top.

Sweet Charity (1969, U.S., 148 mins.) Dir: Bob Fosse; Cast: Shirley MacLaine, Ricardo Montalban, Chita Rivera, Paula Kelly, John McMartin, Stubby Kaye, Sammy Davis, Jr.

This is one of Fosse's musicals. Gwen Verdon, who created the title role on Broadway, lost out to MacLaine in the movie version, but this tale of lowly taxi dancers aspiring to their big break will still break your heart when you're not being knocked out by the tunes and dancing.

Saturday Night Fever (1977, U.S., 119 mins.) Dir: John Badham; Cast: John Travolta, Karen Lynn Gorney, Joseph Cali, Barry Miller, Julie Bovasso, Donna Pescow.

Travolta uses dance (and a slick white suit that had a fashion impact waaay too long . . .) to break out of his small life in Brooklyn, to the big life in Manhattan. Disco never looked or sounded better, and the difficulties fulfilling this American dream are very well portrayed here.

They Shoot Horses, Don't They? (1969, U.S., 121 mins.) Dir: Sydney Pollack; Cast: Jane Fonda, Michael Sarrazin, Gig Young, Susannah York, Red Buttons, Bruce Dern, Bonnie Bedelia, Allyn Ann McLerie.

Oy. Depressing and bleak Depression (1930s, that is) story of marathon dancers. We're talking 24 hours plus at a stretch. Fonda and Sarrazin are compelling as they desperately try to hold themselves together and win the pot that would get them through to the next dance.

The Turning Point (1977, U.S., 119 mins.) Dir: Herbert Ross; Cast: Anne Bancroft, Shirley MacLaine, Mikhail Baryshnikov, Leslie Browne, Tom Skerritt.

Story of aging ballerinas (and the choices they made), but Baryshnikov steals the show. Beautifully detailed friendship and lovely dancing. It was a big hit (in a weak year) and you'll enjoy seeing it once.

The Red Shoes (1948, Great Britain, 133 mins.) Dirs: Michael Powell, Emeric Pressburger; Cast: Moira Shearer, Anton Walbrook.

The mother of all ballet films, you'll want to see this once also. Ballerina must choose between love and her art. Seems overdone these days, but still beautiful to look at.

Zou Zou (1934, France, 92 mins.) Dir: Marc Allegret; Cast: Josephine Baker, Jean Gabin, Yvette Leblon, Illa Meery.

Baker talks! And she also sings and dances, like wow! Great costumes, too. Who cares if you've already heard this story about the girl in the wings waiting for her big chance?

Dirty Dancing (1987, U.S., 97 mins.) Dir: Emile Ardolino; Cast: Patrick Swayze, Jennifer Grey, Jerry Orbach, Cynthia Rhodes.

Jennifer Grey goes to the Catskills and learns about life, love, and how to make her body MOVE, 1960s style. Patrick Swayze helps. Pretty good even if you're not a fan of Mr. Swayze's.

DANCE CARD
■
BEST OF BUSBY

Busby—William Berkeley Enos, that is. His kaleidoscopic choreography, stage pageantry, and innovative camera angles are so remarkable, so fabulous, so kitschy, so absolutely over the top, well, he just deserves a list all to himself. (However, we won't—or maybe we will—comment on the physical discomfort the lovely women of these choruses were often subjected to.) In the depths of the Depression, Busby truly knew how to lift an audience's spirits, despite his use of the same backing-a-Broadway-musical plot over and over again.

Gold Diggers of 1933 (1933, U.S., 96 mins., b/w) Dir: Mervyn LeRoy; Cast: Warren William, Joan Blondell, Aline MacMahon, Ruby Keeler, Dick Powell, Ginger Rogers.

Crooner Powell is "discovered" and a new show is Broadway-bound in this tribute to the girls in the chorus line. Wait till you see "Shadow Waltz" with the bevy of gals in blonde wigs and white gowns playing white neon violins. Fantastic! Fabulous! Also has that resonant ode to Depression-era war heroes, "Remember My Forgotten Man." By the way, this is Keeler's show, though Ginger is here, supporting (don't miss her pig-latin version of "We're in the Money," which she delivers clad only in a gold coin or two).

Gold Diggers of 1935 (1935, U.S., 98 mins., b/w) Dir: Busby Berkeley; Cast: Dick Powell, Ruby Keeler, Adolphe Menjou, Gloria Stuart, Alice Brady, Hugh Herbert, Glenda Farrell, Frank McHugh, Wini Shaw.

Another big show with a slim plot features the pull-out-all-the-stops, Oscar-winning morality musical "Lullaby of Broadway" and the chorus of waltzing grand pianos, complete with the obligatory beautiful girls performing "The Words Are in My Heart."

Million Dollar Mermaid (1952, U.S., 115 mins.) Dir: Mervyn LeRoy; Cast: Esther Williams, Victor Mature, Walter Pidgeon.
■
Busby and Esther. Perfect. We're only disappointed he never connected with Sonja Henie, too. Fictionalized bio of that pioneer of the one-piece suit, aquatic star Annette Kellerman. A little romance with Mature and a lot of great floating Busby choreography. If you're not seasick yet, check out *Easy to Love* also.

Fashions (aka: Fashions of 1934, 1934, U.S., 78 mins., b/w) Dir: William Dieterle; Cast: William Powell, Bette Davis, Verree Teasdale, Reginald Owen, Frank McHugh, Phillip Reed, Hugh Herbert.
∎
Great cast keeps this romp through the the world of the Parisian haute couture lively. Just wait till you get to the Hall of Human Harps (picture a girl as a sort of figurehead for these heavenly harps) and Busby's "Spin a Little Web of Dreams" number.

Dames (1934, U.S., 90 mins., b/w) Dir: Ray Enright; Cast: Joan Blondell, Ruby Keeler, Dick Powell, ZaSu Pitts, Hugh Herbert, Guy Kibbee, Phil Regan.

Yes, it's that Broadway-backers plot again, but it's also the one in which, according to film historian Leslie Halliwell, Busby most fully realized the "decorative possibilities of chorus girls, grand pianos, and optical processes." See it for the heart-shaped beds and "When You Were a Smile on Your Mother's Lips and a Twinkle in Your Daddy's Eye."

Footlight Parade (1933, U.S., 100 mins., b/w) Dir: Lloyd Bacon; Cast: James Cagney, Joan Blondell, Dick Powell, Ruby Keeler, Guy Kibbee, Ruth Donnelly, Hugh Herbert, Frank McHugh.

Jimmy Cagney lets loose as a director of live, spectacular openers for movie theaters. Fast-paced storyline reaches crescendo with three breathtaking Busby attractions—"Honeymoon Hotel," "By a Waterfall" (yes, there's a real waterfall), and the patriotic drill formations of "Shanghai Lil."

42nd Street (1933, U.S., 98 mins., b/w) Dir: Lloyd Bacon; Cast: Dick Powell, Ruby Keeler, Ginger Rogers, Warner Baxter, Una Merkel, George Brent, Bebe Daniels, Guy Kibbee, Ned Sparks, George E. Stone.

Come and see those tapping feet. Wow all the way in this greatest of all backstage, big-break musical extravaganzas, with great tunes by Al Dubin and Harry Warren. You'll be dancing too after you've seen "Shuffle Off to Buffalo" and that grand "42nd Street" finale.

FAMILY
VALUES

A QUESTION OF GENDER

THE FIRST SEX

Women in film. By now we all know that, despite the key role women have always played in the world as we know it, there are still few movies made with females as the pivotal main characters. In this list, the subject is women. How their strengths have been portrayed, how their politics and position have changed throughout film history, and the changing ways film has defined them.

The Lion in Winter (1968, Great Britain, 135 mins.) Dir: Anthony Harvey; Cast: Peter O'Toole, Katharine Hepburn, John Castle, Anthony Hopkins, Jane Merrow.

Back in 1183 there was Eleanor of Aquitane (Hepburn), so fiercely powerful that King Hank (II) felt compelled to imprison her while he decided who should succeed him. Oscar-winning Kate roars back with a spirit and a wit we all too rarely see in movieland. A feast of verbal warfare, with Aquitane presented as a refreshingly unequivocal, dangerous force.

Impromptu (1990, U.S., 109 mins.) Dir: James Lapine; Cast: Judy Davis, Hugh Grant, Mandy Patinkin, Bernadette Peters, Julian Sands, Emma Thompson, Anna Massey.

Leaping ahead to the 19th century, we find that woman's roles are as constricting as their corsets. It's a pleasure, then, to find a woman whose spirit impelled her to break the boundaries. Writer George Sand (as sharply played by Davis) certainly pushed the envelope with her unconventional attire and her unabashed affairs with Chopin and Liszt. And she seemed to enjoy every minute of it. While it's probable that artists had a little more latitude in expressing their individuality, time and again we see these women painted as outsiders and threats. Look at *The Piano, My Brilliant Career,* or *Orlando*—lives sidetracked in a struggle against society's expectation, en route to clearing the always difficult path to self-fulfillment.

Ballad of Little Jo (1993, U.S., 120 mins.) Dir: Maggie Greewald; Cast: Suzy Amis, David Chung, René Auberjonois, Bo Hopkins, Ian McKellen, Carrie Snodgrass.

A specifically American response to an unwed mother's rejection by society. This moody, surprising film explores the true story of a woman who attempts to remake her life in the tough, by any standards, mining settlements of the frontier West. Resorting to her only perceived option to live a full and self-respecting life, she chooses to disguise herself as a man. A fascinating study of limits, resilience, friendship, and betrayal.

Christopher Strong (1933, U.S., 77 mins., b/w) Dir: Dorothy Arzner; Cast: Katharine Hepburn, Colin Clive, Billie Burke, Helen Chandler.

So here's our independent career woman role model who, just like gay characters in years to come, would have to die in order to satisfy even pre-code Hollywood's moralistic requirements. Arzner takes the story of the strong-willed aviatrix (Hepburn), strings us along, and ultimately disappoints us with the wimped-out resolution. As in Michael Curtiz's uneven curio *Female* (the lead is an auto-exec) from the same year, it's all too clear that while women could play, they'd absolutely have to pay.

Adam's Rib (1949, U.S., 101 mins., b/w) Dir: George Cukor; Cast: Spencer Tracy, Katharine Hepburn, Judy Holliday, Jean Hagen, Tom Ewell, David Wayne.

The Tracy-Hepburn show brought to you by Gordon (Ruth) and Kanin (Garson). The battle of the sexes, for women, often comes down to a struggle to maintain one's autonomy—and a successful marriage and career at the same time. Well, nobody does it better than Tracy and Hepburn, in a wild ride as married lawyers representing opposite sides in a murder case. We can't resist a pitch here for Howard Hawks's *His Girl Friday.* Rosalind Russell and Cary Grant as reporter-ex-lovers are just crackling and sharp.

Rosemary's Baby (1968, U.S., 136 mins.) Dir: Roman Polanski; Cast: Mia Farrow, Ruth Gordon, John Cassavetes, Charles Grodin, Maurice Evans, Ralph Bellamy, Sidney Blackmer.

Men seem to have been trying to gaslight women for ages—you just don't see this theme reversed. *Rosemary's Baby* features a particularly enthralling example of the ultimate controlling husband, determined to satisfy his needs at all costs. This theme of woman as psychologically fragile—and subject to the diminishing ploys of their cold and distanced lovers and spouses—is played out repeatedly in such key films as Alfred Hitchcock's *Marnie* and *Rebecca,* and George Cukor's *Gaslight* itself.

The Story of Women (1988, France, 110 mins.) Dir: Claude Chabrol; Cast: Isabelle Huppert, François Cluzet, Marie Trintignant, Nils Tavernier, Louis Ducreux.

In Chabrol's riveting study of an ambitious, disaffected woman, wife, and mother in Nazi-run Vichy France, Huppert is the sacrificial lamb for a society that, using religious dogma as its cudgel, is morally rotten and hypocritical to the core. Interesting, since she is not a political woman—just someone who wants more from her life and has found offering her skills in performing abortions a way to enhance her income.

Alice Doesn't Live Here Anymore (1974, U.S., 112 mins.) Dir: Martin Scorsese; Cast: Ellen Burstyn, Kris Kristofferson, Alfred Lutter, Jodie Foster, Diane Ladd, Harvey Keitel, Vic Tayback, Billy Green Bush, Valerie Curtin.

The pigeonholing of women in domestic roles during the 1950s and 1960s had become so complete that this film was seen as a major feminist statement. Surprisingly it still holds up as a character study, exploring the adjustments a widowed no-career woman and her son make to the single working life. Self-esteem, determination, and raw guts are the principal ingredients, all nicely blended.

Entre Nous (aka: *Coup de Foudre,* 1983, France, 110 mins.) Dir: Diane Kurys; Cast: Miou-Miou, Isabelle Huppert, Guy Marchand.

Kurys gives us another liberation study, WWII vintage in Lyon. As two women who have outgrown their marriages seek self- and professional fulfillment, their deep and abiding friendship evolves into something more. A rich story based on Kurys's family experience.

Swing Shift (1984, U.S., 112 mins.) Dir: Jonathan Demme; Cast: Goldie Hawn, Kurt Russell, Christine Lahti, Ed Harris, Fred Willard.

WWII brought sweeping opportunities for women in what were then nontraditional professions. While *Swing Shift* is a bit uneven, Lahti brings home the plight of the women who found great meaning working outside the home, then were devastated to be laid off once our boys came back. The documentary *The Life and Times of Rosie the Riveter* is a must-see on the same subject.

Daughters of the Dust (1991, U.S., 114 mins.) Dir: Julie Dash; Cast: Cora Lee Day, Alva Rodgers, Adisa Anderson, Kaycee Moore, Barbara O, Eartha D. Robinson, Bahni Turpin, Cheryl Lynn Bruce.

A lyrical and sumptuously photographed look at turn-of-the-century Gullah culture on islands off the shore of South Carolina and Georgia. Isolated from the mainland, they created and maintained a unique African-American way of life that kept close memory of their African heritage. While the movie is slow going at times, the power and strength of this changing matriarchal society is evoked most impressively.

Gap-Toothed Women (1987, U.S., 31 mins.) Dirs: Les Blank, Maureen Gosling, Chris Simon, Susan Kell.

A list of movies about women would not be complete without a film that addresses the beauty myth. One of the most delightful of these is this documentary about lively, interesting, and, indeed, beautiful women—all with that distinctive space between their two front teeth. A look at beauty pageants would be in order as well: *Miss . . . or Myth* or its non-doc counterpart, *Smile,* which has a good time with marriage and suburban ennui, are both of interest here.

The World According to Garp (1982, U.S., 136 mins.) Dir: George Roy Hill; Cast: Robin Williams, Mary Beth Hurt, Glenn Close, John Lithgow, Hume Cronyn, Jessica Tandy, Swoosie Kurtz, Amanda Plummer, Warren Berlinger.

John Irving's raucous novel, interpreted splendidly for the screen, tells the story of Jennie (Close's truly notable screen debut), a firm and clear-eyed feminist, holding unshaken to her principles while living a compassionate and hu-

manistic life. Perceptions of women are challenged throughout, capitalizing on Lithgow's skill and sensitivity in portraying a transsexual football player (fashioned on Renée Richards).

Thelma and Louise (1991, U.S., 128 mins.) Dir: Ridley Scott; Cast: Susan Sarandon, Geena Davis, Harvey Keitel, Michael Madsen, Christopher McDonald, Brad Pitt.

This tribute to friendship, to female bonding if you will, firmly and finally veers away from portraying women in that all too despicable alienating clawing way, as though we view each other as the enemy. This movie shows us two women who thoughtfully, consciously, and with a well-developed sense of the right, pursue their own lives. Wrongly perceived by many as anti-men, this film is a full exploration of women whose choices are too frequently defined by the men in their lives, with the sad message that once they have found true freedom, they also find their options severely limited.

BOYS TO MEN

In the postfeminist era, when political correctness all too often comes in the form of a good swift kick to the nuts and bolts of the average guy's masculinity, when society all but sanctions slicing off his manhood as if it were just a hunk of salami, men have begun to react. This reaction has launched a widespread movement, a crusade, if you will, in which more and more men are reclaiming their male identities . . . or at least putting on a protective cup. Along with weekend warrior workshops— usually cacophonous blends of drumming and chanting, *sturmming und dranging*—the so-called men's movement has spawned a spate of "what it means to be a man" literature. Much of the writing that exists on

the subject is theoretical psychobabble. Movies, on the other hand, render the masculine experience in much more visceral terms. The following films are all, in one way or another, about male rites of passage, initiation, the changing roles of fathers and sons, the codes of behavior that men live and die by, and the search for what Robert Bly has called "the deep masculine."

Deliverance (1972, U.S., 109 mins.) Dir: John Boorman; Cast: Jon Voight, Burt Reynolds, Ned Beatty, Ronny Cox, Billy McKinney, Herbert "Cowboy" Coward, James Dickey.

Four Atlanta businessmen, a typically socialized, citified group of friends, decide to do some manly bonding on a canoe trip through back-country Georgia, which turns into a harrowing rite of passage and an extraordinary journey through the landscape of the masculine psyche. Screenwriter James Dickey, working from his novel, and director John Boorman conjure up image after image of masculine pain, dread, rage, loss, and grief. The Beatty character's squeal-like-a-pig ordeal is a truly terrifying plunge into the dark netherworld between the straight male's greatest sexual fear and latent sexual desire.

The Emerald Forest (1985, U.S., 113 mins.) Dir: John Boorman; Cast: Powers Boothe, Charley Boorman, Meg Foster, Dira Pass.

Powers Boothe is an American engineer building a dam on the edge of the Brazilian rain forest when his young son is abducted by Indians. The boy lives in the jungle for 10 years, is tutored in the ways of the tribe, initiated into manhood as a tribal warrior, and ultimately caught between the "daddy" of his childhood and the spiritual father who raised him. With this stunning visual realization of mythic and mystical notions wrapped in a stir-

ring adventure, director John Boorman transcends what he did in *Deliverance.* Based on a true story.

A Man Called Horse (1970, U.S., 114 mins.) Dir: Elliot Silverstein; Cast: Richard Harris, Judith Anderson, Dub Taylor, Jean Gascon, Manu Tupou.

Richard Harris is an Englishman lost in the American West circa 1825. Captured and tortured by the Sioux, he is eventually initiated into the tribe. Brutal stuff. The sequel, *Return of a Man Called Horse,* with Harris coming back for more, is actually superior and features a Sun Vow ritual performed by a group of Yellow Hand braves.

The Men's Club (1986, U.S., 100 mins.) Dir: Peter Medak; Cast: David Dukes, Roy Scheider, Harvey Keitel, Richard Jordan, Frank Langella, Stockard Channing, Treat Williams, Jennifer Jason Leigh.

Leonard Michaels adapted his own overindulgent novel about a male encounter group, turning the mush into an absolute mishmash. Medak directs with more style than substance but the first-rate cast takes the material somewhat deeper than it seems to be going. Noteworthy as an early example and direct depiction of male consciousness raising as a reaction to feminism in contemporary society.

Reservoir Dogs (1992, U.S., 100 mins.) Dir: Quentin Tarantino; Cast: Harvey Keitel, Tim Roth, Chris Penn, Steve Buscemi, Michael Madsen, Lawrence Tierney, Quentin Tarantino.

Writer-director Tarantino's debut run is a superbly executed, strikingly structured caper film filled with a series of twisted masculine rites and dead-on (but deadly) depictions of modern-day male bonding rituals. Brutal, unflinching portrait of men reduced to the level of rabid dogs as the code they live by is inverted, perverted, and stripped of anything resembling honor. The entire ensemble is astonishing. This film is so full of testosterone and bereft of gynic energy (you'll be hard-pressed to find a female on screen) that it should carry the warning: MEN'S MOVIE—WOMEN BEWARE.

Glengarry Glen Ross (1992, U.S., 100 mins.) Dir: James Foley; Cast: Al Pacino, Jack Lemmon, Ed Harris, Alec Baldwin, Alan Arkin.

David Mamet's Pulitzer Prize-winning play, effectively transferred to the screen, is a superlative example of how the fabric of society can be ripped apart when the codes and standards men live by are thrown to the wind. The men here are a group of real-estate salesmen whose jobs are on the line, but the issue at hand is less about selling than selling out. Like *Reservoir Dogs,* this is a story of male bonding and betrayal. But the brutality here doesn't spring from physical violence; it leaps directly out of the language. The acting is great from top to bottom.

Scent of a Woman (1992, U.S., 137 mins.) Dir: Martin Brest; Cast: Al Pacino, Chris O'Donnell, James Rebhorn, Gabrielle Anwar, Philip S. Hoffman.

Pacino won an Oscar for his portrayal of a blind, irascible, self-pitying retired Army colonel who leads his young caretaker on a voyage of discovery in New York City. While it seems to us that Al's performance is all bombast and bullfeathers, with very little beneath the surface, and the story swings on a rather contrived and obvious plot device, the film has much to say about mentoring, about fathers and sons learning from each other, and about boys becoming men and men getting back in touch with the source of their masculine pride and power.

Dances With Wolves (1990, U.S., 181 mins.) Dir: Kevin Costner; Cast: Kevin Costner, Mary McDonnell, Graham Greene, Rodney A. Grant, Tantoo Cardinal, Charles Rocket, Maury Chaykin.

Overpraised, overlong, big-time Oscar winner about a Civil War soldier who forsakes his own society in favor of the deeper truths he finds in Native American culture, eventually earning his place as a member of the Sioux nation. While the cinematography is breathtaking and the film does resonate with primal energy and deeply masculine spiritual traditions, it is severely undercut by the self-congratulatory attitude and posturing, not to mention one-note performance, of star/director Costner.

A Perfect World (1993, U.S., 135 mins.) Dir: Clint Eastwood; Cast: Kevin Costner, Clint Eastwood, T. J. Lowther, Laura Dern.

Kevin gives a far more textured performance here as an escaped con who takes a young boy (Lowther) hostage and winds up in the role of surrogate father, mentor, and hero—giving the kid a way out from under his mother's overprotective thumb and helping him dissolve the barriers between himself and the man he wants to become. The film manages to be ripe with symbolism and historical perspective without getting heavy-handed. Eastwood's best effort as a director takes a series of unexpected turns and is full of subtle touches.

The Air Up There (1994, U.S., 100 mins.) Dir: Paul M. Glaser; Cast: Kevin Bacon, Charles Gitonga Maina, Yolanda Vazquez, Winston Ntshona, Dennis Patrick.

Bacon is Jimmy Dolan, a college basketball coach with his job on the line, whose search for the next Hakeem Olajuwon takes him all the way to Africa where he not only finds the big man of his dreams (Maina), he discovers his manhood in the process. This slight but entertaining film is built on the premise that overly socialized white men won't ever be able to jump the big jump until they are initiated into the ways of the tribal warrior.

OPENING THE CLOSET

The love that dare not speak its name. Well, while not all gays and lesbians meet their death on their way to celluloid immortality, and, despite Otto Preminger's ground-breaking (and code-changing) efforts in 1962 with *Advise and Consent*, Hollywood hasn't come too far since Mercedes McCambridge and Joan Crawford "symbolically" snorted fire at each other in *Johnny Guitar* and Lawrence Olivier scared Tony Curtis away in *Spartacus*. Filmland in general has been pretty intent on keeping real issues, and real relationships, in the closet. Here are a few that trace these issues, in the closet and out.

Victim (1961, Great Britain, 100 mins., b/w) Dir: Basil Dearden; Cast: Dirk Bogarde, Sylvia Syms, Dennis Price, Peter McEnery, Donald Churchill.

The extreme severity of Britain's homosexual laws in the early '60s brought with them an outrageous incidence of extortion attempts. This tense black-mail thriller tells the story of one man (Bogarde in full command), moved by personal experience and empowered by his upper middle class position as a highly respected barrister, who is impelled to challenge these laws. We see gays and gay issues portrayed realistically for the first time in film—and clearly in too positive a light to win the Code seal-of-approval when it was initially released in the U.S. A sizzler then and now, and a true landmark.

Fox and His Friends (1975, West Germany, 123 mins.) Dir: Rainer Werner Fassbinder; Cast: Rainer Werner Fass-

binder, Peter Chatel, Karlheinz Bohm, Adrian Hoven, Ulla Jacobsson.

Writer/Director Fassbinder casts himself as Franz Biberkopf, a stumble-bum carny character whose act, "Fox the Talking Head," has recently folded. But Franz's fortunes take a prosperous turn when he hits the lottery and falls in love with the handsome and cultured son of a German industrialist. Alternately comic and tragic, it's the first Fassbinder film to take a casual approach to homosexuality. More accessible and "enjoyable" than much of the director's work, but no less tortured.

Les Biches (*The Does*, 1968, France-Italy, 104 mins.) Dir: Claude Chabrol; Cast: Jean-Louis Trintignant, Jacqueline Sassard, Stephane Audran.

Girl meets girl, boy seduces girl, boy drops girl when he is seduced by other girl, girl can't give up either of them. No, it's not that complicated. But the Chabrol take on this involves all the deep, dark, and tragic shades of possession and obsession. And while viewed through a haze of enigma and mirrors, the subtle acts of love and betrayal between the two women reveal why this title has often been (incorrectly) translated as The Bitches.

Torch Song Trilogy (1988, U.S., 121 mins.) Dir: Paul Bogart; Cast: Harvey Fierstein, Anne Bancroft, Matthew Broderick, Brian Kerwin.

Warmly sobby and successful adaptation of Fierstein's brilliant (and he *is* brilliant) Broadway tour de force. Broderick and Bancroft are well cast in story about N.Y. gay man coming to terms with what he wants in life and what he needs to do to get it. A big strong tale of love, family, and the tragedy that sometimes comes with the package.

The Life and Times of Harvey Milk (1984, U.S., 88 mins.) Dir: Robert Epstein; Narrator: Harvey Fierstein.

Sharp and moving documentary about maverick San Francisco board of supervisors member Milk murdered (along with SF mayor George Moscone) by fellow board member Dan White, who became as famous for his Twinkie defense as for the crime itself. Which tells you something. What really moves us here is the inconsolable loss of Milk and the sense of possibility he represented—not just for representation of the gay community but for fair play for the underrepresented of all stripes.

My Beautiful Laundrette (1985, Great Britain, 94 mins.) Dir: Stephen Frears; Cast: Daniel Day-Lewis, Gordon Warnecke, Saeed Jaffrey, Roshan Seth, Shirley Anne Field.

Frears hits the mark with this incisive and funny take on life in Thatcher's racially riven, economically battered London as seen through the efforts of the two positively portrayed lovers in their attempt to start a laundry business. Wonderful performances by the leads go with fine script by ex-pat Pakistani playwright Hanif Kureishi.

Forbidden Love: The Unashamed Stories of Lesbian Lives (1992, Canada, 84 mins.) Dirs: Aerlyn Weissman, Lynne Fernie; Cast: Stephanie Morgenstern, Lynne Adams.

Interwoven with reflective interviews with a number of veterans, these serial-styled vignettes about "the life" in Canada took their inspiration from fifties pulp magazines. Notable for the women's portrayal of how their sexuality defined their perceived success in life. Melodramatic as might be expected, the serial works better as a fun idea than its execution would allow.

Kiss of the Spider Woman (1985, Brazil-U.S., 119 mins., c & b/w) Dir: Hector Babenco; Cast: William Hurt, Raul Julia, Sonia Braga, José Lewgoy.

In this excellent adaptation of Manuel Puig's compelling prison story, set in a brutally repressive Latin American dictatorship, Hurt offers a satisfying (and Oscar-winning) portrayal of the terrified apolitical gay window dresser who is incited to action out of compassion for his radical, straight cellmate, the well-cast Julia. The development of their friendship and commitment is handled with realism and sensitivity.

Sunday Bloody Sunday (1971, Great Britain, 110 mins.) Dir: John Schlesinger; Cast: Glenda Jackson, Peter Finch, Murray Head, Peggy Ashcroft.

A threesome, sort of. A very civilized British rendition of girl loves boy, boy likes girl, but boy likes boy even more. All beautifully acted, especially Finch and Jackson, and very brave at the time (even now) for the male-male screen kisses. Very civilized, but also very moving—and a solid take on the sixties scene.

Okoge (1993, Japan, 120 mins.) Dir: Takehiro Nakajima; Cast: Misa Shimizu, Takehiro Murata, Takeo Nakahara, Masayuki Shionoya.

Another threesome, but Japanese style. An "okoge" is a woman who likes gay men, and mostly this is a charming and poignant tale of the developing friendship between the appealing girl and a male couple struggling with commitment issues. It's also a glimpse into the Japan that still believes in fixed marriages, and it lets us know that gays there face the same negative attitudes as in this country.

Improper Conduct (*Mauvaise Conduite*, 1984, France, 110 mins.) Dirs: Orlando Jiminez-Leal, Nestor Almendros.

Fidel Castro's revolution, touted as the key to a better life for all Cubans, left at least one group behind—Señor Castro couldn't quite reconcile the gay life with his machismo culture. A powerful indictment of the unspeakable methods used to suppress homosexuals and other unwanteds, this documentary by exiled cinematographer Almendros and Jiminez-Leal, is an effective rallying cry against oppression of all kinds.

Longtime Companion (1990, U.S., 96 mins.) Dir: Norman Rene; Cast: Bruce Davison, Campbell Scott, Stephen Caffrey, Mark Lamos, Patrick Cassidy, Mary-Louise Parker, Dermot Mulroney.

Well, *Philadelphia* didn't turn out to be *the* AIDS movie we hoped it would be, and while the disease is far from a gay-only issue, its effects on that community have been hard and specific. *Companion* (originally produced for PBS) honestly and devastatingly traces just those effects on a group of close friends in N.Y.C., from the start of the epidemic in the early eighties. Fine acting and humor-injected Craig Lucas script brighten the grim narrative. See the recent musical *Zero Patience* for the all-stops-pulled look at this issue. Sort of a very whacked *Sarafina!* of AIDS.

JUST LIKE A WOMAN

All of us know that there is a whole strata of society made up of boys who wear lipstick, dresses, and heels. What might surprise you is how many films in some way involve those who do it. And as you will see through the following list, some men seem to cross-dress by nature, some do it by choice, and some have cross-dressing thrust upon them.

Bringing Up Baby (1938, U.S., 102 mins., b/w) Dir: Howard Hawks; Cast: Katharine Hepburn, Cary Grant, Barry Fitzgerald, Charlie Ruggles.

One of the many things Grant gets into during the course of these screwy events is a lace nightgown. When Hepburn's aunt (May Robson) discovers him and asks if he dresses like that all

the time, Cary ad-libs, "No . . . I've just gone gay, all of a sudden . . ."—a line that was not in the script and the first mainstream film use of "gay" to denote homosexuality.

Some Like It Hot (1959, U.S., 122 mins., b/w) Dir: Billy Wilder; Cast: Tony Curtis, Marilyn Monroe, Jack Lemmon, Joe E. Brown, George Raft, Joan Shawlee.

King (or queen) of films on the subject has Lemmon and Curtis as hapless musicians who witness the St. Valentine's Day Massacre and dodge the mob by dressing as dames and joining an all-girls band. Marilyn is at her steamiest, funniest, and most vulnerable. Comic genius of director/co-writer Wilder is at its zenith in this screwball comedy where who's screwing who and who's got the balls are in doubt to the famous last line.

Tootsie (1982, U.S., 110 mins.) Dir: Sydney Pollack; Cast: Dustin Hoffman, Teri Garr, Jessica Lange, Sydney Pollack, Bill Murray.

As actor Michael Dorsey, Hoffman's solution to lack of work is to pose as an actress and go for a woman's role in a popular soap. The scam succeeds, leading to complication piled upon complication in good-but-not-great contemporary comedy that owes a tip of the wig to *Some Like It Hot*. Murray is terrific in role created by Elaine May (one of many uncredited writers). Lange does fine in updated variation of Monroe character—not as steamy but, hey, some like it hotter than others.

Nuns on the Run (1990, Great Britain, 90 mins.) Dir: Jonathan Lynn; Cast: Eric Idle, Robbie Coltrane, Camille Coduri, Janet Suzman, Doris Hare, Lila Kaye.

Things get really hot for Idle and Coltrane as bungling crooks who pick up strange habits in order to avoid the murderous thugs who want them dead. Adding a twist of faith to the Lemmon/Curtis solution, they hide in a convent dressed up as nuns. Absolutely hilarious, it lacks the depth and style of the Wilder, but hey, nobody's perfect.

Pink Flamingos (1973, U.S., 92 mins.) Dir: John Waters; Cast: Divine, Mary Vivian Pearce, Mink Stole, David Lochary, Edie Massey.

If you were remotely put off by the "sacrilege" of *Nuns on the Run,* don't even think of watching this John Waters plunge into perversion and, yecch, excrement. But if you have a taste for mondo trash, this movie where the late, large Divine vies for the title "World's Filthiest Person" might be just your cup of doo-doo. Divine, in case you've never had the pleasure, was a guy named Glenn who built his/her humongous self one heck of a cult-career as the most disgusting woman who ever walked the planet.

Hairspray (1988, U.S., 94 mins.) Dir: John Waters; Cast: Ricki Lake, Divine, Jerry Stiller, Colleen Fitzpatrick, Debbie Harry, Sonny Bono, Ruth Brown, Mink Stole, Pia Zadora.

Waters cleans up his act and steps up in style and budget in this clever, affectionate retro glance at the early '60s teen scene. Lake stars and, though fat, she's no Divine. In fact, she's an actual female and, in her own chunky way, quite the sweetheart. But do not despair, Divine makes his/her swan song as Ricki's mom—a mother-of-another-nature that only a daughter in a John Waters film could possibly love.

Glen or Glenda? (aka: *I Led Two Lives* and *I Changed My Sex,* 1953, U.S., 67 mins., b/w) Dir: Edward D. Wood, Jr.; Cast: Daniel Davis, Dolores Fuller, Bela Lugosi, Lyle Talbot, Timothy Farrell, Charles Crafts, "Tommy" Haynes.

If you thought *Pink Flamingos* was bad, wait till you get a load of this little lovely. Hailed as the worst director of all

time (we think of him as the auteur of awful), the inimitable Edward "Eddie" Wood concocted this boys-will-be-girls docu-fantasy about transvestism, narrated in high Transylvanian style by Bela Lugosi. Some place it in the "so bad it's hysterically funny" category; some find it the ultimate drag. We say, "Huh?"

La Cage Aux Folles (1979, France, 110 mins.) Dir: Edouard Molinaro; Cast: Ugo Tognazzi, Michel Serrault.

Gay couple plays it somewhat straight when Tognazzi's son brings fiancée and her family to town. Serrault's Albin is a female impersonator and hilarity ensues when the father of the bride meets the "mother" of the groom. Foreign film with hugely successful U.S. run spawned two sequels and hit Broadway musical.

In a Year of 13 Moons (1980, West Germany, 129 mins.) Dir: Rainer Werner Fassbinder; Cast: Volker Spengler, Ingrid Craven, Gottfried John, Elisabeth Trissenaar.

Fassbinder's look at the last five days in the life of a despairing transsexual proves that the subject is not the exclusive province of comedy. Spengler is brilliant as Erwin/Elvira, someone who has crossed an absolute border, transgressed the fundamental divide of gender upon which all of society is based. One of the most profound expressions of the human impulse toward self-destruction ever put on film.

The Crying Game (1992, Great Britain, 112 mins.) Dir: Neil Jordan; Cast: Stephen Rea, Miranda Richardson, Forest Whitaker, Jim Broadbent, Jaye Davidson.

Given that writer/director Neil Jordan's cunning conundrum won the Oscar for Best Screenplay and received five additional nominations, including one for Jaye Davidson as Best Supporting

Actor, we won't feel too guilty if we're giving away secrets by including it on this list. Happily, Jordan's brilliantly executed gender trick is far from all the film has to offer. A truly heroic, romantic story, it makes us rethink our notion of what is "normal" and what is "perverse," and ultimately what love and devotion are all about. A genuinely important work of almost transcendent beauty.

Outrageous! (1977, Canada, 100 mins.) Dir: Richard Benner; Cast: Craig Russell, Hollis McLaren, Richert Easley.

Female impersonator Craig Russell's cabaret act—a bagful of fabulous faces and other people's voices—is only one aspect of this very full-bodied movie, beautifully written and directed by Benner. It takes us into a topsy-turvy underground club world where yin and yang dress alike and a man can deal with his fears by confronting the stranger inside himself and making sure her shoes match her purse.

Thunderbolt and Lightfoot (1974, U.S., 115 mins.) Dir: Michael Cimino; Cast: Clint Eastwood, Jeff Bridges, Geoffrey Lewis, Gary Busey, George Kennedy.

Buddy pic has Eastwood come on like a thunderbolt, and Bridges lightfoots it in ladies clothes through much of the film uttering lines like, "We've got to stop meeting like this . . . after all, where there's smoke there's fire." As for Cimino's direction (he wrote it, too), we think it's all smoke and mirrors.

Psycho (1960, U.S., 109 mins., b/w) Dir: Alfred Hitchcock; Cast: Anthony Perkins, Janet Leigh, Simon Oakland, John Anderson, Vera Miles, Martin Balsam, John Gavin, John McIntire.

Calling Norman Bates a transvestite is like calling King Kong a monkey—it's just the beginning of his problems. But let's not overlook the fact that while this Hitchcock masterpiece has much deeper implications, Norman does

spend a lot of time walking around in a dress.

■

NOTE: We'd be remiss if we didn't include films where the pendulum swings the other way; or, rather, where there's no pendulum swinging at all. These are films about criss-crossdressers—women who dress up as men.

Victor/Victoria (1982, U.S., 133 mins.) Dir: Blake Edwards; Cast: Julie Andrews, Robert Preston, James Garner, Lesley Ann Warren, Alex Karras, John Rhys-Davies, Graham Stark.

Blake Edwards's screenplay, based on a rare pre-war German comedy, has raggedy Andrews saving herself from the gutter by passing as a Polish count and becoming the toast of 1930s Gay Paree. Preston is a joy as her gay guru and Garner is suitably confused as an American gangster who can't quite figure out what's up or why. Moving, funny, beautiful-to-look-at film, with Oscar-winning score by Henry Mancini. One of Edwards's best.

Morocco (1930, U.S., 92 mins., b/w) Dir: Josef von Sternberg; Cast: Marlene Dietrich, Gary Cooper, Adolphe Menjou, Francis McDonald, Eve Southern.

The single most memorable scene in von Sternberg's shimmering jewel of a film—Dietrich's first in America—has a sultry Marlene, dressed to the nines in top hat and tails, circulating among the patrons of a Moroccan nightclub and favoring another woman with a kiss. Straddling the sexual fence was a position the actress maintained with mystery, dignity, and unbelievable style for the rest of her life.

Just One of the Guys (1985, U.S., 100 mins.) Dir: Lisa Gottlieb; Cast: Joyce Hyser, Clayton Rohner, Bill Jacoby, Toni Hudson.

Moving from the sublime to the silly,

this teen comedy takes an atypical turn when a pretty high school senior (Hyser), tired of stereotypical treatment, disguises herself as a guy so she can enter a citywide journalism competition. Surprisingly entertaining story has its moments and will definitely make the kiddie set at which it's aimed do some thinking about sexual convention.

LOVE & MARRIAGE

NYMPHETS

From the beginning, Hollywood recognized that youth and desirability went hand in hand. Silent stars Mabel Normand, Mae Marsh, Colleen Moore, and Mary Pickford all rose to fame in their mid-teens. Such undeniably alluring beauties as Liz Taylor and Natalie Wood both got their first break as kids. But while audiences found them attractive, only a moral degenerate would have viewed their films with lust in his heart. In the 1950s, Hollywood, in introducing an alternative to the gamine and the waif, flipped the sweet young thing over and gave us the Baby Doll, the Sex Kitten, the Teenage Temptress, Jailbait. It wasn't long before we had preteen prostitutes and other pretty babies pursing their bee-stung lips and flaunting their nubility, in a conscious attempt to seduce the male audience with what had always been labeled taboo. We're not talking about beach-blanket babes in skimpy bikinis, dancing with boys their own age. To qualify as a nymphet, a young girl must be seen through the lecherous eyes of an older man. The following films feature some of the hottest little girls ever to lick a lollipop or suck a thumb on screen.

Baby Doll (1956, U.S., 116 mins., b/w) Dir: Elia Kazan; Cast: Carroll Baker, Karl Malden, Eli Wallach, Mildred Dunnock.

Carroll Baker received an Academy Award nomination for her performance as the childbride of an over-the-hill, overly possessive cotton-mill owner (Malden), who agrees not to consummate the marriage until the girl's 20th birthday. Question is: Can Baby Doll, who sleeps in a crib and sucks hungrily on her thumb, possibly wait that long? *Time* magazine called it "just possibly the dirtiest American made motion picture that has ever been legally distributed." An exaggeration to be sure, but the film is sexy, funny, superbly shot by Boris Kaufman, and extremely well acted. Baker never did it better. Tennessee Williams based the script on two of his lesser-known plays.

Cape Fear (1991, U.S., 128 mins.) Dir: Martin Scorsese; Cast: Robert De Niro, Nick Nolte, Jessica Lange, Juliette Lewis.

Speaking of thumb sucking, the most titillating and disturbing moment of Martin Scorsese's nerve-jangling remake comes when petulant teenager Juliette Lewis wraps her pouty lips and orthodontures around big bad De Niro's dirty digit in the back of the school auditorium. She's aroused by the man, even though he's a psychopath sworn to reap revenge on her father. He introduces her to Henry Miller. But while she seems anxious to lap it all up, one can't help but feel she's biting off much more than she can possibly swallow.

Husbands and Wives (1992, U.S., 108 mins.) Dir: Woody Allen; Cast: Woody Allen, Mia Farrow, Sydney Pollack, Judy Davis, Juliette Lewis.

Juliette Lewis is a bit more mature in

this one, but not quite mature enough to make her legal. As an underage temptation to a man in the throes of a midlife crisis (Allen), Ms. Lewis serves as an interesting piece in the puzzle that is Woody Allen's psyche. At the time of this movie's release, the Woodman's real-life passion for the young and the restless was front-page fodder for the daily tabloids. The film itself is a literate roundelay of wit and desire. And less self-deluded than you might think.

Lolita (1962, U.S.-Great Britain, 152 mins., b/w) Dir: Stanley Kubrick; Cast: James Mason, Shelley Winters, Peter Sellers, Sue Lyon.

Lolita. Curiously limp adaptation of Nabokov's seminal novel about obsequious Humbert Humbert's obsession with little girls, specifically his wife's nubile daughter, Lolita. Lo-li-ta. The name itself has become a synonym for nymphet. Mason is marvelous as Humbert, but Sue Lyon is icy and autonomous as the obscure object of his desire. Still, while less than the ultimate pedophile dream girl, there is something undeniably sexy in her air of detachment, and the kid can lick a lolly with the best of them.

Return to Peyton Place (1961, U.S., 122 mins.) Dir: José Ferrer; Cast: Jeff Chandler, Carol Lynley, Eleanor Parker, Mary Astor, Tuesday Weld.

Soapy sequel to film based on Grace Metalious's wildly popular novel features pert Carol Lynley as the author's alter-ego Allison Mackenzie, but the real reason for nymphet watchers to see this one is Tuesday Weld. As Selena Cross, Allison's sexually abused best friend, Weld drips with sensuality and vulnerability. The screen seems to fill with moisture every time she appears. If this one makes you thirst for more, you might want to catch *Sex Kittens Go to College*, *Wild in the Country*, and *Lord Love a Duck*.

I Walk the Line (1970, U.S., 97 mins.) Dir: John Frankenheimer; Cast: Gregory Peck, Tuesday Weld, Estelle Parsons, Ralph Meeker.

Tuesday takes a step up here, into the realm of serious actress. Along with the homicidal sweetie pie she plays in *Pretty Poison,* this is her best work. As a moonshiner's daughter used by her pa to seduce middle-aged lawman Peck, she's not quite jailbait, but the smell of forbidden fruit that permeates the film is enough to make a grown man weep.

Butterfly (1981, U.S., 108 mins.) Dir: Matt Cimber; Cast: Pia Zadora, Stacy Keach, Orson Welles, Lois Nettleton, Edward Albert, Stuart Whitman, Ed McMahon, James Franciscus.

Pia Zadora's rich hubby bought his 23-year-old wife the role of Kady, the 16-year-old sexpot who seduces her father (Keach) in this potboiler adapted from one of James M. Cain's smarmier novels. The film is incredibly dumb, but the interesting cast makes it fun. And while Miss Zadorable can't act her way out of a paper bag, her shaggy hair, hungry mouth, and ripe little body give her enough of a "do me now" quality to explain how and why this movie got made.

Kitten With a Whip (1964, U.S., 83 mins., b/w) Dir: Douglas Heyes; Cast: Ann-Margret, John Forsythe, Patricia Barry, Ann Doran, Audrey Dalton.

Ann-Margret's kitten-in-heat performance is the main attraction in this untamed youth, drive-in melodrama about a reform-school runaway who gets fuddy-duddy Forsythe to drive her and her pals to Mexico. A far cry from the all-American girl from Sweet Apple, Ohio, she portrayed in *Bye Bye Birdie*, this role marked Ann-Margret as the quintessential teen tigress . . . the kind of girl who needs a good spanking . . . and the kind of girl who'd spank you back.

Pretty Baby (1978, U.S., 109 mins.) Dir: Louis Malle; Cast: Keith Carradine, Susan Sarandon, Brooke Shields.

Malle's U.S. film debut tells the story of a prepubescent prostitute plying her trade at a Big Easy brothel early in the 20th century. Twelve-year-old Brooke Shields slinks around in sexy lingerie (a body double was used for the nude scenes) and Sven Nykvist's cinematography bathes her in sensual half-light. But Carradine is too wooden as the shutterbug obsessed with the kid, and the result, while palatable, is like Cajun cooking without cayenne—not nearly as hot as it should be.

Taxi Driver (1976, U.S., 114 mins.) Dir: Martin Scorsese; Cast: Robert De Niro, Cybill Shepherd, Harvey Keitel, Peter Boyle, Jodie Foster, Albert Brooks.

Scorsese's descent into the Dante's Inferno that is New York City features Jodie Foster as a 12-year-old pretty baby trapped in the muck, turning tricks for her pimp-lover Keitel until cabby De Niro pulls her out of the mire. Director and actress conspire to reach beyond any conventional nymphet notions and come up with a flesh-and-blood character who never had a chance in hell of having a childhood.

PAGING DR. RUTH

Ever since Edison's *The Kiss* first graced the motion picture screen in 1896, movie-makers have recognized the truth behind one undeniable fact of life—sex sells! The history of the cinema is filled with erotic imagery and sexually charged situations. This list is not a guide to the steamiest moments in the annals of moviedom (though some of these films have some pretty hot spots), but rather to those movies fundamentally devoted, in terms of central theme and basic subject matter, to the exploration of human sexuality.

The Seven Year Itch (1955, U.S., 105 mins.) Dir: Billy Wilder; Cast: Marilyn Monroe, Tom Ewell, Evelyn Keyes, Sonny Tufts, Victor Moore, Oscar Homolka, Carolyn Jones.

Classic Billy Wilder comedy in which the itch in question is the craving a man gets after seven years of marriage, the uncontrollable urge, if you will, to have sex with someone other than his spouse. When Ewell's wife goes away on vacation and Marilyn moves in upstairs, the poor guy practically breaks out in hives. The Wilder/George Axelrod screenplay (from Axelrod's play) is filled with innuendo, and the shot of MM getting a blast of air up her skirt is one of the most memorable sexual images of the 1950s.

Woman in the Dunes (1964, Japan, 123 mins.) Dir: Hiroshi Teshigahara; Cast: Eiji Okada, Kyoko Kishida, Koji Mitsui, Hiroko Ito.

Highly stylized political allegory in which an amateur entomologist, trapped in a sand pit with a beautiful widow, redefines his purpose in life and experiences his sexuality in ways that he never dreamed possible. A cinematic tour de force. The visual blending of sand and flesh, combined with the social themes of the narrative, take the film beyond the simply erotic into the realm of the profound.

In the Realm of the Senses (1976, Japan-France, 105 mins.) Dir: Nagisa Oshima; Cast: Tatsuya Fuji, Eiko Matsuda.

Oshima's watershed film is based on the true story of a prostitute who not only kills her lover, she cleaves his wiener and carries it around with her until she is arrested for the crime. The woman (Matsuda) straddles the fine line between madness and desire, and the film, in its assault on traditional values, stands on the precipice between art and pornography. A genuinely disturbing, erotic work that asks the question: Is death the ultimate orgasm or what?

Last Tango in Paris (1973, France-Italy, 129 mins.) Dir: Bernardo Bertolucci; Cast: Marlon Brando, Maria Schneider, Jean-Pierre Léaud.

Brando and Schneider's rapturous pas de deux in Paris attracted more than a little controversy—and condemnation—when first released. Compared (by Pauline Kael) to Stravinsky's *Rite of Spring*, the film explores human desire as no film ever had before. It holds up now not only because of its sexual frankness, but because it places the sex in the context of all human experience. This is a film about love, torment, death, guilt, rage, beauty, and grace. It is a film about animal passion and exalted dreams. Bertolucci's camera is as sensual as the lovers. A masterpiece.

Swept Away . . . by an unusual destiny in the blue sea of August (1975, Italy, 116 mins.) Dir: Lina Wertmuller; Cast: Giancarlo Giannini, Mariangela Melato.

Giannini is a brutish sailor, a modern-day Robinson Crusoe, marooned on a desert island with the woman who hired his boat (Melato). She, however, is no gal Friday. Rather, she's a wealthy, superficial, self-centered woman begging to be brought down. He rips away at every vestige of pretense until she is stripped literally and figuratively naked, making her his slave, bending her over and giving it to her in the same way that she and her class have always given it to him. Fellini disciple Wertmuller established her reputation with this highly charged parable that is every bit as political as it is sexual.

Henry & June (1990, U.S., 134 mins.) Dir: Philip Kaufman; Cast: Fred Ward, Maria de Medeiros, Uma Thurman, Richard E. Grant, Kevin Spacey.

Biographically based exploration of sex, love, and the literary landscape of 1930s Paris. Ward and de Medeiros are Henry Miller and Anaïs Nin—two writers in love with each other and equally enamored of their mutual muse—Miller's wife, June (Thurman). The film flits around the aesthetic terrain and diddles the erogenous zone between Nin's *Delta of Venus* and Miller's *Tropic of Cancer*. While relatively graphic and undeniably stimulating, on an artistic level it seems content to flit and diddle, and not put it in all the way.

Tie Me Up! Tie Me Down! (1990, Spain, 101 mins.) Dir: Pedro Almodovar; Cast: Victoria Abril, Antonio Banderas, Francisco Rabal, Loles Leon.

Recently released mental patient Banderas makes porno movie star Abril his prisoner, keeping her all tied up while trying to twist her into falling in love with him. An oddly comic, genuinely eccentric, sexually frank film in which writer/director Almodovar tickles, titillates, and finally burrows into the dark regions where we are all prisoners of lust.

The Night Porter (1974, Italy, 115 mins.) Dir: Liliana Cavani; Cast: Dirk Bogarde, Charlotte Rampling, Philippe Leroy.

When the wife of an American symphony conductor checks into a Viennese hotel, she recognizes the night porter (Bogarde) as an officer from the concentration camp in which she was not only a prisoner, but his sexual slave. Haunted by the monstrous memories, the two are pulled into a depraved reenactment of their past. Director Cavani worked with Luchino Visconti, and here she seems to be reducing the monumental sexual decadence of *The Damned* to a much more intimate, insidiously perverse level. Simultaneously sexy, sickening and extremely interesting.

The Mother and the Whore (1973, France, 215 mins.) Dir: Jean Eustache;

Cast: Jean-Pierre Léaud, Bernadette Lafont, Françoise Lebrun.

Léaud, Lebrun, and Lafont are a glib young man, his sweet-faced girlfriend, and his bawdy, middle-aged mistress in this improvisatory marathon that finds them all winding up in bed together. Building around a debauch of monologues and dialogues on matters of the flesh, writer/director Eustache blends long-winded philosophy with an open, honest sexuality into an infuriating but stimulating ménage à trois, which turns out to be well worth the trouble it takes to sit though it. As sullen, scratchy, and soulful as it is sexy.

Belle de Jour (1967, France-Italy, 100 mins.) Dir: Luis Buñuel; Cast: Catherine Deneuve, Jean Sorel, Michel Piccoli, Genevieve Page.

First foray into color by Buñuel is an ambiguous comedy that invites us into what may or may not be the daydreams of the dutiful but dissatisfied wife (Deneuve at her absolute best) of a French med student who relieves her boredom by taking a day job at a most unusual brothel. Structured as a series of whimsical vignettes, this wonderful Buñuelian paradox manages to dissect the bourgeois decay in society while simultaneously delighting in the unadulterated kinkiness of it all. A soaring, surrealistic, erotic fantasy. One of a kind.

The Lover (1992, France, 110 mins.) Dir: Jean-Jacques Annaud; Cast: Jane March, Tony Leung, Frédérique Meininger, Arnaud Giovaninetti.

Adaptation of Margaret Duras's bestseller about sexual awakening and forbidden love in French colonial Indochina maintains the erotic, exotic, confessional tone of the source. The ravaged voice of the author is captured by Jeanne Moreau's narration, while the exquisite, ethereal Jane March is her on-screen embodiment. The sex scenes betweeen Ms. March and Tony Leung are charged with an arresting authenticity and unrelenting passion, and the actress's every gesture, the way she touches her hair, leans on a railing, or walks down a street, conjures the character's inner life with resonating effect.

I DO, I DO

They say that if you can get through the wedding, you can get through anything. And there's something to that. If you think your wedding will be like a spread in *Bride's* magazine, rent one of these films and know that the months before will probably more resemble *Pro Wrestling Digest*.

Father of the Bride (1950, U.S., 93 mins., b/w) Dir: Vincente Minnelli; Cast: Spencer Tracy, Elizabeth Taylor, Joan Bennett, Leo G. Carroll.

The original. The good one. Spencer Tracy is suitably paternal as the overly protective father forced to let his kitten Liz Taylor take up with another man. In fact, Tracy is almost uncomfortably protective of Liz and you sense his wife Joan Bennett enjoys torturing him about it. No one gets off the hook here. A fun watch even if there are no impending nuptials in your family.

Father of the Bride (1991, U.S., 105 mins.) Dir: Charles Shyer; Cast: Steve Martin, Diane Keaton, Martin Short, Kimberly Williams.

The remake. The bad one. It's here because it was so popular that there were obviously some people who liked it and you may be one of them. Among the questions you may ask while watching the film are the following: "Why is there a five-minute father-daughter basketball scene?" and "Why doesn't somebody smack the daughter when she complains about the gift of a blender?" You're warned.

Four Weddings and a Funeral (1994, Great Britain, 118 mins.) Dir: Mike Newell; Cast: Andie MacDowell, Hugh Grant, Kristin Scott Thomas, Simon Callow, Rowan Atkinson.

Little more than a living issue of *Bride's* magazine, this lightweight guide for Sloane Ranger wannabees documents the courtship of Grant and MacDowell as they meet over the course of, yes, four weddings and a funeral. Everything's beautiful and witty and as long as you don't care what all these characters do when they're not in tuxedos and gowns, you'll be fine.

The Catered Affair (1956, U.S., 93 mins., b/w) Dir: Richard Brooks; Cast: Bette Davis, Ernest Borgnine, Debbie Reynolds, Rod Taylor, Barry Fitzgerald.

The wife of a Bronx taxi driver wants to throw a big wedding for their daughter. Gore Vidal adapted the script from Paddy Chayefsky's teleplay and Bette Davis, looking seriously washed out, cracks off her lines as the wife. Like *Marty*, it stars Borgnine and is damn depressing until the possibly happy ending.

A Wedding (1978, U.S., 125 mins.) Dir: Robert Altman; Cast: Carol Burnett, Desi Arnaz, Jr., Mia Farrow, Lauren Hutton, Paul Dooley, Lillian Gish, Howard Duff, Pat McCormick, Dina Merrill, Dennis Christopher, John Considine.

Altman films are like very complicated recipes. Lots of ingredients in exact proportions, heated to a precise temperature and stirred. Serve cool. This look at a ritzy suburban Chicago wedding has all the right elements, but you might find yourself passing on seconds. More amusing to those tying the knot.

The Philadelphia Story (1940, U.S., 112 mins.) Dir: George Cukor; Cast: Katharine Hepburn, Cary Grant, James Stewart, Ruth Hussey, John Howard, Roland Young.

Classy, elegant story of mainline Philadelphia woman whose second marriage is upset by the return of her ex and the arrival of a reporter. Absolutely yawl. If you don't know what that means, watch the film again.

Lovers and Other Strangers (1970, U.S., 104 mins.) Dir: Cy Howard; Cast: Gig Young, Richard Castellano, Anne Meara, Harry Guardino, Bonnie Bedelia, Michael Brandon, Anne Jackson, Marian Hailey, Beatrice Arthur.

A fun and all too real look at the differences that crop up between the members of two families when a couple decide to get married after living together for a while. One of the gems on this list.

Invitation to the Wedding (1973, Great Britain, 89 mins.) Dir: Joseph Brooks; Cast: John Gielgud, Ralph Richardson, Paul Nickolaus.

Improbable attempt at satire about the friend of the bride's brother who falls in love with the bride and tries to block the wedding. Despite a doe-eyed leading pair who look like runaways from a Rick Astley video, this has some amusing moments, all of which take place when either Richardson or Gielgud are on the screen.

June Bride (1948, U.S., 97 mins., b/w) Dir: Bretaigne Windust; Cast: Bette Davis, Robert Montgomery.

Whoever had the idea that Robert Montgomery could be a romantic lead? Affable as he is, he's seriously overmatched here by Bette in this tale of former writer/editor couple reunited to cover wedding styles. Light and diverting, with blissfully little to say about the whole business of getting hitched.

Betsy's Wedding (1990, U.S., 90 mins.) Dir: Alan Alda; Cast: Alan Alda, Molly Ringwald, Madeline Kahn, Joe Pesci, Dylan Walsh, Anthony LaPaglia, Bibi Besch, Ally Sheedy, Burt Young, Joey

Bishop, Nicholas Coster, Catherine O'Hara.

This time Alan Alda plays the daddy who throws a veritable potlatch for his daughter's wedding, but the spin is that she doesn't want it. It's not hard to picture Alda getting in a fuss about floral arrangements, is it?

True Love (1989, U.S., 104 mins.) Dir: Nancy Savoca; Cast: Annabella Sciorra, Ron Eldard, Aida Turturro, Roger Rignack.

A more realistic take on weddings Bronx style à la *The Catered Affair*, but done with verve and humor to balance the uncomfortable truths. Savoca's first film features fine performances, especially from Sciorra as the bride light years beyond her stiff of a groom.

The Wedding Banquet (1993, Taiwan, 111 mins.) Dir: Ang Lee; Cast: Winston Chao, May Chin, Mitchell Lichtenstein, Sihung Lung.

Charming tale of a gay Chinese man whose lover convinces him to marry a tenant so that she can get a green card and the groom-to-be's traditional family will be satisfied that he is wed. Sweetly handled with some definite laughs; the wedding scene itself is the funniest of all on this list.

I DID, I DID

Once the gifts are returned and the honeymoon over, a married couple gets down to the difficult business of living in holy wedlock. Here are 10 films about people trying very hard to live happily ever after.

Barefoot in the Park (1967, U.S., 104 mins.) Dir: Gene Saks; Cast: Robert Redford, Jane Fonda, Charles Boyer, Mildred Natwick, Herb Edelman.

Peppy Neil Simon comedy about newlyweds Fonda and Redford, who move into a shabby New York City apartment and face two of the most trying things in the world: young marriage and New York City real-estate. Solid fun, if you're not looking for wisdom.

Two for the Road (1967, Great Britain, 112 mins.) Dir: Stanley Donen; Cast: Audrey Hepburn, Albert Finney, Eleanor Bron, Williams Daniels, Jacqueline Bisset.

A short drive across France becomes a journey back through 12 years of marriage for Finney and Hepburn, as they decide whether or not to call the whole thing off. With Frederic Raphael's sharp screenplay, some gimmicky '60s editing by Donen that holds up surprisingly well and a great Mancini score, this is as sophisticated and timeless as any film ever made. The longer you're married, the more you'll appreciate it.

The Captain's Paradise (1953, Great Britain, 80 mins., b/w) Dir: Anthony Kimmins; Cast: Alec Guinness, Celia Johnson, Yvonne DeCarlo.

Guinness, the embodiment of the term "mild-mannered," captains the ferry between Gibraltar and Morocco and ferries himself between his two wives—sensible Johnson and spicy DeCarlo. Well, one man's paradise is another man's hell. A diverting English comedy that shouldn't be taken seriously by anyone other than Mormons or Muslims.

The Marriage of Maria Braun (1979, West Germany, 120 mins.) Dir: Rainer Werner Fassbinder; Cast: Hanna Schygulla, Klaus Lowitsch, Ivan Desny, Gottfried John.

Schygulla, wife of a missing Nazi soldier, does everything she has to in order to build a life for herself and the husband she believes will one day return. A gritty tale of marital love transcending all and, even more, a clear metaphor for Germany's post-World War II rebuilding and its secret love of

Nazism. One of Fassbinder's greatest films and probably his most accessible.

L'Atalante (1934, France, 87 mins., b/w) Dir: Jean Vigo; Cast: Jean D'Aste, Michel Simon, Dita Parlo.

Early French film by the influential director Jean Vigo follows two newlyweds as they travel down the Seine on the husband's barge. The troubles they face are hardly new and at times the movie moves as slowly as the barge, but it is beautiful and sweet.

My Favorite Wife (1940, U.S., 88 mins., b/w) Dir: Garson Kanin; Cast: Cary Grant, Irene Dunne, Randolph Scott, Gail Patrick.

Irene Dunne, supposedly dead in a shipwreck, comes back to find hubby Grant rehitched. A sparkling, witty comedy with some wonderful scenes. A special tip of the veil to Gail Patrick, who plays the other woman to perfection here and in many other classic films.

Dodsworth (1936, U.S., 101 mins., b/w) Dir: William Wyler; Cast: Walter Huston, Ruth Chatterton, David Niven, Paul Lukas, Mary Astor, Spring Byington, John Payne, Maria Ouspenskaya.

Brilliant adaptation by William Wyler of Sinclair Lewis's novel about a wealthy, retired American couple who begin to question their lives and their marriage when they take a long trip through Europe. Just about everything and everyone in the film were nominated for Oscars, and Walter Huston's performance shows that John inherited many of his cinematic gifts.

Designing Woman (1957, U.S., 117 mins.) Dir: Vincente Minnelli; Cast: Gregory Peck, Lauren Bacall, Dolores Gray, Sam Levene, Chuck Connors.

Tracy and Hepburn get a fifties remodeling here, as sportswriter Peck and fashion designer Bacall wed, only to find that they can't stand each other's lifestyles. Charming and full of plot twists and complications that cover up the fact that Peck is hardly the master of light humor.

A Kind of Loving (1962, Great Britain, 112 mins., b/w) Dir: John Schlesinger; Cast: Alan Bates, June Ritchie, Thora Hird, Norman Rossiter.

This small, realistic film, one of Schlesinger's first, showed his already sure hand. Bates stars as a young Englishman who gets a girl pregnant, marries her, and then moves in with her and her mother. Considering the period he is not an overly angry young man and in fact seems in a good mood much of the time until mum becomes a serious problem. No sunny, pat ending in this one, but a reaffirmation of sorts that ties it all up well.

Who's Afraid of Virginia Woolf? (1966, U.S., 129 mins., b/w) Dir: Mike Nichols; Cast: Elizabeth Taylor, Richard Burton, Sandy Dennis, George Segal.

What married people in the throes of a blitheringly stupid argument haven't pictured themselves as George or Martha, slugging down drinks and torturing their spouse? The last word on marital bliss. Burton and Taylor perform one of the screen's greatest dances of love and hate in this tremendous adaptation of Edward Albee's play about a failed history professor, his lush of a wife, and the young couple they have over for an evening of booze and bared secrets.

ADULTERIES TO REMEMBER

Working things out in a marriage has provided some good material for films, but not nearly the amount that cheating has. The drama and passion of illicit romance combined with the

guilt and tragedy of breaking one's vows make for some memorable screen moments. Just don't get any ideas.

Unfaithfully Yours (1948, U.S., 105 mins., b/w) Dir: Preston Sturges; Cast: Rex Harrison, Linda Darnell, Rudy Vallee, Lionel Stander, Barbara Lawrence.

Sprightly Sturges romp has conductor Harrison suspecting innocent wife Darnell of adultery and planning her demise during the course of his concert. The sophisticated and hilarious screenplay matches up beautifully with the physical comedy that Harrison executes better than you would ever imagine. A great film.

Men . . . (1985, West Germany, 99 mins.) Dir: Doris Dörrie; Cast: Heiner Lauterbach, Uwe Ochsenknecht, Ulrike Kriener.

Talky German comedy about an advertising executive who moves in with the bohemian artist his wife is having an affair with in order to turn the artist into the kind of person she'll dislike. The friendship between the men is handled with no weepy soul-searching; it's all on target and funny. The one question is whether dressing this badly is mandatory in Germany.

A Letter to Three Wives (1949, U.S., 102 mins., b/w) Dir: Joseph L. Mankiewicz; Cast: Ann Sothern, Linda Darnell, Paul Douglas, Kirk Douglas, Jeanne Crain, voice of Celeste Holm.

Nifty drama about three women who, en route to a boat trip, receive letters telling them that the town hussy has run off with one of their husbands. They spend the whole time wondering who the unlucky one is, flashing back to all the reasons it could be them. With no BIG stars, the strength of this film is in its script and Mankiewicz's direction, both of which won Oscars. A must.

The Baker's Wife (1938, France, 124 mins., b/w) Dir: Marcel Pagnol; Cast: Raimu, Ginette Laclerc, Charles Moulin, Robert Vattier, Robert Brassa.

One of the sweetest, most wonderful films ever made. The people of a small rural village in France love the bread made by a new baker, so when his wife runs away and he becomes too depressed to bake, the town works together to bring her back. A funny, moving film and Raimu as the baker is tremendous.

Fatal Attraction (1987, U.S., 120 mins.) Dir: Adrian Lyne; Cast: Michael Douglas, Glenn Close, Anne Archer, Ellen Hamilton Latzen, Stuart Pankin.

The one-nighter from hell. Michael Douglas thinks his dalliance with Glenn Close was just one of those things, but psychopath Close has other ideas and shares them in quite a violent fashion with Douglas and his family. One of the most popular thrillers ever and probably responsible for more marital fidelity than all the commandments combined.

A Touch of Class (1972, Great Britain, 106 mins.) Dir: Melvin Frank; Cast: Glenda Jackson, George Segal, Paul Sorvino.

Married man Segal goes on a business trip to London and plans to have a little affair. What he ends up with, though, is love. Glenda Jackson is the story here. She won an Oscar for Best Actress as the object of Segal's affections and the play between the two of them is top-notch.

Juliet of the Spirits (1965, Italy, 148 mins.) Dir: Federico Fellini; Cast: Giulietta Masina, Mario Pisu, Sandra Milo, Valentina Cortese, Sylva Koscina.

There's no middle ground on this one; you'll either love it or not get a single minute of Fellini's surrealist journey into the mind of a woman who suspects her husband of cheating. As baffling and inexplicable as it is lovely and beautiful. Giulietta Masina is so demure and sweet compared to Fellini stars like Sophia Loren and Anita Ekberg that it's no wonder she became Mrs. Fellini.

The Bliss of Mrs. Blossom (1968, Great Britain, 93 mins.) Dir: Joe McGrath; Cast: Shirley MacLaine, Richard Attenborough, James Booth.

An odd period piece from sixties London that's somewhere between *Willie Wonka* and *The Collector*. MacLaine, the wife of a wealthy brassiere manufacturer, decides to keep her lover as a permanent guest in their attic. The goofy, Benny Hill-type humor and the groovy art direction keep this entertaining throughout.

Jungle Fever (1991, U.S., 132 mins.) Dir: Spike Lee; Cast: Wesley Snipes, Annabella Sciorra, Spike Lee, John Turturro, Lonette McKee, Anthony Quinn, Samuel L. Jackson.

Spike Lee is in strong form here, but Wesley Snipes is in even stronger form as a black executive who has an affair with a white secretary in his office. Like all of Lee's movies, there are things you can debate forever, but isn't that the point? Say what you will about his personal politics, in his movies Spike Lee tells the truth whether he agrees or not. Samuel Jackson as Snipes's brother deserved an Oscar.

Brief Encounter (1946, Great Britain, 85 mins., b/w) Dir: David Lean; Cast: Celia Johnson, Trevor Howard.

With the turgid Rachmaninoff score and all the clipped, breathless English accents, this simple story of an unfulfilled wife finding love with Trevor Howard wavers between classic melodrama and unwitting humor, depending on how much you like the former. Still, it's the last word on adultery.

DIVORCE, HOLLYWOOD STYLE

Though some couples do manage to keep their marriages going, almost half of all American marriages end in divorce. In years past, divorce was available, but it was nowhere near as accepted as it is now, which explains why so many of the following films are of recent vintage. After watching some of these, you may wonder why married couples don't just stick it out.

The Awful Truth (1937, U.S., 90 mins., b/w) Dir: Leo McCarey; Cast: Cary Grant, Irene Dunne, Ralph Bellamy, Cecil Cunningham.

Watching a sophisticated old film such as this one is something like thinking about your parents having sex: surprising at first, but then heartening and a reminder that we didn't invent sex or, in this case, witty dialogue. Here, Grant and Dunne divorce in order to wed new partners, but each does their best to sabotage the other's wedding plans.

The War of the Roses (1989, U.S., 116 mins.) Dir: Danny DeVito; Cast: Michael Douglas, Kathleen Turner, Danny DeVito, Marianne Sagebrecht, Sean Astin, Heather Fairfield, G. D. Spradlin.

This black comedy about Douglas and Turner battling their way physically and emotionally through their property settlement stops being a comedy after a certain point and just feels black. Not a date movie, unless you're planning for it to be the last one.

Smash Palace (1981, New Zealand, 100 mins.) Dir: Roger Donaldson; Cast: Bruno Lawrence, Anna Jemison, Greer Robson.

Affecting film from New Zealand about a race-car driver who's driven to some very unpleasant acts by his divorce and insufficient visitation rights to his daughter. It goes just a little bit too far, as if no one could quite figure out how to end the movie with anything less than tragedy, but it's definitely worth seeing.

Heartburn (1986, U.S., 108 mins.) Dir: Mike Nichols; Cast: Meryl Streep, Jack Nicholson, Stockard Channing, Maureen Stapleton, Catherine O'Hara, Karen Akers, Jeff Daniels, Richard Masur.

Nora Ephron adapted her own autobiographical novel about her marriage to, and breakup with, journalist Carl Bernstein of *All the President's Men* fame. Aside from the humor and vitriol, both in large doses, the film raises a valuable question: Who makes a better Bernstein, Nicholson or Hoffman?

The Palm Beach Story (1942, U.S., 90 mins., b/w) Dir: Preston Sturges; Cast: Claudette Colbert, Joel McCrea, Mary Astor, Rudy Vallee.

Proof that one of the leading causes of divorce is money. Colbert divorces McCrea, to whom she's been happily married save for their lack of funds, and goes to Palm Beach to find a new, rich husband so that she can funnel bucks back to Joel. A terrific screwball comedy and one of Sturges's best.

Stella Dallas (1937, U.S., 106 mins., b/w) Dir: King Vidor; Cast: Barbara Stanwyck, John Boles, Ann Shirley, Barbara O'Neil, Alan Hale, Tim Holt, Marjorie Main.

A showcase soaper for Stanwyck, who plays a divorced woman who lets her well-to-do ex-husband have custody of their daughter so that the girl can make something of her life. One of the great melodramas, it never gets out of hand. Stanwyck was nominated for Best Actress.

The Good Mother (1988, U.S., 103 mins.) Dir: Leonard Nimoy; Cast: Diane Keaton, Liam Neeson, Jason Robards, Ralph Bellamy, James Naughton.

A divorced mother takes up with a new man, but her custody of her young daughter is challenged by her ex, who accuses her boyfriend of sexual misconduct. Based on the novel by Sue Miller, it has its moments, especially from Keaton, but it's probably not Spock's finest hour as a director.

Kramer vs. Kramer (1979, U.S., 105 mins.) Dir: Robert Benton; Cast: Dustin Hoffman, Jane Alexander, Meryl Streep, Justin Henry.

The custody film to end all custody films and Benton's best. Streep leaves Hoffman and son with vague notions of finding herself, then returns to take the boy back. Wrenching stuff, with great interplay between Hoffman and Justin Henry as the kid. Genuine laughs and genuine tears abound.

An Unmarried Woman (1978, U.S., 124 mins.) Dir: Paul Mazursky; Cast: Jill Clayburgh, Alan Bates, Pat Quinn, Cliff Gorman, Michael Murphy.

A look at divorce provided the high-water mark for this director, too. Mazursky's finest film follows Clayburgh, whose husband has unexpectedly divorced her, as she tries to remake her life. Though it drifts into *Ms.* magazine material at times, overall it's a strong statement about the effects of breaking up and the possibilities of starting over.

The Odd Couple (1968, U.S., 105 mins.) Dir: Gene Saks; Cast: Jack Lemmon, Walter Matthau, Herb Edelman, Carole Shelley.

Unless you've been under a rock the last two decades, you've seen the great Tony Randall/Jack Klugman TV series, but you should absolutely see the film it's based on. Lemmon plays Felix as a depressive obsessive-compulsive rather than as a priss, which gives an edge to the whole thing, as does Matthau's slightly meaner Oscar.

KILLING YOUR SPOUSE

Sometimes divorce isn't the answer. Say your husband is almost satanically evil or your wife is loaded and you're set to inherit it all if she checks out. What else can you do? In truth, next to killing your children or your parents, killing your spouse is one of the most horrific crimes imaginable. So why are there so many great films about it?

Double Indemnity (1944, U.S., 106 mins., b/w) Dir: Billy Wilder; Cast: Fred MacMurray, Barbara Stanwyck, Edward G. Robinson.

Maybe the finest example of film noir has insurance salesman MacMurray sucked into a plot to knock off Stanwyck's husband. Wilder co-wrote the script with Raymond Chandler, based on James M. Cain's novel, and it was so good that Lawrence Kasdan ripped it off years later for *Body Heat.*

How to Murder Your Wife (1965, U.S., 118 mins.) Dir: Richard Quine; Cast: Jack Lemmon, Virna Lisi, Terry-Thomas.

Why cartoonist Jack Lemmon wants to knock off the lovely Virna Lisi is beyond comprehension. So what if he married her while he was drunk; we've all made worse decisions sober. Terry-Thomas's presence indicates that this is a goofy romp and as broad as Lemmon's cartoons in the movie.

Dial M for Murder (1954, U.S., 105 mins., b/w) Dir: Alfred Hitchcock; Cast: Ray Milland, Grace Kelly, Robert Cummings, John Williams, Anthony Dawson.

Killing Grace Kelly makes even less sense than killing Virna Lisi. All Ray Milland wants is her money, though, so

he devises a plot to kill her, not suspecting that Grace is a tougher mark than he thought. Stylish Hitchcock thriller.

Sorry, Wrong Number (1948, U.S., 89 mins., b/w) Dir: Anatole Litvak; Cast: Barbara Stanwyck, Burt Lancaster, Ann Richards, Wendell Corey, Ed Begley.

The tables turn on Stanwyck here, as she plays a rich, bedridden shrew who overhears a plan to kill her. And guess who's behind it all? Great set piece for Stanwyck, who makes this into an almost one-woman show.

Diabolique (1955, France, 107 mins., b/w) Dir: Henri-Georges Clouzot; Cast: Simone Signoret, Vera Clouzot.

The wife of a cruel schoolmaster teams up with his mistress to kill the brutal so-and-so, but did they really kill him? A guaranteed edge-of-your-seat thriller, as Vera Clouzot learns a new meaning for the phrase "Till death do us part."

Divorce—Italian Style (1962, Italy, 104 mins.) Dir: Pietro Germi; Cast: Marcello Mastroianni, Daniela Rocca, Stephania Sandrelli.

Broad Italian comedy about a married baron, in love with his cousin, who tries to instigate an affair for his wife so he can catch her in the act and kill her. Oscar winner for Best Screenplay and Mastroianni is terrific too, but Rocca as his mustachioed wife steals the show.

The Fourth Man (1984, The Netherlands, 104 mins.) Dir: Paul Verhoeven; Cast: Jeroen Krabbé, Renee Soutendijk.

This early effort by Verhoeven is an artsy first draft for *Basic Instinct* and he should have stopped here. Bisexual writer Krabbé falls in the sack with lusty hairdresser Soutendijk, who may or may not have caused the deaths of her three husbands. Lots of weird imagery, symbolism, and sex, along with a strange devotion to the Virgin Mary.

Reversal of Fortune (1990, U.S., 110 mins.) Dir: Barbet Schroeder; Cast: Jeremy Irons, Glenn Close, Ron Silver, Christine Baranski, Stephen Mailer, Uta Hagen, Annabella Sciorra, Fisher Stevens, Julie Hagerty.

Jeremy Irons is brilliant as Claus von Bulow, accused of trying to murder his socialite wife Sunny with an overdose of insulin, and Silver matches him as lawyer Alan Dershowitz, who takes on his case. A very intelligent and compelling look at the real lifestyles of the rich and famous. Irons won an Oscar for his truly eerie performance as the truly eerie von Bulow.

Niagara (1953, U.S., 89 mins.) Dir: Henry Hathaway; Cast: Marilyn Monroe, Joseph Cotten, Jean Peters.

Monroe and her new, slightly nuts husband Cotten honeymoon at Niagara Falls. Things don't go so well, though, and murder appears to be a more viable option than counseling. An offbeat thriller with Hitchcock-like touches and a few surprises.

OBSTETRICS & PEDIATRICS

First comes love. Then comes marriage. Then comes a couple really depressed about the cost of a college education pushing the baby carriage. Though things like test tubes and in vitro fertilization have changed even how babies are made, the struggles and joys we experience in having babies and adjusting to parenthood are timeless.

Father's Little Dividend (1951, U.S., 82 mins.) Dir: Vincente Minnelli; Cast: Elizabeth Taylor, Spencer Tracy, Joan Bennett.

This sequel to *Father of the Bride* is one of the only straightforward views of what to expect when you're expecting. Liz prepares for motherhood and Tracy continues to exhibit some unresolved Oedipal issues by behaving like the only man in history to be unhappy about having a grandchild.

A Taste of Honey (1962, Great Britain, 100 mins., b/w) Dir: Tony Richardson; Cast: Rita Tushingham, Murray Melvin, Dora Bryan, Robert Stephens.

Top of the line English "kitchen sink" movie stars Tushingham as a young woman barely able to care for herself who is helped by a gay friend when a black sailor gets her pregnant. An honest, moving film with great performances. Worth seeing no matter what.

Rosemary's Baby (1968, U.S., 136 mins.) Dir: Roman Polanski; Cast: Mia Farrow, Ruth Gordon, John Cassavetes, Charles Grodin, Maurice Evans, Ralph Bellamy, Sidney Blackmer.

Not recommended if you're expecting. Mia Farrow thinks she's carrying the child of hubby Cassavetes, but maybe one of his new friends from the coven he's joined had something to do with it. One of the all-time best scary movies. Don't worry; the horns would definitely show up on the sonogram.

Penny Serenade (1941, U.S., 120 mins.) Dir: George Stevens; Cast: Cary Grant, Irene Dunne, Beulah Bondi.

Big-time weeper about a couple who adopt after losing one of their own during pregnancy. Grant and Dunne, who teamed up for some wonderful comedies, proved here that they could do the same with drama. Remember, moms and dads-to-be: this is a *tearjerker*.

Three Men and a Baby (1987, U.S., 99 mins.) Dir: Leonard Nimoy; Cast: Ted Danson, Tom Selleck, Steve Guttenberg, Nancy Travis, Margaret Colin.

Three wild and crazy bachelor guys end up sharing their apartment with a baby. Spock shows a deft directing hand in this playful remake of the French comedy *Three Men and a Cradle,* and the trio of unwed fathers transcend their television-level abilities.

The Baby and the Battleship (1956, Great Britain, 96 mins.) Dir: Jay Lewis; Cast: John Mills, Richard Attenborough, Andre Morell, Bryan Forbes.

This solid English comedy is another spin on the "men with a baby" theme. Two British sailors on leave end up with an Italian baby, which they sneak on board ship and do their best to hide from the officers. Mills and Attenborough are good in just about everything they've ever done, and this is no exception.

Raising Arizona (1987, U.S., 94 mins.) Dir: Joel Coen; Cast: Nicolas Cage, Holly Hunter, Trey Wilson, John Goodman, William Forsythe, Sam McMurray, Frances McDormand, Randall "Tex" Cobb.

Where have you gone, Coens? The tremendously talented brothers Ethan and Joel Coen followed up *Blood Simple* with this nonstop comedy about a couple who kidnap a quintuplet after learning that they can't have children of their own. Wacky, heartwarming satire that goes astray a bit when Tex Cobb shows up. Cinematographer Barry Sonnenfeld, who went on to direct *The Addams Family,* gets much credit for keeping this film zipping along.

Look Who's Talking (1989, U.S., 93 mins.) Dir: Amy Heckerling; Cast: John Travolta, Kirstie Alley, Olympia Dukakis, George Segal, Abe Vigoda.

Depending on your tastes, either a laugh riot or a 90-minute commercial for birth control. Alley has a baby by a married man and goes hunting for the right man to be daddy to her son. All the while, the bundle of "joy" makes his own observations via the voice of Bruce Willis. Harmless fun, which is more than can be said for the sequel, *Look Who's Talking Too,* a film that has been proven in laboratory tests to cause brain damage in mice.

Baby Boom (1987, U.S., 103 mins.) Dir: Charles Shyer; Cast: Diane Keaton, Sam Shepard, Harold Ramis, Sam Wanamaker, James Spader.

Hotshot exec Keaton gets saddled with a relative's child and must adjust to motherhood and a new life in Vermont. Though Keaton is as hard to believe as an executive as Nicole Kidman was as a brain surgeon in *Days of Thunder,* the film has its moments and the baby high jinks are amusing.

Bachelor Mother (1939, U.S., 81 mins.) Dir: Garson Kanin; Cast: Ginger Rogers, David Niven, Charles Coburn, Frank Albertson.

Terrific comedy stars Ginger Rogers as a department-store salesclerk who finds an abandoned baby and is cajoled by store-owner Niven to keep the little tyke. Laughs and romance nicely balanced by Kanin, with a minimum of cutesy baby schtick.

OLD AGE

Hollywood's prime market is the demographic between 14 and 24, so it's not surprising that movies about golden agers aren't the studios' first priority. Occasionally, though, mature folks find their way onto the screen, and with some remarkable results. Here's a selection of the best films made about growing old, gracefully and otherwise.

Driving Miss Daisy (1989, U.S., 105 mins.) Dir: Bruce Beresford; Cast: Jessica Tandy, Morgan Freeman, Dan Aykroyd, Esther Rolle, Patti LuPone.

This tale of a cranky old southern woman and the friendship she develops with her black chauffeur features an Oscar-winning performance by Jessica Tandy. The film was named Best Picture, as well.

Cocoon (1985, U.S., 118 mins.) Dir: Ron Howard; Cast: Don Ameche, Wilford Brimley, Gwen Verdon, Brian Dennehy, Steve Guttenberg, Tahnee Welch, Hume Cronyn, Maureen Stapleton, Jessica Tandy.

Tandy shines again, along with real-life husband Hume Cronyn and a cast of other esteemed senior performers in this sweet comedy about a group of retirees finding an alien-created fountain of youth in a neighboring swimming pool. Sniffles and nice sentiments about aging come in equal measure with the laughs.

Wild Strawberries (1957, Sweden, 90 mins., b/w) Dir: Ingmar Bergman; Cast: Victor Sjöström, Ingrid Thulin, Bibi Andersson.

No bittersweet, Hollywood view of aging here. Bergman's slow-moving, cerebral film follows an elderly professor as he journeys through all the mistakes he's made in his life. A must-see for film buffs and more thoughtful viewers; a tough watch for those looking for light entertainment.

Atlantic City (1981, Canada-France, 104 mins.) Dir: Louis Malle; Cast: Burt Lancaster, Susan Sarandon, Robert Joy, Michel Piccoli, Kate Reid.

Burt Lancaster stars as a small-time hood who's seen his best days and Sarandon is the young waitress he falls in love with in this brilliant film by Louis Malle. A sensitive and penetrating view of a man grasping at the last straws of youth.

The Sunshine Boys (1975, U.S., 111 mins.) Dir: Herbert Ross; Cast: George Burns, Walter Matthau, Richard Benjamin.

Neil Simon's comedy about two battling old vaudevillians reuniting for a TV show is memorable for more than just laughs; it's also the film that brought George Burns back onto the screen for the first time since 1939. Jack Benny was originally intended to play Burns's partner, but Matthau is no slouch himself.

On Golden Pond (1981, U.S., 109 mins.) Dir: Mark Rydell; Cast: Henry Fonda, Katharine Hepburn, Jane Fonda, Doug McKeon, Dabney Coleman, William Lanteau.

Fonda finally won an Oscar for this, his last screen appearance as a man fearing his inevitable mortality but who comes to terms with the cycle of life during a summer at the family lake house. Definitely a Hollywood-style lite serious film, sort of like Andre Kostelanetz light classical music, but if the idea of two Fondas and a Hepburn together intrigues you, you'll like it.

Tatie Danielle (1991, France, 106 mins.) Dir: Etienne Chatiliez; Cast: Tsilla Chelton, Catherine Jacob, Isabelle Nanty, Eric Prat, Laurence Fevrier, Neige Dolsky.

Not everybody's taste, but neither is caviar. A very funny black comedy about a seriously mean old woman who moves in with her nephew and proceeds to ruin his life. Tsilla Chelton's performance gives Tatie Danielle a complexity that makes her more than just a nasty caricature; we actually understand why she is so incredibly awful.

Umberto D (1955, Italy, 89 mins., b/w) Dir: Vittorio De Sica; Cast: Carlo Battisti, Maria Pia Casilio.

De Sica's simple story of an old man and his dog about to be thrown out of their apartment is one of the most devastating movies ever made. The honesty and complexity of emotion throughout raise this far above pathos, as does De Sica's ultimate belief in the beauty and hope of life. It's a guaranteed cry and a must-see.

Harry and Tonto (1974, U.S., 115 mins.) Dir: Paul Mazursky; Cast: Art Carney, Ellen Burstyn, Larry Hagman, Geraldine Fitzgerald, Josh Mostel, Barbara Rhoades, Arthur Hunnicutt, Melanie Mayron.

Art Carney plays a man in his seventies who sticks his cat in the car and goes for a drive across country to tie up loose ends and relive memories. Carney joined the group of performers who received belated honors by winning an Oscar for his work in this film. A patient, gentle movie with enough laughs and drama to satisfy everyone.

The Last Laugh (1924, Germany, 72 mins.) Dir: F. W. Murnau; Cast: Emil Jannings, Maly Delschaft.

A monumental and wrenching silent film about a well-known and elderly doorman at a classy hotel who is demoted to bathroom attendant because of his age. Emil Jannings and the groundbreaking cinematography will keep you from noticing that there's no dialogue here.

RELIGION

GOD & THE DEVIL

Either the devil has a better agent than God or else he knows more people in Hollywood, because he's been in some very good movies. If we include all those fourth-rate shock-ers, the devil's also had more work, but God definitely beat him to the punch on a production deal.**

Bedazzled (1967, Great Britain, 107 mins.) Dir: Stanley Donen; Cast: Peter Cook, Dudley Moore, Eleanor Bron, Raquel Welch.

Fry-cook Dudley Moore sells his soul to a swinging London Satan in the form of Peter Cook. Without a doubt the funniest film about the devil and certainly the only one to turn *Faust* into a buddy movie.

The Next Voice You Hear (1950, U.S., 82 mins., b/w) Dir: William Wellman; Cast: James Whitmore, Nancy Davis, Gary Gray.

A strangely disquieting film about God taking to the radio for some divine fireside chats. Why is this film so, well, scary? Is it the threat of imminent Apocalypse coming not from the bomb or space aliens but, for once, from God Himself? Is it the release of all the fury, pain, and fear that's usually hidden beneath the Norman Rockwell image of America? Or is it Nancy Davis, later Nancy Reagan, playing the mother?

The Exorcist (1973, U.S., 122 mins.) Dir: William Friedkin; Cast: Ellen Burstyn, Max von Sydow, Lee J. Cobb, Kitty Winn, Jason Miller, Linda Blair.

All these years later the special effects don't seem that real, but this story of the possession and exorcism of pubescent Linda Blair still has its moments. Actually, the scariest parts don't even show the devil, and that's probably the same reason why *The Next Voice You Hear* gives you the chills too.

The Ten Commandments (1923, U.S., 146 mins.) Dir: Cecil B. DeMille; Cast: Theodore Roberts, Charles de Roche, Estelle Taylor, Rod La Rocque.

The Ten Commandments (1956, U.S., 219 mins.) Dir: Cecil B. DeMille; Cast:

Charlton Heston, Edward G. Robinson, Yul Brynner, Cedric Hardwicke, Debra Paget, John Derek, Anne Baxter.

A dual tour de force for the Almighty, who appears as, among other things, a burning bush and a pillar of fire. What did you expect? He commissioned the project.

The Devil and Daniel Webster (aka: *All That Money Can Buy,* 1941, U.S., 109 mins., b/w) Dir: William Dieterle; Cast: Walter Huston, Edward Arnold, James Craig, Anne Shirley, Jane Darwell, Simone Simon.

Adaptation of Stephen Vincent Benet's tale of a young farmer who sells his soul to the devil and needs Daniel Webster's help to get out of the deal. Walter Huston plays the devil, aka Mr. Scratch. Famous for its visuals and Bernard Herrmann's Oscar-winning score.

The Bible . . . in the Beginning (1966, U.S.-Italy, 174 mins.) Dir: John Huston; Cast: George C. Scott, Ava Gardner, Peter O'Toole, Franco Nero, Richard Harris, John Huston, Ulla Bergryd.

The book is certainly better than the movie, but give John Huston credit for effort. If anything it's too earnest, though it's quite faithful and realistic. Could be a good Sunday school supplement.

The Witches of Eastwick (1987, U.S., 122 mins.) Dir: George Miller; Cast: Jack Nicholson, Cher, Susan Sarandon, Michelle Pfeiffer, Veronica Cartwright.

Out of all the things Satan has ever done to look good, like creating vast and greedy worldly empires and taking on Michael Kinsley on *Crossfire,* sleeping with Susan Sarandon, Michelle Pfeiffer, and Cher in the same film is the only one that is truly convincing. George Miller's version of John Updike's bestseller about the devil coming to a small New England town is full of entertaining touches. Jack Nicholson is all too believable as Satan.

The Green Pastures (1936, U.S., 92 mins., b/w) Dirs: William Keighley, Marc Connelly; Cast: Rex Ingram, Oscar Polk, Eddie Anderson, Frank Wilson, George Reed, Abraham Gleaves, Myrtle Anderson.

God always gets the last word and this list is no exception. This film version of Marc Connelly's Pulitzer Prize-winning play retells biblical stories with an all-black cast. Most of us, save for maybe Orval Faubus and David Duke, would be happy to see Rex Ingram as God on Judgment Day.

CHERUBIM & SERAPHIM

Angels have made a real comeback in popular culture over the last few years, but Hollywood has always liked them. Here are 10 films about angels, arch and otherwise.

Wings of Desire (1987, West Germany, 130 mins.) Dir: Wim Wenders; Cast: Bruno Ganz, Solveig Dommartin, Otto Sander, Curt Bois, Peter Falk.

Many people count this long, lyrical film about angels wandering the streets of Berlin among their favorites. The moody, grainy look comes from Henri Alekan, who shot Jean Cocteau's *Orphée,* among other classics. The movie slows down near the end, but by then you're sold.

It's a Wonderful Life (1946, U.S., 129 mins.) Dir: Frank Capra; Cast: James Stewart, Donna Reed, Lionel Barrymore, Thomas Mitchell, Henry Travers, Beulah Bondi, Gloria Grahame, H. B. Warner, Ward Bond.

If you don't know the plot of this movie, just go out and rent it and consider yourself lucky that you can see it fresh.

The rest of us know why it's a great angel movie and don't want to spoil it for you.

Waiting for the Light (1990, U.S., 94 mins.) Dir: Christopher Monger; Cast: Shirley MacLaine, Teri Garr, Hillary Wolf, Colin Baumgartner, Vincent Schiavelli; Clancy Brown, Jeff McCracken.

Light comedy with dramatic overtones about Garr, her two delinquent kids, and nutty aunt MacLaine reopening a dilapidated diner that starts to take off when an angel appears near it. MacLaine gets all the best bits.

Here Comes Mr. Jordan (1941, U.S., 93 mins., b/w) Dir: Alexander Hall; Cast: Robert Montgomery, Claude Rains, Evelyn Keyes, Rita Johnson, James Gleason, Edward Everett Horton.

Claude Rains plays probably the most elegant angel ever in this splendid old fantasy about a boxer wrongfully taken to heaven, and then sent back in another body.

The Bishop's Wife (1947, U.S., 108 mins., b/w) Dir: Henry Koster; Cast: Cary Grant, Loretta Young, David Niven, Monty Woolley.

Well, maybe Cary Grant is the most elegant angel ever. Here, he comes to help overworked, overwrought Niven deal with his new vicarage, almost stealing wife Young in the process. The story and package make you expect a smarmy film, but you'll be pleasantly surprised by the occasional sharp edges that appear. Niven resists the temptation to play his character as a fool and the romantic tension between Grant and Young is definitely not expected.

Fear No Evil (1981, U.S., 96 mins.) Dir: Frank Laloggia; Cast: Stefan Arngrim, Elizabeth Hoffman, Kathleen Rowe McAllen, Frank Birney.

And you thought your school was tough. Lucifer takes the form of a high school student and does all sorts of gory demonic things until another student, actually the angel Gabriel, takes him on. They must have a great football team.

Miracle in Milan (1951, Italy, 100 mins., b/w) Dir: Vittorio De Sica; Cast: Emma Gramatica, Francesco Golisano, Paolo Stoppa, Brunella Bovo.

A film of political whimsy, as Golisano and the heaven-sent spirit of the old lady who cared for him as a boy help a group of poor people displaced from their village by WWII. It's all about politics anyway, so it doesn't matter if she's not an official angel. A sweetly strange film.

Forever Darling (1956, U.S., 96 mins.) Dir: Alexander Hall; Cast: Lucille Ball, Desi Arnaz, James Mason.

An angel who bears a great resemblance to James Mason comes to Lucy in order to help her bolster her drooping marriage to chemist Desi. Starts strong, but somewhere around Desi's lecture on the value of insecticide it ebbs off. Hard to find a more unusual movie about angels, though.

Gabriel Over the White House (1933, U.S., 87 mins., b/w) Dir: Gregory La Cava; Cast: Walter Huston, Karen Morley, Franchot Tone, Jean Parker, Dickie Moore.

Party hack Huston is elected to the Oval Office during the Depression, but when the angel Gabriel appears to him, he becomes a Capraesque reformer. An odd film with some brilliant moments before it dissolves into rhetoric at the end.

The Horn Blows at Midnight (1945, U.S., 78 mins., b/w) Dir: Raoul Walsh; Cast: Jack Benny, Alexis Smith, Guy Kibbee.

Trumpeter Benny falls asleep and

dreams he is an archangel responsible for ending the world with a blast from his horn, but he's kept from his duties by an attractive woman. A shiny romp of a comedy that never gets sidetracked by Hollywood piety.

MEN OF THE CLOTH

Many have been called to make films about priests and ministers, but few have been chosen to make good ones. Most movies about men of the cloth get dragged down by Hollywood theology and scenery-chomping actors, so it's a miracle that these 11 escaped the usual temptations.

Diary of a Country Priest (1951, France, 120 mins., b/w) Dir: Robert Bresson; Cast: Claude Laydu, Jean Riveyre, Marie-Monique Arkell, Nicole Maurey.

A sickly young priest takes over an unfriendly parish in rural France. It's hard to say which is more depressing—Georges Bernanos's book or this adaptation by Robert Bresson—but the film does have a simple majesty that transcends the novel. A classic film, but a challenge.

Angels With Dirty Faces (1938, U.S., 97 mins., b/w) Dir: Michael Curtiz; Cast: James Cagney, Pat O'Brien, Humphrey Bogart, Ann Sheridan, Huntz Hall, Leo Gorcey, Billy Halop.

Boyhood friends Cagney and O'Brien take different paths as adults: Cagney becomes a hood and O'Brien a priest. Can Father Jerry save Rocky's soul? The kind of brilliant American film that you just assume you've seen and probably haven't. Even the usually annoying Dead End Kids do well, especially in their full-contact basketball scene.

The Shoes of the Fisherman (1968, U.S., 157 mins.) Dir: Michael Anderson;

Cast: Anthony Quinn, Laurence Olivier, John Gielgud, Barbara Jefford, Oskar Werner.

Anthony Quinn as the first Russian Pope. OK, this one does succumb to the usual temptations and it's more than a little dated now, but the Vatican stuff is interesting and fun.

The Night of the Iguana (1964, U.S., 125 mins.) Dir: John Huston; Cast: Richard Burton, Ava Gardner, Deborah Kerr, Sue Lyon.

Speaking of succumbing to temptations . . . Richard Burton stars in this adaptation of Tennessee Williams's play about a defrocked minister leading a tour group in Mexico. Fine performances all around and Huston brings a very stagy play effectively to the screen.

Heavens Above (1963, Great Britain, 105 mins.) Dirs: John and Roy Boulting; Cast: Peter Sellers, Cecil Parker, Isabel Jeans, Eric Sykes.

British satire stars Sellers as an Anglican priest appointed to a new bishopric—outer space. Typically solid Sellers comedy.

Going My Way (1944, U.S., 130 mins., b/w) Dir: Leo McCarey; Cast: Bing Crosby, Barry Fitzgerald, Gene Lockhart, Rise Stevens, William Frawley, Carl "Alfalfa" Switzer.

Everyone's favorite priest movie. Bing Crosby plays a young priest who battles crotchety curate Barry Fitzgerald over his plans to save their poor parish.

Black Robe (1991, U.S.-Canada, 101 mins.) Dir: Bruce Beresford; Cast: Lothaire Bluteau, August Schellenberg, Aden Young, Sandrine Holt, Tantoo Cardinal.

A Jesuit priest in 17th-century Quebec journeys to his new mission among the Huron. Brian Moore wrote the script for this version of his novel. Restrained and realistic, it's an unflinching and intelligent look at the conflict of faiths inherent in missionary activity. The stunning natural backdrops are worth the price of the rental.

The Bishop's Wife (1947, U.S., 108 mins., b/w) Dir: Henry Koster; Cast: Cary Grant, Loretta Young, David Niven, Monty Woolley.

Minister David Niven is so consumed by the demands of his parish that God sends down angel Cary Grant to help him. Niven is convincing as the obsessed vicar and the film gets just close enough to the edge of sappiness to move us without ever going completely over.

Elmer Gantry (1960, U.S., 145 mins., b/w) Dir: Richard Brooks; Cast: Burt Lancaster, Jean Simmons, Dean Jagger, Arthur Kennedy, Shirley Jones, Patti Page.

Burt Lancaster won an Oscar as Best Actor for his performance as the titled southern evangelist who preaches the word of God but does not live it. Based on Sinclair Lewis's novel, this story seems to find renewed relevance every time another Jimmy Swaggart or Jim Bakker comes along.

Open City (1946, Italy, 105 mins., b/w) Dir: Roberto Rossellini; Cast: Aldo Fabrizi, Anna Magnani.

Rossellini's masterpiece about the Resistance movement in Rome during World War II features maybe the best priest ever—a gruff, loving man whose courage lasts to the very end. A terrific film and the kind of priest who would get you to church more often.

Leap of Faith (1992, U.S., 108 mins.) Dir: Richard Pearce; Cast: Steve Martin, Debra Winger, Lolita Davidovich, Liam Neeson, Lukas Haas, Meat Loaf.

Martin plays a conniving con man in the Elmer Gantry mode who learns that maybe there are such things as miracles after all. A big showcase for Martin, who gets to chew the scenery for a reason. The script has the right blend of cynicism and faith, but you soon get the feeling that if it had been done outside of Hollywood, the result would have been absolutely wonderful.

NUNS

If you never had your knuckles smacked by some ruler-wielding Sister Mary Immaculata, you probably don't understand why there's so much fuss about those nice ladies in habits. Here's your chance to learn something about nuns, without spending eight years getting your ears twisted.

The Sound of Music (1965, U.S., 174 mins.) Dir: Robert Wise; Cast: Julie Andrews, Christopher Plummer, Eleanor Parker, Richard Haydn, Peggy Wood, Charmian Carr, Nicholas Hammond, Angela Cartwright, Heather Menzies, Marni Nixon, Anna Lee.

Too-good-to-be-true novice becomes nanny for too-good-to-be-true children of too-good-to-be-true Austrian officer on brink of World War II. Surprise—it's based on a true story. The other surprise is that this quintessential goody-goody musical is one of the only nun movies to acknowledge that not everyone is cut out to join a convent.

Sister Act (1992, U.S., 100 mins.) Dir: Emile Ardolino; Cast: Whoopi Goldberg, Maggie Smith, Harvey Keitel, Bill Nunn, Kathy Najimy, Wendy Makkena, Mary Wickes.

Lounge singer Whoopi Goldberg enters a convent under the witness protection program. *The Singing Nun* for the nineties, this one is surprising for saying that everyone *is* cut out to join an order. Stolen by Kathy Najimy, who plays a sheepish nun. Will we actually start hearing "I Will Follow Him" in church?

The Singing Nun (1966, U.S., 98 mins.) Dir: Henry Koster; Cast: Debbie Reynolds, Greer Garson, Ricardo Montalban, Chad Everett, Agnes Moorehead.

A mid-sixties attempt to pass off guitar-strumming Debbie Reynolds as a "cool" nun who cuts hit records and sings "Dominique" to Congolese natives. Certain to bring back memories of mumbling verse after dirgelike verse of "Kumbaya" at some folk mass in your youth.

The Bells of St. Mary's (1945, U.S., 126 mins.) Dir: Leo McCarey; Cast: Bing Crosby, Ingrid Bergman, William Gargan, Henry Travers, Ruth Donnelly.

The sequel to *Going My Way*. Father Bing moves on to a new parish that lacks money, but boasts maybe the best-looking nun to ever finger a rosary—Ingrid Bergman. The woman could really wear a habit. Fifty years later, the saccharine plot and dialogue can't really disguise a chemistry between Crosby and Bergman that does not seem wholly oriented to a mutual search for the Mystical Being.

The Nun's Story (1959, U.S., 149 mins.) Dir: Fred Zinnemann; Cast: Audrey Hepburn, Peter Finch, Edith Evans, Peggy Ashcroft, Dean Jagger, Colleen Dewhurst.

Audrey Hepburn stars in this *Gone With the Wind* of nun movies, an epic tale of the physical and spiritual travails of a young Belgian nurse who becomes a missionary nun in hopes of ministering to the sick of the Congo. The film takes itself very seriously and shows in great detail the process of entering the convent. Big points for managing to question aspects of the sisterhood while still maintaining respect for it.

The Trouble With Angels (1966, U.S., 112 mins.) Dir: Ida Lupino; Cast: Rosalind Russell, Hayley Mills, June Harding, Gypsy Rose Lee.

Mother Superior Rosalind Russell tries to keep incorrigible students Hayley Mills and June Harding in line at her convent school. Russell makes a great nun; the perfect blend of imperious, idiosyncratic, asexual, scary, and, ultimately, kind. The film has a charming silliness and naïveté—sort of a *Gidget* feel. Mary Wickes dons the habit and does it again later for *Sister Act*.

Agnes of God (1985, U.S., 99 mins.) Dir: Norman Jewison; Cast: Jane Fonda, Anne Bancroft, Meg Tilly.

Psychiatrist Jane Fonda investigates an apparent infanticide by a young nun who became pregnant while cloistered. Adapted from the play, it retains the kind of overheated drama and seriousness that works on stage but numbs us on screen. It is interesting, though, for its exploration of the ecstatic—and erotic—mysticism found throughout history in women's orders.

Lilies of the Field (1963, U.S., 93 mins., b/w) Dir: Ralph Nelson; Cast: Sidney Poitier, Lilia Skala, Lisa Mann, Isa Crino, Stanley Adams.

Sidney Poitier builds a chapel for an order of German nuns. Not a rip-roaring adventure by any means, but Poitier won an Oscar for his role and it's a sweet, if slow, film.

Heaven Knows, Mr. Allison (1957, U.S., 107 mins.) Dir: John Huston; Cast: Deborah Kerr, Robert Mitchum.

Mitchum is a marine, Kerr is a nun, and together they fight the Japanese overrunning the Pacific island they're stranded on. Mitchum, Kerr, John Huston—what more do you want? Semifinalist for Best Nun Movie.

Black Narcissus (1947, Great Britain, 99 mins.) Dirs: Michael Powell, Emeric

Pressburger; Cast: Deborah Kerr, Flora Robson, David Farrar, Sabu, Jean Simmons, Kathleen Byron.

An intense drama based on Rumer Godden's novel about a group of nuns establishing a mission in the Himalayas. A beautiful film, harrowing at times. Absolutely the Best Nun Movie ever and a classic on its own terms. Deborah Kerr in her first, and best, outing as a sister.

THE CHOSEN PEOPLE

The Easter/Passover list should take care of all your biblical epic needs and the Holocaust is a subject in itself, so this list is about Jews in the New World and where they came from. What's not to like about these 10 films?

Yentl (1983, U.S., 134 mins.) Dir: Barbra Streisand; Cast: Barbra Streisand, Mandy Patinkin, Amy Irving, Nehemiah Persoff.

You'd be safe with any film starring Barbra Streisand here, but the combination of her singing 12 songs and an I. B. Singer story of a young woman passing herself as a yeshiva boy in Eastern Europe manages to fulfill every possible criteria for inclusion in this list. And remember—it's StreiSAND.

Fiddler on the Roof (1971, U.S., 180 mins.) Dir: Norman Jewison; Cast: Topol, Molly Picon, Norma Crane, Leonard Frey.

Classic musical based on Sholom Aleichem's stories of 19th-century shtetl life. How can you not like a musical where you know all the words to every song? It's second only because Streisand's not in it, but on the other hand, no one ever sings a number from *Yentl* at a wedding. Too bad Topol and not Zero Mostel (who created the role on Broadway) was cast as Tevye.

Hester Street (1975, U.S., 90 mins., b/w) Dir: Joan Micklin Silver; Cast: Carol Kane, Steven Keats, Doris Roberts, Mel Howard.

A simple, touching tale of immigrant Carol Kane's adjustment to life on New York's Lower East Side around the turn of the century. Valuable for its view of early 20th-century Jewish life and the cultural shock almost all immigrants surely experienced when they first encountered America.

The Apprenticeship of Duddy Kravitz (1974, Canada, 121 mins.) Dir: Ted Kotcheff; Cast: Richard Dreyfuss, Randy Quaid, Jack Warden, Denholm Elliott, Joseph Wiseman, Micheline Lanctot.

Seriocomic tale of a Jewish kid from Montreal who'll do anything to get where he wants to go. Pre-*Jaws* Dreyfuss is great in this adaptation of Mordecai Richler's novel.

Gentleman's Agreement (1947, U.S., 118 mins., b/w) Dir: Elia Kazan; Cast: Gregory Peck, Dorothy McGuire, John Garfield, Anne Revere, Celeste Holm.

Writer Gregory Peck pretends to be Jewish in order to uncover widespread anti-Semitism. Moss Hart wrote the screenplay and Elia Kazan directed. Hard-hitting and controversial in its day, it remains a strong reminder of the way things were, and sometimes still are, for Jews in America.

Enemies: A Love Story (1989, U.S., 118 mins.) Dir: Paul Mazursky; Cast: Ron Silver, Anjelica Huston, Lena Olin, Margaret Sophie Stein, Alan King, Judith Malina, Paul Mazursky.

Another adaptation of a Singer story, this time about the romantic involvements of a Jewish refugee in post-World War II New York. Outstanding performances and a sensitive script capture the feel of Singer's gentle, rich, and often surprising work.

Goodbye, Columbus (1969, U.S., 105 mins.) Dir: Larry Peerce; Cast: Richard Benjamin, Ali MacGraw, Jack Klugman, Nan Martin, Michael Meyers.

Benjamin and MacGraw made their film debuts in this adaptation of Philip Roth's story about nouveau riche suburban Jews in the sixties. You probably know all the words to all the songs on the soundtrack, too.

Bye Bye Braverman (1968, U.S., 94 mins.) Dir: Sidney Lumet; Cast: George Segal, Jack Warden, Alan King, Godfrey Cambridge.
∎
Maybe the strangest road movie ever. Four middle-aged Jewish men encounter adventure of a sort peculiar to New York when they drive to the Bronx for the funeral of a friend. Not for everyone, but definitely your baby if you like old Jewish guy humor.

Dirty Dancing (1987, U.S., 97 mins.) Dir: Emile Ardolino; Cast: Patrick Swayze, Jennifer Grey, Jerry Orbach, Cynthia Rhodes.

For many, this was what summer was about—taking the family up to the Catskills for food, healthy outdoor activities, food, comedians, and food. Here, nerdy guest Jennifer Grey falls for hunky dance instructor Swayze, who teaches her a lot more than the hora. Yeah, it's dreck, but it's good dreck.

The Plot Against Harry (1989, U.S., 81 mins., b/w) Dir: Michael Roemer; Cast: Martin Priest, Ben Lang, Maxine Woods, Henry Nemo.

A great little comedy about a low-level Jewish gangster who gets out of prison to find his world changed. Though he shot the film in 1969 in New York using among his players members of the Temple Emanu El Theater Club, Roemer managed to catch the sly details and nuances that one would expect from a nostalgic look back at the period. Its contemporary feel might explain

why it wasn't released until 1989. A must.

THE AFTERLIFE

What happens after we die? Will it be St. Peter and the Pearly Gates? The River Styx? A big white light with dead Aunt Wanda waiting on the other side? Philosophers have been pondering this question for thousands of years, and lucky for us Hollywood has considered it too.

Jacob's Ladder (1990, U.S., 115 mins.) Dir: Adrian Lyne; Cast: Tim Robbins, Elizabeth Peña, Danny Aiello, Matt Craven.

Extremely disturbing tale of a Vietnam vet having hallucinations about life and death. The script is legendary for having been the best story that for years no one wanted to produce. Once you see the last minute of the film you'll understand why.

All of Me (1984, U.S., 93 mins.) Dir: Carl Reiner; Cast: Steve Martin, Lily Tomlin, Victoria Tennant, Richard Libertini.

Romantic comedy about a lawyer whose body is inhabited by the soul of a deceased, and very cranky, heiress. A perfect role for Steve Martin that allows him to exploit his great talent for physical comedy. The film balances sweet and silly, and knows its limits like the very best of the Ealing Studios comedies.

Stairway to Heaven (aka: *A Matter of Life and Death,* 1946, Great Britain, 104 mins.) Dirs: Michael Powell, Emeric Pressburger; Cast: David Niven, Roger Livesey, Kim Hunter, Raymond Massey, Robert Coote, Marius Goring.
∎
World War II flyer Niven escapes death and then believes that heaven is putting him on trial to defend his right to live. If you choose one film on the list

to watch, make it this one. Despite the dated Anglo-American conflict and its effect on the climax, it's a magical movie.

Defending Your Life (1991, U.S., 110 mins.) Dir: Albert Brooks; Cast: Albert Brooks, Meryl Streep, Rip Torn, Lee Grant, Buck Henry, Shirley MacLaine.

Brooks dies in a car crash and finds the love of his afterlife in Judgment City. Two of Brooks's strengths as a filmmaker come out here. First, he asks simple questions about big issues that make us think more than any pretentious art film does. Second, his characters seem to be schmucks until we realize that they're uncomfortably like us. His vision of the afterlife as a kind of heavenly mall run by a divine corporation is certainly more believable than clouds and harps.

A Guy Named Joe (1943, U.S., 118 mins., b/w) Dir: Victor Fleming; Cast: Spencer Tracy, Irene Dunne, Van Johnson, Ward Bond, James Gleason, Lionel Barrymore, Esther Williams.

If you're tempted to pick up Steven Spielberg's *Always,* stop now and get the film it was based on. Tracy stars as a dead World War II flyer who comes back to help his widow's new suitor. Mind you, this isn't the finest film ever made either, but who would you rather watch for two hours, Spencer Tracy or Richard Dreyfuss?

Truly, Madly, Deeply (1990, Great Britain, 107 mins.) Dir: Anthony Minghella; Cast: Juliet Stevenson, Alan Rickman, Bill Paterson, Michael Maloney.

When husband Rickman dies, Juliet Stevenson takes it so badly that Rickman comes back from the dead to console her. Quite sweet in its way, sort of an Anglo *Doña Flor,* but no one has ever cried as much on film as Stevenson does here.

Here Comes Mr. Jordan (1941, U.S., 93 mins.) Dir: Alexander Hall; Cast: Robert Montgomery, Claude Rains, Evelyn Keyes, Rita Johnson, James Gleason, Edward Everett Horton.

Boxer Montgomery dies before his time and returns to life in a new body. Warren Beatty later remade this classic as *Heaven Can Wait* (1978). Since the Montgomery versus Beatty argument won't convince anyone, choose this one because the screenplay won an Oscar and it's an example of Hollywood at its best.

Flatliners (1990, U.S., 111 mins.) Dir: Joel Schumacher; Cast: Kiefer Sutherland, Julia Roberts, Kevin Bacon, William Baldwin, Oliver Platt.

A slick studio film about a group of med students who kill, and then resuscitate, each other so they can experience death. You'll start exercising and cutting down on unsaturated fats after seeing this, or maybe you'll consider vampirism. A particularly depressing view of the afterlife, unleavened by hope, yet it's well made, so you'll keep watching even after you wish you hadn't.

Heaven Can Wait (1943, U.S., 112 mins.) Dir: Ernst Lubitsch; Cast: Gene Tierney, Don Ameche, Charles Coburn.

Let's end on a happy note. Lubitsch directed this comedy starring Don Ameche as a dead man recounting his many "sins" so he can get into Hell. May death be this witty, charming, and warm.

HISTORY

THE WAY
WE WERE

HAIL CAESAR

The Romans had too much lead in their water and we have TV. There may be other similarities between our culture and Ancient Rome's, but that one seems the most salient. Watch these films and see the glory that was Rome.

Ben-Hur (1959, U.S., 217 mins.) Dir: William Wyler; Cast: Charlton Heston, Stephen Boyd, Haya Harareet, Hugh Griffith, Martha Scott, Jack Hawkins.

The chariot race is one of the all-time best pieces of movie-making ever. Wyler stays pretty close to the original novel by General Lew Wallace and we get to see aspects of the Empire that are overlooked in many other films, like the great galley battle.

Spartacus (1960, U.S., 196 mins.) Dir: Stanley Kubrick; Cast: Kirk Douglas, Jean Simmons, Laurence Olivier, Tony Curtis, Charles Laughton, Peter Ustinov, John Gavin, Nina Foch.

Enormous epic by Kubrick based on the life of a gladiator who led a slave rebellion in the first century B.C. Though most of the films on this list have a gladiator scene, this is the only one that takes a hard look at what it must have been like to be forced to fight in public contests, usually to the death. Supporting performances are strong. Be sure you see the letterboxed director's cut.

Julius Caesar (1953, U.S., 120 mins., b/w) Dir: Joseph L. Mankiewicz; Cast: John Gielgud, Marlon Brando, James Mason, Deborah Kerr, Greer Garson, Edmond O'Brien, Louis Calhern.

Despite all the costumes, money, and stars, Hollywood has rarely examined the Roman Empire with any intelligence. Leave it to Shakespeare to add some real meat. Whatever this straightforward and powerful telling of the story of Caesar's murder lacks in visual impact, it makes up in character and intrigue.

Roman Scandals (1933, U.S., 92 mins., b/w) Dir: Frank Tuttle; Cast: Eddie Cantor, Ruth Etting, David Manners, Edward Arnold, Gloria Stuart, Alan Mowbray.

In a riff on *A Connecticut Yankee in King Arthur's Court,* Eddie Cantor dreams that he is back in a Rome full of song and dance numbers and Busby Berkeley choreography. Certainly not the film you want to watch for historical insight, but light relief from tromping legions and plaster Forums. The story was co-written by George S. Kaufman, who wrote some of the Marx Brothers' best films.

The Fall of the Roman Empire (1964, U.S., 188 mins.) Dir: Anthony Mann; Cast: Stephen Boyd, Alec Guinness, Christopher Plummer, Sophia Loren, James Mason, Omar Sharif.

Massive film with probably the best faux-Rome sets and a top-notch cast. It sounds intelligent, the acting is good, it looks authentic; unfortunately it bears little historical resemblance to the actual facts of the Empire's decline. If niggling details like that don't bother you, go to it.

The Robe (1953, U.S., 135 mins.) Dir: Henry Koster; Cast: Richard Burton, Jean Simmons, Victor Mature, Michael Rennie, Richard Boone.

Sweeping tale of the Roman tribune, played by Burton, who won Christ's robe at the Crucifixion. A good look at everyday life in the Empire. The sequel, *Demetrius and the Gladiator,* follows Burton's slave, Victor Mature, as he is sucked into the royal household and forced to become a gladiator. Both are satisfying entertainment on the Roman Empire level if you haven't burnt out on them from a thousand Easter viewings.

Fellini Satyricon (1969, Italy-France, 120 mins.) Dir: Federico Fellini; Cast: Martin Potter, Hiram Keller, Capucine, Donyale Luna, Lucia Bose, Gordon Mitchell, Alain Cuny.

Not your standard view of Ancient Rome. Fellini loosely, and we mean loosely, adapted Petronius's novel about the adventures, erotic and otherwise, of a young poet to create one strange film. A triumph of style over substance, since there is no discernible substance here, just a series of fascinating, and by turns beautiful and disturbing, images. For special tastes.

The Last Days of Pompeii (1935, U.S., 100 mins., b/w) Dir: Ernest B. Schoedsack; Cast: Preston Foster, Basil Rathbone, Alan Hale, Dorothy Wilson.

An old chestnut, but some awfully good special effects of Pompeii being buried by volcanic ash from erupting Mt.Vesuvius, done by the people who did the effects for *King Kong.* Prior to the grand finale, there's a lot of solid gladiator action. Don't confuse this with the Steve Reeves version, unless, of course, you have a thing for Steve Reeves.

Quo Vadis? (1951, U.S., 171 mins.) Dir: Mervyn LeRoy; Cast: Robert Taylor, Deborah Kerr, Leo Genn, Peter Ustinov.

Another of the Eastertime spectacles that works as Roman history the rest of the year. Here, a Roman noble falls in love with a Christian woman, and you know what happens to Christian women in ancient Rome. A much earlier film, *Sign of the Cross,* has basically the same plot but a considerably different ending. Both films boast great Neros: *Sign of the Cross* (1932) has Charles Laughton and this one has

Peter Ustinov. The earlier version also has Fredric March and better gladiator stuff. Unfortunately, you can't get it on video yet, so stick with *Quo Vadis?* for now.

A Funny Thing Happened on the Way to the Forum (1966, U.S., 99 mins.) Dir: Richard Lester; Cast: Zero Mostel, Phil Silvers, Jack Gilford, Michael Crawford, Michael Hordern, Buster Keaton.

Screen version of Stephen Sondheim's musical about slave Mostel trying to scheme his way to freedom by advancing the amorous plots of his master's son. Directed by Richard Lester, who did the Beatles's movies, this may not be history, but you can't pass up watching Zero Mostel, Buster Keaton, and Jack Gilford on one screen.

■

NOTE: Don't forget *The Epic That Never Was,* the doc about Josef von Sternberg's aborted version of *I, Claudius,* or the *I, Claudius* BBC series based on Robert Graves's masterpiece. It's low on gladiators but high on everything else.

KNIGHTS & CASTLES

Le Morte d'Arthur and all those other great tales of the Middle Ages can strike the adult mind as childish, but that's mostly because we loved them so much when we were children. Following are some reminders that chivalry is not dead.

Ivanhoe (1953, U.S., 106 mins.) Dir: Richard Thorpe; Cast: Robert Taylor, Elizabeth Taylor, George Sanders, Joan Fontaine, Finlay Currie, Felix Aylmer, Guy Rolfe, Basil Sydney, Sebastian Cabot.

Start here, because Walter Scott was largely responsible for the outlandish "thee" and "thou" image we have of the

Middle Ages. Ivanhoe, cast out by his father, wins back the old man's respect—and the love of both Joan Fontaine and Liz Taylor as he battles the Norman occupiers of early England. OK jousting, great costumes for Liz, lots of color.

El Cid (1961, U.S., 184 mins.) Dir: Anthony Mann; Cast: Charlton Heston, Sophia Loren, Raf Vallone, Hurd Hatfield.

Heston stars as the legendary Spanish knight who battled the Moors in the 11th century. Surprisingly smart and, considering its length, well-paced. The jousting scene is by far the best and most realistic you'll see.

The Adventures of Robin Hood (1938, U.S., 106 mins.) Dirs: William Keighley, Michael Curtiz; Cast: Errol Flynn, Olivia de Havilland, Basil Rathbone, Claude Rains.

Kevin Costner's more recent effort may be more historically accurate with all its dark castles and a rather shabby group of Merry Men, but who wants accuracy with one of the best legends of all time? This version is a tremendous storybook outing, probably best accompanied by a tall glass of cold milk and some cookies.

Prince Valiant (1954, U.S., 100 mins.) Dir: Henry Hathaway; Cast: James Mason, Janet Leigh, Robert Wagner, Debra Paget, Sterling Hayden.

He of the terrible haircut romps about the Middle Ages, battling evil knights and calling on King Arthur to help him out of a jam involving his exiled father. Be honest, did you secretly read "Prince Valiant" when you picked up the comics, or did you go right to "Gasoline Alley" and "Peanuts"? Thought so.

Knights of the Round Table (1954, U.S., 115 mins.) Dir: Richard Thorpe; Cast:

Robert Taylor, Ava Gardner, Mel Ferrer, Stanley Baker, Felix Aylmer.

Clearly the challenge here was to see how many of the 64 Crayola colors could be used and director Thorpe did well, getting as far as cornflower and burnt sienna. The acting isn't all that important, nor is the Arthur-Guinevere-Lancelot plot; they're really just excuses for the sets.

Sword of Lancelot (1963, Great Britain, 116 mins.) Dir: Cornel Wilde; Cast: Cornel Wilde, Jean Wallace, Brian Aherne.

A more straightforward approach to Camelot, with solid castle scenery, lots of clanking swords, and a childlike reverence for all things Arthurian. Either this film or Disney's animated *The Sword in the Stone* would be good for the young lords and ladies of the household.

Excalibur (1981, U.S., 140 mins.) Dir: John Boorman; Cast: Nigel Terry, Helen Mirren, Nicol Williamson, Nicholas Clay, Cherie Lunghi, Paul Geoffrey.

Though this is the most faithful retelling of King Arthur's story, its sex and violence rule it out for the kids. Oddly enough, it's also somewhat dated by the quasi-Frank Franzetta look. Still, a must if you're interested in Arthur. Nicol Williamson's slightly off-his-bean Merlin and Helen Mirren as Morgan steal the show, and it's quite a show.

Camelot (1967, U.S., 179 mins.) Dir: Joshua Logan; Cast: Richard Harris, Vanessa Redgrave, David Hemmings, Franco Nero.

Richard Harris and some wonderful tunes are the main reasons to see this screen version of the popular Broadway musical about Arthur and his queen with wandering eyes. It is sadly evident, though, that Harris's singing skills are not on the same level as his abilities as an actor, and you may find yourself in the unusual position of wishing that it were Robert Goulet you were watching as Arthur and not one of the world's greatest thespians.

A Connecticut Yankee in King Arthur's Court (1949, U.S., 107 mins.) Dir: Tay Garnett; Cast: Bing Crosby, Rhonda Fleming, Cedric Hardwicke, William Bendix.

Bing ba-ba-bums his way around Camelot in this cleaned-up, musical retelling of Mark Twain's classic novel about a late-19th-century American transported back to Arthur's England. William Bendix, as usual, makes his character someone to pity rather than comic relief and we get none of Twain's realism or social commentary. Given all that, it's still entertaining and colorful.

Monty Python and the Holy Grail (1975, Great Britain, 89 mins.) Dirs: Terry Gilliam, Terry Jones; Cast: John Cleese, Graham Chapman, Terry Gilliam, Eric Idle, Terry Jones.

A classic comedy about Arthur and his Round Table that takes nothing at all seriously. The fact is, this film is more to the spirit of Twain than the Crosby effort. As in Twain's book, the populace is not uninformed; they are out and out stupid. Death is quick, ever-present, and not regretted and Camelot probably smells bad. It is also hysterically funny.

THE BRITISH RAJ

History may have given us greater empires, but never one as laden with lore and color as the British Raj. The combination of English power and propriety with the exuberant masala of Indian life created a love-hate juxtaposition of worlds that still exists. Given the settings, the florid colors, the drama, and tensions of an empire unable to let go of its most beloved colony, it's no surprise that some wonderful films have been made about the period.

Kim (1950, U.S., 113 mins.) Dir: Victor Saville; Cast: Errol Flynn, Dean Stockwell, Paul Lukas, Robert Douglas, Thomas Gomez.

Generations of teachers have been passing off Rudyard Kipling's novel about a boy entering the Great Game as a children's adventure and this movie has been put in the same pigeonhole. Well, they're wrong. Just because something is supremely entertaining and full of action doesn't mean it's only for kids.

Clive of India (1935, U.S., 90 mins., b/w) Dir: Richard Boleslawski; Cast: Ronald Colman, Loretta Young, Cesar Romero, C. Aubrey Smith, Francis Lister, Colin Clive, Leo G. Carroll.
∎
Entertaining biography of the man who ensured British supremacy in India, Robert Clive. Sturdy and engaging, with a heck of a battle scene matching the Brits against Tippoo Sultan's elephant troops.

Gunga Din (1939, U.S., 117 mins., b/w) Dir: George Stevens; Cast: Cary Grant, Douglas Fairbanks, Jr., Victor McLaglen, Sam Jaffe, Eduardo Ciannelli, Montagu Love, Robert Coote, Abner Biberman, Joan Fontaine.

The English did not have a monopoly on Raj films; in fact most of the great ones are either by the Korda brothers or, like this one, by Hollywood. All stops were pulled for this exciting adventure that follows three pals and their trusty water bearer, fighting for God and Queen versus those heathen Indians. As you may have noticed by now, enjoying these films depends greatly on your ability to shelve all notions of political correctness for about two hours. By the way, it's actually California you're watching, not India.

The Lives of a Bengal Lancer (1935, U.S., 109 mins.) Dir: Henry Hathaway; Cast: Gary Cooper, Franchot Tone, Richard Cromwell, Sir Guy Standing, C. Aubrey Smith, Kathleen Burke.

Another great Hollywood Raj film about three soldiers fighting for God and Queen—you get the picture. Let's face it, the point of most of these is action in exotic settings. You'll get your share of that here, as well as some realistic period flavor.

Wee Willie Winkie (1937, U.S., 75 mins., b/w) Dir: John Ford; Cast: Shirley Temple, Victor McLaglen, June Lang, Cesar Romero.

Shirley Temple stars in another film loosely based, to say the least, on a Kipling story, this one about a little girl who, with her widowed mother, goes to stay with her grandfather the colonel. Worth trying, because if Shirley isn't your idea of entertainment, John Ford probably is.

Drum (1976, U.S., 110 mins.) Dir: Steve Carver; Cast: Warren Oates, Ken Norton, Isela Vega, Pam Grier.

This tale of an Indian prince who helps the English in their battles with tribal chieftains has all the color and excitement of the best Raj films, but its supremely patronizing attitude to everyone who is not English does grate after a while.

The Man Who Would Be King (1975, U.S., 127 mins.) Dir: John Huston; Cast: Michael Caine, Sean Connery, Christopher Plummer.

A movie you can watch over and over again. Buddies Caine and Connery go to Kafiristan to make their fortunes by conquering the fragmented tribes of the area and establishing themselves as rulers. Grand adventure of a sort rarely attempted in these post-Indiana Jones days when "adventure" connotes comic-book exploits. Plus, Huston has the grace to allow the narrative voice of Kipling to finally narrate one of his own stories.

A Passage to India (1984, Great Britain, 163 mins.) Dir: David Lean; Cast: Peggy Ashcroft, Judy Davis, Victor Banerjee, Alec Guinness.

Forster's greatest novel and certainly the greatest to come out of Anglo-India, *A Passage to India,* seems ideal for David Lean with its clash of cultures, rich characters, and colorful settings. Maybe Lean was daunted by the book, but for some reason it feels as though he was afraid to put his own stamp on it. The film fails to express the overwhelming power of India and the tangled relationships between Forster's characters as well as one would expect from Lean. Understand, bad Lean is better than good almost anyone else, but it's too bad Merchant-Ivory didn't get to do this one.

Heat and Dust (1983, Great Britain, 130 mins.) Dir: James Ivory; Cast: Julie Christie, Christopher Cazenove, Sashi Kapoor, Greta Scacchi.

Ruth Prawer Jhabvala wrote the script, based on her own novel, about two generations of Englishwomen and their relationships, sexual and otherwise, with the people of India. For another view of the Raj in its later days, see the fine version of Paul Scott's *Staying On* starring Trevor Howard.

The Four Feathers (1939, Great Britain, 115 mins., originally 140 mins.) Dir: Zoltan Korda; Cast: Ralph Richardson, John Clements, June Duprez, C. Aubrey Smith.

All right, it takes place in the Sudan, but it belongs here. A brilliant film about a man raised in a military family who rejects the martial life, but then must redeem himself when accused of cowardice. One of the best of the Korda films, with the rich colors and production style we are accustomed to from them. A final tip of the topi to C. Aubrey Smith, who is in half of the movies on this list, including this one. Long may his handlebar moustache grow!

THE CIVIL WAR

The fact that many still hail *Gone With the Wind* as a great movie and one of America's favorites is extremely disturbing. Aside from the unashamed racism blithely transposed onto film from the book, the film has helped perpetuate a myth of the Old South with little basis in reality. Margaret Mitchell's novel was a product of nostalgia for an ideal land conjured up by southern apologists in the 1890s. Say all you want about soap opera and romance; if you think that was Mitchell's point in writing her book, you're quite a sucker for propaganda.

The Horse Soldiers (1959, U.S., 119 mins.) Dir: John Ford; Cast: John Wayne, William Holden, Constance Towers, Althea Gibson, Hoot Gibson.

The Civil War would seem like a natural place for John Ford to look for material, but this story of a Federal raiding party deep in Rebel territory is his only film set during the War Between the States. While not prime Ford, there are some great moments between Wayne and Holden, and Ford's attention to detail and understanding of the common soldier hint at what he could have done on the war if he had chosen to.

Friendly Persuasion (1956, U.S., 139 mins.) Dir: William Wyler; Cast: Gary Cooper, Dorothy McGuire, Tony Perkins, Marjorie Main.

An Indiana Quaker family led by Cooper confronts the changes wrought on its members by time, modernity, and the Civil War. Much more amusing and moving than you might think, though Anthony Perkins appears to be in another, more serious movie at times. Not the film you want if you're looking for big battle scenes, but a nice look at the period.

The General (1927, U.S., 74 mins., b/w) Dir: Buster Keaton; Cast: Buster Keaton, Marion Mack.

One of Keaton's best films, about a southern engineer kept out of the service who becomes a hero by thwarting a group of Federal raiders trying to hijack his train. Red Skelton remade it as *A Southern Yankee* in 1948, but definitely see this one first.

Glory (1989, U.S., 122 mins.) Dir: Edward Zwick; Cast: Matthew Broderick, Denzel Washington, Morgan Freeman, Cary Elwes, Jihmi Kennedy, Andre Braugher, Cliff DeYoung.

A tremendous film about an all-black regiment and its complex white colonel. Great performances, realism, and an avoidance of any excessive piety about its themes help make this one of the best movies about the Civil War.

The Red Badge of Courage (1951, U.S., 69 mins., b/w) Dir: John Huston; Cast: Audie Murphy, Bill Mauldin, Douglas Dick, Royal Dano, John Dierkes.

The other truly great film about the Civil War. John Huston does a fine job adapting Stephen Crane's novel and gives us very credible views of cowardice and the horrors of battle.

Dark Command (1940, U.S., 94 mins.) Dir: Raoul Walsh; Cast: John Wayne, Claire Trevor, Walter Pidgeon, Roy Rogers.

Interesting film based on the murderous raider Quantrill and his reign of terror in the Kansas territory. The movie doesn't hold to the actual facts of the story, but Pidgeon and Wayne are good in the leads and it's a valuable look at a little-known theater of the war.

Shenandoah (1965, U.S., 105 mins., b/w) Dir: Andrew McLaglen; Cast: James Stewart, Glenn Corbett, Doug McClure, Katharine Ross.

Virginia planter Stewart, a widower with several children, tries not to take sides in the war, but as his family is drawn into the conflict, so is he. One of the few evenhanded takes on the war, which allows it to accurately portray the pain the war inflicted on everyone involved.

Johnny Shiloh (1963, U.S./MTV, 90 mins.) Dir: James Neilson; Cast: Kevin Corcoran, Brian Keith, Eddie Hodges, Darryl Hickman, Regis Toomey.

Sort of a Civil War *Johnny Tremain,* loosely based on the story of one of the war's youngest combatants. Originally two episodes on the television show *The Wonderful World of Disney* and still a good treatment of the war for younger viewers.

The Birth of a Nation (1915, U.S., 157 mins., b/w) Dir: D. W. Griffith; Cast: Lillian Gish, Henry B. Walthall, Mae Marsh.

One of the most controversial films of all time. When, before you see it, you hear over and over how prejudiced this film is, it's hard to believe that it could actually be that repellent. It is. Yes, Griffith may have invented the grammar of film here and built some extremely entertaining and moving scenes, but it's difficult to watch them without asking what they were in service to. While it's a remarkable achievement in filmmaking terms, it's an achievement that deserves a very big asterisk after it.

Gettysburg (1993, U.S., 254 mins.) Dir: Ronald F. Maxwell; Cast: Martin Sheen,

Jeff Daniels, Tom Berenger, Sam Elliott, Stephen Lang, Richard Jordan.

Based on Michael Shaara's Pulitzer Prize-winning novel *The Killer Angels,* this epic film focuses on the fulcrum battle of the Civil War. What sets it apart is the involvement of over 5,000 reenacters, whose presence and knowledge lend it a realism that goes all the way down to the smallest role. Look for Ted Turner himself in a cameo. (True to form, he plays a Rebel.)

Sherman's March (1986, U.S., 155 mins.) Dir: Ross McElwee.

Not a film for hard-core Civil War buffs and battlefield visitors. Documentary filmmaker McElwee gets a grant for a film about Sherman's march through Georgia, but what he ends up making is a meditation about southern women and his relationships with them. A very funny and moving documentary that subtly makes some important points about life, love, and the South.

COWPERSONS & INDIGENOUS PEOPLES

"When the legend becomes the fact, print the legend." Once upon a time in the western, that adage, taken from John Ford's *The Man Who Shot Liberty Valance*, was the rule of thumb. Western movies like *Stagecoach*, *Red River*, and *Shane* all stressed the mythic aspects of America's past. But with the coming of political correctness, filmmakers stopped resting on the laurels of legend and started looking for ways to uncover the facts, to expose the racial prejudice and the obsession with manifest destiny that led to the systematic annihilation of Native Americans, and to take a more honest look at the significant role women played—and the oppression they faced—in the development of the West. These are the best of the

revisionist westerns, the films that debunk the myths. Our title for this list may be flip, but the films themselves are deadly serious in their intent to set the record straight.

Cheyenne Autumn (1964, U.S., 145 mins.) Dir: John Ford; Cast: Richard Widmark, Carroll Baker, Karl Malden, Dolores Del Rio, Sal Mineo, Edward G. Robinson.

While numerous John Ford westerns feature sympathetic portrayals of Native Americans, the Indians are, as a whole, misguided savages hell-bent on war making. In this, his last western, Ford attempts to atone—the Cheyenne, exiled from their Oklahoma reservation in 1878, are not the villains here, the U.S. government is. "I've killed more Indians than Custer, Beecher, and Chivington put together," Ford said. "I wanted to show their point of view for a change." Visually gorgeous and sympathetic to its subject, the film is more an act of conscience than good movie-making. Interesting on many fronts, but tedious.

Little Big Man (1970, U.S., 147 mins.) Dir: Arthur Penn; Cast: Dustin Hoffman, Faye Dunaway, Richard Mulligan, Chief Dan George.

Penn, working from a book by Thomas Berger, blends outrageous comedy, serious tragedy, and revisionist history to tell the life story of 121-year-old Jack Crabbe (Hoffman), an adopted Indian who claims to have survived Custer's last stand. The film exposes the traditional Hollywood view of the West as part of a massive cultural cover-up that attempted to wash over a hundred years of human rights violations. Exceptionally ambitious and much of it hits home.

Dances With Wolves (1990, U.S., 190 mins.) Dir: Kevin Costner; Cast: Kevin Costner, Mary McDonnell, Graham Greene.

Serious, lyrical account of the plight of Native Americans after the Civil War as seen through the eyes of a renegade soldier who finds a new life among the Sioux. Winner of numerous Academy Awards, it brought a revised, more honest version of the way it was to a large audience. For this, the film deserves much praise. And while we know that the sight of Kevin Costner do-si-do-ing with a wolf around a glowing fire makes half of America moist, we think he's a big, dumb, ineffectual stiff on the screen—a cactus has more emotional range. All in all, a worthy effort, but less than meets the eye.

Buffalo Bill and the Indians, or Sitting Bull's History Lesson (1976, U.S., 125 mins.) Dir: Robert Altman; Cast: Paul Newman, Joel Grey, Shelley Duvall, Geraldine Chaplin, Burt Lancaster, Kevin McCarthy, Harvey Keitel.

Altman's view of the Old West is just what it claims to be—a history lesson—revisionist history whose subject is, more than anything else, the historical process. Newman is Buffalo Bill Cody in this angry satire that concerns itself not with how the West was won, but with how the myths were made. When Joel Grey as the producer of Buffalo Bill's Wild West Show says "I'm going to Codyfy the world," he's elucidating the pop-culture approach to history: manufacture a myth, sell it as truth, and the gullible public will buy it.

The Left-Handed Gun (1958, U.S., 102 mins., b/w) Dir: Arthur Penn; Cast: Paul Newman, John Dehner, Hurd Hatfield.

The story of Billy the Kid is presented as a stylized, exaggerated psychological inquiry into the nature of violence—it's about an immature, unbalanced boy, trapped by his own mythology. Newman's Billy is an angry, brooding, misunderstood adolescent, a child of the fifties rather than the Old West—a rebel with no discernible cause. The actor is using "the Method" to get at the madness. Director Penn and screenwriter Leslie Stevens, working from a play by Gore Vidal, are much more interested in dismantling the myth than in perpetuating it.

The Missouri Breaks (1976, U.S., 126 mins.) Dir: Arthur Penn; Cast: Marlon Brando, Jack Nicholson, Harry Dean Stanton, Kathleen Lloyd.

Jack is a horse thief, Marlon a fat hired gun, in what amounts to an anti-western set in 1880s Montana. Original reviews were beyond negative—critics destroyed it. So we'll step out on a limb here and claim that even though director Penn had to kowtow to Brando's whims, and Thomas McGuane's script was bent beyond recognition, the result is strangely satisfying. Brando takes enormous risks, making his character an actor who slips in and out of various skins, playing head games with his adversaries—it's almost as if he'd rather blow Nicholson's mind than blow him away. Definitely worth a look.

Doc (1971, U.S., 122 mins.) Dir: Frank Perry; Cast: Stacy Keach, Faye Dunaway, Harris Yulin.
■
The classic American view of the gunfight at the OK Corral comes from John Ford's *My Darling Clementine:* Wyatt Earp and Doc Holliday were heroes, plain and simple; the Clantons were as bad as bad can be. *Doc* debunks the myth. Liberal journalist Pete Hamill's script paints Holliday (Keach) and Earp (Yulin) as men of questionable character, representatives of a corrupt social system; the Clantons are seen as virtual victims. Well-made, well-acted, but sour tasting. More recent re-tellings of the saga include *Tombstone* and *Wyatt Earp*—each less concerned with revising our view of history than exploiting it emptily.

McCabe and Mrs. Miller (1971, U.S., 107 mins.) Dir: Robert Altman; Cast: Warren Beatty, Julie Christie, Shelley Duvall, Keith Carradine, René Auberjonois, William Devane, Michael Murphy.

Beatty and Christie are the title characters—a wilderness pimp and a westward ho—who, in their isolated, self-absorbed, calculating ways, stand quite apart from most of the romantic couples that rode the range in westerns that came before. Altman's view of westward expansion is decidedly unheroic—it disturbs us because all of the comforts of convention are gone, all of the myths we cling to are covered with mud. The dialogue comes in layers, like real people speak; the characters are multidimensional; the atmosphere is palpable; the truth is painful. One of the important films of the seventies.

Heartland (1979, U.S., 95 mins.) Dir: Richard Pearce; Cast: Rip Torn, Conchata Ferrell, Lilia Skala.

Torn and Ferrell (her film debut) give strong, understated, naturalistic performances as a sullen rancher and the young widow he hires as his housekeeper in old Wyoming. Beth Ferris based her screenplay on the diaries of Elinore Randall and the director, Richard Pearce, fuses rigorous authenticity with a genuinely romantic vision, tapping into the reality of pioneer life while capturing the essence of frontier spirit. Made by a company called Wilderness Women Productions, this is the first "womanist" western.

Unforgiven (1992, U.S., 127 mins.) Dir: Clint Eastwood; Cast: Clint Eastwood, Gene Hackman, Morgan Freeman, Richard Harris, Frances Fisher, Jaimz Woolvett.

The lure of reward money pulls reformed gunfighter Eastwood (who also directed) away from his family, into a bloody range war—a conflict caused when a frontier hooker laughs at the size of a cowpoke-john's Jeremiah Johnson. Part old-fashioned shoot em up, part down-and-dirty, tell-it-like-it-was revisionism, the film manages to have it both ways and succeed on many levels. It won Oscars for Best Picture, Director, Screenplay, Editing, and an especially well-deserved one for Hackman's supporting performance.

W W I

The indisputable evil of the fascist opposition gives World War II films a fairly clear-cut good guys/bad guys approach to war, but the morality of World War I was more complicated. The introduction of new technologies like planes, tanks, and poison gas, and the deadly pointlessness of trench warfare meant the bloody birth of a new age, and films about the First World War tend to show the confusion and fear it engendered. Because the conflict was so blurry and incomprehensible, most World War I films address war in general and not the specifics of taking on Kaiser Wilhelm. To be sure, there are many great World War II movies, but the proportion of landmark World War I movies is much higher.

Grand Illusion (1937, France, 111 mins., b/w) Dir: Jean Renoir; Cast: Jean Gabin, Pierre Fresnay, Erich von Stroheim, Marcel Dalio, Julien Carette, Dita Parlo.

French POWs and their sympathetic German commandant. Often named as one of the greatest films ever made: memorable scene after memorable scene and the best film at expressing the transition from 19th-century codes of honor to the realities of the emerging modern world.

All Quiet on the Western Front (1930, U.S., 130 mins., b/w) Dir: Lewis Milestone; Cast: Lew Ayres, Louis Wolheim.

German boys in World War I, based on Erich Maria Remarque's novel. The best antiwar film, with battle scenes that perfectly depict the harrowing, otherworldly quality of combat in all wars, but especially World War I.

The Big Parade (1925, U.S., 126 mins., b/w) Dir: King Vidor; Cast: John Gilbert, Renee Adoree, Hobart Bosworth, Claire McDowell, Karl Dane.

King Vidor's very poignant World War I film. *Grand Illusion* and *All Quiet on the Western Front* have a European angle, but Vidor gives the American experience of the war, which was no less frightening. Again, strong battle scenes. It's a silent.

Paths of Glory (1957, U.S., 86 mins., b/w) Dir: Stanley Kubrick; Cast: Kirk Douglas, Ralph Meeker, Adolphe Menjou, Wayne Morris, George Macready.

Based on the true story of three French soldiers tried for cowardice after their hopeless attack on an enemy position ends in retreat. Absolutely brilliant. You don't watch the battle; the camera puts you in it. Counts as a superior trial movie as well. Kubrick wrote the screenplay with Calder Willingham (*Ramblin' Rose*) and hard-boiled novelist Jim Thompson.

Gallipoli (1981, Australia, 110 mins.) Dir: Peter Weir; Cast: Mark Lee, Mel Gibson, Robert Grubb, Tim McKenzie, David Argue.

Another film on the absurdity of war, centering on one of the worst blunders in military history—the British assault on Gallipoli and the Ottomans. The formula is familiar—young men in a battle they can't possibly win—but post-Vietnam, the theme regained its resonance.

Sergeant York (1941, U.S., 134 mins., b/w) Dir: Howard Hawks; Cast: Gary Cooper, Walter Brennan, Joan Leslie,

George Tobias, Stanley Ridges, Margaret Wycherly, Ward Bond, Noah Beery, Jr., June Lockhart.

Bio of American war hero Alvin York, a pacifist, who came to accept the necessity of war. Like most World War I films, *Sergeant York* does not glorify war, but, produced before Pearl Harbor, it clearly calls for American intervention in World War II. Irrespective of the political background, it's a fine movie.

THE GREAT DEPRESSION

If unemployment goes above six percent and growth slows down a bit, all of a sudden we're told that we're plunging into a recession and nearing the end of civilization as we know it. Talk about short memories. Watch some of these films about the Great Depression and get some perspective on the leading economic indicators.

They Shoot Horses, Don't They? (1969, U.S., 121 mins.) Dir: Sydney Pollack; Cast: Jane Fonda, Michael Sarrazin, Gig Young, Susannah York, Red Buttons, Bruce Dern, Bonnie Bedelia, Allyn Ann McLerie.

Sleeper classic about marathon dancing during the thirties in which contestants dance themselves nearly to death for the prize money. A sad, moving film that shows the real pain that people went through during the period. Gig Young won the Oscar for Best Supporting Actor as the promoter.

Paper Moon (1973, U.S., 101 mins., b/w) Dir: Peter Bogdanovich; Cast: Ryan O'Neal, Tatum O'Neal, Madeline Kahn, John Hillerman.

Father-daughter team of Ryan and Tatum O'Neal play a con man and the little girl he takes on as his accomplice in the Depression-ravaged Midwest.

Black-and-white cinematography and attention to detail express the period well and, as one would hope, the chemistry between Ryan and Tatum elevates the otherwise middling talents of each.

Bonnie and Clyde (1967, U.S., 111 mins.) Dir: Arthur Penn; Cast: Warren Beatty, Faye Dunaway, Estelle Parsons, Gene Hackman, Michael J. Pollard.

Classic film about bank robbers Bonnie Parker and Clyde Barrow and how they became folk heroes during the Depression, even though they were stealing money from the common people who idolized them. Dunaway and Beatty have never been better and Parsons won an Oscar.

The Grapes of Wrath (1940, U.S., 128 mins., b/w) Dir: John Ford; Cast: Henry Fonda, Jane Darwell, John Carradine, Charley Grapewin, Dorris Bowden, John Qualen.

You can stop here if you like. John Ford's adaptation of John Steinbeck's novel about a family displaced by the dust bowl is one of the greatest films in cinematic history and the last word on the Depression. Fonda is tremendous as Tom Joad, as is Jane Darwell as his mother. True Americana and a must-see.

Bound for Glory (1976, U.S., 147 mins.) Dir: Hal Ashby; Cast: David Carradine, Ronny Cox, Melinda Dillon.

Carradine does a great job playing Woody Guthrie, American's greatest folk singer and certainly one of the defining voices of the Depression. Haskell Wexler's cinematography won an Oscar and the dust-storm scene is a frightening and effective bit of special-effects work.

Ironweed (1987, U.S., 135 mins.) Dir: Hector Babenco; Cast: Jack Nicholson, Meryl Streep, Carroll Baker, Michael O'Keefe, Diane Venora, Fred Gwynne,

Margaret Whitton, Tom Waits, Joe Grifasi.

Long and downbeat, though highly atmospheric, version of William Kennedy's novel about a boozy drifter in Depression-era Albany trying to come to terms with his past. Streep shows off her considerable singing skills in one of her memorable scenes as Nicholson's fellow drinker and companion. They don't call it the Depression for nothin', folks.

My Man Godfrey (1936, U.S., 90 mins., b/w) Dir: Gregory La Cava; Cast: Carole Lombard, William Powell, Eugene Pallette, Mischa Auer, Gail Patrick, Alan Mowbray, Alice Brady.

Maybe the best screwball comedy and one of the few films from the Depression that makes the growing gap between the classes a central concern. Lombard is a young socialite who hires "forgotten man" Powell as butler for her wacky family, then falls in love with him. The foibles, indulgences, and cruel ignorance of the period's rich come under fire, but in only the most enjoyable ways.

Pennies From Heaven (1981, U.S., 107 mins.) Dir: Herbert Ross; Cast: Steve Martin, Bernadette Peters, Christopher Walken, Jessica Harper.

Here's a surprise—a Hollywood film that surpasses the original it was based on. Dennis Potter's sluggish BBC series about the struggles of a not-very-nice man during the Depression, intercut with musical numbers of peppy period songs lip-synched in realistic settings, is concentrated here and given extra life through fabulous cinematography inspired by Edward Hopper and other painters of the time. Martin and Peters are up to the challenge of this difficult, entertaining, and disturbing film.

Sounder (1972, U.S., 105 mins.) Dir: Martin Ritt; Cast: Cicely Tyson, Paul Winfield, Kevin Hooks, Carmen Mathews, Taj Mahal.

A moving film about a black family sharecropping in the rural South, hit hard by the Depression but never defeated by it. Sensitive and beautiful, and the theme of the young son growing up makes it great family viewing.

Our Daily Bread (1934, U.S., 74 mins., b/w) Dir: King Vidor; Cast: Tom Keene, Karen Morley, Barbara Pepper, John Qualen.

King Vidor's ode to Depression-era farmers may make for better history now than it does entertainment, but this story of a couple who inherit a farm and do their best to make it succeed has some fine sequences.

WARS IN HISTORY

As we know, Hollywood is not a primary source for historical research, so other criteria come into play when discussing movies about wars throughout history. Entertainment value, costumes, and the battle scenes are key in thinking about war epics, but the single greatest test is this: How good is it to watch on a Sunday afternoon when you're lying on the couch and the game is really boring?

Zulu (1964, Great Britain, 138 mins.) Dir: Cy Endfield; Cast: Stanley Baker, Jack Hawkins, James Booth, Michael Caine.

The king of all lying-on-the-couch movies. The true story of a small British outpost in 1879 that faced slaughter from an attack by an overwhelming number of Zulu warriors. Unlike most, this is actually fairly accurate history. Make sure you have the snacks nearby, because you won't want to miss any of the long and terrific battle scene.

El Cid (1961, U.S., 184 mins.) Dir: Anthony Mann; Cast: Charlton Heston, Sophia Loren, Raf Vallone, Hurd Hatfield.

Heston stars as the legendary Spanish hero El Cid, who defeated the Moors at Valencia in 1094. A great joust and some nice swordplay help build up to the massive battle that closes out the film; the best big-scale knights vs. infidels fight on film. The characters are well drawn and acted, so you'll keep watching when people are talking, too.

The Vikings (1958, U.S., 114 mins.) Dir: Richard Fleischer; Cast: Kirk Douglas, Janet Leigh, Tony Curtis, Ernest Borgnine.

If this was Viking life, sign us up. Kirk Douglas and Tony Curtis invoke the name of Odin as they ravage both Northumbria and Janet Leigh. Shot on location with some attention paid to accuracy, it's a visually beautiful, realistic movie with neat battles and requisite Orson Welles voiceovers. The faux Wagner score is a bit much, though.

Lawrence of Arabia (1962, Great Britain, 222 mins.) Dir: David Lean; Cast: Peter O'Toole, Omar Sharif, Alec Guinness, Anthony Quinn, José Ferrer, Jack Hawkins.

It's a prissy thing to say that this is best seen on the big screen—you *want* to watch it on your duff, that's why you're renting it—but if you haven't see it in a movie house, it really is too bad. At least it's letterboxed. This is one of the greatest movies ever made. Period. David Lean's biography of T. E. Lawrence sweeps you into the desert and you'll stay there for days afterward. Adventure, heroism, charging camels, and not a woman in sight. The ultimate action movie.

Ran (1985, Japan-France, 160 mins.) Dir: Akira Kurosawa; Cast: Tasuya Nakadai, Satoshi Terao, Jinpachi Nezu, Daisuke Ryu.

Kurosawa's enormous interpretation of *King Lear* has two, count 'em, two rousing battles scenes between warring factions in feudal Japan. The armor, weapons, and other aspects of waging war are so foreign to Western eyes as to appear otherworldly. Kurosawa's penchant for long, talky scenes discounts this for on-the-couch honors, but it's an electrifying film.

Potemkin (1925, U.S.S.R., 65 mins., b/w) Dir: Sergei Eisenstein; Cast: Alexander Antonov, Vladimir Barski, Grigori Alexandrov, Mikhail Gomorov.

You've probably heard so many reverent things said about this Eisenstein classic about Russian sailors taking over their ship for the 1905 Revolution that you think it belongs to the musty world of film scholarship. Well, it's certainly brilliant propaganda, but it's also great action. *Potemkin* cracks along until those big guns lower to face St. Petersburg. Let's face it, the tsar wasn't such a nice guy either.

Waterloo (1970, Italy-U.S.S.R., 123 mins.) Dir: Sergei Bondarchuk; Cast: Rod Steiger, Christopher Plummer, Jack Hawkins, Orson Welles, Virginia McKenna.

Meticulous re-creation of Napoleon's swan song at the hands of Wellington. The buildup takes a while, but once the fight gets going it may be the best battle scene in the movies. Bondarchuk cares as much about the details as he does about giving us a sense of the broad scope of Waterloo.

War and Peace (1967, U.S.S.R., 373 mins.) Dir: Sergei Bondarchuk; Cast: Lyudmila Savelyeva, Sergei Bondarchuk.

OK, the six plus hours of this make it tough to watch in one sitting and if you're in a war-movie mood you might not want Tolstoy, but it *is* Bondarchuk. He applies the same brilliance evident in *Waterloo* to Napoleon's failed invasion of Russia, and that's definitely worth your time.

The Charge of the Light Brigade (1936, U.S., 115 mins., b/w) Dir: Michael Curtiz; Cast: Errol Flynn, Olivia de Havilland, David Niven, Donald Crisp, Henry Stephenson, Patric Knowles, C. Henry Gordon, Nigel Bruce, Spring Byington.

An alleged re-creation of the famed charge by British lancers during the Crimean War made even more famous by Tennyson's poem. Unfortunately the movie has little to do with the Crimea, so don't expect to learn much about the mid-19th-century conflict. The charge of the 600 packs a wallop, though. Leave it to the Brits to glorify a disaster.

Henry V (1945, Great Britain, 137 mins.) Dir: Laurence Olivier; Cast: Laurence Olivier, Robert Newton, Leslie Banks, Leo Genn, Renée Asherson, Esmond Knight, Ralph Truman.

Henry V (1989, Great Britain, 135 mins.) Dir: Kenneth Branagh; Cast: Kenneth Branagh, Paul Scofield, Derek Jacobi, Ian Holm, Alec McGowen, Judi Dench, Brian Blessed, Emma Thompson, Robbie Coltrane.

If you think Shakespeare is boring, rent one of these and then see if you feel the same way. *Henry V* tells the story of the English invasion of France in the 15th century climaxed by the battle of Agincourt. Olivier's version is more polished and considered by some the best movie ever made, while Kenneth Branagh's recent one captures more of the period feel. Either way you can't go wrong. The battles in both are terrific. Shakespeare truly understood the emotions of battle and Henry's speech before Agincourt will stiffen your spine. Orson Welles's 1966 *Chimes at Midnight* (aka *Falstaff*) also features a wonderful battle scene with young Hal that works as action and humor at the same time.

SUBMARINES

There's no other way to say this—submarines are neat. Though the plotlines are fairly limited by what can happen on a mission, submarine movies tend to be neat too, with lots of action, tense moments, and special effects. The following are some of the best. Dive! Dive!

Ice Station Zebra (1968, U.S., 148 mins.) Dir: John Sturges; Cast: Rock Hudson, Ernest Borgnine, Patrick McGoohan, Jim Brown.

If it was good enough for Howard Hughes, it's good enough for you. There are reasons why the crazed billionaire could watch this over and over, especially Patrick McGoohan and the very cool under-the-polar-ice journey the submarine takes.

The Hunt for Red October (1990, U.S., 137 mins.) Dir: John McTiernan; Cast: Sean Connery, Alec Baldwin, Scott Glenn, Sam Neill, James Earl Jones, Joss Ackland, Richard Jordan, Peter Firth, Tim Curry, Jeffrey Jones.

Top-notch action, as Soviet sub commander Connery tries to defect to the West, submarine and all. High-tech adventure and a far cry from all the World War II sub films of the forties and fifties. It's the kind of movie where you have to remind yourself to breathe once in a while.

Run Silent, Run Deep (1958, U.S., 93 mins.) Dir: Robert Wise; Cast: Clark Gable, Burt Lancaster, Don Rickles.

A submarine *Moby Dick,* as commander Gable defies all orders, sense, and second-in-command Burt Lancaster by pursuing the Japanese ship that sunk the last sub he was in charge of. Good Gable and Lancaster interplay and a better than average crippled sub scene.

Destination Tokyo (1943, U.S., 135 mins., b/w) Dir: Delmer Daves; Cast:

Cary Grant, John Garfield, Alan Hale, John Ridgely, Dane Clark, Warner Anderson.

Though Cary Grant would never be at the top of a list of Men's Men, he makes a solid sub captain in this excellent film. The crew members are well drawn and while the special effects were clearly done in either the shallows off Venice Beach or in someone's pool they still look cool, sort of like watching model trains.

Das Boot (*The Boat,* 1982, West Germany, 150 mins.) Dir: Wolfgang Petersen; Cast: Jurgen Prochnow, Herbert Gronemeyer, Klaus Wennemann, Hubertas Bengsch.

Very realistic film about a German U-boat in World War II, probably the best for sheer detail on submarine life. The strange part is that no matter how much we empathize with the individual characters, they *are* trying to sink Allied boats, which makes for some split loyalties for the viewer. Though some have called this an antiwar film, it's about as antiwar as Admiral von Doenitz.

Hell Below (1933, U.S., 105 mins., b/w) Dir: Jack Conway; Cast: Robert Montgomery, Walter Huston, Madge Evans, Jimmy Durante, Eugene Pallette, Robert Young, Sterling Holloway.

■
Rare, pre-World War II sub film about captain Huston and his clashes with seaman Montgomery. Heavier on drama than it is on special effects and a fun look at early submarines.

Operation Petticoat (1959, U.S., 124 mins.) Dir: Blake Edwards; Cast: Cary Grant, Tony Curtis, Dina Merrill.

Grant takes command of another sub, but under slightly different circumstances. This one's in bad shape, and scheming Curtis—along with some fetching Navy gals—help him make it seaworthy again. Blake Edwards's

direction and fine performances all around make this a classic comedy, and it's nice for once to not sneak into Tokyo Bay.

Torpedo Run (1958, U.S., 98 mins.) Dir: Joseph Pevney; Cast: Glenn Ford, Ernest Borgnine, Dean Jones.

Glenn Ford is a submarine captain who is forced to sink the Japanese transport carrying his wife and daughter. Better than average special effects help take the edge off of this depressing premise.

The Day Will Dawn (1942, Great Britain, 99 mins., b/w) Dir: Harold French; Cast: Hugh Williams, Griffiths Jones, Ralph Richardson, Deborah Kerr, Roland Culver, Francis L. Sullivan, Finlay Currie.

A landlubber's sub film, but taut British suspense good for any sub fan. Young Deborah Kerr plays a Norwegian girl who assists a reporter trying to blow up a secret Nazi sub base near her home. Terence Rattigan worked on the screenplay.

The Enemy Below (1957, U.S., 98 mins.) Dir: Dick Powell; Cast: Robert Mitchum, Curt Jurgens, David Hedison.

A gripping game of cat and mouse as destroyer captain Mitchum and U-boat *kapitan* Jurgens chase each other through the Pacific. No-frills excitement. Jurgens's presentation as a "good Nazi" who hates Hitler brings up the same issue as *Das Boot,* but if you're convinced of his intrinsic goodness you'll be rooting for each guy in turn.

W W I I
■
EUROPE & THE ATLANTIC

It seems that World War II films are second only to westerns in quantity, but they are certainly their equal in the number of stereotypical charac-

ters and situations. **Some filmmakers, however, have managed to make realistic, engrossing films about WWII; the following are the medal winners from the effort to chronicle the war against the Nazis.**

The Longest Day (1962, U.S., 169 mins., b/w) Dirs: Andrew Marton, Bernhard Wicki, Ken Annakin; Cast: John Wayne, Henry Fonda, Robert Ryan, Red Buttons, Richard Burton, Richard Todd, Mel Ferrer, Alexander Knox, Curt Jurgens.

The mother of all war films tells the story of the mother of all invasions—the Allied landing at Normandy in 1944. Every few minutes another star pops up and something else explodes. Long, but consistently gripping and full of enough action for three movies.

Battleground (1949, U.S., 118 mins., b/w) Dir: William Wellman; Cast: Van Johnson, John Hodiak, Ricardo Montalban, James Whitmore, George Murphy.

Solid retelling of the Battle of the Bulge from the soldier's eye view. Good battle scenes, but the character details are what set this apart from the run-of-the-mill WWII films. Whitmore is the best in a medium-name cast; he looks straight out of a Bill Mauldin "Up Front" cartoon.

Hell Is for Heroes (1962, U.S., 90 mins.) Dir: Don Siegel; Cast: Steve McQueen, James Coburn, Robert Darin, Bob Newhart, Fess Parker.

Steve McQueen is a heroic, but troubled, soldier assigned to a new squad that finds itself responsible for holding down a position against heavy odds. McQueen leads the way with a silent, grizzled performance that predates Eastwood and Bob Newhart brings up the rear with some genuinely funny moments when he actually gets to do his phone routine during battle. Excellent action and Fess Parker, too.

Patton (1970, U.S., 170 mins.) Dir: Franklin Schaffner; Cast: George C. Scott, Karl Malden, Stephen Young, Michael Strong.

George C. Scott somehow actually became General George Patton in this film bio—there's no other explanation for this tremendous performance. Everything else around him is great too, from the battle scenes to Willie the Pit Bull. See it again.

Sink the Bismarck! (1960, Great Britain, 97 mins., b/w) Dir: Lewis Gilbert; Cast: Kenneth More, Dana Wynter.

Off to sea with the British Navy, as they hunt down the dreaded German battleship, the *Bismarck*. The best WWII naval adventure, it's sure to send you down to the basement to find your copy of *Battleship*.

In Which We Serve (1942, Great Britain, 115 mins., b/w) Dirs: Noel Coward, David Lean; Cast: Noel Coward, John Mills.

Even though you might only think of Noel Coward in connection with frothy, fey comedies and musicals, he wrote, co-directed, scored, and starred in this classic film about a British ship. David Lean, in his first outing, was the other director. Full of the stiff-upper-lip English pride that you have to like, especially in a war movie.

The Guns of Navarone (1961, U.S., 159 mins.) Dir: J. Lee Thompson; Cast: Gregory Peck, David Niven, Anthony Quinn, Anthony Quayle, Irene Papas, James Darren, Gia Scala, Stanley Baker, Richard Harris.

Best of all the special-mission films. Peck and Niven lead a detachment of men against a huge German gun emplacement on the Greek coast. It takes a while, but the payoff is worth it.

A Walk in the Sun (1945, U.S., 117 mins., b/w) Dir: Lewis Milestone; Cast:

Dana Andrews, Richard Conte, John Ireland.

A simple and honest film that follows a company as it makes its way up from the beaches to its farmhouse objective. Even more painful than the injuries from bullets are the emotional wounds that the well-cast characters sustain. Like many of the other great war-film directors, Milestone hates war but appreciates the bravery and character it breeds. The only problem is the syrupy theme song, but you'll get past it.

The Big Red One (1980, U.S., 113 mins.) Dir: Samuel Fuller; Cast: Lee Marvin, Mark Hamill, Bobby DiCicco, Robert Carradine, Kelly Ward.

Sam Fuller serves up a winner with this tremendous film about a unit that served in virtually all the campaigns of the European theater. Marvin's grizzled face was meant for the role of a hard-boiled sergeant, and there are few movies that capture the experience of war as well as this one.

The Young Lions (1958, U.S., 167 mins.) Dir: Edward Dmytryk; Cast: Marlon Brando, Montgomery Clift, Dean Martin, Maximilian Schell, Hope Lange, Mai Britt.

A sprawling, cynical film about the end of the war in Europe. Brando leads a fine cast in this adaptation of Irwin Shaw's novel. All the characters are complex, considered people; unlike so many WWII movies, there are no easy answers and not all the Americans are good guys doling out candy bars.

WWII
■
THE PACIFIC & ELSEWHERE

Fighting on the other side of the world against a culture we knew nothing about gave rise to some par- ticularly panicked reactions from America. Though films about the war in Europe are loaded with propaganda messages, they don't come close to the depths of jingoism that the Pacific films sink to. Still, there are some classic war movies among them if you can get past the sometimes embarrassing anti-Japanese screeds.

They Were Expendable (1945, U.S., 135 mins., b/w) Dir: John Ford; Cast: John Wayne, Robert Montgomery, Donna Reed, Jack Holt.

John Ford made a big, moving film about some small boats—the PT boats that acted as quick attack vehicles in the Pacific. The Duke takes the romantic lead here with Donna Reed, while Robert Mongomery—the Ed Harris of the forties—shows the Navy just how tough his little boats are. Ford takes as much care with his supporting characters as he does with his battle scenes, which makes for a great film.

Objective Burma! (1945, U.S., 142 mins., b/w) Dir: Raoul Walsh; Cast: Errol Flynn, William Prince.

Solid action film based on the true story of soldiers dropped into the jungles of Burma where they secured a key spot, but then weren't relieved until they were nearly wiped out. Try to avoid the colorized version, which makes everything a sort of washed-out, seasick green. If you like Sam Fuller, you should also find *Merrill's Marauders*, which tells the same story from the darker, tougher, Fuller perspective.

Sands of Iwo Jima (1949, U.S., 109 mins., b/w) Dir: Allan Dwan; Cast: John Wayne, John Agar, Forrest Tucker.

One of John Wayne's best moments here, as he plays a tough marine sergeant trying to whip his boys into shape. It's what we think of as quintessential Duke, with an even harder edge than he has in his great roles in John Ford movies. Fine battle footage of the taking of Iwo Jima, too.

Guadalcanal Diary (1943, U.S., 93 mins., b/w) Dir: Lewis Seiler; Cast: William Bendix, Lloyd Nolan, Preston Foster, Richard Conte, Anthony Quinn, Richard Jaeckel.

Two things keep this from being one of the very best films about the war in the Pacific. First, the voiceover narration is annoying, intrusive, and pious; the story tells itself well enough. Second, William Bendix. The most you can say for him here is that he's not a simpering boob, he's a tough boob. His presence in a film guarantees you at least one scene of him blathering on about "dem Bums" (except maybe in *The Babe Ruth Story*) and sadly this is something of a showcase for him. Aside from these two quibbles, it's a fine war movie.

Wake Island (1942, U.S., 78 mins., b/w) Dir: John Farrow; Cast: Brian Donlevy, William Bendix, Robert Preston, Macdonald Carey.

The problem here is that it takes forever for things to get started. Once the Japanese attack, the action is strong and nonstop, but get ready for some fairly standard and seemingly endless character development up to that point. Maybe it's because this was one of the first World War II films about the Pacific and they were working out the kinks. Later filmmakers could telegraph a character with a line or two—or just the way he or she held a cigarette; but they needed *Wake Island* first.

From Here to Eternity (1953, U.S., 118 mins., b/w) Dir: Fred Zinnemann; Cast: Burt Lancaster, Montgomery Clift, Deborah Kerr, Philip Ober, Frank Sinatra, Ernest Borgnine, Jack Warden, Donna Reed.

This isn't wall-to-wall combat like some of these films, but this classic about military life in Hawaii before Pearl Harbor is one of the great films about the period. It won Best Picture and just about every other award in 1953 and it was the film that resuscitated Frankie's moribund career. The Japanese attack on Pearl Harbor is done extremely well, as is Lancaster's beach attack on Deborah Kerr.

Tora! Tora! Tora! (1970, U.S., 142 mins.) Dirs: Richard Fleischer, Toshio Masuda, Kinji Fukasaku; Cast: Jason Robards, Jr., Martin Balsam, Joseph Cotten, James Whitmore.

So what if there's no story? If you want a story, watch *From Here to Eternity*. If you want to watch straight military stuff with lots of things blowing up and no smooching, this is your film. Great special effects and a strong view of the Japanese side give this the kind of verisimilitude that made those epic sixties and seventies World War II films so watchable. *Midway* aspires to this and has a better cast, but somehow it falls short. Maybe you need to equip yourself with "Sensurround," one of Hollywood's dumbest gimmicks and *Midway*'s only real claim to fame.

Thirty Seconds Over Tokyo (1944, U.S., 138 mins., b/w) Dir: Mervyn LeRoy; Cast: Van Johnson, Spencer Tracy, Robert Walker, Robert Mitchum, Phyllis Thaxter.

Winner about the first bomber raids on Tokyo stars a sturdy Johnson, along with Tracy as General James Doolittle. Written by Dalton Trumbo, it's definitely a product of the war, but worth seeing all the same.

Sahara (1943, U.S., 97 mins., b/w) Dir: Zoltan Korda; Cast: Humphrey Bogart, Dan Duryea, Lloyd Bridges, J. Carrol Naish, Rex Ingram, Bruce Bennett.

On to Africa, where Bogey and his armored unit are forced to take on the

Afrika Korps when they're stranded in the desert. Nice acting by Bogart combined with good battle scenes make this a must-see among WWII films. Need we say, don't confuse this with the Brooke Shields movie of the same title.

The Desert Fox (1951, U.S., 88 mins., b/w) Dir: Henry Hathaway; Cast: James Mason, Jessica Tandy, Cedric Hardwicke, Luther Adler.

Not too much in the way of battle scenes, but Mason's performance as Panzer pioneer and eventual Hitler enemy Erwin Rommel makes this a classic. Interesting postwar treatment of Rommel, who is lionized as a "good Nazi" for his involvement in the plot to assassinate the Führer, despite all his years of service to the Reich. An intense psychological drama. Mason plays Rommel again in *The Desert Rats*, a more action-oriented movie about the war in North Africa.

WWII
■
THE HOMEFRONT

The war effort was more than just sending the boys over to Europe and the Pacific. It was buying bonds, Rosie the Riveter, and dreading a telegram from the War Department. Here are some films that show how the war was fought at home, whether home was in the U.S. or behind Nazi lines.

Mrs. Miniver (1942, U.S., 134 mins., b/w) Dir: William Wyler; Cast: Greer Garson, Walter Pidgeon, Richard Ney, Dame May Whitty, Teresa Wright, Helmut Dantine.

Greer Garson probably could have been canonized by the Church of England after her portrayal of this brave, plucky Englishwoman keeping her family

going during the Blitz. Propaganda of the highest sort, it won seven Oscars, including Best Picture and Best Actress.

Hangmen Also Die (1943, U.S., 131 mins., b/w) Dir: Fritz Lang; Cast: Brian Donlevy, Walter Brennan, Dennis O'Keefe, Anna Lee.
■
Co-written by Lang and Bert "Call Me Bertolt" Brecht, this is a tense thriller about how the assassination of the notorious Nazi known as Heydrich the Hangman released a wave of Nazi terror in occupied Czechoslovakia. Brechtian images and characters abound and the exaggerated portrayals of the Nazis are arguably the best the screen has ever seen in that they expose both how vicious they were and how ludicrous. A brilliant nail-biter.

Saboteur (1942, U.S., 108 mins., b/w) Dir: Alfred Hitchcock; Cast: Robert Cummings, Priscilla Lane, Otto Kruger.

In sort of a run-through for *North by Northwest,* Hitchcock sends munition worker Cummings, accused of sabotage, across the country as he tries to escape the authorities and the real bad guys. A strange movie with great touches all the way through.

The Human Comedy (1943, U.S., 118 mins., b/w) Dir: Clarence Brown; Cast: Mickey Rooney, Frank Morgan, Marsha Hunt, Van Johnson.

Rooney's performance as a Western Union delivery boy who must bring the news of death in battle to waiting families is one of the high points of his career. William Saroyan's novel is faithfully transformed into a complex and sentimental homage to small-town America during wartime.

The More the Merrier (1943, U.S., 104 mins., b/w) Dir: George Stevens; Cast: Jean Arthur, Joel McCrea, Charles Coburn.

Charming, bright comedy about the Washington, D.C., housing crunch. Arthur is forced to share her apartment with crusty Coburn and stubborn McCrea, whom she can't decide whether she loves or can't stand.

To Be or Not to Be (1942, U.S., 99 mins., b/w) Dir: Ernst Lubitsch; Cast: Jack Benny, Carole Lombard, Robert Stack, Sig Ruman, Stanley Ridges, Lionel Atwill.

To Be or Not to Be (1983, U.S., 108 mins.) Dir: Alan Johnson; Cast: Mel Brooks, Anne Bancroft, Charles Durning, Tim Matheson, José Ferrer.

Both versions of this dark comedy about the impact the Nazi invasion has on a Polish theatrical troupe are enjoyable. Lubitsch has Benny and Lombard and doesn't get schmaltzy, but the Brooks edition is funnier and features Anne Bancroft doing a wonderful turn as Brooks's straying wife.

Watch on the Rhine (1943, U.S., 114 mins., b/w) Dir: Herman Shumlin; Cast: Paul Lukas, Bette Davis, Beulah Bondi, George Coulouris, Lucile Watson.

Lillian Hellman and her main man Dashiell Hammett did the adaptation of her play about Nazis in Washington coming after Resistance fighters who eluded their grasp back in Europe. Lukas won the Oscar for Best Actor. An intelligent and exciting film.

Mission to Moscow (1943, U.S., 123 mins., b/w) Dir: Michael Curtiz; Cast: Walter Huston, Eleanor Parker.

Interesting, pre-Cold War curiosity about the American ambassador to the Soviet Union. Clearly an exercise in hands across the water popular diplomacy, it's a great look at attitudes toward the U.S.S.R. before the Bomb and McCarthy.

This Land Is Mine (1943, U.S., 103 mins., b/w) Dir: Jean Renoir; Cast:

Charles Laughton, Maureen O'Hara, Walter Slezak, George Sanders, Kent Smith.

Cowardly schoolteacher in occupied France faces up to the Nazi oppressors. This dream match-up of Renoir and Laughton is hampered by the restraints of wartime propaganda, but some wonderful scenes still result. Lose the final speeches and you'd have a solid film.

Swing Shift (1984, U.S., 112 mins.) Dir: Jonathan Demme; Cast: Goldie Hawn, Kurt Russell, Christine Lahti, Ed Harris, Fred Willard.

With her husband at war, Goldie Hawn becomes a blonde version of Rosie the Riveter. Period detail is very good and though the print released got mixed notices, Demme's cut was shown later and revealed a more complex and interesting film. But if it's wartime America you want, either one will do.

KOREA:
THE FORGOTTEN WAR

Lost between World War II and Vietnam, the Korean War has been called "the forgotten war," and the same fate has befallen the films it produced. Anyone who thinks the movies on this list are simply retreads from the last war hasn't seen them. These films show the realities of combat, but without the political overlay of Vietnam films and the gung-ho-ism of World War II movies. What we're left with are almost existential war films; distillate stories of men in deadly, confusing battle with no clearly defined reason for being there.

Retreat, Hell! (1952, U.S., 95 mins.) Dir: Joseph H. Lewis; Cast: Frank Lovejoy, Richard Carlson, Anita Louise, Russ Tamblyn.

The one real gung-ho, WWII-like film in

the bunch and the guiding hand of the Marine Corps is clear. Still, this telling of the heroic retreat (it's not an oxymoron to these guys) from the Changjin Reservoir has some strong moments. It is the exception though, especially in its congratulatory tone toward the young and murderous Russ Tamblyn.

The Steel Helmet (1951, U.S., 84 mins., b/w) Dir: Samuel Fuller; Cast: Gene Evans, Robert Hutton.
■
From the start of the credits, you know you're seeing a new kind of war film. Director Sam Fuller isn't interested in patriotism or apple pie; he cares about survival and the relationships between men under fire. Gene Evans towers over an already strong cast as a tough-as-nails sergeant who hooks up with a Korean boy and a lost outfit. A brilliant film.

The Manchurian Candidate (1962, U.S., 126 mins., b/w) Dir: John Frankenheimer; Cast: Frank Sinatra, Laurence Harvey, Janet Leigh, Angela Lansbury.

Psychological and political thriller about a platoon of men who may have been brainwashed by their captors while prisoners during the Korean War—and the one who may be an assassin. The highly stylized aspects of its production seem prescient now. Based on a story by Richard Condon, it also has one of Sinatra's best performances.

Men in War (1957, U.S., 104 mins., b/w) Dir: Anthony Mann; Cast: Robert Ryan, Aldo Ray, Vic Morrow.

At first this looks like just another story of a decimated company trying to get back to friendly lines. But as it goes on, the isolation, the danger, and the fact that many of these men had just fought a war create a harrowing atmosphere that heightens the action. Robert Ryan deserves more credit than he ever gets for his acting, and here he's perfect as

a lieutenant reaching the end of his rope. Much common Vietnam War imagery was born here.

Sayonara (1957, U.S., 147 mins.) Dir: Joshua Logan; Cast: Marlon Brando, Miyoshi Umeki, Red Buttons, James Garner, Ricardo Montalban.

Brando stars as an Army major in the Korean War who falls in love with a Japanese woman, over the protests of everyone around him, including the Army. The lush production doesn't get in the way of its solid message about anti-Japanese bigotry in the armed forces and healing between the U.S. and Japan. From a story by James Michener.

The Bridges at Toko-Ri (1954, U.S., 110 mins.) Dir: Mark Robson; Cast: William Holden, Grace Kelly, Fredric March, Mickey Rooney.

Another Michener tale brought to the screen. Holden plays a promising lawyer unwillingly pulled back into the Naval Air Corps by the Korean War. The first half hour or so is a long set piece on a carrier that feels like a big wet kiss for the Navy, but by the end this is a serious antiwar film about the absurdity of war. Again, no happy ending. The seeds of dissatisfaction with American militarism were obviously brewing long before Vietnam.

The Rack (1956, U.S., 100 mins., b/w) Dir: Arnold Laven; Cast: Paul Newman, Wendell Corey, Edmond O'Brien, Anne Francis, Walter Pidgeon.
■
Brainwashing again, with Paul Newman as its victim, on trial for treason. Adapted from a script by Rod Serling and featuring his usual gutsy realism.

M*A*S*H (1970, U.S., 116 mins.) Dir: Robert Altman; Cast: Donald Sutherland, Elliott Gould, Tom Skerritt, Sally Kellerman, Robert Duvall, Jo Ann Pflug, Gary Burghoff.

Altman's classic film about army doctors in Korea is wonderful, but in comparison to some of these others, it's certainly not the toughest take on the war. It's also not the first about M*A*S*H units; Bogart's inferior *Battle Circus* was there before (1953).

Field of Honor (1988, France, 87 mins.) Dir: Jean-Pierre Denis; Cast: Cris Campion, Pascale Rocard, Eric Wapler.

Instead of the standard focus on the American experience of the war, here is a view through the eyes of a Dutch combatant serving in the United Nations forces. A good reminder that we weren't the only people fighting in Korea.

Pork Chop Hill (1959, U.S., 97 mins., b/w) Dir: Lewis Milestone; Cast: Gregory Peck, Rip Torn, George Peppard, Harry Guardino.

Lewis Milestone made some tremendous war films in his day and this is one of his best. Peck stars as an officer forced to continue a hopeless attack on the Chinese despite an impending peace agreement. Cowardice, racism, and the true behavior of men in combat get honest play along with the powerful battle scenes.

THE RED MENACE

In 1947 the House Un-American Activities Committee (HUAC) began a series of inquisitions to ferret out Hollywood pinkos hell-bent on Communizing, Stalinizing, and subverting American movies. The "red scare" reached its zenith between 1950 and 1954 when demagogue Senator Joseph McCarthy whipped the witch hunters into a paranoid frenzy. Victims of the HUAC degradation ceremonies who refused to "name names" of supposed communists faced the possibility of imprisonment and the probability of political exile. Hundreds of writers, directors, and actors were blacklisted. It was a time of choosing up sides in Hollywood, and many films made during and after the period reflect the fears on both sides of the fence. Polemics were often obvious, sometimes painfully so, but some messages—both pro- and anti-McCarthy—were buried in allegorical conceits, with fascists and fellow travelers hiding where you least expect to find them.

Cornered (1945, U.S., 102 mins., b/w) Dir: Edward Dmytryk; Cast: Dick Powell, Micheleine Cheirel, Walter Slezak, Nina Vale, Morris Carnovsky, Luther Adler.

Made two years before the blacklist, this tough, midlevel, postwar film noir about ex-POW Powell tracking his wife's killer to Buenos Aires contains a number of anti-fascist speeches that director Edward Dmytryk acknowledged were written along Communist Party lines. Dmytryk, producer Adrian Scott, writer John Wexley, and actors Adler and Carnovsky were all eventually blacklisted.

Force of Evil (1949, U.S., 78 mins., b/w) Dir: Abraham Polonsky; Cast: John Garfield, Beatrice Pearson.

Brilliant, brutal film noir about slick lawyer Garfield helping the syndicate set up a numbers racket rip-off is a thinly veiled critique of capitalism and the connection between gangsterism and government. First and only film directed by screenwriter Polonsky before he was blacklisted; it was 22 years until he would direct again. Garfield, also marked red for refusing to cooperate with HUAC, died of a heart attack soon after.

Guilty by Suspicion (1991, U.S., 105 mins.) Dir: Irwin Winkler; Cast: Robert De Niro, Annette Bening, George Wendt, Patricia Wettig, Sam Wanamaker, Martin Scorsese.

Somber look back at what it was like to be branded a Bolshevik in McCarthy-era Hollywood. Abraham Polonsky wrote first draft of the screenplay, which emphasized suppression of freedom inherent in HUAC handling of communists; director Winkler rewrote the script and eliminated all traces of red in the characters, painting them as victims by association. High-minded fare on the surface avoids deeper political implications and is ultimately a moral cop-out.

Pickup on South Street (1953, U.S., 80 mins., b/w) Dir: Samuel Fuller; Cast: Richard Widmark, Jean Peters, Richard Kiley, Thelma Ritter.

Pickpocket Skip McCoy (Widmark) stumbles into a nest of Stalinist vipers and more trouble than he bargained for when he inadvertently lifts a roll of microfilm from the purse of a communist spy's mistress (Peters). Commies are portrayed as much lower than the lowlifes—a thief, a prostitute, and a stool pigeon—who do them in. Red-baiting angle makes it historically interesting; Fuller's cinematic audacity makes it art.

The Thief (1952, U.S., 85 mins., b/w) Dir: Russell Rouse; Cast: Ray Milland, Rita Gam, Martin Gabel, Harry Bronson.

Unusually high budget and fascinating gimmick set this apart from bulk of anti-communist propaganda coming out of Hollywood at the time. Entire story of atomic scientist Milland selling secrets to the reds and running from the FBI is told with no dialogue. Wordless script works surprisingly well in conjunction with good location photography and excellent Milland.

My Son John (1952, U.S., 122 mins., b/w) Dir: Leo McCarey; Cast: Helen Hayes, Robert Walker, Van Heflin, Dean Jagger.

Reactionary director McCarey concoct-ed this Oscar-nominated story about havoc raised in apple pie American family when parents Hayes and Jagger discover that their number one son (Walker) is a lefty and react as if he were a leper. Fundamental purpose here is to pit communism against the Catholic Church and caution God-fearing citizens against the godless pink peril attempting to worm its way into the sinew of American society.

The Miracle of Our Lady of Fatima (1952, U.S., 102 mins.) Dir: John Brahm; Cast: Gilbert Roland, Frank Silvera, Susan Whitney, Sherry Jackson.

Moving religious drama of Portuguese farm children visited by the Virgin Mary, who delivers a stern and fearful warning about the state of the world and the terrible things that will happen if God is not embraced by the people of all nations. At the height of HUAC hysteria even the Holy Mother served as a source of anti-Soviet propaganda.

The Thing (aka: *The Thing From Another World*, 1951, U.S., 87 mins., b/w) Dir: Christian Nyby; Cast: Kenneth Tobey, Margaret Sheridan, Robert Cornthwaite, James Arness.

Scientists on Arctic expedition are set upon by creepy creature made of vegetable matter, the first movie monster from outer space. Critics generally lump this in with 1950s spate of alien invaders as metaphor for commie conspiracy films, but uncredited co-writer Ben Hecht saw it as an attack of McCarthyism—"the thing" is simply Senator McCarthy as a blood-sucking carrot. So-so sci-fi produced by Howard Hawks. Too bad he didn't direct.

Invasion of the Body Snatchers (1956, U.S., 80 mins., b/w) Dir: Don Siegel; Cast: Kevin McCarthy, Dana Wynter, Larry Gates, Carolyn Jones, King Donovan, Virginia Christine.

This time the invading veggies come

in the form of giant pea pods that swallow up humans and replicate them as cold, soulless, authoritarian pod people—just like the Ruskies. Patently anti-communist allegory sets the standard against which all alien takeover movies must be measured. Tight, controlled direction by Siegel quickly overcomes the eau de camp engendered by the dated dialogue, and you get caught in the web of paranoia and suspense.

Johnny Guitar (1954, U.S., 110 mins.) Dir: Nicholas Ray; Cast: Joan Crawford, Sterling Hayden, Mercedes McCambridge, Scott Brady.

Director Nick Ray's aggressively offbeat, Freudian western, fraught with homoerotic tension, is also a strong reaction to McCarthyism. The outlaws are the commies, guitar-strumming Hayden is a former outlaw/commie and member of the entertainment industry; Crawford, who cozies up to the outlaws, is a fellow traveler, and McCarthy-like McCambridge manipulates others to "name names." Important, intriguing film that works extremely well on many levels.

On the Waterfront (1954, U.S., 108 mins., b/w) Dir: Elia Kazan; Cast: Marlon Brando, Eva Marie Saint, Karl Malden, Lee J. Cobb, Rod Steiger.

Writer Budd Schulberg and director Kazan were both members of human rights organizations that HUAC labeled as commie cells. Both were called to testify and both named names. This film, a scathing indictment of union corruption, contains some of the most memorable characters and powerful acting in all of cinema. Its plot, with Brando's Terry Malloy doing his moral duty by finking on fellow hoods, is a clearly articulated justification by Kazan and Schulberg of their own political turnaround.

The Bridge on the River Kwai (1957, Great Britain, 161 mins.) Dir: David Lean; Cast: William Holden, Alec Guinness, Jack Hawkins, Sessue Hayakawa.

British POWs led by misguided colonel (Guinness) cooperate with Japanese captors to build a bridge during WWII. Holden is the American who escapes and returns to blow it up. Fertile script has much to say about human nature; as a political parable, the Guinness character is like a witness cooperating with HUAC, while proletarian Holden spits in their faces. Blacklisted writers Michael Wilson and Carl Foreman received no credit for the film, which won seven Oscars including Best Screenplay.

The Front (1976, U.S., 94 mins.) Dir: Martin Ritt; Cast: Woody Allen, Zero Mostel, Andrea Marcovicci, Joshua Shelley, Georgann Johnson.

Illuminating comedy drama looks back at this dark and frightening period in Hollywood history and chronicles the practice of blackballed writers using "fronts"—like the schlemiel played by Woody—to represent their work. Writer Walter Bernstein, director Marty Ritt, actor Zero Mostel, and others in the cast were all done in by the witch-hunt, and their credits at the end are all followed by the dates on which they were blacklisted.

Miracle on 34th Street (1947, U.S., 96 mins., b/w) Dir: George Seaton; Cast: Edmund Gwenn, John Payne, Maureen O'Hara, Natalie Wood.

Hard to imagine Santa as part of a commie plot? Well just look at it this way: A guy in a red suit convinces the populace that crass commercialism and capitalist competition are unsound and unsavory economic theory. The paranoid powers that be haul him into a circus-like hearing to find out if he is now, or has ever been, a menace to society. It seems clear to us that, aside from this beloved film's obvious other well-known delights, it was tossing one big snowball at HUAC.

VIETNAM

No war has ever divided our country as Vietnam did and for a long time many thought the rift was permanent. Thirty years later it seems we may finally be moving on and if that's so, we owe Hollywood thanks and blame—blame because Vietnam movies often worried wounds on the way to mending; thanks because some drew out the poison.

Go Tell the Spartans (1978, U.S., 114 mins.) Dir: Ted Post; Cast: Burt Lancaster, Craig Wasson, Marc Singer.

An underrated early entry into the post-Vietnam film explosion about a group of fresh soldiers sent grudgingly by commander Lancaster to scout a town suspected of Vietcong activity. Free of pompous statements, pathos, criminal indictments of the system, etc., it is first and foremost a strong war movie, and second a considered view of Vietnam. The only drawback is a slightly TV movie feel in the direction and production values.

The Ugly American (1963, U.S., 120 mins.) Dir: George H. Englund; Cast: Marlon Brando, Eiji Okada, Arthur Hill, Jocelyn Brando.

A look at the policies and mindset that got us there. Brando plays a new ambassador to an unnamed Asian nation whose right-wing views stir up communist sentiment. It smacks of typical 1970s Monday-morning quarterbacking until you realize that the film was made in 1963 and based on a book written even earlier, giving it an eerie prescience.

Hearts and Minds (1974, U.S., 110 mins.) Dir: Peter Davis.

This documentary about our effort to win over the people of Vietnam came out right after the war ended and it still carries the sharp pain of a fresh wound.

Extremely controversial in its day, it will probably start a few discussions in your house even now.

The Green Berets (1968, U.S., 141 mins.) Dirs: John Wayne, Ray Kellogg; Cast: John Wayne, David Janssen, Jim Hutton, Aldo Ray, Raymond St. Jacques, Bruce Cabot, Jack Soo, George Takei, Patrick Wayne, Richard Pryor.

Less a movie than a political screed, this film has value only as a perverse document and unwitting self-parody of the period's gung-ho right. It took a long time to watch *Stagecoach* again after seeing the Duke make such a fool of himself here. Plus, it's boring. You'd think a film extolling the war could give us some good action scenes.

BAT 21 (1988, U.S., 100 mins.) Dir: Peter Markle; Cast: Gene Hackman, Danny Glover, Jerry Reed.

By 1988 some of the emotions had died down and it was becoming possible to make Vietnam films like this one, films that didn't drip with politics. Here, desk-jockey Hackman is shot down behind enemy lines and Glover has to get him out before the Vietcong capture him or the U.S. bombing run slated for the area hits. Good, solid action.

Platoon (1986, U.S., 120 mins.) Dir: Oliver Stone; Cast: Tom Berenger, Willem Dafoe, Charlie Sheen, Francesco Quinn, Johnny Depp, Keith David, Kevin Dillon.

This great Oliver Stone movie about the war is one of the best war movies ever. Stone takes us down to the grunts and with them through the paddies and klicks. A powerful film, with Academy Award-winning editing by Claire Simpson.

Apocalypse Now (1979, U.S., 153 mins.) Dir: Francis Ford Coppola; Cast: Martin Sheen, Marlon Brando, Robert Duvall, Dennis Hopper, Frederic Forrest.

Sure, the Brando stuff at the end could have been cut down, but there are those *Classics Illustrated* fans who say that *Moby Dick* could stand to lose 200 pages. This is not a flawed film, as some would have you believe; it is a towering masterpiece. There are five or six unforgettable scenes, any one of which would make another film worth seeing. Brando resembles Welles in *Othello* as he plays with the dark and the light. If you like the film, you'll also like *Hearts of Darkness*, a documentary about its making.

Full Metal Jacket (1987, U.S., 120 mins.) Dir: Stanley Kubrick; Cast: Matthew Modine, Dorian Harewood, Adam Baldwin, Vincent D'Onofrio.

Another of the big boys weighs in with a great film. Here, Kubrick presents a split story—one half about the hell of basic training and the other about the hell of Vietnam itself. Though the in-country scenes work very well, and Kubrick has made some of the best war films ever, it's the first half centering on a brutal drill instructor trying to turn a special case into a soldier that knocks you over. It's no surprise this same director made *A Clockwork Orange*.

The Deer Hunter (1978, U.S., 183 mins.) Dir: Michael Cimino; Cast: Robert De Niro, Meryl Streep, Christopher Walken, John Cazale, John Savage.

A long, rich, and affecting film about what Vietnam did to a group of friends in a Pennsylvania steel town. This came out the same year as *Coming Home*, Hal Ashby's painfully soppy and skewed vision of Vietnam, and got a rep as a right-wing, violent film. Time has told and this has emerged as a classic—the one film here that can really make you cry. Instead of running a sensitivity seminar, Cimino gave us our first chance to mourn together.

Born on the Fourth of July (1989, U.S., 144 mins.) Dir: Oliver Stone; Cast: Tom Cruise, Raymond J. Barry, Caroline Kava, Willem Dafoe, Kyra Sedgwick, Abbie Hoffman, Tom Berenger.

Stone doesn't make wishy-washy films. People either love them or hate them, and while many loved this version of Ron Kovic's memoir of his transformation from rabid marine to paralyzed antiwar vet, we're on the other side. It's one thing to manipulate our emotions about a character or a story, but when we're manipulated about politics under the pretense of the former we get polemic. Kovic doesn't become a better person here; he merely joins the correct voting bloc. Other films on this list make Stone's points with greater art and sensitivity.

BLACK IN AMERICA

The black experience in America covers territory from the insult and derogation of slavery through the special ongoing pressures encountered by minority populations in this country. Here is a film response to a culture whose identity has been shaped and developed by two centuries of living in—and contributing richly to—this separate and not-so-equal society.

Nothing But a Man (1964, U.S., 92 mins., b/w) Dir: Michael Roemer; Cast: Ivan Dixon, Abbey Lincoln, Julius Harris, Gloria Foster, Yaphet Kotto, Moses Gunn.
■
Austerely powerful and moving drama with knockout performances, and almost documentary-like realism to the script and settings. Dixon and Lincoln struggle to hold onto their marriage and their dreams in the oppressive 1960s deep South context of limited opportunities for blacks.

Visions: The Images, Words, and Music of Gordon Parks (1991, U.S., 60 mins.) Dir: Gordon Parks; Cast: Gordon Parks, Avery Brooks, Roscoe Lee Browne, Joe Seneca.

The Learning Tree (1969, U.S., 107 mins.) Dir: Gordon Parks; Cast: Kyle Johnson, Alex Clarke, Estelle Evans, Dana Elcar, Mita Waters.

Pure poetry from Parks, in impressionistic documentary tracing events from mid to late 20th-century America, as viewed from his unique perspectives as a youth in rural Kansas, a barrier-breaking internationally known *Life* photographer, and as a successful writer, filmmaker, and composer. Parks's feature adaptation of his autobiography, *The Learning Tree,* is a beautifully photographed dramatization of the early Kansas years.

Mississippi Blues (1983, U.S., 96 mins.) Dirs: Bertrand Tavernier, Robert Parrish.

The blues—a form that is a direct lyrical and musical extension of life in the American South. From the Delta to downtown, having grown from a gospel tradition, the blues are now a basic part of the American musical vocabulary. Come along in this documentary's joyous jaunt across the southern heartland, as seen through the eyes of the French Tavernier and American writer Robert Parrish, killer soundtrack included.

The Color Purple (1985, U.S., 155 mins.) Dir: Steven Spielberg; Cast: Whoopi Goldberg, Danny Glover, Rae Dawn Chong, Margaret Avery, Oprah Winfrey.

Somewhat overly sentimental treatment of Alice Walker's stirring Pulitzer-winning novel about the life of a black woman in Georgia in the first half of the 20th century. Beautiful photography (Allen Daviau), Quincy Jones score, and an exceptional performance by Goldberg help hold together this gut-wrenching tale of oppression and survival.

The Autobiography of Miss Jane Pittman (1974, U.S./MTV, 102 mins.) Dir: John Korty; Cast: Cicely Tyson, Richard Dysart, Odetta, Michael Murphy, Collin Wilcox.

Tyson outdoes herself in this superlative made-for-TV adaptation of Ernest J. Gaines's novel about a former slave who lives to take part in the civil rights demonstrations of the 1960s. Catch her in *Sounder* as well—a beautifully made saga of a Louisiana sharecropper family during the Depression.

Mississippi Burning (1988, U.S., 127 mins.) Dir: Alan Parker; Cast: Gene Hackman, Willem Dafoe, Frances McDormand, Brad Dourif, Lee Ermey.

This roaring re-creation of a time and place is nevertheless a questionably fictionalized account of the FBI investigation of the murders of three young civil rights workers (one black and two whites) in 1964 Mississippi. Well worth a look, but not for the weak—it's almost as if Oliver Stone was looking over Parker's shoulder when he made this.

The Bingo Long Traveling All-Stars and Motor Kings (1976, U.S., 111 mins.) Dir: John Badham; Cast: Billy Dee Williams, James Earl Jones, Richard Pryor.

Baseball before Jackie Robinson became the first black player allowed into the white majors. This is an original comedy-drama about breakaway ball players who leave the Negro National League in 1939 to form their own team, taking us along on their antic tour of rural America.

Shaft (1971, U.S., 106 mins.) Dir: Gordon Parks; Cast: Richard Roundtree, Moses Gunn, Charles Cioffi.

The original blaxploitation movie, and a different challenge for Parks. Like *Superfly* and the rest that followed, this is the other side of the black experience, that is, the Eastwood-Bronson fantasy version, as embodied by the well-cast Roundtree, playing a private eye here. Rip-snorting action-thriller, loaded with drugs, sex, and violence and great music by Isaac Hayes. *Shaft* finally led to good character roles for blacks in this action genre—notably Danny Glover in the *Lethal Weapon* series and even Eddie Murphy in the *Beverly Hills Cop* films.

The Brother From Another Planet (1984, U.S., 110 mins.) Dir: John Sayles; Cast: Joe Morton, Darryl Edwards, Dee Dee Bridgewater, John Sayles, David Strathairn.

Morton is terrific in a subtle and cleverly scripted story of his arrival from outer space (at the shore of pre-renovated Ellis Island, with memorable scenes inside); his silence is eloquent as we watch how he begins to understand how being black is perceived in N.Y.C. Watch for Sayles in a good bit as a cop pursuing from the other planet.

Malcolm X (1993, U.S., 201 mins.) Dir: Spike Lee; Cast: Denzel Washington, Angela Bassett, Albert Hall, Al Freeman, Jr., Delroy Lindo, Spike Lee, Theresa Randle, Kate Vernon, Lonette McKee, Tommy Hollis, Giancarlo Esposito.

Vibrant and controversial story of Malcolm X's rise to charismatic radical leader stops short of exploring his later, more conciliatory message that held tighter to the tenets of Islam. Lee's view has been taken to task for being too glossy on the facts and too soft on Malcolm's character, but it's well worth viewing for the basic rudiments on the activities and beliefs of this key figure in modern black history.

Boyz N the Hood (1991, U.S., 107 mins.) Dir: John Singleton; Cast: Ice Cube, Cuba Gooding, Jr., Morris Chestnut, Larry Fishburne, Angela Bassett, Nia Long, Tyra Ferrell.

South Central L.A.: Singleton's auspicious debut as writer and director zeroes in on the concerns of a black community that too often finds itself victimized by its own members. Shattered families, shattered lives—carefully tied into a message of hope. A deeply affecting movie.

Jungle Fever (1991, U.S., 132 mins.) Dir: Spike Lee; Cast: Wesley Snipes, Annabella Sciorra, Spike Lee, John Turturro, Lonette McKee, Anthony Quinn.

While this tough drama concerns an interracial affair (between an on-target Snipes as an architect, and the luminous Sciorra), its real story is in the exploration of what it means to be black in American society. Lee lays out the territory with sharp editing and lively dialogue, with all sides telling their version of the truth as the film heads toward a seemingly inevitable conclusion.

■

NOTE: One of the quirkier footnotes to our separatist culture were the all-black musical casts. Of them, *Stormy Weather,* is worth checking out while we're waiting for the films that cast blacks without the stereotypes, in the roles they play in areas like education, medicine, and throughout the music and entertainment industry.

BLACK & WHITE

Why can't we just be friends? We don't pretend to understand, but here are some films that look at different sides of this difficult issue.

Guess Who's Coming to Dinner? (1967, U.S., 112 mins.) Dir: Stanley Kramer; Cast: Spencer Tracy, Katharine Hepburn, Sidney Poitier, Katharine Houghton, Beah Richards, Cecil Kellaway, Isabel Sanford.

This old chestnut is graced with the last joint Tracy-Hepburn performance. Poitier and Houghton are also quite charming. The story of impending mixed marriage, though dated, was quite shocking at the time.

Cry the Beloved Country (1951, Great Britain, 105 mins., b/w) Dir: Zoltan Korda; Cast: Canada Lee, Charles Carson, Sidney Poitier, Geoffrey Keen, Reginald Ngeabo, Joyce Carey.

In this first film exploration of apartheid, Alan Paton's novel is brought to terrible and grueling life. It's a close-in exposé of the appalling living conditions in the black ghettos of South Africa, as told via the moving story of a rural black minister seeking his now-criminal son. The cinematically less successful, but still powerful *Cry Freedom* is also worth a look for its 1987 update on the same subject, covering nonviolent anti-apartheid leader Steven Biko, and the aftermath of his murder.

Do the Right Thing (1989, U.S., 120 mins.) Dir: Spike Lee; Cast: Danny Aiello, Spike Lee, Ossie Davis, Ruby Dee, John Turturro.

Lee gives us another winner—difficult, but definitely a winner. Aiello and Lee are super in this movie about the deep-rooted and festering conflicts between Italians and blacks in a Brooklyn neighborhood. The subtleties of their interactions against this background are brilliantly played.

Odds Against Tomorrow (1959, U.S., 96 mins., b/w) Dir: Robert Wise; Cast: Harry Belafonte, Robert Ryan, Shelley Winters, Ed Begley, Gloria Grahame.

Crackerjack cast in character drama about a crime caper jeopardized by racial tension between the ill-matched partners, Ryan's bigoted career crook and Belafonte's debt-ridden jazz musician. Smoky score by John Lewis.

In the Heat of the Night (1967, U.S., 110 mins.) Dir: Norman Jewison; Cast: Rod Steiger, Sidney Poitier, Lee Grant, Warren Oates.

Sizzling acting and script heightened with humor, style, and seething racial tension between the terminally redneck sheriff (Steiger at his best) and the Philadelphia detective (Poitier is perfect) who comes south to help solve a murder. Five well-deserved Oscars and a notable Quincy Jones score to boot.

Shadows (1959, U.S., 87 mins., b/w) Dir: John Cassavetes; Cast: Lelia Goldoni, Ben Carruthers, Hugh Hurd.
■
Cassavetes does a sort of cinema vérité, heavily improvised, and jazz-inflected version of the beat N.Y. experience, with a clear-eyed (in very smoke-filled rooms) and compassionate view about the different experience of siblings from a mixed marriage.

The Landlord (1970, U.S., 114 mins.) Dir: Hal Ashby; Cast: Beau Bridges, Lee Grant, Pearl Bailey, Diana Sands, Lou Gossett, Susan Anspach, Bob (Robert) Klein, Patricia (Trish) Van Devere.
■
Ah, urban renewal. Out-of-touch rich white boy (Bridges) buys Brooklyn tenement with plans to gussy it up for himself. Sharp and bright satire in Ashby's directorial debut as militant black tenants give Bridges a run for his money.

Driving Miss Daisy (1989, U.S., 105 mins.) Dir: Bruce Beresford; Cast: Jessica Tandy, Morgan Freeman, Dan Aykroyd, Esther Rolle, Patti LuPone.

Huge Oscar success details a critical slice of mid-20th-century southern Americana. Great casting subtly reveals the depths of the relationship between Freeman's superbly fine-tuned, unprepossessing chauffeur and his wealthy employer (Tandy, incandescent as always). Aykroyd, despite the odd makeup, is fine as Tandy's son.

The Intruder (aka: *Shame* and *I Hate Your Guts,* 1961, U.S., 84 mins.) Dir: Roger Corman; Cast: William Shatner, Frank Maxwell, Beverly Lunsford.

Shatner does well as bigotry incarnate, simple and repulsive, as he is seemingly compelled to travel throughout the South inciting anti-school-desegregation riots. Surprisingly successful Corman-with-a-message. Solid script was supplied by *Twilight Zone* writer Charles Beaumont.

A Soldier's Story (1984, U.S., 102 mins.) Dir: Norman Jewison; Cast: Howard E. Rollins, Jr., Adolph Caesar, Denzel Washington, Larry Riley, Art Evans.

Theatrically satisfying murder mystery-drama, adapted from Charles Fuller's Pulitzer-winning Negro Ensemble Company play, exposes racial hatred in the WWII-era segregated military. Compellingly restrained performance by Rollins as the first black officer the soldiers have ever seen, in his role as Captain Davenport, sent from Washington to investigate the murder of a black sergeant.

PRIDE & PREJUDICE

The place where anyone can be "the other."

Mississippi Masala (1992, U.S., 118 mins.) Dir: Mira Nair; Cast: Denzel Washington, Sarita Choudhury, Roshan Seth; Sharmila Tagore; Joe Seneca.

Rich and vibrant contemporary American love story between southern Afro-American and East Indian (by way of Uganda). While it sounds like people of all nations, it's the same old racist story—the lovely Choudhury's family won't have anything to do with the affair. Wonderfully drawn mix of cultures, and very entertaining, while dismaying in its message.

Come See the Paradise (1990, U.S., 132 mins.) Dir: Alan Parker; Cast: Dennis Quaid, Tamlyn Tomita, Sab Shimono, Shizuko Hoshi.

This first movie about the unconscionable internment of Japanese Americans during WWII is beautiful to look at, but that may be a key flaw. While Tomita is radiantly well cast (as are the rest of her family), Quaid, her eventual husband, is never a real character, just a plot advancer and factoid-server. So while we learn a lot, despite certain liberties, we wish the film had been smaller, tougher, and more focused.

West Side Story (1961, U.S., 155 mins.) Dirs: Robert Wise, Jerome Robbins; Cast: Natalie Wood, Rita Moreno, Richard Beymer, George Chakiris, Russ Tamblyn.

Exhilarating music (Leonard Bernstein! Stephen Sondheim!) and dance (Jerome Robbins!) make this Latino-Anglo *Romeo and Juliet* affair of the N.Y. tenements soar. The star-crossed tragedy of Maria (Wood) and Tony (Beymer) emphasizes the meaninglessness of gang rivalry and all too painfully counterpoints the clash of reality challenging the hopes and dreams of the new Puerto Rican immigrants. Still holds up after all these years. For the Gordon Parks Latino/Afro-American version of *R&J*, check out the not bad *Aaron Loves Angela,* with tunes by José Feliciano.

Crossover Dreams (1985, U.S., 86 mins.) Dir: Leon Ichaso; Cast: Rubén Blades, Shawn Elliot, Tom Signorelli.

Blades is very convincing as a Latino singer (which he is) whose career heats up along with his tantalizing salsa music. Alas, ego supersedes reality and as it looks like the big breakout might not happen, he faces the loss of those he abandoned on the way up. Seemingly small story has a real tang.

Incident at Oglala (1992, U.S., 89 mins.) Dir: Michael Apted; Narrator: Robert Redford.

Riveting documentary questions Native American Leonard Peltier's conviction for murder of FBI agents sent to investigate A.I.M. terrorist activities at the Oglala Sioux reservation in South Dakota. Slow pacing is mitigated by overall impact of the interviews with the imprisoned Peltier and careful use of re-enactments for the shooting scenes.

Thunderheart (1992, U.S., 118 mins.) Dir: Michael Apted; Cast: Val Kilmer, Sam Shepard, Graham Greene, Fred Ward, Fred Dalton Thompson, Sheila Tousey.

Powerhouse action and performances in an era where we finally have real Native Americans playing non-stereotyped characterizations of same. Part-Sioux FBI agent (played well by Anglo Kilmer), investigating a tribal murder with Shepard, becomes immersed in the spiritual traditions of his ancestry.

The Boy With Green Hair (1948, U.S., 82 mins.) Dir: Joseph Losey; Cast: Pat O'Brien, Dean Stockwell, Robert Ryan, Barbara Hale.

That war (WWII that is) orphan Dean Stockwell sure is cute, but when he wakes up one morning with green hair, well, call him the town pariah. Despite a sort of strange production with little song segues, the generally light touch works in favor of this fable. While Clairol could fix him right up, he must choose whether his "mark" and its inherent message (we'll save that for you to discover) is a burden he can bear.

To Kill a Mockingbird (1962, U.S., 129 mins.) Dir: Robert Mulligan; Cast: Gregory Peck, Mary Badham, Philip Alford, Robert Duvall, Brock Peters.

Brilliantly acted and powerfully resonant version of Harper Lee's novel about another neighborhood outsider, with the incomparable Duvall as recluse Boo Radley. A must-see.

El Norte (1984, U.S., 139 mins.) Dir: Gregory Nava; Cast: Zaide Silva Gutierrez, David Villalpando, Lupe Ontiveros.

The American Dream draws desperate refugees from embattled Guatemala through Mexico and across the border into a land they hope will shelter them. In this compelling story a young brother and sister, facing the dehumanizing difficulties of illegal aliens with spunk and remarkable fortitude, struggle to create a new life.

Stand and Deliver (1988, U.S., 102 mins.) Dir: Ramon Menendez; Cast: Edward James Olmos, Lou Diamond Phillips, Rosana de Soto, Andy Garcia.

Olmos's bravura performance, as real-life high school teacher Jaime Escalante, galvanizes this very special fact-based story about East L.A. students inspired to exceed their limited barrio expectations and come up aces in a key calculus exam. Definitely *Rocky* theme-music time—but also a lot more.

Crossfire (1947, U.S., 86 mins., b/w) Dir: Edward Dmytryk; Cast: Robert Ryan, Robert Mitchum, Robert Young, Gloria Grahame, Sam Levene.

Gay-bias story, white-washed (as it were) to anti-Semitic theme for cold-feet Hollywood, is nonetheless a hot drama involving police pursuit of bigoted ex-soldier wanted for murder. Based on *The Brick Foxhole* by Richard Brooks.

Gentleman's Agreement (1947, U.S., 118 mins., b/w) Dir: Elia Kazan; Cast: Gregory Peck, Dorothy McGuire, John

Garfield, Anne Revere, Celeste Holm, June Havoc, Albert Dekker, Jane Wyatt, Dean Stockwell, Sam Jaffe.

Black Like Me (1964, U.S., 107 mins, b/w) Dir: Carl Lerner; Cast: James Whitmore, Clifton James, Roscoe Lee Browne, Lenka Peterson, Sorrell Booke, Will Geer.

WASP writer Peck masquerades in upper-class circles as a Jew, and guess what he finds out. Laura Z. Hobson's novel-turned-film was major Oscar winner, but a little pat nowadays. Almost 20 years later white reporter turns to skin-color-altering drugs to have the *black* experience. His findings were also about what you'd expect. While the book *Black Like Me* is based on a true story, and the movie deals with the ever timely issues of prejudice and white-black relations, it's dated too.

Before Stonewall: The Making of a Gay and Lesbian Community (1984, U.S., 87 mins.) Dirs: Greta Schiller, Robert Rosenberg; Narrator: Rita Mae Brown.

June 27, 1969—the turning point in the history of gay rights. When the Stonewall bar in Greenwich Village was raided that night, the police encountered major resistance and the days of passive response to persecution were over. *Before Stonewall* makes potent use of archival footage and interviews to trace, from the 1920s on, the attitudes—and legislative history—that led to this boiling point.

The Last Temptation of Christ (1988, U.S., 164 mins.) Dir: Martin Scorsese; Cast: Willem Dafoe, Harvey Keitel, Barbara Hershey, Harry Dean Stanton, David Bowie, Verna Bloom, Andre Gregory, Juliette Caton, Roberts Blossom.

Written by Paul Schrader, and adapted from the novel by Nikos Kazantzakis, this movie is a powerful exploration of the human nature of Jesus Christ's struggle to accept his divine mission. Interesting that the story of a man persecuted for his religious beliefs was attacked most vociferously by religious fundamentalists who felt the film should be suppressed for its—most respectfully presented—point of view.

THINGS TO COME

ALIEN PRESENCE

The first movies to come to mind in this category are the superb and seminal *Alien, Aliens, Close Encounters of the Third Kind, Star Wars, Return of the Jedi, The Empire Strikes Back,* and of course all of the *Star Treks* and the irresistible *E.T.* These movies epitomize the fear of the unknown, tied irrevocably with the lure of the same, and often not just a little bit of the urge to conquer.

A Trip to the Moon (*Le Voyage dans la Lune,* 1902, 14–21 mins., b/w, silent) Dir: Georges Méliès; Cast: Georges Méliès, Victor André, Bleuette Bernon, Corps de Ballet du Châtelet.
∎
Wonderfully perky first sighting—the first film aliens were charming little moon people who were inclined to explode when tapped with an umbrella. Strikingly imaginative effects from a director (with a great sense of humor) who was a magician by trade, with tips of the space helmet to Jules Verne and H. G. Wells.

The Day the Earth Stood Still (1951, U.S., 92 mins., b/w) Dir: Robert Wise; Cast: Patricia Neal, Michael Rennie, Hugh Marlowe, Sam Jaffe.

An alien comes to warn the Earth about the dangers of the Bomb. One of the best, and not just for the glimpse of monolithic 1950s Washington, D.C., and its Cold War trappings. A moving and effectively acted picture about how our national psyche is so rooted in fear we risk not hearing what we need to hear. The effects are great too.

The Man Who Fell to Earth (1976, Great Britain, 140 mins.) Dir: Nicolas Roeg; Cast: David Bowie, Candy Clark, Buck Henry, Rip Torn, Bernie Casey.

International businessman is really an alien on a mission. Starring a genuine alien. But this isn't only about aliens—it's about Big Business and Success in America, and is as absorbing as it is offbeat. Wonderful footage of New Mexico. There are a few different cuts of this around—in fact, the fully restored version has some stuff they might as well have kept out. Note: Based on the novel by Walter Tevis, author of *The Hustler.*

Solaris (1971, U.S.S.R., 165 mins.) Dir: Andrei Tarkovsky; Cast: Natalya Bondarchuk, Yuri Jarvet.

Cult repertory favorite. This time scientists are sent into space to a new world, where they confront sentient counterparts from their past. Visually stunning knockout; try to see it on a big screen.

The Thing (aka: *The Thing From Another World,* 1951, U.S., 87 mins., b/w) Dir: Christian Nyby; Cast: Kenneth Tobey, Margaret Sheridan, Robert Cornthwaite, James Arness.

So the Air Force goofs and blows up a flying saucer, then melts down its occupant with an electric blanket. Unlike so many Cold War sci-fi films, this one is not too concerned with alien (or capitalist) hegemony. So while the people on the screen would like to cook the alien invader (oh yeah, the "thing" is a high-intelligence tuber of some kind), it's all done with a light hand but very skillfully—as you might expect

with a screenplay by Charles Lederer *(The Front Page)* and production by Howard Hawks (though contrary to rumor, he did not direct). This is a great movie that brings up all kinds of "visitor" issues without beating us up about them, and still admonishing us to "watch the skies."

Invaders From Mars (1953, U.S., 78 mins.) Dir: William Cameron Menzies; Cast: Arthur Franz, Helena Carter, Jimmy Hunt, Leif Erickson, Hillary Brooke, Milburn Stone.

This one, however, brings out all the artillery (and we mean *everything*—looks like WWII and the Korean . . . uh . . . conflict, all in one) for one little flying saucer whose inhabitants are determined to replace humans with mutants (you know, they look just like us . . . but not quite). You'll not only watch the skies, but you'll be feeling the back of your neck for that telltale crystal implant they're threatening you with. Cold War phobia at its best. Beware: The 1986 update of this is pathetic.

UFOria (1981, U.S., 100 mins.) Dir: John Binder; Cast: Cindy Williams, Harry Dean Stanton, Fred Ward, Robert Gray, Darrell Larson.

Adam and Eve *were* astronauts and Jesus *did* come to earth in a flying saucer, right? This is one for all you believers out there. Cindy believes, and Brother Bud (our favorite, Harry Dean, but not as great as he can be), a sleaze-ball evangelist, knows a crowd-pleaser when he sees it. So, done up like Aimee Semple, Williams and her Waylon Jennings-pretender beau (Ward) take it on the road, to mixed results.

Repo Man (1984, U.S., 92 mins.) Dir: Alex Cox; Cast: Emilio Estevez, Harry Dean Stanton, Tracey Walter, Olivia Barash, Dick Rude.

Now here's Harry Dean in his element, with a terrific movie that's as totally quirky as he is. He's the repo-man mentor to young Emilio, and their escapades include close encounters of all kinds in an L.A. junkyard of odd characters, including a genuine (technically speaking) alien or two. Grand finale is the ultimate car-repossession effect.

Forbidden Planet (1956, U.S., 98 mins.) Dir: Fred McLeod Wilcox; Cast: Walter Pidgeon, Anne Francis, Leslie Nielsen, Earl Holliman.

Before Nielsen was the hysterical *Airplane!* passenger he was an astronaut, and while he doesn't get to do much here aside from some discreet elevator-eyeing of Anne Francis, he does fly us to the land of the Krel—an apparently not-quite-extinct alien world where we find that SF writers of the 1950s were up on their psychoanalytical reading. The planet features friendly robots (who make great sour-mash whiskey), and you have nothing to fear but your id. Nice beam-us-up-Scotty type special effects.

Five Million Years to Earth (aka: *Quatermass and the Pit; The Creeping Unknown;* and *Enemy From Space,* 1967, Great Britain, 98 mins.) Dir: Roy Ward Baker; Cast: James Donald, Andrew Keir, Barbara Shelley, Julian Glover.

This is the penultimate, and arguably the best, in an immensely popular series originally made for British TV by writer Nigel Kneale. The respected Dr. Quatermass (Keir) investigates a mysterious capsule uncovered during an excavation of a London street. Its contents reveal Martian intervention at early stages of human evolution. Powerful stuff.

2001: A Space Odyssey (1968, U.S.-Great Britain, 139 mins.) Dir: Stanley Kubrick; Cast: Keir Dullea, Gary Lockwood, William Sylvester, Daniel Richter, Douglas Rain.

Possibly wasted on a small screen—you're guaranteed to get lost in it in the right viewing situation—but it's a mesmerizing experience any way you watch it. We visit our past and our future, embryo to archetype. What does it all mean? Is Mankind Really Ready To Know? The startling message to do with aliens comes at the end, so we won't spoil it for you.

ROBOTS, 'DROIDS & OTHER SENTIENT BEINGS

It's hard being a robot—or a cyborg, android, bionic being, or an automaton or deconstructed humanoid of any stripe. And as much as they're assumed to be better for not having feelings, they all seem to have them anyway. Look at Frankenstein's monster—not a happy creature. And the burdens they have—in *The Day the Earth Stood Still* the robots from another planet assume they're responsible for ensuring peace in the galaxy. But some of them do have fun, like Robby in *Forbidden Planet,* a swell robot, and a good friend, too.

Star Wars (1977, U.S., 121 mins.) Dir: George Lucas; Cast: Mark Hamill, Harrison Ford, Alec Guinness, Carrie Fisher, Peter Cushing, Anthony Daniels, David Prowse, voice of James Earl Jones.

The Empire Strikes Back (1980, U.S., 118 mins.) Dir: Irvin Kershner; Cast: Mark Hamill, Harrison Ford, Carrie Fisher, Billy Dee Williams, Alec Guinness, Frank Oz, David Prowse, Anthony Daniels, voice of James Earl Jones.

Return of the Jedi (1983, U.S., 133 mins.) Dir: Richard Marquand; Cast: Mark Hamill, Carrie Fisher, Harrison Ford, Alec Guinness, Billy Dee Williams, Denis Lawson, voice of James Earl Jones.

This series has the zaniest and most wonderful pack of creatures who wouldn't know from DNA, at least not the earthly variety: the loyal and humble Chewbacca; that charming quirk of prelingual metal, R2-D2, and his somewhat prissy multilingual counterpart, C-3PO; the fabulous Ewoks; all the fearsome war machines in *Empire;* and of course the bionic Darth Vader. Well, you don't want to miss any of them. You especially want to see the wonderful intergalactic barroom scenes in the original, where each patron was truly a fresh and inspired creature from another planet (or two).

Making Mr. Right (1987, U.S., 100 mins.) Dir: Susan Seidelman; Cast: John Malkovich, Ann Magnuson, Glenne Headly, Ben Masters, Laurie Metcalf, Polly Bergen, Jeff Hoyt.

What every woman dreams of—her own personal android. Used to be just a young houseboy was enough. Loopy comedy—without quite the punch we expect from *Desperately Seeking* Seidelman—has some really good bits and bright performances. Malkovich, who does do comedy, and well, is twice-cast as the 'droid *and* his inventor, and performance artist Magnuson is the android's tough-cookie P.R. chief and love interest.

Blade Runner (1982, U.S., 122 mins.) Dir: Ridley Scott; Cast: Harrison Ford, Rutger Hauer, Sean Young, Edward James Olmos, Joanna Cassidy, Daryl Hannah.

The movie that asks, are androids really a metaphor for feelings? Story taken from Phillip K. Dick's *Do Androids Dream of Electric Sheep?* has re-enlisted cop Ford hunting renegade androids in 21st century L.A.—and Daryl's really found herself, as one of them. The richly layered sets and action make the future look very much like Tokyo meets Times Square. Lots of fuss about the new director's cut available (no voice-

over; tougher ending), but this is powerful stuff whichever version you see.

The Stepford Wives (1975, U.S., 115 mins.) Dir: Bryan Forbes; Cast: Katharine Ross, Paula Prentiss, Tina Louise, Patrick O'Neal, Nanette Newman.

The boys in the 'burbs whip up (with the help of modern robotics in the form of a former Disney tech) their idea of the perfect wife—brain numb, but oh so eager to please. While interpretable as a cautionary tale with fem political overtones, it's a pretty successful thriller, as in "Who's been replacing the nice wives of Stepford?" *The Perfect Woman*, a vintage 1949 plum from the U.K., plays the lighter side of female robotics—here, the boys just want to have fun.

Terminator 2: Judgment Day (1991, U.S., 136 mins.) Dir: James Cameron; Cast: Arnold Schwarzenegger, Linda Hamilton, Edward Furlong, Robert Patrick.

OK all you bionic boys and girls. This is a warmer and friendlier *Terminator*—a cyborg actually, for you tech types. The action's rousing, the effects a wow, and Arnold is getting more endearing all the time—but don't worry, he never loses his punch. Hamilton's musculature (and character) are pretty good, too.

Sleeper (1973, U.S., 88 mins.) Dir: Woody Allen; Cast: Woody Allen, Diane Keaton, John Beck, Don Keefer, Mary McGregory, John McLiam.

A Woody-fest of gimmicks and gadgets help him spoof the early 1970s when he defrosts in 2173 after 200 years of cryogenic sleep and gets involved with poet-revolutionary Luna (Keaton is delightful). You'll love his robo-butler and orgasmatron (in Jane Fonda's comic-strip *Barbarella* they had one of these too, but called it an "excessive machine"), and you'll especially like the clone job he's got to do as part of the rebel plot—all he's got to work with is the guy's nose . . . and shoes. It's *very* funny.

Metropolis (1926, Germany, 120 mins., silent, b/w) Dir: Fritz Lang; Cast: Brigitte Helm, Alfred Abel, Gustav Frohlich, Rudolph Klein-Rogge.

Based on a novel written by Lang's wife, screenwriter Thea von Harbou, this heavyweight Gothic parable about the literally underground working class and the despotic surface rulers features an incandescent performance by Helm as both Maria the reformer and her robot self, created for unclear reasons to lead a revolt of the workers—at the behest of the rulers. Powerful, striking set designs and effects are enhanced further by the mesmerizing Giorgio Moroder score in the color-tinted and shorter 1984 release.

Robocop (1987, U.S., 103 mins.) Dir: Paul Verhoeven; Cast: Peter Weller, Nancy Allen, Ronny Cox, Kurtwood Smith, Dan O'Herlihy.

Devastating damage to brain and body leaves Detroit patrolman Weller with the cyborg solution as his only chance for continued life on this planet. His digital vision (and other zippy powers) are great for crime control, but he's still a torn man, somehow still subject to memories of former hearth and home. And maybe that's part of the appeal of this meaningless (though, some felt, humorous), ultraviolent, super-effects venture into the mechanical cure.

Dark Star (1972, U.S., 83 mins.) Dir: John Carpenter; Cast: Dan O'Bannon, Brian Narelle, Dre Pahich.

Dark Star is a hilariously out-of-this-world sci-fi satire about a tuckered-out space crew whose job is to go around blowing up unstable planets. One of the bombs in their hold is a master of phenomenological reasoning, and, shades of *2001*'s HAL (though unrelated, writ-ers Carpenter and O'Bannon [*Alien*] say), it's up to our loyal crew of surfers and other odd-fits to talk it down from premature explosion. In *2001*, HAL the computer had a mind of its own as well, but it just wouldn't listen to reason, with appropriately weightier results. Maybe HAL and *Dark Star*'s bomb should have had a chat.

CAUTIONARY TALES

The world is too much with us—and we just keep trying to get rid of it, it seems. Herewith, The Bomb . . . and a few other select sources of global apocalypse.

Dr. Strangelove: Or, How I Learned to Stop Worrying and Love the Bomb (1964, U.S., 93 mins.) Dir: Stanley Kubrick; Cast: Peter Sellers, Sterling Hayden, George C. Scott, Keenan Wynn, Slim Pickens, Peter Bull.

Brilliant, biting satire. WWIII gets started by demented U.S. Air Force general Jack D. Ripper (Hayden), who's convinced the Russians have polluted his "vital bodily fluids" and sends a squad of B-52s loaded with nukes to blast the Russkies away. Sellers is priceless in three roles, but Scott, Hayden, and Pickens are also swell as they each hear the music of their particular character's insanity. Kubrick, as always, is brilliant with his scoring, especially in the Vera Lynn-accompanied tour de force ending. Terry Southern and Peter George (*Red Alert* author) co-wrote the screenplay with Kubrick.

Fail Safe (1964, U.S., 111 mins., b/w) Dir: Sidney Lumet; Cast: Henry Fonda, Dan O'Herlihy, Walter Matthau.

Once again an American bomber is mistakenly ordered to target Moscow—this time, however, because of a mechanical malfunction, confronting the U.S. with the horrifying necessity of self-imposed damage control. Effectively acted and tightly wound.

The Quiet Earth (1985, New Zealand, 91 mins.) Dir: Geoff Murphy; Cast: Bruno Lawrence, Alison Routledge, Peter Smith.

A global energy grid gone awry seems to have created the "effect" that caused all the earth's inhabitants to vanish, aside from this odd-lot of three, featuring *Smash Palace*'s Lawrence as project scientist Zac. Lushly produced film is most interesting when it explores Zac's adventures in adapting when he thinks he's the only one left. Film blames Americans, who were joint developers of the project with New Zealand, for not disclosing key info—a timely slam at the U.S. for our sanctions against N.Z. for establishing itself as a nuclear-free zone. Sort of a remake of the 1959 *The World, the Flesh, and the Devil* with two male and one female holocaust survivors and their inherent sexual and racial tensions, but here we've traded a Maori tribesman (Smith) for the black (Harry Belafonte), a redhead (Routledge) for a blonde (Inger Stevens), and Mel Ferrer for Lawrence.

On the Beach (1959, U.S., 134 mins., b/w) Dir: Stanley Kramer; Cast: Gregory Peck, Ava Gardner, Fred Astaire, Anthony Perkins.

Nevil Shute's global atomic-war novel brought to devastating life. Melbourne, Australia, 1964: the nuclear radiation fallout is now reaching this last corner of the planet. This is done exceptionally well, with characters and situations realistically rendered. Gives us chills to think about it.

The Day the Earth Caught Fire (1962, Great Britain, 90 mins., b/w) Dir: Val Guest; Cast: Edward Judd, Janet Munro, Leo McKern, Michael Goodliffe, Bernard Braden, Arthur Christiansen, Michael Caine.

Anything you can split, I can split better. . . . Well, this one's just as hard as *On the Beach*. Don't let the sensationalist title fool you—this is a very tough and realistic enactment of the cataclysmic results of A-bomb testing as dramatized via the newsroom reporting of the *Daily Express* in London (Christiansen, who plays the editor-in-chief, is a former editor of the actual *Express*). The reporters' lives and the unfolding events are well balanced, to make this ever-more powerful. Definitely a nonglitzed Hollywood production; those ban-the-Bomb demonstrators, beatniks, and everyone else on the street look just like you and me. Whew.

The Bed Sitting Room (1969, Great Britain, 91 mins.) Dir: Richard Lester; Cast: Rita Tushingham, Sir Ralph Richardson, Spike Milligan, Sandy Nichols.
■
We wish this was available on video. This is the British *Goon Show*'s view of the apocalypse. Their lighter-side (if there can be such a thing) version involves the post-apocalyptic mutation process. You know, humans turn into all kinds of other creatures, even pets and the like. Some nice, weird photography of floating St. Peter's among other submerged monuments.

Fat Man and Little Boy (1989, U.S., 126 mins.) Dir: Roland Joffe; Cast: Paul Newman, Dwight Schultz, Bonnie Bedelia, John Cusack, Laura Dern, John C. McGinley, Natasha Richardson, Del Close.

Desert Bloom (1986, U.S., 106 mins.) Dir: Eugene Corr; Cast: Jon Voight, JoBeth Williams, Ellen Barkin, Annabeth Gish, Allen Garfield.

The Atomic Cafe (1982, U.S., 88 mins.) Dirs: Kevin Rafferty, Jayne Loader, Pierce Rafferty.

The Manhattan Project and how we got the Bomb. *Fat Man and Little Boy* is fictionalized and simplified, but still compelling in its telling of the ethical and moral dilemmas facing the elite group of handpicked Los Alamos, N.M.-based scientists, led by Robert Oppenheimer (Schultz), who were responsible for bringing us into the Atomic Age. *Desert Bloom* is a real knockout that tells the compelling story of the people in Nevada who were affected by the radioactive fallout that these boys and their successors created with the testing of their new toys. And *Atomic Cafe* is a must-see for its incredibly wry look at the paranoia induced by the government propaganda of the 1950s Cold War era. Duck and cover.

Koyaanisqatsi (1983, U.S., 87 mins.) Dir: Godfrey Reggio.

In *Koyaanisqatsi* fabulously majestic images, filmed from mind-boggling angles, contrast aspects of American life and survival with its geological wonders. Tightly edited, enhanced by a brilliantly soaring score by Philip Glass, the beauty of this mesmerizing film—whose title is Hopi for life out of balance, or, a state of life that calls for another way of living—may seem to negate its negative message. The sequel, *Powasqqatsi,* as powerful in its imagery, scoring, and impact, looks at exploited cultures in Third World countries.

WarGames (1983, U.S., 113 mins.) Dir: John Badham; Cast: Matthew Broderick, Ally Sheedy, Dabney Coleman, John Wood, Barry Corbin.

We've really advanced now. David (appealing Broderick) is an all-too-realistic young computer-hacker who accesses the new game "Thermonuclear War." Turns out it's the Defense Department version, though, not Nintendo's. Well-paced and believable action-thriller.

The China Syndrome (1979, U.S., 123 mins.) Dir: James Bridges; Cast: Jane Fonda, Jack Lemmon, Michael Douglas, Peter Donat, Scott Brady, Wilford Brimley.

Silkwood (1983, U.S., 131 mins.) Dir: Mike Nichols; Cast: Meryl Streep, Cher, Kurt Russell, Craig T. Nelson, Diana Scarwid, Henderson Forsythe, Fred Ward.

The China Syndrome is even more believable. Riveting story, with super performances by all, is based on various incidents at nuclear-power plants. A news crew gets involved with the attempted cover-up of a post-earthquake nuclear "accident" causing a perilously low water-shield level, critically exposing the nuclear rod pile . . . and threatening meltdown. *Silkwood,* Nichols's well-done adaptation of the real-life Karen Silkwood story, also deals with nuclear-plant accidents (and their cover-ups) with wonderfully developed characters, especially Cher as Karen's best friend Dolly and La Streep herself as Silkwood, a factory worker who died suspiciously as she was en route to delivering some potentially damaging info about her employer to the *New York Times.*

The Rapture (1991, U.S., 102 mins.) Dir: Michael Tolkin; Cast: Mimi Rogers, Patrick Bauchau, David Duchovny, Kimberly Cullum, Will Patton.

This list would not be complete without some basic Armageddon. Rogers goes for broke in her portrayal of a woman whose search for meaning in her life has been left unsatisfied until she is literally carried away by her new-found religious enlightenment.

■

NOTE: Two special mentions for here. In the "fear of annihilation" category we have Joe Dante's entertaining Atomo Vision-Rumble Rama visit to the Bay of Pigs near-calamity in his 1993 *Matinee.* And in the apocalypse-noir category we have Robert Aldrich's *Kiss Me Deadly,* so dated it's almost a B, but it still has its own unique punch.

POST-APOCALYPSE

We're in the Future now. What happened—nukes, meteors, the unknowable, or, certainly, more of What Man Does Not Want to Know—doesn't really matter. Here are some scenarios about what it will be like.

Fahrenheit 451 (1966, Great Britain, 111 mins.) Dir: François Truffaut; Cast: Oskar Werner, Julie Christie, Cyril Cusack.

Double whew. It could happen here. Thinking and literature are verboten, and the renegades devote their lives to memorization of the outlawed texts. A must-see.

Brazil (1985, U.S.-Great Britain, 131 mins.) Dir: Terry Gilliam; Cast: Jonathan Pryce, Bob Hoskins, Katherine Helmond, Ian Holm, Robert De Niro, Michael Palin.

Surely inspired by *1984,* another vision of our future with the Brain Police. Some hated this film, but with its potent imagery and scale, stunning sets, and clear message, it's powerful stuff. And there's just enough Pythonesque attitude to make you laugh. (You'll hum the title song for a week.)

The Illustrated Man (1969, U.S., 103 mins.) Dir: Jack Smight; Cast: Rod Steiger, Claire Bloom, Robert Drivas.

A trip into the unknown through the graphics tattooed over every inch of Steiger's body. Three separate stories are told; the future-vision one takes place in the African veldt, where just wishing your parents would disappear can make it so. Not quite as good as the original Ray Bradbury book, but you always feel like it really could happen.

A Clockwork Orange (1971, Great Britain, 137 mins.) Dir: Stanley Kubrick; Cast: Malcolm McDowell, Patrick Magee, Adrienne Corri, Aubrey Morris, James Marcus, Steven Berkoff, David Prowse.

A future of alienation, milk bars, and the ultimate in mindless violence in a fractured society. Based on Anthony Burgess's novel, sans the last chapter, we are subjected to visual terrorism— the images here will stick with you, and though it's slow at times, this is a pill worth taking once.

A Boy and His Dog (1975, U.S., 87 mins.) Dir: L. Q. Jones; Cast: Don Johnson, Susanne Benton, Jason Robards, Alvy Moore, Helene Winston, Charles McGraw.

Harlan Ellison fans alert! Totally weird picture, with some good twisted zing, of Our Future After the Bomb. The middle class goes underground (literally) and comes out looking like Raggedy Ann meets the Stepford wives.

Alphaville (1965, France, 100 mins., b/w) Dir: Jean-Luc Godard; Cast: Eddie Constantine, Anna Karina, Akim Tamiroff.

Private eye Lemmy Caution, played by the wonderful Eddie Constantine, takes a car trip through Nuevo Wavo intersidereal space to a city that just might be Paris, where he confronts a society that is controlled by computer central, all with a very 1950s noir attitude.

1984 (1984, Great Britain, 123 mins.) Dir: Michael Radford; Cast: John Hurt, Richard Burton, Suzanna Hamilton, Cyril Cusack.

The ultimate totalitarian society. Big Brother is watching and now you can ring him back if you get Call ID. Nothing can match George Orwell's book for pure prescient terrorism, but the movie does a pretty good job.

The Handmaid's Tale (1990, U.S., 118 mins.) Dir: Volker Schlondorff; Cast: Natasha Richardson, Faye Dunaway, Aidan Quinn, Elizabeth McGovern, Victoria Tennant, Robert Duvall.

Margaret Atwood's novel about a not-too-future fascist society that's found God and a sexist solution to the rampant infertility caused by our toxic atmosphere is stylishly told and attention-holding, but vaguely low on impact. Nice cast does what it can with Pinter's limited screenplay; but Duvall's Commander is still disappointing.

Death Race 2000 (1975, U.S., 80 mins.) Dir: Paul Bartel; Cast: David Carradine, Sylvester Stallone, Louisa Moritz, Mary Woronov.

Bloody but catchy parable about the innately violent nature of humankind thinly disguised as an intracontinental road-race action flick, features Sly in a ha-ha funny role. This wry Roger Corman production is the granddaddy of the slew of future-road movies that followed, most notably the Mad Max series, with its classic *The Road Warrior.*

THX-1138 (1971, U.S., 88 mins.) Dir: George Lucas; Cast: Robert Duvall, Maggie McOmie, Donald Pleasence.

Lucas's remarkable first feature film based on a graduate-school short of his, and partly filmed in the then-unfinished San Francisco BART subway tubes. Shades of *Brave New World,* the movie asks, "Are you sedated enough?" in this apocalyptic vision of a world moved underground, where the cops look like C-3P0 precursors, and everyone has a vanity license plate instead of a name. There's work, videos, and sleep, and until THX's roommate LUH dares to alter their pill intake, almost no one's awake enough to think much further beyond that.

Planet of the Apes (1968, U.S., 112 mins.) Dir: Franklin J. Schaffner; Cast: Charlton Heston, Roddy McDowall, Kim Hunter, Maurice Evans, James Whitmore, James Daly, Linda Harrison.

While Heston is stiff as a board as usual and the ape make-up, so lauded in its day, is not so impressive anymore, who could knock a concept that has our future hanging on a reevaluation of the course of evolution? Chuck is one of a trio of surviving crash-landed astronauts on a planet inhabited by a ruling class of linguistically (and otherwise) evolved apes. Of course, Mr. Heston couldn't quite accept the symmetry of the situation and ends up taking this still quite moving indictment of man and human nature rather personally.

INDEX

A

A Bout de Souffle, *see* Breathless *(1959)*
Abe Lincoln in Illinois, 48
Absent-Minded Professor, The, 69, 103
Accidental Tourist, The, 183
Adam's Rib *(1949)*, 30, 195, 226
Adorable, 132
Adventures of Milo and Otis, The, 112
Adventures of Picasso, The, 185
Adventures of Robin Hood, The, 263
Adventures of Robinson Crusoe, 170
Advise and Consent, 45, 230
African Queen, The, 83, 134
After Hours, 71, 187
Age of Innocence, The, 175
Agnes of God, 255
Agony and the Ecstasy, The, 184
Aguirre, the Wrath of God, 85
Air Up There, The, 104, 229
Airplane!, 67
Alamo, The, 145, 147
Alfie, 78, 197
Ali—Fear Eats the Soul, 161
Alibi Ike, 121
Alice Doesn't Live Here Anymore,
    164, 226
Alien, 292
Aliens, 292
All of Me, 257
All Quiet on the Western Front, 270
All That Jazz, 220
All the King's Men, 47, 51, 175
All the President's Men, 49, 72
All the Right Moves, 105
Alphaville, 299
Amadeus, 203
Amazing Dr. Clitterhouse, The, 135
American Dream *(1989)*, 5
American Gigolo, 96
American Graffiti, 199, 207
American Hot Wax, 198, 207
American in Paris, An, 79, 130, 192, 218
American Me, 41
American Werewolf in London, An, 78
Anastasia, 20
Anatomy of a Murder, 30, 205
Angel at My Table, An, 24

Angel Face, 144
Angel Heart, 75
Angels Over Broadway, 138
Angels With Dirty Faces, 139, 141, 253
Anna Karenina, 179
Antarctica, 85, 112
Apartment, The, 3
Apocalypse Now, 285
Apprenticeship of Duddy Kravitz,
    The, 256
Arise, My Love, 133
Arthur, 9, 89
Article 99, 14
Artists and Models, 157
As You Desire Me, 20
Ash Wednesday, 18
Asphalt Jungle, The, 28
At Long Last Love, 195
At Play in the Fields of the Lord, 84
Atlantic City, 90, 124, 249
Atomic Cafe, 297
Autobiography of Miss Jane Pittman,
    The, 287
Avalon, 58
Awakenings, 13
Awful Truth, The, 244

B

Babette's Feast, 87
Baby and the Battleship, The, 248
Baby Boom, 248
Baby Doll, 235
Baby Face, 149
Bachelor and the Bobby Soxer,
    The, 103
Bachelor Mother, 248
Bad and the Beautiful, The, 211
Bad News Bears, The, 103
Badlands *(1974)*, 26
Bagdad Cafe, 188
Baker's Wife, The, 88, 243
Ball of Fire, 128, 134
Ballad of Little Jo, 225
Band Wagon, The, 190, 219
Bang the Drum Slowly, 102
Bank Shot, 28
Barabbas, 57
Barbary Coast, 76
Barefoot in the Park, 241
Barfly, 89
Barton Fink, 212

Basileus Quartet, 203
BAT 21, 285
Battle of the Sexes, The, 122
Battleground, 276
Battling Bellhop, The, *see*
    Kid Galahad *(1937)*
Baxter *(1991)*, 112
Bear, The, 116
Becky Sharp, 171
Bed Sitting Room, The, 297
Bedazzled, 250
Beethoven *(1936)*, 203
Beetlejuice, 61
Before Stonewall, 292
Being There, 73, 209
Belle de Jour, 239
Bells of St. Mary's, The, 255
Belly of an Architect, The, 188
Ben-Hur *(1959)*, 261
Best Man, The, 43
Betsy's Wedding, 240
Bible . . . in the Beginning, The, 251
Bicycle Thief, The, 81
Big Broadcast, 206
Big Combo, The, 129
Big Deal on Madonna Street, 27
Big Easy, The, 74
Big Heat, The, 35
Big Parade, The, 270
Big Red One, The, 277
Big Sleep, The *(1946)*, 32
Big Store, The, 97
Bingo Long Traveling All-Stars and
    Motor Kings, The, 102, 287
Bird, 95, 196
Bird Man of Alcatraz, The, 42
Birds, The, 116, 159
Birth of a Nation, The, 267
Bishop's Wife, The, 252, 254
Black Like Me, 292
Black Narcissus, 255
Black Orpheus, 84
Black Robe, 253
Black Stallion, The, 115
Blackboard Jungle, The, 7, 197
Blade Runner, 36, 295
Blaze, 47
Bliss of Mrs. Blossom, The, 244
Blithe Spirit, 60
Blob, The, 214
Blonde Bombshell, *see* Bombshell
Blonde Venus, 150

Blow-Up, 78, 99, 187, 200
Blue Velvet, 95
Bluebeard's Eighth Wife, 98, 133
Boat, The, *see* Das Boot
Bob le Flambeur, 29, 91
Bob Roberts, 43
Body and Soul *(1947)*, 106, 125
Bombshell, 149
Bonnie and Clyde, 25, 146, 271
Bonnie Parker Story, The, 26
Boomerang *(1947)*, 47
Boomerang *(1992)*, 6
Border Incident, 129
Born Free, 117
Born on the Fourth of July, 286
Born to Dance, 194
Born Yesterday *(1951)*, 74
Bound for Glory, 271
Boy and His Dog, A, 299
Boy With Green Hair, The, 291
Boyz N the Hood, 288
Brazil, 299
Break the News, 194
Breakfast at Tiffany's, 72, 110, 176
Breaking Away, 109
Breathless *(1959)*, 26, 80
Breathless *(1983)*, 26
Brewster McCloud, 68
Brian's Song, 105
Bridge on the River Kwai, The, 284
Bridges at Toko-Ri, The, 281
Brief Encounter *(1946)*, 244
Bringing Up Baby, 117, 232
Broadcast News, 73
Broadway Melody of 1940, 193
Broken Noses, 107
Brother From Another Planet, The,
    71, 288
Brothers Karamazov, The, 180
Buddy Holly Story, The, 67, 198
Buffalo Bill and the Indians, or Sitting
    Bull's History Lesson, 268
Bull Durham, 102
Bulldog Drummond, 39, 127
Bullitt, 76
Bunny Lake Is Missing, 40, 200
Burden of Dreams, 211
Burroughs: The Movie, 94
Butterflies Are Free, 17
Butterfly, 236
Bye, Bye Birdie, 210
Bye Bye Braverman, 257

C

Cabinet of Dr. Caligari, The *(1919)*, 151
Cal, 57
Call Northside 777, 38
Camelot, 263
Cameraman, The, 186
Camille Claudel, 185
Can-Can, 157, 195
Candidate, The, 42
Canterville Ghost, The *(1944)*, 61
Cape Fear *(1991)*, 143, 235
Captain's Paradise, The, 241
Caravaggio, 184
Carefree, 219
Carny, 216
Carousel, 217
Carpetbaggers, The, 153
Carrie *(1952)*, 175
Casablanca, 141, 146, 191
Casino Royale, 136
Cat From Outer Space, The, 111
Cat People *(1942)*, 110
Catch Us If You Can, *see* Having
    a Wild Weekend
Catered Affair, The, 240
Caught, 152, 153
Champagne Waltz, 133
Champion, 107
Chan Is Missing, 76
Change of Habit, 155
Charade, 80
Charge of the Light Brigade, The
    (1936), 115, 274
Chariots of Fire, 109
Cheyenne Autumn, 268
Children of Paradise, 79
Chilly Scenes of Winter, 183
Chimes at Midnight, 167
China Syndrome, The, 298
Chinatown, 33
Chocolat, 82
Christine, 208
Christmas in Connecticut *(1945)*, 62
Christmas in July, 98
Christmas Story, A, 62
Christopher Strong, 68, 225
Cincinnati Kid, The, 91
Cinderella *(1950)*, 101
Cinema Paradiso, 214
Circus, The, 216
Circus of Horrors, 19
Citadel, The *(1938)*, 14

Citizen Kane, 4, 127, 142, 150
Citizens Band, *see* Handle With Care
City Lights, 17
City of Hope, 48
Clive of India, 264
Clockwork Orange, A, 173, 299
Close Encounters of the Third Kind, 292
Closely Watched Trains, 65
Clowns, The, 216
Coal Miner's Daughter, 201
Cocoon, 249
Color Purple, The, 182, 287
Come See the Paradise, 290
Comfort and Joy, 208
Coming Up Roses, 214
Commitments, The, 57
Competition, The, 204
Connecticut Yankee in King Arthur's
    Court, A *(1949)*, 264
Conrack, 8
Contempt, 211
Conversation, The, 34, 76
Convoy, 202
Cool Hand Luke, 41, 87
Corky, 108
Cornered, 282
Country, 12
Coup de Foudre, *see* Entre Nous
Cover Girl, 100, 217
Crack-Up, 37
Crazy People, 7
Creeping Unknown, The, *see*
    Five Million Years to Earth
Crossfire, 291
Crossover Dreams, 290
Crowd Roars, The, 108
Cry Freedom, 83
Cry of the City, 36
Cry the Beloved Country, 289
Crying Game, The, 57, 233
Cyrano de Bergerac *(1950)*, 178

D

Dames, 222
Damn Yankees, 103
Damsel in Distress, A, 191
Dances With Wolves, 229, 268
Dangerous Liaisons *(1988)*, 177
Dark Command, 266
Dark Passage, 18
Dark Star, 296
Dark Victory *(1939)*, 15

Darkman, 19
Darling, 99
Das Boot, 70, 275
Daughters of the Dust, 227
Dave, 74
Day for Night, 211
Day of the Jackal, The, 52
Day of the Locust, The, 182, 211
Day of the Triffids, 18
Day the Earth Caught Fire, The, 297
Day the Earth Stood Still, The, 73, 142,
    292, 294
Day Will Dawn, The, 275
Days of Heaven, 12
D.C. Cab, 73
Dead, The, 56
Dead Calm, 70
Dead Heat on a Merry-Go-Round, 92
Dead Poets Society, 8
Dead Ringers, 13
Death Becomes Her, 19
Death Race 2000, 300
Deathwatch, 210
Deep Cover (1992), 35
Deer Hunter, The, 286
Defending Your Life, 258
Delicatessen, 88
Delicious, 191
Deliverance, 228
Desert Bloom, 297
Desert Fox, The, 279
Design for Living, 137
Designing Woman, 100, 242
Desperately Seeking Susan, 20
Destination Tokyo, 274
Devil and Daniel Webster, The, 251
Devil and Miss Jones, The, 4, 97
Devil Is a Sissy, The, 162
Devil's Disciple, The, 60
Diabolique, 8, 246
Dial M for Murder (1954), 40, 246
Diamond Jim, 131
Diary of a Chambermaid (1964), 9
Diary of a Country Priest, 253
Die Hard, 36
Diner, 87, 105
Dirty Dancing, 221, 257
Dirty Harry, 35, 76
Discreet Charm of the Bourgeoisie, The, 86
Distinguished Gentleman, The, 46
Divorce—Italian Style, 246
Do the Right Thing, 71, 289

Doc, 269
Doctor, The, 14
Doctor in the House, 13
Doctor Zhivago, 180
Dodge City, 141
Dodsworth, 242
Does, The, see Les Biches
Dog-Pound Shuffle, 113
Doña Flor and Her Two Husbands, 60, 84
Don't Knock the Rock, 197
Double Indemnity (1944), 37, 246
Downhill Racer, 110
Dr. Ehrlich's Magic Bullet, 15
Dr. Jekyll and Mr. Hyde (1932), 13
Dr. Strangelove: Or, How I Learned
    to Stop Worrying and Love the
    Bomb, 296
Driving Miss Daisy, 248, 289
Drugstore Cowboy, 94
Drum, 265
Drums Along the Mohawk, 60
Duel in the Sun, 144

E

Each Dawn I Die, 42
Easter Parade, 58
Easy Living (1937), 88, 131
Easy Rider, 64
Eating Raoul, 87
Eddie and the Cruisers, 152
Edison the Man, 214
Educating Rita, 8
Egg and I, The, 11
8½, 210
Eight Men Out, 90, 102
8 Million Ways to Die, 34
El Cid, 263, 273
El Norte, 291
Eleanor and Franklin, 49
Eleanor and Franklin: The White House
    Years, 49
Elephant Boy, 116
Elephant Man, The, 16
Elevator to the Gallows, 205
Elmer Gantry, 254
Elvis, 155
Emerald Forest, The, 228
Emil and the Detectives (1931), 132
Emil und die Detektive, see
    Emil and the Detectives (1931)
Empire Strikes Back, The, 294

Employees Entrance, 97
Enemies: A Love Story, 256
Enemy Below, The, 275
Enemy From Space, *see* Five Million
    Years to Earth
Enforcer, The *(1951)*, 38
Entre Nous, 226
Epic That Never Was, The, 262
Equus, 115
Erendira, 85
E.T., 292
Everybody's All-American, 105
Ex-Lady, 149
Excalibur, 263
Executive Suite, 4
Exorcist, The, 73, 250
Experiment in Terror, 38
Eyes of Laura Mars, The, 186

F
F for Fake, 92
Fabulous Baker Boys, The, 197
Face in the Crowd, A, 47, 210
Fahrenheit 451, 299
Fail Safe, 296
Fall of the Roman Empire, The, 261
Fallen Idol, The, 10
Falling From Grace, 202
Falstaff, *see* Chimes at Midnight
Family Way, The, 205
Fanny and Alexander, 62
Fantasia, 203
Fantastic Voyage, 14, 159
Farewell to Arms, A *(1932)*, 181
Fashions, 222
Fashions of 1934, *see* Fashions
Fast and Loose, 130
Fast Break, 104
Fat City, 106
Fat Man and Little Boy, 297
Fatal Attraction *(1987)*, 243
Father of the Bride *(1950)*, 239
Father of the Bride *(1991)*, 239
Father's Little Dividend, 247
Fear No Evil, 252
Fear Strikes Out, 103
Fellini Satyricon, 262
Fellini's Roma, 82
Female, 149
Fiddler on the Roof, 256
Field, The, 12

Field of Dreams, 102
Field of Honor *(1988)*, 282
Fish Called Wanda, A, 93, 113
Fistful of Dollars, A, 160
Fitzcarraldo, 69, 84
Five Corners, 124
Five Easy Pieces, 87
Five Million Years to Earth, 294
Flaming Star, 154
Flatliners, 258
Flipper, 114
Flying Down to Rio, 68, 218
Follow the Fleet, 218
Footlight Parade, 222
For Whom the Bell Tolls, 181
Forbidden Love *(1992)*, 231
Forbidden Planet, 169, 294
Forbidden Quest, 86
Force of Evil *(1949)*, 30, 282
Foreign Correspondent, 67, 122, 139
Forever Darling, 252
Fortune Cookie, The, 105
42nd Street, 191, 222
Fountainhead, The, 183
Four Feathers, The *(1939)*, 265
Four for Texas, 156
400 Blows, The, 163
Four Weddings and a Funeral, 240
Fourth Man, The, 246
Fox and His Friends, 230
Frances, 22
Frankenweenie, 113
Frantic *(1957)*, *see* Elevator to the Gallows
Freaks, 216
French Connection, The, 35
Freud, 21
Frida, 185
Fried Green Tomatoes, 183
Friendly Persuasion, 266
Fritz the Cat, 111
From Here to Eternity *(1953)*, 278
Front, The, 213, 284
Front Page, The *(1931)*, 152
Full Metal Jacket, 286
Funny Face, 100, 186, 192
Funny Thing Happened on the Way
    to the Forum, A, 262

G
Gabriel Over the White House, 49, 252
Gallipoli, 270

Gambit, 28
Gap-Toothed Women, 227
Gaslight *(1944)*, 22
Gay Divorcee, The, 193, 219
Gay Purr-ee, 111
General, The, 66, 266
Genevieve, 108
Gentleman Jim, 106
Gentleman's Agreement, 256, 291
Get Crazy, 55
Getaway, The *(1972)*, 26
Gettysburg, 267
Ghost, 60
Ghost and Mrs. Muir, The, 61, 188
Gig, The, 196
Ginger and Fred, 219
Girl Can't Help It, The, 198
Girl Most Likely to . . ., The, 19
Glass House, The, 41
Glass Key, The *(1942)*, 46
Glen or Glenda?, 233
Glengarry Glen Ross, 4, 229
Glory *(1989)*, 266
Go Tell the Spartans, 95, 285
Godfather, The, 147
God's Little Acre, 12
Godspell, 58
Going My Way, 253
Gold Diggers of 1933, 221
Gold Diggers of 1935, 221
Gone With the Wind, 10, 141
Good Morning, Vietnam, 207
Good Mother, The, 245
Good Neighbor Sam, 6
Goodbye, Columbus, 257
Goodbye, Mr. Chips, 7
Gorillas in the Mist, 117
Grand Illusion, 270
Grand Prix, 108
Grapes of Wrath, The, 128, 271
Great Escape, The, 28
Great Expectations *(1946)*, 171
Great Gatsby, The, 181
Great McGinty, The, 46, 130
Greatest Show on Earth, The, 216
Green Berets, The, 285
Green for Danger, 39
Green Pastures, The, 251
Greyfriars Bobby, 112
Grifters, The, 93
Group, The, 182
Guadalcanal Diary, 278

Guess Who's Coming to Dinner?, 288
Guilty by Suspicion, 282
Gun Crazy *(1949)*, 25, 146
Guncrazy *(1992)*, 25
Gunga Din, 138, 264
Guns of Navarone, The, 145, 276
Guy Named Joe, A, 258
Guys and Dolls, 90

H

Hail Mary, 63
Hail the Conquering Hero, 43
Hairspray, 233
Hamlet *(1948)*, 168
Handle With Care *(1977)*, 207
Handmaid's Tale, The, 300
Hangmen Also Die, 125, 279
Happy New Year *(1973)*, 55
Hard-Boiled, 36
Hard Day's Night, A, 77, 199
Hardcore, 160
Harder They Fall, The, 38
Harlan County U.S.A., 5
Harry and Tonto, 65, 250
Harvey, 90
Hatful of Rain, A, 94
Haunting, The, 61
Having a Wild Weekend, 200
He Ran All the Way, 125
He Walked by Night, 129, 147
Heart Is a Lonely Hunter, The, 183
Heartbreak Hotel, 155
Heartburn, 73, 245
Heartland, 269
Hearts and Minds, 285
Hearts of Darkness: A Filmmaker's
    Apocalypse, 211
Heat and Dust, 265
Heaven Can Wait *(1943)*, 258
Heaven Knows, Mr. Allison, 255
Heavens Above, 253
Heiress, The, 174
Hell Below, 275
Hell Is for Heroes, 276
Hell's Angels, 153
Help!, 199
Henry & June, 238
Henry V *(1944)*, 167, 274
Henry V *(1989)*, 167, 274
Here Comes Mr. Jordan, 252, 258
Hero, 210

Heroes for Sale, 95
Hester Street, 256
High and the Mighty, The, 145
High Anxiety, 22
High Heels *(1991)*, 101
High Hopes, 78
High Noon, 145
High Sierra, 135
High Society, 194
His Girl Friday, 121, 139
History Is Made at Night, 69
Hoffa, 5
Hold Back the Dawn, 134
Hold On!, 200
Holiday, 55
Holiday Affair, 62
Holiday Inn, 55
Holly and the Ivy, The, 63
Home Alone, 164
Honeymoon in Vegas, 90, 155
Honeysuckle Rose, 201
Honkytonk Man, 202
Hoosiers, 104
Horn Blows at Midnight, The, 252
Horse in the Gray Flannel Suit, The, 116
Horse Soldiers, The, 266
Horse's Mouth, The, 172, 189
Hospital, The, 14
Hot Rock, The, 28
House Calls, 14
House Divided, A, 134
House of Games, 22, 92
House of Usher *(1960)*, 173
How Green Was My Valley, 5, 163
How to Get Ahead in Advertising, 7
How to Murder Your Wife, 246
How to Succeed in Business Without
    Really Trying, 3
Howards End, 172
Howards of Virginia, The, 60
Huckleberry Finn *(1939)*, 174
Hucksters, The, 6
Human Comedy, The, 279
Humoresque *(1947)*, 203
Hunchback of Notre Dame, The *(1939)*, 177
Hunt for Red October, The, 274
Husbands and Wives, 235

I

I Am a Fugitive From a Chain Gang, 41
I Changed My Sex, *see* Glen or Glenda?

I Confess, 144
I Hate Your Guts, *see* Intruder, The *(1961)*
I Led Two Lives, *see* Glen or Glenda?
I Never Promised You a Rose Garden, 23
I, the Jury *(1953)*, 130
I, the Jury *(1982)*, 33
I Walk the Line, 236
Ice Station Zebra, 86, 153, 274
Idiot, The *(1951)*, 180
Ikiru, 16
Illustrated Man, The, 299
I'm All Right Jack, 5
Imitation of Life *(1959)*, 10
Impromptu, 184, 204, 225
Improper Conduct, 231
In a Lonely Place, 212
In a Year of 13 Moons, 233
In the Heat of the Night *(1967)*, 289
In the Line of Fire, 52
In the Realm of the Senses, 237
In Which We Serve, 276
Incident at Oglala, 291
Incredible Mr. Limpet, The, 114
Incredible Shrinking Man, The, 158
Informer, The, 56, 140
Inherit the Wind *(1960)*, 31
Innocents, The, 174
Inserts, 211
Intermezzo *(1939)*, 203
International House, 208
Into the West, 116
Intruder, The *(1961)*, 290
Invaders From Mars *(1953)*, 293
Invasion of the Body Snatchers
    (1956), 283
Invasion of the Body Snatchers *(1978)*, 77
Invisible Man, The *(1933)*, 158
Invitation to the Wedding, 240
Ironweed, 271
Ishtar, 64
It *(1927)*, 98
It Happened One Night, 64
It Should Happen to You, 6
It's a Wonderful Life, 251
It's Alive, 143
Ivanhoe *(1953)*, 262

J

Jacob's Ladder, 257
Jailhouse Rock, 42
Jane Eyre *(1944)*, 171

Jason and the Argonauts, 142
Jaws, 113
Jazz on a Summer's Day, 196
Je Vous Salue Marie, *see* Hail Mary
Jean de Florette, 12
Jesus Christ Superstar, 58
Jesus of Montreal, 58
Jezebel, 135
JFK, 50, 75
Joe Macbeth, 169
John Meade's Woman, 151
Johnny Guitar, 230, 284
Johnny Handsome, 18
Johnny Shiloh, 267
Johnny Tremain, 59
Juarez, 136
Jubal, 170
Judge Priest, 44
Juliet of the Spirits, 243
Julius Caesar *(1953)*, 168, 261
June Bride, 240
Jungle Book *(1942)*, 117
Jungle Fever, 244, 288
Just One of the Guys, 234

K
Kansas City Bomber, 109
Kennel Murder Case, The, 39
Kentucky, 115
Kentucky Fried Movie, 209
Kid, The, 162
Kid Galahad *(1937)*, 106
Kid Galahad *(1962)*, 154
Kids Are Alright, The, 200
Killer, The, 36
Killers, The *(1946)*, 181
Killing, The, 29
Kim *(1950)*, 264
Kind of Loving, A, 242
King Creole, 154
King Kong *(1933)*, 67, 140, 158
King of Comedy, The, 209, 215
King of Kings *(1961)*, 57
King of Marvin Gardens, 208
King's Row, 125
Kiss Me Deadly, 33, 298
Kiss Me Kate, 169, 194
Kiss Me Stupid, 193
Kiss of Death *(1947)*, 137
Kiss of the Spider Woman, 84, 214, 231
Kitten With a Whip, 236

Knife in the Water, 70
Knights of the Round Table, 263
Knock on Any Door, 30
Knute Rockne—All American, 106
Koko—A Talking Gorilla, 117
Koyaanisqatsi, 298
Kramer vs. Kramer, 245
Krays, The, 78
Kwaidan, 175

L
La Bamba, 67, 198
La Bête Humaine, 178
La Cage Aux Folles, 233
La Dolce Vita, 81
Lady Eve, The, 92, 130
Lady Sings the Blues, 196
Lady Vanishes, The *(1938)*, 65
Landlord, The, 289
Lassie Come Home, 112
Last Action Hero, The, 148
Last American Hero, The, 107
Last Boy Scout, The, 34
Last Days of Pompeii, The *(1935)*, 262
Last Exit to Brooklyn, 5
Last Hurrah, The, 44
Last Laugh, The, 250
Last Picture Show, The, 213
Last Supper, The, 58
Last Tango in Paris, 80, 238
Last Temptation of Christ, The, 58, 292
Last Tycoon, The, 182
Last Year at Marienbad, 178
L'Atalante, 242
Late Show, The, 111
Laura *(1944)*, 35, 188
Law and Order *(1932)*, 135
Lawrence of Arabia, 273
Le Chat, 111
Le Mans, 108
Le Plaisir, 178
Le Voyage dans la Lune, *see*
    Trip to the Moon, A
Leap of Faith, 254
Learning Tree, The, 186, 287
Left-Handed Gun, The, 268
Legal Eagles, 189
Lenny, 94, 152, 215
Les Biches, 230
Les Enfants du Paradis, *see*
    Children of Paradise

Les Girls, 194
Les Miserables *(1935)*, 127, 177
Let's Get Lost, 196
Let's Make Love, 195, 215
Letter, The *(1940)*, 141
Letter From an Unknown Woman, 204
Letter to Three Wives, A *(1949)*, 243
Life and Times of Harvey Milk, The, 230
Life Is Sweet, 88
Life of Her Own, A, 99
Lifeboat, 70
Light That Failed, The, 17
Like Water for Chocolate, 87
Lili, 217
Lilies of the Field, 255
Lilith, 21
Lion in Winter, The, 62, 225
Little Big Man, 268
Little Foxes, The, 128
Lives of a Bengal Lancer, The, 265
Lola Montes, 216
Lolita, 176, 236
Long Good Friday, The, 77
Long Goodbye, The, 33
Long Voyage Home, The, 128, 151
Longest Day, The, 276
Longest Yard, The, 105
Longtime Companion, 15, 232
Look Who's Talking, 248
Lookin' Good, *see* Corky
Lord of the Flies *(1963)*, 173
Lorenzo's Oil, 16
Lost Horizon *(1937)*, 67, 144
Lost in America, 7
Lost Squadron, The, 68
Lost Weekend, The, 88
Lost World, The, 158
Love in a Taxi, 11
Love in the City, 82
Love Is on the Air, 206
Love Me Tonight, 189
Loved One, The, 173
Lover, The, 239
Lover Come Back *(1961)*, 6
Lovers and Other Strangers, 240
Lower Depths, The *(1936)*, 180
Lust for Life, 184

M
Macao, 147
Macbeth *(1948)*, 168

Mad Love, 150
Madam Satan, 148
Madame Bovary *(1991)*, 178
Magnificent Seven, The, 160
Mahogany, 99
Maids, The, 9
Making Mr. Right, 295
Malcolm X, 288
Maltese Falcon, The *(1941)*, 32, 77, 134
Man and a Woman, A, 108
Man Called Horse, A, 228
Man Facing Southeast, 24
Man I Love, The, 192
Man in the Gray Flannel Suit, The, 6
Man in the White Suit, The, 3
Man on the Eiffel Tower, The, 80
Man Who Fell to Earth, The, 293
Man Who Shot Liberty Valance, The, 44, 267
Man Who Would Be King, The, 265
Manchurian Candidate, The, 51, 281
Manhattan, 71, 193
Manon of the Spring, 12
Man's Favorite Sport?, 113
Margaret Bourke-White, 186
Marnie, 24
Marriage of Maria Braun, The, 241
Marriage on the Rocks, 157
Mary Poppins, 77
M*A*S*H, 13, 104, 281
Matewan, 4
Matinee, 298
Matter of Life and Death, A, *see* Stairway to Heaven
Matter of WHO, A, 15
Mauvaise Conduite, *see* Improper Conduct
Mazeppa, 115
McCabe and Mrs. Miller, 96, 269
Medium Cool, 210
Meet John Doe, 47, 92
Meet Me in St. Louis, 162
Melvin and Howard, 68, 153
Men . . . *(1985)*, 243
Men in War, 281
Men's Club, The, 228
Metropolis *(1926)*, 296
Metropolitan, 63
Mickey One, 215
Midnight, 10, 133
Midnight Cowboy, 95
Midnight Lace *(1960)*, 40

Midsummer Night's Dream, A *(1935)*, 162, 167
Million Dollar Mermaid, 221
Miracle of Morgan's Creek, The, 130
Miracle in Milan, 252
Miracle of Our Lady of Fatima, The, 283
Miracle on 34th Street *(1947)*, 72, 163, 284
Miracle Worker, The, 16
Mirage, 20
Misfits, The, 116, 123
Missing, 85
Mission to Moscow, 280
Mississippi Blues, 287
Mississippi Burning, 287
Mississippi Masala, 290
Missouri Breaks, The, 269
Mo' Better Blues, 196
Moby Dick *(1956)*, 70, 114, 174
Moderns, The, 182
Mogambo, 83
Molly Maguires, The, 126
Mona Lisa, 96
Monkey Business *(1931)*, 70, 139
Monsieur Hulot's Holiday, 109
Monty Python and the Holy Grail, 264
Monty Python's Life of Brian, 58
More the Merrier, The, 74, 279
Morocco, 101, 234
Moscow on the Hudson, 59, 98
Mosquito Coast, The, 70
Mother and the Whore, The, 238
Moulin Rouge, 185
Mountains of the Moon, 82
Mr. and Mrs. Bridge, 176
Mr. Lucky, 91
Mr. Peabody and the Mermaid, 114
Mr. Saturday Night, 215
Mr. Smith Goes to Washington, 44, 59, 72
Mrs. Miniver, 279
Much Ado About Nothing, 168
Murder, My Sweet, 32
Murder on the Orient Express, 66
Murders in the Rue Morgue *(1932)*, 135
Music in the Air, 133
Music Man, The, 59
Music of Chance, The, 91
My Beautiful Laundrette, 78, 231
My Dinner With Andre, 87
My Fair Lady, 78
My Favorite Wife, 242
My Favorite Year, 209
My Left Foot, 15, 100

My Man Godfrey *(1936)*, 8, 272
My Own Private Idaho, 169
My Son John, 283

N
Naked and the Dead, The, 175
Naked Lunch, 175
Nanook of the North, 86
Narrow Margin, The *(1952)*, 34, 66
Nashville, 51, 202
National Velvet, 114, 163
Natural, The, 103
Network, 208
Never Cry Wolf, 117
Never So Few, 157
Next Voice You Hear, The, 206, 250
Niagara, 247
Night and Day *(1946)*, 193
Night at the Opera, A, 121, 151
Night Moves, 34
Night of the Iguana, The, 253
Night on Earth, 11
Night Porter, The, 238
Nightmare Alley, 217
1984 *(1984)*, 172, 299
Ninotchka, 133
No Way Out *(1987)*, 46
Norma Rae, 5
North by Northwest, 67, 143
North Dallas Forty, 105
Not as a Stranger, 14
Nothing But a Man, 286
Nothing Sacred, 92, 137, 204
Notorious, 138
Number One, 106
Nuns on the Run, 232
Nun's Story, The, 255

O
Objective Burma!, 277
Oblomov, 179
Obsession *(1976)*, 160
Ocean's Eleven, 29, 56, 156
Odd Couple, The, 109, 245
Odds Against Tomorrow, 289
Of Mice and Men *(1992)*, 12
Official Story, The, 85
Okoge, 231
Old Man and the Sea, The, 113, 181
Old Yeller, 112

Oliver Twist *(1948)*, 171
Olympia, 110
Olympische Spiele, *see* Olympia
On a Clear Day You Can See Forever, 21
On Dangerous Ground, 17, 142
On Golden Pond, 249
On the Beach, 297
On the Road Again, *see*
    Honeysuckle Rose
On the Town, 71, 219
On the Waterfront, 5, 205, 284
One Day in the Life of Ivan Denisovich, 180
One False Move, 93
One Flew Over the Cuckoo's Nest, 23
One Plus One, 201
Only Angels Have Wings, 69
Open City, 81, 254
Operation Petticoat, 70, 275
Orlando, 172
Orpheus, 207
Othello *(1951)*, 167
Our Daily Bread, 272
Our Modern Maidens, 150
Out of Africa, 82
Out of the Past, 33
Outlaw, The, 153
Outrageous!, 234
Overboard, 20

P
Pale Rider, 160
Palm Beach Story, 245
Panic in Needle Park, The, 94
Panic in the Streets, 15, 74
Paper Lion, 105
Paper Moon, 93, 163, 271
Papillon, 41
Parallax View, The, 50
Paris Blues, 79, 196
Paris Is Burning, 99
Paris, Texas, 124
Parnell, 56
Passage to India, A, 265
Passport to Pimlico, 79
Patch of Blue, A, 17
Paths of Glory, 270
Patterns, 4
Patton, 276
Pennies From Heaven *(1981)*, 272
Penny Serenade, 247
Perfect Furlough, The, 86

Perfect World, A, 229
Pet Sematary, 111
Peter's Friends, 55
Petrified Forest, The, 121
Philadelphia Story, The, 240
Pickup on South Street, 283
Picture of Dorian Gray, The, 171, 188
Pink Flamingos, 233
Piranha, 114
Pirate, The, 194
Pixote, 84
Places in the Heart, 11
Planet of the Apes, 300
Platoon, 285
Play Misty for Me, 207
Playboys, The, 56
Player, The, 212
Playtime, 80
Plot Against Harry, The, 257
Poltergeist, 209
Polyester, 214
Porgy and Bess, 192
Pork Chop Hill, 282
Portrait of Jennie, 188
Poseidon Adventure, The, 55
Possessed *(1931)*, 149
Potemkin, 273
Power and the Glory, The, 131, 150
President's Analyst, The, 21, 73
Pretty Baby, 75, 96, 237
Pretty Woman, 96, 98
Pride and Prejudice *(1940)*, 171
Pride of the Marines, 18
Pride of the Yankees, 103
Prime of Miss Jean Brodie, The, 7
Prince of Tides, The, 21
Prince Valiant, 263
Prisoner of Second Avenue, The, 23
Prisoner of Shark Island, The, 52
Prisoner of Zenda, The *(1937)*, 125
Private Life of Sherlock Holmes, The, 40
Professional Sweetheart, 206
Proof, 17, 186
Protocol, 45
Psycho, 143, 234
Public Eye, The *(1992)*, 186
Pump Up the Volume, 207
Punchline, 214
Pure Country, 202
Purple Rose of Cairo, The, 213
Pursued, 126
Putney Swope, 6

Q

Quadrophenia, 200
Quatermass and the Pit, *see*
  Five Million Years to Earth
Queen of Spades, The, 179
Quick Change, 71
Quiet Earth, The, 297
Quiet Man, The, 56
Quo Vadis? *(1951)*, 262

R

Rabid, 18
Rack, The, 281
Radio Days, 208
Raging Bull, 106
Raising Arizona, 248
Ran, 169, 273
Random Harvest, 19
Rapture, The, 298
Raw Deal *(1948)*, 129
Rear Window, 185
Red Badge of Courage, The *(1951)*,
  174, 266
Red-Headed Woman, 149
Red Planet Mars, 207
Red Pony, The *(1949)*, 116
Red River, 144
Red Shoes, The, 101, 221
Ref, The, 62
Regarding Henry, 20
Reign of Terror, 129
Remains of the Day, The, 9
Rembrandt, 184
Remember the Night, 132
Repo Man, 293
Requiem for a Heavyweight *(1962)*, 107
Reservoir Dogs, 29, 228
Retreat, Hell!, 280
Return of the Jedi, 294
Return to Peyton Place, 236
Reversal of Fortune, 247
Rhapsody in Blue, 192
Ride the Pink Horse, 37
Rififi, 27
Right Stuff, The, 68
Ring-a-Ding Rhythm, 199
Ring of Bright Water, 117
River of No Return, 69
River Runs Through It, A, 114, 177
Road to Hong Kong, 157
Road Warrior, The, 64, 108

Robe, The, 261
Roberta, 219
Robin and the Seven Hoods, 156
Robocop, 296
Rock Around the Clock, 197
Rock, Rock, Rock, 198
Rocking Horse Winner, The, 91, 172
Roger & Me, 3
Rollerball, 110
Roman Holiday *(1953)*, 81, 140
Roman Scandals, 261
Roman Spring of Mrs. Stone, The, 81, 96
Romantic Englishwoman, The, 124
Rome Adventure, 80
Romeo and Juliet *(1936)*, 168
Roof, The, 81
Rose Tattoo, The, 126
Roseland, 219
Rosemary's Baby, 226, 247
Round Midnight, 195
Royal Wedding, 219
Ruby *(1992)*, 50
Rules of the Game, The, 151
Ruling Class, The, 23
Run Silent, Run Deep, 274
Run Wild, Run Free, 115
Runaway Train, 41, 67
Rush, 93, 206
Ryan's Daughter, 57

S

Sabotage, 214
Saboteur, 279
Sahara *(1943)*, 278
Saint Jack, 95
Salt and Pepper, 157
Samba Traore, 83
San Francisco, 77
Sands of Iwo Jima, 277
Sarafina!, 83
Saturday Night and Sunday Morning, 173
Saturday Night Fever, 72, 220
Sayonara, 281
Scarface: The Shame of the Nation
  (1932), 137
Scarlet Letter, The *(1973)*, 174
Scenes From a Mall, 98
Scent of a Woman *(1992)*, 18, 229
Scott of the Antarctic, 85
Scoundrel, The, 138
Scrooged, 10, 63

Searchers, The, 142
Seconds, 19, 126
Secret Honor, 49
Seduction of Joe Tynan, The, 45
Semi-Tough, 105
Senator Was Indiscreet, The, 45
Sergeant York, 136, 270
Sergeants 3, 156
Servant, The, 9, 123
Set-Up, The, 107
Seven Days in May, 51
7 Faces of Dr. Lao, 216
Seven Year Itch, The, 237
1776, 59
Shadows, 289
Shaft, 287
Shall We Dance, 191, 217
Shame (1961), see Intruder, The (1961)
Shame of the Nation, The, see Scarface:
    The Shame of the Nation (1932)
Shane, 267
Shanghai Express, 67
Shark!, 114
She Done Him Wrong, 149
Sheltering Sky, The, 83
Shenandoah, 267
Sherman's March, 267
Ship of Fools, 69
Shock Corridor, 24, 38
Shocking Miss Pilgrim, The, 192
Shoes of the Fisherman, The, 253
Shoeshine, 101
Shop Around the Corner, The, 98
Short Cuts, 176
Short Eyes, see Slammer
Show Boat (1936), 189
Silk Stockings, 195, 218
Silkwood, 298
Simple Gifts, 63
Singin' in the Rain, 218
Singing Nun, The, 255
Sink the Bismarck!, 276
Sister Act, 161, 254
Sister Kenny, 15
Six Degrees of Separation, 91, 187
Sky's the Limit, The, 190
Skyscraper Souls, 148, 188
Slammer, 42
Slap Shot, 109
Slaughterhouse-Five, 176
Sleeper, 206, 295
Slightly Scarlet, 130

Smallest Show on Earth, The, 213
Smash Palace, 108, 244
Smash-Up: The Story of a Woman, 89
Smiles of a Summer Night, 170
Snake Pit, The, 23
Sneakers, 28
Snows of Kilimanjaro, The, 181
S.O.B., 88
Solaris, 293
Soldier's Story, A, 290
Some Came Running, 157
Some Like It Hot, 65, 232
Somebody Up There Likes Me, 107
Something of Value, 83
Something Wicked This Way Comes, 66
Something Wild, 64
Song of Love, A, 204
Songwriter, 202
Sons and Lovers, 172
Sorry, Wrong Number (1948), 246
Sound of Music, The, 254
Sounder, 272
Spartacus, 230, 261
Spellbound, 20
Spirit of St. Louis, The, 67
Spirit of the Beehive, 213
Spot, see Dog-Pound Shuffle
Stagecoach (1939), 139, 151, 267
Stairway to Heaven, 67, 257
Stand and Deliver, 8, 291
Star 80, 100
Star is Born, A (1937), 121, 139
Star is Born, A (1954), 190
Star Trek IV: The Voyage Home, 77
Star Wars, 159, 294
State Fair (1945), 12
State of Siege, 85
State of the Union, 43
Stay Tuned, 209
Steel Helmet, The, 281
Stella Dallas, 245
Stepford Wives, The, 295
Sting, The, 92
Store, The, 97
Stormy Weather, 288
Story of Women, The, 226
Stranger, The (1946), 40, 147
Stranger Than Paradise, 65
Strangers on a Train, 102
Streetcar Named Desire, A (1951), 74
Streetwise, 97
Strictly Ballroom, 220

Strictly Dishonorable, 131
Stunt Man, The, 212
Suddenly, 52
Sullivan's Travels, 130, 212
Summer Stock, 190
Sun Valley Serenade, 67
Sunday Bloody Sunday, 231
Sunrise at Campobello, 48
Sunset Boulevard, 9, 212
Sunshine Boys, The, 249
Sure Thing, The, 161
Swann in Love, 178
Sweet Charity, 97, 220
Sweet Dreams, 201
Sweet Smell of Success, 122, 126
Swept Away . . . by an unusual destiny
    in the blue sea of August, 238
Swimmer, The, 176
Swing Shift, 226, 280
Swing Time, 190, 218
Sword of Lancelot, 263
Sympathy for the Devil, see
    One Plus One

T

Taking of Pelham One Two Three, The, 72
Talk Radio, 207
Tall Blond Man With One Black Shoe, The,
    101
Tampopo, 87
Tanner 88, 43, 210
Taste of Honey, A, 247
Tatie Danielle, 249
Taxi! (1932), 11
Taxi (1953), 10
Taxi Blues, 11
Taxi Driver, 10, 51, 96, 143, 159, 237
Tempest (1982), 170
Ten Commandments, The (1923), 250
Ten Commandments, The (1956), 57, 250
Tender Mercies, 201
Terminator 2: Judgment Day, 295
Terms of Endearment, 16
Terror in a Texas Town, 160
Thank You, Jeeves, 9
That Darn Cat!, 111
That's Entertainment, 219
Theatre of Blood, 170
Thelma and Louise, 27, 64, 227
Thelonious Monk: Straight, No Chaser,
    196

These Three, 127
They Live by Night, 25
They Shoot Horses, Don't They?, 220, 271
They Were Expendable, 277
Thief, The (1952), 283
Thief of Bagdad, The (1940), 158
Thieves Like Us, 26
Thin Man, The, 39, 89, 125
Thing, The (1951), 86, 283, 293
Thing From Another World, The, see
    Thing, The (1951)
Third Man, The, 102, 205
Thirty Seconds Over Tokyo, 278
36 Hours, 145
This Is My Life, 215
This Land Is Mine, 280
This Sporting Life, 109
Those Wonderful Men With a Crank, 213
Thousand Clowns, A, 210
Three Cases of Murder, 187
Three Comrades, 146
Three Faces of Eve, The, 23
3 Godfathers, 63
Three Lives of Thomasina, The, 111
Three Men and a Baby, 247
Three Sisters, The (1970), 180
Three Strangers, 136
3 Women, 187
Thrill of It All, The, 100, 209
Throne of Blood, 169
Throw Momma From the Train, 65
Thunder Road, 88
Thunderbolt and Lightfoot, 234
Thunderheart, 291
THX-1138, 210, 300
Tie Me Up! Tie Me Down!, 238
Tightrope, 75
Time of Their Lives, The, 60
T-Men, 37, 129
To Be or Not to Be (1942), 280
To Be or Not to Be (1983), 280
To Have and Have Not, 181
To Kill a Mockingbird, 31, 183, 291
To Sir, With Love, 7
Tom Brown's School Days, 171
Tom Jones, 123, 170
Tomorrow Is Forever, 19
Tootsie, 147, 232
Top Hat, 190, 217
Topkapi, 27
Topper (1937), 61
Tora! Tora! Tora!, 278

Torch Song Trilogy, 230
Torpedo Run, 275
Touch of Class, A, 243
Trading Places, 91
Treasure of the Sierra Madre, The, 134, 141
Tree of Wooden Clogs, The, 11
Trip to the Moon, A, 292
Trouble Man, 206
Trouble With Angels, The, 255
True Believer, 31
True Colors, 45
True Love, 241
True Romance, 27, 155
Truly, Madly, Deeply, 258
Tucker: The Man and His Dream, 3, 152
Tune in Tomorrow . . ., 75
Turning Point, The (1977), 220
Twelve O'Clock High, 68
Twentieth Century, 66, 131, 137
20,000 Leagues Under the Sea, 114
20,000 Years in Sing Sing, 42
Twilight Zone—The Movie, 68
Two for the Road, 64, 241
Two-Minute Warning, 105
2001: A Space Odyssey, 159, 294

U

UFOria, 93, 293
Ugetsu, 61
Ugly American, The, 285
Umberto D, 113, 249
Unbearable Lightness of Being, The, 186
Under the Roofs of Paris, 79
Under the Volcano, 90
Undercover Man, The (1949), 37
Underworld (1927), 136
Unfaithfully Yours (1948), 203, 243
Unforgiven (1992), 269
Uninvited, The, 61
Union Pacific, 66
Unlawful Entry, 161
Unmarried Woman, An, 245
Untouchables, The, 123
Up the Down Staircase, 8
Urban Cowboy, 202
Utz, 187

V

Verdict, The (1982), 31, 89
Vertigo, 76, 143

Victim, 230
Victor/Victoria (1982), 234
Vikings, The, 273
Vincent and Theo, 184
Visions: The Images, Words, and Music
    of Gordon Parks, 286
Viva Las Vegas, 154
Von Ryan's Express, 66
Voyager, 67

W

Wagner, 204
Wait Until Dark, 17
Waiting for the Light, 252
Wake Island, 278
Walk in the Sun, A, 276
Walk on the Wild Side, 75
Wall Street, 3
War and Peace (1956), 179
War and Peace (1967), 273
War of the Roses, The, 244
War Room, The, 43
WarGames, 298
Watch on the Rhine, 280
Waterloo, 273
Waterloo Bridge (1940), 121
We Live Again, 127, 131
We Think the World of You, 112
Wedding, A, 240
Wedding Banquet, The, 240
Wee Geordie, 110
Wee Willie Winkie, 162, 265
Werner Herzog Eats His Shoe, 101
West Side Story, 169, 290
Westerner, The, 128
What About Bob?, 22
What Price Hollywood?, 212
What's New, Pussycat?, 22
What's Up Doc?, 161
When Harry Met Sally, 55
When Worlds Collide, 158
Where the Sidewalk Ends, 35, 137
While the City Sleeps, 38
White Fang (1991), 113
White Men Can't Jump, 104
Who's Afraid of Virginia Woolf?, 89, 242
Who's That Knocking at My Door?, 198
Wild in the Country, 154
Wild in the Streets, 49, 94
Wild Strawberries, 249
Wilson, 48

Wings of Desire, 251
Winning, 108
Winter Kills, 50
Wise Blood, 182
Witches of Eastwick, The, 177, 251
Witness for the Prosecution *(1957)*, 31
Wizard of Oz, The, 101, 162
Wolf at the Door, 185
Woman in the Dunes, 237
Woman in the Window, 40
Women, The, 99
Working Girl, 4
Working Girls, 95
World According to Garp, The, 227
Wuthering Heights *(1939)*, 122, 127

X Y Z
Yankee Doodle Dandy, 59
Yellow Cab Man, The, 11
Yentl, 256
You and Me, 205
You Can't Take It With You, 122
You Only Live Once, 25
Young Lions, The, 277
Young Mr. Lincoln, 30, 48
Zazie dans le Métro, 80, 178
Zebrahead, 289
Zentropa, 67
Ziegfield Follies, 219
Zou Zou, 221
Zulu, 82, 272

ABOUT THE AUTHORS

LYNNE ARANY, a writer and designer, is the founder of the book development firm, Ink Projects. Her credits include the *Born to Shop* travel series for Bantam and the forthcoming cookbook, *Patio Daddy-O!: The Golden Age of Barbecue* for Chronicle Books. She remembers with fondness needing to leave the movies early to get to her orthodontist appointments on time. She still plans to see the end of *Huckleberry Finn* (1939) someday, though not, alas, at Flushing's Prospect Theater.

TOM DYJA is a writer and editor living in New York. One of his earliest memories is of playing sick in the second grade so he could watch *A Taste of Honey* on the morning movie.

GARY GOLDSMITH writes for film and television. He has written documentaries on subjects ranging from rock 'n' roll to JFK, and while he wrote and co-directed a series of films for the Ronald Reagan Presidential Library, he claims to have had no knowledge of any arms for hostages trade, maintaining he was at the movies when the deal went down.